THE SOVIET UNION IN THE HORN OF AFRICA

Soviet and East European Studies: 71

Editorial Board

Soviet and East European Studies

Series list continues on p. 408

THE SOVIET UNION IN THE HORN OF AFRICA

The diplomacy of intervention and disengagement

ROBERT G. PATMAN

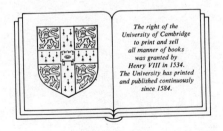

The right of the
University of Cambridge
to print and sell
all manner of books
was granted by
Henry VIII in 1534.
The University has printed
and published continuously
since 1584.

CAMBRIDGE UNIVERSITY PRESS

Cambridge
New York   Port Chester   Melbourne   Sydney

Published by the Press Syndicate of the University of Cambridge
The Pitt Building, Trumpington Street, Cambridge CB2 1RP
40 West 20th Street, New York, NY 10011, USA
10 Stamford Road, Oakleigh, Melbourne 3166, Australia

First published 1990

Printed in Great Britain at the University Press, Cambridge·

·*British Library cataloguing in publication data*
Patman, Robert G.
The Soviet Union in the Horn of Africa: the
diplomacy of intervention and disengagement.
– (Soviet and East European studies; 71)
1. Horn of Africa. Political events. Role of
Soviet Union & United States, 1950–1988
I. Title   II. Series
967'.7

Library of Congress cataloguing in publication data
Patman, Robert G.
The Soviet Union in the Horn of Africa: the diplomacy of
intervention and disengagement / Robert G. Patman.
        p.   cm. – (Soviet and East European studies: 71)
Revision of the author's thesis (PhD.) – University of
Southampton, 1986.
Bibliography.
Includes index.
ISBN 0-521-36022-6
1. Africa. Northeast – Foreign relations – Soviet Union.
2. Soviet Union – Foreign relations – Africa. Northeast.
3. Ethiopia – Foreign relations – Soviet Union. 4. Soviet
Union – Foreign relations – Ethiopia. I. Title.   II. Series.
DT367.63.S65P38 1990
327.47063 – dc20   89-15826 CIP

ISBN 0 521 36022 6

CE

To my mother and father

Contents

Maps

Tables

Preface

Events in the Horn of Africa in the 1970s were even more striking than those of the Italian–Ethiopian War in the 1930s and at least as far-reaching in their international repercussions. In the space of just four years, the USSR concluded a treaty of Friendship and Co-operation with Somalia, Ethiopia experienced a revolution in 1974 that was as thoroughgoing as any African upheaval, the Soviet Union dramatically shifted massive support from Somalia to Ethiopia and then played a key part in the military defeat of its former ally in the Ogaden conflict of 1977–8. For much of the following decade, these historic events broadly determined the shape of Soviet policy in the region.

The purpose of this study is to analyse the paradoxes of Soviet involvement in the Horn. This concern grew out of a nagging question: if the Soviet Union was one of the most powerful states in the world, and able to project military force in distant places like Ethiopia, why did it find it necessary to disengage in Somalia, a country where Soviet interests had apparently been firmly established? The search for an explanation involves a detailed examination of the interaction of Soviet power and influence in the Horn of Africa.

The structure of the book reflects this central objective. It is divided into four parts. The introductory section provides the theoretical framework in which the substance of Soviet involvement is cast. It explores, in general terms, the concepts of intervention and dis-engagement in international politics, distinguishing between the motive to intervene and the opportunity to do so. Part I, embracing two chapters, examines how Soviet motives toward the Horn were fashioned by history and the perception around 1970 of a shift in the global 'correlation of forces' at the expense of the West. The second part of the book, consisting of three chapters, traces the actual development of Soviet policy from close Soviet–Somali ties in the early

1970s to Soviet–Cuban intervention on behalf of Ethiopia in 1977–8. The Conclusion weighs the Soviet experience in the region and relates it to events there in the post-war period after 1978. This section includes an assessment of the change in Soviet policy in the Horn under Mikhail Gorbachev. For convenience of reference, Appendix A and Appendix B present the texts of the Soviet–Somali Treaty of Friendship and Co-operation, signed 11 July 1974, and the Soviet–Ethiopian Treaty of Friendship and Co-operation, signed 20 November 1978.

This study does not seek to present a fully comprehensive picture of the developments and complexities of the Eritrean conflict. That is a major issue in its own right. Instead the reader will find that the Eritrean question is only discussed inasmuch as it forms the context of Soviet relations with Ethiopia and Somalia.

A wide variety of published sources have been consulted in the preparation of this study. As the notes attest, I have tried to use Soviet primary sources whenever possible. Such sources include Soviet government publications, academic monographs, periodical articles, newspaper reports and radio broadcasts. This research has been supplemented by African materials. But, and this is a problem familiar to many students of Soviet foreign policy, hard evidence for Soviet policy in the Horn has often been scant. While there has been an 'explosion of intellectual activity' in the Soviet mass media after the 'revolutionary changes'[1] of the Gorbachev era, glasnost', according to Eduard Shevardnadze, the Soviet Foreign Minister, has not yet taken firm hold in the area of foreign policy. Besides, the main focus of this study falls within the Brezhnev years when there was little official encouragement of public discussion in any shape or form. The secrecy of Soviet government, moreover, has been compounded by the closed decision-making process characterising the Ethiopian and Somali regimes. To reduce the information gap, therefore, I have consulted Western publications, unpublished Ph.D dissertations, specialist journals and newspapers. Furthermore, I obtained invaluable information from interviews and discussions with acknowledged experts and individuals who were directly involved at some stage in the events under review.

The book does, I believe, shed some new light in the field of Soviet studies. By looking at the relatively neglected relationship between Soviet disengagement and Soviet intervention in the region – the tendency among Western observers has been to generalise about particular aspects of Soviet activity – the book challenges several prevailing assumptions. Firstly, it undermines the notion, held by many analysts, that countries like the 'People's Democratic Republic of Ethiopia' and 'The Somali Democratic Republic' are, by virtue of a proclaimed allegiance to Moscow, simply a geographical extension of the Soviet model. This study demonstrates that Soviet relations with Ethiopia and Somalia have always been marked by considerable national and political differences as well as by certain similarities. Secondly, the book indicates that the Soviet literature on the Horn of Africa cannot be safely ignored by Western or African specialists. While sometimes bland and polemical in content, Soviet writings are important in that they have mirrored a long-term Soviet interest in Ethiopia, and occasionally contained illuminating differences of view in relation to the problems of the Horn. Thirdly, the study provides an alternative perspective in the 'Africanist' versus 'Globalist' debate, which developed out of Soviet involvement in the Horn. The 'Africanist' school emphasises that Soviet policy in the region lacked coherence and was essentially 'reactive and opportunistic'[2] in the face of a local conflict that was not of Moscow's making. In contrast, the 'Globalist' school of thought argues that Soviet behaviour in the Horn was consistent with a grand design to undermine Western (and Chinese) influence wherever possible through the cynical manipulation of local grievances. It is shown, however, that both of these approaches are equally deficient. Our discussion reveals that while Moscow did not deliberately engineer the Ethiopian–Somali conflict for the sake of global ambitions, it definitely had long-term political objectives in the Horn. The fact that Moscow pursued these objectives in an opportunistic fashion did not mean they were non-existent. Rather, it meant that 'calculated opportunism' was perhaps a more appropriate description for Soviet activities in the Horn.

The Soviet Union in the Horn of Africa evolved from a doctoral dissertation, written in fulfilment of the requirements for a Ph.D in Politics at the University of Southampton. The dissertation was completed in December 1986. Additional research on the Gorbachev period and a revision of the original manuscript were needed to transform the dissertation into a book. During the course of this study, I have received considerable assistance from many people and institutions which I wish to acknowledge – though, of course, the responsibility for the views expressed in the book belongs only to me. My first thanks go to my Ph.D supervisors, Professor Karen Dawisha, of the University of Maryland, and Professor Peter Calvert, University of Southampton. Karen Dawisha helped me get the research off the ground through constant encouragement, shrewd advice and intellectual inspiration. To add to this, she continued to take an active interest in the research after taking up a teaching post in the United States. I owe her much. At the same time Peter Calvert greatly helped by consistently offering wise and judicious counsel. He also made some important points during the preparations for publication. In addition, I would like to thank my long-suffering Russian language teachers, David Jones, of the University of Southampton and Jeffrey Garnett, of the Rayleigh Sweyne School. David had the difficult task of introducing me to Russian and was always a generous and responsive teacher. Jeffrey, a family friend, checked some of my translations and generally took a keen interest in the study.

Four other individuals deserve special thanks: Paul B. Henze, of the Rand Corporation, had a marked impact on this project. He not only inspired me to persevere in the research, but also generously made available many of his published as well as unpublished writings on the Horn. Furthermore, he made many helpful suggestions on the manuscript and graciously shared his insights with the author during an interview in London in June 1988. Patrick Gilkes, of the BBC, painstakingly read the manuscript and provided a number of constructive and detailed comments. Professor Christopher Clapham, of the University of Lancaster, read the manuscript at various stages and gave me the benefit of his profound knowledge of the Horn, especially in relation to the final chapter. Moreover, I am indebted to my ex-colleague and friend, David Morison, the editor of *USSR and Third World*. He kindly helped me as an informal adviser and I found his perceptive observations on Soviet policy in our discussions to be most useful. His comments on the manuscript were greatly valued. To each of these men I am deeply grateful.

I should also like to thank the following for their readings of the manuscript: Professor I. M. Lewis, of the London School of Economics and Political Science; Colin Legum, editor of the *Africa Contemporary Record*; W. M. Dickinson, the Director of *Africa Research Bulletin*; Harold Jenkins, of the Research Department of the British Foreign and Commonwealth Office; and Professor Fred Halliday, of the London School of Economics and Political Science. I derived invaluable information from a number of people connected with events in the Horn of Africa, who shared information with me on a confidential basis. I take pleasure in thanking them again. It must be added that this book would not have been undertaken without the aid of three people: Rodney Cole, of Brentwood High School, played a major part in encouraging me to pursue a university education; Professor Peter Nailor, of the Royal Naval Staff College, Greenwich, taught me to appreciate the intellectual power of relating theory to practice and supported my application for graduate work; and Professor Philip Reynolds, of Lancaster University, heightened my awareness of analytical thinking and astutely advised me to seek a research place at the University of Southampton.

There are institutional debts to acknowledge: to the Economic and Social Science Research Council for funding the first three years of the Ph.D; to the Richard Newitt Foundation for awarding me a travel scholarship to visit the USSR; to the British Council for making arrangements for and also helping to defray the costs of my visit to the USSR. To the staff of the Department of Politics, University of Southampton, especially Phil Williams, Dr John Simpson and Dr Alan Brier, for making my stay at Southampton a very happy and rewarding one. I wish to thank the librarians at the University of Southampton, all of whom cheerfully tolerated incessant requests for books, interlibrary loans, microfilm and xerox copies. A special thanks must also go to the efficient staff of the Press library at the Royal Institute of International Affairs. In a similar vein, I would like to express my appreciation to the librarians of the Central Asian Research Centre, the Schapiro Library in the London School of Economics and Political Science, the School of Slavonic and East European Studies and the School of Oriental and African Studies.

I was fortunate to have the assistance of the staff of Cambridge University Press, notably the editor of the Soviet and East European Series, Michael Holdsworth, who brought helpfulness, commitment and patience to this project. And I owe a debt of gratitude to Ms Krysia Campbell for her excellent secretarial assistance. She accepted the complexities of typing the manuscript with resourcefulness and humour.

Finally, and most importantly, I should especially like to thank my family, particularly my parents. Throughout the long haul of this study they were supportive in every possible way. If nothing else, this book is a tribute to their faith.

Abbreviations

ACDA	Arms Control and Disarmament Agency
ALF	Afar Liberation Front
BGN	The United States Board on Geographic Names
CELU	Confederation of Ethiopian Labour Unions
CIA	Central Intelligence Agency
CMEA	Council for Mutual Economic Assistance
COPWE	Commission for Organising the Party of the Working People of Ethiopia
CPSU	Communist Party of the Soviet Union
EDU	Ethiopian Democratic Union
EEC	European Economic Community
ELF	Eritrean Liberation Front
EPDA	Ethiopian People's Democratic Alliance
EPLF	Eritrean People's Liberation Front
EPRP	Ethiopian People's Revolutionary Party
FESM	Free Ethiopian Soldiers Movement
IDA	International Development Agency
IISS	International Institute for Strategic Studies
IMF	International Monetary Fund
KGB	Soviet State Security Service
MAAG	Military Assistance Advisory Group
MEISON	All-Ethiopian Socialist Movement
NATO	North Atlantic Treaty Organisation
OAU	Organisation of African Unity
OECD	Organisation for Economic Co-operation and Development
OLF	Oromo Liberation Front
PCGN	The Permanent Committee on Geographical Names
PMAC	Provisional Military Administrative Council

POMOA	Political Office of Mass Organisational Affairs
RDF	Rapid Deployment Force
RRC	Relief and Rehabilitation Commission
SAASC	Soviet Afro–Asian Solidarity Committee
SNM	Somali National Movement
SRC	Supreme Revolutionary Council
SRSP	Somali Revolutionary Socialist Party
SSDF	Somali Salvation Democratic Front
TPLF	Tigrean People's Liberation Front
USSR	Union of Soviet Socialist Republics
WPE	Workers Party of Ethiopia
WSLF	Western Somali Liberation Front

NOTE ON TRANSLITERATION OF RUSSIAN WORDS

In this study, I have adopted the BGN/PCGN system for the transliteration of the Russian cyrillic alphabet. The scheme is designed for the convenience of readers who are unacquainted with the Russian language.

Except in cases where names are more recognisable in a traditional variation (e.g., Moscow), I have attempted to transliterate according to the following pattern:

Russian	Roman	Russian	Roman	Russian	Roman
А, а	a	К, к	k	Х, х	kh
Б, б	b	Л, л	l	П, п	ts
В, в	v	М, м	m	Ч, ч	ch
Г, г	g	Н, н	n	Ш, ш	sh
Д, д	d	О, о	o	Щ, щ	shch
Е, е	e, ye	П, п	p	Ъ	"
Ё, ё	e, ye	Р, р	r	Ы, ы	y
Ж, ж	zh	С, с	s	ь	'
З, з	z	Т, т	t	Э, э	e
И, и	i	У, у	u	Ю , ю	yu
Й, й	y	Ф, ф	f	Я, я	ya

Source: The Permanent Committee on Geographical Names, The Royal Geographical Society, Kensington Gore, London.

Introduction

1 From intervention to disengagement: a framework

Intervention is a very central and a very old subject in the study of international relations, and there is a sense in which there is nothing new that can be said about it. But at the same time it is one of those subjects which we have constantly to reassess, in relation to changing circumstances: the underlying questions may be the same, but they keep arising in new forms.

(Preface in Hedley Bull, ed. *Intervention in World Politics*, Oxford, Oxford University Press, 1984)

The last decade has reaffirmed that intervention and its close relative, disengagement, remain both important and very topical issues in international politics. A couple of examples will suffice. In January 1979, the Vietnamese army entered Kampuchea and overthrew the Pol Pot regime. At the end of the same year, Soviet troops crossed the border into Afghanistan and deposed the government of President Hafizullah Amin. Both Vietnam and the USSR denied they had intervened. The Vietnamese claimed they were 'liberating' the Kampuchean people from a tyrannical government, whilst the Soviets said they had simply responded to a repeated request for military assistance against 'armed intervention by imperialist forces'.[1] Now, nearly a decade later, Vietnam and the USSR have begun the process of extricating themselves from these military entanglements. In June 1988, Hanoi announced its intention to withdraw all its 100,000-strong troop contingent from Kampuchea by 1990. Meanwhile, the USSR, under the terms of a UN-mediated accord signed on 15 April 1988, had withdrawn all 115,000 of its troops from Afghanistan by February 1989. In each case, the disengaging power has tried to square its decision to leave with its original commitment to 'go in'. Thus, Vietnam claims that its withdrawal from Kampuchea was prompted, not by the weight of Third World opposition to its occupation, but by the fact that 'the national-democratic forces in the country [opposed to

Pol Pot] had gained the upper hand'.[2] Similarly, notwithstanding the fierce resistance of the mojahedin in Afghanistan, the USSR declares that 'Soviet generals do not think that they have lost the war' as the Geneva accords provide 'the indispensable legal foundation . . . for an end to the interference in the internal affairs of Afghanistan'.[3] Such explanations, of course, are partisan and self-serving. But they are fairly representative of the level of controversy and disagreement which so often surrounds the term intervention.

The problem of definition

Despite the fact that intervention is a ubiquitous feature of modern world politics, there appears to be little agreement on the meaning of the term. In W. B. Gallie's terms, intervention is an 'essentially contested concept'.[4] Such a concept involves fierce disputes about the proper application on the part of its users. This has given the concept a certain vagueness. The literature is pervaded with military interventions, propaganda interventions, symbolic interventions as well as highly specific actions such as customs interventions or foreign-aid interventions.[5] Indeed, intervention is frequently defined in such diverse ways that it seems virtually indistinguishable from concepts like aggression, imperialism or other non co-operative features of international relations.

For clarity's sake, however, it is necessary to delineate the subject more closely. Several notable attempts have been made in this direction. First, a classic definition by L. Oppenheim restricts intervention to those acts which constitute 'dictatorial interference'[6] by an outside party or parties in the sphere of the domestic jurisdiction of a sovereign state. This definition forms the basis of Article 2 Paragraph 7 of the United Nations Charter which upholds the principle of non-intervention in international society. In practice, this legal formulation has done little to stem the outbreak of state-sponsored intervention. Between 1945 and 1988, at least 150 separate conflicts took place around the world, the vast majority of which involved developing countries.[7] The limitations of the legalistic approach are considerable. For one thing, it is not really clear what constitutes 'dictatorial interference'. In the long-running debate in the UN on South Africa's policy of apartheid, for example, representatives from Pretoria have often held such an all-encompassing conception that even verbal condemnation is deemed 'dictatorial interference' in the domestic affairs of the Republic.

In addition, the notion of domestic jurisdiction is obscure. If, as generally seems to be the case under the UN Charter, member states are free to define their own domestic jurisdiction, the chances of international agreement on the boundaries of the term are correspondingly slim. In the pre-Gorbachev era, for example, adherence to the class principle gave the USSR a distinctive understanding of the scope and meaning of Article 2 Paragraph 7 of the UN Charter. Thus, during the Hungarian uprising of 1956 and the events in Czechoslovakia of 1948 and 1968, the Soviet government took the view that discussion of these issues in the UN was a flagrant interference in the internal affairs of those countries.[8]

Finally, intervention so conceived is plagued by a double-standards problem. Oppenheimer's definition strongly implies that sovereign states have the moral right to have their spheres of jurisdiction respected, and that 'dictatorial interference' abridges that right. The reality of intervention, however, is not so clear cut. It was possible, for instance, both to condemn Soviet intervention in Czechoslovakia in 1968 as a violation of human rights and to applaud the Tanzanian intervention in Uganda in 1979 for restoring human rights by toppling the brutal Idi Amin regime. Clearly, the morality of interventionary behaviour will depend on the objective towards which it is directed.

A second definition of intervention has been advanced by James Rosenau. He contends that 'all kinds of observers from a wide variety of perspectives seem inclined to describe the behaviour of one international actor toward another as interventionary whenever the form of the behaviour constitutes a sharp break with then-existing forms and whenever it is directed at changing or preserving the structure of political authority in the target society'.[9] While this formulation tries to narrow the subject from other forms of international activity, it does so in an overly restrictive way. It has a built-in bias toward the examination of military interventions. The latter are the most obvious departures from existing patterns of behaviour which are directed towards the authority structures of target states. Yet, it is not always clear when a conventional mode of behaviour has been broken. Nor is it always plain whether authority structures are the target of such unconventional behaviour. Activities like foreign aid are excluded from consideration although they can indeed fall within the boundaries of the definition. For example, the arms deal between the Soviet ally, Czechoslovakia, and Egypt in 1955 represented a sharp break with the existing norms of behaviour, but whether it aimed at preserving or changing the political authority structure in Cairo can be verified only by assessing the motives of Soviet decision-makers, something which Rosenau explicitly seeks to avoid. In short, Rosenau's definition seems to omit a great deal of behaviour that seems relevant to the subject.

A third perspective is provided by Richard Little. Concerned to avoid the limited focus of Rosenau's approach, Little offers a three-sided conception of intervention: 'An interventionary situation exists when an actor responds to an intervention stimulus. The stimulus emerges when conflict develops between the units in a bifurcated actor, creating a potential for system transformation. Maintaining a relationship with one side of a bifurcated actor constitutes an intervention response: maintaining a relationship with both sides of a bifurcated actor constitutes a non-intervention response.'[10] For Little, then, internal division, conflict and the potential for system transformation are the three conditions necessary to describe a situation in which intervention develops. This formulation, however, encounters substantial problems. In a sense, it is both too narrow and too broad. Too narrow in that Little specifically links the act of intervention to conflict within a bifurcated target state. Such a perspective strains the commonsense usage of the word. For example, under Little's definition, activities like the Bay of Pigs incursion of 1961 or the Israeli–French–British operation against Egypt in 1956 would not be classified as interventions because neither Cuba nor Egypt were bifurcated actors at the time. Too broad in that the definition is vague in distinguishing interventionary behaviour from other types of international action. Intervention is couched in terms of 'response'. This suggests a lack of volition on the part of the intervener. Moreover, one is tempted to ask what type of 'response' is an interventionary response? 'Maintaining a relationship with one side of a bifurcated actor' seems woolly in the extreme. It does not tell us anything about the power relationship between the intervener and intervened. Further, it implies that intervention is synonymous with any inter-action involving a state and one side of a bifurcated target state.

In view of these difficulties, there is no need to pile definition upon definition. Plainly, the term intervention suffers from a lack of conceptual clarity. But there is little sign that the concept is falling into disuse. That is because it has an empirical existence as well as an evaluative one. Interventions touch on moral and legal issues, but they also find expression in the activities of identifiable human beings. The Soviet Union for instance, until the Soviet–Yugoslav declaration of March 1988,[11] maintained a *de facto* doctrine of intervention. For Soviet observers, intervention (Russian: interventsiya) generally connoted an authoritative interference by a state(s) 'in affairs within the domestic jurisdiction of another state'.[12] But, while Moscow consistently argued that Soviet activities in the international arena fell outside the scope of this definition, it nevertheless recognised the validity of intervention in certain circumstances. One such circumstance was when 'forces that are hostile to socialism' tried to promote 'the restoration of a capitalist regime' in a socialist country. This, it was said, 'becomes not only a problem of the people concerned, but a common problem and concern of all socialists'.[13] The Brezhnev doctrine, as it became known, was first propounded as an *ex post facto* justification for the Soviet intervention in Czechoslovakia in August 1968.

The Soviet example has two important ramifications. One is that we cannot afford to ignore intervention since what is represented by the term will not go away (however much we may wish it). The other is because intervention is used to describe such a diverse range of activities in international politics it is unlikely that any single definition can capture the entire reality. Therefore, the search for an all-encompassing definition acceptable to all reasonable persons will remain an elusive one. From our discussion, however, we can at least identify some of the major features of the concept. These are outlined below, not as a stack of fully developed elements, but as a set of guidelines in need of further empirical elaboration:

1 If a state intervenes in the affairs of another, it wants to achieve some political, moral or legal objective(s). The act is an instrument of action, a means, not an end.
2 The power relationship between the intervening state and the target society is perceived to be unequal. The intervener believes its power to be superior than that of the object of the intervention.
3 Intervention represents a clear departure from the existing pattern of relations both for the intervener and the target society.
4 From the perspective of the intervener, intervention is intended to be limited in scope and time.
5 The objective of the intervener is more often than not connected with changing or preserving the structure of political authority in the target society. Such an aspiration may or may not involve the use of military force.
6 The dividing line between intervention and non-intervention is not marked by objective criteria. The difference rests on intention.[14]

We are dealing, therefore, with a situation where a state or a combination of states deviate from the norm of existing relations and attempts to impose its will on a nation, perceived as being weaker, in order to realise some political, moral or legal objective within a limited period of time.

Intervention as an instrument of policy

For a state to intervene in the affairs of another, there must be both the motive and opportunity to do so.[15] The motives of a state are shaped by a broad range of interests. At the domestic level, these include: defence interests such as the protection of a state and its citizens against the perceived threat of physical violence from outside; ideological interests such as the promotion or preservation of a set of values which the people of a state share; economic interests such as a concern to acquire or to preserve access to resources; institutional and elite group interests such as the projection of organisational goals in a state's policy-making process by entities like the Foreign Ministries, political parties, trade unions and military establishments. At the external level, there are: strategic or world order interests such as the maintenance of a state's security in the context of the global distribution of power; regional interests such as a concern with contiguous areas perceived as having a bearing upon the well-being of a state.

Taken together, these interests form the broad context within which the motive to intervene evolves. The extent to which they are present will vary from one state to the next. Their definition or interpretation, however, will also depend in some measure on the emotional disposition[16] of the policy-maker(s). Certain factors have been known to affect the inclination to intervene. One is the susceptibility of the policy-maker to historical analogy. In 1956, Anthony Eden, the British Prime Minister, developed a psychological commitment to intervention in Egypt. This was because Eden's experience as Foreign Secretary during the 1930s, when Britain pursued an unsuccessful policy of appeasement towards Nazi Germany, predisposed him to perceive a strict parallel between Nasser's charismatic leadership and that of the Hitler dictatorship.[17] In addition, domestic difficulties such as poor economic performance or political divisions can hasten the search for a foreign distraction. The Argentinian intervention in the Falkland Islands in April 1982 was, amongst other things, an attempt to disarm domestic opposition to military repression and rally the nation behind the new junta led by President Galtieri. Furthermore, there may be the perceived need to respond to an action or gesture on the part of one state which has belittled or humiliated another. In April 1980, following the failure of negotiations to secure the release of American hostages seized by student supporters of Ayatollah Khomeini, the Carter administration felt it necessary to mount an abortive attempt to free the hostages through military intervention.[18]

These motives provide a necessary but not a sufficient condition for intervention. How a state 'goes in', when a state 'goes in' and whether in fact it will 'go in' depends usually on another factor. This factor is the opportunity to intervene. And, whilst some policy-makers may act blindly on their emotions, it is fair to assume that some kind of rational assessment will be made before doing so. This assessment will be based on the objective conditions in which the action will take place. Some conditions conducive to intervention can be pinpointed:

The possession of recognisable power

Interventions are characterised by unequal power structures. If a state is to intervene, it must have power resources that are both superior and clearly apparent to policy-makers in the target environment. But what is power? Power is generally defined as the ability to affect the will and mind of others irrespective of their wishes. The term can be distinguished from that of influence which may be seen as the ability to induce others, through non-military means, to do what we wish them to do.[19] Thus, power can be exercised simply on the initiative of one side and, for this reason, is central to intervention. However, attempts to influence events may be found before and after the initial act of intervention. Most states have two types of capability at their disposal. The first is physical. It includes elements like geography, demography and economic development. The second is qualitative, that of political culture. This refers to the structure of values and norms which give coherence to the operation of political institutions and organisation within a society.[20]

Dependency

Extreme dependence of one state upon another may provide a springboard for intervention. Although nominally sovereign, a state may be dependent for a variety of reasons such as the inadequacy of its resources or the inadequate nature of internal support for the regime. In all cases, however, the effect is to limit, to differing degrees, the freedom of manoeuvre of the state's policy-makers. The experience of the Marxist government of Salvador Allende is instructive. Allende's attempts to reduce Chile's economic dependence on the US by nationalising American-owned copper mines and increasing trade with several Communist states drew a hostile response from the Nixon administration. Interventionary measures included a credit blockade and substantial Central Intelligence Agency (CIA) funding to the major opponents of Allende.[21] Such measures had the intended effect. In September 1973, with the Chilean economy reduced to chaos, President Allende was overthrown in a military coup.

Political crisis in the target state

There are at least three kinds of political crisis likely to serve as stimuli for intervention:

Overt crisis This depicts a situation where 'rival political forces have arisen willing and able to use violence'[22] without being strong enough, individually, to give the government decisive support or to overthrow it. In such crisis, legitimate authority is absent and force becomes the norm for implementing decisions. As we shall see, Ethiopia experienced an overt crisis after the deposition of Emperor Haile Selassie in September 1974. A combination of violent power struggles inside the revolutionary government and widespread rebellions brought the country to the verge of chaos by early 1977. These were the circumstances in which the besieged government of Lieutenant Colonel Mengistu Haile Mariam looked to and received, in the form of Soviet–Cuban military intervention, external assistance for the resolution of internal problems.

Latent crisis The term refers to a situation wherein a political or social minority rule in a way which the mass populace detests but which they are too weak to overthrow.[23] The antagonism typically reveals itself when the government becomes embroiled in a conflict with another party, but gets only limited support from its own populace, thereby necessitating outside intervention. A case in point was South Vietnam following the outbreak of a communist-backed insurrection in 1959. Unable to rally much support from the indigenous, largely peasant population, the corrupt regimes of Ngo Dinh Diem and its successor, Nguyen Van Thieu, depended on

American military intervention to prosecute the war with North Vietnam.

Power vacuum   This occurs when there has been a rapid dismantlement of the traditional political order with no nationally based political movement ready to fill the breach.[24] The result is likely to be civil war with little or no prospect of a decisive outcome, short of foreign intervention on the side of one of the contending political groups. A situation of this type was evident in Angola after the unexpectedly swift collapse of the Portuguese dictatorship in 1974. During the transitional period to independence, fighting broke out between the Popular Movement for the Liberation of Angola (MPLA), on the one hand, and the Union for the Total National Liberation of Angola (UNITA) and the Front for the National Liberation of Angola (FNLA), on the other.[25] All three drew their support from the ethnic–linguistic cleavages dividing Angola. As a consequence, the Soviet–Cuban military intervention in 1975–6, and the parallel lack of US support for the FNLA and UNITA, proved decisive in determining the outcome of the civil war.

Popularity of the intervener

Policy-makers may be inclined towards intervention if they believe it would be popularly received in the target society. Several things may affect such judgements. First, a history of cultural, religious, ethnic or ideological links may make a relationship 'special' (at least to the intervener) and engender optimistic expectations. Second, a belief that the ruling regime in the target society is widely unpopular. Third, the perception of an identity of interest between the intervener and the general political opposition in the target society. If some or all of those factors are present, the intervener may view its role as that of national 'saviour' or 'deliverer'. In this connection, the American decision to intervene in Grenada in October 1983 probably reflected the expectation that such an action would be broadly welcomed by a people with memories of a democratic mode of government. Suffice it to say, the populist hopes of the intervener are not always realised.

So far we have discussed, in somewhat abstract terms, the motivation to intervene and the circumstances that favour it. We must now consider the inter-play between the subjective and objective elements characterising the interventionary situation.

The calculus of intervention

The use of intervention as a policy tool involves some risk. That is, there is a measure of uncertainty about the consequences of taking such an action. A willingness to engage in a risk situation assumes a high degree of belief about the likely gains or losses from the projected act and an estimate of the policy-makers' reaction in the target state or states allied to it. The first part of the formula centres on the notion of probability. This implies rational decision-making. It is necessary, however, to be clearer on what we mean by rationality in an interventionary context. How can a potential intervener measure its resources when some are physical, some ambiguous, some constantly changing and others are intangible? If one is to 'cumulate the components of power one must assess the relative importance of each component, and such an assessment can only be made by referring to the goals which power is designed to serve'.[26] It is the policy-makers who make such assessments. We can only assume rationality, therefore, insofar as these individuals may be 'misinformed, adventurous, primitive, reckless, overcautious or appeasing' but they share the characteristic that 'they do not want to lose'.[27]

Why, then, is it difficult for policy-makers to estimate the consequences of intervention? The answer largely lies in the complex nature of power. Power is a very general concept and has many dimensions, one of which is force. The ability of a state to impose its will upon another may or may not be advanced by the possession of military force. This will depend on whether the military instrument can be related to the particular ends of policy and also how this capability relates to that which others possess. With regard to the former point, it must be said that the refinement and accumulation of military might does not by itself ensure a freedom to intervene. The superpowers, for example, have a profound difficulty in relating their nuclear weapons to concrete political objectives, other than mutual deterrence. On the one hand, fear of anything approaching a nuclear war has encouraged the superpowers to some extent to avoid situations which might otherwise bring them to the brink of hostilities. On the other hand, because mutual destruction is assured in the event of a nuclear war, the superpowers believe that the possibility of such a war can be more or less discounted and that they now have greater scope for intervention than obtained previously.[28]

The paradox of superpower has been clearly evident in the Third World. This area has been coveted by both great powers. The many

Third World states that have been comparatively weak, unstable and riven by internal conflicts and tensions have presented 'targets of opportunity'. Yet, for all their nuclear muscle, the superpowers have not always been able to convert their might into an effective basis for influence, threats or prescription.[29] Several things have stood in the way. First, because of the far-flung alliances of each superpower and because of the presumed effects that such actions would have on nuclear proliferation, neither superpower has employed physical nuclear compellence against non-nuclear states. Secondly, there has been a glaring disproportion between the stakes involved and the threatened measures. As one observer notes 'it is common wisdom that mosquitoes are not most effectively killed with heavy artillery',[30] particularly since the effort will make the giant look worse than its challenger(s). Thirdly, the global spread of nationalism has reinforced the will of many less developed states to resist external intervention. The experiences of the superpowers in Vietnam and Afghanistan have underlined that point. Other small states like Libya and Iran have also shown precious little restraint in relations with the major nuclear powers. Clearly, while military force is often important in the act of intervention, it is not, even in its nuclear form, without its limitations as an instrument of policy.

This takes us to the second part of the equation. The utility of military force must be put in the context of other forms of power. Here, several developments have challenged traditional thinking. One concerns the changing balance of economic power within the international system. The 1970s witnessed the emergence of the Organisation of Petroleum Exporting Countries (OPEC) in the world economy. The political repercussions were far–reaching. Many OPEC nations and their allies were able to use their newly swollen oil revenues to finance technological and educational transformations, and import substantial quantities of sophisticated military hardware from the West and the USSR.[31] In this way, a number of Third World countries not only reduced their vulnerability to external intervention but also developed regional aspirations of their own. In addition, America's economic power relative to others has waned in the last decade. Compared to the fifties and sixties, when US economic pre-eminence was unassailable, the gap between Washington and her major economic competitors has now narrowed significantly.[32] The European Economic Community (EEC) has emerged as a serious rival in the fields of aviation and space technology while Japan has become a world leader in electronics and a near equal in car manufacturing and computers. Furthermore, and not unrelated to this, international life has seen a steady growth in economic interdependence. This has found expression, for instance, in the increasing involvement of socialist countries in what was once regarded as a repugnant international order. During the 1970s and 1980s, Soviet bloc countries have imported substantial quantities of Western technology, capital and, in the Russian case, American and Australian grain. For its part, the Soviet Union dramatically increased the export of oil and energy-related products to Western Europe.[33] Such a trend has recently intensified since, in the words of Gorbachev, 'all of us are in the same boat, and we must behave so that it does not capsize'.[34]

Thus, the importance of these developments is that they complicate the logic of military power. In particular, the proliferation of international links has increased the scope for disagreement within the two main Alliance systems. For example, in 1983, the Reagan administration's attempt to impose sanctions to delay or prevent the construction of the Yamal natural-gas pipeline, bringing Soviet gas to Western Europe from Urengoy, Siberia, was effectively resisted by America's allies, West Germany, France and Britain, all of whom had a financial stake.[35] Such an example indicates that the ability of a state to impose its will upon another frequently requires a diversity of resources. If a state has a mix of capabilities, we can expect it to shape its target environment. Often, though, recourse to intervention is born out of a failure to influence – and this is why it presents grave risks for policy-makers. The ability to embark on an intervention is not the same as the capacity to sustain the venture. The former usually requires a predominantly military capability, the latter involves a military capability plus a wide range of other resources (economic, administrative, political etc.) to neutralise or win the support of the population in the target state. Conquest, then, is not automatically control.[36]

Finally, the issue 'to intervene or not to intervene'[37] is affected, in some degree, by an assessment of the policy-makers' reaction in the target state, and those states allied to it. In many cases, interventions are launched in the belief that the adversary state will not respond or only respond in a minimal fashion (i.e., verbal condemnation). At the state level, two factors tend to shape policy-makers' assessments. First, there is the impact of ideology upon perceptions. Adherence to Marxism–Leninism certainly affected the decision of the Soviet government to make what was an unsuccessful intervention in Poland in 1920. The action was based on the false assumption that the Polish workers would support the intervention on class grounds. Secondly, the quality of information available to policy-makers will affect their perceptions. Time pressures, inadequate communications, censorship, lack of competent advisers or intelligence sources may produce faulty information and hence misperception. In April 1961, the Kennedy administration sent an interventionary force of 1,200 Cuban exiles to the Bay of Pigs, Cuba. According to the CIA, the intervention would trigger a general uprising in the country and the eventual overthrow of the Castro regime. This intelligence proved to be disastrously wrong. The exiles were defeated within days of landing.[38]

The international climate also figures in policy-makers' assessments. The relationship, however, between the international atmosphere and the risks of intervention is not a simple one. For instance, a co-operative international mood like Soviet–American *détente* may encourage a state to embark upon a 'low-risk' intervention where the adversary state has only an indirect interest. Although the action may not be dangerous in the specific instance, it may leave a 'residue which increases the risk-taking readiness of the opponent'[39] in future situations. Of course, the 'residue of resolve' may not be known to the intervening state and this, combined with the apparent success of the 'low-risk' action, will also produce a heightened risk-taking propensity. Consequently, the seeds of a future confrontation will have been sown from one event or a succession of events which, in themselves, are of a 'low-risk' nature. To some extent, the tough American reaction to Soviet intervention in Afghanistan developed along these lines.

Therefore, for the policy-maker contemplating intervention, optimal conditions – low risk and minimal cost – are rare. This fact moved one observer to note that 'nobody enters a risk situation without calculating what to do if the situation worsens'.[40] Yet, this is only true in the most general sense. It may be prudent for a policy-maker to draw up scenarios that include worst-case possibilities, but such projections have a limited utility. They are based on partial information and may, therefore, rest on erroneous assumptions. In short, it is impossible for the intervener to calculate the element of surprise out of the interventionary equation. The decision to 'go in' rests on political judgement.

The path to disengagement

In analytical terms, it is difficult to separate the notion of disengagement from intervention. It is almost a *doppelgänger* idea which fits on the back of intervention.[41] It is a derivative term used to describe the point where intervention ends. In practice, disengagement usually involves the withdrawal or substantial reduction of the intervener's personnel, whether they be troops, technicians, military/political advisers, from or in the target state.

There are three senses in which we speak of a state disengaging. First, the process may occur after the objective(s) of intervention have been achieved. In 1984–5, for example, the US systematically reduced its military presence in Grenada after intervening to overthrow the revolutionary government and initiating steps to restore multi-party democracy in that country.[42] Secondly, disengagement can refer to 'an essentially defensive technique for tactically avoiding the worst consequences of perceived failure'.[43] A case in point was South Africa's decision to cut its losses in the Angolan civil war in January 1976. The strength of the Soviet–Cuban-backed MPLA offensive and the Western unwillingness to back Pretoria's 'struggle against communism'[44] convinced South Africa that Angola was a 'no-win' situation. Thirdly, disengagement depicts situations where withdrawal has become a necessity. On the one hand, this may include states who originally requested external involvement but subsequently had a change of mind and expelled the foreign mission. The exodus of something like 15,000 Soviet advisers from Egypt in July 1972 falls into this category. On the other hand, obligatory disengagement may cover situations where the intervening force has collapsed or experienced military defeat. This included, for instance, the fruitless efforts of the Libyan army on behalf of the Idi Amin government during the Ugandan–Tanzanian conflict of 1979.

But if, as we have argued, intervention is primarily the product of two factors – motivation and opportunity – it follows that disengagement, at least in its negative meanings, is due to the erosion of one or both of these factors. Several variables can be said to have an adverse effect on these elements:

Bureaucratic pressures

The act of intervention requires a relatively sophisticated level of administration. Planning is essential to the formulation of the operation. Equally, co-ordination and communication are vital after the act. Nevertheless, bureaucracy can be something of a 'necessary evil' for policy-makers. Bureaucratic forces may subvert the goals of an intervention. For one thing, if military force is involved, the commitment can be enlarged beyond original expectations.[45] Let us imagine, for example, an initial shipment of heavy weaponry to a seriously threatened, but weak target state (or to one of the actors within it). Once enacted, this decision involved a back-up service of spare parts and replacements. But, since the recipient has only limited technical expertise, it is necessary for the intervener to send technicians to perform the service. This, in turn, raises the question of the security of the foreign personnel and equipment. Gradually, the intervention begins to outgrow its original purpose(s) as the policy-makers become the passengers rather than the drivers of a bureaucratic machine carried forward by the momentum of its own procedure. In some ways, US involvement in Vietnam conformed to this pattern. In June 1963, the Kennedy administration had about 14,000 non-combat military personnel in South Vietnam. Their purpose was to provide training in anti-guerrilla warfare techniques. By April 1969, four months after Nixon had assumed the Presidency, the US commitment had stretched to the deployment of 543,000 combat troops in Vietnam.[46]

Moreover, intervention is subject to goal displacement. This is not the same as bureaucratic drift in that these objectives are derived from a conscious identity associated with membership of a particular organisation. If an organisation's definition of an interventionary situation differs from that of the policy-makers', then, it may use its resources (assuming they are relevant) to impose its viewpoint. In interventions, we might expect institutions like military establishments, intelligence agencies and certain governmental ministries to assert their interests. This happened, for example, during the Russian civil war. Although Lloyd George, the British Prime Minister, initially expressed sympathy for the new Bolshevik regime, his views were not shared by the Foreign Office. Consequently, when Lloyd George tried to terminate a military intervention originally designed to protect some Czechoslovakian divisions from German attack behind Russian lines, he encountered resistance. Instead, the War Office (who shared the Foreign Office view) suggested that Allied troops be used against the Bolsheviks. Thus, the 'intervention was transformed from an anti-German to an anti-Bolshevik venture'.[47]

Political impermeability

It is easy to over-estimate the impact of an intervening nation upon a target society. As noted, the use of external force alone rarely achieves political objectives. For a state to legitimise its intervention, it must win or build political support in the target environment. Ideally, this should be a political party or institution. In this vein, the USSR, following its intervention in Afghanistan, sought to construct a 'progressive' infrastructure by, amongst other things, training some cadres of the Afghanistan People's Democratic Party. Failing this, the intervener might cultivate a political faction or group to serve as a 'puppet' regime. Such arrangements however, do not always facilitate effective penetration. First, if the target state has an independent tradition, the act of intervention may only serve to unify otherwise divided political groups, thus isolating the new 'puppet' regime. Secondly, if the intervention is a unilateral one, it is possible that the action will not be supported by the intervener's allies and may be subject to international condemnation. This, in turn, will strengthen political opposition in the target country. Thirdly, societal differences such as race, language, religion and culture may severely restrain the activities of the intervener and, by association, its 'puppet' regime. If, for example, the mere appearance of foreign troops or personnel provokes a hostile response the loyalties of 'fellow travellers' are likely to be shaken or divided. Such supporters may become untrustworthy in the eyes of the intervening power.

The manipulation of an external presence

In cases where intervention is genuinely at the request of the target country, the intervener finds itself in a paradoxical position: it can pursue its objectives without having to worry about legitimising its presence, but the terms of entry are defined by the host country. In effect, this means that the activities of the intervener are constrained by the requirements of the target state which can withdraw the legitimacy it has bestowed if it so wishes. To avoid this constraint, the intervener may try to establish a power-base in the target environment that is independent of the existing regime there. Such 'meddling', however, is extremely risky and can result in the very sanction which the intervener is trying to insure against, namely, expulsion from the target state. The Soviet experience in Egypt during the early 1970s seems relevant here. Having established a desperately needed air-defence system in Egypt in 1970, the USSR gained substantial military privileges and had nearly 15,000 troops stationed there. Yet, despite all this, the Soviets had relatively few links with the domestic political scene in Egypt. That point assumed critical importance after the death of Nasser in September 1970. The new President, Anwar Sadat, initiated a dialogue with Washington, strengthened his internal position by dismissing the pro-Soviet Vice-President Ali Sabry and then, in July 1972, expelled the Soviet contingent from Egypt.[48]

When pieced together, these three factors demonstrate how an intervention can become something of a blunt instrument. On such occasions, however, there is no automatic switch to disengagement, for policy-makers are generally reluctant to pull out once committed. The view could be taken that a government should keep all its commitments, however ill-chosen in the first place. From that standpoint, it would be very difficult to reverse an interventionary commitment because this constitutes a 'symbolic demonstration of a country's dedication to principles'.[49] Vacillation may follow as policy-makers postpone a decision in the hope that future events will improve the situation. This was evident to some extent in America's involvement in Vietnam. By 1968 it was clear that domestic discontent over the conflict in the US inhibited the single-minded pursuit of the original goal – to 'save South Vietnam from communism'. But considerations like 'selling out' an ally and the lingering belief that the conflict might somehow be won delayed a termination of the commitment until 1973.

Despite the constraints, disengagement does take place. At some point, the initial assumptions supporting the intervention break down, and a new definition of the situation is introduced. This process does not happen overnight. Those policy-makers with a behavioural commitment,[50] that is one motivated primarily by political expediency, will be the most likely to revise their position first. But those who are psychologically committed[51] to the intervention may continue to rationalise discordant information until a threshold is reached where the sheer weight and volume of this information 'unfreezes' the rationalisation process, and re-evaluation takes place. Clearly, when both de-commitments coincide, disengagement becomes a distinct possibility for the intervener.

What factors, therefore, tilt policy-makers toward disengagement? There are at least four:

The recovery of costs Disengagement becomes an option if the probability exists that the costs incurred by withdrawal will be recovered elsewhere. This element was almost certainly present in Soviet calculations about Iran in 1946. In May of that year, the USSR finally withdrew its troops from northern Iran, some two months after the deadline for the evacuation of all foreign troops from the country. The move was prompted by strong pressure from Britain and the US, who had completed their troop removal from Iran. At that stage, Stalin did not want to jeopardise his plans for Soviet influence in Eastern Europe by straining East–West relations to breaking point. From the Soviet standpoint, the costs of leaving Iran in 1946 were offset by the prospect of securing Eastern Europe.[52]

Mutual agreement   The possibility of an arrangement on the basis of mutual agreement strengthens the case for disengagement. Admittedly, this condition is rarely present. Intervening states pull out often because they are forced to, or else because they perceive they will be forced out at some future date. However, when withdrawal is carried out on a reciprocal basis, the costs are decreased for both parties. For the state who has been on the receiving end, the arrangement is likely to reduce the chances of another incursion in the future. The Austrian State Treaty of May 1955 is an example of a lasting, negotiated withdrawal involving four countries, the USSR, USA, Britain and France. For the intervener, the benefits include a lowering of political costs in that it does not compromise credibility and makes for favourable relations with the post-intervention regime in the target country. Moreover, this type of agreement may bring considerable prestige when linked to other issues (i.e., 'our intervention brought them to the negotiating table to discuss the border problem').

The political imperative   The belief that the political system of the intervener is capable of functioning or might function better after disengagement enhances the prospects for a withdrawal. This issue is a vital one since it can involve the life of a government. In 1958, for example, a nationalist rebellion in what was then French Algeria occasioned a political crisis in France. The rebellion, coming in the wake of French withdrawals from Indochina and Suez, strengthened the resolve of the French Army, many French Algerians and some Paris-based politicians, that France must remain in Algeria.[53] Consequently, when the French government appeared to be on the verge of ordering a disengagement in May 1958, the Army seized control of Algeria and precipitated the fall of the Fourth Republic. Nevertheless, disengagement may be seen as an essential step to improve the workings of the intervener's political system. In this regard, there was widespread concern in the US during the late 1960s that intervention in Vietnam was tearing America apart and actually threatening the democratic process. President Nixon recognised this and gradually steered the US to the 1973 disengagement.

The learning process The process of learning from historical situations may shape the decision to disengage. The process has been explained in terms of 'the economy of cognition' whereby 'the trial and error explorations of one member serve to save others the trouble of entering the same blind alleys'.[54] While it is doubtful that the process has advanced this far in a foreign-policy setting, there are indications that it is present. For example, President Reagan sometimes justified military aid to the 'Contra' rebels, opposed to the Sandinista regime in Nicaragua, on the grounds that it would prevent deployment of US troops and hence a repetition of another 'Vietnam'. Equally, in the case of the USSR, there have been signs of ideological feedback. After the sometimes unproductive military entanglements in the Third World under Brezhnev, Gorbachev's government has revived the Leninist notion that the cutting-edge of Soviet foreign policy now depends as much on the performance of the Soviet economy as it does on military strength.[55] The impact of the learning process, however, should not be exaggerated. Differing historical, cultural, ideological and social traditions retard the exchange of experiences. In this vein, it is instructive that Gorbachev has categorically rejected any parallel between Soviet intervention in Afghanistan and US intervention in Vietnam as 'artificial'.[56]

Thus the path to intervention and from intervention to disengagement is rarely a smooth one. More often than not it is a tortuous one. Policy-makers in the intervening state may agonise over the decision to go in. Moreover, having intervened, a government may then face a protracted period in which there are oscillations between times of severe doubt and renewed optimism for the operation. Eventually, the logic of getting out asserts itself. To point up some of the features of this course, as we have, is not to advance a theory or a model of intervention and disengagement. Rather, it is simply to provide a conceptual framework through which to view Soviet activities in the Horn of Africa between 1970 and 1978.

Part I

Motivational Aspects

2   The evolution of a Soviet interest

Historical tradition in the context of international relations is a poorly
explored subject ... Even so, it is not something intangible. On the
contrary, one has to accept as 'weighty' those feelings – often noted
in history – of traditional friendship and sympathy between countries
which contribute to their mutual trust, understanding and co-
operation.

Ethiopia and the Soviet Union (formerly Russia) are bound by this
kind of longstanding and deep-rooted friendship. Its origins go well
beyond the Great October Revolution.

(A. Khrenkov, 'Deep Roots', *Asia and Africa Today*, no. 1,
1985, p. 59)

The Horn of Africa is a metaphor rather than a political entity. It has no
precise boundaries but is often thought to comprise Ethiopia, Somalia
and Djibouti, the tiny, former French colony. These territories lie
between the Middle East and black Africa, forming a bridge between
the two. The geo-political significance of the area should not be
understated. The Horn flanks the oil states of Arabia, controls the Bab
el Mandeb Straits which are a busy international shipping lane,
dominates part of the Gulf of Aden through which oil tankers pass,
and overlooks the passages where the Red Sea, the Gulf of Aden and
the Indian Ocean converge (see Map 1).

A Russian interest in the Horn dates back to very early times. An
awareness of Ethiopia began with the translation of certain Greek
works such as Epiphanius's *Periplus of the Erythrean Sea* into Old
Slavonic and the Caucasian languages.[1] In the fourteenth century
contacts between Ethiopian monks and Copts, as well as Armenians,
were established through various religious communities in Jerusalem.
These clerical links were reinforced in the fifteenth century when
Armenians journeyed to Ethiopia, and played a prominent role in the
political and diplomatic affairs of the country.[2] The same century also

25

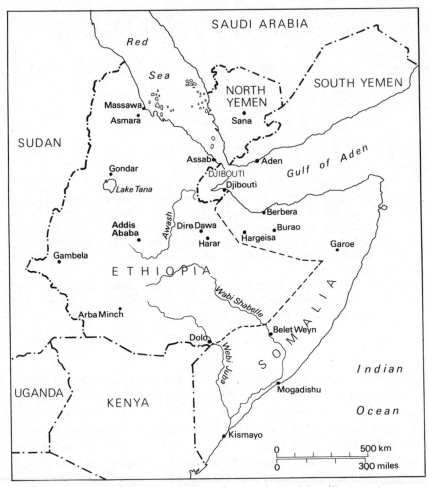

Map 1. The Horn of Africa. *Source*: Central Intelligence Agency, Washington D.C., USGPO, 1987.

saw the first visit of a Great Russian to the Horn of Africa: the merchant Afanasy Nikitin of Tver spent a few days in Somalia on his way back from India in the 1470s.[3] Further information about Ethiopia was gained though a succession of Russian visitors to Jerusalem where they observed the Ethiopian colony's religious services.[4] By the eighteenth century Ethiopia found its way into some Russian general travel and geography books.[5] Then, during the 1850s, a Russian monk, Porfify Uspensky, who headed the Russian Orthodox Mission in Jerusalem, enthusiastically wrote about the prospects that Christian

Ethiopia offered the tsarist empire as a base for expanding Russian influence in Africa.[6]

The tsarist period

However, it is not until the second half of the nineteenth century, when the European powers extended their influence into the Horn of Africa, that Russia began to pay serious attention to Ethiopia. In particular, tsarist Russia was concerned with British penetration of the area. In 1868 Britain defeated Ethiopia in the Battle of Magdala. Seven years later, London purchased a controlling share in the Suez Canal Company. This caused the Russians considerable anxiety about maintaining free access to the Canal. Such fears were fuelled by the closing of the Canal during the Russo–Turkish war of 1877. The British military occupation of Egypt in 1882 confirmed British dominance over Suez. For Russia, these reverses in the Canal region underlined the strategic case for access to the Red Sea via Ethiopia. This objective held out the possibility of thwarting Britain's ambition of carving out a swath of imperial territory from the Cape of Good Hope to Cairo and, at the same time, maintaining a secure Suez lifeline to India. Moreover, Russian influence over the source of the Nile – Ethiopia – was potentially a powerful lever against British control of Egypt. By manipulating the Nile's sources, Egypt could be turned into a desert.[7]

Russia's interest in Ethiopia also had an economic aspect. Unlike the other European powers, imperial Russia was convinced that Ethiopia – or Abyssinia, as it was then known – had vast economic potential. A memorandum addressed to the Ministry of Foreign affairs listed the country's products as cotton, coffee, grain, butter, honey, hides and meat, and observed that 'the abundance of these products' as well as 'their low price, the plenitude of labour, the unusual richness of the soil . . . an extremely favourable position on the international trade route from Europe to the Orient, relative proximity to the sea with the construction of a railroad (the distance from Addis Ababa . . . to the sea is the same as that between Moscow and Petersburg) . . . should make Abyssinia a country of great world importance'. In short, Ethiopia was regarded as 'a country where the cream has yet to be skimmed'.[8]

The desire to make Ethiopia a Russian protectorate – 'Russia has the same right to it as others'[9] – led to a policy of support for Ethiopian nationalism as a means of undermining the rival European powers in the area. Such support took various forms. First, Russia was a generous supplier of arms and military advisers (usually Russian army officers) for Emperor Menelik II's army. This role began clandestinely before 1890, when Ethiopia was subject to an 1886 Anglo–French arms ban, but was regularised during the early 1890s. In 1891 Lieutenant V. F. Mashkov visited Ethiopia. Mashkov, a 'scientific' emissary of the Imperial Russian Geographic Society, reaffirmed Russian support for Ethiopian independence and made overtures to Menelik with respect to economic, military and religious 'protection'.[10] Thus, Mashkov had the distinction of being the first Russian to hold official talks with an African head of state. By doing so, he provided assurances that were instrumental in the development of Menelik's nationalist strategy.

This found expression in the stiffening of Menelik's resolve to resist foreign encroachment. Tension had developed between Ethiopia and Italy over the Treaty of Ucciali (1889). Italy interpreted the Treaty as legal grounds for declaring a protectorate over Ethiopia. Menelik's rejection of such claims culminated in a military confrontation at Adowa in March 1896. The outcome was a total victory for Menelik's army. Russian arms, as well as the strategic advice of Captain N. S. Leontev, who had come to Ethiopia in 1895 as part of an expedition headed by Captain A. N. Eliseyev, made a vital contribution.[11] Adowa marked a high spot in Russian–Ethiopian relations: Leontev was accorded an Ethiopian title and represented Menelik in post-war negotiations with the Italians. Russia, along with France who also supplied arms to Ethiopia, established a fully accredited diplomatic mission at Menelik's court.

Russian military aid also facilitated the massive expansion of the Ethiopian Empire. In 1887 Ethiopia annexed Harar, following the Egyptian withdrawal, and then absorbed the Somali-populated lands of the Haud and the Ogaden, both of which were officially under British protection.[12] By 1897, Ethiopia's new frontiers were codified, at least theoretically, through treaties with Britain and Italy. These treaties, however, were signed without the consent of the Somali clansmen (who had earlier placed themselves under British protection) and left a legacy of confusion for future Ethiopian–Somali relations (see Map 2).

In addition, Russia gave humanitarian assistance to Ethiopia. During the Italian–Ethiopian war, the Russian Red Cross Society dispatched a first-aid unit and subsequently established a hospital, the Menelik II, staffed by Russian doctors. This assistance, as Emperor Haile Selassie later confirmed, made a lasting impression on the Ethiopian people.[13] Russia also provided technical aid in gold mining operations and geological surveys in the Wollega Province as well as

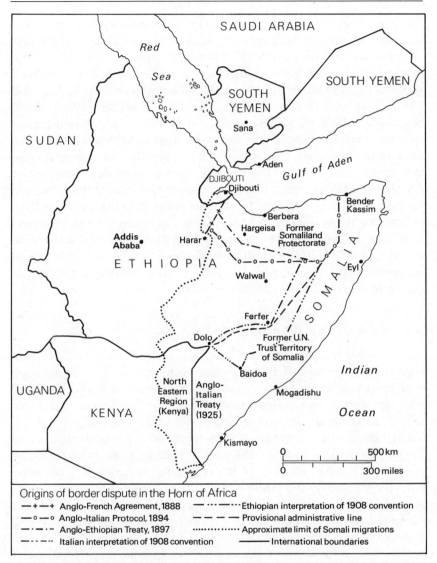

Map 2. The imperial partition of the Horn. *Source*: John Drysdale, The Somali Dispute. London: Pall Mall Press 1964, p. 24.

educational training for some Ethiopian students. Tekle Hawariat, who later pleaded the cause of Ethiopia before the League of Nations, was one of these students. In 1888, a *Beginner's Abyssinian–Russian Dictionary* was published in St Petersburg.[14]

Furthermore, Ethiopia became the scene of a large number of

Russian expeditions. Adventurers like the Cossack, N. I. Ashinov, scientists like the ethnographer N. N. Miklukho-Maklay and soldiers like the aforementioned V. F. Mashkov visited, investigated and reported on various parts of the country. Other expeditions included those of A. Gudzenko in 1896, A. K. Bulatovich in 1896–7, 1898 and 1899, L. K. Artamonov in 1898, K. N. Arnoldi in 1897–9, P. V. Shchasev in 1898, A. M. Dragomirov in 1899–1900 and N. Kurmakov in 1904.[15] While many of these missions had a political as well as an exploratory character, Ethiopia benefited directly and indirectly from the information derived. For example, topographic data supplied by Russian specialists strengthened the military position of the Ethiopian Empire. And, less tangibly, these missionary activities increased the international prestige of Addis Ababa. For many of the explorers wrote accounts of their travels, and this, in turn, aroused the attention of the academic world. A prolific Jewish scholar, B. A. Turayev, edited and published texts, articles and monographs on Ethiopia throughout the early years of the twentieth century.[16]

Soviet rule: the early period

After the revolutionary upheaval of 1917, the new Bolshevik regime initially showed little interest in Ethiopian affairs. Confronted with huge problems like the consequences of the First World War, civil war, revolution and Allied intervention, the Bolsheviks had every reason to distance themselves from the Ethiopian intrigues of the Tsars. There was, moreover, something of a political obstacle to Soviet–Ethiopian relations. Ethiopia had become a sanctuary for many prominent Russian émigrés – doctors, engineers, lawyers – evacuated from the Crimea by the White Army in 1920. Some of these specialists served as advisers to the Ethiopian government. A Russian lawyer compiled the first Ethiopian law codexes. The extent of the White Russian presence was reflected in the fact that Emperor Haile Selassie received Grand Duke Aleksander Mikhaylovich as his personal guest ('He liked to hear my stories of the reign of my relations because they helped him to decide what he should not do').[17]

Despite the difficulties, the Bolsheviks did not altogether discard their predecessors' concern with the Horn of Africa. Faced with the perceived threat of armed invasion by Britain and France, the Soviet government devised a strategy of undermining 'imperialism from the rear'.[18] The Bolsheviks calculated that by encouraging nationalist unrest in the colonies of the European powers they would undermine the 'imperialists'' ability to attack the USSR. This policy, however, necessitated a widening of the diplomatic net. In the 1920s, Moscow established diplomatic relations with Saudi Arabia and Yemen, and expressed a willingness to extend ties to the countries on the other side of the Red Sea, in the Horn. But when the Prince-Regent of Ethiopia in 1924 responded to this overture, efforts to start negotiations on restoring diplomatic relations were blocked by Britain and Italy.[19] A year later, in November 1925, the Ethiopian Consul, in a conversation with his Soviet counterpart, expressed a desire to start such talks but requested that their conversation 'remains absolutely secret in order to avoid a campaign on the part of the Entente'.[20]

In the early 1930s, Soviet diplomacy in the Horn began to bear some fruit in the sphere of trade. At the end of 1931, a representative of the Soviet foreign-trade corporation, Soyuzneftexport, conducted negotiations in French Somaliland and Addis Ababa with representatives of the Ethiopian government. These talks resulted in Moscow agreeing to sell Ethiopia a large consignment of oil products.[21] A year later, A. A. Yurev, a representative of the USSR People's Commissariat for Foreign Trade, held further negotiations in Ethiopia and noted a positive change in Ethiopia's attitude to the Soviet Union. Yurev reported that 'Ethiopia is taking a great interest in the USSR'.[22]

Moscow also established commercial ties with the then Italian colony of Eritrea. In the spring of 1931, A. E. Stupak, a representative of the Soviet trade organisation, Vostgostorg, in the Yemen, visited Eritrea. As a result of this, the USSR shipped 250 tons of sugar, 450 tons of wheat, 75 tons of flour, 100 crates of kerosene, 700 crates of petrol and 30 tons of coal to Eritrea.[23] In 1932 the USSR provided Eritrea with a third of all Eritrea's wheat imports for that year and a fifth of all its sugar imports. Stupak remained in Eritrea for three years, and made contacts with local firms in Djibouti, British Somaliland, Aden and Ethiopia. This paved the way for the export of Soviet goods (including sugar and flour) to Djibouti and Italian Somaliland.

The establishment of commercial ties in the Horn of Africa, although modest, was significant insofar as it served the interests of the Soviet state. However, by the mid-1930s, events in Europe reshaped Moscow's world view. The rise to power of Adolf Hitler in Germany, and the growth of Fascism elsewhere, changed the USSR's policies toward France and Britain. The 'united front from below' strategy was abandoned in favour of the pursuit of broad anti-Fascist coalitions.[24] This new policy manifested itself in the Soviet response to the Italian invasion of Ethiopia 1935–6, following the Walwal incident in 1934.

While the USSR was one of the first states to denounce Italian aggression and support Haile Selassie in the League of Nations – indeed it initially championed strong sanctions against Italy – it soon moderated its position once it became clear that neither Britain nor France would take decisive measures against Mussolini. Thus, Soviet support, apart from respecting the League's somewhat ineffective export ban on iron, ore, manganese and chromium to Italy, was largely verbal. Stalin did not make any major policy statements on the Italian Fascist occupation nor did he break Soviet ties with Italy. In fact, the only material support rendered was a Soviet gift of $5,000 to Ethiopia through the Red Cross.[25] In contrast, and despite its declared sympathies, the USSR supplied certain quantities of aid for Mussolini's war machine. During the conflict in Ethiopia, it shipped to Italy 91 per cent of her imported oats, some coal and slightly increased its exports of oil.[26] Moreover, ships of the Soviet merchant marine were hired for Italy's African transport. Altogether, trade with Italy constituted 5 per cent of the total Soviet trade exchange. Such an equivocal role was rationalised by the Soviet foreign minister in the League of Nations Assembly:

> The peoples of the Soviet Union cherish nothing but the greatest respect and sympathy for the Italian people. They are interested in the uninterrupted development and consolidation of their existing political, economic and cultural relations with Italy. Nevertheless, the Soviet government expressed its readiness to take part in general international action against Italy in defence of a country with which the Soviet Union had not even any relations whatever. At every stage of discussion of the Italo-Ethiopian conflict, my Government has declared that it would participate in any action provided for under the Covenant and adopted and executed jointly by other Members of the League.[27]

In practice, therefore, the USSR was unwilling to go it alone and sacrifice its relations for the sake of Ethiopia. There was, in Soviet eyes, a vast difference between Mussolini and Hitler, who was regarded as the main threat. And if, as became evident during the Abyssinian crisis, it was not possible to build an anti-Fascist coalition, local advantages were to be preserved, not sacrificed.

Covert support for Italy was not inconsistent with such considerations. The Italian colonies, Eritrea and Italian Somaliland, were the USSR's most reliable trading partners in the Horn during the 1930s.[28] Thus, the Soviet stand was nominally anti-Fascist, no more than that and, much less, anti-colonialist.

It was the Second World War rather than the Abyssinian crisis which changed the image of the USSR in Ethiopia. Faced with a Nazi onslaught, which at one point took the Germans to just twelve miles from Moscow, the Stalin government, now allied with Britain and the United States, rallied its people by identifying with the Russia of the great tsars. Saints and warriors of Imperial Russia were recalled and the Army regulations of Peter the Great were cited as a model. In April 1943, Stalin formally de-emphasised the international class struggle by disbanding Comintern. Five months later, on 4 September 1943, in what was a politically consonant act, Stalin rehabilitated the Russian Orthodox Church.[29] These measures impressed Emperor Haile Selassie and his White émigrés friends. Suspicion gave way to sympathy. On 1 July 1943 diplomatic relations between Ethiopia and the USSR were established. The tradition of mutual interest revived as Moscow established a sizeable diplomatic legation in Addis Ababa.

As far as the Emperor was concerned, a widening of diplomatic options was timely. After the Italian defeat and Haile Selassie's return in 1941, the pre-war borders of Ethiopia were not immediately restored. This proved to be a cause of considerable irritation in Addis Ababa. For under the terms of the Anglo–Ethiopian agreement of 31 January 1942, Britain recognised Ethiopian sovereignty over the Ogaden, but retained administrative control over the strategic city of Jijiga, the agricultural areas around it (the Reserve Areas) and the Haud, and the railway from Dire Dawa to the border of French Somaliland.[30] This British control was prompted by two factors. First, there was the need to prosecute the war still raging in northern Africa and Europe. Second, Britain had ideas of its own for the Ogaden and Haud territories. It should be recalled that Ethiopian control of these territories was not recognised, internationally, until the Treaties of 1897, and the Ethiopian–Italian Convention of 1908. And all of these agreements were ambiguous in the extreme (see Map 2).

The first treaty concluded between Britain and Ethiopia established the southern boundary of British Somaliland. While the position of the boundary was clear enough, the Treaty stipulated that the grazing rights of nomads from British Somaliland were to be respected in the Haud and the Reserved Area 'in the event of a possible occupation by Ethiopia'.[31] In effect, Britain obtained Ethiopian recognition for the new boundaries of British Somaliland without recognising Ethiopian sovereignty[32] over the territory which she had unilaterally relinquished.[33] As for the border between Italian Somalia and Ethiopia, neither the Ethiopian–Italian Treaty of 1897 or the Convention of 1908 succeeded in defining its exact location; the predictable result was that the Ethiopians claimed the border was closer to the coast than the Italians were willing to concede. This indeterminacy, temporarily superseded by the Italian conquest of Ethiopia, introduced serious strains into the British–Ethiopian relationship after 1941.

Many of the territories under British military administration, the Haud, the Ogaden and the former Italian colonies, Italian Somaliland and Eritrea, experienced a dramatic upswing in political activity during the war years. This was possible because the British permitted a measure of freedom of speech and association, previously denied. Moreover, in the Somali territories, the administration took an explicit pro-Somali stand. On 13 May 1943, the first Somali political organisation, the Somali Youth Club, was established in Mogadishu.[34] By 1946, it was estimated that the Club had no less than 25,000 affiliates. At the same time, in the Ogaden, and despite Ethiopian moves to win Somali favour, a campaign developed against the surrender of that territory to Ethiopia. Meanwhile, in Eritrea, where Britain had committed itself to eventually settling the status of the former colony through respecting the wishes of the majority of its people, political activities intensified.[35] By the end of 1945, three political parties had emerged: the Eritrean Independence Party, the Islamic League and the Unionist Party.

Viewed from Addis Ababa, the stirrings of Somali and Eritrean nationalism was a most unwelcome development. The British were said to have inspired it. The initial agreement to leave the Ogaden and the Haud under British control was dictated by the need of Haile Selassie to reestablish his control over the centre of the country. But by 1944 his position was more secure and he demanded the return of the Haud and the Ogaden, two areas which Ethiopia had never fully administered. In addition, the Emperor claimed all the adjacent colonies of Italy. For the moment, Britain did not cede to these demands. A further Anglo–Ethiopian agreement, signed in 1944, returned the Franco–Ethiopian railway to its pre-war status along with the British military cantonments in Ethiopia, but allowed the British military administration to continue in the Ogaden and Haud without prejudice to Ethiopia's ultimate sovereignty. This, however, did little to reassure the Emperor about British intentions in the area. The search for new allies began.

The cold war and the Horn of Africa

Encouraged by the discord between Ethiopia and Britain, the Soviet Union was quick to declare an interest in the fate of the former Italian colonies, then under British administration. When the question was raised at the summit meetings of allied leaders at Teheran, Yalta and Potsdam, the USSR sought a trusteeship over the territories in question.[36] This manoeuvre, however, was strongly opposed by Britain whose own proposal, the 'Bevin Plan', suffered a similar fate at the hands of the US, USSR and France. These powers, along with Britain, were charged with the responsibility of disposing of Libya, Eritrea and Italian Somaliland after Italy formally renounced its rights to the colonies at the Paris peace conference in June 1946.

Following its initial failure to establish a foothold in the Horn of Africa, Soviet involvement during Stalin's time was minimal. This was due to both internal and external factors. By 1947, the Kremlin's view of the world was sharply divided into two irreconcilable camps, that of socialism and capitalism.[37] Accordingly there could be no middle ground between the two camps. Short of aligning itself with the socialist world, a developing country was, by definition, reactionary and an ally of the 'imperialists'. Such a negative attitude won few friends in the developing world. The Horn was no exception. There was, however, an additional consideration. Ethiopia, then the only independent state in the region, gravitated toward America in the post-war period.[38]

In 1944, the US and Ethiopia established full diplomatic relations. Within months, an American citizen, John Spenser, was appointed as Emperor Haile Selassie's foreign-policy adviser. In 1945, an American company, Trans World Airlines, signed an agreement with the Ethiopian government for setting up Ethiopian Airlines.[39] And, despite the British presence in the Ogaden, the first concession for oil exploration there was granted to a US company, Sinclair.[40] The Ethiopian–American connection grew out of mutual need. For the Emperor, the absence of a direct say in the settlement of the old Italian colonies, and the need to dislodge the British from the Ogaden and the Haud, made Washington the most likely guardian of its local interests. To the United States, Ethiopia appeared to be an important buffer in Africa against the perceived global threat of Soviet communism. It had several attractions. Firstly, it had potential location and physical characteristics needed for a major communications centre. Secondly, it could serve as a convenient link in the air routes towards India and the

Far East. Thirdly, Ethiopia, as the oldest independent African country, was seen as a useful point of contact between the United States and a continent long dominated by the European colonial powers.[41]

The convergence of Ethiopian and US interests had a profound effect on the post-war settlement in the Horn of Africa. In September 1948, Britain bowed to joint Ethiopian–American pressure and withdrew from the Ogaden. Amongst other things, Emperor Haile Selassie skilfully exploited Washington's economic interest in the area to pressurise Britain. Without the support of its closest ally, and lacking the financial wherewithal to continue the military occupation, Britain decided to leave despite the known strength of Somali feeling on the matter. The President of the Somali Youth League, formed in 1947, had already formulated a programme of Somali reunification that was to include the Ogaden. When the British decision to 'return' the territory to Ethiopia was announced, a riot ensued in which twenty-five Somalis lost their lives. The eventual transfer of the territory was eased through a British disbursement of £91,000 amongst the Ogaden clansmen.[42]

The future of the Italian colonies was not decided until 1950. The whole issue had been placed in the hands of the United Nations' (UN) General Assembly after the Four Powers failed to reach any agreement. It was decided to grant Libya independence and place Somaliland under a ten-year Italian trusteeship, after which it too would become independent. But the UN found it more difficult to settle Eritrea's future. Opinion on Eritrea was sharply divided between those who favoured union with Ethiopia, the Unionist Party, and those seeking independence, the Muslim League. Eventually, a second UN commission of inquiry produced a majority report recommending close association with Ethiopia. This verdict, coupled with the diplomatic support of the US and its allies, resulted in United Nations Resolution 390 A (V), passed on 2 December 1950. According to the resolution, Eritrea was to be an autonomous unit federated with Ethiopia under the sovereignty of the Ethiopian Crown.[43]

From Ethiopia's standpoint, the US connection had 'delivered'. In 1951, the Emperor demonstrated his gratitude by sending a battalion of his well-trained Imperial Bodyguard to fight on the American side in the Korean war.[44] A year later the implementation of the UN resolution on Eritrea and the withdrawal of the British military-assistance mission paved the way for a strategic alliance. An agreement signed in May 1953 gave Washington a 25-year lease on a communications station near Asmara, Eritrea. This station, known as

Kagnew, became the 'linchpin'[45] in the Ethiopian–American relationship. In the words of one US observer, Kagnew was 'important to the worldwide network of US communications through the Philippines, Ethiopia, Morocco, Arlington and important as well for the NATO communications within Western Europe itself when electrical and magnetic disturbance upset communications in these'.[46] And, as John Foster Dulles, then US Secretary of State, made clear, such strategic considerations took precedence over local rights:

> From the point of view of justice, the opinion of the Eritrean people must receive consideration. Nevertheless, the strategic interest of the United States in the Red Sea basin and considerations of security and world peace make it necessary that the country has to be linked with our ally, Ethiopia.[47]

In return for access to the Kagnew Station, the US agreed to train and equip three Ethiopian military divisions of 6,000 men and agreed to pay Ethiopia about $7 million per year in 'rent'. Over the next two decades, Addis Ababa received 20 per cent of all US economic aid ($350 million) and 50 per cent of all US military aid to black Africa ($278.6 million).[48]

In 1954, the remaining obstacle to a post-war settlement in the Horn was cleared. Britain decided to end its administration in the Haud and Reserve Areas, and return these vital grazing lands to Ethiopian control. However, when the Anglo–Ethiopian agreement of 29 November 1954, providing for the complete withdrawal of British authority, became public knowledge, there was an immediate and widespread Somali outcry. A belated British attempt to redress the situation by buying back the disputed territory from Ethiopia failed. Faced with increasing nationalist agitation in British Somaliland and an outrageous Ethiopian claim to sovereignty over all of the Horn, the British administration indicated it would support the union of the protectorate with Somalia when it became independent if desired.[49]

Seen from Moscow, events in the Horn of Africa during the early post-war period simply confirmed the fact that the area had fallen victim to 'Anglo–American imperialism'. The outlandish claim that 'only the victory of the armed forces of the Soviet Union over the Italo–German fascist coalition secured the successes of the Ethiopian people in the struggle with the Italian colonialists' was tempered by the conclusion that 'Anglo–American imperialism came to take the place of Italian imperialism'.[50] This process allegedly began with the British military administration during the war. According to Moscow, the Anglo–Ethiopian Treaty of 1942 symbolised Ethiopia's new dependency and coincided with the plunder of the country: 'Italian property was taken out of Ethiopia on the pretext of using it in the war against the states of the fascist bloc'; 'the British seized control over the country's finances and foreign trade' and used the railways for their own purposes without regard for Ethiopian exports. Furthermore, in the Ogaden and Haud, Britain 'used the most cruel methods' to consolidate its rule ('Britain soldiers and officers robbed the inhabitants, raped the women and drove away their animals').[51]

Nevertheless, the growing Ethiopian indignation caused by the British presence provided an opportunity 'which the USA hastened to take advantage of'. Ethiopia's 'raw materials, resources and important strategic position' occupied 'a far from secondary place in the aggressive plans of the USA' and was 'an important link in the attack of American capital on the positions of Britain and France in the Mediterranean'.[52] The advance of US 'imperialism', at the expense of its British rival, was said to be evident in at least two ways. First, the US financed the conversion of Ethiopia's currency. The old East African shilling was changed over to the Ethiopian dollar which was based on the US currency. Secondly, the British manager of the Ethiopian State Bank was replaced by an American. The latter was said to have used his position to encourage exports to the USA at low prices and imports from the USA at high prices, which 'undermined the basis of Ethiopia's trade with other countries'.[53] This uneven struggle between the capitalist rivals was, in Soviet eyes, the determining factor of the politics of the region.

The crudeness of the Soviet perception revealed itself during the disposal of the old Italian colonies. Moscow characterised Bevin's initial plan to unify the Somali people as an attempt to create 'a state dependent on her of the type of Transjordan'.[54] Andrey Gromyko, then the Soviet representative in the UN, had little doubt about British intentions: 'It is not difficult to understand that the proposals had been derived from the United Kingdom's desire to improve its position in North and North East Africa at the expense not only of defeated Italy but also of Ethiopia.'[55] The British plan was also depicted as a manoeuvre to limit US influence in the Ogaden. In the view of one Soviet writer the British resented the US Sinclair Petroleum Company prospecting for oil in the area, and asked it to desist for security reasons. When the Americans refused, the British 'organised an attack by Somali tribesmen'.[56]

Moscow's own position *vis-à-vis* the former Italian colonies constantly changed. At the beginning of the Paris peace conference of

June 1946, Moscow, like the USA, favoured international trusteeship. Yet within days of the opening of the conference, the USSR came to support the idea of Italian trusteeship for the four territories.[57] The change was based on the expectation that the Italian Communist Party would win the Italian General Election of April 1948. When the communists failed to win, Moscow promptly revived the idea of international trusteeship. However, the communist bloc did not see its volte-face as inconsistent. The Ukraine delegate said his government 'had hoped the former Italian colonies might be placed under the administration of a democratic Italy freed from fascism'. The present government of Italy, however, had 'delivered that country bound hand and foot into the hands of the capitalists'. His government had, therefore, 'realised the impossibility of allowing Italy to administer any of its former colonies'.[58]

However, by mid-1948, the three Western powers categorically rejected the option of international trusteeship. The Soviet Union saw some design behind Western 'intransigence':

> Three states had dragged out discussions until after the time-limit for solution had lapsed so that the matter would automatically be transferred to the General Assembly where they were sure of a majority of votes. The delay was used by the governments of these states to hold separate talks in which agreements had been reached for the partition of the territories.[59]

The administering powers, Britain and the US, were said to be determined to transform 'the former Italian colonies into strategic military bases for the armed forces of the United States and the United Kingdom. The Western Powers sought to maintain this hold on the former Italian colonies at any cost in order that they might be utilised as strategic bases for any possible military action against the Soviet Union and the people's democracies'.[60]

In view of the West's alleged intentions, the subsequent UN decision to grant Somalia independence after a limited trusteeship was hailed as a Soviet victory: 'the Soviet Union unfailingly spoke out in defence of the interests and rights of the small peoples and decisively opposed the colonialist desires of the imperialist powers. It was only thanks to the firm position of the Soviet Union that a fixed period for the trusteeship over Somalia was set'.[61] For the Italians 'did not want to relinquish willingly their establishment in Somalia of a regime of colonial exploitation' but were forced to do so through a change in the balance of forces in the UN to the advantage of the socialist countries.[62] With an equal indifference for the facts, the same writer depicted a similar image of a reluctant imperialism in British Somaliland. Here, 'the development of the previously splintered Somali national liberation movement ... seriously frightened the British colonialists'[63] and eventually forced them to grant independence.

Beyond this, Soviet concern for the cause of Somali national liberation was sparse. There was little coverage of tension in the Ogaden other than the assertion that Britain was still 'doing everything possible' to hinder the Ethiopians in the area. Nor was any serious attention given to the incidents involving Ethiopian soldiers and Somali nomads after the controversial surrender of the Haud in 1954. If there was tension it was whipped up by the 'imperialists'. It was noted, for example, that in November 1955 the British provoked a bloody conflict between nomads from British Somaliland and tribes in the Ogaden and then used the incident to campaign for the dissolution of the 1954 agreement.[64] The logic of the Soviet position was such that it actually brought it into opposing Somali aspirations. Thus, the extension of the Ethiopian administration to the Haud was applauded as 'an unconditional success for Haile Selassie's government'.[65] Moreover, when the question of a 'Greater Somalia' was raised at the Foreign Ministers' Conference in Paris, 1956, it was 'only the firm position of the Soviet Union' which prevented Britain from realising her plans.[66]

Finally, the disagreement over the future of Eritrea also had an East–West dimension. The USSR, along with some Arab states, advocated complete independence for Eritrea. In a speech to the UN, the Soviet delegate rejected the federalist 'compromise' solution advocated by the US: 'How is it possible to talk about a compromise if it has been adopted without the consent of the peoples concerned, that is, without the participation of Eritrean peoples? Furthermore, it has been adopted, notwithstanding the Eritrean people's wishes, against their interests and in violation of their most vital, fundamental right – the right of self-determination.'[67] Yet the Soviet stand was less about Eritrean rights than it was preventing the Western powers from improving their strategic position in the Horn. Commenting on British military administration in Eritrea, some Soviet writers noted that the British 'colonial regime' was worse than Italian rule had been.[68] The Soviet commitment to Eritrean self-determination was put into perspective in 1954. In a major work on Africa, two Soviet scholars backed Ethiopia's claim to Eritrea both on historical and economic grounds, and noted that the USSR had favoured Ethiopian access to the Eritrean port of Assab as early as 1946 (although they declined to point out that this proposal was part of a package which envisaged Eritrea under Italian trusteeship). Their objection to the federalist solution was that it did not strengthen Ethiopian sovereignty enough and was 'only a convenient cover for the virtual rule of British and American imperialism'.[69]

Having played little or no role in the Horn after 1945, Moscow assumed, up to 1955, that Ethiopia was part of the Western camp. While never criticising Haile Selassie directly, Soviet pessimism about his country was unmistakable. Ethiopia was one of those 'formally independent' states which 'fell into the rapacious claws of American and British monopolies'. As a result, her independence was more symbolic than real. The economy had a 'semi-colonial character' with no heavy industry or engineering and was 'turned into an agricultural raw-material appendage of foreign monopolies'.[70] In short, Ethiopia was 'a backward feudal state . . . still under the yoke of the foreign imperialists'. Nor could Haile Selassie's domestic reforms 'bring Ethiopia out on the wide road of independent development'. For the 'anti-imperialist democratic forces' were weak and the US had acquired important military privileges (such as the May 1953 defence agreement) 'which created a threat to the country's sovereignty'.[71]

The thaw in Soviet–Ethiopian relations 1955–1960

A significant revision in Moscow's attitude toward Ethiopia occurred in the mid-1950s. The ground was prepared by a gradual relaxation of the two-camp thesis. In 1952 the first signs began to appear that the USSR might drop its reservations about the new bourgeois nationalist regimes. At the International Economic Conference in Moscow, Soviet officials expressed an awareness of the economic and political problems facing Third World governments, and stated that the Soviet Union was prepared to enter into full trading relationships with these countries based on the principle of complete equality.[72] A year later the Soviet Union announced its intention to contribute to the United Nations' programme of technical assistance for developing countries. However, Stalin's death and the subsequent succession struggle postponed a new policy initiative for a further two years.

The turning point for Soviet foreign policy was the first Non-Aligned Conference of Africa and Asian States at Bandung in April 1955. On the eve of the conference, the Soviet government declared that it 'would support any steps . . . towards strengthening the national independence of these countries and consolidating peace and friendly co-operation among the people'. This new approach acknowledged the non-aligned states as a 'group of peace-loving European and Asian states which have proclaimed non-participation in blocs as a principle of their foreign policy' and constituted, along with the socialist states, 'a vast peace zone'.[73] Thus, in what was a departure from Stalin's policy, Khrushchev revived the Leninist concept of a historical symbiosis between the socialist states and the developing countries. The reevaluation was said to be prompted by radical changes in the international situation brought about by the strengthening of the socialist camp and the progressive collapse of the colonial system, as well as the frank admission that previous Soviet analysis of the developing countries was less then adequate. According to Anastas Mikoyan, in a report to the 20th C.P.S.U. Congress, 'many of the most vital problems in studying the East have been avoided completely or considered from erroneous positions'.[74]

After 1955, Soviet–Ethiopian relations began to take on a more positive note. While Moscow retained reservations about the Ethiopian polity, it found certain aspects of Ethiopia's policy praiseworthy. A great deal of prominence was given to Emperor Haile Selassie's post-war 'economic, social and political reforms' such as the abolition of slavery, tax reforms, land distribution and education. The new Constitution of 1955 was hailed as 'a step forward on the path of the country's democratisation',[75] and even the Emperor's acceptance of large-scale aid from the US was rationalised as conscious policy dictated by economic necessity. But the main element behind Moscow's new-found enthusiasm was Ethiopia's 'anti-imperialist' posture in foreign affairs. Ethiopia attended the Bandung Conference of 1955 and thereafter came out strongly in support of the Pan-African movement. Soviet commentators interpreted this stand as a genuine attempt to preserve Ethiopia's independence from 'the imperialists', and endorsed Addis Ababa's efforts to diversify foreign trade: 'in recent years ... the Ethiopian Government, trying to show some resistance to American monopolies, tries to attract capital from other countries too',[76] including the socialist states – Czechoslovakia, Bulgaria and the USSR. But the major seal of Soviet approval was earned in April 1958 when Ethiopia aligned herself with the other African states against colonialism and imperialism at the Accra Conference of African states.

The Soviet reappraisal of Ethiopia was opportune. By 1956, Haile Selassie had reasons of his own for widening diplomatic contacts.

Many of these seemed to centre on Washington's indifference for Ethiopia's local interests. In the mid-1950s, the US offered financial support to Egypt, a traditional adversary of Ethiopia, to help build the Aswan dam. And, although the US offer came to nothing, the Soviets financing the project instead, Haile Selassie was upset by what he regarded as Washington's high-handed behaviour.[77] No less irritating was the level of US military assistance at a time when the Emperor became concerned about nationalist fervour in the Ogaden and Eritrea.

As related, Somali unrest intensified after the controversial return of the Haud to Ethiopia in 1954. And with no avenue open in the Ogaden for the expression of Somali grievances, the number of rebellious incidents increased. Ethiopian tax-collecting forays were often resisted, sometimes forcibly, and subsequent Ethiopian attempts to make Somali nomads accept Ethiopian citizenship only heightened anti-Ethiopian feeling. The situation was not helped by the failure of Ethiopia and Somalia, (formerly Italian Somaliland) to reach agreement on their mutual frontier which, in practice, remained the provisional administration line left by the British in Somalia in 1950. After the failure of direct negotiations, the UN General Assembly recommended arbitration in 1957. However, neither Ethiopia nor Italy, representing Somalia, could agree on an 'independent' person to draw up the tribunal's terms of reference. Eventually, on the initiative on the UN, Trygve Lie was appointed. He failed, however, to secure any agreement, and no resolution was passed on the eastern frontier before Somalia's independence.[78]

Meanwhile, in Eritrea, Emperor Haile Selassie's policy of systematically subverting the region's autonomy had unintended consequences. The Ethiopian leader never made any secret of his contempt for the UN-sponsored federation arrangement. His representative in Eritrea, Andargachew Mesai, declared on 22 March 1955, 'there are no internal or external affairs, as far as the Office of His Imperial Majesty's Representative is concerned, and there will be none in the future'.[79] In 1952, the Emperor suspended the Eritrean constitution and acquired the power to veto the decision of the Eritrean Assembly. In 1956, the Eritrean National Assembly was suspended. A year later, the locally spoken languages of Tigrinya and Arabic were replaced by Amharic as the official language. In 1959, the Eritrean flag was finally removed. Such expansionism, however, provoked increasingly organised opposition. The turning point came in 1958 when the Ethiopian government brutally suppressed a general strike led by the officially banned Trade Unions. That act pointed up the impossibility of open protest and, within a year, an underground organisation, the Eritrean Liberation Movement, had formed to oppose Ethiopian imperialism.

Viewed from Addis Ababa, the late 1950s had raised the spectre of Muslim encirclement. The unwillingness or inability of the United States to share this fear exasperated the Ethiopian Emperor:

> The US has assisted us and we hope it will continue to do so ... Ethiopia has received military aid from the US and a request for further aid in aviation and naval fields in addition to financial aid has been made ... Negotiations on this request have been going on for the last two or three years, but satisfactory results have not been forthcoming.

Furthermore, in the same breath, Haile Selassie made it clear that Ethiopian needs would not be defined by broader ideological considerations: 'Ethiopia wishes to live in peace and have good relations with both East and West'.[80] The Emperor was not bluffing. In June 1959, the Ethiopian leader became the first African Head of State to visit the Soviet Union. The visit, a significant landmark in relations between the two countries, had been preceded by a steady increase in contacts. In June 1956, the USSR and Ethiopia had raised their respective diplomatic missions to full Embassy status. Almost exactly two years later, the Ethiopian Minister of Foreign Trade was received in Moscow. In September 1958, the Soviet Union extended relief aid to Ethiopian flood victims.[81] All this prompted one Soviet writer to speak of 'the essentially new relations developing between the socialist countries and Ethiopia'.[82]

The Emperor's visit was a personal triumph in more ways than one. After a two-week visit of industrial and agricultural show places, the Emperor received one of the USSR's highest military decorations, the Order of Suvorov, and negotiated trade, cultural and credit agreements including a $100 million loan; the latter was the largest credit extended to a black African nation and, at the time, was one of the largest single Russian credits in the Third World.[83] Such generosity reflected Moscow's desire to detach Ethiopia from the West. According to a Soviet writer, 'while the Soviet Union is pursuing a policy of peace and friendship with respect to Ethiopia, the Western powers continue to regard her as an object of colonial policy'.[84] It also reflected Moscow's appreciation of Ethiopia's commitment to the 'Bandung principles': 'In the Soviet Union, they value highly the peace-loving foreign policy of Ethiopia, its constructive position in the Afro–Asian community, and its consistent stand in defence of the enslaved peoples of Africa.'[85]

For his part, the Emperor had a tactical interest in the first Soviet concern and an unqualified willingness to identify with the second. Although essentially anti-communist in outlook, the Emperor played the Soviet card ostensibly to prompt more generous US military aid. In this, he was successful. A combination of political skill – he described the USSR as 'the world's greatest power' at a time when Washington was very sensitive about Moscow's technological prowess – and a generous Soviet offer of military assistance[86] elicited the desired response from the US. In a secret agreement of 1960, the US revised its military-assistance programme by agreeing to equip and train a 40,000-strong Ethiopian Army; it 'also re-affirmed its continuing interest in the security of Ethiopia and its opposition to any activities threatening the territorial integrity of Ethiopia'.[87] As for Moscow's efforts to promote the Emperor as the champion of the African liberation movement, this was essentially a case of doing the Emperor's work for him. And, while the timing of the USSR's support was probably related to strains in the Soviet–Egyptian relationship in 1959, Emperor Haile Selassie welcomed the chance to improve his standing amongst 'progressive' international opinion. In doing so, he hoped to 'roadblock' any possible Somali attempt to enlist support from that quarter for its position in the territorial dispute with Ethiopia.

Thus, by 1960, relations between the Soviet Union and Ethiopia had expanded considerably since their modest beginnings in 1943. According to Moscow, these relations were a graphic example of the Leninist policy of peaceful co-existence:

> Ethiopia is a monarchy. The Soviet Union is a socialist country. They are far from one another, but friendly ties inspired by mutual respect and trust have been established and are growing stronger between the Ethiopian and Soviet peoples.[88]

Yet, in reality, the scope for 'mutual respect and trust' was limited by the acknowledged political differences of the two sides. The abortive coup by the Neway brothers in Ethiopia in December 1960 was instructive in this respect. The Soviet press remained silent until the outcome was clear, and then firmly condemned the revolt as US inspired.[89] Clearly, Soviet sympathy for Ethiopian foreign policy did not amount to unequivocal support for the Emperor's regime itself.

The period of escalation 1960–1967

1960 was an important year for the Horn of Africa. It marked the end of a period of relative tranquillity and the beginning of a phase dominated by strife and tension. The catalyst in this transformation was the birth of an independent Somalia. The country was formed on 1 July 1960 through the unification of the former British Somaliland Protectorate and the former Italian Trust territory. Yet such independence did not fully correspond to the aspirations of Somali nationalism. For over a million Somali, sharing a common language, a common religion, a common culture and a common understanding of themselves as a political community, were left outside the borders of the new state. These Somali lived in three contiguous regions: French Somaliland (later to become Djibouti), the Northern Frontier District of Kenya and the Ogaden region of Ethiopia (see Map 3).

From the very beginning of its existence, Somalia refused to accept the existing borders as valid. These were seen as artificial and arbitrary, and simply a legacy of the colonial era. The task thus confronting the new Republic in 1960 was to expand the boundaries of the state so that they coincided with those of the 'nation'. This fundamental goal was enshrined both in the new state's constitution ('The Somali Republic shall promote, by legal and peaceful means, the union of Somali territories')[90] and a five-pointed star flag, with each point representing one of the segments into which the colonial powers had divided Somalia. But, if the realisation of the Somali nation-state depended on a revision of existing frontiers, it was equally true that the survival of the Ethiopian state was seen to depend on their preservation. Being a multi-ethnic state, Ethiopia feared that if the right to secede be granted in the Ogaden, such a grant would stimulate secessionist demands from other groups and thus culminate in the disintegration of the state itself.[91] In other words, Ethiopian and Somali approaches to the border question were irreconcilable. There was little or no room for compromise. Somali self-determination could only be exercised at the expense of Ethiopian territorial integrity and vice versa.

Fighting in the border region erupted almost immediately after Somali independence. On 1 January 1961, in the confused aftermath of the abortive coup in Ethiopia, there was a brutal clash between armed Somali tribesmen and Ethiopian soldiers in Damot (near the Ethiopian–Somali border).[92] In what was a portent for future clashes, the US-equipped and US-trained Ethiopian forces emerged triumphant. This, however, did not stop the Somali President, Aden Abdullah

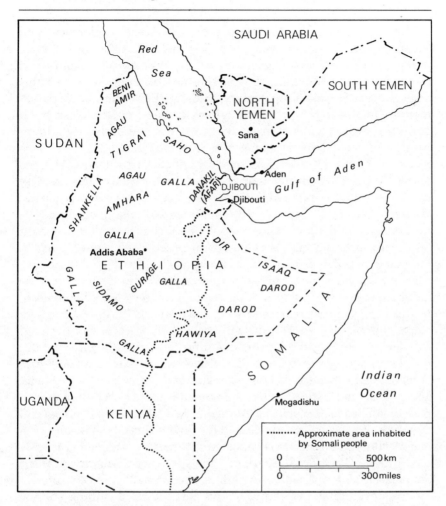

Map 3. Ethnic groups in the Horn. *Source*: Central Intelligence Agency, Washington D.C., USGPO, 1980.

Osman, from threatening war if Ethiopian mistreatment of indigenous Somalis did not cease. For its part, Ethiopia demanded an end to armed Somali infiltration into the Ogaden. A meeting between the two sides at the Monrovia Conference of May 1961 did not produce any serious negotiations on the border issue. Further incidents were reported. And 1961 ended the way it had begun – shrouded in mutual suspicion. In December 1961, the Somali government was shaken by an attempted coup which aimed to divide the two Somalias again. Ethiopian complicity was suspected.

The rising tension in the Horn presented Soviet diplomacy with fresh opportunities, as well as new problems. Like most newly independent countries, Somalia faced the problem of forming and training a professional army. Unlike other countries, however, this objective was Somalia's top priority. Initially, the Western-style parliamentary regime in Mogadishu sought assistance from the West. But it got little encouragement. In January 1961 the new Kennedy administration rejected a Somali request for $9 million in military aid.[93] This response reflected Washington's concern not to jeopardise its relations with Ethiopia, its main ally in black Africa, for the sake of an extremely poor and thinly populated country. There was also a more general Western fear that its military aid would be used to support Somalia's irredentist ambitions. Finally, most Western countries were reluctant to embarrass Britain, who was then in the process of bringing Kenya to independence. The Soviet Union, however, had no such inhibitions.

Following the 'very warm reception' accorded to its delegation at the independence celebrations in Mogadishu, Moscow assured Somalia of its full support in overcoming the 'colonial legacy'.[94] Almost immediately afterwards, Czechoslovakia, presumably with Soviet backing, offered arms to Somalia.[95] Mogadishu turned down the offer but did not discourage Soviet friendship. In September 1960, the USSR and Somalia established full diplomatic relations. Six months later, a Soviet government delegation visited the Somali Republic. Within a month the Somali Prime Minister, Dr Abdirashid Ali Shermarke, and several members of his cabinet, travelled to the Soviet Union; the result was a major economic and technical assistance agreement signed in Moscow on 2 June 1961. Under the terms of the agreement, Moscow granted Somalia a long-term credit of 40 million roubles at 2½ per cent interest for the development of industry and agriculture, including specific projects to be built with Soviet assistance, and a short-term loan of 7 million roubles for trading purposes.[96] The USSR also gave free assistance to the Somali government in a number of other areas.

While this agreement, which was then the largest per-capita credit given to a foreign state, boosted Soviet standing in Mogadishu, the impact of the USSR was initially limited by the competition of other aid donors. Somalia received direct assistance in the form of annual grants from the colonial powers, Britain and Italy; it also received aid and loans from America and Egypt, as well as generous assistance through various UN agencies. Moscow regretted the 'sometimes, shackling' agreements with the West: 'The Somali people may have finished with political colonialism but economic colonialism is still alive.'[97] Nevertheless, Moscow remained confident that its economic assistance would have a political effect. A Soviet economic adviser in Somalia, Sarukhanyan, observed: 'The enterprises we are building will be the property of the Somali state, thereby giving rise to a state sector of the economy'.[98] Such optimism was reinforced by the conviction that the Somalis were 'socialist by nature', even if their notions of socialism were 'naive'.[99]

But there was nothing naive about the Somali rationale for the economic agreement with Moscow:

> The US had already given aid but not enough and not quickly enough. For this reason the Somali Republic has turned to the Soviet Union for credit assistance. The US was just too slow for us. You do not give us military aid, yet the Ethiopians continue to get it because of the Eritrean base.[100]

Between 1961 and 1963 Somali politicians played the 'Soviet card' in a continued attempt to win military assistance from the West:

> Our problem is to unite this country and this makes the border problem critical. Our whole people are behind us in this and the masses are getting an unfriendly idea of the United States because you won't help us, yet you help Ethiopia. I haven't asked the Soviets for arms because we want them from the West but I know they would give them to us.[101]

Dr Shermarke's prediction was remarkable both for its accuracy and for the light it shed on the Soviet role in the Horn.

In November 1963, Mogadishu refused a tripartite offer of Western military assistance, valued at $10 million and, instead, accepted Soviet military aid, said to be worth $35 million. The Western proposal, put together by the US, Italy and West Germany, envisaged training a force of 5,000 to 6,000 men with a heavy emphasis on domestic security and civic action. In the Somali view, the Western offer had quantitative and qualitative 'inadequacies' but was rejected, above all, because of the 'political conditions which accompanied it'.[102] In contrast, the Soviet arms offer was free of formal conditions.[103] And, while it was a modest deal by Soviet standards, it was a substantial one in local terms; it provided for the expansion of the Somali Army, from 2,000 to 10,000 and included an assortment of MiG-15 aircraft and T-34 tanks. In addition, Somali cadets were to be trained in the USSR (600 were reported there in 1966) and a Soviet military mission in Mogadishu (estimated at 250 in 1966) was established. Altogether, the Soviet arms package was ten times greater than the estimated total of Somalia's defence budget for 1964 (£3,900,000).[104]

The Soviet-Somali arms deal certainly increased tension in the Horn of Africa. It represented not so much a definite change in policy but a growing realisation that a strategic interest could not be sustained outside the parameters of the Ethiopian–Somali dispute. The evolution of the Soviet attitude toward the dispute requires some elaboration. Prior to and immediately after Somali independence the Soviet position was one of strict neutrality. The assumption being that 'imperialism' was responsible for the Ethiopian–Somali conflict, and that with the advent of Somali independence, the main obstacle to good relations would be removed. Before 1961, there was little or no Soviet recognition of centrifugal forces within Ethiopia such as the Somalis in the Ogaden. Indeed, Moscow blandly asserted that the nationalities problem was already being resolved within the existing state framework. For example, D. A. Ol'derogge and I. I. Potekhin argued that the ethnic differences within Ethiopia were gradually being obliterated through living together in one territory for a period of time. Six years later, in 1960 M. V. Rayt and Ye G. Titov reached a similar conclusion. After noting the mutual inter-action between Amhara culture and that of the other peoples of Ethiopia, they contended that 'in the near future the peoples of Ethiopia are likely to merge into a single Ethiopian nation'.[105]

However, by 1961, escalating violence along the Ethiopian–Somali border prompted a Soviet reassessment. Moscow began to accept, tacitly at first, that the 'imperialists' were not entirely to blame for the ill-feeling between the two countries. Commenting on the 3rd African Peoples Conference in Cairo, 1961, S. Kondrashov conceded that 'there were clashes between some of the delegations, for instance, between the Somali and Ethiopian over Ethiopia's border regions populated by Somali tribes' and that this is one of the facts 'indicative of the complex political situation in Africa'.[106] A year later, a Soviet publication referred to 'the clash between Ethiopian forces and Somali nomads.' By 1963, it was frankly admitted that Ethiopian–Somali relations were impaired by 'territorial disputes'.[107]

This transition, though, was not a smooth process. Between 1961 and 1963, Soviet thinking was obscure and, at times, confused. For example, in what was an apparent departure from previous Soviet writing, A. M. Khazanov traced the birth of Somali nationalism to an uprising led by Sayid Mohammed Abdille Hassan (known to the British as 'The Mad Mullah') during the first two decades of the twentieth century. The uprising 'from the very beginning had the character of a national liberation movement'. And, although it eventually failed,

Sayid Mohammed Abdille Hassan performed a 'historical service' in that he was 'the first Somali who not only became prominent but also tried practically to realise the idea of the creation of a Somali state'.[108] Yet, depite the fact that the uprising encompassed the Ogaden, the author resisted the obvious conclusion, namely, that the 'Greater Somalia' concept had an indigenous basis. On the contrary, Khazanov argued that the uprising was simply a reaction to the British 'imperialist' presence and was not directed against the Ethiopians since they were not hostile to the Somalis.[109]

A comparable inconsistency characterised the Soviet attitude towards the federal arrangement linking Eritrea to Ethiopia. D. R. Voblikov and I. D. Levin considered the union to be a proper, constituted arrangement.[110] But other Soviet writers reached the opposite conclusion. For instance, G. B. Aleksandrenko argued that the federation was 'imposed artifically from above' by the 'governing clique of Ethiopia' in order to avoid 'feudal fragmentation and civil war'.[111] This was evident, he maintained, in 'the absence of representation of Eritrea in those organs which according to the Act of Federation of 11 September 1952, were to fulfil the functions, of an all union authority for certain affairs'. Thus, Eritrea fell victim to the 'unitary tendencies'[112] of the Ethiopian state.

Yet if Moscow was less than clear on these issues, such vagueness was, in part, intentional. The USSR wanted good relations with both Ethiopia and Somalia. It was less interested in assigning guilt for local disputes than obtaining military facilities in a strategic area. Consequently, when Emperor Haile Selassie terminated the federal arrangement and annexed Eritrea in 1962, the Soviet Union's response was the same as the United States, which had its Kagnew interest to consider, namely, one of official silence. The fact that Ethiopia's action violated the provision specifying that only the UN General Assembly had the power to change the status of the Federal Act[113] was apparently deemed not sufficient reason for objection.

A desire to remain aloof from local rivalries also expressed itself in a Soviet concentration on the 'progressive' foreign policies of both Ethiopia and Somalia. The domestic shortcomings of both countries were passed over relatively quickly. Thus, while the then ruling Young Somali League 'expresses fundamentally the interests of the well-to-do sections of the population', Moscow praised Somalia's 'policy of neutrality based on the Bandung principles',[114] its support for 'the speediest ending of colonialism on the black continent', 'the liquidation of foreign military bases', the rejection of 'aggressive military pacts' and its support for 'full disarmament and the banning of nuclear weapons'.[115] Similarly, in Ethiopia, where 'the feudal class is in power'[116] and despite 'the grim situation of the peasants who form about 90 per cent of the population',[117] it was noted with satisfaction that the country continues to follow 'a neutralist policy'. Ethiopia, it was said, had no desire to participate in 'pro-imperialist groupings' and 'considers herself as belonging only to one group, the African group'.[118]

By 1963, it became clear that Moscow's strategic attempt to ingratiate itself with both Ethiopia and Somalia was not working. Relations with Ethiopia stagnated, particularly in the sphere of economic collaboration. The initial projects under the 1959 agreements were not spelt out until 1962. And Haile Selassie had only used a fraction of the Soviet credit extended to him. At the same time, Ethiopia's relations with the US recovered from the low point of 1959. According to a series of secret agreements signed in 1962, 1963 and 1964, the US agreed to speed up the delivery of arms contained in the 1960 commitment, provided 'civic action equipment' and accepted an Ethiopian request for a squadron of twelve F-5 aircraft.[119] Reassured by Washington's support, the Emperor had little need for developing relations with the USSR. In 1963 the Ethiopian leader rejected A. Grechko's offer ('we will give you all the arms you need, much more than to the Somalis')[120] to replace US as its arms supplier.

That failure presented the Kremlin with a dilemma. On the one hand, the pressures for actively supporting Somalia in its dispute with Addis Ababa had become very great in 1963. The worsening border situation only intensified Mogadishu's efforts to obtain arms. And the USSR was not the only possible donor. As related, Somalia negotiated with the West. It also had a dialogue with the People's Republic of China which had no conflicting commitments in Ethiopia. In June 1963, Dr Shermarke visited China and signed trade and aid agreements. Speculation mounted that there was also a Somali–Chinese arms deal in the offing.[121] Nor could the USSR remain indifferent to the enormous domestic political pressures on the Somali government. Accused of providing inadequate leadership over the Northern Frontier District issue and failing to win international support for its Ogaden claim, the Somali government sought some dramatic action to restore its popularity before the municipal elections in November 1963. In the circumstances, it would take more than Soviet expressions of sympathy – in March 1963 V. Kudryavtsev observed that the Somali people were divided into five parts 'and naturally when Somalia became independent, its government saw as its task the unification of all Somalis into an independent Somali state'[122] – to meet Somali needs and secure a strategic foothold in the area.

On the other hand, Soviet willingness to identify with the Somali cause was tempered by Ethiopia's success on the diplomatic front. As the self-appointed natural ally of the developing countries, the USSR could not ignore Haile Selassie's standing as an African statesman. A founder member of the Organisation of African Unity (OAU), a fact symbolised by the location of the organisation's headquarters in Addis Ababa in May 1963, the Emperor used his prestige to translate Ethiopian state interests into the OAU charter. In the debate prior to the adoption of the charter, and despite Somali objections, the Ethiopian Prime Minister won overwhelming support from the major-ity of Heads of State present (many of whom had their own fears of balkanisation) for the proposition that 'it is in the interests of all Africans now to respect the frontiers drawn on the maps, whether they be good or bad, by the former colonisers'.[123] As a result, the OAU pledged itself to defend the member states' 'sovereignty, their terri-torial integrity and independence' (Article 3) and upheld this commit-ment as a principle of the organisation.[124] This represented a diplo-matic rebuff for Somalia. But the USSR had wider interests to consider. In a message to the Heads of State at the OAU Conference, General Secretary N. S. Khrushchev observed that the 'lofty and noble goals set by the charter meet with full support in the Soviet Union'.[125]

The Soviet–Somali arms deal of November 1963 represented the first step in a Soviet attempt to square these conflicting pressures into a coherent policy. Although the size and the timing of the agreement was due primarily to Somali initiative – witness the immediate and beneficial effect of this for the SYL in the November municipal elections where the government party won 665 of the available 904 seats (74 per cent)[126] – it opened the door for a Soviet presence in Somalia. The second step came on 31 December 1963, when N. S. Khrushchev sent a lengthy memorandum to all Heads of State in the world. This outlined a proposal to renounce force in territorial dis-putes. And, while the document was not written with the problems of the Horn of Africa exclusively in mind, a reference to 'recent events in North Africa'[127] left little doubt about its relevance.

In the memorandum, Khrushchev distinguished between territorial disputes concerned with ending 'colonial oppression' and 'other territorial claims'. In the latter, the difficulty of disentangling such claims made force impermissible; 'In justifying their claims the parties to these disputes advance arguments and considerations having to do with history, ethnography, consanguinity, religion and so forth ... How can one tell which side is right, who occupies a just position and who an unjust one?' Furthermore, in the present time of 'ramified systems of alliances' such disputes had more than a 'purely local character': 'we must not fail to take into account that wars that begin with the use of simple weapons could at the present time grow into a world war with the use of thermo-nuclear weapons'. Accordingly, Khrushchev endorsed the stand of the OAU which 'affirmed the impermissibility of settling differences and disputes between African states by means of force', and urged all governments to conclude an international treaty banning the use of force in all territorial disputes 'having to do with the established borders between states'.[128]

The importance of Khrushchev's proposal was political rather than practical. The distinction between colonial territorial disputes and 'other territorial disputes' was meaningless, in operational terms, without specifying criteria. Yet, in political terms, this 'distinction' performed two useful functions. First, it preserved the USSR's image as staunch supporter of the national liberation movement and those who considered themselves victims of colonial oppression (i.e., Somalia). Secondly, it enabled Moscow to publicly align itself with the principle, championed by Ethiopia and supported by the majority of African states, concerning the retention of existing frontiers at independence. That this now constituted a major strand in official Soviet policy soon became clear.

Khrushchev's initiative was followed by a spate of publications which broadly echoed the thrust of the memorandum. Writing in January 1964, V. A. Zorin and V. L. Israelyan observed: 'There can be no doubt, that the resolution of territorial disputes through force contradicts the fundamental interests of the peoples, bringing irreparable damage to world affairs, democracy and socialism.'[129] The danger of escalation into nuclear war, the authors argued, made negotiation, based on the observance of the territorial status quo, the best short-term solution. In the long term, however, only a socialist federation, involving the disputing parties, would provide a lasting solution. Under socialism, the authors continued, the right to secede would be freely available (sic) but ethno-graphic frontiers were only temporary once capitalist oppression had been eliminated. This had been demonstrated by the example of 'the multi-national family of Soviet peoples'.[130] The writers, Y. Tomilin and I. I. Potekhin concurred, with this analysis.[131]

In the context of the Ethiopian–Somali dispute, then, Soviet policy evolved from detached neutrality to what might be termed permissive neutrality. That combined a formal acceptance of the principle upholding the inviolability of territorial borders at independence with a willingness to supply arms to a state dedicated to undermining that very principle. Such duplicity was expressed publicly in February 1964, following the outbreak of full-scale fighting between Ethiopia and Somalia in the border area. In an identical message to the Emperor of Ethiopia and the President of Somalia, Khrushchev observed that 'it is the conviction of the Soviet government that in our time there are not, and there cannot be any territorial disputes that have to be settled with the use of arms'.[132] The Soviet leader called for a peaceful settlement, and sent Deputy Foreign Minister Yacov Malik to the two countries concerned, offering mediation. The US and China also pledged neutrality.

The border war continued until 30 March 1964 when both Ethiopia and Somalia agreed to respect an OAU cease-fire resolution. This, however, had little more than a short-term impact on the Ogaden problem. In view of the consequences of the war, it could not be otherwise. After seeing her army virtually routed by the larger Ethiopian forces, Somalia experienced yet another diplomatic reverse. In July 1964, a Tanzanian resolution, at the OAU Summit in Cairo, to reaffirm the principle concerning the preservation of the existing territorial frontiers at independence, was passed by the overwhelming number of the Heads of State present. And while Somalia declared she did not feel bound by the resolution, it was undoubtedly a set-back for any hopes she had of pressing her territorial claims through peaceful means. In March 1965, for instance, a Somali request for the dispatch of an OAU 'fact-finding commission' to examine the causes of the unrest in the Ogaden was ignored after Ethiopia objected. Between 1964 and 1966, a number of armed skirmishes involving Ethiopian forces and Ogaden nomads were reported. Attempts, moreover, to resume negotiations in accordance with the Khartoum cease-fire agreement ran into repeated difficulties.[133]

Tension over the Ogaden was exacerbated by Ethiopian–Somali rivalry over the future of French Somaliland. Following riots during President de Gaulle's visit there in August 1966, and the subsequent French promise of a referendum to decide the future of the territory, Ethiopia and Somalia revived longstanding claims to the area. The event itself took place on 19 March 1967 in rather suspicious circumstances.[134] A majority of the population voted for continued association with France. Somalia, whose calls for international supervision of the referendum were ignored by the French authorities, denounced the result as a fraud. Ethiopia quietly accepted it.

The prolonged conflict in the Horn placed an increasing strain on Soviet 'neutrality'. Moscow's public opposition to 'the threat or the use of force, against the territorial inviolability or political independence of any state'[135] and its contention that because 'the main enemy is imperialism, the task ahead is to strengthen sovereignty, and to avoid any complication between African states which might weaken the front of anti-imperialist struggle'[136] cut very little ice in Addis Ababa. Soviet arms continued to reach Mogadishu despite periodic denials.[137] And Soviet aid projects in Somalia outpaced those in Ethiopia. By September 1964, Moscow had built two hospitals, a secondary school and a printing plant, all free of charge.[138] Furthermore, during the period 1960–7, the volume of Moscow's trade with Somalia was about 25 per cent higher than with Ethiopia (see Table 5).

Nor could Emperor Haile Selassie be persuaded of Soviet disinterest in the Eritrean rebellion. This suspicion was founded on Moscow's close ties with Syria, a close ally of the Eritrean Liberation Front (ELF) Established in 1961 as a separate liberation organisation from the disintegrating ELM, the ELF began military operations against Ethiopian forces the same year. Initially, though, the impact of the ELF was limited by an inability to win external support and the effectiveness of an Israeli-trained Ethiopian counter-insurgency force. But, in 1964, Syria became the first country to grant the ELF direct material assistance. This help was a tremendous boost. Between 1964 and 1967 ELF forces grew from a few hundred with antiquated weapons to about 2,000 men with relatively modern weapons (Kalashnikov automatic rifles, Czech Stens, British Enfields, some Soviet AK-47s, an assortment of captured US M-ls, Chinese rockets and mortars).[139] Just how important Syria was to the ELF was indicated by the location of the organisation's headquarters in Damascus.

While Syria had reasons of its own for supporting the Eritrean struggle – the Ba'athist regime championed the ELF as an Arab liberation movement (which it was not) fighting a reactionary pro-Israeli regime – its actions probably had the indirect support of Moscow. Two circumstantial factors pointed to this conclusion. First, many of the weapons the ELF received via Syria originated from the USSR or Czechoslovakia. It would seem unlikely that Moscow did not know about the eventual destination of some of its arms given to Syria. Secondly, the next major arms donor after Syria was China.[140] This suggested that Peking, Moscow's arch ideological rival, perceived a

Soviet–Syrian connection in Eritrea, and was anxious not to leave the USSR an unrivalled field to establish its credentials as a supporter of the national liberation movement there.

In 1966, Ethiopian displeasure with Soviet activities in the Horn of Africa was publicly stated. During a visit to Addis Ababa in May 1966, the first Deputy Foreign Minister, Yakov Malik, was warned by the Emperor that continued arms shipments to Somalia were 'likely to harm'[141] the hitherto cordial relations. The Government newspaper, the *Ethiopian Herald* was blunter:

> The USSR has commenced taking steps that adversely effect the interests of the Ethiopian people . . . it is one thing to give arms to meet a country's security needs and quite another to conduct a traffic in heavy weapons above and beyond the defence needs of that country.[142]

The Soviet reaction was swift. Within a week of Malik's visit, G. Dzotsenidze of the USSR's Supreme Soviet visited Addis Ababa to reassure the Emperor of Moscow's friendly intentions.[143] Moscow repudiated the 'fabrication' that 'the Soviet Union is allegedly abetting the "annexationist" plans of the Somali Republic'. Rather it was 'colonialism' which sowed the 'seeds' of the 'territorial disputes and animosities between individual East African states': 'The imperialists are making use of this for subversive activity and are intensifying their military infiltration into East Africa – they are equipping proving grounds, creating bases under the guise of "tracking stations", stationing troop contingents, conducting manoeuvres etc.'[144]

Despite the rhetoric, and an apparent concern about the level of hostilities in the Horn, it was clear by 1966 that Moscow valued its relations with Somalia more highly than those with Ethiopia. Soviet writers condemned the 'powerful' and 'reactionary' role of the Ethiopian Church and observed, scornfully, that 'the Ethiopian Government has adopted the course of promoting private enterprise in every way.'[145] Foreign policy alone remained the single positive factor in the Soviet appraisal of Ethiopia. In contrast, Soviet commentary about Somalia was optimistic, sometimes to the point of inaccuracy. In a country, where most of the population were nomadic tribesmen, one writer claimed that 'the working class is growing far faster than the national bourgeoise'.[146] Another claimed that the first five years of the Somali Republic 'demonstrated that its economy is viable'[147] despite the fact that the country experienced 0.4 per cent real decline in per-capita income, and only managed to implement about 50 per cent of the projects envisaged by the first five-year plan (1963–7).[148]

3   Entering the 1970s: The Soviet disposition

> Having evaluated the overall balance of forces in the world, we
> arrived at the conclusion a few years ago that there was a real
> possibility for bringing about a fundamental change in the inter-
> national situation.
>
> (Leonid I. Brezhnev, General Secretary of the CPSU, in *Pravda*,
> 15 June 1974)

The signing of the Nuclear Non-Proliferation Treaty in 1968 and the
initiation of the Strategic Arms Limitation Talks (SALT) heralded the
beginning of *détente* (razryadka). For Soviet commentators, the ending
of the cold war marked a new stage in the global struggle between the
opposed social systems of capitalism and socialism, the linchpin of
which was the relationship between the USA and USSR. Washington,
it was argued, was forced to accept a political dialogue principally
because its previous policy, the threat of military 'diktat', was no
longer feasible. The years 1969–70 were identified as ones in which
there had been a major shift in the 'correlation of forces' (sootnoshenie
sil) in favour of socialism. The implication of this analysis was clear.
The general direction of Soviet foreign policy remained unaltered. But
its potentialities for realising long-standing objectives had enormously
increased. Washington, therefore, had simply been compelled to
recognise these new realities, and make a retreat of historic proportions.

The Soviet explanation for *détente* is important not necessarily for the
realities it unveiled but for the attitudes and perceptions it suggested.
Had Soviet policy entered a new phase? How was the situation
'qualitatively new'? Did the USSR genuinely feel the US was undergo-
ing a steady decline of power? Or was the Soviet assessment simply
propaganda to cover domestic economic shortcomings? Was there a
new pattern of Soviet assertiveness? This chapter will explore these
elusive issues of Soviet motivation insofar as they affected Moscow's

policy in the Horn of Africa. We are particularly concerned with the extent to which Soviet motivation was subject to change during the late 1960s, the period immediately prior to Soviet involvement in the Horn. The task is not an easy one. Outside knowledge of Soviet intentions has been sparse. Churchill's characterisation of Soviet Russia as 'a riddle wrapped in a mystery inside an enigma'[1] was just as valid then as it had been before. Two obstacles stood in the way of understanding. First, the Soviet decision-making process was obscured by an almost impenetrable fog. The deliberations of the Politburo remained a secret. Secondly, Soviet 'watchers', faced with a dearth of information and encouraged by impressive developments in satellite technology, tended to infer intentions from observed military capabilities. But, while there was probably a relationship between the two, it was never one so simple or precise. It told us very little about the aspirations guiding Soviet power.

As a starting point, therefore, it is necessary, however imperfect the result, to reconstruct Moscow's view of the world in the late 1960s. Soviet foreign policy, as before, was said to be the product of Marxist–Leninist ideology. This holistic doctrine combined economic, social and political aspects in a dialectical theory of history which, it was claimed, gave Soviet policy a scientific basis. While subject to modifications over the years, the intellectual continuity of Marxism–Leninism lay in its 'class essence'. The axiom that class conflict was inevitable (at least, for the foreseeable future) and that a state's policy, domestic or foreign, was determined by the class nature of its government found expression in the apparent consistency of Soviet foreign-policy objectives. In March 1966, at the 23rd Congress of the CPSU, it was decided that the strategic objectives 'to ensure peaceful conditions for building a communist society in our country'[2] made four goals paramount. First, the foreign policy of the USSR was aimed at securing favourable international conditions for the building of socialism and communism. Secondly, it sought to strengthen the unity and cohesion, the friendship and fraternity of the socialist countries. Thirdly, the USSR pledged its support for the national liberation movements and to maintain all-round co-operation with the young, developing countries. Finally, it upheld the principle of peaceful co-existence of states with different social systems, firmly repelling the aggressive forces of imperialism, and delivering mankind from the threat of a new world war. This formulation followed almost word for word the line of Soviet foreign policy as laid down in the *Official History of Soviet Foreign Policy* in 1956.[3] An almost

Table 1. A comparison of Soviet and American nuclear strike forces in 1970

Category	United States		Soviet Union	
	Type	Number	Type	Number
Land-based missiles				
ICBM	LGM-25C Titan 2	54	SS-7 Saddler }	220
	LGM-30B Minuteman 1 }	990	SS-8 Sasin }	240
	LGM-30F Minuteman 2 }		SS-9 Scarp	800
	LGM-30G Minuteman 3	10	SS-11	
			SS-13 Savage	40
IRBM			SS-5 Skean	100
MRBM			SS-4 Sandal	600
SRBM	MGM-31A Pershing	250	SS-1b-d Scud AC }	300
	MGM-29A Seargent	500	SS12 Scaleboard }	
Cruise missiles			SSC-1 Shaddock	100
Sea-based missiles				
SLBM	UGM-27B Polaris A2	208	SERB	45
	UGM-27C Polaris A3	448	SS-N-6	160
SLBM			-SARK	75
Cruise missiles			-Shaddock	310
Cruise missiles			-Shaddock	52

Long-range bombers	B52 C–F	250	Mya-4 Bison	40
	B52 G/H	255	TU20 Bear	100
Medium-range bombers	FB–111	35	TU16 Badger	500
Strike aircraft (land-based)	F 105 D F–4 F–111A/D A–7D }	1200	TU 22 Blinder Yak 28 Brewer SU 7 Fitter MiG 232 Foxbat }	1000
Strike aircraft (carrier-based)	A–4 A–6A AS–7A RA–5C }	900		

Aircraft

Note: ICBM Inter-continental ballistic missile(s)
IRBM Intermediate range ballistic missile(s)
MRBM Medium-range ballistic missile(s)
SLBM Submarine-launched ballistic missile(s)
SRBM Short-range ballistic missile(s)

Source: *The Military Balance, 1970–1971*, London, International Institute for Strategic Studies, 1970, p. 105

Table 2. Historical changes in Soviet and American launcher strength, 1960–1970

	Category	1960	1961	1962	1963	1964	1965	1966	1967	1968	1969	1970
USA	ICBM	18	63	294	424	834	854	904	1,054	1,054	1,054	1,054
	SLBM	32	96	144	224	416	496	592	656	656	656	656
USSR	ICBM	35	50	75	100	200	270	300	460	800	1,050	1,300
	SLBM	0	some	some	100	120	120	125	130	130	160	280

Source: *The Military Balance, 1970–1971*, London, Institute for Strategic Studies, 1970, p. 106

identical formulation was repeated in turn by Leonid Brezhnev in his opening speech at the 24th CPSU Congress in 1971.

However, it would be unwise to assume a correspondence between Soviet rhetoric and actual policy. In the USSR, the class principle (and the objectives it prompts) was and still is operationalised, in current policy terms, through the application of the 'correlation of forces'. This concept was described by Lenin as being 'the core of Marxism and Marxist tactics'.[4] In foreign politics as in politics in general 'one must be able to calculate the balance of forces ... What are the forces involved? How are they grouped? And only when we are able to estimate these forces correctly and quite soberly, irrespective of our sympathies and desires, shall we be able to draw the proper conclusions concerning our policy in general, and immediate tasks in particular'.[5] Unlike the Western balance-of-power notion which confines itself to a comparison of military might, the 'correlation of forces' is concerned with all elements affecting the aggregate relationship, to use Soviet jargon, of contemporary class forces. That subsumes, as Lenin acknowledged, qualitative as well as quantitative factors,[6] and thus gives Soviet leaders considerable scope for interpretation. In this way, the 'correlation of forces' is both diagnostic, as description of power relations, and prescriptive, a calculus for the furthering of the international class struggle.[7]

Given the extensive nature of the 'correlation of forces' concept, the Soviet assessment around 1969–70 will be examined here by reviewing trends at three levels: the global; the regional; and the local (the Horn of Africa). The interaction of these trends will also be considered. With these trends established, some continuities in Soviet foreign policy will finally be considered in order to place the Soviet disposition in perspective.

Global trends

Soviet perceptions of America and China were fundamentally altered during the late 1960s. The reevaluation was closely related to the attainment of rough parity in strategic nuclear weapons between the super-powers (see Table 1), and to the impact of the Vietnam war. The tremendous growth in the Soviet nuclear armoury was incontestable. Between 1962 and 1970, Soviet strategic capabilities underwent a numerical leap (see Table 2). By 1965 Moscow had succeeded in largely ensuring the survivability of its strategic forces in the event of a Western 'first-strike'. In strategic terms, the USSR established true, if limited, counterforce power. In addition, the 1960s saw considerable improvements, both quantitative and qualitative, in the Soviet Navy. In 1970 the Soviet Navy conducted its first worldwide exercise, 'Okean', thus registering the intention to act on distant seas and shores.

Soviet writers interpreted the erosion of American nuclear superiority as a turning point in international relations:

> Important developments have taken place in recent years in Soviet–US competition in the sphere of military technology. In spite of the US's crash rate of development of nuclear missile armaments at the beginning of the 1960s, the Soviet Union, as US sources recognise, quantitatively and qualitatively strengthened its own defense (in particular, in general megatonnage in intercontinental ballistic missiles, in strategic bombers, in orbital weapons, in anti-missile defense etc.).[8]

> The attempts of US imperialism to strengthen its influence in the world by means of the strategic armaments race have been neutralised in both political and strategic terms by the adequate measures which the Soviet Union has taken to strengthen its defence capability.[9]

> The beginning of the 1970s has been marked by important new shifts in the global balance of forces. The most essential of these is the further strengthening of the might of the USSR and the other countries of the socialist community. They now . . . have the ability to guarantee inevitable annihilating retribution for any aggressor, if he should decide on world war.[10]

Implicit in these remarks was the assertion that the USSR, and not the US, was becoming the dominant global actor. This assessment was linked to the fact that the Soviet military build up took place at a time when American society was experiencing profound difficulties.

Tumultuous events – racial violence, student unrest, political assassinations, growing unemployment, poverty, crime, drug abuse and, above all else, the growing anti-Vietnam war movement – convinced many Soviet commentators that Washington had suffered a serious loss of political confidence. G. Arbatov (the then Director of the USA & Canada Institute in Moscow) noted that there was a 'growing uneasiness [in Washington], doubt with respect to the correctness of the policy that is being pursued and anxiety concerning the fact that the USA is entering a period of profound and dangerous internal convulsions'.[11] Another Soviet writer went further: 'the popular masses are demanding increasingly, decisively and loudly the renunciation of military adventures abroad',[12] and quoted the then US

Vice-President Spiro Agnew on the seriousness of the domestic situation – 'Will the government of this country remain in the hands of its elected officials or will it descend to the street?'[13]

Seen from Moscow, the 'American crisis' had important foreign-policy repercussions. First, the 'collapse of confidence in the very government of the US'[14] undermined its ability to use force as an instrument of policy. It was argued that 'the failure in Vietnam gave rise to talk about the post-Vietnam non-intervention syndrome predicting that Washington would now show greater restraint in new international crises and conflicts, would strive to avoid involvement in some situations, and would soften its traditional principle of using force as the main instrument in conducting US policy'.[15] Secondly, because of the demonstrable linkage between involvement in Vietnam and the upheaval in American society 'imperialism' had experienced a set-back of global proportions. For now, more than ever before, it was clear that the strength and the international influence of 'imperialism', 'requires first of all concern for the stability of its own rear'.[16] This appeared to be an oblique reference to the inherent constraints of a democratic system fighting unpopular foreign wars.

Thirdly, it was claimed that Vietnam radically reshaped Washington's world outlook. The relative ineffectiveness of US military might alienated many of the so-called traditional supporters of the 'military option'. Many members of the US business community, with the exception of a small number of military–industrial complexes, came to realise 'that they could have earned much larger profits if part of federal military expenditures had been switched over to finance domestic programs'.[17] As a result, 'moderate bourgeois politicians' were in the ascendency by the late 1960s. The latter were said to recognise the need for 'a new approach to many traditional policy concepts such as national security and national power because it [the US] can no longer base its foreign policy assumptions on the premise that it has one and only one enemy in the shape of the USSR . . . and that any harm inflicted on that enemy automatically signifies an equivalent profit for the US'.[18]

As far as Moscow was concerned, the 'growth of realism' in Washington had several results. One was Nixon's apparent acceptance that the US could no longer fulfil the function of a world policeman. The promulgation of the Guam Doctrine, with its stress on stimulated self-help, was not confined to Vietnam. Kissinger's remarks in this vein were noted: the 'US is no longer in a position to operate programs globally . . . Regional groupings supported by the

US will have to take over major responsibility for their immediate areas'.[19] Another manifestation of the new realism was Nixon's willingness to accept Moscow as a co-equal superpower. The measured tones of Nixon's inaugural address, with its pledge for 'strategic sufficiency'[20] was favourably compared with the proud almost strident speech of President Kennedy some eight years earlier ('Let every nation know, whether it wishes us well or ill, that we shall pay any price, bear any burden, meet any hardship, support any friend, oppose any foe to assure the survival and the success of liberty').[21]

These changes in America's global perspective were, in Moscow's view, inextricably interwoven with the 'general crisis of capitalism' in the West: 'For the capitalist system the 1960s were a decade of unchecked disintegration of the hierarchy of international relations formed as a result of the second world war and characterised by the undisputed dominance of American imperialism in all spheres – political, economic, military and ideological.'[22] Militarily, such 'disintegration' was discerned in the French decision to leave the military wing of NATO in 1966, and the refusal of Britain, traditionally America's staunchest ally, to actively back the 'Vietnam gamble'. Ideologically, Moscow drew comfort from the growth of convergence theories in the West at the expense of what it termed the bellicose right. Talk of 'rolling back' communism and of defending the 'free world' had less currency by the late 1960s. And, while Moscow firmly rejected the convergence notion since 'socialist foreign policy is inconceivable without its unswerving fidelity to its revolutionary liberation ideals',[23] the arrival of Henry Kissinger in Washington probably symbolised a more accommodating intellectual trend. Kissinger argued that certain common state interests transcended ideological differences.

As for the political sphere, the Western demise was epitomised by its muted response to Soviet intervention in Czechoslovakia in August 1968. The intervention came just a month after the USSR, US and Britain signed the Treaty of Non-Proliferation of Nuclear Weapons. But while the NATO Foreign Ministers, in December 1968, denounced both the invasion and its concomitant, the Brezhnev Doctrine, they were prepared by May 1969 to announce their readiness to explore possibilities for negotiations with the USSR and the East European countries. These negotiations centred on European security and were tentatively agreed before the invasion. A willingness to resume these negotiations in so short a time must have reinforced an image of

declining political will. It also implied tacit aceptance of Soviet dominance in East Europe and all that that entailed, including the assertion
that there was no formal sovereignty outside the international class
struggle.[24] Certainly Moscow derived some satisfaction from Western
inaction:

> The crushing defeat inflicted on the anti-socialist counter-
> revolutionary forces and international imperialist reaction, which
> jointly launched a serious offensive on socialist Czechoslovakia, once
> again demonstrated to the world the strength and stability of the
> socialist countries and the steadfast will of their people to defend
> their revolutionary gains.[25]

Interestingly, though, while Soviet writers documented the ideological, political and military weakening of capitalist society, no
immediate upheaval in the overall economic system itself was anticipated. Some comments were made about war-fuelled inflation in the
US, its serious balance of payments problem and the almost 'obligatory' intensification of capitalist contradictions.[26] But, in general,
Soviet commentary was characterised by respect for the Western
economies. The then Director of the Institute for World Economy and
International Relations, N. Inozemtsev, singled out the US economy
as 'the mightiest and most highly-organised production mechanism in
the capitalist world . . . being especially strong in power equipment,
nuclear reactors, aircraft, wheat, corn and foreign investment
capital'.[27] Such technological pre-eminence, of course, was considered
to be temporary. Yet, at least, one Soviet observer cautioned against
undue optimism on this front:

> it would . . . be incorrect to assume that the American bourgeoise has
> exhausted all of its potentials and reserves and that, therefore, there
> is nothing left for it but to sag under the weight of its vices and
> sicknesses. The US is the most powerful and richest capitalist country
> which still possesses considerable economic and political reserves.[28]

Such respect was an admission, of sorts, that the Soviet economic
performance was less than satisfactory. In December 1969, *Pravda*
identified the key problem as one of production.[29] It conceded that the
old extensive methods of the 'command' economy were no longer
adequate. Beyond that, *Pravda* did not elaborate. However, a Western
analyst identified at least six problems facing the Soviet economy.[30] Of
these, the cumulative strain imposed by the massive build up in the
military sector was probably the most serious. Brezhnev contended
that 'socialism was powerful enough to secure both reliable defence

and the development of the economy' but he admitted in the same breath that 'the Soviet economy would have advanced more quickly, had it not been for large defence expenditures'.[31]

Soviet outlay in defence might have been less had it not been for 'the harmful influence of the Mao Tse-tung group'.[32] The late sixties witnessed a sharp deterioration in Sino–Soviet relations. In part, this was related to the beginnings of a new Sino–American relationship. The Peking leadership, alarmed by the Soviet invasion of Czechoslovakia, came to the conclusion that only the US could serve as an effective 'counter-weight' to the growing Soviet threat. Consequently, the twelfth plenary session of the Chinese Communist Party in October 1968 decided to seek improved relations with Washington. This move was reciprocated. Even before taking office, Nixon signalled his intention to get a new China policy: he maintained that 'we simply cannot afford to leave China forever outside the family of nations'.[33] After taking office in 1968, Nixon asked the State Department, the Defense Department and the CIA to consider new policy options towards China. For Nixon and Kissinger, China was central to the strategy of ending the Vietnam war 'with honour'.

In November 1968 China proposed the resumption of ambassadorial talks with the US in Warsaw. The Soviet reaction was swift. Moscow charged that the Warsaw talks were aimed at 'combining forces against the Soviet Union'.[34] Tensions along the Soviet–Sino border increased. In March 1969 violent clashes erupted between Soviet and Chinese troops on Damansky Island in the Usurri river region. These skirmishes marked a hardening in the Soviet attitude toward China. The latter was increasingly depicted as an ally of 'imperialism'. It was argued that China 'devotes active efforts (effectively operating on parallel lines with the imperialists) toward weakening the vanguard liberated countries' links with the USSR and the brotherly socialist states'.[35] Moscow made a half-hearted attempt to resume border negotiations with Peking. This initiative, however, broke down after it became apparent that Kosygin had visited India in early May to discuss their 'mutual border problem with China'.[36] A month later, at the International Meeting of Communist and Workers' Parties in Moscow, Brezhnev proposed a 'system of collective security in Asia'.[37] Although nominally directed at the regional designs of the Western powers, the proposal was clearly aimed at 'containing' the People's Republic of China.

By mid-1969, Sino–Soviet strains threatened Moscow's strategy in the Vietnam war. The latter consisted of maintaining an uninterrupted flow of materials to the North Vietnamese, Viet Cong, Pathet Lao and Khmer Rouge. By controlling the flow of arms, Moscow could dictate the pace of the war. This held out the prospect of undermining the Chinese claim to leadership of the communist world, thwarting an American–Chinese accommodation by creating conditions inimical to it, and furthering the ensnarement of the US in Vietnam. Such a strategy, however, was jeopardised by China's refusal 'to establish unity of action with other socialist countries'.[38] Of the three major logistical routes for transporting weaponry from the USSR to South-east Asia, two transversed China or its territorial waters. The first route was from the Siberian port of Vladivostok to Haiphong via the China Sea. The second route ran from the Trans-Siberian railway through China's Sinkiang province to the North Vietnamese rail and road system. In the spring of 1969, China 'created obstacles to the transportation of arms and supplies across Chinese territory'[39] and held up deliveries of Soviet hardware into South-east Asia. With the Suez Canal closed to shipping after the 1967 Israeli–Arab war, the third route running from the Black Sea, around the African continent, through the Indian Ocean to North Vietnam became enormously important. Unless Moscow could safeguard this route it might lose its position as the dominant ally of Hanoi (between 1965 and 1971 Soviet military aid estimated at US$1,660 million was nearly three times as great as Chinese aid during the same period)[40] and the initiative in the conflict would switch to America. In terms of global strategy, there-fore, there was every reason for a Soviet interest in naval facilities in the Indian Ocean.

It is interesting to note that these potentially unfavourable global trends, the Sino-Soviet split and paramountcy of Western economic power, were not among the 'objective' conditions which the Soviets claimed were responsible for the development of *détente* during this period. Such an omission, however, did not amount to an outright falsehood, important though these factors undoubtedly were. The Soviet global view was dominated by the irreconcilable struggle between East and West. As a consequence, any perceived deterior-ation in the Western position such as the loss of its preponderance in military strength was likely to be interpreted as a Soviet advantage: 'Each new step along the road of advancement of economic, political and military power of the socialist states limits the capacity of imperial-ism to manoeuvre, narrows the sphere of its dominance, and in this way alters the correlation of forces in the world arena to the detriment of imperialism and reaction.'[41] Thus, while the Soviet leadership was obviously aware of negative trends, it was cognitively inclined to attach greater significance to trends which confirmed ideological preconceptions. The result was a view of *détente* which held no concessions to Western interests.

Détente, on this view, was primarily an instrument of war avoidance. But it did not change 'the laws of the class struggle'. Brezhnev made that quite plain:

> Of course, comrades, all this does not mean that the antagonism between the two social systems, socialism and capitalism has disappeared ... The whole matter is simply a case of preventing this process from developing into armed conflicts and wars between countries and into the application of force in relations between them, and to prevent its hindering the development of mutually advantageous collaboration between states with differing social structures.[42]

An instance of such 'mutually advantageous collaboration' was the Treaty of Moscow concluded on 12 August 1970 between the USSR and the Federal Republic of Germany. The agreement, the cornerstone of the Ostpolitik concept, formed the basis of what amounted to a *de facto* European peace settlement. Moscow hailed the agreement as 'a major result of the struggle for the fundamental improvement of the situation in Europe and for the acknowledgement of post-war realities'.[43]

Other agreements followed. In September 1971 the USSR signed the Quadripartite Agreement on Berlin. Two months later the first practical steps for holding a European conference took shape. NATO drew up an agenda for discussions with their Warsaw Pact counterparts. And sandwiched between these agreements in October 1971 was a Soviet invitation to President Nixon to visit Moscow. It was to be the first ever visit to the Soviet Union by a US President. Significantly, it followed the announcement in July 1971, that President Nixon was to visit Peking.

However, while the USSR welcomed stability in its relationship with the US, it did not envisage that this would prevent it from pursuing a more active policy in peripheral areas – a policy more in line with its ideology and its enhanced military capabilities. In this regard, General Secretary L. Brezhnev made a distinction between inter-state relations and class struggle:

> The Communist Party of the Soviet Union and other Marxist–Leninist Parties sharply distinguish the sphere of operation of the principle of peaceful co-existence from that of national liberation war.

They base this on the fact that there is not and cannot be peaceful co-existence between oppressed and oppressors, between imperialist states and their colonies. There is not and cannot be peaceful co-existence where it is a matter of the processes of class struggle and national liberation struggle in capitalist countries and in colonies.[44]

Regional trends

By the late 1960s, North-east Africa began to figure prominently in Soviet thinking. A series of events such as the Six Day War of June 1967, the British decision to withdraw its navy from stations 'East of Suez', the expansion of the Soviet Navy and London's willingness in December 1966 to lease the British Indian Ocean Territory (BIOT) to America for defence purposes, succeeded in focussing the USSR's attention on a part of the world where, hitherto, it had played little part. This new interest, in part, was related to Moscow's revised perception of its 'internationalist duty' in the Third World. Historically, the Soviet attitude towards the developing countries owed much to Lenin's theory of imperialism. Stated briefly, Lenin argued that capitalist states were impelled by the nature of their economic systems to seek cheap sources of labour and raw materials abroad. Consequently, the less developed regions, Africa, Asia, the Middle East and Latin America were seen as prime targets for imperialist expansion. And, while, this expansion could do little to prevent the inevitable triumph of socialism, Lenin believed that the historical process could be accelerated through an alliance of the developing countries and the socialist states. This alliance, it was argued, would enable the developing countries to follow a non-capitalist path of development.

For Lenin and his successors, the common interest of the USSR and the developing countries in opposing imperialism was expressed through the concept of 'Proletarian Internationalism'. Defined as 'the solidarity of the working class and of Communists in all countries',[45] proletarian internationalism was not regarded as an abstract principle but, rather, a 'scientific' tool for the promotion of the world socialist revolution. It was claimed that the concept is both dynamic and yet unchanging. Dynamic in that it develops in accordance with the world revolutionary process; that is, 'its concrete context, principles, forms and scope are enriched, developed and extended'[46] in relation to circumstances and each particular stage of history. Unchanging in that the class essence of the policy is deemed to be permanent.

It was certainly true that Soviet internationalism in the late 1960s retained a number of features bearing the Leninist stamp. First, Moscow continued to interpret regional developments through a global framework:

> ... the Party constantly emphasizes the need in our day always to bear in mind, in practical foreign policy work, that the international stage is an area of collision of two foreign policy courses, that of the socialist states and that of the imperialist states. If we were to lose this criterion for the analysis of the foreign policy of the socialist states, we should discard and lose the point of reference for our forward march.[47]

Indeed, this point of reference was common to Soviet Third World policy from Lenin through to Brezhnev. And, while there were changes during the Khrushchev era, these were changes in scope rather than in objectives.

Secondly, Moscow, perhaps curiously, did not equate the perceived decline in Western power with any basic change in the nature of 'imperialism': 'Its aggressive essence remains unchanged, and as a result menacing military-and-political sallies have not been dropped from its agenda'.[48] Moreover, 'with the radical changes in the world strategic situation, the military doctrines of the imperialist blocs have been revised, and the centre of gravity has been transferred to so called "local wars"'.[49]

Thirdly, while Moscow denied any conflict between the interests of Soviet socialism and those of the revolutionary liberation movements, it was clear that in the event of divergence, Soviet interests took precedence. A *Pravda* editorial, 'The Supreme Internationalist Duty of a Socialist Country', did not pull any punches. After noting the USSR had become 'the stable centre of the world revolutionary movement' and bore the chief brunt in the struggle against 'imperialism', *Pravda* declared 'that the best way to fulfil our internationalist duty to the working people of the entire world is the successful construction of socialism and communism in the socialist countries'.[50] The inference was that Third World countries should accept the Soviet assessment of their material requirements in the form of aid.

Fourthly, and not unrelated to the last point, the Soviet government conferred upon itself the ultimate right to define 'real internationalism' and 'scientific socialism'. A policy of 'ideological independence',[51] as expressed in the concept of 'national socialism' favoured by some African countries, was regarded as a heresy: 'The authors of national socialism make their mistake in overstressing the special features of their countries.' But, here lay the weakness of such arguments. Only 'scientific socialism' could keep these African or Asian states' 'national socialism' from sliding backward into capitalism: 'Does a particular kind of algebra exist for Kenya? Or some other kind of zoology for Senegal? Then why should these be different socialisms?'.[52] The rider, then, of this perspective was that Soviet internationalism had a universal applicability.

Beyond these basic tenets, however, Soviet internationalism changed significantly during the 1960s. On the one hand, Khrushchevian optimism about the ability of Third World leaders to effect radical change evaporated. The much-heralded theory of non-capitalist development in which 'after winning political independence . . . the people begin to see that the best way to abolish age-long backwardness and improve their living standards is that of non-capitalist development'[53] did not live up to expectations. The fact that between 1965 and 1968, four 'revolutionary democratic' leaders in Indonesia, Algeria, Ghana and Mali were toppled by military coups provided food for thought:

> History knows examples of regressive phenomena in the relations between some young states and the socialist countries, when as a result of reactionary coups, or the entrenchment of pro-imperialist circles in a country's leadership, economic and cultural relations, already well established, have been damaged through no fault of the socialist countries themselves.[54]

By 1970–1, it was admitted that the process of non-capitalist development in Africa was 'very complicated' and would in all probability be 'extremely long'.[55]

On the other hand, the USSR's confidence in its own ability to influence events in the Third World had markedly increased:

> With the balance of the world forces now obtaining, superiority in military, and in particular the nuclear capacity of the United States and of other powers, have in practice lost their importance, as an instrument for resolving local conflicts. Local anti-imperialist forces (the national liberation movement, and the young national states), relying on the support of socialism can be successful in combat struggle both against insecure puppet regimes and against American forces operating on alien or hostile territory thousands of kilometres from the United States.[56]

It was now claimed that the USSR could project 'mobile armed forces appropriately trained and equipped . . . where the need arises for military support of peoples fighting for their freedom'. Moreover, 'in some situations the mere fact of a Soviet military presence in an area where a conflict is coming to a head or developing could exert a restraining influence on the imperialists and on local reaction, preventing their suppression of an insurgent people.'[57]

It was against this background – a gradual acceptance of Third World disarray and the growing conviction that Soviet power could turn events Moscow's way – that a new theory of 'states of socialist orientation' advanced. First enunciated in November 1967, this approach, unlike the earlier theory of non-capitalist development, was fairly explicit about the non-socialist features of many developing countries. States of 'socialist orientation' are 'countries which, while not yet socialist, reject capitalism as the system for their further social development and regard socialism as their goal'.[58] The internal and external policies of these states are 'directed toward anti-imperialist, anti-feudal and partially anti-capitalist reforms, the aim of which consists in the creation of state-political, socio-economic and scientific prerequisites for the gradual approach in the future toward socialism'. But, 'in most of the liberated countries these prerequisites are non-existent'.[59]

Moscow's new realism was based on several factors. First, the USSR recognised 'the problem of so called "strong personalities"' in developing states. While such leaders might be generally radical, 'the system of personal rule as such has serious negative aspects', the major one being a reluctance to democratise public life. Secondly, Moscow distinguished between 'purely verbal radicalism' and the reality of political parties' organisational shortcomings in the Third World. Parties were often marked by 'motley social composition, their lack of any strong discipline and of any political and ideological unity, the low educational level of most members of the party and, often, their political passivity'. Thirdly, even in those countries pursuing a non-capitalist path, the masses, by and large, were 'mentally not equipped to absorb the ideology of the revolutionary democrats'.[60]

Thus, the theory of 'states of socialist orientation' was prompted, not by the intrinsic merits of the developing countries themselves, but by the enhanced ability of the Soviet Union to aid non-capitalist development:

> The material and technical support of the socialist countries further the development of the young independent countries and serves them as a socio-political guarantee of the success of their progressive reforms and as a safeguard against the encroachments of imperialism. In effect, assistance from the socialist community which actively

opposes imperialism, is the foundation of non-capitalist development and the factor making this development possible'.[61]

Furthermore, Moscow came to regard military aid as the most important form of support for 'the forces of national liberation'. Unlike the
Khrushchev era when Soviet economic potential was seen as pivotal,
the Brezhnev regime increasingly stressed the military component in
the 'correlation of forces' assessment. This was evident, for example,
in a discussion of the mechanics of projecting force: 'The problem of a
military presence, like any other big military-strategic problem, is first
of all an economic and political problem, and then *beyond that a strictly
military problem.*'[62] Another writer was even more emphatic:

> ... economic might does not of itself ensure a leading position ...
> Not only does victory of the socialist system depend on its economic
> achievements but also the defensive power of the socialist commu-
> nity which has become the chief bulwark of the worldwide liberation
> movement.[63]

The focus on the military factor in Soviet regional thinking reflected
the growing conviction that the 'socialist' military instrument had an
independent utility. In considering the question of a Soviet 'military
presence' or military intervention (to de-Leninise this phrasing) a
Soviet writer observed that:

> ... one cannot fail to observe that the USSR is pursuing its own policy
> in this which is in principle distinct from US policy. Unlike the United
> States, the USSR has its own particular historical, economic and
> geographic features which neither gave it the possibility nor occa-
> sioned the need for it to secure a military presence in areas of the
> world distant from the USSR. In the present situation the Soviet
> Union finds that the need has arisen ... in response to the global
> aggressive policy of imperialism.[64]

The latter, it was said, makes 'wide use of the provision of weapons' to
its 'satellites'.[65]

And, since, in Moscow's view, at least, it had never initiated local
wars, it followed that 'socialist' military aid had distinct advantages.
First, Soviet-backed liberation movements, irrespective of means,
purportedly had greater moral strength than their adversaries. Such
morality was based on 'the alignment of the real forces of all classes in
all countries' and not 'abstract morals':

> The wars waged by the peoples of Korea, Algeria and Vietnam, were
> just wars of liberation, fought for their freedom and independence,

which gave them an enormous advantage over the aggressors who were pursuing aggressive and imperialist aims.[66]

Soviet support, therefore, was nothing but an alignment with natural justice. Secondly, the upsurge of Vietnam-inspired anti-Americanism in the developing countries during the late 1960s convinced Moscow that the Third World had become a peculiarly receptive place for its own military aid. This was because the USSR had, through the Vietnam conflict, demonstrated the effectiveness of its 'assistance' in a part of the world where 'as a rule', there is only 'a modest level of industrial production, science and technology' and where 'states do not manufacture conventional weapons'.[67] Thirdly, Soviet military aid was said to be distinguished by 'its revolutionary character'. Freed of colonial inclinations.

> the Soviet Armed Forces are serving as a source of military experience for the armies of the young states . . . Today, when questions of the armed defence of the national liberation revolution are of special importance for the struggle against foreign and internal reaction, this experience is exceptionally important . . . in that Soviet experience in military work and practice is militarily and technologically the most advanced.[68]

By emphasising the political and military role of the USSR, the theory of 'socialist oriented' states assumed, unlike Khrushchev's theory of non-capitalist development which claimed that the people themselves would advocate such a path, that the developing state itself would promote socialism and prepare the masses for 'popular' decision-making. This new doctrine entailed a significant broadening of what constituted a 'progressive' regime in the Third World:

> In our opinion 'progressive' in present day conditions means a policy of resolute opposition to neo-colonialism, struggle for the strengthening of the sovereignty and independence of young states and their economic liberation from imperialism, and the struggle for peace, for social progress and for the strengthening of solidarity with the leading forces of our time, and in the first place with the socialist countries.[69]

There appeared to be only one essential criterion for a regime or a movement to receive active Soviet support. Namely, a willingness to adopt an anti-Western position. A Soviet writer quoted Lenin as saying that the political complexion of a national liberation movement may be 'bourgeois republican, and in some cases dynastic and religious, so long as it is anti-imperialist in content'.[70] Next to that, Third

World allies were expected to favour an anti-Chinese stance. That involved 'non-acceptance of the theories of "rich" and "poor" nations and of "two super powers" founded on a repudiation or deliberate distortion of the contradictory class nature of the two world systems'.[71]

Beyond these minimum requirements, most developing countries were now eligible for Soviet 'internationalist' assistance. Neither the existence of a private-enterprise sector or institutionalised religion were seen as insurmountable barriers to a 'socialist orientation'. Even more striking, however, was Moscow's permissiveness toward Third World military regimes. The old Leninist dictum that an army was either revolutionary or reactionary, depending on the class that it served, was shelved. It was now asserted that military elites were relatively independent from class:

> Although representatives of the propertyless toilers are rare among the officer corps, it is, as a whole well acquainted with the needs and sentiments of the 'common people' and better still with the views and temper of the petty bourgeoise and professional sections.[72]

With their greater awareness, the military, as opposed to other institutions in developing countries, were not only consistent advocates of modernisation but also, because of their 'incomparably' more rigorous organisation and discipline, the most effective managers of the process. This applied particularly to the young, multi-ethnic societies where the military might be the single national institution.[73]

But this was more than just a pragmatic acceptance of military coups. Moscow also stressed the positive virtues of the military as a potential ally:

> The advantages of the army as against political parties is obvious if one compares the sources for financing the parties, which are limited and not always reliable, with the resources allocated to maintaining the army. The army is a state organisation, which receives the funds for its support entirely from the state budget. It does not need to worry about the business situation in the country, nor about the financial power of the bourgeoisie.[74]

And while this writer, and others, insisted on the need for 'progressive control' of the army by a vanguard party to guard against 'Bonapartism', it is significant that even more skeptical observers like Professor G. Mirskiy[75] shared the conviction that Soviet 'assistance' could push a Third World military regime in a 'progressive' direction when no such party existed. Clearly, the acknowledged risks of backing military governments were outweighed by the perceived advantages. One was political. By reaching an understanding with strongly nationalist and often strongly anti-Western regimes, Moscow could claim a widening of the 'progressive' umbrella. Another consideration was economic.

The theory of 'socialist-oriented' states emphasised the principle of economic rationality. Rather than trying to use economic aid to win political influence, Moscow asserted that:

> Assistance from the socialist countries necessarily bears the character of mutually beneficial co-operation because the resources of one side obviously cannot satisfy the acute and growing requirements of the countries that have taken or are prepared to take the road of non-capitalist development.[76]

Put bluntly, Moscow was telling the developing countries it could not finance their social transformations *in toto*, and that its aid should not be interpreted as an 'obligation'. Instead:

> Our co-operation with them [the developing countries] based on the principles of equality and respect for mutual interests is acquiring the character of stable distribution of labour, contrary to the system of imperialist exploitation in the sphere of international economic relations. At the same time, by expanding trade with the developing countries, the Soviet Union will gain the opportunity of satisfying more fully the requirements of its own national economy.[77]

This last requirement, coupled with the anticipated economic conflict between the West and the developing countries, reinforced a somewhat tolerant attitude toward many regimes in the Third World who had little in common, ideologically, with the Soviet Union.

The changing nature of Soviet internationalism influenced, and was influenced by, developments on the ground in North-east Africa. In the period from 1967 to 1970 traditional power structures in the area were in a state of flux. That the USSR emerged as the chief beneficiary of this new climate was not a coincidence. Fundamental to an understanding of Soviet progress during this period is the impact of the Suez Canal closure in July 1967. The economies of Egypt, the Sudan, South Yemen, Ethiopia and Somalia were among those severely hit by the loss of foreign revenues from portage and bunkering fees. The loss of hard currency was compounded by a concomitant increase in the cost of exports. After the closure of the Canal, it took, on average, three weeks more for these countries to send their goods to Western Europe.[78] This, in turn, led to a drop in foreign demand

and hence higher prices, all of which had important political implications.

In Egypt, the humiliating defeat of its Soviet-equipped Army at the
hands of the Israelis and the resultant loss of £100 million or more in
foreign earnings per annum – £80 million in Suez Canal revenues and
£20 million in profits from the Sinai oil fields – had the effect of making
General Abdul Nasser's government even more dependent on Soviet
aid. And Moscow, anxious to repair the damage to its own prestige in
the area, responded generously. By 1969, a massive Soviet airlift
resulted in the replacement of 80 per cent of all Egyptian aircraft, tanks
and artillery lost during the Six Day War.[79] Nasser publicly thanked
Moscow for its efforts.[80]

In the Sudan, Moscow benefited from the growing identification of
Mohammed Ahmed Mahgoub's government with the Arab cause.
Plagued by economic stagnation and ethnic dissension, Mahgoub's
regime sought to restore its domestic standing through a new orientation in its foreign policy in the wake of the Six Day War. In July 1967,
Khartoum severed diplomatic relations with two of its traditional arms
suppliers, the US and the UK, both of whom were allies of Israel.
Moscow promptly stepped into the breach, and within a year had
established itself as the major arms supplier to Sudan. According to an
agreement of 1968, Moscow provided MiG–21 fighters, T–34 and T–54
tanks, an assortment of modern artillery and large quantities of light
arms. Altogether, the arms package was said to be worth £50 million.[81]

Yet while Mahgoub's government was commended for 'strengthening its ties with all anti-imperialist and anti-colonialist forces', Moscow
did not hesitate to welcome its overthrow. A military coup by the
Revolutionary Council headed by Colonel Ja'far an-Numeiry on 25
May 1969 was described by *Pravda* as a 'logical completion of the
Sudanese revolution of October 1964'. Six months later, the *coup d'état*
was depicted as a full-blown 'revolution' directed 'against a bourgeois-
landowner regime'.[82] Thus, a regime once considered acceptable was
subsequently denigrated in order to accommodate the new military
regime. Such was the *Realpolitik* of Soviet Third World policy.

Soviet–Sudanese relations developed strongly after the May 'revolution'. A new aid agreement providing credit for development
projects, reportedly worth $42 million,[83] was signed in November
1969. Trade links were expanded and debt rescheduling arrangements
were agreed. By 1970 Sudan ranked in first place among the USSR's
trading partners in black Africa. Moreover, Soviet arms transfers to
Khartoum increased and provision was made for expanding the

Sudanese Army from about 30,000 to 50,000. Despite Numeiry's public reservations about the level of Soviet economic aid,[84] the USSR's enthusiasm for the new military regime remained undaunted. It was praised for the 'profound social changes' at home and for its 'position of leadership in the anti-imperialist struggle'[85] in the Arab world. As for Sudan's then most pressing domestic problem, the secessionist movement in the South, Moscow endorsed the military government's commitment to preserve the territorial integrity of the country. It was argued that the secessionist movement was artificially created by the British during the colonial era, and could be solved on the basis of 'regional autonomy, as advocated by the Sudanese communists'.[86]

Meanwhile, in Aden, a major bunkering port with a poorly developed hinterland, the closure of the Suez Canal brought food shortages, labour unrest and persistent civil strife. Such conditions served to radicalise the political options facing the country. In consequence, the British decision to withdraw from Aden in November 1967, after a 128-year presence, paved the way for the creation of the People's Democratic Republic of South Yemen (PDRY). In January 1968, Prime Minister Harold Wilson announced the withdrawal of all Royal Navy units 'East of Suez'. These events were watched with much interest in the Kremlin. In March 1968, a Soviet military mission visited South Yemen to assess the weapons requirements of the new nation's army. Within a few months, the USSR agreed to provide military aid and advisers to South Yemen.[87] But if Moscow's immediate impact on the country was limited by factional disputes in the PDRY's revolutionary government, its 'progressive' potential – in 1969 the PDRY severed diplomatic ties with the US – convinced Moscow that the 'national liberation movement in the Persian Gulf countries and in the southern Arabian peninsula were notably strengthened after the creation of the PDRY'.[88]

This assessment, though, was related, in part, to the decline of the Soviet position in North Yemen. Paradoxically, this reverse began at a time, in 1968, when Soviet weapons deliveries to the Republican government, engaged in a protracted civil war against Royalist forces, reached their peak. The flow of arms had increased after Moscow found itself having to directly sustain the Republican regime, following the Egyptian disengagement from North Yemen in late 1967. Nevertheless, several factors contrived to cool Soviet–North Yemeni relations. First, Soviet interest in neighbouring South Yemen, a bitter rival of North Yemen even before the British withdrawal, was prob-

Table 3. *The Soviet naval presence in the Indian Ocean, 1960–1983*

Year	Total ship days
1960	200
1961	0
1962	100
1963	100
1964	0
1965	0
1966	0
1967	200
1968	1,200
1969	4,100
1970	4,900
1971	4,000
1972	8,900
1973	8,900
1974	10,500
1975	7,100
1976	7,300
1977	6,700
1978	8,500
1979	7,600
1980	11,800
1981	10,700
1982	10,200
1983	8,800

Source: adapted from Mark A. Carolla, 'The Indian Ocean Squadron' in Bruce W. Watson and Susan M. Watson, eds., *The Soviet Navy: Strengths and Liabilities*, Boulder, Colorado, Westview Press, 1986, p. 242

ably interpreted in Sana as a sign of the Kremlin's limited commitment to the Republican cause. This suspicion was reinforced by the tentative Soviet attempts to persuade Premier al-Amri to negotiate a settlement with the Royalists.[89] Secondly, Moscow's role was increasingly challenged by Saudi Arabia. In the wake of the 1967 Arab–Israeli war, the Saudis provided generous financial support for the North Yemeni government in an effort to lessen Soviet influence. The strategy worked. By 1970, North Yemen had moderated its international stance sufficiently to reopen diplomatic relations with several Western governments.

But North Yemen still seemed the exception rather than the rule for

Soviet diplomacy in North-east Africa between 1967 and 1970. As well as greatly expanding its ties with the states of this region, the USSR also established what was to become a permanent naval presence in the Indian Ocean (see Table 3). A contingent of warships moved into the Indian Ocean for the first time from their Pacific fleet stations, visiting Mogadishu in April and Aden in June 1968. This initial deployment consisted of approximately eighteen ships, about one-third of which were combatants.[90]

The entry of the Soviet Navy into the Indian Ocean had a political and a geo-strategic rationale. Politically, a naval presence was seen by Moscow as a valuable instrument for consolidating ties with the littoral states. Soviet naval doctrine, as articulated by Commander in Chief, Admiral S. G. Gorshkov, emphasised the peacetime military–political role of the Navy in 'protecting state interests',[91] including Soviet state economic, political and military interests in the Third World. This task was 'especially important' in the Indian Ocean region, 'the epicenter of the national liberation movement'.[92] According to Soviet writers, there had been a 'significant weakening of the West's positions in the Indian Ocean basin':

> The new political situation in the Indian Ocean is above all char-
> acterised by a significant strengthening of the national liberation
> movement and the role of the liberated countries . . . The growth of
> the national liberation movement and the development of non-
> capitalist trends in a number of countries of the Indian Ocean is
> proceeding side by side with the expansion of most of these coun-
> tries' links with the Soviet Union, and with the whole socialist
> community.[93]

One way of forging these 'links' was through 'showing the flag' (see Table 4):

> Of no small importance for strengthening friendly relations with the
> peoples of the Indian ocean basin countries are the visits of ships of
> the Soviet Navy to ports of friendly countries (Indian ocean countries
> visited by Soviet naval vessels in recent years include Egypt, Tan-
> zania, Pakistan, Ethiopia, India, Somalia, Kenya, Yemen Arab
> Republic, People's Democratic Republic of Yemen, Iran, Iraq, Mauri-
> tius and others).[94]

On several occasions, moreover, the Soviet Navy was able, in Gorsh-kov's words, 'to put pressure on potential opponents without direct use of its weapons'.[95] For instance, in 1967, the Soviet Navy ferried South Yemeni troops from Aden around the coast to staging areas

Table 4. *Pattern of Soviet operational ship visits in the Indian Ocean 1967–1976*

Country	1967	1968	1969	1970	1971	1972	1973	1974	1975	1976	1967–76
Somalia	0	0	2	7	22	20	42	61	54	75	283
S. Yemen	0	0	4	5	15	7	14	37	34	18	134
Iraq	0	0	4	1	2	8	15	17	8	12	67
Sri Lanka	0	1	2	1	0	6	2	5	6	6	29
Mauritius	0	0	1	7	1	9	1	2	2	1	24
India	0	0	1	6	2	0	3	2	4	2	20
Kenya	0	0	1	4	0	0	2	4	1	0	12
N. Yemen	0	0	1	2	0	0	0	1	2	3	9
Pakistan	0	0	5	2	0	0	0	0	0	0	8
Maldives	0	0	0	0	3	0	0	0	1	1	5
Iran	0	0	2	0	0	0	0	0	1	1	3
Tanzania	0	0	0	2	0	0	0	0	0	0	2
Ethiopia	0	0	1	0	0	0	0	0	0	0	1
Kuwait	0	0	1	0	0	0	0	0	0	0	1
Madagascar	0	0	1	0	0	0	0	0	0	0	1
Seychelles	1	0	0	0	0	0	0	0	0	0	1
Sudan	0	0	0	1	0	0	0	0	0	0	1
Totals	1	1	26	38	45	50	79	129	113	119	601

Note: visits by naval noncombatants such as hydrographic vessels are not included in this table.
Source: adapted from Bradford Dismukes and James McConnell, eds., *Soviet Naval Diplomacy*, New York, Pergamon, 1979, Table 2.7 p. 69

from which it is assumed they crossed the border to support the
Dhofar rebels; in 1970, the Soviet Navy played an important part in the
transfer and maintenance of Soviet air defence contingents dispatched
during the War of Attrition; in the same year, in Somalia, the
announcement of an abortive coup attempt at the time of a Soviet port
visit prompted an extension of a stay originally scheduled for only five
days. These examples confirmed Moscow's tacit acceptance of the
Western view that 'a naval vessel has always been an important power
symbol for the peoples of this region'.[96]

At the same time, the Soviet Indian Ocean Squadron served
broader, strategic purposes. While Soviet commentators seemed to
acknowledge the British departure from the region, this did not
prevent them from asserting that 'imperialism' was intensifying its
efforts to militarise the Indian Ocean. A *Tass* statement of 3 March 1968
accused the US and British of 'hatching plans for knocking together a
military bloc' among the Persian Gulf countries. Moreover, in view of
the USSR's geographical proximity ('the attention of imperialist strategists, and above all of aggressive US circles, is attracted by [the Indian
Ocean's] northern regions which lie in proximity to the USSR')[97]
Soviet writers suggested that the region had attained a new significance in the 'correlation of forces' estimate:

> In the opinion of foreign politicians and military specialists, the
> Indian Ocean and the countries bordering it are gradually acquiring
> the status of an independent geopolitical complex. The importance of
> the Indian Ocean as a theater of military and naval activities is
> growing.[98]

One reason for the geographical focus was the perceived threat of a
US strategic strike from the Indian Ocean:

> Since the Polaris A–2 and A–3 missiles with which US submarines are
> now armed have an operational range of from 3,000 to 4,500 kilo-
> metres, they represent a definite threat to the security of many states,
> including the Soviet Union, regardless of what ocean these sub-
> marines are in ... In terms of distance, the Soviet Union's southern
> borders from the Indian Ocean are only 1,200 to 1,500 kilometres,
> which means that a large part of Soviet territory is within range of
> Polaris missiles ... these considerations strongly attract US strate-
> gists to the Indian Ocean; they look on it as a convenient launching
> area for submarine-carried strategic missiles. With the replacement of
> the Polarises by the Poseidons [in 1966], whose range is up to 5,000 to
> 6,000 kilometres, the strategic value of the Indian Ocean from this
> point of view will be even greater.[99]

Furthermore, attempts to counter the Polaris and Poseidon developments through diplomacy bore little fruit. In December 1964, Moscow
launched an initiative at the United Nations to make the Indian Ocean
a nuclear-free zone. The idea met a cool response in Washington.
Apart from a reluctance to squander a strategic advantage, the United
States was also sceptical about Soviet motives. The Soviet UN memorandum made no mention of other oceans apart from the Mediterranean.

A second consideration for Moscow was the establishment of a US
communications, air and naval base on the island of Diego Garcia in
the late 1960s. This followed a defence agreement between the United
States and Britain in December 1966. According to the terms of the
deal, Britain agreed to lease the Chagos Islands, otherwise known as
the British Indian Ocean Territory, the largest of which was Diego
Garcia, to Washington for defence purposes for fifty years, with the
option of a further twenty years if required.[100] In Moscow's eyes, the
Diego Garcia development demonstrated the 'aggressive character' of
US intentions in the region:

> It should be noted that the US military command selected Diego
> Garcia for its central stronghold in the Indian Ocean because it was
> felt that this island could ensure dominance in the Indian Ocean with
> a minimum of armed force. And this fully corresponds with the
> Nixon doctrine on the nature of US armed forces participation in
> establishing a 'balance of power' in Asia.[101]

The last point gave the clue to Moscow's immediate concern about the
Diego Garcia base. It was feared that this 'island strategy' was
connected with plans to 'squeeze' Soviet support for North Vietnam.
This much was admitted by another commentator who observed that
'the permanent "military presence" of the imperialists in this region
[the Indian Ocean] threatens the Soviet Union's sea communications
through it, connecting the ports of the Baltic and the Black Sea with the
Pacific coast'.[102]

A third reason for Soviet interest was Western economic dependence on the Indian Ocean region: 'With the establishment of the Diego
Garcia base, US strategists at the same time reckon on solving the
problems of the Persian Gulf' through exerting '"indirect influence"
by means of regular visits of US ships from the Indian Ocean to the
Persian Gulf'.[103] These 'problems' were substantial:

> The Persian Gulf region's proven reserves of oil constitute over 60 per
> cent of the capitalist world's reserves; and over half Western Europe's

oil supplies come from the region. Middle East oil is widely used by the US Navy. The countries of the Indian Ocean are also principal suppliers of natural rubber and tin.

By pointing out the dimensions of Western dependence, Moscow reached conclusions which implied and justified a Soviet naval presence in the region:

> The strategic situation of the Persian Gulf is of immense importance for the imperialists. The one who has the mastery of the Gulf has the control of the biggest oil artery in the world; and thereby he also controls the economic life of the Arab Shaykhdoms, oil being their principal export. [104]

The final aspect in the strategic equation was the growth of Sino–Soviet competition in the Indian Ocean region. While Moscow was obviously aware of Chou En-lai's remark in Mogadishu in February 1964 concerning the 'excellent revolutionary situation in Africa',[105] such 'adventurism' only became a serious challenge after the Cultural Revolution. In the Sudan, a country where Moscow established strong ties during this period, Chinese diplomacy had to be reckoned with. After the military coup, a series of government exchanges culminated in the signing of a fifteen-year credit agreement in June 1970. The credit was reportedly worth $34.8 million,[106] making it one of the largest Peking had extended prior to this date. In South Yemen, the USSR's close links with the Secretary-General of the National Liberation Front were partially offset by a military coup in June 1969 which established Salim Rubayi Ali as President. Ali favoured the Chinese model of development, namely self-reliance and minimal foreign assistance. Meanwhile, across in North Yemen, the eclipse of the Soviet position was also affected, although not determined, by China. Here, Peking's main achievement was to confirm itself as a steadfast ally during the civil war. For example, the Chinese embassy in Sana was the only foreign embassy not to evacuate its staff during the Royalist siege of Sana in December 1967.[107] Thus, the challenge for Moscow was not that China would surpass it as a supplier of arms, food or technical personnel – the Chinese position remained in comparative terms, quantitatively weak – but rather that the states in the region would acknowledge the CPR as the ideological model for the Third World.

Whatever the political and strategic motivations behind the new Soviet naval presence, such a presence had one manifest requirement, namely, the need for shore-based support. Yet Moscow apparently remained confident that the region could satisfy its requirements: 'On the Indian Ocean there are up to 27 operational and 10 former naval bases and basing points, which is in excess of the needs of the naval forces of littoral states.'[108]

Local trends 1967–1970

In the Horn of Africa itself, the impact of the Arab–Israeli war was something of a mixed blessing for the Soviet Union. All governments and national liberation movements in the area experienced economic hardship in one form or another as a result of the closure of the Suez Canal. But these effects were uneven, and did not work out to the immediate political advantage of the USSR. In fact, during the period from June 1967 until the military coup in Somalia in October 1969, the Soviet position in the Horn actually stagnated.

To some extent, this trend was self-imposed. Moscow's main priority, after the Six Day War, was to rebuild the devastated armies of Egypt and Syria, the objective being to restore Soviet credibility as an ally at a time when the Israeli victory 'trivialized Arab interest in events on the periphery of the Middle East'.[109] And given that Arab funds and arms to the ELF, from Syria, and to Somalia, from Egypt and the Sudan, virtually dried up, the USSR found it politic to scale down its own involvement in the Horn. In doing so, Moscow was able to demonstrate to some of its more sceptical Arab friends its dedication to the Arab cause. This meant, in the case of the ELF, effectively terminating Soviet aid altogether.[110]

In addition, there was an increasing Soviet concern about the level of hostilities in the Horn of Africa. This had manifested itself as early as March 1967 when the Soviet government informed Emperor Haile Selassie that it did not support Somali self-determination through military means.[111] Presumably, after the 1967 war, Moscow was even more wary of escalation in the Horn. In particular it was probably anxious to avoid placing itself again in a situation of failing to prevent the defeat of an ally. Moreover, with new openings elsewhere, in South Yemen and the Sudan, there was less need for Moscow to run such risks. As a consequence, the USSR significantly reduced its military and economic assistance to Somalia.[112]

However, Moscow's reduced role in the Horn was not entirely of its own making. Not only were there very real logistical difficulties in re-supplying Somalia after the Suez Canal closure but it was also the case that Moscow's friends in the area were the chief victims of the resultant economic dislocation. Ethiopia, whose links with Moscow were marginal in political terms, emerged as the least scathed party. For while it now cost Addis Ababa about 50 per cent more to ship a ton of coffee to Western Europe, this did not compare with the damage sustained by her internal and external adversaries.

For the ELF, the consequences were nearly catastrophic. Already weakened by Haile Selassie's diplomatic success at the beginning of 1967 in persuading the Sudan to limit its support of the ELF in return for curtailing Ethiopian–Israeli assistance to the Anyana rebels in Southern Sudan, the ELF found itself on the receiving end of a massive Ethiopian offensive in September 1967. The assault, involving for the first time regular Ethiopian troops, routed both the ELF and Eritrean civilians alike. Nearly 300 villages were destroyed, more than 28,000 Eritreans were driven across the border to the Sudan, and an ELF leader, Waldaye Kassaye, surrendered to the Ethiopian authorities.[113] By early 1968, the Eritrean rebels appeared to be on the verge of total defeat.

Meanwhile, the Somali guerrilla campaign to 'free' the Ogaden was hampered by an increasing shortage of Soviet weapons and the economic consequences of the Suez Canal closure. A drastic decrease in Somali foreign-exchange earnings from bananas and livestock, the two main exports, as well as higher shipping rates, markedly increased the burden of the military effort in the Ogaden. All this, however, was not immediately apparent. The insurgents in the Bale/Ogaden region had been sufficiently armed to maintain a military struggle even with the slowing of Mogadishu's logistical support. But, by early 1969, the guerrillas began to feel the pinch. In 1968, Addis Ababa launched a campaign to divide the rebels from the indigenous population in the Ogaden by attacking corruption and tackling peasant grievances.[114] Gradually, the local population, whose lives had been continuously disrupted by the insurgency, ceased to provide the guerrillas with the support they required.

Faced with the fact that a policy of confrontation had done little to realise the pan-Somali goal, the new Somali government of President Abdirashid Ali Shermarke and Prime Minister Mohammed Ibrahim Egal, formed in July 1967, decided to see what might be achieved by more conciliatory diplomacy towards Ethiopia. After encouraging exchanges with the Ethiopian delegation at the OAU Heads of State meeting in Kinshasa in September 1967, a Somali ministerial team arrived in Addis Ababa five days later for talks. Within days, a series of agreements were announced. These included the normalisation of diplomatic relations, the reactivation of the Ethiopian–Somali joint military commission (in accordance with the Khartoum agreement of 1964), the convening of periodic meetings of regional administrators to discuss frontier problems and a pledge to remove the 'conditions which affect adversely relations between the two countries'.[115]

Over the next two years further agreements followed. Air and telecommunications links were restored between Ethiopia and Somalia. Trade was resumed, and both countries agreed to end hostile propaganda broadcasts. All this was achieved, however, without any progress on the major issues originally causing the border dispute. Ethiopia interpreted the new agreements as fully consistent with the preservation of its territorial integrity. Somalia, on the other hand, rationalised the *détente* strategy in terms of economic expediency ('No country in the world, no matter how big or powerful, can stand alone either politically or economically')[116] but vigorously denied there had been any compromise on the principle of Somali unification. Indeed, the Somali Prime Minister characterised *détente* as a gain for the Somali position.[117] In short, *détente* simply meant that Ethiopia and Somalia no longer saw their dispute as an obstacle to the improvement of relations.

Moscow initially welcomed the improvement in Ethiopian–Somali relations. This was evident just two months after the beginning of the new dialogue, when domestic opponents of the policy in Somalia accused the Somali Prime Minister of a 'sell-out'. Moscow countered with a spirited defence of the new government's initiative. It condemned Abdirazak Haji Hussein's (the former Prime Minister) government for 'squandering' 30 per cent of the national income 'on dead-end policy' which 'antagonised neighbouring states' and violated 'the decisions of the OAU on the settlement of disputes'. The new Somali government, in contrast, was praised for reversing this course through a new popular policy which enabled it 'to tackle domestic problems'.[118] Clearly, Moscow did not believe *détente* would damage its interests in the region. Such confidence was probably related to the fact that Dr Abdirashid Ali Shermarke, the new Somali President, commanded considerable respect in Moscow. As Prime Minister, Shermarke concluded the military-aid agreement of November 1963, and was 'known for his honesty and anti-colonial activity'.[119]

But Moscow's enthusiasm for the new policy was short lived. The benefits of Ethiopian–Somali *détente* were soon overshadowed, in Soviet eyes, by the concomitant *rapprochement* between Somalia and the West. Discouraged by the ineffectiveness of Soviet military aid during the Six Day War, the Somali government under Egal, a leader with a British political pedigree, used *détente* to extend the hand of friendship to Ethiopia's Western allies. In December 1967, Somalia restored diplomatic relations with Britain. A month later, US Vice-President Hubert Humphrey was warmly received in Mogadishu. In March 1968, Egal himself was the guest of President Lyndon Johnson in Washington where he was praised for being 'enormously constructive in a troubled area of Africa'.[120] The Somali Prime Minister also met leading US businessmen with a view to encouraging investment in Somalia. In September 1968, Egal journeyed to Paris in an attempt to reach an understanding with de Gaulle over the Djibouti question. During this period of hectic foreign-policy making, Prime Minister Egal also visited Rome, Bonn, Brussels, London, Lusaka and Nairobi.

This brand of shuttle diplomacy was interpreted in the USSR as an abandonment of Somalia's policy of non-alignment. Soviet writers accused Egal, but not Shermarke, of 'openly supporting a pro-Western policy'.[121] Signs of coolness between the two countries appeared. No Soviet press coverage was given to the accords signed by Ethiopia and Somalia between 1967 and 1969. This was a significant omission. In the field of trade, figures for 1969 indicated that exports from the USSR to Somalia decreased and were lower than at any point since 1962 (see Table 5). Moreover, attempts to reverse this downward trend came to nothing. For example, the Soviet–Somali economic agreement of August 1968 called for a rescheduling of certain outstanding loans and an actual write off by the Soviet government of other obligations.[122] Yet, within nine months, the two governments were involved in 'acrimonious negotiations' over the very question of debt rescheduling.[123] In July 1969, the strained relationship resulted in the cancellation of a state visit by Shermarke and Egal to Moscow. The rift widened in September 1969. Confronted with the threatened cut-off of all US foreign aid unless the passage of 'flag of convenience' vessels into Haiphong was halted, the Somali government opted to reduce its merchant traffic into Vietnam.[124] Such acquiescence must have angered the USSR. The reduction of neutral cargo carriers came at a time when Moscow was feeling the logistical squeeze applied by the US and China in South-east Asia.

The USSR fared little better in its dealings with Ethiopia. *Détente* in the Horn failed to narrow the distance between the two sides. For its part, Ethiopia remained suspicious of Soviet motives. In Eritrea, for instance, the revival of ELF operations in the second half of 1968 took place, in Haile Selassie's view, with Soviet connivance. As before, this

Table 5. *Soviet trade with Ethiopia and Somalia, 1960–1969 (millions of roubles)*

	1960			1961			1962			1963			1964		
	Exp.	Imp.	Turn.	Exp.	Imp.	Turn.	Exp.	Imp.	Turn.	Exp.	Imp.	Turn.	Exp.	Imp.	Turn.
Ethiopia	0.8	0.4	1.2	0.8	0.6	1.4	0.8	1.1	1.9	1.0	1.8	2.8	3.0	2.1	5.1
Somalia	0	0	0	0	0	0	0.8	0.3	1.1	6.1	0.2	6.3	7.5	0	7.5

	1965			1966			1967			1968			1969		
	Exp.	Imp.	Turn.	Exp.	Imp.	Turn.	Exp.	Imp.	Turn.	Exp.	Imp.	Turn.	Exp.	Imp.	Turn.
Ethiopia	7.0	2.3	9.3	4.7	2.7	7.4	1.9	3.5	5.4	1.9	1.9	3.8	2.2	3.6	5.8
Somalia	6.2	0	6.2	7.8	0	7.8	5.1	0.1	5.2	3.2	0.1	3.3	1.9	0	1.9

Note: Exports (Exp.) are from the USSR; Imports (Imp.) are to the USSR; Turnover (Turn.) refers to the total volume of trade between the two countries.

Source: *Vneshnyaya Torgovlya za SSSR*; Moscow, Statistika, various years

suspicion rested on Moscow's links with several of the Arab states who resumed their support for the ELF. Quantities of Soviet arms were given by Syria, South Yemen, and also, after the May 'revolution' of 1969, by the Sudan. Moreover, all of these states, to a greater or lesser degree permitted ELF personnel to attend training courses for Palestinian fedayeen, some of which were given by Soviet instructors.[125]

That this assistance created problems for Ethiopia is undeniable. From mid-1968, the Ethiopian Army in Eritrea was challenged by a more tactically aware, as well as better-armed adversary. Rather than engage in conventional military operations which they could not win, the ELF resorted to hit and run tactics. In August 1969, in two separate ambushes, the ELF killed 113 soldiers in the Massawa area. Outside Ethiopia, the ELF initiated a series of bombings and hijackings aimed at Ethiopian Airlines (EAL). On 11 March 1969, the ELF bombed and badly damaged an EAL jet at Frankfurt airport, West Germany. On 18 June 1969 the ELF struck again at Karachi airport, badly damaging a second jet. Similarly, on 13 September, three ELF members hijacked an EAL jet to Aden, interrupting an Addis Ababa–Djibouti flight.[126]

Angered by the publicity generated through these incidents, the Ethiopian government blamed the 'Syrian Liberation Front of Eritrea' for the disturbances. The then Governor General of Eritrea, Prince Asrate Kassa asserted that 'there is no nationalist movement inside Ethiopia'; the ELF was nothing but 'an organised syndicate of bandits, a Mafia with Marxist cadres'. The Ethiopian government also saw the 'foreign hand of communism'[127] behind the growth of student unrest in the country. In March 1969, the Haile Selassie I University was closed, and two Soviet journalists and three Czechoslovakian diplomats were expelled in connection with student agitation in Addis Ababa. This action followed demonstrations outside the Ethiopian Embassy in Moscow led by radical Ethiopian students demanding 'an end to the rule of Emperor Haile Selassie'.[128] According to Paul B. Henze, the Soviets penetrated the Ethiopian student movement at around this time in a bid to discredit the Haile Selassie regime. They apparently provided the students with 'money, tactical encouragement and help in preparing propaganda materials'.[129]

Certainly, the USSR made little effort to improve relations with Addis Ababa. Stung by Haile Selassie's comprehensive condemnation of the Soviet invasion of Czechoslovakia in August 1968,[130] Soviet writers refined old grievances about Ethiopia. A commentary of February 1969 observed that Ethiopia's 'economic backwardness' preserved a 'feudal–landlord regime' which has on the one side 'an absolute monarchy, a dominance of the clergy, large feudal landlords, a military-police bureaucratic state apparatus' and on the other 'masses of landless Ethiopian peasants whose life changed little through the last hundreds of years'.[131] Another writer asserted that the US was tightening its grip over Ethiopia, displacing other foreign military advisers in the country (from Sweden, India, Britain, Norway and Israel) with its own. This process of political subordination, it was argued, was symbolised by 'the well known American base at Kagnew'. Not only was this 'the most powerful radio station in Africa' but it also served as a US propaganda centre, thus earning the local nickname, 'Little America'.[132]

The hardening of the Soviet attitude can be gauged by the fact that Ethiopian foreign policy, previously regarded as the single positive factor in Soviet writings on the country, was no longer exempt from criticism. Reflecting, perhaps, the anger of some of its Arab allies, Moscow complained, with respect to the 1967 war, that Ethiopia 'was extremely reticent in evaluating Israeli aggression'.[133] This, it was claimed, was confirmed by Addis Ababa's inconsistent voting performance at the UN Security Council and at the Extraordinary Session of the UN General Assembly, one month later. As in Somalia, the decline in Soviet relations with Ethiopia during this period found expression in the field of trade. Notwithstanding the establishment of a permanent Soviet Trade Mission in Addis Ababa in 1967, and the signing of a technical agreement of June 1968, Soviet–Ethiopian trade fell sharply. The volume of trade between the two countries in 1970 was lower than at any time since 1962 (see Tables 5 and 11).

However, the Soviet eclipse in the Horn only proved to be temporary. The turning point was a military coup in Somalia during the early hours of 21 October 1969. The immediate triggering event was entirely unexpected. On 15 October 1969, President Shermarke was assassinated by one of his police guards. The motives for the killing were not clear. Before Prime Minister Egal and other members of the ruling Somali Youth League could elect a successor as President, the Army intervened. A Supreme Revolutionary Council (SRC) headed by Major General Mohammed Siad Barre, commander of the Armed Forces, took control of the country. Egal and many other politicians were arrested. The constitution was suspended, parliament dissolved and all political parties were declared illegal. The country was officially renamed the Somali Democratic Republic (SDR).

Having pledged itself to fight corruption, tribalism and nepotism, and build a society based on social justice, the new government embarked on a series of radical measures. In May 1970, the SRC nationalised a number of foreign businesses. These included all banks (Bank di Roma, Banko di Napoli, the British National and Grindleys Bank), insurance companies, petroleum companies (AJIP and Shell) and the import–export sector.[134] In addition, steps were taken to abolish private education, set up a nationwide literacy campaign and improve food production through the introduction of a number of agricultural co-operatives. Finally, the new military government expelled all US Peace Corps volunteers from Somalia in December 1969 and about half of the US Embassy staff, including the military attaches.[135] It also revoked the ousted government's decision to reduce its merchant traffic into Vietnam. None of these decisions endeared the new Somali regime to Washington. On 1 June 1970, the US terminated further economic assistance to Mogadishu, thereby ending an aid programme which had provided $70 million in assistance since 1954.[136]

But if the new military government alienated the US, its effect on Moscow was exactly the opposite. Within three days of the coup, *Pravda* welcomed the new Somali government and compared it with the revolutionary regimes in Sudan and Libya.[137] Links between the two countries quickly developed. The first contingent of USSR representatives to visit the new SDR was from the Soviet Navy. Between 26 November and 12 December Soviet warships made port calls in both Mogadishu and Berbera, and Soviet officers met with representatives of the SRC.[138] Meanwhile, on 2 December, a team of fourteen economic specialists led by A. Aretemev, Chief of the African Department of the USSR State Committee for Foreign Economic Relations, arrived in Mogadishu.[139] This delegation reversed the USSR's earlier economic stand; it reportedly offered financial assistance and wrote off some of the old unpaid loans. This prompt action was bound to make a favourable impression in Mogadishu.

Over the next year, Soviet support for Siad's government steadily increased. In April 1970, in a gesture of solidarity, the Soviet Navy extended a diplomatic call at Mogadishu as the military government foiled a 'counter-revolutionary plot' allegedly involving Major General Jama Ali Khorsel, the first Vice-President of the SRC, 'to create a puppet regime serving the purposes of the imperialists'. In June of the same year, Brezhnev forewarned Siad Barre of another coup against his regime.[140] A month later, a Soviet specialist on East Africa proclaimed that the new Somali leaders had accomplished more in seven months than their predecessors had in as many years.[141] The final seal of Soviet approval came on the first anniversary of the coup when Siad proclaimed Somalia's allegiance to 'scientific socialism'. This announcement, foreshadowed by the retrospective transformation of the coup into a revolution in both Soviet and Somali media alike, suggested the pursuit of Soviet-style socialism in Somalia. At least, Soviet observers understood this to be the case.

Politburo member and first Deputy Premier D. S. Polyanskiy, who led the Soviet delegation at the anniversary celebrations in Mogadishu, described Siad Barre as 'an outstanding leader and devoted patriot'. He also praised Somalia's 'progressive' stand on a number of international issues including 'US aggression in Vietnam and in the Middle East, support for the national liberation movement and establishing diplomatic relations with the GDR'.[142] Another Soviet observer, present at the celebrations, was equally enthusiastic: 'The national democratic forces of Somalia ... made a choice of the non-capitalist path of development and lead an anti-imperialist policy. Progressive social-economic reforms are implemented' with the 'moral, political and material support' of the USSR.[143] In fact, in the year after the coup, Soviet aid to Somalia totalled about $80 million. Of this, around $40 million was devoted to military assistance. The remainder went on economic-aid credits; this placed Somalia fourth among African recipients of Soviet loans and first on a per-capita basis. At the same time, the number of Soviet advisers in the country grew from 190 to approximately 900. These included an estimated 300 military advisers, something like 100 economic advisers and 500 engineers, technicians and teachers.[144] By the end of 1970, Moscow was able to declare that 'the Somali revolution was a heavy blow at the imperialists' positions in Africa'.[145]

The rapid expansion of Soviet–Somali ties fuelled speculation concerning the origins of the coup. Christopher Clapham, Gary Payton and Paul Henze were among those Western observers who credited Moscow with a possible role in the military take-over in Somalia.[146] That possibility cannot be easily dismissed. For it was clear, by mid-1969, that the USSR had a lot to lose, in strategic terms, if a more sympathetic regime in Mogadishu did not emerge. The Egal government had already shown itself susceptible to US pressure and, therefore, was unlikely to grant the Soviet Naval Squadron in the Indian Ocean the regular access to local port facilities that it required. Without such facilities, the task of protecting the remaining logistic route, in the face of the growing US–Chinese accommodation and the new US base at Diego Garcia, to South-east Asia would be extremely difficult.

If Moscow had a strategic motive for subverting the Egal government, it also had some opportunity to do so. As noted, from 1963 to 1969, hundreds of Somali officers travelled to the USSR for military training and teaching in Marxism–Leninism. This did not necessarily mean that they returned home pro-Soviet or Marxist but they were probably more receptive to Soviet influence than they otherwise would have been. In this vein, it is interesting to note that Soviet visitors in 1970 professed surprise at the large number of Somali officers who spoke Russian.[147] Furthermore, owing to the substantial number of Soviet military advisers in Somalia during the 1960s, it is reasonable to assume that Moscow had acquired a broad knowledge of Somali politics and economics. This meant that, for example, the Soviet intelligence apparatus was aware of 'dissatisfaction in army circles',[148] as evidenced by an abortive military plot prior to the elections of March 1969, and other signs of domestic turmoil. In the circumstances, it was relatively easy for Moscow to convey a promise of further support to rebellious elements in the Somali military.

Several aspects of the coup would seem to support this idea. First, following the March 1969 election, Moscow abandoned its agreed position on Somali debt repayments and adopted a new hardline approach.[149] This reversal in policy appeared to be a deliberate attempt to exacerbate the already severe economic problems of Mogadishu, thus undermining the credibility of Egal's regime, particularly in the eyes of the Somali military. Secondly, while the USSR's subsequent denunciation of the overthrown government may have simply been a rhetorical device to ingratiate itself with the new military regime, it also betrayed an early recognition that the USSR would benefit from the coup. Within days of the coup, *Pravda* praised the military take-over as a pre-emptive measure to forestall efforts by Somali 'reactionaries to take power and arrest progressive reformers'. The 'reactionaries', identified as 'Egal's entourage' were linked with 'Shermarke's murder' and were trying to promote as his presidential successor, Hajmoussa Boger, 'who is known for his pro-American views'. Hence, 'Washington's obvious dissatisfaction with the coup'.[150] Thirdly, and more concretely, in the days immediately after the 21 October coup the first official contacts between the SDR and the USSR took place through military channels. These contacts, preceding by days the arrival of the Soviet economic delegation, would seem to indicate a degree of understanding inconsistent with an entirely spontaneous upheaval.

The Soviet Union, however, did not orchestrate the Somali coup. It was one thing to anticipate, even encourage military intervention, but quite another to contrive the local conditions which caused the Somali military to contemplate it. In Somalia, there was little need for contrivance. For Egal's policy of *détente* was as divisive at home as it was accommodating abroad. Irredentism, after all, had been the major unifying factor in a country where separate colonial experiences, clan differences and economic inequities were compounded by a complex electoral system of Italian-style proportional representation. And, since Egal and Shermarke had nothing to put in its place except the vague promise of peaceful Somali reunification, the new initiative encountered much opposition. This extended even to the ranks of the ruling Somali Youth League (SYL) party itself. For example, in November 1967, the Central Committee of the SYL expressed its displeasure by expelling Prime Minister Egal from the party.[151] The Somali government, however, preserved its freedom of action by manipulating the multi-party system. Using the financial resources at its disposal, the government literally traded on the diverse loyalties of Somalia's political representatives to secure a balance of support in the National Assembly. Such was the commercialisation of Somali politics that between January and October 1969 the Prime Minister reportedly dispensed £500,000 in public funds to members of the National Assembly which 'had been turned into a sordid marketplace'.[152] The degeneration of Somalia's democracy was epitomised by the general election of 26 March 1969. A record number of candidates, 1,002, representing 62 parties, contested 123 seats. Voting was accompanied by street violence (as many as 40 people, including members of the security forces, were killed). Moreover, the election result – the SYL were returned with an overwhelming majority – left a bitter legacy of discontent. Opposition groups charged, and with a high degree of credibility, that Shermarke and Egal were guilty of electoral fraud and intimidation.

The other dangerous consequence of *détente* with Ethiopia was that it seemed to deprive the army of its *raison d'être*. Having been built up to the recover the 'lost' Somali lands, the military were suddenly told that there would be no fighting for such a purpose. That prospect could not but alarm the Somali military. As the largest and most cohesive organisation in Somalia, as well as the fourth most powerful army in Sub-Saharan Africa,[153] the military had good reason to equate its own 'health' with the active pursuit of the pan-Somali objective. By putting this goal on ice, Egal was downgrading the role of the army in Somali national life, and thus undermining the very bonds of professional patriotism which had held the army together. In the circumstances, the potential for military opposition to Egal's government was extremely high.

Lastly, *détente* did not fulfil its economic promise. Some progress was achieved, most notably in the development of trade links between Somalia and Ethiopia (and Kenya) but, generally, the Egal government was unable to overcome the economic malaise which had bedevilled Somalia since independence. The main problem was the lack of a clear economic strategy. In part, this was due to the natural poverty of the country. Like his predecessors, Egal was heavily dependent on foreign aid. This had at least two negative consequences. First, while Somalia had attracted as much as $320 million in aid before 1969 from a variety of sources (including $59 million from the USSR) the economy became something of a mish-mash in the process.[154] Secondly, by injecting more capital into Somalia than could be absorbed, foreign donors fostered extravagance and widespread corruption amongst state officials.

Such conditions were particularly challenging to the Egal administration. Unlike its predecessors, this government relegated the irredentist issue ostensibly to promote economic development. But the second development plan (1968–70), drawn up as an interim measure to correct the imbalances of the first five-year plan, fell victim to the political requirements of the March 1969 election. For six months or so before the election, the central institutions of the government were geared to the political, rather than the economic battles ahead. This meant, for instance, at the district level the administration was transformed to accommodate political appointees. Consequently, Egal's development plan made little headway in completing projects (some of which were started during the first five-year plan), developing the agricultural sector or reversing Somalia's balance of trade deficit which at the end of 1968 amounted to 335 million Somali shillings (about $65 million).[155]

Clearly, whatever part the Soviets played in the events immediately before 21 October 1969, the Somali coup was staged for local reasons by local forces. The point is worth establishing since it had an important bearing on the Soviet–Somali relationship. By most accounts, the new military regime initially enjoyed overwhelming popular support.[156] The SRC's early claim that 'intervention by the

Armed Forces was inevitable'[157] and that it had 'retrieved and restored the nationhood of the Somali people',[158] was, therefore, not totally without substance. Certainly, it was instructive that Siad chose to define the 'vanguard role' of the military in national rather than strictly ideological terms:

> Our soldiers are not the products of a privileged class. They are the sons of farmers, nomads, small craftsmen and ordinary workers, and they draw the smallest salaries in the Republic . . . In Somalia, there are no classes in the Marxist sense.[159]

Inspired essentially, then, by a sense of nationalist destiny, a fact recognised by at least one Soviet writer,[160] the new military regime was more independent than it seemed. In foreign affairs, the old principle of non-alignment 'which has proved suitable' in the past was reaffirmed:

> We will seek the friendship of all nations which are prepared to accept us and to show us their friendship. We will support world peace and oppose imperialism and all kinds of colonialism, whether from our brothers here or abroad.[161]

But it was stressed that this policy 'of positive neutrality by no means signifies that we treat as equals our sincere friends and those who are hindering our efforts to achieve independence and democracy by taking actions hostile to us'.[162] In short, the Somali concept of non-alignment was framed by perceived national interests, and not vice versa. Accordingly, close relations with the USSR were neither precluded or obligatory. The dominant Somali attitude was one of pragmatism.

From the outset Siad Barre emphasised, during an interview with a *Pravda* correspondent, that Soviet–Somali relations were a two-way street.[163] Just what this amounted to in practice was made plain during the visit of the powerful Soviet economic delegation in December 1969. After welcoming the delegation, Mogadishu Radio, with an eye obviously to the future, pointedly remarked that there had been 'big losses in Soviet aided projects'[164] in the past. The Somali rule of thumb, then, as far as relations with the USSR were concerned, was essentially utilitarian: 'If socialism has no benefits for us, then we must throw it away and take something else instead. But if it has value, we must adopt it.'[165] And, while Siad had apparently decided that 'socialism' was worth adopting by the first anniversary of the military coup, it was not an unqualified commitment. For example, a key sector in the Somali economy such as the profitable banana plantations remained in private hands because there 'must be a whole range of intermediate stages of social development' before the 'transition to the construction of socialism'[166] could take place.

It was also noteworthy that while the Siad regime backed the Soviet position on international issues where its own interests were not directly at stake, it was quite prepared to adopt an independent line where they were perceived as being so. Relations with Communist China were a case in point. These steadily expanded after the coup. In June 1970, an SRC delegation visited China. In the same month, a large Chinese agricultural delegation visited Somalia. Four months later, a sizeable CPR delegation attended the celebrations commemorating the first anniversary of the coup.

Nearer home, the Somali coup was a source of deep concern in Addis Ababa. Relations between the two countries had become strained even before Egal's overthrow. During the summer of 1969, there were a number of armed skirmishes between Ethiopian security forces and Somali nomads. And, while the new military government pledged to continue the policy of *détente*, it also declared that it regarded 'the Somali people's right to self-determination as a sacred right' and could not 'ignore the aspirations of the Somali people in whichever territory they lived'.[167] The portent of these words, as far as Ethiopia was concerned, was confirmed by other developments. In 1970, an organisation called the Western Somali Liberation Front (WSLF), which almost certainly had links with Mogadishu, began to canvass the Arab world for support. A WSLF delegation visited Kuwait, Sudan, Libya and Algeria to explain the programme for freeing 'West Somalia' from 'Ethiopian colonialism'. Furthermore, in October 1970, Siad Barre officially raised the question of Somalia's 'occupied' lands and said it was 'high time' a solution was found.[168] The Sudanese newspaper, Al Ayam, agreed and openly supported Somalia's claim to the Ogaden.[169]

Meanwhile, in Eritrea, Ethiopia's security problems continued. A district governor was killed in Serai in August 1970. Then, on 21 November, the commander of the Ethiopian Second Division, General Teshome Erghetu, was assassinated during an inspection visit to the province. That particular incident prompted a new hardline strategy in Addis Ababa. Prince Ras Arate Kassa who, as Governor General of Eritrea had urged political reconciliation, was replaced by Lt-Gen. Debbebe Haile-Mariam. A State of Emergency was declared on 17 December, thus placing much of Eritrea under martial law. At the same time, Ethiopia launched a massive air and ground offensive against ELF-held areas. The destruction was immense. Large numbers of Eritrean civilians were killed and hundreds of villages razed.[170] Whatever its military merits, this operation made a political settlement in Eritrea more, rather than less difficult.

Nevertheless, there were some encouraging signs for Emperor Haile Selassie. First, as the ELF grew during the late 1960s, internal divisions based on ideology, religion and personality surfaced. In 1970, at least two factions detached themselves from the ELF. The first group, the Popular Liberation Forces (ELF–PLF), led by Osman Saleh Sabbe, was basically non-socialist in outlook and saw the Eritrean independence war as an integral part of the Middle-Eastern struggle to fulfil Arab nationalism. The second group, the Eritrean Liberation Forces – Obel (Obelyan), led by Issayas Aferworki, initially attracted Christian highlanders and tended to be Marxist in orientation.[171] Suffice it to say, the rivalry between these organisations was such that by the end of 1970 they were sometimes fighting each other as well as the Ethiopian forces stationed in Eritrea.

Secondly, the Ethiopian Emperor had a measure of success in limiting external support for the rebels. On 2 December 1971, Addis Ababa officially recognised the Peoples Republic of China as 'the sole legal Government representing the entire Chinese people',[172] and fully supported China's admission to the UN. In return, China, a spasmodic arms supplier to the ELF since 1967, terminated all arms aid to the rebels shortly thereafter. In addition, Ethiopia seemed to check the PDRY's enthusiasm for the Eritrean cause by warning Aden that the large population of Yemeni traders in Ethiopia existed only at the Emperor's sufferance.[173] Attempts, though, to enlist Soviet help in restraining other Arab arms suppliers came to nothing.

On the basis of these admittedly mixed trends, then, there was little sign of any imminent change in the local balance of power. In 1970, Ethiopia was still the dominant power in the Horn of Africa. In strictly military terms, Somalia was inferior, both quantitatively and qualita-tively (see Table 6). Two factors stand out in this equation. Firstly, the Ethiopian Armed Forces were over three times as large as their Somali counterparts. Secondly, Ethiopia had overwhelming superiority in the air. In fact, with the exception of South Africa, the Ethiopian Air Force, thanks to US assistance, was considered to be the best and strongest in sub-Saharan Africa.[174] Thus, even taking into account that about 15,000–20,000 Ethiopian soldiers (nearly half of Ethiopia's Armed Forces) were deployed in Eritrea,[175] there did not appear to be, in any objective sense, any immediate threat to the territorial integrity of Ethiopia.

Table 6. *The military balance in the Horn of Africa 1969–1970: A breakdown*

Category	Ethiopia	Somalia
Population	25,200,000	2,925,000
Estimated GNP 1969	US$1.6 billion	$0.2 billion
Total armed forces	45,400	12,000
Estimated defence budget 1969–70	US$ 35,948,000	$9,008,000
Army Total strength	41,000	10,000
	48,000 infantry brigades	7 mechanised battalions
	1 tank battalion	3 infantry battalions
	About 50 M-41 Walker Bulldog and M-24	1 battalion of mobile scouts
	Chaffee light tanks	About 150 Soviet T-34 tanks
	About 40 Armoured Personnel Carriers	some Ferret Scout Cars
	(APCs)	60 Soviet APCs including BTR-152s
	1 armoured car squad.	
	4 artillery battalions	
	1 engineer and 8 training battalions	
Navy Total strength	1,400	250
	1 training ship (ex seaplane tender)	6 patrol boats
	5 patrol boats	
	2 motor torpedo boats	
	4 landing craft	

Air Force

Total strength	3,000	1,750
	43 combat aircraft	18 combat aircraft
	1 bomber squad. with 6 Canberra B2	18 MiG–15/17 fighters
	1 fighter-bomber squad. with 12 F8–6F	20 Yak–11 and 6 MiG–15/17 UTI trainers
	1 ground-attack squad. with 8 SAAB–17	Transports include C–45, C–47 and
	1 fighter squad. with 8F–5A	1AN–24
	1 reconnaissance squad. with 6T–28 and 3T–33	
	1 transport squad. with 6 C–47, 2 C–54, 3 Doves & 1 Ilyushin 14	
Other aircraft	15 SAAB, 19 Safirs & 8 T–28 trainers and 3 Alouette helicopters	
Defence expenditure as % of total GNP in 1970	2.1	4.6

Source: Adapted from Richard Booth, *The Armed Forces of African States*, Adelphi Paper no. 67, International Institute for Strategic Studies, London, May 1970, pp. 18–27 and *The Military Balance 1970–1971*, London, International Institute for Strategic Studies, 1970, pp. 43–52

In the longer term, however, the impact of the Somali coup and the shifting pattern of alliances accompanying it, was less reassuring. In particular, the implications of Moscow's enthusiastic embrace of Siad Barre's military regime could not but disturb Addis Ababa. Officially, the Soviet position *vis-à-vis* the territorial dispute was unchanged, despite the Somali coup. It was one of 'neutrality', but this 'neutrality' took a rather unusual form. During 1970, Moscow sympathised, in a discrete fashion, with both of the respective stands of Somalia and Ethiopia. To Somalia, the USSR expressed its readiness to 'co-operate in the struggle against imperialism, colonialism and neo-colonialism and for self-determination [a phrase suggesting Soviet support for Somali territorial aspirations], national independence and social progress'.[176] To Ethiopia, Moscow maintained that 'relations between the Soviet Union and Ethiopia were friendly and developed on the basis of complete equality, mutual respect for sovereignty, territorial integrity [a phrase which could be interpreted as an assurance that Moscow was against Somali expansion], national independence and non-interference in each other's domestic affairs'.[177] However, there was one 'consistent' note in these joint communiqués. On both occasions, the USSR emphasised its support for a peaceful resolution of the Ethiopian–Somali border dispute.

Certainly, by 1970, Moscow appeared to be fully aware of the potential explosiveness of the situation in the Horn of Africa. The border dispute was described, with a minimum of ideological verbiage, as 'one of the most complex questions of international relations' in Africa.[178] It was recognised that 'all causes of tense relations between Somalia and its neighbours are still not liquidated.' These 'causes' include 'a non-correspondence of state frontiers with the distribution of peoples, the complexity of political circumstances, the unresolved nationality question and religious discord' as well as a 'definite influence on the inter-state relations of these countries by extra-continental links'.[179] Of these factors, however, the 'major influence' was 'the aspirations of the Somalis toward reunification into a single state'. Consequently, most Soviet commentators agreed that 'on the whole . . . relations between Somalia and neighbouring countries [i.e., Ethiopia] will be largely determined by the development of Somalia's internal policies'. This point was reflected in the Soviet recognition that 'the military revolution in Somalia prompted definite anxiety in Addis Ababa' where it was 'feared that . . . Mogadishu will not change its policies in relation to the frontiers of African countries'.[180]

Nevertheless, there were definite signs, with the most obvious being expanded Soviet aid, that the USSR believed the Barre military government had 'qualitatively changed' the situation in the Horn. For one thing, a sharp distinction was now being drawn between Somali 'self-determination' and the 'separatist activity'[181] in Eritrea. The latter, it was implied, was unjustified since Eritrea was historically part of Ethiopia. That is why 'the Eritrean assembly decided to repeal itself and to enter complete integration with Ethiopia [*sic*]'. And, while 'not all of the Eritreans were for unification . . . far more were for complete integration'.[182] That view was echoed by Georgiy Tsypkin, a Soviet historian who in 1969 clearly identified Eritrea as an integral part of Ethiopia.[183]

The tone of Soviet writings also changed. Under Egal, when relations with Somalia were strained, Soviet commentators tended to take negative attitudes toward Mogadishu's territorial claims. Writing in 1968, G. V. Fokeyev noted that the 'nationalistically inclined Republic of Somalia' had 'territorial claims' on the 'important Ethiopian province, the Ogaden' and had armed the nomads involved in border clashes with Ethiopian troops. Such 'subversive activity', it was argued, made the imperialist role in the Horn's troubles almost 'superfluous'.[184] After the coup, though, Soviet commentary about Somalia's policy toward its neighbours became less critical. For example, it was noted that 'the new [Somali] government declared that it deliberately intends to strengthen in the future friendly ties with Kenya and Ethiopia'.[185]

The perception of a 'new' situation in the Horn masked a basic division amongst Soviet writers. On the one hand, there were those like Maria Rayt who apparently assumed that with the establishment of a 'progressive' regime in Mogadishu, Somalia would relinquish its longstanding territorial claims: 'The essence of the Ethiopian–Somali and Kenyan–Somali conflicts is similar. They consist *until recently* of Somali claims to significant territories (forming parts) of Ethiopia and Kenya . . . ' In Rayt's view, such claims foundered on 'the difficulty of determining the frontier of settlement of the Somali population in Ethiopia'. First, 'in many localities of Harar [the province which includes the Ogaden] where Somalis live, there also live other peoples – Galla-Kottu, Amhara, Harari and Arabs'. Secondly, 'the Somalis wander far beyond' the Ogaden; 'it is reckoned that the Somalis wander over approximately one fifth of the Ethiopian territory'. Thirdly, 'as concerns the entire region inhabited by Somalis – the province Harar, on the whole is very important for Ethiopia. A railway passes through the district linking the capital of Ethiopia with the central industries and the sea port of Djibouti (French Somalia).' Fourthly, 'the Ethiopian Somalis themselves have differing attitudes toward the question concerning the unification of this territory [the Ogaden] with Somalia'. Some of them, according to Rayt, feared that they would lose their fertile lands to Somali immigrants: 'In April 1962 these Somalis submitted a petition to the Emperor of Ethiopia demanding to prohibit the residents of Somalia crossing the frontier and herding their cattle in the territory of Ethiopia.' However, it was also conceded that 'some of the Somali nomads, on the contrary, come out for unification with Somalia'.[186] The logic of the Rayt position, therefore, would seem to point to the conclusion that expanded Soviet economic and military aid could be used as a means of disarming domestic advocates of Somali unification, and thus nudging the new revolutionary regime in the direction of the OAU dictum, concerning the immutability of territorial boundaries at independence.

On the other hand, writers like Ye Etinger seemed to argue that Mogadishu's conversion to 'scientific socialism' had fundamentally altered the nature of Somali irredentism. According to Etinger, Somalia's 're-unification aspirations' were different from other irredentist movements in Africa. In the first place, the Somalis 'appear as a homogenous ethnic group' which is an 'unusual phenomenon in Africa'. Moreover,

> the most active advocates [of reunification] are precisely the most anti-imperialist and radically inclined circles of Somalian society, regarding the movement towards reunification of their peoples in the same light as the struggle against the legacy of colonialism in Africa, against imperialism and the influential circles of some African countries who have orientated themselves against it

– a side-swipe at Ethiopia. Thus, Somalia was unlike the 'majority of cases' in Africa where 'state nationalism', 'irredentism' and 'separatism' complicates 'co-operation between individual countries'.[187] The corollary of this standpoint was that Somali irredentist objectives deserved the political, economic and military support of the USSR.

Whether these nascent divisions over Somalia were linked to a power struggle in the Kremlin remains a point for further research. There was, however, an additional factor obscuring the new direction of Soviet policy around 1970, namely, a political reassessment of Ethiopia. The long-held view that the 'best representatives' of the Ethiopian intelligentsia ('teachers, students, writers, and poets, artists and scholars') would eventually play an 'active part'[188] in the country seemed to lose ground. Instead, Moscow began to look to the Ethiopian Army as 'an important political force'.[189] Historically, it was argued, the Imperial Army had played a key role in preserving the Empire's territorial integrity. Not only had it been used to repel foreign threats ('The Ethiopian Army covered itself with glory in 1896 at Adowa when the forces of Menelik II totally defeated the army of the Italian colonialists') but also it had been used with 'maximum effect' to suppress periodic peasant revolts within the Empire. Consequently, given the still backward nature of Ethiopian society, the power of Haile Selassie 'was determined in the final analysis by the power of his army'.[190]

All this, of course, was rather academic as far as Emperor Haile Selassie was concerned. It is unlikely that he read Moscow's published analysis[191] of the region or was aware of the nuances behind the USSR's ambiguous policy. To the Emperor, the Soviet–Somali *rapprochement* was a threat, pure and simple. But, unlike previous threats, Ethiopia, by 1970, could no longer count on continued US support to counter it. America's policy toward Ethiopia was revised in light of its Vietnam experience: 'It is another lesson of the 1960s . . . that African defence against subversions, like African development, must be born most directly by Africans rather than by outsiders.'[192] This view was buttressed by Dr Kissinger's optimism, that with the beginnings of international *détente*, Soviet 'interference' in the developing world could be curtailed by tying Moscow to the status quo through a network of trade and commercial agreements. As an upshot, President Nixon redefined the US's role as seeking a 'co-operative and equal relationship' with African countries. He emphasised that: 'We want no military allies, no spheres of influence, no big power competition in Africa.' Ethiopia was to be no exception.[193]

During a visit to Ethiopia in February 1970, Secretary of State William Rogers indicated Washington was not interested in getting embroiled in the local controversy in the Horn of Africa. The Emperor's request to arm a fifth division of the Ethiopian Armed Forces to combat the perceived increase of Soviet influence in Somalia was politely refused. Rogers also belittled the challenge of the Eritrean guerrillas by publicly asserting that the ELF held no territory in the province. Addis Ababa was also reminded that the Nixon administration was more inclined to give economic assistance, rather than military aid, to African countries in order to help them help themselves.[194]

Dissatisfied, but sensing perhaps that Washington could still be cajoled into meeting Ethiopia's military needs, Emperor Haile Selassie resorted to a familiar ploy – the Soviet 'card'. In May 1970, the Emperor, at his own initiative, journeyed to Moscow. The visit had a dual purpose. First, the Emperor hoped, by including in his entourage the governors of Eritrea and Bale (part of the Ogaden), to persuade the USSR to limit its support for Addis Ababa's local adversaries. This objective, however, foundered on Ethiopia's unwillingness to cut its close links with Israel.[195] Secondly, the Emperor tried to signal to Washington that Ethiopian friendship could not be taken for granted. With this in mind, the Emperor lined up with the USSR in favouring 'the unconditional withdrawal of foreign troops from Indo–China'[196] (a barely disguised reference to the US role in Vietnam). He also observed, somewhat poignantly, that African states could rely on the assistance of the USSR against colonialism.[197]

This manoeuvre made little impression in Washington (or, for that matter, in Moscow). It had worked in the past when the Kagnew communications base was deemed vital to the US but, by the late 1960s, this was no longer the case. A combination of rapid advances in satellite communications technology and the availability of an alternative facility at Diego Garcia effectively ended America's need for Kagnew. In the view of the Pentagon, the Diego Garcia site had a decisive advantage in that it would permit an exclusively American presence.[198] That prospect had considerable political appeal given the mounting Congressional unrest about the US presence in Eritrea. Senator Stuart Symington expressed the fears of many of his colleagues when he said:

> Everywhere we go we are the ones to stay. The Italians have left this part of the world, the French have left, the Soviets haven't come in, but we are there with a very sizable military contingent . . . I just don't like to see another Vietnam come up overnight.[199]

The Nixon administration had no such wish either.

In October 1970, David Newson, the Assistant Secretary of State for African Affairs spelt out US policy toward Addis Ababa. He reaffirmed that Ethiopia occupied a 'special place in the United States African relations' but added 'we have no security commitment to Ethiopia'. That is to say, the US would use its 'good offices in the UN in the event of an attack on Ethiopia' but there was 'no implication here of any commitment to defend Ethiopia with American forces'.[200] Ethiopia was thus placed in a difficult position. Despite attempts to diversify its military-assistance programme, Ethiopia, by 1969–70, derived almost half of its military aid ($35 million per annum) from the US. At the same time, the Emperor was reluctant to advertise his dependence on Washington by publicly pleading the case for a greater US commitment. Like much of the developing world, Ethiopia, particularly its students, became infected with growing anti-Americanism at the end of the sixties. That the Emperor was conscious of the dangers inherent in this for his own position was indicated by his reluctant acceptance of the American decision to withdraw the Peace Corps from Ethiopian provinces at around this time for security reasons.[201] Thus, looking to the future, the ageing Emperor faced the uncomfortable prospect of neither being able to rely on Washington nor renounce the connection.

The Soviet disposition in perspective

The above trends confirm that the late 1960s/early 1970s was an extremely significant period in the development of the Soviet foreign-policy posture. The period seemed to be one of change in the sense not so much of conception but of range. The most decisive ingredient in this metamorphosis was a consciousness of enhanced military might,[202] arising from the attainment of rough parity in strategic nuclear weapons with the US. This development, in Moscow's view, facilitated a more active Soviet role in the Third World including, of course, the Horn of Africa.

Unlike the Khrushchev era when Soviet support for the Third World allies was constrained by US nuclear preponderance, the Brezhnev regime, in effect, neutralised the constraint:

> At present the main factor which restrains the imperialist aggressors in all regions of the world is the ability of the USSR to reach any point on the world's surface with nuclear weaponary. This way of restraining the military expansion of imperialism is extremely important from the point of view of averting a general nuclear war.[203]

By eliminating the risk of nuclear blackmail, the USSR was now able to exert its growing 'political authority and military might'[204] on 'those events that might be territorially remote but that touch on our security and also on the security of our friends'.[205] It was now claimed that 'support for revolutionary liberation movements is one of the *basic constants* of the Soviet Union's now more active and resourceful foreign policy'[206] and that it had become a 'permanently operating factor in world politics'.[207] In short, Moscow was asserting its status as a global power.

But how confident was Moscow about its self-proclaimed status? Did Soviet spokesmen really believe their largely self-congratulatory accounts of Soviet achievements? These questions are important. Communist partisanship is an established principle of Soviet historiography. And revolutionary assertiveness is not an entirely new characteristic of Soviet foreign policy, either. Thus, the Soviet claim regarding a shift in the 'correlation of forces' must be set against the continuities of Soviet policy. The fact is that there had been no transformation in Soviet domestic politics nor any significant decline in ideological rigidities (peaceful co-existence was described as 'a specific form of class struggle between socialism and capitalism')[208] during the period in question. This meant that while the substantial, relative power increase of the USSR could be harnessed to residual, universalist goals, it might also be subject to traditional Soviet traits such as caution:

> It goes without saying that the question of the character and form of a Soviet military presence in this or that region can be decided only with full consideration both of the concrete situation in the said region and of the international situation as a whole.[209]

In other words, Moscow was tacitly conceding that its willingness to intervene, militarily, would still be influenced by the attitude of the West in any given case.

This applied to the Horn of Africa as much as anywhere else in the Third World. Located in an area where Soviet global and regional ambitions converged, the Horn of Africa in 1970 must have inspired a distinctly forward-looking attitude in the Kremlin. For, in a period of less than a year, Moscow had been able to politically exploit a military coup in Somalia at Washington's expense, and then learn of America's declining interest in its old ally, Ethiopia. The latter development not only suggested that Washington had lost interest in the Horn generally, but also strengthened the hand of those in the USSR who saw support for Mogadishu's irredentism as part and parcel of the USSR's 'internationalist duty'.

Part II

The Horn of Opportunity

4 The budding alliance: Marx, Lenin and Mohammed

> Although the Soviet Union and Somalia lie on different continents thousands of kilometres apart there is much in common that brings the two countries together and makes them comrades-in-arms and friends. They are at one in the struggle against imperialism and colonialism and have been acting unitedly in the struggle for lasting world peace.
>
> (V. Sofinsky, 'Somalia on the Path of Progress', *International Affairs* (Moscow), no. 11, November 1974, p. 65).

Between 1971 and 1974, the initial enthusiasm of the USSR for the Somali revolution was converted into a major commitment. Moscow, in the words of President Siad, became 'Somalia's greatest helper'.[1] In the economic sphere, Soviet technical and financial assistance covered more than twenty projects in the country. Altogether, Soviet economic assistance was valued at $100 million.[2] This figure, when compared with that made available to other African states was, by Soviet standards, substantial. However, in the military field, the Soviet contribution was even more impressive. Estimates vary but even the most conservative suggest a ten-fold increase of Soviet military aid to Somalia during this period.[3] By 1974, the Somali military inventory reportedly included large numbers of MiG fighter planes, T-54 tanks and a vast assortment of heavy arms. In return, the USSR obtained a major naval facility at Berbera and access to a number of Somali airfields. As a result of these arrangements, about 3,600 Soviet advisers, of whom roughly 1,400 were military personnel, had flocked into Somalia by 1974.[4] Then, on 11 July 1974, the Soviet–Somali relationship reached a 'qualitatively new and higher stage'[5] with the signing of a Treaty of Friendship and Co-operation. The treaty, the first of its kind between the USSR and a black African state, was said to demonstrate the 'permanent character'[6] of Soviet–Somali friendship.

Few Western commentators challenged *Pravda*'s assessment. In the view of one writer, the scale of Soviet involvement merely confirmed Somalia's status as a fully fledged Soviet satellite.[7] Certainly, on the face of it, President Siad's espousal of 'scientific socialism' reinforced the impression of an alliance based on a common ideology, and a pro-Soviet one at that. Yet the reality of the relationship was not always the same as its image.

The expansion of Soviet–Somali ties

In the early 1970s, Moscow's geo-political ambitions in North-east Africa received a couple of major set-backs. In July 1971, an abortive pro-communist coup in Sudan seriously damaged relations between Khartoum and Moscow. For a brief time, the government of General Numeiry was overthrown and replaced by a left-wing alliance, dominated by the strong and well-organised Sudanese Communist Party. The Soviet Union welcomed the coup. But within three days a counter-coup, strongly backed by Egypt and Libya, restored Numeiry to power. In the crackdown that followed, the coup leaders and many prominent members of the Sudanese Communist Party, including its General Secretary, Ahmed Mahgoub, were executed. Moscow reacted by condemning the 'repressions' and 'bloody massacres'[8] in the Sudan. For his part, Numeiry accused the USSR and Bulgaria of complicity in the abortive coup.[9] Relations, however, while strained were not broken. About a month after the July events, Moscow moderated its position and resumed aid to Khartoum, albeit on a much smaller scale. Then, twelve months later, on 18 July 1972, the Egyptian President, Anwar Sadat, angered, amongst other things, by the USSR's reluctance to supply offensive weaponary to Cairo, demanded the withdrawal of all Soviet military advisers and experts, estimated to number about 15,000. The withdrawal, which was largely completed within a month, coincided with the loss of important strategic facilities; the USSR lost the use of Egyptian airfields and had its privileged access to a number of Egyptian ports such as Alexandria, Port Said and Mersa Matruh severely curtailed.

These reverses served to emphasise to Moscow the importance of relations with Somalia. In August 1971 Somalia offered its good offices to improve relations between Sudan and the Soviet Union. This initiative was probably calculated to improve Somalia's standing with the USSR. At the same time, Mogadishu made it clear that it was not short of diplomatic options. In the early 1970s, there was a significant upsurge in Chinese aid to Somalia. A loan in June 1971 estimated at

$110 million[10] was then the largest Chinese loan in Africa apart from
the funding of the Tanzam railway. Projects covered by this credit
included a 650-mile North–South highway, a stadium in Mogadishu,
agricultural and fishing enterprises and the development of light
industry. The protocols for many of these schemes were signed during
President Siad's successful visit to Peking in May 1972. According to
Premier Chou En-lai, the visit 'made important contributions to the
enhancement of the friendship between the Chinese and Somali
peoples and the strengthening of friendly relations and co-operation
between the two countries'.[11]

   The USSR was not disposed to take Chinese competition in Somalia
lightly. Peking had already profited from the Soviet–Sudanese quarrel
by signing a $34.8 million aid agreement with Khartoum in August
1971.[12] Moscow, therefore, hastened to reinforce its ties with Mogadishu. In November 1971, President Siad and a ministerial-level
delegation arrived in Moscow for talks, at the invitation of the Soviet
government. A number of accords were signed including agreement
'on co-operation in the building of a dam and power station on the
Juba River [a significant reversal of an earlier Soviet refusal to help in
this project], on delivery of farm machinery to Somalia, on co-
operation in the fishing industry' as well as 'measures to improve the
broadcasting system in the SDR'.[13] It was also announced that 2
million of the 1961 47 million roubles' loan was to be written off, and
that repayment of existing loans due in 1971 was to be extended for a
further five years.[14]

   In addition, the USSR apparently agreed to increase its military aid
to Somalia. A joint communiqué issued during Siad's visit expressed
inter alia Somalia's 'profound appreciation for the assistance rendered
by the Soviet Union . . . in strengthening its defence potential'.[15]
Clearly, Siad made a good impression in Moscow. The Somali leader
told his hosts that Somalia was certain to benefit from the Soviet
experience in constructing a classless society. Both sides rated President Siad's visit an important success. Moscow said it reaffirmed the
USSR's 'internationalist policy' and demonstrated to 'African patriots
. . . how important it is to rely on the Soviet Union and other socialist
countries' at a time when Africa's enemies – the 'imperialists' and
'other external forces operating with pseudo-revolutionary slogans'[16]
(i.e., China) – sought to undermine such co-operation. The Somali
media was no less enthusiastic. Some 'reactionary countries . . . hated
to see her [Somalia] enjoy deep friendship with the Soviet Union' but
'their hopes were dashed when the outcome of the [November] visit

turned out to be the most significant ever'. President Siad, it was contended, 'had scored a major victory by his visit'.[17]

The next milestone along the way occurred in February 1972. The Soviet Defence Minister, Marshal A. Grechko, paid a four-day visit to Somalia at the invitation of the Somali government. After discussing 'Somali–Soviet military co-operation and its further development, as well as some other vital issues', both parties agreed 'on practical measures' for the 'further consolidation' of these military ties.[18] These 'practical measures', it subsequently emerged, involved a specific exchange arrangement between the two countries. The Soviet Union committed itself to helping Somalia carry out a major military build-up. This included an extensive modernisation programme for Mogadishu's Army (for details see below) and the development of existing air and harbour facilities. In return, the USSR obtained access to the port of Berbera, the right to expand military facilities there, and the use of Somali airfields for purposes of naval reconnaissance.

The timing of this new agreement seemed to owe more to Moscow's changing strategic requirements than to the perceived merits of the Siad regime. A number of considerations pointed to this. First, Grechko's visit, which came fourteen months after the cancellation of an earlier planned visit, coincided with the emergence of strains in the Soviet–Egyptian relationship. Secondly, there was a certain similarity between the new range of naval port facilities at Berbera and those which the USSR then had under construction at Mersa Matruh in Egypt.[19] Thirdly, it was during the Grechko visit that the Soviets first raised the question of a Friendship Treaty, along the lines of that signed with Egypt. At that time, however, the Siad regime resisted the idea, apparently because it did not wish to alienate some of the conservative Arab regimes. Fourthly, it was probably not a coincidence that Grechko journeyed straight on to Egypt, following his successful trip to Somalia.[20] Such a manoeuvre was probably intended to remind Egypt that the Kremlin had other well-placed friends in North-east Africa.

Subsequent events confirmed Somalia's position as a strategic standby to Egypt. On 10 July 1972, two days after Moscow first learned of Sadat's expulsion decision,[21] the Somali Defence Minister and Commander in Chief of the Somali Armed Forces, General Mohammed Ali Samantar, was invited to Moscow for talks. He was given a red-carpet welcome. During the visit, Marshal Grechko appeared to signal yet another increase in military aid to Somalia by noting the 'favourable prospects' for the 'further strengthening' of Soviet–Somali relations in 'the military sphere'.[22] While careful to avoid any specific statement of support for Somalia's territorial claims, Moscow generally asserted that the USSR 'consistently supported and does support peoples fighting for their liberation, national independence and social progress'.[23]

After the February and July agreements of 1972, Soviet arms began to pour into Somalia. According to the International Institute of Strategic Studies (IISS), the Soviets supplied MiG-15 and MiG-17 fighter aircraft, IL-28 bombers, Yak trainer planes, Antonov transport aircraft, T-34 and T-54 tanks, armoured personnel carriers, P-5 torpedo boats and large quantities of automatic guns and artillery.[24] Furthermore, the number of Soviet military advisers and technicians present in Somalia rose from less than a thousand to around 3,600. This was an unusually large figure even allowing for the fact that the mainly Soviet-equipped and Soviet-trained Somali Army increased in size by almost 50 per cent during this period.

At the same time, the Soviets developed extensive military facilities in Somalia. In October 1972, Soviet engineers and construction crews started to expand the port of Berbera. A three-section floating pier was assembled and an oil pipeline, linking the port with the site of a new military airfield, was built.[25] In addition, a floating barracks-machine shop, similar to those that had appeared when the Soviets moved into Alexandria in June 1969, was towed down from Vladivostok.[26] This significantly improved the ability of the Soviet Navy in the Indian Ocean to supply and repair its units and rest its crews. As a consequence, the number of visits by Soviet naval vessels to Berbera sharply increased[27] (see Table 4). In early 1973, the USSR installed a long-range communications station at Berbera. This facility, established at a time when its American counterpart in Ethiopia was being phased out, was used to help co-ordinate the movement of Soviet warships throughout the Indian Ocean. Also, at around this time, a missile-handling facility and a 13,000–15,000 ft surfaced runway were built at Berbera. The airfield enabled Soviet Tu Bear and Il-38 May ASW reconnaissance aircraft to stage periodic flights over the Indian Ocean region.[28]

The Soviet media, somewhat characteristically, offered no detailed comment on Moscow's military activities in Somalia. Instead, it asserted that Soviet assistance in the 'defence spheres' was linked to Somalia's efforts to build a 'society on socialist lines'.[29] The precise nature of this ideological connection, however, was a matter of dispute. N. Khokhlov, for example, observed nothing less than the creation of full 'scientific socialism'[30] in Somalia. In this vein, Siad Barre was quoted as saying 'there could be no African socialism' but 'only one socialism, namely scientific socialism, and only one reasonable way for Somalia's development, namely the road chartered by scientific socialism'.[31] But other Soviet observers were less convinced:

> Of course, it is impossible to completely identify the declarations of the Somali leaders concerning scientific socialism with Marxism. This, for the time being, is the typically revolutionary democratic opinion in which socialism is combined with Islam and nationalism. However, elements of Marxism are already present here.[32]

Despite the ideological nuances, Soviet writers found much to admire in the development of the Somali revolution. The Supreme Revolutionary Council (SRC) led by Siad was praised for ushering in an era of 'profound transformation in the social, economic and political spheres'[33] of society. This assessment, although an exaggeration, was in one sense apt. The first phase of Siad's rule up to 1974, notwithstanding the military build-up, was one of concentration on domestic affairs. That is, local development and the consolidation of the regime's authority. And Soviet civilian advisers were actively involved in what was generally acknowledged to be a time of considerable advance. About 1,400 Soviet experts served with Somali ministries or government agencies, a fact which prompted one Western newspaper to conclude in 1973 that the Soviets had penetrated 'nearly every level of the Somali Government'.[34]

In practice, though, scientific socialism developed more slowly than the size of the Soviet presence suggested. In political–institutional terms, Somalia experienced relatively little change during this period. With all political parties banned, the army remained the very centre of power. The ruling group, the SRC, was essentially a committee of top military officials, many of whom, like the President, General Mohammed Siad Barre, had held prominent positions under the old civilian administrations. Originally a 25-man body, the SRC was reduced to 21 by 1974 as Siad's political dominance asserted itself. The SRC ran the country through a conventional system of Ministries, each headed by a Secretary of State. These Secretaries, generally young civilian technocrats, had executive powers and were responsible for conducting the day to day business of government. Moscow treated the SRC leadership as a communist hierarchy. Officials were invited to the USSR for the twenty-fourth Party Congress, ceremonial occasions, anniversaries and to study the principles of scientific socialism.[35] In short, the Soviet Union did all within its power to include Somalia amongst the group of 'progressive' African and Asian countries who had taken the path of 'socialist orientation'. Clearly, the Soviets felt confident the military could initiate a process of change in Somalia. This perception was due both to Moscow's new brand of internationalism and Siad's political skill.

From 1971 Moscow was under the impression that the Somali government would reform itself 'on the basis of party and public organisation'.[36] In 1972 E. Denisov observed that the SRC leaders 'are convinced of the fact that it is impossible to guarantee the stable social–economic and political position of the country without the creation of a political vanguard and progressive public organisation . . .'.[37] But whatever assurances were given to the Soviets in private, President Siad was not, in any formal sense, desperate to form a ruling political party. It was not until the fourth anniversary of the Somali revolution, on 21 October 1973, Siad publicly announced the intention to set up a political organisation, based on the ideas of scientific socialism. Even then, the announcement was not without qualification: 'Such a political organisation, indispensable for our future development, can only be created by the will of the masses'.[38]

Siad's announcement, although vague, did enough to ensure the continuation of Soviet support. As intimated, Moscow was pressing for the formation of a vanguard party. Experience elsewhere, not least in the Sudan and Egypt, indicated Soviet military aid, by itself, could not secure a permanent foothold in a developing state. In Somalia, therefore, the Soviets sought to institutionalise its position through the establishment of party to party relations. However, Siad's decision to embark on this path was not down simply to Soviet pressure – there was also a domestic angle. As the public enthusiasm which initially greeted the coup in Somalia diminished, it became increasingly important for President Siad's regime to legitimise itself through an official ideology. To do this, however, required an organisational framework to mobilise the population in support of the government's objectives. Thus, if a party is seen here simply as a mobilising agent, rather than as a source of power independent of the army, President Siad had good reasons for wanting a party. Amongst other things, it would serve as a vehicle for the Somali leader to create a pervasive personality cult.[39]

The process of socialist construction was controlled by the SRC. While President Siad was open to Soviet advice – 'we cannot turn a blind eye to the experience of countries that have adopted socialism before us' – he made it plain that socialism in Somalia would be applied 'in accordance with our specific conditions'.[40] In 1972, the political office of the SRC, known as the Bureau of Public Relations and renamed the National Political Administration in 1973, was expanded into a national organisation. Branches were established in all permanent settlements of any size throughout the country. This was the skeleton of the projected party. These local branches set up Orientation Centres which were responsible for inculcating the population with socialist ideals.[41] The Soviet attitude to the Orientation Centres was mixed. There were those, like V. Sofinsky, who praised them for 'conducting important ideological work among the population, involving broad masses of people in political affairs and mobilising the working people to participate actively in building the new Somalia'.[42] Other Soviet commentators were less enthusiastic. Writing in 1973, A. Rachkov acknowledged that 'the ideas of a socialist orientation are being widely propagated' through Orientation Centres but added in the same breath, 'it is true that up to now they work with little success'.[43] The main impediment, it was argued, was the high rate of illiteracy in Somalia.

Alongside the National Political Administration, the SRC, with Soviet help, constructed two other organisations. Both were chiefly concerned with maintaining revolutionary discipline and surveillance. The first body was called the Victory Pioneers. The organisation was a kind of youth militia, modelled on the lines of Komsomol, the Soviet Communist Youth organisation. Formed in the summer of 1972, the Victory Pioneers were responsible for drumming up local support for 'voluntary' work and monitoring the activities of foreigners in Somalia. The organisation impressed Soviet visitors. The Victory Pioneers, it was observed:

> are very active in helping the new regime to consolidate and safeguard the gains of the revolution. We watched groups of young men and women of this organisation, performing their duties in maintaining law and order ... They wear green shirts and red ties which, the leaders of the organisation told us, symbolise loyalty to Leninist principles.[44]

The second organisation was the dreaded National Security Service (NSS). This was responsible for state security and enjoyed wide-ranging powers including the power of arbitrary arrest. The NSS, headed by Siad's son-in-law, Colonel Ahmed Suleiman Abdulle, was principally concerned with preventing the emergence of opposition groups and uncovering possible plots. Established after the coup in 1969, the NSS was built up with Soviet and East German assistance.[45]

In 1972, Yu. Andropov, the then head of the KGB, paid a little publicised visit to Somalia to see that the organisation was on the right lines. A year later, Colonel Suleiman turned up in Moscow to study KGB operations.[46]

Nonetheless, the KGB–NSS connection was not a one-way street. While the arrangement undoubtedly provided Moscow with access to an extraordinary amount of hard intelligence, it also provided President Siad with an increasingly watertight security service. As related, the USSR supported Siad's regime during two previous coup attempts in 1970. In 1971, Moscow once again appeared to play a part in thwarting a coup against the military government. On 4 May, Vice-President Brigadier Mohammed Ainanshe and another SRC member, Salah Gavere Kedie were arrested for plotting to overthrow the government. According to a Soviet writer, the 'anti-government plot' was prepared 'by a group of pro-Western officers' whose plans 'had received prior approval in the West'.[47] In any event, Siad rode out the immediate crisis with the comfort of an allied Russian naval ship riding at anchor on the horizon beyond Mogadishu.[48] A year later, in July 1972, Ainanshe and Kedie were publicly executed for treason, apparently on the strong advice of a visiting Soviet delegation who argued that an example should be made of Siad's political opponents.[49] Many Somalis were unhappy about the executions but the message got home. President Siad's word was law and brooked no defiance. By the end of 1972 a Soviet commentator was able to assert that the Somali government was now 'confident in the stability of the revolutionary regime's position in the country'; and that with regard to Somalia's path of development, a victory had been gained 'in conditions of acute political struggle ... for the side of the non-capitalist path of development'.[50] Evidence of President Siad's growing confidence was expressed in his 1973 decision to release from detention many of the politicians arrested on 21 October 1969. Thus, the consolidation of Siad's regime was in no small way due to Soviet help, a point acknowledged by the Head of the Soviet Foreign Ministry Press Department. The USSR, he said, had *inter alia* helped Somalia 'to more effectively resist the internal reactionary forces'.[51]

But, if there was only a modest degree of political change in Somalia during this period, the same was less true for the realm of social and economic policy. Here, very real advances were made. Unlike its civilian predecessors, Siad's military regime made a determined effort to ameliorate the worst aspects of the country's dreadful poverty. In the words of *Pravda*, Somalia was 'one of the most backward countries in Africa [with] three quarters of the population leading nomadic lives'.[52] The 'transition to a settled way of life' (according to *Pravda*, Somalia's main problem) was hampered by the predominantly agrarian nature of the economy ('based on nomadic cattle-breeding') and the lack of industry. There was, in addition, 'virtual universal illiteracy' and 'a severe lack of local specialists'.[53] All of which led to the conclusion that 'breaking with the old traditions' in Somalia will 'involve large financial expenditure'.[54]

In the circumstances, there was inevitably a gap between the rhetoric and the economic practice of 'scientific socialism' in Somalia. The Siad government pursued what the International Labour Office called a 'basic needs'[55] strategy. On the one hand, the SRC expanded the role of government in the economy. First, following the nationalisations of May 1970, the government revamped the country's financial structure. In late 1972 a decision was taken to centralise the budget system. By 1973, Somalia, for the first time in its history, had a unified budget, incorporating the former central and regional budgets. This measure, Moscow observed, was a prerequisite for the discipline of a planned economy.[56] Secondly, Somali agriculture was diversified. The Siad regime, with Soviet support, established a number of state farms. It also promoted agricultural co-operatives. On 27 July 1973 the SRC announced a scheme whereby government finance was made available to farming enterprises which organised themselves into co-operatives.[57] The results of the co-operative movement, however, were mixed.[58] In addition, the SRC introduced National Marketing Agencies for products like grain, bananas and certain types of livestock. These agencies obtained monopoly control over the purchase and sale of the products, with a view to eliminating the role of the self-seeking middleman in the economy. Further, the Somali government sought to supplement the traditional exports, livestock and bananas. Sugar, rice, dates, cotton, sorghum, maize, wheat and tomatoes were among the crops either introduced or increased. A fishing industry was also developed and in mid-1973, a joint Soviet–Somali fishing company was set up, after a fruitful joint fishing expedition off Somalia's northern coast.[59]

Thirdly, and most importantly, the Siad regime introduced nationwide crash programmes and self-help schemes. These methods epitomised the 'bootstrap' spirit for which Somalia became renowned during this time. Under the self-help programme, the urban population was mobilised to contribute as much as seven hours per week of their spare time to construct government-designed projects such as roads, hotels, office buildings, schools and housing.[60] As for the crash programmes, the most impressive of these were in education and public health. In 1973, the SRC initiated a mass urban literacy campaign. This followed President Siad's historic decision of 1972 to adopt the Latin alphabet as the official script for the national language, Somali.[61] The campaign was highly successful. By 1974, illiteracy had almost been eliminated in the towns. Other significant measures included the decision in October 1972 to abolish private education in Somalia. As an upshot, there was a substantial expansion of the school population at primary, secondary and university level. On the public-health front the SRC phased out all private medicine and launched a nationwide immunisation programme. The incidence of malaria, tuberculosis and other endemic diseases fell sharply.[62] In 1973, a new Faculty of Medicine was established at the National University, Mogadishu.[63] This meant Somali doctors could now qualify at home. Hospital services were extended. There was also a concerted effort to improve animal health care. A network of veterinary stations was set up to improve the condition of the nomad's livestock. Vaccination against animal diseases was provided freely by the State. According to a Soviet observer, the innoculation of cattle increased by 100 per cent after the 1969 revolution.[64] In 1972 a training Institute for Animal Health Assistants was established in Mogadishu. All this prompted Julius Nyerere, an authority on African socialism, to remark in 1974: 'The Somalis are practicing what we in Tanzania preach.'[65]

At the same time, Siad's government did not attempt to fundamentally alter the balance of Somalia's mixed economy. Despite a pledge to extend the public sector to 'the commanding heights of the economy', the two mainstays of Somalia's export economy, livestock and bananas, remained in private hands. The nomads, with their privately owned herds of camels, cattle and goats, continued to sell much of their surplus livestock to the Arab and Persian Gulf market.[66] Equally, the bulk of the banana crop was produced on privately owned plantations, although it was exported exclusively through a national marketing agency which instituted a fixed price for producers. In fact, the SRC actively encouraged private investment in agriculture. The nationalised banks, for example, were authorised to grant credit facilities to individuals, including plantation owners, for the purpose of agricultural mechanisation.[67] Moreover, in April 1972, Siad reassured Somali businessmen that wholesale nationalisation was not on the political agenda:

> Private ownership is allowed in scientific socialism to be practiced in
> Somalia, provided that such wealth is not used against the interests
> of the Somali people, politically or economically. If a man conducts
> his business in a clean manner which is not detrimental to the
> interests of the masses, then the Revolution has no cause to inter-
> vene.[68]

Clearly, Siad was unwilling to force the pace of socialist development in Somalia. Several factors seemed to be at work here. In the
first place, the military government probably feared that sweeping
changes such as land nationalisation would decrease agricultural
production and thus bring a drop in export earnings. Furthermore,
such a radical measure would have almost certainly alienated the
nomadic majority from the regime. As it was, enthusiasm for Siad's
government was not exactly uniform.[69] Also, for all Siad's stress on
the concept of self-reliance, Somalia's economic progress was critically dependent on the need to attract foreign aid. In the 1971–3
Development Plan, described by Moscow as 'a realistic evaluation of
internal resources',[70] it was proposed that 80 per cent of the required
investment would be externally funded. To meet this need Siad
solicited aid from a variety of sources, non-communist as well as
communist.

One source was Italy. Linked by the colonial past – Siad at one time
served as a professional soldier in the Italian Army[71] – Italy remained,
in net terms, Mogadishu's biggest trading partner during this period,
and provided significant support. Amongst other things, Rome
helped the SDR create the Somali National Bank in 1971, rendered
'considerable assistance'[72] in the financing of the National University
in Mogadishu and backed a number of construction projects such as
the People's Hall, a building originally earmarked to house the
Parliament, and the modernisation of Kismayo airport. Another aid
donor was Iraq. In 1971, Baghdad extended a 38 million shilling loan at
low interest.[73] This was repayable over eight years, partly in cash and
partly in goods. A third source of aid derived from multilateral donors.
As an associate member of the European Economic Community
(EEC), Somalia received substantial support from the European Development Fund (EDF). This included grants for drought relief, the
development of a telecommunications centre, the building of secondary schools and the financing of automatic telephone exchanges at
Kismayo and Mogadishu. The EDF, along with the World Bank, also
provided 175 million Somali shillings to modernise and expand the
Mogadishu port.[74]

The USSR, therefore, was just one of several important donors of non-military assistance to Somalia. But this did not shake Moscow's conviction that Somalia had adopted a 'socialist orientation'. On the contrary, Somalia's mixed economy was cited as evidence of the Somali leadership's ability to distinguish between the 'strategic and tactical aspects' in the transition to socialism. The 'strategic' question related to 'the complete expulsion of foreign and even national private capital' whereas 'tactics' referred to how to pursue these objectives 'on a scale acceptable for the given conditions'. Moreover

> As a rule, at the stage of revolutionary democratic transformation the appropriate tactics are not so much the expulsion but the attraction of foreign capital, making use of it under control of the state in the most important spheres of economic construction ... in the interests of speeding up national reconstruction. Just such a line is adhered to by the Somali leaders.[75]

The same writer quoted Siad as saying 'our basic aim consists of creating a completely socialist economic structure' but 'the reality of the present situation, and also the organisation of our administrative–economic base compels the preservation of a mixed economy as an inevitable transitional step'.[76]

The Soviet analysis, leaving aside the clear inconsistency of Siad's remarks on the role of the private sector, rested on several elements. One was the perception that the Somali state sector, where Soviet aid was channelled, was 'occupying an increasingly important place in the economic life of the country'.[77] It was estimated, for instance, that budget revenue from state enterprises rose from just 2 per cent in 1969 to 17 per cent in 1973.[78] And most of these enterprises (which included the few large industrial concerns in Somalia) were built with Soviet assistance. Reviewing Soviet economic aid in 1974 a commentator noted that the USSR constructed:

> ... a milk factory at Mogadishu, a deep sea port in Berbera, and a fish-canning plant at Las Khoreh. The Soviet Union has built a boarding school, a radio station, a printing works and two hospitals as gifts to the Somali people. A meat-packing plant at Kismayo constructed in 1967 was one of the major projects of Soviet–Somali co-operation. It is a state enterprise with highly mechanised techno-logical processes ... In 1973 alone ... it turned out 20 million tins of high quality foods and processed nearly 63,000 head of cattle ... Construction has been started on the Juba River in the Fanole district of a dam, a 5,000 kw. hydro-electric power station and an irrigation canal.

In addition it was reported that:

> Soviet specialists – doctors, engineers and technicians – have been contributing to the complicated and difficult task of building the new Somalia . . . The Soviet Union has extended considerable assistance to the SDR in education, and in the training of skilled national personnel . . . At present, over 1,000 Somalis are studying in the USSR; over 1,500 young specialists have already graduated from Soviet educational institutions and are working with great effect in various branches of Somalia.[79]

All this was accompanied by a steady increase in Soviet–Somali trade, albeit with the balance heavily in Moscow's favour. In 1971 the volume of trade between the two countries was worth 7.3 million roubles. By 1974 that figure jumped to 18.8 million roubles[80] (see Table 11). No doubt this trend was assisted by the establishment of a permanent Soviet trade mission in Mogadishu in July 1972.[81]

The other main ingredient which in the Soviet view distinguished Somalia as a country of socialist orientation was the 'character' of its 'socio-economic transformation'. Soviet writers stressed the 'massive support' from 'workers, farmers, soldiers and nomadic cattle breeders' for the new measures introduced by the 'revolutionary democratic regime' in Somalia.[82] Several of these were singled out for praise. With regard to the campaign to combat illiteracy, it was noted that the decision to introduce a Somali script not only enabled 'hundreds of thousands of Somalis in an amazingly short time' to learn 'how to read and write', but also was an important political step in that it provided 'a powerful means of deepening revolutionary–democratic reform'.[83] That is, the new script 'greatly facilitated the successful mobilisation of the masses for the construction of the national economy and aided the growth of national consciousness'.[84]

Moscow also applauded President Siad's efforts to stamp out tribalism. In November 1970, the titles of sultans and all other chiefs were abolished, and a number of measures were adopted to stop inter-clan strife.[85] In 1971 a crash campaign against tribalism culminated in demonstrations where effigies (representing tribalism) were symbolically burnt or buried in centres throughout Somalia. Soviet visitors to the country were duly impressed. A Soviet member of the Soviet–Somalian Scientific Expedition of 1972 noted the 'quick overcoming of tribal dissensions' after the 'Revolution of 21 October 1969' both because of 'the law aimed at liquidating tribal conflict and regarding any propaganda of tribalism as a State offence'; and because 'their economic roots are also being exterminated'.[86] This optimistic line on the anti-tribal campaign was echoed by other Soviet commentators, although there was at least one dissenting voice.[87]

More generally, Soviet writers seemed to assume that Somalia's 'growing political consciousness' coincided with the weakening of 'the conservative Islamic course' in the country. During this period, it was noted that the Somali 'revolutionary democrats' curbed 'religious fanaticism' and 'put a stop to the counter-revolutionary activity of individual Islamic leaders'.[88] The same observer also attached special significance to the construction of statues to honour heroes of the past struggle against the 'colonialists': 'One should bear in mind that the Koran, the Moslem Holy Book, prohibits the making of human images in stone or in canvas.'[89] The new statues, therefore, were 'a reflection of the change in thinking of the Moslem' and 'only became possible in a period of revolutionary change'.[90] Similarly, E. F. Chernenko interpreted a new willingness to work on Friday, a holiday according to the Islamic calendar, as evidence that the Somali 'people are not frightened to anger God'.[91]

The ambiguities of Somalia's 'socialist orientation'

It was difficult, however, to square this Soviet analysis with local realities. Despite the closeness of Soviet–Somali relations during this period, the claim that the Somali leadership was 'strictly'[92] adhering to the Soviet model of non-capitalist development was hardly convincing. There was, for example, little sign that the SDR's decision to diversify its foreign support was purely 'tactical' – for Soviet economic aid was not without its problems. The meat-packing plant at Kismayo and the fish-canning factory at Los Khoreh were unable to operate at full capacity, while the Fanole irrigation scheme (the Somali 'Aswan') was still at the drawingboard stage by 1974.[93] And, on occasions, Siad publicly voiced his dissatisfaction with Soviet aid projects.[94] Consequently, Moscow was probably more nervous about its economic rivals in Somalia that it cared to admit. Certainly, this may have accounted for its derisive treatment of Western aid in the country,[95] and also its even more abusive attacks on China's 'primitive'[96] African assistance.

In addition, Siad's socio-economic strategy was inextricably intertwined with what was called 'Somalisation'. Unlike Moscow, Siad never assumed in advance that there was an identity of interests between the two states. For instance, in what was a reference to the large Soviet contingent in the country, Siad conceded Somalia's need for foreign experts but insisted that 'they should do for us what we want, and not what they want'.[97] Such an attitude could explain why even in major Soviet-backed projects, like the successful deep-sea-fishing project, Soviet influence was largely confined to 'how it should be done' rather than 'what should be done'.[98] By the same token, the Soviets were not involved in drawing up the country's development plans. Nor were there any Russian advisers serving in the key economic and financial institutions such as the Central Bank and Treasury. It was also instructive that President Siad's public appeals for the implementation of 'scientific socialism' were sometimes coupled with warnings against imitating foreign ideas like Marxism, Leninism and Christianity.[99] In this connection, it is interesting to note in the aforementioned literacy campaign that Siad, in contrast to the Soviets, stressed its benefits primarily in terms of national unity:

> The key . . . is to give everybody the opportunity to learn reading and writing . . . It will be the weapon to eradicate social balkanisation and fragmentation into tribes and sects. It will bring about an absolute unity and there will be no room for any negative foreign cultural influences.[100]

Finally, the Soviet assessment grossly underestimated the persistence of traditional forces in Somalia. The assertion that the revolution curbed tribalism was directly contradicted by the large number of prison sentences handed out for this offence. Indeed, an authority on Somalia observed that the political principle of clan representativeness was reflected in the composition of the SRC itself.[101] Even President Siad, in one of his franker moments, admitted the scale of the problem in 1972:

> Tribalism looms over all other factors. It is unfortunate that our nation is rather too clannish, if all Somalia are to go to Hell, tribalism will be their vehicle to reach there.[102]

As for the Soviet claim that socialism would advance at the expense of Islam, this found no favour with the Somali government. Siad repeatedly stressed that scientific socialism was fully compatible with Islam:

> Historically, our people, strongly believing in Islam, have unanimously fought all threats against their faith and their country. Today their faith is stronger than ever. As far as socialism is concerned, it is not a heavenly message like Islam but a mere system for regulating the relations between man and his utilisation of the means of production in this world. If we decide to regulate our national wealth, it is not against the essence of Islam.[103]

Siad acknowledged differences with the USSR on this question
('Those who have applied socialism before us maintain that socialism
and religion cannot go together')[104] but was unyielding:

> Both the ones who teach that scientific socialism has no place in Islam
> and those who teach that Islam has no place in scientific socialism are
> liars and are not working for the interests of the Somali people.[105]

On balance, then, the coincidence between Somalia's mixed
economy and the Soviet prescription, that African countries opting for
socialism should adopt a mixed economy as a necessary transitional
step, was not particularly striking. Somalia's brand of scientific socialism, attempting as it did to reconcile Mohammed and Marx, was
basically a locally adapted doctrine. 'Scientific Siadism'[106] might have
been a more appropriate description of the Somali experience at this
time. Thus, Soviet interest in Mogadishu, expressed in substantial
military and economic aid and the elevation of Somalia to the status of
a country of 'socialist orientation', was not wholly related to the
country's internal arrangements. There was also the question of
Somalia's 'active anti-imperialist foreign policy course'.

According to a Soviet writer the

> basic principles of [Somalia's] foreign policy was the declaration of
> support for the national liberation movement, struggle with colonial-
> ism and neo-colonialism, peaceful co-existence with other states,
> peaceful regulation of differences with neighbouring countries, faith
> in the ideals of the UN and OAU.[107]

The Somali leaders 'were among the first in the developing world to
resolutely condemn anti-Sovietism and anti-communism'. In short,
there was 'a radical change in the assessment of international developments' by Somalia after the 1969 revolution. This new foreign-policy
approach 'won the Somali Democratic Republic the respect of the
progressive public'.[108]

But in reality Siad's foreign policy was almost as ambiguous as his
domestic policy. It was certainly true that Somalia and the USSR
shared similar positions on a number of international questions. Siad
expressed support for broad Soviet initiatives such as the proposed
European Security Conference and the World Disarmament Conference; he also endorsed the Soviet line on Indo-China, categorically
denounced 'Israeli aggression against the Arab countries'[109] in the
Middle East and condemned the Anglo–American decision to establish a communications base on Diego Garcia in the Indian Ocean.[110] In
African affairs, the military regime in Somalia, much to the delight of

Moscow, established itself as an active member of the radical grouping within the Organisation of African Unity (OAU) and as a peacemaker on the continent. Siad used the OAU forum to vigorously oppose any dialogue with South Africa and to rally support for African liberation movements such as the MPLA in Angola and SWAPO in Namibia.[111] In 1971, Somalia hosted what was generally acknowledged to be a successful Central and East African Summit. And when, in 1973, Tanzania and Idi Amin's regime in Uganda teetered on the brink of war, it was Siad who mediated between them. 'These progressive steps', according to Moscow radio, boosted Somalia's 'international prestige'.[112]

Nevertheless, it would be wrong to attribute this measure of foreign-policy agreement solely to Soviet influence. In at least two of the above issues, Somalia had a distinctive interest in pursuing the line that it did. In seeking a more prominent African role, Siad sought both to legitimise his government and create a more favourable climate of African opinion *vis-à-vis* the aspirations of Somali nationalism. Equally, the SRC's close identification with the Arab cause, the high point being reached during the October 1973 war,[113] was rationalised less in terms of 'anti-imperialism' than by Islamic solidarity. The logic was simple. By stressing its religious links with the Arab world, Somalia hoped to focus Arab attention on its own national grievance with Ethiopia, a traditional adversary of the Arabs. The strategy was effective. During the course of 1973, Somali Embassies opened in Algeria, Syria, Libya, Kuwait, Iraq and Abu Dhabi. Military contacts also expanded. In March 1973 Somali Defence Minister Mohammed Ali Samatar visited Egypt. Four months later the Egyptian Defence Minister returned the visit. And economic co-operation increased – Mogadishu signed new trade agreements with South Yemen, Syria and Jordan.[114]

Beyond this, Somalia's foreign policy was conspicuous for its diversity. As noted, Siad succeeded in attracting foreign aid from a variety of sources. Foreign policy was adjusted accordingly. Thus, while Siad insisted that 'capitalist ideology has no future', he maintained cordial relations with Italy and the EEC on the grounds 'that it is possible to combat economic exploitation without necessarily alienating foreign investment'.[115] The SRC also managed to combine excellent relations with both the USSR and its allies – Somalia received considerable economic assistance from the GDR, Bulgaria, North Korea and Cuba during this period[116] – and China. In this regard, the Somali leader commented: 'You all know that the USSR and the

Peoples Republic of China are among our greatest socialist friends. They might have their differences but let us not involve ourselves in the internal conflict between friends'.[117]

Yet, there was too clear a pattern to conclude that Somali foreign policy was shapeless. Siad seemed determined to maximise foreign support for his country and for what he saw as his country's central foreign-policy objective, namely, the unification of all Somalis under one flag. Throughout this period, President Siad repeatedly declared that Ethiopian–Somali differences over 'the occupied territories' should be settled by peaceful means only. However, he made it clear that the problem had to be settled.[118]

For a time, Ethiopian–Somali relations remained outwardly cordial. In June 1971 Siad attended the OAU Summit in Addis Ababa. He was accorded an exceptionally warm welcome by the Ethiopian Emperor and his government. In October 1971, the Emperor himself was warmly received when he attended the Central and East African Summit in Mogadishu. After extensive talks with President Siad, Haile Selassie declared that friendship between the two countries had been strengthened. He admitted, though, that the political commitments of the two were irreconcilable in respect of Somalia's claim to unite all Somalis.[119] And, in what was seen as an attempt to improve relations, Siad cut off the support Somalia traditionally gave to the Western Somalia Liberation Front (WSLF) operating in the Ogaden.[120] This, it should be stressed, did not halt the WSLF activities in the area. In addition, the Somali leader periodically jailed militant Ogadeni Somalis within the Somali government or Armed Forces whose activities threatened to embarrass the SRC.[121] As a result, it was reported in July 1972 that the Ethiopian–Somali border talks, initiated by Siad's predecessor, Egal, and the Emperor, continued 'in a spirit of brotherhood and understanding'.[122]

All this, however, began to crumble toward the end of 1972. In December, a US oil company, Tenneco, announced the discovery of substantial quantities of natural gas in the Bale region of the Ogaden. The discovery, made only 30 miles from the Somali border, was sufficient to suggest the strong likelihood of oil deposits nearby. Mindful of the massive Soviet-sponsored military build up in Somalia, the Ethiopian government took the opportunity to deploy a sizeable military contingent along the border, ostensibly to ensure the security of drilling operations. Somalia countered by deploying troops on its own side of the border. This increasingly tense situation took a turn for the worse in January 1973. A face to face meeting in Mogadishu between the Ethiopian Foreign Minister, Dr Minassie Haile and his Somali counterpart, Omar Arteh, arranged to cool the diplomatic temperature, produced nothing except a vitriolic shouting match. Shortly after, both sides concentrated more troops along the Ogaden border. At least one military skirmish was reported to have occurred sometime in March or April 1973.[123]

By the time of the OAU Council of Ministers Summit in May 1973, the Ethiopian–Somali dispute took on the character of a full-blown diplomatic confrontation. The Somali call for a solution 'of the territorial dispute' was vigorously rejected by the Ethiopian Foreign Minister on the grounds that no such dispute existed.[124] The crisis was exacerbated on 26 May when Siad accused Ethiopia of massing half of her Army along the border; as a consequence, he said, he could not attend the Summit. The Ethiopian Minister of Information, Dr Tesfaye Gebre Egzi, subsequently called Siad 'a liar' and added that his country would not yield 'even one inch'[125] to Somalia. President Siad eventually attended the Summit but Ethiopia and Somalia remained at loggerheads. An OAU 'good offices' Committee set up by the then OAU Chairman, General Y. Gowon, failed to reconcile the two neighbours, despite energetic efforts. These included visits by President Numeiry to Mogadishu and Addis Ababa in June 1973 on behalf of the Committee and a special mission led by Nigeria's Dr Arikpo in August 1973.[126] At the end of the day, however, neither side was willing to make concessions. Siad stressed that Somalia would never give up its claim on the Ogaden while Emperor Haile Selassie described the region as 'an inseparable part of Ethiopia'.[127]

Notwithstanding the diplomatic stalemate and the odd border incident, neither side seemed eager to go to war in 1973 to settle their differences. President Siad was quoted as saying:

> I will never be party to Africans killing Africans and will never attack our neighbours. I believe this dispute can be resolved by peaceful negotiations, perhaps through the OAU.[128]

To emphasise the point, the Somali government noted that the border crisis was inflamed by 'war-mongering foreign media'.[129] As for Ethiopia, the situation was altogether different. Favoured by the territorial status quo, Addis Ababa had every reason to avoid war. It could not, however, but be concerned by the more belligerent stance of Mogadishu.

The breakdown of the Ethiopian–Somali *détente* cast an interesting light on Soviet policy. Without doubt Somalia's new assertiveness was linked to massive Soviet military backing. By 1973, Somalia was beginning to close the gap in the regional military balance. There were a number of indicators. First, Somalia's armed forces were built up from 12,000 in 1970 to 17,300 in 1973, an increase of nearly 50 per cent. On the other hand, Ethiopia's armed forces, estimated at 44,570, remained roughly at the 1970 level, despite the need to contain a guerrilla war in Eritrea. Furthermore, in terms of heavy weapons and tanks, Somalia's Army actually achieved superiority over its Ethiopian counterpart.[130] Secondly, Somalia's airforce acquired MiG-15s, MiG-17s and MiG-19s without a commensurate response from Addis Ababa.[131] Thirdly, Somalia's spending on defence, as a proportion of GNP, rose from 4.6 per cent in 1970 to 16 per cent in 1973, a staggering increase.[132] In comparison, Ethiopia's defence budget remained, according to *The Military Balance 1973–74*, relatively static. It rose from 2.1 per cent in 1970 to just 2.8 per cent in 1973 (see Table 7).

The extensive arming of Siad's regime, with all its destabilising implications, was not matched by official Soviet endorsement of Somali ethnic nationalist claims. In part, this was due to a Soviet reluctance to publicly offend the OAU principle concerning the immutability of colonial borders bequeathed at independence. For, while Siad's African diplomacy undoubtedly improved Somalia's standing in the OAU, it failed, with odd exceptions such as Colonel Gaddafy's Libya,[133] to win over many African countries to the Somali cause. There was, however, another consideration. In the previous chapter, we noted a disagreement between Soviet writers like Ye Etinger who apparently believed that Soviet support for the new 'progressive' regime should include its irredentist aspirations, and those such as M. Rayt who argued it should not. Sometime in 1972 someone (Podgorny?) seemed to have knocked the pundits' heads together. The result was the emergence of an approach which recognised that Somalia 'like all progressive countries' was 'a target for imperialist expansion'[134] and deserved Soviet military support, and at the same time continued to question the validity of Somali claims on Ethiopia. For example, R. N. Ismagilova in 1973 repeated many of the earlier arguments used by the skeptical M. Rayt:

> In Ethiopia the Somalis live in the province of Harar, Bale and Sidamo, districts historically and economically connected with Ethiopia. The Ethiopian Somalis have various views toward the question of reunification with Somalia. Part of them on the strength of a series of economic and political reasons are not interested in annexation . . . But some of the Somali nomads support incorporation into the

Table 7. *The military balance in the Horn of Africa 1973–1974: A breakdown*

Category	Ethiopia	Somalia
Population	26,500,000	3,000,000
Estimated GNP 1972	$US 2.07 billion	$182 million
Total armed forces	44,570	17,300
Estimated defence budget 1972	$US 40.5 million	$11.4 million
Army Total strength	40,940	15,000
	4 infantry divisions of 8,000 men each	4 tank battalions
	1 tank battalion	9 mech. infantry battalions
	1 airborne infantry battalion	1 commando battalion
	4 armoured car squadrons	2 field art. battalions
	4 artillery battalions	5 A A art. battalions
	5 air defence batteries	About 150 T-34 med. tanks
	2 engineer battalions	60 BTR-40 and 250 BTR-152 Armoured
	50 M-41 med. tanks	Personnel Carriers
	20 M-24 lt. tanks	
	About 40 Armoured Personnel Carriers	
	30 M-9, M-20 and 56 AML-25 arm. cars	

Navy

Total strength 1,380

1 coastal minesweeper
1 training ship
5 patrol boats
4 harbour defence craft
4 landing craft

300

4 P-6 and 6 P-4 MTB (ex-Soviet)

Air Force

Total strength 2,250

37 combat aircraft
1 bomber squad. with 4 Canberra B-2
1 fighter-bomb. squad. with 12 F-86F
1 squad. with 6 T-28A
1 fighter squad. with 15 F-5A
1 transport squad. with 6 C-47, 2 C-54,
5 C-119G and 3 Dove
3 train. squads. with 20 Safir, 15 T-28A
and 11 T-33A
5 Alouette II, 2 Mi-6, 2 Mi-8 and 5 AB
204B helicopters

2,000

21 combat aircraft
Some Il-28 light bombers
2 MiG-15 and 19 MiG-17 fighters
Transports include 1 C-45, 3 C-47, 3
An-2 and 1 An-24
2 MiG-15/-17, 10 Piaggio P-148 and Yak
trainers

Defence expenditure as
% of GNP 2.8% 16%

Source: adapted from *The Military Balance, 1973–1974*, London, Institute for Strategic Studies, 1973, pp. 39–41.

Somali Republic. The imperialist powers, using the nationalistically inclined officials and some organisations are inflaming the inter-state conflict on ethnic grounds.[135]

Other Soviet writers were equally unsympathetic. N. Kosukhin and L. Obukhov noted that 'right-wing nationalist forces' in Somalia were seeking to impede the 'further deepening of the national democratic revolution'. While E. F. Chernenko also conceded that: 'narrow nationalistic prejudices which have retarded [political] consciousness have been preserved by part of the population and are still hindering the movement forward'[136] in the SDR.

The key element in this otherwise contradictory approach was the Soviet conviction that it could firmly control the Somali military. It was reported that Moscow kept Somalia low on spare parts, ammunition and military fuel.[137] Moreover, with a large military contingent of advisers built into the Somali military machine, the Soviets were probably confident that Mogadishu would be unable to launch a major operation without their involvement. Thus, as far as the USSR was concerned, the very real risk of fuelling a Somali attack on Ethiopia was contained by its perceived operational control over the Somali Army.

Soviet perceptions of an emperor in decline

Ethiopia continued to figure prominently in Soviet thinking. Unlike Somalia, where the general picture in the first half of the 1970s was one of cohesion and guarded optimism, Haile Selassie's Ethiopia was increasingly divided and demoralised. Two major factors were responsible for this. First, in 1970, a devastating drought hit the Ethiopian provinces of Tigre and Wollo and, eventually, affected most of the country (as well as Somalia). By 1972, the harvest was meagre and Ethiopia found itself in the grip of a disastrous famine. Something like 100,000 peasants died of starvation or related diseases.[138] But the tragedy of drought was not new to Ethiopia: the important difference this time was that the standard government practice of covering up such disasters was shattered by a BBC film crew. Unable to deny the problem, Haile Selassie's government then compounded its moral ineptitude by presenting inaction as the official policy response.[139]

The drought crisis brutally exposed the limitations of Haile Selassie's government. Amongst other things, the failure to enact a programme of land reform (first mooted in 1966) and an inability to resolve the issue of political succession probably magnified the impact of the disaster. This, along with rising inflation caused by sharply increased costs of oil imports in 1973,[140] unleashed a wave of popular discontent. In particular, many students and urban intellectuals were outraged by the authorities' handling of the situation. Moreover, by the end of 1973, there were ominous rumblings of unrest within the ranks of junior Army Officers.[141]

Secondly, the rebellion in Eritrea widened despite a period of considerable rebel weakness. Between 1971 and 1974 the ELF and the more recently formed EPLF were embroiled in a bloody civil war in an effort to enforce unity. Acts of assassination and full-scale military clashes became commonplace. In addition, Emperor Haile Selassie achieved a notable diplomatic success in reducing Sudan's support for the Eritrean movement. In March 1971, Ethiopia and the Sudan agreed to desist from helping subversive movements in the other country. A year later, in February 1972, the two countries signed a treaty recognising each other's territorial integrity. In July 1972 another agreement settled the question relating to the demarcation of the Ethiopian–Sudanese border.[142] Taken together, these developments seriously weakened the guerrillas' ability to challenge the Ethiopian presence.

However, in 1973, the Eritrean rebels managed to step up their military operations against the Ethiopian Army. There was a new wave of attacks on Ethiopian personnel and government installations in Asmara, the province's capital, in September. Such activities were largely the result of increased Arab support. Increasingly convinced that the Red Sea should be an 'Arab Lake'[143] and that Ethiopia's close ties with Israel – Tel Aviv maintained a small group of counterinsurgency advisers in Eritrea – were an obstacle to this pan-Arab objective, Syria and Iraq expanded financial and armed assistance to the ELF while Libya asserted itself as the main backer of the EPLF. As a result, Ethiopia, no longer so confident of Washington's support, found itself under heavy pressure to break its ties with Israel. At the OAU Heads of State Summit in May 1973, Libya accused Emperor Haile Selassie of 'occupying a territory [Eritrea] and dispersing a people with American support',[144] and demanded, in view of Ethiopia's close ties with Israel, that the OAU headquarters be moved from Addis Ababa. Threats and promises from other Arab states, including Saudi Arabia,[145] followed.

The Soviet Union reacted to Haile Selassie's predicament with a mixture of ideological hostility and traditional political interest. On the one hand, the Imperial regime in Ethiopia was depicted as a variant of what Lenin called 'local imperialism' (a tendency in weak and backward states 'dependent on major imperialist vultures to conduct "their own" imperialist policies in some particular region').[146] Writing in 1972, A. Kokiev described Ethiopia as 'the citadel of feudalism on the African continent'; there had been 'comparatively little change' in the country since 'the Middle Ages'. The 'predominant productive relations are feudal' and Ethiopia, 'according to the standard of national income per head . . . holds one of the worst places in the world'.[147]

Such backwardness was linked to the fact that 'the real power in the country is found in the hands of the old feudal nobles and churchmen'.[148] Together, these two groups owned about 80 per cent of Ethiopia's land and dominated a Parliamentary system in which each candidate had to pay 800 dollars to register to stand. Consequently, for the landless peasants who made up the vast bulk of the population, Ethiopian elections were essentially 'unrepresentative'.[149] This, according to G. Tanov, was confirmed by the Parliament's stubborn refusal to pass the government's Land Tenure Bill whereby rents would be paid in cash to the landowner instead of the feudal payment-by-service system prevailing in Ethiopia.[150]

Soviet writers also condemned the 'active penetration of foreign monopolies' in the Ethiopian economy. The small industrial sector, accounting for about 8 per cent of the country's GNP, was said to be dominated by Western concerns. K. Gerasimov observed that companies like Total, Mobil and Shell 'still monopolise trade in oil products in the country'. At the same time, the predominant agricultural sector was becoming increasingly 'the object of attachment of direct foreign [Western] investment'.[151] This was a reference to the fact that US and Dutch companies developed coffee and sugar plantations respectively. But, while Soviet commentators exaggerated the level of Western investment,[152] the emergence of commercial relations in what was a basically subsistence agrarian economy apparently made one thing clear. The Ethiopian government seeks 'to effect a gradual transition of the feudal economy on to the tracks of the capitalist development path' whereby 'the basic costs for the modernisation of agriculture are intended to be piled on the peasants'. As a consequence, the further development 'of capitalism in its most grotesque form'[153] was envisaged in Ethiopia.

On the other hand, the Soviet media continued to stress the 'fruitful and mutually advantageous co-operation'[154] between Ethiopia and the USSR. A variety of contacts were reported during the period under review. In September 1971 the two states signed an agreement concerning the establishment of air-routes between Moscow and

Addis Ababa.[155] In March 1972, the USSR opened a permanent trade centre in Addis Ababa.[156] It was claimed that Soviet–Ethiopian trade 'increased considerably' in the early 1970s through the delivery of Soviet tractors, trailers, bulldozers and trucks and the purchase of Ethiopian coffee, oil seeds, pulse crops and leather,[157] but this claim was contradicted by the USSR's own trade statistics (see Tables 5 and 11). In September 1972, the Soviet Union donated medicine to an Ethiopian orphanage and, a month later, exchanged Red Cross delegations with Ethiopia.[158] In January 1974, a visit to Ethiopia by Patriarch Pimen, ostensibly to consolidate the traditional fraternal relations between the Ethiopian and Russian Orthodox Churches, 'promoted a further strengthening of friendly relations between Ethiopia and the Soviet Union'.[159]

It was also pointed out that the USSR gave Ethiopia 'considerable assistance in economic and social development'.[160] Summarising Soviet aid to Addis Ababa in 1973, V. Shmarov listed some of the achievements:

> The oil refinery built with Soviet assistance in Assab in 1967 – the first enterprise of Ethiopia's national industry – is saving the country a great deal of money: instead of oil products it is importing crude oil, which is much cheaper. The Soviet hospital in Addis Ababa where Soviet doctors have treated thousands of people has earned a good reputation in the country. Young Ethiopians who have acquired a higher education in the Soviet Union and graduated from the polytechnical institute built with Soviet assistance at Bahr Dar are reinforcing the ranks of national specialists and helping the country in its economic development.[161]

The accent on the positive in Soviet–Ethiopian relations was probably linked to two important geo-political considerations. One concerned the faltering relationship between Emperor Haile Selassie and the United States. Confronted by a steady military build-up in Somalia, the Emperor looked to Washington to redress the balance. However, the Nixon administration seemed determined to avoid deepening its involvement in the Horn. In May 1973, the Ethiopian leader travelled to Washington in an attempt to extract a massive increase in military aid (he presented a $450 million shopping list). The US response was restrained. It agreed to supply another squadron of F5-E fighter-bomber aircraft, some M60 tanks and naval patrol boats on a credit and cash basis. But Washington politely rejected the Emperor's other requests which included air-to-ground missiles and an increase in the US military-aid grant.[162]

In addition, the US decision to phase down the Kagnew communications centre was officially confirmed by Ethiopia in October 1973.[163]
It was agreed that US personnel at the station would be reduced to
one hundred by 1 July 1974, and that its functions would be gradually
transferred to the Diego Garcia base in the Indian Ocean. The
Ethiopian Foreign Ministry stressed that the initiative for the phase
down was taken jointly and was due to 'advances in the fields of
communications technology'.[164] But this was essentially a case of
putting a brave face on the matter. For, while the phase down was in a
sense a technical matter, it also signalled, in the words of a US
observer, that 'the dominant element of the rationale given to Congress for military assistance to Ethiopia had been removed'.[165] The
point was not lost on Moscow. Tass described the move as 'contributing to international *détente*'.[166] Moreover, in economic terms, the US
withdrawal from Kagnew was a severe blow. It was estimated that the
station contributed $4 million to $6 million a year to the Ethiopian
economy,[167] most of it concentrated in Asmara, and was a major
source of local employment.

A final blow to the Ethiopian–American relationship in 1973 was
dealt by the US Congress. The latter decided to cut back its defence
loans appropriations to a somewhat meagre $25 million for the whole
of Africa.[168] Since Ethiopia received $12.1 million in military-aid grants
in 1973, and was one of the largest recipients of defence grants in the
past, this measure raised serious difficulties for a country which could
not afford to pay cash for its arms requirements. The clear implication,
once again, was that Ethiopia had been relegated in the order of US
defence priorities. It is worth pointing out that by 1970 the US had
established a 107-man Military Assistance Advisory Group (MAAG) in
Ethiopia. This contingent provided instructions for the Debre Zeit
parachute-training centre and the Harar Military Academy.[169]

The other important consideration for Moscow was the growing
rapprochement between Emperor Haile Selassie and China. This owed
much to Peking's own reaction to the Soviet role in Somalia and Haile
Selassie's determination to counteract the pro-Chinese wing of the
ELF. In October 1971, the Ethiopian Monarch made a highly successful
state visit to China. The visit produced an $84 million interest-free loan
from the PRC to cover road building, rural electrification, irrigation,
animal husbandry and other agricultural projects in Ethiopia.[170] China
also agreed to send engineers and technicians to Ethiopia to participate in the above projects. Furthermore, as if to emphasise Chinese
goodwill, the Foreign Minister Chi Peng Fei took the unusual step, on

the occasion of Ethiopia's National Day in 1971, of praising the 'Imperial Government'.[171] By 1973, there were reports that China, a state whose foreign policy assumed 'the character of global opposition to everything the Soviet Union does',[172] had offered Ethiopia arms.

Soviet sensitivity to these trends, however, might have been less had it not been for its own enduring sense of identification with Ethiopia. Certainly, close relations with revolutionary Somalia failed to diminish it. In February 1973, shortly before the thirtieth anniversary of Ethiopian–Soviet diplomatic relations, G. Tsypkin emphasised Ethiopia's role in the anti-colonialist movement by recalling its famous victory over Italy at Adowa in 1896:

> It is impossible to overestimate the historic significance of the battle of Adowa where the hand picked colonial troops were routed. Ethiopia triumphed and it was practically the only independent country in Africa.[173]

Other Soviet commentators discerned parallels in the historical development of the two countries. It was noted that Ethiopia, like tsarist Russia, had economic potential (K. Gerasimov referred to the 'possible presence of oil in the country'), a largely peasant population and a multi-ethnic society.[174] Such similarities, an Ethiopian writer told a Soviet visitor in 1972, meant that: 'The problems of Russia in the 19th century as it were illuminate contemporary Ethiopian society.' The same Soviet visitor said that Ethiopians recognised the friendly attitude of the USSR toward their country, and quoted another Ethiopian writer as saying: 'Our ancient links must be strengthened and developed on a new basis'.[175]

This, it would seem, is precisely what Soviet diplomacy sought to achieve. Having eroded Ethiopian military dominance by generously arming Somalia, Moscow then tried to capitalise on the new situation by acting as an intermediary in the Horn. Between 1972 and 1973, the USSR was involved in a series of behind-the-scenes moves. In May 1972, S. Tsarapkin, roving ambassador of the USSR, visited Addis Ababa for undisclosed talks with the Ethiopian government.[176] In June 1972, Dr Menassie Haile, the Ethiopian Foreign Minister, made a little publicised visit to Moscow.[177] A year later, in August 1973, S. Tsarapkin paid another secret visit to Ethiopia.[178] In September 1973, V. Kudryavstev, Deputy Chairman of the Soviet Afro-Asian Solidarity Committee, led a delegation in a visit to Ethiopia.[179] A month later, in October 1973, M. A. Samantar, the Somali Defence Minister, interrupted his vacation in the USSR to have talks with President Podgorny and A. Grechko, the Soviet Defence Minister.[180] Once again, the subject(s) of the talks was not revealed.

Despite the secrecy, it was reasonable to assume these negotiations explored the possibility of a Soviet-backed deal for the Horn. The prospects for such a deal had clearly emerged. By 1973, the Ethiopian government was sufficiently weak, for a variety of domestic and external reasons already outlined, to turn closer to the Soviet Union in the hope that the Kremlin might put a brake on Somalia and also to persuade Arab states to reduce their support for the Eritrean liberation movements. As for the USSR, it was confident of its ability to restrain Somalia if it felt so inclined and had only a tactical interest in the Eritrean cause. While it was true that Soviet arms still reached the Eritrean rebels via Arab states, Moscow was careful to publicly distance itself from the guerrillas' struggle. In 1971, the authoritative Soviet journal, *New Times*, reaffirmed that Eritrea was an integral part of Ethiopia. An article declared that 'Ethiopia, with its several hundred kilometres of Red Sea shoreline and its two ports (Assab and Massawa) cannot be said to be landlocked.'[181] Another Soviet commentary attacked the 'ultra-nationalist liberation front' in Eritrea as an 'obstacle' to Ethiopian development. However, Moscow stressed that Addis Ababa would have to shed its pro-Western stance if it wished to make progress on the Eritrean issue: 'Ethiopia's attempts to improve relations with its Arab neighbours were unlikely to succeed while there were still US bases in the country'.[182]

In October 1973, two events occurred which suggested Emperor Haile Selassie might heed Moscow's advice. The first, the announcement concerning the phasing out of the US communications station at Kagnew, has already been discussed. The second event was a by-product of the Yom Kippur war. On 23 October Ethiopia severed diplomatic relations with Israel. This move, foreshadowed by an announcement that the Emperor would journey to the USSR for a 'business'[183] visit, ended what had been an extremely close relationship with Tel Aviv. Indeed, Israel was known to have acted as a lobbyist for Ethiopian interests in Washington.[184] The decision to break relations, therefore, was both a desperate attempt to keep within the mainstream of OAU and non-aligned thinking on the Middle East and to improve relations with the Arab world, particularly those states sympathetic to Somali and Eritrean nationalism.

But, if the Ethiopian government hoped these moves would secure some sort of deal with the USSR, it met with disappointment. As arranged, Emperor Haile Selassie visited the Soviet Union on 29–30

October 1973. Talks took place in 'an atmosphere of candour and mutual understanding'.[185] That, according to the conventions of Soviet political parlance, indicated disagreement. A joint communique observed:

> that relations of traditional friendship exist between the USSR and Ethiopia. Soviet–Ethiopian co-operation is being carried out ... on the basis of the principles of independence, sovereignty, equality and non-interference in each other's internal affairs.[186]

However, the phrase 'territorial integrity', the key principle in the Ethiopian case against Somali territorial claims, and one which appeared in the May 1970 Soviet–Ethiopian statement, was not mentioned in the 1973 communique. This omission, given the zero-sum diplomacy of the Horn, seemed to the Ethiopians at least to signal Soviet support for the Somali position. But the Soviet political purpose was probably more subtle than that.

The joint communique was careful to stress the need for long-term Ethiopian–Soviet co-operation because it was 'in the interests of the Soviet and Ethiopian peoples' and 'contributes to the consolidation of peace on the African continent'.[187] But there was a recognition, in the words of President N. Podgorny, that Soviet–Ethiopian relations were developing against the background of a 'qualitatively new situation'[188] in Africa. That is to say, Moscow was aware of the increasingly difficult situation facing the Emperor's regime. Accordingly, the Soviet refusal to endorse Ethiopian 'territorial integrity' appeared to be a calculated snub against Haile Selassie at what was perceived to be a politically opportune time. Suffice it to say, the Moscow trip did nothing to relieve Ethiopia's sense of isolation, abandonment and weakness.

The year 1974: the treaty

On 11 July 1974, Presidents Podgorny and Siad, 'prompted by a desire to reinforce and consolidate the existing friendly relations between the USSR and the SDR',[189] signed a Treaty of Friendship and Co-operation on behalf of their respective states. This treaty, along with the events immediately preceding it, marked 1974 as a momentous year in the Horn of Africa. It began with the climax of Somalia's Arab diplomacy. On 15 February 1974 Somalia joined the Arab League. Her admission was sponsored by conservative Saudi Arabia. The Saudis calculated that Somalia's entry would weaken its commitment to scientific socialism and the USSR. For its part, Somalia stressed that its decision to join was based on its historical ties with the Arab world. President Siad even claimed that Arab aspirations would henceforth take precedence in Somali foreign policy:

> The problem of liberation and unification of the other parts of Somalia had been relegated to second place now that Somalia had regarded herself as one of the frontline countries against the enemy [Israel].[190]

Despite the hyperbole, there was little doubt the Somali leadership regarded its Arab League membership as an important gain. In the words of Siad:

> It was based on wisdom and far-sightedness. I can say that the Somalis had many times missed the point but I sincerely believe that this step is one of the very few times we have really hit the point.[191]

The 'point' was both political and, more specifically, economic. As a new member of the Arab League, Somalia rapidly developed its links with the Arab states and, in doing so, attracted substantial foreign assistance. This included an Iraqi pledge to construct a refinery, supply crude oil and provide a three-year loan to cover Somalia's half of the cost; grants totalling 234 million Somali shillings from Saudi Arabia and Kuwait, announced in September 1974; a loan of US $7.3 million from the Kuwaiti Fund for Arab Economic Development, which also agreed in December 1974 to finance the construction of a new power station in Mogadishu at a cost of over 140 million Somali shillings; finance from Abu Dhabi worth £28 million to construct an abattoir, canning factory and irrigation scheme at Bardera; and a number of shipping and agricultural agreements with Libya, concluded in February 1974.[192]

Moscow, however, did not welcome Somali participation in the Arab League. The issue received scant attention in the Soviet media at the time but what was said betrayed a certain unease. One commentary, for example, was moved to claim that Somali membership was prompted by the desire 'to develop relations with the progressive Arab regimes'.[193] Such a claim had two implications. First, a tacit Soviet recognition that Somalia had joined an organisation which included the 'reactionary circles' of the Arab world within its ranks. Secondly, a Soviet concern that Mogadishu was now vulnerable to the petrodollar pressure of anti-Soviet elements in the League, notably Saudi Arabia. It was no secret that in early 1974 the Saudi Arabian government firmly tied an aid offer of $75 million to the systematic contraction of Soviet activities in Somalia.[194]

Other developments reinforced the USSR's sense of uncertainty. At the end of February 1974, Emperor Haile Selassie's government was paralysed by a domestic crisis of enormous proportions. The crisis was triggered by a mutiny of the Fourth Brigade of the Army at Negelle in South-west Ethiopia in January 1974. Within weeks, the 'Negelle flu' spread throughout the Ethiopian Army and to the rest of the country. On 28 February 1974, the Emperor, confronted with nationwide strikes and radical political demands from the military, accepted the mass resignation of his Cabinet. Having made that concession, the Emperor proceeded to lose his authority and ultimately his throne. But these events will be more fully discussed in the next chapter. It will suffice here to note that while the USSR took a keen interest in the Ethiopian political crisis and soon indicated where its sympathies lay – within a month of the first disturbances in Ethiopia, Moscow depicted the situation as a conflict between 'the forces of democracy and progress against those of reaction'[195] – it seemed unsure of the eventual outcome. A Soviet analysis in mid-1974, just three months before Haile Selassie's dethronement, declared that 'the unrest in Ethiopia is gradually subsiding'.[196] In the meantime, Ethiopian–Somali relations continued to deteriorate. In January 1974 Ethiopia accused Somalia of publicly advocating its dismemberment.[197] In June, the OAU Heads of State Summit in Mogadishu was again disrupted by the Ethiopian border controversy. The Ethiopian Foreign Minister claimed that Somalia used the occasion to 'launch a propaganda campaign against Ethiopia'. Such resentment was fuelled by the Somali authorities' decision to permit the distribution of a book condemning the Ethiopian 'occupation' in the Ogaden and to allow representatives of the ELF and WSLF to mix on the fringes of the conference.[198]

In the circumstances, the USSR found itself under pressure to act merely to maintain existing facilities in Somalia. For, in the short term, at least, Moscow did not appear to have an alternative ally in the Horn. Moreover, Somalia's political standing as an African ally was considerably boosted by new gains on the diplomatic front. As related, Mogadishu was the venue in 1974 for the annual meeting of the OAU Heads of State. And, following tradition, President Siad, as leader of the host country, was elected as Chairman of the OAU for the succeeding year. Furthermore, the Somali Foreign Minister, Omar Arteh Ghalib, bolstered by the support of the Arab members and many of the predominantly Muslim black African states, only narrowly lost the contest for the vacant OAU post of Secretary-General.

Apparently convinced that Somalia was now its top priority in black Africa, the USSR responded to these developments by increasing the pressure for a treaty to codify bilateral relations and give them a more binding character. President Siad resisted for a while but, by mid-1974, consented, asking only to delay signature until after the June OAU conference. Thereupon, on 8 July, shortly following the announcement of a Soviet gift of 7 MiG-21s to Somalia,[199] President N. Podgorny, the most senior Soviet politician ever to visit a black African country, arrived in Mogadishu. He was accompanied by a high-powered 60-man delegation that included senior ministers and officials.[200] After several days of talks, on 11 July 1974 President Podgorny signed a twenty-year Treaty of Friendship and Co-operation with Somalia. A protocol to the Soviet–Somali agreement of June 1961 on economic and technical co-operation was also signed.

In its published provisions, the treaty fell short of binding the parties to a full military alliance. Instead, it declared that the Soviet Union and Somalia 'will co-operate in every way' to ensure 'the preservation and deepening of their people's socio-economic achievements' (Article 1).[201] The two sides also pledged to expand economic and scientific–technical co-operation (Article 2). As a palliative, Moscow wrote off Somalia's military and economic aid debts, amounting to $80 million and $45 million respectively.[202] Both governments committed 'to develop co-operation in the military sphere . . . in the training of Somali military personnel and in the mastering of weapons and equipment supplied to the SDR for the purposes of enhancing its defence potential' (Article 4). This provision coincided with a fresh influx of MiGs, Ilyushin-28 bombers, SA-2 and SA-3 surface-to-air missile systems, T-54 tanks and artillery into Somalia.[203] In addition, the two parties opposed 'imperialism and colonialism in all its forms and manifestations' (Article 7) and agreed to consult each other regularly (Article 8), something they were already doing. Finally, both countries proclaimed they would 'not be party to military alliances . . . or to actions . . . directed against the other' (Article 10).[204]

Izvestiya hailed the treaty as a 'firm foundation for the further development of friendly relations between the USSR and the SDR'.[205] But the wording of the document suggested otherwise. It was ambiguous and permitted wholly inconsistent interpretations. Thus, the Soviet Union could claim the document placed Somalia squarely in the 'progressive' camp. The treaty made no specific concessions to Somalia's territorial claims, while Articles 1 and 9 seemed to imply a Soviet right to take an interest in Somalia's internal and external affairs. Also, Article 10 could be understood as a Somali obligation not to have close ties with the Western states, China or Arab 'reactionary circles'. On the other hand, it was possible for Somalia to interpret the treaty as a formal endorsement of its territorial aspirations. Article 7 proposed to oppose 'imperialism and colonialism ... on the basis of ... self-determination of the peoples'. By the same token, Somalia was free to consider Article 10 as an injunction against Soviet support for its longstanding adversary, Ethiopia.

Nevertheless, the treaty was definite in one respect. It reaffirmed that the Soviet Union would continue to arm and train the Somali armed forces. The point did not escape Ethiopia where the Soviet–Somali agreement provoked expressions of resentment. In what was a thinly veiled warning about the future of Ethiopian–Soviet relations, Addis Ababa radio commented:

> ... no diplomatic jargon can hide the ambivalence of the Soviet mission to Somalia and at this time it poses the question as to whether this mission and the agreement figure under the umbrella of *détente* or of the cold war. One is impressed by the fact that African diplomacy is a two-headed thing – and much more since the Soviet Union professes friendship with both Ethiopia and Somalia.[206]

Both the USSR and Somalia denied that the treaty was aimed against a third party (i.e., Ethiopia). But the denial was not made for the same reasons.

Moscow assessed the significance of the treaty primarily in broad political terms. It was asserted that the Soviet–Somali agreement 'was simultaneously Soviet–African friendship because assistance to a progressive country like Somalia should be regarded as assistance to all the progressive forces of Africa fighting for liberation and for complete independence of the African continent'.[207] The USSR regretted that 'imperialist quarters and their flunkeys' had sown doubts about the treaty in 'neighbouring African countries' like Ethiopia:

> ... some Western newspapers have in fact gone so far as to allege that the Soviet Union is building military bases in Somalia and that its military assistance to this country pursues 'expansionist objectives'. President S. Barre has categorically refuted such imperialist propaganda fables. In its relations with the neighbouring African states, he had declared, Mogadishu guides itself by the principles of peace and brotherhood and seeks to settle all disputes on the basis of these principles.[208]

To stress the point, *Izvestiya* declared that Soviet–Somali military co-operation 'is being carried on exclusively for purposes of ensuring Somalia's self-defence' and was consistent with a policy of prompting 'friendship and international co-operation'[209] in the Horn of Africa.

However, the Soviet analysis of the treaty, with regard to Somalia, was a rather selective one. Whatever else he may have said, President Siad's principal justification for the agreement was national interest. The Somali leader emphasised that the treaty had 'far-reaching bene-fits for his people', a people whose lands, President Podgorny was informed, are 'still under colonial domination, both black and white', and that Soviet aid had no strings attached to it.[210] No country, Siad explained, 'could influence the policies of fully independent Soma-lia'.[211] And this included Moscow, as well as Saudi Arabia (who expressed its displeasure at the growing Soviet–Somali connection by withdrawing its ambassador from Mogadishu).[212]

It was significant that Siad chose to praise the Chinese leader, Mao Tse-tung, in the very speech celebrating the signing of the Friendship Treaty.[213] This gesture, coming as it did so soon after sharp attacks on Peking's foreign policy by Podgorny in Mogadishu, had a couple of implications. First, it was a stark reminder that the Somalis were not completely on the Soviet side. Secondly, and not unrelatedly, it underlined the fact that the treaty was concluded on the initiative of the USSR. According to one source, the treaty issue prompted stormy debates in the ruling SRC both before and after the signing cere-mony.[214] Certainly, it was true that Moscow's ratification of the document followed quickly, while Somalia's was delayed for three months. Moreover, a three-man Somali military delegation was dis-patched to China[215] before the instruments of ratification were finally exchanged on 29 October 1974. Clearly, the passage of the treaty in Somalia was not without its complications.

In many ways, then, the Soviet–Somali treaty was a fitting finale to relations between the two countries during this period. It symbolised a relationship based on the rhetoric but not the substance of Marxist–Leninist ideology. Attracted by 'Somalia's advantageous geographical location' (which 'had long attracted the special attention of imperialist countries'),[216] Moscow dubbed Somalia 'one of the most progressive states'[217] in Africa and, for its support, obtained extensive strategic facilities. By 1974, Somalia had become the major centre for Soviet operations in the Indian Ocean and Red Sea.[218] At the same time, President Siad's regime proclaimed its dedication to Marxism–Leninism and elicited substantial military support from the USSR but insisted that scientific socialism was the servant of Somali nationalism and, as such, was compatible with Islam and close relations with China. In short, the Soviet–Somali alliance was one coated with the ideological sugar of political expediency. But this arrangement worked well enough while Moscow's 'progressive' options in the Horn of Africa were limited. After 1974, however, the Ethiopian revolution changed all that and, as we shall see, eventually undermined Soviet–Somali relations.

5 The Ethiopian revolution and the quest for a Pax Sovietica

Now that revolutionary transformations and progressive socio-economic changes are taking place in Ethiopia our peoples will have greater opportunity to impart a new and richer meaning to Soviet–Ethiopian co-operation in the political, economic, cultural and other spheres.

(Soviet Foreign Minister, Andrey Gromyko, in Yu Ivanov, 'Strengthening Friendship' *New Times*, no. 30, July 1976)

In spite of the historical contradictions between Somalia and Ethiopia, there are progressive forces in both able to sort out their political and economic problems. Here we are optimists: we think it is possible to have a Marxist–Leninist confederation in the Horn of Africa.

(Anatoly Gromyko, Director of the Africa Institute, Moscow, and son of the former Soviet Foreign Minister, *The Manchester Guardian*, 10 July 1977)

The years from 1974 to early 1977 witnessed a gradual but definite shift in Soviet policy in the Horn of Africa. Having formalised its close ties with Somalia through a Treaty of Friendship and Co-operation, Moscow proceeded to expand the range of its policy in the region. In 1976, in what was a significant departure, Moscow began to pursue a policy which sought to combine good relations with both Somalia and its traditional adversary, Ethiopia. To this end, the USSR proposed that the 'brother enemies' sink their differences in a Marxist–Leninist confederation. Clearly, the USSR hoped to establish itself as the dominant external power in the Horn and thus realise what had been a latent, yet historic Russian ambition.

The event that served as the main catalyst in the transformation of Soviet policy was the Ethiopian revolution of 1974. Unlike Somalia, Ethiopia experienced a social upheaval, not only in the rhetoric of its leaders, but in practice as well. In a relatively short period of time, the power of Haile Selassie's feudal regime (which traced its ancestry to

King Solomon and the Queen of Sheba)[1] was broken; a sweeping land reform, the most radical in Africa, was enacted and practically all of the country's important industries were nationalised. The Soviet media followed these events with keen interest and, from the outset, insisted that 'the deposition of the Emperor [on 12 September 1974] was not just an ordinary military coup'. Rather, it was 'a landmark in the revolution'.[2]

Despite this initial Soviet approval, relations between the two countries did not gain momentum until 1976. The breakthrough came in July when Moscow hosted a high-level Ethiopian delegation led by Captain Moges Wolde Michael. Five months later, the Dergue, against a background of mounting internal security problems and deteriorating relations with the United States, signed a secret arms agreement with the USSR. The deal was reportedly worth $100 million.[3] Finally, on 3 February 1977, the Soviet commitment to the Dergue was cemented by the accession to supreme power of Lieutenant-Colonel Mengistu Haile Mariam, a long-time favourite of the Soviet press, following a bloody shootout at the PMAC's headquarters in Addis Ababa. Within twenty-four hours of his victory, Mengistu was given an assurance of full Soviet backing from Anatoly Ratanov, the Soviet ambassador in Addis Ababa.[4]

But, as intimated, Moscow did not equate its support of Ethiopia with a sacrifice in relations with Somalia. For much of the period under review Somalia seemed well installed as the USSR's closest ally in black Africa. Amongst other things, Moscow signed a $55 million economic-aid agreement with Somalia in June 1975[5] and maintained a level of military aid that surpassed anything the Dergue received from the US. At the same time, the SDR championed the Soviet–Cuban intervention on behalf of the MPLA in the Angolan civil war (1975–6) and, in July 1976, became, in Moscow's words, 'an inalienable part of the world revolutionary movement'[6] when it dissolved the SRC, the erstwhile ruling military body, and transferred its functions to a new Soviet-style vanguard party, the Somali Revolutionary Socialist Party (SRSP).

Encouraged by the decline of 'the imperialist factor' in the Horn, the new Soviet policy thrust peaked in March 1977. At a secret summit held in Aden, attended by both Mengistu and Siad, President F. Castro of Cuba presented a Soviet proposal to form a Marxist–Leninist confederation of Ethiopia, Somalia, Djibouti (destined to become independent in June 1977) and South Yemen. It was a failure. The Somali President rejected the proposal out of hand. He argued that there was no room for international solutions until Somalia's national aspirations were satisfied. Thus, the Kremlin's dream of a Pax Sovietica in the Horn was, in effect, buried in the contested sands of the Ogaden. Unable to produce an agreed settlement, the Soviets were increasingly forced to take sides in the escalating Ethiopian–Somali border dispute. And that, as far as the Soviet–Somali alliance was concerned, marked the beginning of the end.

The course of the Ethiopian revolution 1974–1976

After many years in the making, the rising tide of popular discontent in Ethiopia finally broke the mould of Emperor Haile Selassie's *ancien régime* in early 1974. The upheaval started on 12 January with a revolt over pay and conditions by NCOs and soldiers at Negelle, in the province of Sidamo. This unrest soon spread to other military units. In February 1974, mutinous troops took over the Massawa naval base, the Debre Zeit air base, the Asmara garrison in Eritrea and most of Addis Ababa's strategic points.[7] While the soldiers' demands were initially economic in character, they were quickly politicised by the almost simultaneous outbreak of civil unrest. On 14 February 1974, students and teachers staged major demonstrations against the government's proposed education reforms. Four days later, the teachers and taxi drivers, angered by a 50 per cent rise in petrol prices, went on strike. Confronted with virtual chaos throughout the country, the Imperial regime responded by making concessions. On 23 February, the Emperor's government agreed to reduce petrol price increases for taxi drivers, and on 24 February, announced a substantial wage rise for privates in the Ethiopian Army. But the military wanted more – namely, the removal of the Prime Minister, Aklilu Habte Wolde. Once again, the Emperor retreated. On 28 February, the Emperor accepted the resignation of his cabinet *en masse* and appointed Endelkachew Makonnen, formerly Minister of Communications, Telecommunications and Posts, as his Prime Minister.[8] Thus began the 'revolution by instalments'.[9]

Alexis de Tocqueville once observed that 'the most perilous moment for a bad government is one when it seeks to mend its ways' since 'a grievance comes to appear intolerable once the possibility of removing it crosses men's minds'.[10] So it proved in the case of the Haile Selassie regime. From the very outset, the political authority of Endelkachew's administration was crippled by a flood of long-suppressed grievances and demands. Despite the promise of liberal reform, Endelkachew's government was on the receiving end of a successful general strike (7–10 March); a teachers' strike which closed Ethiopia's schools for a month; and a nationwide protest movement that included even the lower clergy of the Ethiopian Orthodox Church.[11]

With the country in disarray, radical elements in the Ethiopian Armed Forces gradually moved into the vacuum created by Endelkachew's political weakness. A decisive step in this process occurred on 23 April 1974. Disgusted by the refusal of the Emperor and Endelkachew to authorise the arrest of former Ministers and officials suspected of corruption, the Army's Fourth Division took matters into their own hands. They detained about 200 senior dignitaries including the ex-Prime Minister, Aklilu Habte Wolde.[12] Other arrests followed. On 30 April 1974, the Communications' Minister, General Assafa Ayene, became the first member of Endelkachew's government to fall victim to the Army's anti-corruption purge.

Toward the end of June, the Ethiopian Army began to exercise power in a more direct fashion. On 27 June, the formation was announced of a Co-ordinating Committee of the Armed Forces, the Police and the National Guard. This committee, usually known by its Amharic term, the Dergue, was initially a secret body consisting of 126 members (all were below the rank of Lieutenant-Colonel) representing each of the forty units within the armed forces. Almost immediately after its establishment a new wave of arrests followed. Prominent victims included the Defence Minister, General Abiye Abebe and the Emperor's grandson and Commander of the Ethiopian Navy, Prince Iskander Desta. The Army action was virtually a *coup d'état*. On 3 July, the Emperor, reduced by events to a mere cipher, acceded to the Dergue's demand concerning the right to maintain 'close contact with Government officials for the sake of the country's unity'.[13] On 22 July, the Dergue brought Endelkachew's premiership to a close by forcing his resignation. He was replaced by Michael Imru, an aristocrat distinguished by both opposition to the monarch and his liberal views.

The change in government, however, was purely cosmetic. The Dergue was effectively in power in everything but name. And, by mid-August, it became evident the Dergue had decided to end that anomaly. Emboldened by the report of a Constitutional Commission which recommended the establishment of a Constitutional Monarchy,[14] the Army launched a campaign to isolate and discredit Emperor Haile Selassie. Amongst other things, it abolished three key institutions of the Imperial regime – the Ministry of the Pen, the department responsible for channelling the Emperor's orders to all state organs, the Crown Council, the Emperor's personal military staff and the Special Court of Justice (the 'Chilot'). The Dergue also orchestrated a massive media offensive against the integrity of the Emperor himself. As part of this, Haile Selassie was publicly described as 'an expensive and unnecessary luxury'.[15] All this prepared the Ethiopian people for the final *coup de grâce*.

On 12 September 1974, the Dergue deposed Emperor Haile Selassie and formally assumed the mantle of government under the title of the Provisional Military Administrative Council (PMAC). The constitution was suspended and the parliament dissolved. Initially, the PMAC seemed dominated by Lt.-General Aman Andom. Distinguished by a brilliant military career and widely admired for his long-time defiance of the Emperor, Aman was appointed Prime Minister and chief 'spokesman' of the new military regime.[16] But, apart from being committed to the vague notion of 'Ethiopia Tikdem' (Ethiopia First), the PMAC had little ideological cohesion when it came to power. Indeed, differences soon developed between Aman and the younger officers in the PMAC, led by Major Mengistu Haile Mariam, the First Vice-Chairman, and Major Atnafu Abate, the Second Vice-Chairman. These differences related to both policy and personal ambition. Areas of dispute included civil–military relations, the tempo of revolutionary change and the future of the Eritrean province.[17] Matters came to a head on 17 November 1974, when Aman, an Eritrean by birth, rejected Mengistu's demand to send an additional 5,000 troops to Eritrea and resigned as acting Head of State, apparently in a bid to rally Dergue opinion behind him. But it was Mengistu who prevailed. On 22 November, Aman was killed at his residence while allegedly resisting arrest. Within twenty-four hours, fifty-seven officials of the *ancien régime* and two PMAC members who supported Aman were summarily executed. The executions provoked an international outcry. In particular, the US reacted by briefly reviewing its programme of military aid and economic assistance to Addis Ababa, worth $59 million in 1974, before resuming it in late December.[18] All the same, Brigadier-General Teferi Bante, Commander of the 2nd Division and Mengistu's choice as Aman's successor, was confirmed as the new Chairman of the PMAC on 28 November 1974.

Teferi's appointment coincided with the radicalisation of Ethiopian policy. On 20 December 1974, PMAC issued a proclamation in which it introduced the concept of 'Ethiopian socialism' (hebrettesebawinet). This involved, *inter alia*, a commitment to establish a one-party socialist state based 'on national lines rather than along those imported from abroad',[19] the extension of state control over the key sectors of the economy and the essential maintenance of Ethiopia's existing foreign policy. Shortly afterwards, the PMAC launched the National Campaign for Development Through Co-operation, or Zemacha, to popularise the revolution in the countryside. In what was, in part, an echo of the Somali experience, the Ethiopian government closed down the universities and senior high schools, and sent about 60,000 students into rural areas. Their task was to help eradicate illiteracy and administer the new land reform.[20] Other major reforms followed. On 1 January 1975, all banks and the largest insurance companies were nationalised. On 3 February, seventy-two industrial and commercial enterprises were fully nationalised, and the Ethiopian state took overall control in twenty-nine others. Then, on 4 March, the most significant reform, a land reform, was promulgated: all rural land was nationalised, tenancy was abolished and the peasantry were given the right to till land up to a maximum of 10 hectares.[21] In one stroke, the PMAC dismantled the feudal edifice of the old regime and boosted the income of millions of peasants by eliminating the exorbitant rents they had been paying.

However, the PMAC's attention was not confined to the countryside. On 26 July 1975, all urban land and all houses and flats not occupied by their owners were nationalised.[22] The measure was directed against wealthy property speculators. In addition, the Dergue extended its grip over the Trade Union movement. On 6 December 1975, following a crackdown on CELU and the imposition of martial law, a tough new Labour code was enunciated. The new union structure was arranged hierarchically, on the basis of 'democratic centralism', so that each level was accountable to the one immediately higher, with the All-Ethiopian Trade Union (AETU) at the top.[23] As a consequence, the unions' role was reduced to that of transmission belts between the PMAC and the workers. Then, in what was yet another important change, the military government, on 21 March 1975, formally abolished the Monarchy and proclaimed Ethiopia a Republic.

Finally, Ethiopia's radical evolution was capped on 20 April 1976 by the announcement of a detailed political programme, the National Democratic Revolution (NDR). The latter became the charter of the Ethiopian revolution. Couched in Soviet-style political parlance, the NDR officially marked the beginning of a working alliance between the Dergue and a pro-Soviet, left-wing civilian group, MEISON (an Amharic acronym for the All Ethiopian Socialist Movement). In essence, the programme called for the creation of a 'people's democratic republic' and the building of 'a firm foundation for the transition to socialism' under the guidance of a 'party of the proletariat'.[24] To facilitate this, the NDR programme mandated the establishment of a body called the Provisional Office for Mass Organisational Affairs (POMOA) to prepare the ground for a political party of the workers. It also recognised the right of every nationality in Ethiopia to 'regional autonomy', but promised to uphold the nation's unity by arming the 'broad masses' against 'internal and external enemies'. Equally, the programme committed Ethiopia to a foreign policy of non-alignment, but envisaged all-round co-operation between Addis Ababa and the 'progressive forces' struggling against 'imperialism'.[25]

Suffice it to say, these new policies generated considerable internal opposition. On the left, the most militant opposition came from the Ethiopian People's Revolutionary Party (EPRP). Founded in August 1975 and drawn from urban-based students and Trade Union radicals, the EPRP was a Marxist–Leninist group which insisted that the military was a 'petty bourgeoise' body and had usurped a popular revolution.[26] The Dergue countered by brutally crushing the EPRP's public demonstrations, accusing it of anarchism and counter-revolution.[27] The breach between the two became all but final in the spring of 1976 when MEISON, the EPRP's arch rival on the civilian left, decided to work with the Dergue. Sensing it would be the first victim of this unholy alliance, the EPRP took up the option of armed struggle. On the right, the PMAC faced armed resistance from the Ethiopian Democratic Union (EDU). Established in March 1975, this organisation was a broad coalition of the non-Marxist opposition. Its membership included former high-ranking officials of the Haile Selassie regime, dispossessed feudal lords and liberal modernisers. While the EDU aspired to create a democratic state with civil rights in Ethiopia, its guerrilla operations were mainly confined to the northern provinces of Begemder, Tigre and Wollo.[28]

Moreover, the revolution, inasmuch as it weakened the hold of central government in the country, led to the growth of nationalist movements in multi-ethnic Ethiopia. In Eritrea, after a certain lull in hostilities, the situation rapidly declined after the killing of General Aman, the PMAC leader who was personally identified with the search for a negotiated settlement, and the consequent dispatch of an extra 5,000 troops to the province in late November 1974 to enforce a military solution. The two main Eritrean movements, the ELF and the Eritrean People's Liberation Front (EPLF), no doubt boosted by a new influx of arms from Red Sea and Persian Gulf states like Saudi Arabia, Egypt, Sudan and Kuwait, responded in kind. In February 1975, the two rebel groups, in what was a co-ordinated switch to conventional warfare, launched a joint offensive on Asmara, provincial capital of Eritrea.[29] From then on, the war escalated.

By the spring of 1976, the PMAC had devised a 'carrot and stick' strategy to deal with the Eritrean insurrection. The 'carrot' was a nine-point peace plan, announced on 16 May 1976. The plan offered 'immediate autonomy' to Eritrea, amnesty, compensation, rehabilitation and the lifting of the state of emergency which was in force.[30] However, these proposals cut very little ice with any of the Eritrean organisations. For, at precisely this time, the PMAC mobilised a 40,000-strong peasant militia, ill equipped and poorly trained, to march into Eritrea and unleash a kind of 'holy war' against the rebels, who were depicted in Addis Ababa as foreign-backed Arab puppets. But the so-called 'Red March' turned out to be a disaster for the Dergue. In fact, this rag-tag militia was crushingly defeated before it even entered Eritrea.[31]

The second major regional challenge to the Dergue came from the Ogaden. In 1975, the WSLF re-emerged as a potent guerrilla force. This development was linked to a major restructuring of the organisation. With the growth of disorder in Ethiopia after 1974, the Siad regime came under intense pressure from both the tribal coalition which supported his regime and his general staff to plan for the liberation of the Ogaden.[32] As a consequence, the WSLF was reorganised so that its efforts would be co-ordinated with those of the Somali regular army. The process was assisted to some extent by the effects of a terrible drought in the Ogaden in 1974–5. The concentration of many Ogadeni nomads in Somali government famine-relief camps facilitated a WSLF recruitment drive. The revamped WSLF began to receive arms and training from Somalia. The latter also arranged for some WSLF members to receive instruction abroad – in the Soviet Union, Cuba and North Korea.[33]

The revival of the WSLF virtually ended what little chance there was of a negotiated solution to the Ogaden problem. To be sure, in the wake of the 1974 revolution, both Ethiopia and Somalia made conciliatory noises. In December 1974, the Dergue's Minister of Information declared that Ethiopian–Somali relations were at their 'very best'.[34] For its part, Mogadishu publicly welcomed the emergence of a fellow socialist regime and denied it had any designs on Ethiopia.[35] Nevertheless, once it became clear the Dergue was as uncompromising as its

Imperial predecessor over Ethiopia's territorial integrity, Somalia went ahead with its programme of covert aid to the WSLF, as well as to other rebel movements in Ethiopia. By early 1976, the WSLF reportedly had several thousand well-trained and well-armed guerrillas placed throughout the Ogaden. With increasing frequency, Ethiopian army convoys, police stations and army bases came under attack. In January 1976, the Dergue sent a memorandum entitled 'War Clouds in the Horn of Africa' to a number of African leaders.[36] This spelled out in great detail a Somali planned 'war of subversion' to annexe both the Ogaden and what was then known as the French Territory of Afars and Issas (FTAI) or Djibouti.

The latter issue had become an additional bone of contention after a sudden reversal of policy by France. On 31 December 1975, Giscard's government officially recognised Djibouti's right to independence within the next two years. From the outset, its viability as an independent entity seemed in doubt. Sandwiched between Ethiopia and Somalia, tiny Djibouti consisted of a modern port, which was linked by rail to Addis Ababa, and a small piece of desert, sparsely populated by two ethnically distinct and historically antagonistic peoples. These were the Somali-speaking Issas, who constituted the majority group in Djibouti, and the Afars, a tribe whose members for the most part lived in Ethiopia. But while Ethiopia had officially abandoned all territorial claims to Djibouti on 31 July 1975,[37] it was unwilling to accept Somalia's claim to a territory which in 1975–6 handled 60 per cent of Ethiopia's export–import traffic.[38] Thus, both Ethiopia and Somalia publicly welcomed the prospect of Djibouti's independence, but each accused the other of wanting to usurp it.

It was evident, though, that regional opposition to the PMAC was not confined to Eritrean secession or Somali irredentism. In April 1976, the then First Vice-Chairman of the PMAC, Major Mengistu Haile Mariam, acknowledged that 'our surroundings do not favour our revolution' and admitted to armed rebellions in eight of the fourteen Ethiopian provinces excluding Eritrea and the Ogaden[39] (see Map 4). Not all of these ethnic-based movements were equally threatening or well organised, but three of them were potentially serious for the Dergue. In the north, in the province of Tigre, bordering Eritrea, a Marxist guerrilla group called the Tigrean People's Liberation Front (TPLF) fought to advance national self-determination. Founded in February 1975, the TPLF gained control of some parts of the province and played an important part, along with its ally, the EPLF, in defeating the Dergue's 'Red March' on Eritrea in May 1976. Further

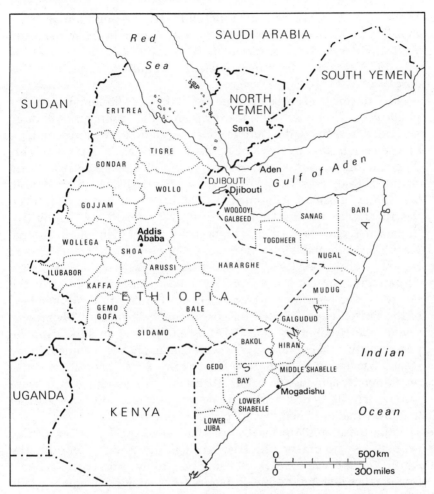

Map 4. Administrative regions in Ethiopia and Somalia. *Source*: Central Intelligence Agency, Washington D.C., USGPO, 1977.

east, in the Dankalia area of southern Eritrea, the traditionalist Afar community led by Sultan Ali Mireh took up arms to oppose the PMAC's programme of land reform. Established in March 1975, the Afar Liberation Front (ALF) was backed by Somalia and Saudi Arabia, and co-operated with the ELF and the EDU in guerrilla activities along the strategic road linking the Eritrean port of Assab to Addis Ababa.[40] Meanwhile, in the provinces to the south and west of Addis Ababa an atavistic nationalism awoke among the Oromo (Galla), Ethiopia's most populous group. In October 1974, a group of left-wing intellectuals formed the Oromo Liberation Front (OLF). This organisation called for the establishment of a 'People's Democratic Republic of Oromia'. And while this demand only attracted modest support initially, the OLF, by July 1976, was able to launch guerrilla operations in pursuit of its aim.[41]

Nor, during this period, was the PMAC itself immune to the political and ethnic divisions gripping the country. Although shrouded in secrecy, the Dergue consisted of military representatives whose background in terms of class and ethnic affiliation was highly disparate. In this sense, the membership of the Dergue was a microcosm of Ethiopian society.[42] The first major clash, which resulted in the killing of Aman Andom in November 1974, has already been described. Six months later, in April 1975, the PMAC survived a 'right-wing plot' to oust it. The security chief, Lieutenant Colonel Neguissie Haile and another top intelligence official, Captain Debessu Beyene, were among those arrested for involvement in the conspiracy. Apparently, the coup attempt was linked with opposition to the Dergue's land-reform programme.[43] In late January 1976, six members of the PMAC were arrested for corruption.[44] Then, on 23 February, seven cabinet members – no PMAC member held an administrative post directly until February 1977 – were dismissed and detained. In the week that followed, the PMAC arrested 2,000 people for 'anti-revolutionary activities' in Addis Ababa.[45] As the political temperature rose, sharp differences within the Dergue even found expression in the government-owned newspaper, *Addis Zemen*.[46]

While these splits in the Dergue had ideological overtones, they were also symptomatic of a basic struggle for power. Certainly, by April 1976, it became clear, following his promulgation of a 'National Democratic Revolution' in Ethiopia, that Major Mengistu Haile Mariam was emerging as a dominant figure in the military regime. Indeed, according to one source, the Chairman of the Council, Teferi Bante, only learnt of the programme's contents over the radio.[47] But Mengistu's ascendancy did not go unchallenged. On 10 July 1976 an alleged plot to remove Mengistu was discovered. On 13 July, Major Sisay Habte, the Chairman of the Dergue's Political Committee, Getachew Nadew, the Commander-in-Chief in Eritrea and seventeen accomplices were executed for participation in the coup attempt. Officially, the latter was said to be backed by the EPRP and the CIA. Whatever the facts, Sisay and Getachew, like others before them, were disenchanted with the military resolution of the Eritrean question and also favoured more emphasis on a return to civilian government.[48]

The executions caused considerable unrest in the Ethiopian Army and, despite stern warnings, did not inhibit further opposition to Mengistu within the PMAC. Finally, as if the Dergue's authority had not been shaken enough already, there was a record number of government officials who, between 1974 and 1976, abandoned their posts and sought political asylum abroad. The list included Kifle Wodajo, the Ethiopian Foreign Minister; Commodore Tassew Desta, Ambassador to North Yemen; Getachew Mekasha, Ambassador to Egypt; and Major Negash Tesfatsion, a prominent member of the Dergue.[49]

By mid-1976, Ethiopia appeared to be on the verge of disintegration. Two and a half years of revolutionary upheaval, multifarious internal challenges and the looming military threat of the Somali Republic had drastically weakened the PMAC's hold over the country. With the survival of Ethiopia's existing borders in doubt, the Dergue quickly found itself in need of a major infusion of arms and advisers to train the additional troops required to deal with the situation. At first, the Dergue, like Haile Selassie's regime, looked to the United States as its military main-stay. But, for a variety of reasons elaborated below, American arms supplies did not come close to meeting Addis Ababa's rapidly escalating needs. Desperate for arms and also increasingly Marxist-oriented, the PMAC widened its diplomatic net and found a more logical alternative – the Soviet Union.

The Ethiopian revolution through Soviet eyes

From the early days of the revolution, the Soviet media covered events in Ethiopia with great interest. Within a month of the first army mutiny, *Pravda* stressed the significance of the changes underway:

> Ethiopia, one of the most ancient states on the African continent, is passing though an important stage in its history. The political system, which seemed stable until recently is today experiencing a major crisis . . . The strike of teachers and taxi drivers that erupted in the capital, followed by disturbances in the army . . . led to the fall of the government that had ruled continuously for almost 13 years. The result was the formation of a new government, in which none of the former Ministers were included. This fact is itself unprecedented for Ethiopia.[50]

Moscow also applauded the success of 'the first general strike of working people in Ethiopia's history'. This act, which forced the government to introduce reforms such as 'a minimum wage for workers and ... their right to a pension', enabled 'the Ethiopian working people to secure their first victory'. Moreover, 'with the acceptance of their demands and with the subsequent legislative embodiment to those demands, the country will take a big step toward the democratisation of the social order'.[51]

While Soviet commentators did not conceal their political sympathies during this unfolding drama, there was a certain hesitancy about the future direction of events in Ethiopia. At the end of February 1974, for example, *Pravda* declared that the situation in Addis Ababa was 'quickly returning to normal'[52] following the Emperor's decision to rescind petrol price increases. Several months on, and despite continued unrest, *New Times* compounded the error: 'The unrest in Ethiopia is gradually subsiding. The authorities have met some of the demands made by army units, workers and students.'[53] Such assessments were not simply the product of excessive caution. Rather, they reflected an initial division of opinion in Moscow over the Ethiopian situation. On the one hand, there was what might be termed the 'conservative' response. This argued that 'almost no one could have foreseen that disturbances in the [Ethiopian] army would result in such serious political consequences. But the fact is that these events only revealed the social crisis that had come to a head in society.'[54] Moreover, subsequent 'events in Ethiopia in February, March and April showed the working masses, above all the urban proletariat of the country, are the main motive forces . . . despite its youth and small numbers'.[55] On the other hand, there was a body of opinion which paralleled the new emphasis on the role of the military in Soviet Third World thinking. In this connection, V. Petrov observed in May 1974: 'To be frank, for me these events hardly came as a surprise. I know well the hardships endured by Ethiopia's soldiers, who are paid a pittance for their difficult military service. It was they who initiated the first demands for improved material conditions. I could compare their actions with a spark that lit up in the hearts of other Ethiopians.'[56]

This initial disagreement in the diagnosis of the Ethiopian revolution may have been related to what V. G. Solodovnikov, then the Director of the Institute of Africa, frankly acknowledged as 'different (Soviet) views on the problem of non-capitalist development'[57] in the Third World. In any event, by July 1974, some three months before the Dergue formally took power, Moscow had evolved a sufficiently coherent position to line itself up behind the Ethiopian military. The Soviet press now observed that the army was 'the most powerful force in the country', was actively involved 'in the country's internal political life', was resolved 'to achieve the fastest possible implementation of the reforms promised to the people by the government' and was 'relying on the support of the masses'[58] in doing so.

It came as no great surprise, therefore, that the USSR expressed satisfaction when its 'old friend', Emperor Haile Selassie was deposed in September 1974. According to Moscow, the Emperor's government had been one of 'the regimes that serve as conductors of imperialist influence'[59] and subjected its people to a system of 'constitutional absolutism' where 'corruption, bribery, embezzlement of public funds and the abuse of power become standard practice of everyday life'.[60] More specifically, the old regime was deemed responsible for 'the death of 200,000 peasants from famine at a time when the gentry kept hundreds of millions of dollars in Swiss banks'. Consequently, the Dergue's seizure of power was nothing less than a revolutionary step which was 'welcomed by the population at large'[61] in Ethiopia. As far as Moscow was concerned 'only Western propaganda keeps on claiming there was a coup'.[62]

The Soviet attitude toward the new military regime was extremely sympathetic. The Soviet media ignored the almost immediate demonstration in Addis Ababa against the PMAC by thousands of students and CELU activists. Instead, Soviet commentators insisted that many 'progressives' in Ethiopia recognised that necessary measures such as land reform could be implemented 'only by a strong military government capable of quelling resistance on the part of the feudals [sic]'.[63] In an article prepared for the 25th Congress of the CPSU, a Soviet authority on Ethiopia rationalised the Soviet stance at some length:

> In his time, F. Engels wrote: 'In political life there are only two decisive forces: the organised force of the state, the army, and the non-organised, spontaneous force of the mass of the people.' In Ethiopia, the interests of these forces coincided at a given stage of development and support for the existing regime collapsed. Considering the peculiarities specific to Ethiopia, one can say that if there had not been massive dissatisfaction in the country with the regime, backed up by energetic and, for the most part, spontaneous anti-government actions, then a 'total' take-over on the part of the army would scarcely have been possible.
>
> In the conditions of an absence of parties, a weak Trade Union movement and a fragmented student movement, the army came forward as the political representative of a coalition of social strata – petty and middle bourgeoise, peasantry, intelligentsia, workers, low and middle level bureaucrats and others. The Armed Forces move-

ment in effect became the vehicle of the aspirations and hopes of the majority of a people which had been oppressed by an absolute monarchy, by landlords, by nobility, by the church elite and by foreign monopoly capital, that is to say it acted as an all-nation force.[64]

As Moscow saw it, the 'authority of the PMAC' among the Ethiopian workers was 'substantially reinforced' by the proclamation of Ethiopia's socialist orientation (December 1974) and the implementation of 'a number of radical reforms'.[65] Some of these were given considerable prominence. First, Soviet writers hailed the Dergue's decision to nationalise nearly all of Ethiopia's commercial and industrial sector, as well as certain private property. Such measures not only significantly strengthened the 'anti-capitalist oriented public sector'[66] but also demonstrated the state's willingness 'to make effective use of economic levers ... to protect the country ... from such intrinsic capitalist diseases as crisis and unemployment and to put an end to exploitation of man by man.'[67]

Secondly, Moscow discerned 'fundamental changes in the character and status of Trade Union organisation' in Ethiopia. In 1975, the Dergue, for all intents and purposes, closed down CELU by arresting its 'pro-Western leadership' and severing its links with the International Confederation of Free Trade Unions, a body 'under strong imperialist influence'.[68] It was replaced by the centralised AETU, which was created in the wake of the Labour code of December 1975. Furthermore, for the first time in Ethiopian history, 'the working people ceremoniously observed May 1 – the international day of labour'[69] in 1975.

Thirdly, Moscow spotlighted the Dergue's efforts to deal with unemployment ('a social evil inherited from the old regime'). It was noted Ethiopia had 'set up a board to provide jobs for the unemployed. With a view to drawing them into useful labour, a large centre to aid the homeless and the workless [sic] has been opened, offering general educational and vocational training. As a result of this endeavour thousands of people have received jobs in recent times.'[70]

Fourthly, Soviet observers emphasised the Dergue's concern for the development of education. After the revolution, there had been 'the gradual introduction of free education in all types of educational establishments' and 'an important increase in the number of teachers and schools especially in the countryside'. Moreover, with the nationalisation of all private learning institutions at the start of the 1975–6 school year, 'many buildings which had belonged to members of the

Imperial family, the nobles, the burearcratic hierarchy and the church, were handed over to the Ministry of Education'.[71]

Fifthly, the attempts of the military regime to improve medical services in Ethiopia were highly assessed. A Soviet writer in 1977 declared that 'a vast programme to combat infectious diseases is under way'. For example, 'in a country which only two years ago recorded dozens of thousands of smallpox cases, now jointly with the World Health Organisation, a programme for an overall onslaught on the world's only persisting seat of smallpox has been developed'.[72]

None of these steps, however, was significant to the USSR as the Dergue's agrarian reform of March 1975. The latter was variously described as 'the most radical in the revolutionary history of Africa',[73] the 'major achievement of the Ethiopian revolution'[74] and an event of 'great importance for the fate of the country'.[75] Behind the epithets lay the Soviet conviction that the land reform had ended 'the centuries old feudal system' by 'having liquidated private land ownership, the basis of exploitation of millions of tillers'. The reform 'showed that the new powers of Ethiopia had seriously undertaken the breaking up of the old conditions' in a country where 'land is power'.[76] And this, in Moscow's view, would help to secure the long-term future of the Ethiopian revolution.

Soviet observers were impressed both by the political and administrative dimensions of the land reform. Politically, it was 'a major merit of Ethiopia's revolutionary leaders' to enact a measure which would give land to about 12 million peasants. In this way, the PMAC attracted to its side 'the most downtrodden sector of the country's population – the peasantry – which previously had no rights'.[77] At the same time, this measure delineated the Dergue's class enemies: 'the progressive character of the agrarian reform is revealed in the fact that the land is being confiscated from the estate owners without compensation payments and given free to the peasants'.[78] Administratively, the Dergue, by establishing a system of peasant associations, had 'foreseen' the need for an organisation with 'wide-ranging full powers' to oversee 'the confiscation and the redistribution of landed estates'. The Dergue was also praised for sending 60,000 students into the countryside to explain the new land reform to the peasants: 'the [Ethiopian] military have made use to a certain extent of the experiences of the cultural revolution in Cuba and the campaign for the elimination of illiteracy in Somalia'.[79] Thus, while Moscow had no illusions about 'reactionary resistance' to the agrarian reform – the 'feudals [sic] are not inclined to give away the land without a fight'[80] –

it seemed convinced the Dergue had taken a strategic step toward ensuring lasting change in Ethiopia.

Within a year of the agrarian reform, the USSR declared itself satisfied that Addis Ababa's 'progressive transformations' had reached 'a more profound stage'. The precipitating factor was the PMAC's programme of the National Democratic Revolution (NDR), promulgated in April 1976. As related, this programme heralded the formation of a 'people's democratic republic' in Ethiopia. But 'unlike previous general statements' by the military regime, Moscow maintained that the NDR programme 'defined more precisely the goals of revolutionary social reorganisation and the role of different groups and classes in the reorganisation'.[81] In particular, three aspects of this 'reorganisation' appealed to the USSR.

The first concerned the refinement of Ethiopia's commitment to socialism. According to a Soviet writer, the NDR programme decided 'to build [Ethiopian] society on the basis of the principles of scientific socialism as the only way of resolving complicated, existing problems'.[82] This new emphasis was confirmed by a leading member of the PMAC at around this time: 'Our irreversible aim is socialism and when we speak of socialism we mean scientific socialism based on the principles of Marxism–Leninism and the doctrine of proletarian dictatorship which, I need hardly say, will take into account the concrete conditions of Ethiopia.'[83] To a Soviet reader, well-versed in the subtleties of political parlance, the phrase 'scientific socialism' clearly had a pro-Soviet connotation. That being so, the NDR programme was seen as a welcome departure from the 'peculiar emphasis on "Ethiopian socialism"' which initially characterised the country 'after the overthrow of the monarchist regime'.[84]

In addition, and not unrelated to the last point, the NDR programme appeared to recognise the Leninist principle that 'the vanguard of the revolution ... is to be a party of the working class'. It should be recalled that the programme set up a body called POMOA. This was to conduct the preparations for the creation of a vanguard party by organising the political education of the population, disseminating socialist concepts in Ethiopia and generally mobilising support. For the Soviets, such a development was, at last, proof that the Ethiopian leadership believed 'the people's revolutionary gains can be consolidated only if the revolution is headed by a working-class party'.[85] Whether this Soviet perception coincided with the reality of the situation is another matter. Certainly, the USSR had shown a consistent interest in the question of party development in revolutionary Ethiopia. As early as December 1974, *New Times* spoke of the PMAC's intention to establish a ruling 'progressive political party conforming to Ethiopia's socialist orientation'.[86] Then, in August 1975, a full month before the Dergue officially announced the imminent formation of a 'political organisation', and again in November 1975, *Pravda* reported progress being made towards the construction of a national political party in Ethiopia.[87] However, when expectations were not matched by results, several Soviet writers expressed their impatience over what they saw as an important issue. V. S. Yag'ya, for example, writing about Ethiopia in late 1975, pointedly observed: 'A democratic society [the USSR] has more than once already spoken out for the creation of a progressive party in the country.'[88] Similarly, a Soviet visitor in February 1976 noted: 'The present stage is a difficult one in Ethiopia's life, there being no progressive political party and not enough functionaries dedicated to the cause of revolution.'[89] Clearly, the NDR programme did not end Soviet concern about the pace of party development in Ethiopia. But it went some way to assuage the feelings of those commentators who insisted 'that a vanguard party is indispensible' both for the unity of 'all progressive members of the working class, the peasantry and the intelligentsia' and to 'maintain friendly ties with other vanguard communist parties'.[90]

Also, the NDR programme, in the words of one Soviet commentator, 'commenced most important steps' in the 'basic resolution of the ethno-religious problems' facing Ethiopia. The NDR document 'says that "special attention" will be paid to peoples living on the national outskirts of former monarchic Ethiopia ... to raise the political, economic and cultural life of these nationalities' and 'to equalise these nationalities with the other nationalities of Ethiopia'.[91] With this in mind, the programme recognised that: 'all Ethiopia's peoples have the right to self-determination, with the most progressive and effective vehicle thereto at this present stage being "regional autonomy", deriving from the interests of faster development, the consolidation of multinational unity and the preservation of territorial integrity'.[92]

Seen from Moscow, the Dergue's concept of regional autonomy was a timely answer to what was described as the growth of 'centrifugal tendencies'[93] in post-Imperial Ethiopia. While the 1974 revolution undoubtedly hastened 'the process of ethnic integration' in the country, it was admitted there were a number of obstacles in the way of 'nation-formation' in Ethiopia. In 1976, G. Galperin listed some of them:

> ... the national market still does not guarantee the necessary mutual
> dependence of the separate regions of the country ... It is impossible
> also to speak of a stable community, with a state (Amharic) language,
> especially outside the town centres. We must not forget as well the
> fact that the territory of present day Ethiopia was formed com-
> paratively recently, at the end of the previous and at the start of the
> present century.[94]

Furthermore, 'a policy of forced Amharisation' had been conducted by
the old 'monarchic regime'. For instance, Amharas made up 'more
than 60 per cent of the government officials, 75 per cent of the officer
corps and 70 per cent of the district governors in the southern
non-Amharic regions, who at the same time were the biggest land-
owners there'. Moreover, the non-Christian population was 'severely
exploited ... Muslims were not allowed to own land, were deprived of
many civil rights and comprised the bulk of the unemployed and
low-paid categories'.[95] All this, according to Galperin, left the PMAC a
legacy of nationalist and religious discontent, the worst of which was
in Eritrea and the Ogaden.

Nevertheless, the USSR indicated that the Ethiopian revolution had
fundamentally altered the complexion of these problems:

> Scientific socialism has never viewed secession as a political fetish, as
> an aim in itself, stripped of class-mindedness and social expediency.
> Marxist–Leninists emphasise not the close interconnection between
> the solution of problems of national statehood and the attainment of
> socialism, but also the point that socialism comes first. Which means
> that the nationalities should be resolved in the context of the vital
> interests of the working masses. As Lenin pointed out, the right to
> self-determination 'is not the equivalent of a demand for separation,
> fragmentation and the formation of small states. It implies only a
> consistent expression of struggle against all national oppression.[96]

Thus, the fact that the Dergue's notion of regional autonomy
eschewed the possibility of separation and independence for nationalities that wanted it did not worry Moscow. Rather, the important
thing was the 'Ethiopia's revolutionary democrats' regarded the
nationalities issue 'as an organic part of the overall question of class
struggle'. At stake, then, was 'not the liberation of colonies but the
development of nationalities within a revolutionary Ethiopia'.[97]

Endorsement of the Dergue's principle of regional autonomy coincided with sympathetic treatment in the Soviet media of Addis
Ababa's handling of the 'so-called Eritrean problem'. This issue was
fraught with implications for the Soviet position in the Horn. It should

be recalled that Moscow refrained from publicly supporting the
Eritrean insurgents during the last years of Haile Selassie's regime.
Indeed, the Eritrean question received very little attention, in any
shape or form, in the Soviet press. But, after the 1974 revolution,
Moscow lost its reserve. It quickly identified with the PMAC's efforts
'to solve the problem through peaceful means, following the principles of preserving national unity and the territorial integrity of the
state'.[98]

In early 1975, *Pravda* reported a sharp escalation of 'terrorist attacks'
and 'acts of sabotage' in Eritrea by forces 'who demand full independence for this province'.[99] Such activity 'impedes the implementation
of progressive reforms in the country' and took no account of the new
political system there. Unlike the 'feudal–imperial regime' which
'depended on the fomentation of ethnic and religious conflicts' and
'carried out a policy of internal colonisation in Eritrea', the PMAC
'attributes great significance to resolving the Eritrean problem'.[100]
Even 'in the first hours of the Ethiopian revolution' the PMAC
appealed 'to the separatists to come and sit at the negotiating table'.
And while the USSR expressed reservations about some aspects of the
Dergue's policy – it recommended 'foreign policy steps' to improve
'relations with the Arab countries, a part of which is supporting the
Eritrean rebels' – it argued that 'peaceful negotiations represent the
sole way to a settlement in Eritrea',[101] a position nominally shared by
the Dergue. In this vein, Moscow 'greeted with satisfaction' the
initiative of the Sudan's President Numeiry on 8 February 1975 which
called for an immediate ceasefire, and also urged the Ethiopian
government to grant 'a general amnesty for everyone who has been
doing his national duty in the ranks of the liberation movement in
Eritrea'.[102] The new assumption was, of course, that this 'national
duty' was no longer necessary.

According to Moscow, 'claims made by separatist cliques' concerning 'a separate developed Eritrean nation' were 'manifestly
groundless'. Eritrea was historically part of Ethiopia ('one of the most
important provinces of ancient Ethiopia')[103] and had a population
which was 'a conglomeration of at least 10 nationalities and related
tribes'. Besides, in the wake of the 1974 revolution, the Eritrean
movement suffered from a certain political 'poverty': 'Only one
purpose has been designated – separation from Ethiopia, separation
by any means and under any conditions.'[104] As a consequence, the
Eritrean revolt allegedly experienced a 'reactionary degeneration' after
1974. That is, it 'objectively' served the interests of 'imperialist

circles'.[105] The latter, it was argued, sought to weaken the revolutionary government's efforts 'to liquidate the foreign military presence' in
Ethiopia, a country of 'great strategic importance in Africa'. To this
end: 'the US press was putting out rumours about the situation in
Eritrea that were calculated to widen the dispute between the Arab
countries and Ethiopia. It is significant that under the former Ethiopian regime, when the USA had absolute control over the military
base in Asmara, US officials were unanimous about the need to
suppress the liberation movement in Eritrea'; now, however, they
wanted to exploit the problem 'to create disputes among the peoples
of that area in order to weaken their unified front against imperialist
infiltration'.[106]

The new Soviet attitude toward Eritrea puzzled Moscow's main ally
in the region, Somalia. As noted, the Somalis and the Eritrean rebels
were linked by their respective territorial claims on the common
Ethiopian enemy. In a sense, then, Moscow's indifference toward the
Eritrean cause could not but raise doubts in Mogadishu about the
Soviet commitment to Somali aspirations in the Ogaden. But, if the
USSR was aware of Somali sensibilities, it showed little sign of it. In
mid-1976, about a month after the proclamation of the NDR programme, Moscow signalled its strongest expression of support yet for
the Dergue's policy toward Eritrea. This was occasioned by the
PMAC's nine-point peace plan of May 1976. While the Eritreans, the
Somalis and most Arab states swiftly rejected the new initiative, the
Soviet Union warmly welcomed it. These proposals, Moscow
observed, 'answered the hopes and dreams of the provinces' population'[107] by seeking 'to satisfy the basic right of the people of the
administrative region of Eritrea' – such a phrase was a mortal sin in the
eyes of Mogadishu and the Eritrean liberation movement – and thus
'knocked the poisoned weapons from the hands of counter-
revolution' in Ethiopia.[108]

But, to Soviet commentators, the Eritrean problem was only one
manifestation of a deep and inevitable political process in the new
Ethiopia: 'Like any social revolution, the revolution in Ethiopia
delineates the bridgeheads and hinterland of the opposing classes and
forces ever more clearly. And like any social revolution it also
unmistakedly tells friends from foe outside the country.'[109] The
principal 'foe' Moscow had in mind was Western 'imperialism'. It was
alleged that 'imperialist propaganda' began 'to raise its voice' as soon
as the Ethiopian revolution gained momentum. The Western news
media fabricated 'news in order to smear the Ethiopian revolution'.[110]

For example, in October 1975, the Western press reported clashes between left-wing and right-wing groupings at a time when Addis Ababa was 'living an absolutely normal life'.[111] Equally, the Western media were 'full of the grimmest pessimistic forecasts' about the future of Ethiopia under its new government. In the circumstances, Moscow felt obliged to warn the Dergue that 'one cannot exclude the possibility of direct imperialist intervention in the course of events in Ethiopia'.[112] After all, *Pravda* noted, the US had 'one of its biggest African bases'[113] in Ethiopia.

Western hostility was said to be aroused, amongst other things, by the PMAC's 'realistic foreign policy'. This was characterised as 'anti-imperialistic, anti-colonialist' and based 'on the principles of active neutrality and non-alignment'.[114] Such a posture was perceived to be the product of twin imperatives. The first was the PMAC's pledge 'to destroy the dominance of foreign capital' in Ethiopia and 'to do away with the influence of the USA[115] in the country. The second concerned the Dergue's desire 'to extend its links with the socialist countries'. In this connection, Soviet writers approvingly quoted the government newpaper, *Ethiopian Herald* as saying: 'Ethiopia can learn a great deal from the socialist countries, making use of, in particular, the great experience and knowledge of these countries in the building of a new society in the social and economic spheres, in the sphere of industriali-sation and agriculture'.[116] It was no coincidence, therefore, that 'one of the first foreign policy agreements of post-Imperial Ethiopia was the agreement on cultural co-operation with the Soviet Union'.[117] The agreement, which was signed at the beginning of January 1975, was valid for a year; it provided for the exchange of students, teachers, musicians, radio and TV programmes, and was, in the words of a Soviet observer, part of the PMAC's campaign to purge 'the Western course' from the 'Ethiopian consciousness'.[118] At the same time, Moscow expressed its satisfaction with Ethiopia's decision to support 'the Angolan "patriots" [the MPLA's] just cause' in early 1976. For its part, the USSR declared in April 1976 that 'the friendly people of Ethiopia could rest assured that the Soviet public would always be on their side in the struggle against imperialism and neo-colonialism, for lasting peace and the people's security'.[119]

The initial phase of the Ethiopian revolution was thus seen as one of cumulative promise. Writing around this time, A. Kokiev and V. Vigand summarised the Soviet perspective: 'The most essential feature of the Ethiopian revolution is that beginning as a bourgeoise-democratic movement against feudal relations, for general democratic reforms, it has grown into an anti-imperialist democratic revolution paralleled by a struggle to achieve anti-capitalist changes.'[120]

The reality of Soviet caution

From the prominence given to Ethiopia in the Soviet media, one would have thought the USSR occupied a special position in the country. But the facts were rather more stark. Between 1974 and mid-1976, Soviet–Ethiopian relations remained decidedly low-key. While a number of official exchanges took place, these were generally low-level or symbolic affairs. A résumé makes interesting but thin reading.

In May 1974, on the anniversary of the Ethiopian victory over Italian Fascism, the two governments exchanged telegrams stressing the strengthening of the traditional friendship between the countries. A year later, the Soviet Afro–Asian Solidarity Committee marked the same occasion by sending a congratulatory message to the PMAC extolling the historic triumph of Ethiopian 'unity and independence' and wishing it 'future success'[121] in the construction of a new life. Meanwhile, in the spring of 1974, a CELU delegation led by Ato Tesfay Tadesse visited the USSR. During the visit, the Ethiopian side 'expressed the hope that the friendly relations between Ethiopia and the Soviet Union . . . would continue to grow'. The compliment was returned in the summer of 1975 when a Soviet Trade Union delegation made a little publicised trip to Ethiopia.[122]

At an unofficial level, Moscow was equally cautious. In September 1974, shortly after the military government came to power, the Soviet ambassador in Addis Ababa, Anatoly Ratanov, indicated to the PMAC that the USSR was prepared to replace the US as Ethiopia's arms supplier.[123] This initiative, however, apparently took Ratanov beyond his authority. For, while the PMAC at this stage did not wish to sever the US arms connection, it did express an interest in diversifying its arms sources. But when the Ethiopian government made an approach, the Soviet ambassador was unable to respond.[124] Nevertheless, in March 1975, a Soviet General turned up in Addis Ababa and gave briefings on the types of weapons that might be available in the event of a close relationship.[125] These briefings served to wet the appetite of some Dergue members. In the spring of 1975, the PMAC secretly sent a delegation to Moscow to explore the prospects of military assistance. The delegation met with Grechko, Kosygin and a number of lower-ranked officials.[126] The Soviets did not seem enthu-

siastic about supplying arms but were willing to continue the dialogue. According to several sources, the Soviets hinted that the
presence of a number of pro-Western people in the PMAC made it
difficult for them to provide many weapons.[127] Moscow promised to
send a military delegation but it did not arrive until September. The
visit was a secret one. The delegation's first reaction to a detailed
Ethiopian request for arms was that 'it is on the big side'.[128] Once
again, Soviet officials alluded to the presence of 'certain elements' in
the Ethiopian military which inhibited their ability to supply arms.
Ambassador Ratanov continued to propound this line after the delegation had returned home. The USSR made no formal reply to the
Ethiopian arms request until early 1976, and then only offered non-
lethal equipment such as earth-moving equipment and small transport planes. The PMAC communicated its disappointment in no
uncertain terms. It refused to send another delegation to Moscow for
more arms discussion.[129]

But Moscow quietly persevered in maintaining contacts with the
Dergue. In January 1976, the month in which the aforementioned
Soviet–Ethiopian cultural co-operation agreement was due to expire, a
delegation representing the mass information media led by Lieutenant-
Colonel Asrate Desta visited the USSR. The delegation was received
by candidate member of the Politburo and Minister of Culture,
P. Demichev. At the end of the visit, *Pravda* reported that the delegation had 'expressed a desire to develop friendly relations in every
possible way between the USSR and Ethiopia in various spheres of
ideological, cultural and educational work'.[130] The upshot was a new
two-year Soviet–Ethiopian agreement, signed in June 1976. As well as
facilitating co-operation in science, technology and fine arts, this
agreement granted 400 Soviet studentships, which was more than
double the previous number.[131] In between these events, Moscow
sent another 'unofficial' delegation of its own to Ethiopia. In mid-
February, a group of representatives from the Soviet Afro–Asian
Solidarity Committee headed by Malek Fazylov, Foreign Minister of
the Kazakh Soviet Socialist Republic, visited the country. The delegation met with the Ethiopian Foreign Minister twice (16 and 20
February) during its stay. However, the Soviet visitors returned home
with mixed impressions. In an interview in the Soviet foreign affairs
journal, *New Times*, Fazylov praised the revolutionary 'enthusiasm' of
the Ethiopian masses but conceded the Dergue faced formidable
problems in that the peasants 'sometimes fall under the influence of
feudals' who 'are supported by imperialist states'.[132] Yet again

Moscow was intimating that the PMAC was susceptible to pro-Western pressures.

Furthermore, while the Soviet Union gave some economic assistance to the Dergue, the amount was initially very modest. Modest, that is, in comparison with both the aid Addis Ababa received from the US and Moscow's own economic contribution in neighbouring Somalia over the same period. These issues, however, are dealt with below. It will suffice here to note that the old 1959 Soviet–Ethiopian aid agreement remained in force and that Soviet aid at this time largely consisted of the provision of drought relief. This included a gift of 4,000 tons of wheat in June 1974, a donation of 3,000 tons of fertiliser in January 1975, a large consignment of medicines from the Soviet Red Cross and the dispatch of teams of Soviet doctors to work in drought stricken parts of Ethiopia.[133] At the same time, the level of trade between the USSR and the new military regime in Ethiopia was minimal. After an encouraging start in 1974 when the figures doubled (see Table 11), Soviet–Ethiopian trade stagnated. In fact, the volume of trade between the two countries in 1976 was virtually the same as it had been in 1971.[134] In statistical terms, Moscow took about 1 per cent of Ethiopian imports. By way of contrast, the revolution notwithstanding, the US, Japan and the EEC together accounted for 49 per cent of Ethiopian exports and supplied 59 per cent of Ethiopian imports.[135] Nor was this dismal trading performance typical for the USSR in the region. In trade with Somalia in 1975 and 1976, the USSR achieved record turnover levels – the figures were 26.5 million roubles and 23.4 million roubles respectively[136] – which were roughly five times as great as the Ethiopian equivalents.

The Soviet reserve toward Ethiopia was epitomised by the absence of any mention of the country in Brezhnev's main address at the 25th Congress of the Soviet Communist Party in February 1976. Instead the Soviet leader stressed that 'our close relations with the Somali Democratic Republic' were being 'sealed still more dependably'.[137] The point seemed to be confirmed by President Siad's attendance at the Congress. All this was a source of frustration for those PMAC leaders who hoped to enlist Soviet support. Mengistu is reported to have explained Ethiopia's reliance on US arms to disgruntled radicals at Debre Zeit air base in June 1976 by saying, 'What else can we do, the Soviets will not provide them!'[138] How, then, can we explain the disparity between the very real reticence of Soviet policy towards Ethiopia and the lively Soviet media interest in the country? Several factors stood out as possible explanations.

In the first place, Moscow was unsure for a considerable period what the relationship would be between the new military regime and the US. As related, the US had begun to reassess its position in Ethiopia well before the 1974 upheaval. In 1973, Washington decided to gradually phase out the Kagnew communications centre. Then there was a further complication. In January 1974, the US Ambassador, Ross Adair, became ill and left Ethiopia for America. He was not replaced until March 1975. During that critical fifteen-month period, the US was only represented in Addis Ababa by a chargé d'affaires.[139] Such a situation owed a lot to the distractions of the Watergate affair and apparently more pressing foreign-policy concerns elsewhere. For a while, though, US diplomacy seemed unaffected. In September 1974, the US established friendly relations with the new Head of State, General Aman. He reassured Washington that the PMAC 'will never nationalise foreign property and investments in Ethiopia'[140] and had no intention of obtaining military equipment from any new sources. Such sentiments, however, were soon undermined by the killing of Aman and the leftward lurch of the Ethiopian revolution thereafter. The US became 'deeply troubled' by what the PMAC did and said. The fact that the PMAC nationalised a number of US enterprises without offering immediate compensation caused resentment in Washington.[141] To add insult to injury, the Ethiopian press, in 1975, began to feature regular denunciations of 'US imperialism' and suggestions that the CIA were supporting the 'enemies of the revolution'.[142]

Relations were also strained by the intensification of the Eritrean war in February 1975. The Dergue asked the US for an emergency airlift of $30 million worth of small arms and ammunition to enable it to continue the war. After a considerable delay, the US State Department informed the PMAC that it was only prepared to sell Ethiopia $7 million worth of ammunition.[143] The refusal to meet the Ethiopian request in full reflected the American fear that a substantial involvement in the Eritrean conflict might jeopardise American access to the Eritrean sea ports at Massawa and Assab, and might draw adverse reaction from the Arab countries like Saudi Arabia which were supporting the Eritreans. The US decision angered the PMAC. According to a PMAC supporter, the offer of reduced military aid was symptomatic of an innate hostility in Washington toward the Ethiopian revolution:

> Ever since the signature of a military assistance pact in 1953, the United States Government had provided Ethiopia with equipment, training and logistical support and never once had seriously and

publicly queried Ethiopia's general policies, particularly in regard to Eritrea. Now, however, with revolutionary development sweeping through Ethiopia, Washington began to raise questions about the conflict in northern Ethiopia [Eritrea].[144]

To the majority of Dergue members, therefore, the US was a dubious ally which was not above using its arms aid as a lever to interfere in Ethiopia's domestic affairs.

Nonetheless, and much to Moscow's consternation, Ethiopia and the US remained partners, despite themselves, for the whole of the period under review. This was due, above all, to the coalition of interests that had built up between the two countries over the previous three decades. The Ethiopians, for reasons already outlined, had in their own words a 'desperate need for arms and spare parts'.[145] Initial contacts with Moscow were disappointing. And there was still no sign of the USSR withholding military aid from Addis Ababa's old adversary, Somalia. There was also the question of logistics. At a time when Ethiopia was already experiencing turmoil through revolutionary political changes, the Dergue probably recognised it was not a good idea to rush into swapping suppliers in the military sphere. As for the US, it believed, on balance, that its geopolitical interests were still served by arming Ethiopia. This conviction rested on at least two elements. First, Washington feared that an arms embargo 'would only strengthen the hands of radical elements among the military and further frustrate the moderates, perhaps leading them to concur in more radical initiatives'[146] such as an arms link up with Moscow. Secondly, the US was determined to counter the Soviet arms build up in Somalia. Concern centred especially on the rapid expansion of Soviet facilities at the port of Berbera in northern Somalia. On 10 June 1975, the US Secretary of Defence, James Schlesinger, told the Senate Armed Services Committee that aerial reconnaissance had revealed the existence of a 'very substantial'[147] Soviet missile installation at Berbera. But if Schlesinger's assessment was exaggerated for domestic political reasons – on 27 July 1975 the Senate approved $100 million in funds for the development of Diego Garcia[148] – it was equally true that blanket denials by both the USSR and Somalia over the Berbera facilities left many observers, and not just American ones, sceptical. Unease over Soviet activities in Somalia, for example, almost certainly led to the abrupt cancellation of the Arab League Summit, scheduled for Mogadishu in June 1975.[149] To Henry Kissinger, the Secretary of State, it was essential, therefore, to arm Ethiopia as a regional counterweight to Soviet-backed Somalia. Failure to do so, it was

Table 8 *Ethiopian and Somali arms imports 1961–1979 (millions of current US $)*

Year	Ethiopia	Somalia
1961	9	1
1962	11	2
1963	10	2
1964	6	18
1965	10	12
1966	11	5
1967	13	0
1968	19	4
1969	12	6
1970	10	10
1971	10	0
1972	10	20
1973	10	40
1974	10	90
1975	30	70
1976	50	100
1977	440	80
1978	1,100	170
1979	210	30
Total 1961–74	151	210
Total 1961–76	231	380
Total 1974–76	90	260
Total 1977–79	1,750	280
Total 1961–79	1,981	660

Source: adapted from Paul B. Henze, 'Arming the Horn 1960–1980', Washington DC, Working Paper 43, International Security Series, Woodrow Wilson Center for Scholars, Smithsonian Institution (July 1982), p. 653

argued, would undermine US credibility as a friend throughout the world.

Paradoxically, then, US military supplies to Ethiopia soared in the first three years after the revolution. From an average of about $10 million a year between 1969 and 1974, US military deliveries reached a total value of $18.5 million in 1974–5, $26 million in 1975–6 and almost $135 million in 1976–7.[150] This increase was almost entirely on a cash-sale basis. Military equipment purchased included M-60 tanks, F5-E fighter-bomber aircraft and the Maverick and Sidewinder missiles to go with them, and at least one squadron of second-hand F-5A Freedom Fighters from Iran with US approval.[151] Even so, these arms shipments did not match the weaponry which the Soviet Union was pumping into Somalia (see Table 8). Altogether, from 1974 to 1977, Moscow supplied Somalia with more than $300 million in arms. That was far in excess of the approximately $180 million worth of arms which the US sent to Ethiopia during the same period.[152] It should be added that there was little relation between the reasons why the US decided to supply arms and the reasons why Ethiopia wanted them. The Dergue wanted US arms to ensure its own survival. The US provided arms to offset the threat of Soviet influence in the region. Thus, the partnership between the Dergue and the United States was a marriage of convenience, and a fragile one at that. Just how fragile became evident in May 1976 when the US warned the Dergue that arms shipments would be affected if it went ahead with the intended human-wave attack by peasant militia on Eritrean rebels.[153] In the event the 'peasant march' was abandoned.

Meanwhile, the USSR seemed perplexed and, to some extent, repelled by the Dergue's choice of foreign friends. In March 1975, *Pravda* admitted that 'it is still impossible to surmise what form the future development of Ethiopia will take'.[154] Although 'serious observers cannot but see that, while the restoration of the extremely reactionary monarchy and feudal bureaucracy is unlikely, there is still a possibility that Ethiopia may be pushed into the path of lopsided development along the lines of what is known as "capitalism Africa style"'.[155] It would appear that one of the Soviet preconditions for a significant upgrading in relations with Addis Ababa was that Ethiopia terminate its links with the United States. In this vein, a Soviet observer in May 1976 tempered praise of the PMAC's NDR programme with a demand for 'a more careful and realistic appraisal of the [Ethiopian] situation by the authorities as well as of the unity of the anti-feudal and anti-imperialist forces'.[156]

To a lesser degree, Soviet caution was also prompted by the perception of Maoist tendencies within the PMAC. Initially, at least, the PMAC seemed to derive some revolutionary inspiration from the PRC. The second Vice-Chairman Colonel Atnafu Abate was rumoured to be pro-Chinese and, when the regime adopted a socialist orientation in December 1974, it had certain Maoist strands. The notion of 'Ethiopian socialism', for instance, appeared to mirror the Chinese idea of revolutionary self-sufficiency.[157] Equally, the Ethiopian land reform drew on Chinese experience. In January 1975, the PRC sent technicians and personnel to Addis Ababa to provide advice on agrarian reform.[158]

From 1974 to December 1976, the PRC maintained an active but low-profile role in Ethiopia. It provided relatively small but important programmes of non-military aid, some of which started under the Emperor's rule. They included a major Chinese road-building project in northern Ethiopia, drought-relief aid, the installation of electricity generators and a medical-assistance programme.[159] There was, in addition, a number of official exchanges between the two countries. In March 1976, an Ethiopian goodwill delegation led by Captain Moges Wolde Michael, Chairman of the Dergue's economic committee, visited China and, following talks with the Chinese Vice-Premier, Ku Mu, signed an economic agreement with Peking.[160] Eight months later, a Chinese economic and trade exhibition opened in Addis Ababa.[161]

It would be wrong, to exaggerate Peking's influence on the PMAC. A major limitation was the PRC's unwillingness to supply substantial military aid to Addis Ababa. In the summer of 1976, the PMAC sent a secret arms mission to Peking. Apparently, the only result of these talks was the delivery of a 200-ton consignment of small arms.[162] Yet this was cold comfort to Moscow. For, one of the main reasons for China's reluctance to sell major weapons was a concern not to endanger its already cordial relationship with the USSR's erstwhile ally, Somalia. As it was, the PRC used its modest foothold in Ethiopia (and, for that matter, in Somalia) to denounce 'Moscow's imperialist designs in the Horn and Red Sea'.[163] It warned the African states not to accept Soviet air and naval bases in exchange for the 'modern tsars' military assistance.[164] But while, in propaganda terms, Moscow gave as good as it got, it is safe to assume the USSR remained suspicious of the Dergue for flirting with such flagrant 'anti-Sovietism'.

The third and perhaps most substantial constraint on Soviet policy towards Ethiopia was the Kremlin's stake in Somalia. After the Treaty of Friendship and Co-operation in July 1974, Soviet–Somali relations, according to one Soviet writer, became a model example 'of the relationship between a country of developed socialism and a state of socialist orientation'.[165] Co-operation was said to be 'diverse' and 'taking on an even more stable, friendly and brotherly character'.[166] The Soviet Foreign Minister, Andrey Gromyko, reportedly alluded to this in a conversation with the Ethiopian Ambassador in Moscow in the summer of 1975, when he said that supplying arms could create problems for the Soviet Union in Somalia.[167]

In the economic sphere, Soviet assistance to Mogadishu markedly increased during this period. The increase coincided with one of the worst ever droughts in Somali history. Between 1974 and 1975 a vast area of northern Somalia, with a population of not less than a million, mostly pastoral nomads, was severely affected. The nomads' livestock was decimated. But, unlike Haile Selassie's regime during the earlier Ethiopian famine, Siad's government, to its credit, did not attempt to conceal the scale of the disaster. Rather, it declared a state of emergency, established famine relief camps and launched a series of appeals for international aid. The Soviet response was both impressive and unusually generous. In June 1975, Moscow concluded a new economic co-operation agreement with Somalia. Under it Somalia was to receive aid totalling $52 million for development projects.[168] The USSR also agreed to support Mogadishu's ambitious plan to resettle many of the drought victims. Convinced the scheme was 'truly revolutionary in scope and significance',[169] the Soviet Union provided air and road transport on a massive scale to carry it out. It supplied twelve AN-12 transport planes and 165 heavy lorries, with pilots and drivers (at the end of the operation the lorries were donated to Mogadishu). Furthermore, the USSR sent fully equipped portable hospitals, foodstuffs, medicaments, medical personnel and thousands of tents to the resettlers' camps in Somalia. As a result, between June and August 1975, the USSR helped to evacuate some 90,000 nomads to southern Somalia.[170] Many of these nomads were settled in three new farming townships at Dujumo, Sablabeh and Kurtun Waarey, each of which were developed with the aid of Soviet land-excavating machines, building materials and agricultural equipment. The remainder, some 15,000 nomads, joined Soviet-sponsored fishing co-operatives situated on the southern coastline.[171] Moscow provided the co-operatives with modern trawlers and training, and co-ordinated their activities through the 'highly profitable'[172] Soviet–Somali commercial fishing company, Somalfish.

By the end of 1975, the Somali government had managed to effectively contain the worst consequences of the drought. Something like 20,000 people died in the process. But there was a general recognition that this figure would have been much higher were it not for the dynamism of the Siad regime, and the 'internationalist assistance' of its ally, the USSR. Certainly, Moscow took the view that its assistance 'at the time of the re-settlement campaign reinforced even more strongly the friendly relationship with the Soviet Union'.[173] Soviet visitors to Somalia around this time were struck by the gratitude

of local officials. Mohammed Isse Salwe, the Commissioner of the new
Kurtun Waarey township, told a Soviet journalist:

> We would have never been able to do this without the help of the
> Soviet Union. The Russians were real brothers to us. We shall never
> forget this. Ask any resident of the township and he will tell you that
> he owes his very life to the Soviet Union.[174]

Another official, Egal, the Commissioner for the Brava region, spoke
of Soviet popularity amongst the nomads and roundly declared, 'we
trust the Russians'.[175] Such comments pinpointed what Moscow
considered to be the essential political point.

It was argued that Soviet drought aid demonstrated Somalia had
'friends who have already confirmed their reliability at this extremely
difficult time for the nation'.[176] The implication was obvious. Not all of
Somalia's friends had shown themselves to be so reliable. And here
the target of Soviet criticism seemed to be Mogadishu's 'brothers' in
the Arab League. In February 1975, the Foreign Ministers of the Arab
League promised Somalia $100 million in emergency drought assist-
ance. However, while Libya fulfilled its original pledge of 61,890,706
Somali shillings, as did Bahrain and Abu Dhabi (3,115,000 Somali
shillings and 34,650,000 Somali Shillings respectively), the bulk of the
Arab relief effort simply never materialised.[177] Basically, there were
two reasons for this. First, and as previously noted, some of the
wealthy Arab states became increasingly disenchanted with Mogadishu's Soviet connection. Second, Saudi Arabia and other League
members were shocked by the summary execution in January 1975, at
the height of the Somali famine, of a group of religious leaders who
opposed Siad's decree on sexual equality as being contrary to the
Koran. But if Moscow did not acknowledge the reasons for the Arab
shortfall, it was quick to make political capital out of it by contrasting
its own economic role in a Somalia which was 'going forward': 'Today
90 per cent of the country's specialists had been trained in the USSR;
over 1,000 young Somalis were now studying in the Soviet Union; and
Soviet teachers, doctors, geologists, construction specialists, engineers, agronomists and fishery experts could be found in remote spots
throughout the country.'[178]

What Moscow did not say, however, was that military aid continued
to be the main instrument of its policy. Between 1974 and 1976, Soviet
largesse transformed little Somalia into the fourth most heavily armed
state in black Africa after Nigeria, Zaire and Ethiopia. The 1976
inventory revealed a marked expansion in nearly all categories of

Table 9. *The military balance in the Horn of Africa 1976–1977: A breakdown*

Category	Ethiopia	Somalia
Population	28,620,000	3,250,000
Estimated GNP 1975	US$ 2.9 billion	$0.3 billion
Total armed forces	50,800	25,000
Estimated defence budget	US$ 84 million	$15 million
Army Total strength	47,000 1 mech. division 3 infantry divisions 1 airborne infantry battalion 4 art. battalions 2 engineer battalions 4 Armoured Car Squadrons 24 M-60 tanks 54 M-41 lt tanks 90 M-113 Arm. Personnel Carriers 56 AML-245/60 armoured cars	22,000 6 tank battalions 9 mech. infantry battalions 5 infantry battalions 2 commando battalions 6 field, 5 AA art. battalions 200 T-34, 50-54/55 med. tanks 60 BTR-40, 250 BTR-152 Armoured Personnel Carriers
Navy Total strength	1,500 1 coastal minesweeper 1 training ship 5 large patrol craft (ex-US) 4 coastal patrol craft 4 landing craft (ex-US) 1 Kraljevica-class patrol boat	300 2 Osa-class FPBG with Styx SSM 6 P-4 & P-6 MTB (ex-Soviet) 4 medium landing craft (ex-Soviet)

Air Force

Total strength	2,300	2,700
	36 combat aircraft	66 combat aircraft
	1 bomber squad. with 4 Canberra B2	1 light bomber squad. with 10 Il-28
	1 fighter attack squad with 11 F-86F	2 fighter attack squads. with 44 MiG- 15
	2 fighter attack squads. with 16 F-5A/E	UTI and MiG-17
	1 reconnaisance squad. with 5 T-28A	1 fighter squad. with 12 MiG-21
	1 transport squad. with 12 C-47, 2 C-54, 12	1 transport squad. with 3 An-2, 3
	C-119G, 3 Dove	An-24/-26
	3 transport squads. with 19 Safir, 13	Other aircraft – 3 C-47, 1 C-45, 8 P-148, 20
	T-28A/D, 11 T-33A	Yak-11
	1 helicopter squad. with 10 AB204 and 6	1 helicopter squad. with Mi-2, Mi-4 and
	UH-1H	Mi-8
Defence expenditure as		
% of GNP	3.6%	20%

Source: adapted from *The Military Balance, 1976–1977*, London, Institute for Strategic Studies, 1976, pp. 42–44.

conventional military power; the Somali armed forces totalled 22,000, a jump of 30 per cent on the 1974 figure; in terms of armour, Somalia acquired an additional 100 T-34 and T-54 tanks to give it an overall force of 250 medium tanks and approximately 300 armoured personnel carriers; the Somali air force, which formerly consisted of about 21 combat aircraft, trebled in size thanks to an infusion of 24 supersonic MiG-21s, as well as MiG-17s, MiG-15s and Ilyushin bombers. On paper, Somalia in 1976 had probably the strongest air-strike capacity in black Africa. However, the operational availability of Somalia's aircraft and other weaponry was uncertain since, in the words of the 1976 Survey of the International Institute for Strategic Studies, Soviet 'spares are short and not all equipment is serviceable'.[179]

While Somalia's arms requirements were hardly a crushing burden on Moscow, the net effect as far as the Dergue was concerned was to create a security nightmare. The local military equation had shifted further in Mogadishu's favour. In the first place, Ethiopia's traditional advantage in manpower was sapped by losses in Eritrea, by the use of forces to counter domestic opposition throughout the country and by the decimation of the senior officer corps as a result of the Dergue's political purges in the Ethiopian Army.[180] In other areas, too, Ethiopia found itself at a distinct disadvantage. With regard to air-power, for instance, Somalia established a quantitative edge over Ethiopia for the first time. This gain was admittedly, somewhat tempered by the quality of Ethiopia's air force. As related, in April 1976 the Dergue acquired American F-5E fighter bombers, a sophisticated aircraft which could more than hold its own against the Somali MiGs. There was, though, a more dramatic difference in armour strength. According to the aforementioned 1976 survey, Ethiopia had 75 medium tanks and about 146 armoured personnel carriers which together was less than half the size of Somalia's arsenal in the same department[181] (see Table 9).

Moscow maintained that its military aid to Somalia was purely defensive in character. A Soviet official in Somalia was quoted as saying: 'It is natural that a young republic with a new political system should want a good army to guarantee its security. That is what we are providing at its [Somalia's] request.'[182] In other words, the USSR was not prepared to explicitly endorse the Somali territorial claim in the Ogaden. But it was prepared to supply the Siad regime with a range of weapons for which there was no other possible use. Thus, Somalia, unlike Ethiopia, obtained a capability for rapid, deep penetration in the best blitzkrieg style.[183] Presumably, powerful figures in the

Kremlin calculated that given Somali dependence on Soviet arms Moscow could ensure that this military capability served Soviet political ends. But, with the unravelling of the Ethiopian revolution, a number of Soviet commentators began to question the logic of their country's policy toward Somalia. This dissent, which had never been too far beneath the surface of Soviet policy in the Horn, was expressed in a number of ways. At a cursory glance, the ideological positions of the two countries appeared to be closer than ever. In February 1976, President Siad attended the 25th Congress of the CPSU. In his speech at the Congress, Siad, *inter alia*, identified Somalia as 'an inseparable part of the world revolutionary movement', warmly thanked the USSR for its drought-relief assistance and enthusiastically endorsed Soviet–Cuban military intervention on behalf of the MPLA in the Angolan civil war of 1975–6.[184] The speech, by all accounts, pleased the Soviets.[185] It is not clear, though, whether the same could be said about President Siad's subsequent talks with President Podgorny and other Soviet officials during what was an extended stay in the USSR. A short *Tass* statement at the end of the visit, merely stating that the discussions covered future links between the SRC and the CPSU and 'the situation in some parts of Africa',[186] seemed to indicate disagreement. It is known that there were four main areas of Soviet discontent.

First, some Soviet observers voiced scepticism about Siad's 'shoot from the hip'[187] ideology. On the one hand, the Somali leader persisted with the notion that 'there is only one socialism, namely scientific socialism'. On the other hand, Siad insisted that 'a Soviet socialist cannot tell me about Somalian problems, which must be put in an African context'.[188] A Soviet specialist on Somalia, Evgeny Sherr, seemed to rationalise such inconsistency in the following way: 'the President of the SRC speaks in a language which is understandable to all the [Somali] people. His speeches are saturated with graphic national expressions, derived from folklore.'[189] However, in the eyes of other Soviet observers, Somalia's ideological confusion was compounded by its very slow progress in the basics of Marxism–Leninism. Here, the question of party development loomed large. Sherr himself, during a 1974 visit to Somalia, drew attention to the absence of a 'vanguard' party: 'During tours around the country one repeatedly heard, sometimes from the leaders, sometimes from the rank and file workers, regrets in the Republic concerning the acutely felt lack of a party and its guiding influence.'[190] Yet, at the time of the 25th Congress of the CPSU in February 1976, there was still no clear indication that President Siad would respond to such 'regrets'. The

Somali leader admitted to his Soviet hosts the 'need for a political organisation' but insisted that 'the formation of a party is a long process'.[191]

By the same token, Soviet commentators questioned the ideological veracity of Somali economic policy. G. V. Kazakov, for one, highlighted the survival of capitalist tendencies in Somali society:

> Notwithstanding the implementation in 1970 of partial nationalisation the activity of the private sector did not lessen. The financing by the banks of the activity of the private sector at the beginning of 1971 exceeded its deposits in the bank by 49% [sic]. This is the characteristic feature, indicating the activity but not a reduction of 'activities' of the private sector in Somalia after the revolutionary overthrow of 1969.[192]

A related but more fundamental criticism centred on Mogadishu's economic capacity to sustain a path of socialist orientation. The majority of Soviet writers acknowledged Somalia's 'deep socio-economic transformations', but several argued that these 'transformations' faced 'great difficulties' in a country of such 'extreme economic backwardness'. The problems included 'a shortage of financial and material resources, the struggle with obsolete traditions, ignorance, lack of culture and so on'.[193] This meant, apart from anything else, 'the [Somali] government is not narrowing the sphere of application of private capital because it does not have at its disposal sufficient financial resources which could completely guarantee the development of even the leading branches of the economy'.[194] In a similar vein, A. Dolgov noted that many Somali peasants and nomads, after receiving a professional training from the government, joined private enterprises 'because the national government for the time being cannot pay them so much'.[195]

Secondly, Moscow was frustrated by the presence of Islam in President Siad's Somalia. Contrary to Soviet expectations, the revolution did not weaken the influence of the Muslim faith on the Somali people. This was brought home in January 1975, when Siad introduced a law on equality of women. *Pravda* welcomed the move as a 'progressive' measure which 'finds full support from the Soviet Union'.[196] But in Somalia the new law was not well received. In fact, it occasioned considerable anti-Soviet sentiment when ten Muslim leaders, who protested that the new legislation transgressed the Koran, were executed. An Italian, who was mistaken for a Russian, was stabbed, while a mid-air collision of two Soviet MiGs over Mogadishu on the day of the execution was celebrated locally as a case of divine retribution.[197] It was difficult, therefore, for the Soviets to have much contact with the Somali people. Known as the 'Godless' ones, Soviet personnel, despite official denials, were often subject to popular abuse.

Aware of the domestic standing of the Soviets, and concerned to reassure his conservative Arab allies about his rule, President Siad delivered a blunt message to the USSR in early 1976: 'To attain our strategic goal – building a socialist society – we must take account of the realities'. One of the 'realities' was the Somali population's 'devotion to Islam'. Siad added: 'In our country religion is not just a matter of faith: it is inherent in our culture and has its own social structure.' And because 'imperialism has always tried to use religion as an instrument against communist ideas, we decided that in our country there should be no struggle between religion and socialism.'[198] In other words, Siad was saying that Islam – a serious problem in Soviet eyes – was here to stay.

Thirdly, the USSR was increasingly concerned about the 'narrowness' of Somali nationalism. Like his predecessors, President Siad operated within a political framework which was to some extent defined by the founding father of the Somali nation, Sayid Mohammed Abdille Hassan. The latter specified, amongst other things, that Somalis should not compromise national sovereignty by taking 'coins'[199] from foreigners. But, while Siad was prepared to disregard this dictum in accepting Soviet 'coins', his regime remained conscious of the need to demonstrate that Somali sovereignty was not being infringed in doing so. Just how conscious was made plain during the Berbera 'missile crisis' of summer 1975. In a bid to kill US allegations that the Soviets were establishing a missile base at Berbera, the Somali President invited an international group of journalists and delegations from the US Senate and Congress to inspect the facilities themselves. As a preliminary to the visits, Mogadishu issued a vigorous public defence of its position, with scant regard to Soviet sensibilities. The Somali Foreign Minister, Omar Arteh Ghalib, declared: 'The Soviet Union has never asked us to give them a base in Somalia and, even if they did, we will never allow it because it is against our policies.'[200] To support its case, the Siad regime argued that the Horn region should be 'free of big power rivalry', and that Mogadishu 'in the near future' would repeat its 1974 offer of naval facilities to the US. Thus, the purpose of the above invitation was in Siad's words 'to clear away the clouds and this means we want American friendship'.[201]

However, the inspection visits which took place in early July 1975 failed to reassure Washington. And, what is more, President Siad experienced a stunning humiliation into the bargain. Having promised Senator Dewey Bartlett, who headed a delegation from the Senate Armed Services Committee, unrestricted access to the Berbera complex, Siad had his orders promptly overturned by the Soviets who refused to allow Bartlett's group see a key area in and around their Communications Centre.[202] As an upshot, Senator Bartlett said on his return to Washington that his trip to Berbera 'absolutely confirms' the Pentagon's contentions about Soviet-built facilities. Nonetheless, he was convinced of Mogadishu's desire to improve relations and recommended an expansion of US drought-relief assistance to Somalia.[203]

For the Soviet Union, the episode was a disturbing one. While, in the last analysis, it was able to slap down Siad over the specific issue of the Berbera Communications Station visit, the USSR was certainly unhappy about the general circumstances which made the incident possible. By making what were perceived to be 'anti-Soviet' noises and drawing world attention to the Soviet military presence in Somalia, President Siad had shown himself to be an unreliable ally and an opportunist. After all, Siad showed few qualms about embarrassing the Kremlin when he saw the chance to undercut the position of Somalia's adversary, Ethiopia, through playing the American 'card'.

Fourthly, Soviet observers were irritated by Mogadishu's dissatisfaction with Soviet economic aid. Despite receiving a relatively liberal dose of Soviet support, President Siad indicated this fell short of his expectations:

> We are promoting all-round co-operation with the Soviet Union and receive economic and political aid from it . . . *This co-operation may not have yet reached the level we would like*, for our revolution is still young and the socialist countries have to be convinced of our consistency in pursuing our chosen line.[204]

The latter qualification can be taken with a pinch of salt. In reality, Siad, as before, sought to maximise Soviet aid through a deliberate policy of economic diversification. As a Soviet commentator put it, 'Somalia is receiving aid from many states' although its socialist orientation 'presupposes . . . the reduction of dependence upon foreign capital'.[205] Two aid donors, in particular, served to fuel Somalia's economic demands on the USSR.

One was the PRC. Unlike the Soviets, whose projects sometimes had the reputation for delays and rising costs,[206] the Chinese made themselves popular in Somalia by maintaining a simply conceived but well-implemented aid programme. As in Ethiopia, the Chinese focussed on rural development and road building. Amongst other things, Peking successfully installed a water-supply system at Hargeisa, sunk numerous boreholes to provide water for the largely nomadic Somali tribesmen, completed the Belet Uen-Galcaio section of the Belet Uen-Burao highway, despatched additional medical personnel and donated 4,000 tons of maize to Somalia to help the drought victims.[207] Furthermore, Somali delegations in the fields of livestock, forestry and health visited the PRC during this period. While the Chinese never sought the diplomatic limelight in Somalia, it is interesting to note that its economic-assistance programme was not matched by the Soviets until 1975.[208]

The other source of aid, with challenging implications for Moscow, was the conservative Arab bloc led by Saudi Arabia. Earlier, we mentioned how the USSR seemed to contrast its own response to Somalia's greatest hour of need, the drought of 1975, with the meagre efforts of the oil-rich 'reactionary' Arab states. But there was little sign the Somali government drew the same political conclusion as Moscow. On the contrary, the drought episode, along with Siad's own Arab diplomacy – in May 1975 he visited Saudi Arabia, Iraq, Syria, Libya, Egypt and the Sudan[209] – probably persuaded him that the Soviet connection was in many respects an obstacle to more economic aid for Somalia. Certainly, it was confirmed in May 1976 that Saudi Arabia had offered to finance a substantial economic and military package for Somalia if it broke with Moscow.[210] Nothing came of the proposal at the time. But such an overture, coupled with a larger input of aid from Kuwait and the Arab Fund for Economic Development in 1976, undoubtedly toughened Mogadishu's attitude towards Soviet aid.

For its part, the Soviet Union reminded Somalia that 'in the general volume of foreign aid, Soviet aid is without doubt the most significant and effective'.[211] While it grudgingly acknowledged 'international organisations are rendering Somalia comparatively small, but occasionally sufficient effective assistance'[212] in drought relief, Moscow also emphasised the distinctive character of its bilateral aid. A. Dolgov, for example, compared the willingness of Soviet specialists to train Somali workers with the American record in the construction of the Kismayo port in the late 1960s, where they 'had not trained a single qualified Somalian worker'. At the same time, Moscow hinted at a lack of gratitude on the part of the Somalis. A Soviet writer, discussing 'the preparatory work' of the planned hydro-electric scheme at Fanole, said that while 'compatriots from Moscow are always happy there' the site itself 'is no paradise':

> On the banks of the Juba there are many malaria carrying mosqui-toes. The builders in Fanole go to sleep to the roar of the lion, the fighting of hyennas and other inhabitants of the savannah. Our specialists are already used to working in heat approaching 50 Centigrade, sometimes, if necessary for 10 to 12 hours, occasionally without days off.[213]

Clearly, while these strains did not endanger the Soviet commit-ment to Somalia in 1976, they could not but reinforce Moscow's awareness of political opportunities elsewhere in the region.

The new drive towards a Pax Sovietica

The month of July 1976 brought several seemingly disparate events relating to the Horn of Africa which, in retrospect, precipitated the birth of a new Soviet approach to the region.

On 1 July, Somalia's top decision-making body, the Supreme Revolutionary Council (SRC), officially surrendered power to the new Somali Revolutionary Socialist Party (SRSP) and disbanded. This reform, however, was not as sweeping as it seemed. The most powerful figures of the old military regime continued to be the most prominent in the new ruling party. President Siad was 'elected' Secretary-General of the SRSP, and also held the posts of Prime Minister and Chairman of the vital Political Bureau. The four other members of the Political Bureau were also key men in the SRC – three Vice-Presidents and the head of both the National Security Service and Army Intelligence. Moreover, the SRSP Central Committee, which had seventy-four members, included all the members of the former SRC.[214] Thus, while the number of people involved in official policy-making was enlarged, it was clear the transition to civilian rule in Somalia was achieved without effectively disturbing the old leader-ship. This fact, along with the evident haste with which the SRSP was eventually formed, strongly suggests that the reform was designed, above all, to satisfy Soviet requirements for additional aid. It is interesting to note that the establishment of the new party closely followed a Soviet decision to freely supply Somalia with food pro-ducts, construction materials, oil products, motor vehicles and other commodities.[215]

Whatever the case, Moscow was quick to warmly welcome the formation of the SRSP. In a message of congratulations, Soviet leader,

Brezhnev, told President Siad that 'Soviet Communists regard the establishment of the Somali Revolutionary Socialist Party as a major landmark in the development of the Somali revolution and evidence of the Somali people's determination to fight for the ideals of national independence, freedom and socialism'.[216] More specifically, the new reform indicated Somalia had 'turned to the experience in party-building amassed by the socialist countries', and had succeeded in overcoming 'narrow nationalistic'[217] approaches. In short, Moscow saw the creation of a vanguard party as making Somalia safe for socialism and, by implication, ripe for Soviet influence.

The second development was the visit to Moscow of a high-level Ethiopian state delegation between 6 and 12 July 1976. Headed by the chairman of the PMAC economic committee, Captain Moges Wolde Michael, who three months earlier led a party to the PRC, the delegation held meetings with Premier A. Kosygin, Foreign Minister Andrey Gromyko, Central Committee Secretary B. Ponomarev and Vice-Chairman of the Soviet Council of Ministers I. Arkhipov. According to *Pravda*, the talks were conducted in a 'friendly atmosphere' and had 'positive results'. A joint communique remarked that 'favourable new conditions are presently taking shape for expanding relations between the Soviet Union and Ethiopia and developing all round co-operation'.[218] As a step in this direction, it was agreed that 'a group of Soviet experts' would go to Ethiopia to study 'the lines of mutually beneficial economic and technical co-operation'. In addition, the USSR decided to render Ethiopia assistance in the fields of skill training and education. (By late summer, it was reported that Soviet lecturers had started arriving at Addis Ababa University, mainly to teach newly inaugurated courses in Marxist–Leninist ideology.)[219] Furthermore, the leader of the Ethiopian delegation hinted he had received a Soviet pledge of future aid: 'Ethiopia finds in the USSR the necessary support in the progressive transformation of its society.'[220] In Moscow, the impact of the visit was symbolically expressed in the Soviet press. For the first time since the 1974 revolution, *Pravda* referred to Addis Ababa as 'Socialist Ethiopia'.[221] It was striking that the Soviet media had never described neighbouring Somalia in such fulsome terms.

Thirdly, and most significantly, there was the crushing of a plot to oust Major Mengistu Haile Mariam from the PMAC. As previously noted, on 13 July 1976, Major Sisay Habte, the political head of the Dergue and number three man in the regime, and eighteen accomplices were executed for alleged participation in 'anti-revolutionary activities'. This outcome pleased the USSR. The latter was, in the words of a Mengistu supporter, one of the 'outside powers' who 'watched the ongoing [July] crisis with keen interest'.[222] And Sisay Habte, although a convinced Marxist, had a pragmatic reputation for insisting on Ethiopia's continued connection with the US. A graduate of an American University and chief spokesman for the Air Force within the Dergue, Sisay was responsible for secretly negotiating the resumption of Israeli aid to Ethiopia in 1975.[223] He was also reportedly close to the US Embassy in Addis Ababa.[224] Indeed, the possibility of international involvement in the abortive coup against Mengistu cannot be excluded.

One of the official PMAC charges against Sisay was his refusal 'to go to the Soviet Union, the founder of socialism at the head of a high-level delegation, to discuss urgent matters related to the country's urgent needs'.[225] In other words, Sisay opposed the visit of the Ethiopian delegation to the USSR just outlined. At the same time, the US expressed surprising concern over the demise of a radical like Sisay. For example, during the US Senate Sub-Committee hearings on the Horn of Africa 1976, John H. Spencer, one-time foreign-policy adviser to Emperor Haile Selassie, berated the 'assassination' of Sisay whom he described as 'pro-Western'.[226] In contrast, Moscow applauded the execution of the July conspirators 'caught red-handed' and linked with 'terrorists and the reactionaries' backed 'by external forces, including the US Central Intelligence Agency'.[227]

But, to understand the importance of this episode in Soviet eyes, it is necessary to consider what was a key variable in the Soviet–Ethiopian relationship, namely, the Soviet assessment of the political balance within the Dergue. For, while Moscow had no objection in principle to military rule in Ethiopia, it had very definite views on the type of military leadership it wished to see. According to Soviet writers, the 'class variations'[228] inside the PMAC initially ranged from 'bourgeoise-reformist forces' which 'were struggling for a capitalistic path' to 'revolutionary democrats . . . who had come out for a progressive path of development'.[229] As a consequence, between 1974 and 1976, the USSR worked quietly behind the scene to strengthen the 'revolutionary-democratic wing' of the Dergue[230] – 'From the first days of their arrival in power, the revolutionary democratic forces in Ethiopia felt the brotherly help and support of the Soviet Union and other socialist countries'[231] – and thus fashion an Ethiopian leadership which was perceived to be consistent with Soviet interests.

The process of penetrating the Ethiopian military may have begun before the 1974 revolution. Paul Henze, a specialist on the Horn of Africa who served at the US Embassy in Addis Ababa in 1968–72, reported that the Soviets were making contact with junior officers in the Ethiopian Army in the early 1970s.[232] Intriguingly, Henze's claim coincided with Soviet reports that 'in the 1960s – beginning of the 1970s a lot of people came into the [Ethiopian] army convinced of the necessity of destroying the feudalist–monarchist edifice', and these included 'Marxist units, among a part of the middle and junior officers and rank and file sergeants'.[233] It was also noteworthy that in December 1973, the month in which Moscow – unlike most Western countries – first got wind of a serious mutiny in the Ethiopian Army,[234] a new Soviet Ambassador, A. Ratanov, previously Ambassador to 'progressive' Guinea,[235] was appointed to Ethiopia. At least one Soviet writer implied that the Dergue's subsequent rise to power was achieved with the help of external guidance.[236] Beyond this, however, one thing was clear. At an early stage in Ethiopia's national revolution and, it must be stressed, before Mengistu had fully consolidated his power, the Soviet Union decided he was the main horse to back in the Dergue.

The Soviet media was quick to champion Mengistu's cause. Just two months after the overthrow of the Emperor, *New Times* identified Mengistu as 'an influential leader of the Armed Forces Movement'.[237] Other commentaries referred to him as 'one of the chief organisers of the anti-monarchial coup' and the head of the 'revolutionary democratic' nucleus[238] within the PMAC. Equally, Moscow fully endorsed the Mengistu-inspired decision to eliminate the first leader of the PMAC, General Aman Andom. The latter, it was alleged, 'came out against the revolution' and participated in the preparation 'of a state coup of a pro-American orientation'.[239] But the USSR gave Mengistu more than just verbal support. In early 1975, Mengistu and other selected PMAC members attended short political training courses in the Soviet Union.[240] Over the next two years, similar courses were extended to hundreds of soldiers in the Ethiopian Army in the USSR and Eastern bloc countries like Bulgaria, Czechoslovakia and East Germany (see Table 10). Most of those sent were known to be followers of Mengistu.[241] Moreover, and not unrelated to this, it is likely that Mengistu received the assistance of the Soviet intelligence services in the struggle with his political adversaries in the PMAC.[242]

Thus, while the relationship between Mengistu and the USSR during this time was by definition a shadowy one, there was a relationship. However, it was difficult to say whether Mengistu was

Table 10   *Training of Ethiopian and Somali military personnel in Soviet-bloc countries 1955–1979*

	Total	USSR	Eastern Europe
Ethiopia	1,790	1,290	500
Somalia	2,585	2,395	160

Source: adapted from US Central Intelligence Agency, *Communist Aid Activities in Non-Communist Less Developed Countries, 1979*, ER 80-10318U, October 1980, p. 16

'Moscow's man' out of ideological conviction or political opportunism or both. It will suffice here to note that the USSR may have been attracted by Mengistu's reputation for anti-Americanism. It was claimed he was radicalised by two visits to the USA in the late 1960s for military training. A combination of exposure to the Vietnam anti-war movement and the personal experience of racial insult allegedly embittered Mengistu towards the US.[243] But there was little evidence of his radicalism prior to the 1974 revolution. An alternative and more plausible interpretation of Mengistu's pro-Soviet stance was political expediency. Confronted with the social and ethnic convulsions created by the revolution, Mengistu coolly grasped the need for an ideological rationale to preserve Ethiopia's territorial integrity and, in doing so, legitimise his own political ambitions. The solution he found was Marxist–Leninism. This doctrine established Mengistu's revolutionary credentials at a time when his main rivals inside and outside the PMAC were Marxists, provided a ready-made scapegoat for existing troubles ('US imperialism') and held out the promise of a new source of external aid which was both more reliable and more interested than the US.

Despite the obscure nature of the Soviet–Mengistu connection, it was fair to assume the demise of Sisay Habte sent an important signal to Moscow. With the removal of two leading figures in the PMAC (General Aman Andom was the first), Moscow probably calculated that Mengistu, increasingly bolstered by the return of Soviet-trained military 'cadres', was odds-on favourite to win the power struggle in Addis Ababa. As a result, the Kremlin believed it was now in a position to reach for what it had always regarded as the major prize in the Horn – Ethiopia.

From July 1976 onwards, the USSR embarked on the ambitious

strategy of courting 'Socialist Ethiopia' without disturbing its friendship with Somalia. The new approach evolved in what was a bloody
setting. In the autumn of 1976, Ethiopia was plunged into a state of
virtual civil war. Isolated by the Dergue–Meison alliance of April 1976,
the main left-wing civilian opposition group, the EPRP, which
demanded the immediate establishment of a civilian regime, went
underground and launched an urban guerrilla war against the 'fascist'
Dergue. A wave of organised assassinations struck a succession of
prominent figures linked to the Dergue. In October and November,
the victims included Fikre Merid, a senior political adviser to the
PMAC and a Vice-Chairman of POMOA, Gebre Egziabher Hagos,
Minister of Education, an Assistant Professor at the Yekkatit 66' school
for the dissemination of Marxist ideology and Guetenet Zewde, the
Permanent Secretary of Labour and Social Affairs. Mengistu himself,
then Vice-Chairman of the PMAC, barely escaped an armed ambush
on 23 September 1976.[244]

The Dergue responded to these attacks with its own brand of 'red
terror'. In September 1976, the Ethiopian government introduced a
campaign of summary executions for 'counter-revolutionaries'.
Throughout October, November, December and well into 1977, Addis
Ababa radio regularly announced the execution of 'anarchists' and
'reactionaries' (meaning members of EPRP). Many killings, however,
went unreported, a trend, incidentally, which sharply increased after
the arrival of the Israeli-trained Fifth Division in the capital in mid-
November 1976. Known as the Nebalbal, and reportedly loyal to
Mengistu, this division was split into special units – 'Flame Squads' –
and given extensive powers to enter and search people's homes for
weapons. The result was sheer carnage. Thousands of people, even
children, were gunned down, sometimes for simply having anti-
Government leaflets in their possession or because they attended
demonstrations.[245]

To Moscow, the bloodbath in Addis Ababa was something of a
political opening.[246] Keenly aware of American embarrassment over
this turn of events – William Schaufele, the US Secretary of State for
African Affairs, was prompted to condemn the Dergue as 'unstable,
prone to violations of human rights, incapable of managing Ethiopia's
deteriorating economy, and beset by insurgencies and incipient
insurgencies'[247] – Moscow stepped up its vocal support for the
beleaguered Dergue. According to Soviet reports, the progressive
regime in Addis Ababa, faced with an inevitable 'intensification of the
class struggle',[248] was successfully 'liquidating counter-revolutionary

bands'. It was asserted that these 'decisive measures' enjoyed the support of the 'broadest layers' of Ethiopian society. Reaction had resorted to terrorist acts, sabotage, provocative rumours 'and demagogy' in a bid to 'hinder the implementation of deep socio-economic transformations'[249] in Ethiopia.

On 7 October 1976, the Soviet Ambassador called on Vice-Chairman of the PMAC, Mengistu, and conveyed the Soviet people's 'indignation'[250] at the attempt on his life. And, in what was an even more striking gesture of solidarity, the USSR, for the first time, condemned all civilian opposition to the Dergue as 'reactionary'. The 'remnants of the former exploiting class' and the 'so called EPRP', whose members were derisively listed as 'pro-Maoist leftists', 'Trotskyists' and 'paid agents of the CIA', were simply lumped together as tools of 'international imperialism'.[251] But, if the 'undefeated forces of reaction' were causing the PMAC 'significant difficulties',[252] *Pravda*, by October 1976, was adamant that 'the revolutionary process, which had begun in Ethiopia in September 1974, will not be reversed'.[253]

This pledge was not without substance. In December 1976, an Ethiopian military delegation (which may have included Mengistu) travelled to Moscow where it signed a secret arms deal. Under the agreement, which was the first of its kind between the two countries, Ethiopia was to receive second-line Soviet equipment like third generation T-34 tanks and artillery, estimated to be worth a total of $100 million.[254] In view of the fact that previous requests from the Mengistu faction for Soviet arms had been turned down, it is fair to assume this arms deal had some conditions attached to it. These are unknown, but it is likely the Soviets sought and were given an assurance that Ethiopia would sever the US military connection.[255] The change in the Soviet attitude was linked, amongst other things, to a new appointment in Moscow.

In December 1976, Anatoly Gromyko, formerly head of the foreign-policy section of the American Institute of the Soviet Academy of Sciences and son of the Soviet Foreign Minister, was appointed Director of the Institute of Africa. Unlike his predecessor, Vasily Solodovnikov (whose tolerance of internal disagreement over the issue of non-capitalist development implied a relatively cautious estimate of Soviet interests in Africa), Gromyko junior came to the job with a reputation for tough-mindedness, based on an uncompromising view of US 'imperialism':

> US foreign policy is wholly determined by the general interests of all th monopoly capital groups and these can be roughly summarised

as follows: Fight the socialist countries and progressive ideas; support the most reactionary, anti-popular regimes; suppress national liberation movements by means of the old colonialist methods and the newer more flexible tactics of neo-colonialism.[256]

The corollary of this view, then, was a belief in the necessity of a harder policy against the US, especially in areas where Washington's interests were seen as declining. The decision to arm Ethiopia must be seen in this light. Faced with a 'lame duck' Ford administration seeing out its time in Washington and backed by pro-Ethiopian sentiment in the Soviet Foreign Ministry establishment, the younger Gromyko was exceptionally well-placed to argue that arming Ethiopia was an essential step in making the USSR the dominant power in the Horn.

By displacing the US as Ethiopia's arms supplier, Gromyko junior and other Soviet observers believed that the USSR would be in a position to sponsor a political solution to the Ethiopian–Somali dispute: 'It is well known that the colonial partition of the Horn of Africa caused territorial-border disputes between Somalia and Ethiopia which were kept on the boil by the neo-colonialists.'[257] But with the elimination of the 'imperialist factor' from 'this important region', the prospects for reconciliation were seen as bright:

> The choice by both countries [Ethiopia and Somalia] of a non-capitalist path of development with an orientation towards socialism has for the first time after many years of alienation and hostility inspired the hope of a peaceful, friendly settlement of differences between brotherly African nations.[258]

It was admitted the two countries had 'different ethnic or religious and cultural features' but such differences, Moscow insisted, 'do not appear antagonistic'.[259] As a consequence, Anatoly Gromyko declared: 'We think it is possible to have a [Marxist–Leninist] federation in the Horn of Africa.'[260]

The Soviet media certainly tried to foster an improvement in Ethiopian–Somali relations. Reporting Siad's attendance at the extraordinary assembly of the OAU in Addis Ababa in January 1976, *Pravda* noted that Siad had 'fruitful, business-like meetings with the Ethiopian leaders'. During his stay, Siad was said to have paid tribute to 'progressive changes' in Ethiopia, and congratulated the new military regime on taking 'the right path'. He reportedly declared that Ethiopia and Somalia were 'geographically and historically closely linked' with 'much in common'.[261] Moscow also emphasised that in its bilateral dealings with Addis Ababa and Mogadishu both countries had publicly reaffirmed their commitment to peace in the Horn. For example, in the joint communique released at the end of the visit to Moscow by the Ethiopian delegation in July 1976, the Ethiopian side indicated 'its interests in strengthening relations of friendship and good neighbourliness among all the nations of the African Horn'.[262] Similarly, in August 1976, 'at a time when imperialism tried to create a new hotbed of tension in East Africa', a visiting Somali delegation told its Soviet hosts of its 'desire to bring about a situation whereby all countries of Eastern Africa will build their relations on the basis of peace, friendship and good-neighbourliness'.[263]

But the new Soviet approach took very little account of local realities. Between mid-1976 and early 1977, Ethiopian–Somali relations deteriorated rapidly. Unlike the USSR, Somalia seemed to actually welcome the chaos and anarchy that engulfed the Dergue, not least because it gave Mogadishu a chance to press its claim on the Ogaden. On 25 September 1976, President Siad accused Ethiopia of blocking a peaceful solution to 'the land and population issues'[264] dividing the two countries. He revealed the Ethiopian government had rejected his proposal in January 1976 to form a federation between Somalia and Ethiopia – the tabling of the proposal was confirmed by a Soviet source[265] – and warned the Dergue that, 'if we were provoked, there is no doubt that we would fiercely defend ourselves'.[266] The hardening of the Somali attitude must be seen against a backdrop of two important regional developments.

First, a major quarrel between Ethiopia and the Sudan left Addis Ababa desperately short of friends in the area. The starting point in this dispute was a Libyan-backed attempt to overthrow President J. Numeiry in July 1976. The attempt failed but Numeiry, who had earlier publicly endorsed the Dergue's nine-point peace plan for Eritrea, charged the Dergue with complicity in the conspiracy and retaliated by pledging support for Addis Ababa's enemies. In January 1977, Khartoum announced that the ELF and the EDU were among the opposition groups receiving Sudanese arms and training.[267] At the same time, the episode had the effect of strengthening ties between the Sudan and Somalia. In early 1977, the Somali government expressed full support for the Sudanese side by backing Numeiry's call to remove the OAU headquarters from Addis Ababa.[268] Second, and partly because of the Ethiopian–Sudanese rift, the military position of the Dergue in Eritrea worsened. Backed by a coalition of Arab states – Saudi Arabia, Egypt, Syria and North Yemen – the ELF and the EPLF inflicted a series of defeats on Ethiopia's demoralised army. It must be

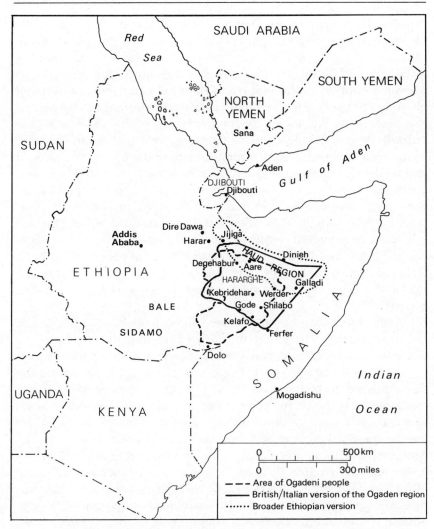

Map 5. The Ogaden. *Source*: Central Intelligence Agency, Washington D.C., USGPO, 1980.

stressed that the availability of the Sudan as a sanctuary for the Eritrean guerrillas played no small part in this success. From July 1976, practically all of the Ethiopian garrisons in Eritrea found themselves under active siege. On 5 January 1977, Karora became the first Eritrean town to be captured by the EPLF. About a month later, Um Hager fell to the ELF. Then, on 23 March 1977, the EPLF, for the first time, extended nationalist control over a district capital, Nacfa, in the Sahel province.[269]

In the circumstances, the Dergue was in no mood to listen to Siad's plea to 'humanly trust us'. On 14 October 1976, the Ethiopian Foreign Ministry accused Somalia of 'harbouring, arming and training reactionary and subversive elements' – a thinly veiled reference to Somalia's support of the WSLF and the ELF – and roundly declared 'there is no denying the fact that Somalia still has not abandoned its expansionist ambitions'.[270] By the beginning of 1977, Addis Ababa officially described Mogadishu as an 'enemy' of the revolution and one of the 'reactionary forces planning to invade the country.' The Siad regime dismissed these allegations as 'malicious propaganda'[271] and countered with its own charges. Nevertheless, it became plain there was some 'fire' behind this rhetorical 'smoke'. In December 1976-January 1977, major clashes between the Somali-backed WSLF and Ethiopian government troops in the Ogaden were reported.[272] More seriously, the first indications began to emerge in February 1977 of a series of Somali tank incursions into the Ogaden in support of the WSLF guerrillas.[273] The battle for the Ogaden was beginning (see Map 5).

Clearly, in trying to build a united front amongst its allies in the Horn, the USSR was either unable or unwilling to recognise the consequences of its past policy there. Having supplied the Somalis with sufficient arms to make a reasonable attempt at 'reuniting the dismembered Somali people and ... restoring the integrity of her territory'[274] (in the words of one-time Foreign Minister Omar Arteh Ghalib), the Soviet Union suddenly expected Somalia to trim its by now vibrant nationalism for the sake of ideological unity with its 'worst enemy'.[275] It was a prospect which positively alarmed Mogadishu. In early August 1976, just a month after the departure of the Ethiopian delegation, Vice-President and Defence Minister, Mohammed Ali Samantar paid an official visit to Moscow 'to cement' Soviet–Somali co-operation. The visit, however, fell short of its stated purpose.

Moscow tried to reassure Samantar about the Soviet–Ethiopian *rapprochement* by pledging that arms supplies would be maintained, possibly even increased, and that 'bilateral relations would continue to rest on principles of full equality, mutual respect and revolutionary solidarity.'[276] But these promises did not fully satisfy the Somalis. For one thing, they were communicated by a Soviet negotiating team which, in contrast to the one which received the Ethiopian delegation, lacked officials with the stature of Andrey Gromyko, the Foreign Minister, or A. N. Kosygin, the Chairman of the Council of Minis-

ters.[277] Furthermore, the Samantar delegation failed to win any statement of support for Somalia's claim on the Ogaden. Rather, Moscow
cast the blame on the 'forces of imperialism and reaction'[278] for any
possible conflicts in the Horn of Africa. The subsequent Soviet–
Ethiopian arms deal of December 1976 probably confirmed Mogadishu's worst fears about the shift in Soviet policy. Thus, while the
USSR seemed to understand Somali nationalism in the abstract – a
Soviet adviser in Mogadishu was quoted as saying any attempt to tell
the Somalis what to do would be met with the reply, 'Go to Hell'[279] – in
practice it attached greater weight to the attenuation of Western
interests in the Horn. And the final piece in this particular jig-saw was
about to fall into place.

On 3 February, Colonel Mengistu established himself as the undisputed leader of the PMAC. The method was both brutal and dramatic.
The Head of State, Brigadier-General Teferi Bante, and six prominent
members of the Dergue were killed in an armed confrontation at the
PMAC's headquarters. All of these victims were known opponents of
Mengistu. Four supporters of Mengistu also died in the fighting. The
showdown, which is still inadequately understood, may have centred
on the Soviet demand that the PMAC cut its military ties with
Washington.[280] This notion seemed to encounter fierce resistance
inside the Dergue. On 31 December 1976, the PMAC issued a proclamation announcing that its organisation was being formally restruc-
tured. Under the new arrangements, power was to be shared among a
Congress comprising all members (then thought to be about 100
strong), a Central Committee of 40 members and a 17-man Standing
Committee.[281] This new tripartite system of authority effectively
undermined Mengistu's power base by conferring new responsibili-
ties on his rivals (and future victims) within the Dergue. Amongst
other appointments, Teferi Bante, previously figurehead chairman of
the PMAC, was made Commander-in-Chief of the Armed Forces
while Captain Alemayehu Haile took over the key post of Secretary-
General of the PMAC. The reform, therefore, was a severe blow for
Mengistu and his supporters in the Kremlin. On top of this, on 29
January 1977, General Teferi Bante delivered what was widely
regarded as an anti-Mengistu diatribe on Ethiopian state radio. In his
speech, Teferi extended an olive branch to the EPRP by making an
impassioned appeal for the reconciliation of all 'progressive' forces in
the country.[282] Coming, however, after Mengistu had already taken
an extremely hard line against the EPRP, Bante's speech seemed to be
part of a manoeuvre to isolate Mengistu and then oust him from the

ruling Military Council. But, if this is true, it was Mengistu, not Teferi, who was able to strike first.

The USSR lost no time in recognising Mengistu's triumph. On 4 February, the Soviet Ambassador to Ethiopia, A. Ratanov, met with Mengistu to convey his congratulations and assure him of full Soviet backing. In the following days all Eastern European countries, as well as Cuba, sent messages of support to the new Ethiopian leader. At the same time, the Soviet media praised the 'revolutionary measures' taken on 3 February 'against groups of plotters inside the PMAC, who had prepared a counter-revolutionary coup along the lines of the Chilean model'.[283] *Pravda* added that the victory of Colonel Mengistu Haile Mariam, 'who in fact had been at the head of the revolutionary movement since February 1974',[284] coincided with new positive moves in Ethiopia. These included an 'important decree' in mid-February 1977 whereby the 'terms of reference' of the Dergue's Chairman were 'significantly broadened', a pledge by the Mengistu regime to follow 'the principles of scientific socialism', a renewed commitment to establish 'a party of the working class' and a declaration 'that the revolution was changing from the defensive to the offensive'.[285] Not on this list, but no less important to Moscow, was the Dergue's announcement, on 11 February 1977, that in future it would only buy arms from the 'socialist countries'.[286] The speed of the Soviet response, all the more remarkable after years of official caution, strongly implied that the Soviets knew of Mengistu's plans before 3 February. Indeed, an enigmatic observation by two Soviet commentators later in 1977 seems to point to the possibility of even deeper Soviet involvement in these events:

> The ability of the Ethiopian revolutionary democrats to form the leading force of social progress is due to the relationship between the Ethiopian revolution and more socially mature contingents of the world revolutionary process, which exercises a profound effect on the content and prospects of this revolution.[287]

With Mengistu installed as Head of State in Addis Ababa, Moscow felt the time was ripe to implement its Pax Sovietica strategy. In March 1977, the USSR launched a diplomatic initiative to resolve the Ethiopian–Somali conflict. The go-between in this effort was Cuba's President Fidel Castro, who visited Somalia on 13 March and Ethiopia on 14 March, and convened a joint meeting of Presidents Siad and Mengistu in Aden on 16 March 1977.[288] At the meeting, Castro presented a Soviet proposal that the two countries put aside their national differences and join a Marxist–Leninist confederation consisting of Ethiopia, Somalia, South Yemen and Djibouti (which was earmarked for independence in June 1977). Under this plan, which was underwritten by a Soviet guarantee of economic and military support,[289] the trouble spots Eritrea and the Ogaden, following minor frontier rectifications in the Hararghe province, would be granted the status of autonomous regions within the existing border arrangements of Ethiopia.[290] From a Soviet standpoint such a formula had obvious advantages. Not only would it have sustained Soviet influence in both Ethiopia and Somalia, it also denied the possibility of Eritrean independence and thus put the USSR in a unique position to dominate the strategically important Straits of Bab el Mendeb. All this, however, counted for nothing.

While Mengistu welcomed what was basically a pro-Ethiopian solution, President Siad angrily rebuffed the Soviet proposal. The Somali leader argued that a federation was fruitless unless all peoples within it had been granted the right to national self-determination. On this view, Eritrea was entitled to be a member of the federation in its own right and the Ogaden or 'Western Somalia' should have the option of joining either as an independent unit or as part of Somalia. The Aden meeting ended, somewhat predictably, on a note of bitter recrimination with, amongst other things, Siad accusing Mengistu of having a colonial mentality.[291]

The failure of the Pax Sovietica plan was a watershed for Soviet policy in the Horn. Not for the first time, Moscow had become a victim of its own Marxist–Leninist ideology. By assuming an absolute connection between perceived global trends – in the mid-1970s the Soviet Foreign Minister flatly declared that 'socialism is now the most dynamic and influential force on the world scene'[292] – and the local situation in the Horn, the USSR disastrously underestimated the national and ethnic rivalries peculiar to the region. To many observers in the Third World, the idea of a Marxist–Leninist confederation was doomed from the outset. It was variously described as 'misconceived',[293] 'based on inaccurate information'[294] and yet another example of the Soviet Union 'trying to create an Africa after her own image'.[295] But, if the failure of the Castro mission did not appear to shake Moscow's immediate confidence in a Pax Sovietica solution, it certainly relieved the Soviet leadership of any lingering illusions about Mogadishu's commitment to 'scientific socialism'. By rejecting the Soviet peace plan, President Siad made it plain that Moscow would not be able to avoid the burden of choice if it wished to retain a foothold in the Horn of Africa. As will soon be apparent the USSR was not slow to give its answer.

6   War, realignment and the enforcement of proletarian internationalism

> When Somali troops invaded the territory of Ethiopia, the USSR sided with the victim of aggression, proceeding from the fundamental principles of its foreign policy, and at the request of Ethiopia is giving the country the appropriate material and technical assistance.   (*Pravda*, 22 January 1978)

> We will teach the Somalis a lesson they will never forget. They will be pushed back from the Ogaden and we will be back in Somalia – we will bring them to their knees.
> (Georgiy Samsonov, Soviet Ambassador to Somalia, quoted in
> *Newsweek*, 13 February 1978, p. 14)

In the space of just one year, Soviet policy in the Horn underwent a complete somersault. After the failure of the Marxist–Leninist confederation proposal in March 1977, Moscow made the critical decision that if a choice had to be made between Somalia and Ethiopia, it would opt for the latter. On 23 April 1977, the leader of the Dergue, Lt.-Col. Mengistu Haile Mariam, cleared the way for Moscow by expelling all US military advisers from Ethiopia and closing the Kagnew Communications Station and other US facilities in the country. Two weeks later, the new Soviet–Ethiopian alliance assumed a formal shape. On 6 May, during an official visit to the USSR, Mengistu signed a 'Declaration on the Foundations of Friendly Relations and Co-operation'[1] between the USSR and Ethiopia. At the same time, the Soviet government concluded its second major arms package with Mengistu, reportedly worth $385 million.[2] The agreement coincided with reports that a substantial number of Cuban military advisers had arrived in Addis Ababa.

These developments alarmed Somalia. On 17 May, President Siad publicly characterised Soviet military aid to Ethiopia as a 'danger' to his government. The Soviet media ignored this charge, except to say 'imperialist' efforts to divide Somalia from the USSR were 'doomed to failure'.[3] But Moscow's stubborn attempt to play both sides in the Horn was finally sunk by the full-scale Somali invasion of the Ogaden on 23 July 1977. Few options were left for Moscow. On 17 August, the Soviet Union for the first time openly took a pro-Ethiopian stance toward the conflict. It accused Somalia of 'armed intervention in Ethiopia's internal affairs'[4] and subsequently announced the cessation of all arms deliveries to Mogadishu. The latter reacted sharply. Accusing the USSR of 'brazen interference' in the Horn of Africa, Somalia, on 13 November 1977, expelled all Soviet military advisers and abrogated the 1974 Tready of Friendship and Co-operation.

Thirteen days later, on 26 November, the Soviets launched a huge air and sealift of equipment and personnel to Ethiopia. Altogether, the USSR ferried in over one billion dollars worth of arms, some 12,000 Cuban combat troops and about 1,500 Soviet military advisers.[5] Predictably, this massive intervention – given the absence of any equivalent Western support for Somalia – changed the course of the war. By January 1978, the Ethiopian–Cuban forces, under the direction of the Deputy Commander-in-Chief of Soviet Ground Forces, were strong enough to mount a counteroffensive. The back of Somali resistance was soon broken. On 5 March 1978, the Ethiopians regained control of the key town, Jijiga. And, on 9 March, President Siad announced the withdrawal of what was left of his army from the Ogaden. The Ethiopian–Somali war was officially over.

Thus, Soviet-backed Ethiopia had prevailed against Soviet-armed and Soviet-trained Somali forces. In effect, Moscow established the parameters of the conflict and then assured an outcome considered favourable to Soviet interests.

The Soviet disengagement

Following the failure to reconcile Ethiopia and Somalia by diplomatic means, the USSR boldly adopted what might be termed a 'first among equals' strategy in the Horn. That is to say, while Moscow still hoped the Somalis would in the end come round to accepting its Pax Sovietica plan, it decided in the meantime to make Ethiopia its top priority in the region. This strategy was apparently based on the assumption that Somalia's military reliance on Moscow would eventually force President Siad to come to terms with the new Soviet–Ethiopian alliance. After all, the Somali leader had told President Castro 'that they would never invade Ethiopia, that they would never carry out a military attack'.[6]

In the spring of 1977, the USSR moved swiftly to complete its displacement of the US in Ethiopia. On 24 February 1977, the new Carter administration angered Addis Ababa by publicly confirming the cancellation of military-aid grants to Ethiopia, worth $6 million, because of consistent violations of human rights. The Dergue countered by ordering the closure of four US organisations and expelling more than 300 American officials on 23 April. The facilities affected were the 100-man Military Assistance Advisory Group (MAAG), the Kagnew Communications Station, the Naval Medical Research Unit and the US Information Service. In addition, the PMAC ordered the US and five of its allies to close their consulates in Asmara, and ejected three resident Western correspondents. The US retaliated against these 'unwarranted' actions on 28 April by halting all arms deliveries and terminating the $100 million military sales credit programme under which Ethiopia was to have received more F-5E Tiger jet aircraft, M-60 tanks and ammunition.[7]

Moscow welcomed the 'resolute steps' taken in Ethiopia against Western 'subversion'. The Dergue, it was noted, had 'put an end to the activity of the American military advisers and other organisations serving as a cover for the CIA destabilisation operation in Ethiopia'.[8] But, while Mengistu claimed the break with the US was a matter of principle, it was instructive that he only moved against Washington after tangible proof of the Soviet commitment. In March 1977, Ethiopia received its first consignment of Soviet arms. These included about thirty elderly T-34 tanks, forty armoured personnel carriers and some anti-aircraft guns. It was also reported that General Arnaldo Ochoa, Cuba's Deputy Minister of Defence, had arrived in Addis Ababa accompanied by 200 Cuban advisers to help train the Ethiopians to use Soviet weapons.[9]

With the Americans finally out of the picture, the Soviets were free to consolidate their new position in Ethiopia. On 3 May, Mengistu was received with full honours in Moscow. The Soviet media gave the Ethiopian leader's first official trip abroad extensive coverage. Hailed as 'an outstanding leader of the Ethiopian revolution',[10] Mengistu held talks with President N. Podgorny, General Secretary of the CPSU, L. I. Brezhnev and Foreign Minister, Andrey Gromyko. The discussions took place 'in an atmosphere of friendship and complete mutual understanding'. A number of agreements were concluded. The two sides signed a protocol on economic and technical co-operation, an agreement on cultural and scientific co-operation and a consular convention. More importantly, a 'Declaration on the Principles of Friendly Relations and Co-operation' and the joint communique, issued on 9 May, revealed firm Soviet political and military support for 'Socialist Ethiopia'.[11]

If the form of the declaration showed a Soviet concern for Somali sensitivities – a declaration was still a level lower than the Soviet–Somali Treaty of Friendship – its substance certainly did not. Amongst other things, the document repudiated Somali claims to the Ogaden by stressing respect for 'the territorial integrity of states and the inviolability of state boundaries'.[12] The communique went further. The Soviet side 'supported the moves undertaken by the PMAC for the democratic solution of the nationalities question' and condemned, without mentioning Somalia by name, 'the intrigues of the imperialist and other reactionary circles' in the Horn of Africa. These very same forces, according to Podgorny, were 'seeking to exploit' Ethiopia's nationalities problem in order 'to create some kind of exclusive military–political bloc'[13] in the Red Sea area. This was almost certainly an allusion to Saudi and Sudanese efforts to detach Somalia from the USSR and involve it in a regional security pact. The communique also hinted at the expansion of Soviet military aid to Ethiopia. It was noted that the USSR 'expressed solidarity with the efforts of the people and leadership of Ethiopia defending revolutionary gains'. This statement followed the disclosure that both General S. L. Sokolov, the Soviet Deputy Defence Minister, a key figure in the Somali military aid programme, and Defence Minister D. Ustinov participated in talks with the visiting Mengistu delegation.[14] No details of the discussions were printed in the Soviet press but, according to Western reports, the USSR concluded a second major arms deal with Ethiopia, worth around $385 million. The agreement apparently consisted of 48 MiG-21 interceptors, up to 200 T-54 and T-55 tanks, an unknown number of SAM-3 and SAM-7 anti-aircraft missile batteries and Sagger anti-tank missiles. Mengistu himself all but confirmed such an arms deal. On his return home on 10 May (via Bulgaria and possibly Libya) Mengistu said 'all the socialist countries were ready to give the necessary support for the bitter revolutionary struggle of the broad masses of Ethiopia'.[15] In subsequent weeks, the Cuban presence in Ethiopia steadily increased and the delivery of Soviet arms began to gather momentum. At first, Soviet arms were shipped to Ethiopia from South Yemen via the port of Djibouti. However, after the establishment of a direct air link between Moscow and Addis Ababa on 21 July 1977, the Soviet arms build up accelerated. By late summer, it was

Table 11. *Soviet trade with Ethiopia and Somalia, 1970–1978 (millions of roubles)*

	1970			1971			1972			1973			1974		
	Exp.	Imp.	Turn.	Exp.	Imp.	Turn.	Exp.	Imp.	Turn.	Exp.	Imp.	Turn.	Exp.	Imp.	Turn.
Ethiopia	1.3	0.8	2.1	1.3	2.9	4.2	1.6	2.1	3.7	1.6	2.2	3.8	2.6	3.6	6.2
Somalia	2.8	0.4	3.2	5.5	1.8	7.3	11.7	2.9	14.6	11.5	1.1	12.6	16.8	2.0	18.8

	1975			1976			1977			1978		
	Exp.	Imp.	Turn.	Exp.	Imp.	Turn.	Exp.	Imp.	Turn.	Exp.	Imp.	Turn.
Ethiopia	3.2	2.1	5.3	3.6	0.7	4.3	22.4	1.5	23.9	64.2	4.3	68.5
Somalia	22.2	4.3	26.5	18.7	4.7	23.4	20.1	2.9	23.0	0	0	0

Note: exports (Exp.) are from the USSR; imports (Imp.) are to the USSR; turnover (Turn.) refers to the total trade between the two countries

Source: *Vneshnyaya Torgovlya za SSSR*, Moscow, Statistika, various years

reported that five planeloads of arms shipments were arriving at Addis Ababa airport each week.[16]

Moscow expanded its links with Ethiopia in other spheres. On a humanitarian level, the Soviet Red Cross organisation announced on 25 May 1977 that it was to reconstruct and enlarge the Russian hospital in Addis Ababa.[17] It was also agreed to send more Soviet doctors to assist their Ethiopian counterparts. Political and cultural contacts were likewise extended. On 10 June, the USSR and Ethiopia signed a television and radio co-operation agreement. On 6 July, the formation of an Ethiopian–Soviet Friendship and Solidarity committee in Addis Ababa was announced.[18] In between these events, the head of the Ethiopian Church attended a conference of Church leaders in Moscow. The visit apparently convinced him that freedom of religion existed in the USSR.[19] Then, on 22 July 1977, the USSR and Ethiopia signed a new trade agreement, replacing the existing trade agreement which had been in force since 11 July 1959. Details about the new arrangement were scarce, but it would appear Moscow substantially increased the export of agricultural machinery, building materials, medicines and cultural products to Ethiopia in return for a relatively small increase in the import of traditional Ethiopian goods like coffee, oil seeds and pulses.[20] As a consequence, the volume of Soviet–Ethiopian trade grew from 4.3 million roubles to 23.9 million roubles[21] (see Table 11). This was more than a 500 per cent increase. Moreover, in the space of just one year, Soviet trade with Addis Ababa had overtaken that with Somalia, Moscow's long-time ally in the region.

Needless to say, President Siad did not share Moscow's enthusiasm for the Dergue. In the first half of 1977, the fighting in the Ogaden province rapidly escalated. The WSLF, taking advantage of the Dergue's preoccupation with the Eritrean crisis and sensing that the power of the Ethiopian Army would soon be enhanced by Soviet arms deliveries, stepped up its operations. Something like 6,000 well-armed and highly mobile guerrillas carried out a concerted campaign of sabotage and harassment throughout the Ogaden. Targets included key transportation routes, Ethiopian army convoys, police stations and army bases. The worst blow was delivered on 1 June, when WSLF guerrillas destroyed five bridges on the Addis Ababa–Djibouti railway and thus cut Ethiopia's only direct rail link to the sea. Ethiopia blamed this incident and other attacks in the province on 'Somali-trained infiltrators'.[22]

Mogadishu vehemently denied Ethiopian charges. The Siad regime claimed the Ogaden was simply witnessing a local liberation struggle waged by the WSLF against Ethiopian colonial occupation. The same statement was repeated again and again. Such an explanation, however, had a hollow ring to it. The Somali government admitted that regular Somali troops 'on leave' were being allowed to 'volunteer' for duty with the WSLF guerrillas. Nor did Mogadishu attempt to conceal its hostility towards the Mengistu regime. Unlike Moscow, President Siad saw the Dergue as 'neither Marxist nor Leninist, neither socialist nor democratic'.[23] While Siad categorically disavowed any intention to invade Ethiopia, he warned that Mogadishu could not accept Ethiopia's 'continued colonisation of Somali territory'.[24]

The growing tension between Ethiopia and Somalia worried Moscow. On 2 April 1977, President N. V. Podgorny, who was in Africa visiting Tanzania, Zambia and Mozambique, paid a short 'unofficial visit' to Mogadishu. The talks centred on 'questions of the development of Soviet–Somali relations' and 'an exchange of views on current international problems and especially about the situation on the African continent'[25] (meaning the Horn of Africa). Apparently, Podgorny urged Siad to be patient. But this advice did not impress the Somali leader: 'Who can guarantee us that once his regime is consolidated and his army strengthened, Mengistu will consent to negotiate the territorial conflict between us so as to find a solution that complies with the wishes of the Somali people in the Ogaden?'[26] The Soviet–Somali negotiations ended in failure.

After Mengistu's visit to Moscow in May, the rift between the USSR and Somalia visibly widened. Siad publicly warned Moscow that Somalia would make 'a historic decision' if the Soviet Union continued to arm Ethiopia. 'We would not,' he said, 'be able to remain idle in the face of the danger of the Soviet Union's arming of Ethiopia.' At the same time, Vice-President and Defence Minister, Mohammed Ali Samantar summoned the ambassadors of the Warsaw Pact countries and made it plain that continued Soviet and Cuban aid to the 'false regime'[27] in Addis Ababa would endanger Somalia's relations with these countries. Somali anger further increased when it became known that Soviet military advisers, some of whom were transferred directly from Mogadishu, had arrived in Addis Ababa. Old signs of Soviet–Somali friendship quickly disappeared. Posters in Mogadishu showing a white hand shaking a black one over a hammer and sickle were removed. There were also reports of assaults on Soviet and Cuban personnel by Somali citizens.[28] Moreover, Somalia now began to explore its options of support elsewhere.

One option was China. In January 1977, Siad sent a congratulatory message to Chairman Hua saying that 'the militant friendly relations and bonds of co-operation and understanding between Somalia and China would without doubt be further consolidated'. Six months later, Vice-President Ismail Ali Abokor led a Somali government delegation to Peking. The delegation had talks with senior Chinese officials including Chairman Hua. The Chinese reportedly offered spare parts for some of Somalia's older Soviet weapons, and agreed to supply Mogadishu with some quantities of small arms.[29] In addition, Somalia cultivated her links with the Arab states. On 22–3 March 1977 (after the meeting with Castro in Aden), President Siad attended a summit meeting in Taiz, North Yemen, with the leaders of the Sudan and both North and South Yemen. Though formally arranged by the Sudan, the conference was strongly backed by Egypt and, in particular, by Saudi Arabia. The purpose of the meeting was to discuss ways of making the Red Sea an 'Arab Lake', free of Soviet and Israeli influence. Siad took the opportunity to publicly endorse this scheme and, as a result, contacts between Somalia and Saudi Arabia increased thereafter. On 5 and 6 April 1977, Siad played host to the Saudi Foreign Minister, Prince Saud al-Faisal. The latter reaffirmed an earlier offer to grant $300–350 million in assistance,[30] including funds for the purchase of arms from the West, if Somalia ended its military ties with the USSR. On 12–13 July, Siad visited Riyadh for talks on 'the security of the Red Sea'. Somalia also bolstered its ties with several other pro-Western Middle Eastern states. In April 1977, the Somali Minister of Culture and Higher Education, Omar Arteh Ghalib (a former Foreign Minister) toured the United Arab Emirates (UAE), Qatar, Bahrain and Kuwait. In May, a month in which the Sudan upset the USSR by expelling all ninety of the Soviet military advisers there, Somalia demonstrated its solidarity with Khartoum by sending Vice-President Hussein Kulmi Afrah to attend the eighth anniversary celebrations of the Sudanese revolution.[31] Several weeks later, on 25 May 1977, the Iranian Foreign Minister, Abbas Ali Khalatlari arrived in Mogadishu to discuss the provision of oil supplies and the possibility of ending Somalia's oil dependence on the USSR. This was followed by the visit of an UAE delegation to Somalia in early June, and a return trip by Siad himself to the UAE on 23–4 June for 'urgent discussions' on the regional situation. Altogether, during the first six months of 1977, visits between government officials of Somalia and conservative Arab states totalled around sixty.[32]

Furthermore, the Somalis sought arms from the West. The first feelers were put out to the United States in February 1977.[33] The Carter administration, however, did not respond until after the decline in Ethiopian–American relations in the spring of 1977. On 6 April, President Carter told his aides 'to move in every possible way to get Somalia to be our friend'.[34] For its part, the Somali government began to relax its anti-Western stance. Siad received technical aid missions from the US, Britain and the EEC, and signed contracts with companies like Hawker Siddely and the Westinghouse Corporation. On 16 June, Carter received a formal request for arms from the Somali Ambassador in Washington, Ahmed Addou. According to a US official who was present at the meeting, Carter replied that the US could only provide defensive weaponry, and even this provision would depend upon the existence of a genuine threat to Somali security.[35] At roughly the same time, Dr Kevin Cahill, Siad's personal physician and an American citizen, conveyed a message to the Somali President that was allegedly from the State Department. Siad was told that Washington was 'not averse to further guerrilla pressure in the Ogaden' and was willing to consider Somalia's 'defence needs'.[36] On 1 July, the US Secretary of State, Cyrus Vance, also sent what may have been viewed as a positive signal to Somalia. Vance said that 'we will consider sympathetically appeals for assistance from states which are threatened by a build up of foreign military equipment and advisers on their borders, in the Horn and elsewhere in Africa'.[37] On 26 July, the US State Department announced that Washington (with Britain and France) was 'in principle' prepared to provide 'defensive weapons'[38] to Somalia. But this was not the end of that particular story.

In a sense, Somalia's maverick diplomacy justified Soviet involvement in Ethiopia. For one thing, Siad's participation in the Taiz summit angered Moscow. According to one Soviet writer, the proposal for an 'Arab lake' 'plainly smells of nationalism, particularly since not all the littoral countries are Arab – not to mention the matter of the national affiliation of the ships which pass through the Red Sea'. Such a scheme, therefore, was intended to 'incite the Arab countries against Ethiopia, which itself has a Red Sea coastline of 625 miles' and had 'anti-Soviet motives'[39] as well. Consequently, Siad's presence at Taiz fuelled the Soviet suspicion that he was 'a petty bourgeoise nationalist' and a 'parasite'[40] trying to exploit both sides. This suspicion plus the desire to resist Soviet exclusion from the Red Sea area led to strong expressions of concern about Ethiopia's growing security problems.

Officially, Moscow portrayed the threat to 'progressive' Ethiopia as coming from US imperialism and its 'local accomplices', Saudi Arabia, Sudan and Eritrean 'separatists'.[41] However, the USSR also made it clear, in a series of tough but coded warnings, that it was aware of Somali-backed strife in the Ogaden. On 28 April 1977, the Soviet Afro–Asian Solidarity Committee, 'on behalf of the multi-million Soviet public', condemned 'acts of aggression' against Ethiopia as 'a gross violation of the universally accepted norms of international law'.[42] Then, on 6 June 1977, with the Ogaden guerrilla campaign in full swing, Moscow cautioned those 'circles which are preparing to undertake an aggression against Ethiopia' that they risked 'playing with fire'.[43] Despite the strains, Moscow wanted to preserve its friendship with Somalia. The same was true for Mogadishu. But each side wanted friendship on its own terms. In the ensuing tug of war, several new agreements emerged. These included a two-year co-operation agreement between the Soviet Association for Friendship with African People and the International Department of the SRSP and an extension of Somali naval facilities to the Soviet fleet in the Indian Ocean Region.[44] In addition, the Soviet media went to great pains to generally project a positive image of Soviet–Somali relations. The Somali leadership was quoted as saying the two countries were linked by 'a common ideology', that the USSR was a 'reliable and true friend' of the Somalis, and that the two sides enjoyed increasingly 'fruitful co-operation'.[45] In this vein, a Somali visitor to Moscow observed that Soviet aid had helped Mogadishu achieve 'substantial successes in all sectors of the national economy'.[46] President Siad himself showed a willingness to play this strange double game:

> The USSR has the sovereign right to aid whoever it wishes. But we think that we can still explain to our Soviet friends our appreciation of the situation and tell them that we cannot remain indifferent to the strengthening of a regime which is hostile to us and which is colonising part of our national territory. But this policy of the USSR in no way calls into question our agreements and the close relations we have with it.[47]

Towards the end of May 1977, the Somali Vice-President and Defence Minister, M. A. Samantar, travelled to Moscow in another bid to patch things up. He had talks with L. Brezhnev, Andrey Gromyko and B. Ponomarev, the Secretary of the CPSU Central Committee and in charge of the International Department. According to one account, Samantar emphasised to the Soviet leaders that they could not befriend both Somalia and Ethiopia.[48] A Soviet statement simply confirmed the talks 'devoted much time to the issues concerning the

Horn of Africa' where 'imperialist and reactionary forces have stepped up their aggression in the region with the aim of starting another war'.[49] But the Somalis did not share this analysis. The talks proved to be largely unproductive. While Moscow expressed confidence 'that relations between the two countries are developing well',[50] the fact remained that Samantar's visit yielded no conclusions and no joint communique.

With Moscow unwilling to withdraw its support for Ethiopia, Somalia decided to present the USSR (and the rest of the world) with a *fait accompli* solution to the Ogaden problem. Concerned that Somalia's recent military superiority over Addis Ababa would soon be nullified by the arrival of Soviet arms, conscious of Ethiopia's stunning reverses in Eritrea in July 1977, encouraged by Arab and Western promises of help and, lastly, fearful of ignoring the groundswell of nationalist sentiment inside Somalia, the Siad regime resolved to exploit a 'historic opportunity'[51] to recover the 'lost lands'. On 23 July 1977, the Somali Army launched a general offensive in the Ogaden in support of the WSLF insurgents (see Map 6). Between July and September 1977, the Somali campaign in the Ogaden was extremely successful. Through a series of lightening strikes, the Somali forces captured virtually all of the important towns in the southern part of the Ogaden. These included Degahabur, Kebridehar, Werder and Gode. On 15 August, Ethiopian aircraft reportedly bombed towns in northern Somalia. Ethiopia and Somalia were now engaged in full-scale war. Diplomatic relations were severed on 7–8 September; and Mengistu ordered a national mobilisation against the 'open invasion' by Somalia. By mid-September 1977, the Somali side had gained control, even by Addis Ababa's own admission, of 90 per cent of the disputed area.[52] The most telling blow came on 13 September when the Somalis overran Jijiga, Ethiopia's main tank and radar base and gateway to Dire Dawa and Harar, two strategic towns in the Hararghe region. At this stage, Ethiopia appeared to be facing defeat. But, if Somalia was winning the war on the battlefield, the opposite was true on the diplomatic front.

Mogadishu's repeated claim that it was 'not implicated'[53] in the fighting failed to impress the eight-nation OAU mediation committee. Convened in Libreville between 5 and 9 August 1977, the committee passed a resolution which reaffirmed the inviolability of African frontiers and, in effect, upheld the Ethiopian position. The inability to establish the justice of the Somali case in Africa undermined Siad's efforts to secure foreign support. In early August 1977, the US,

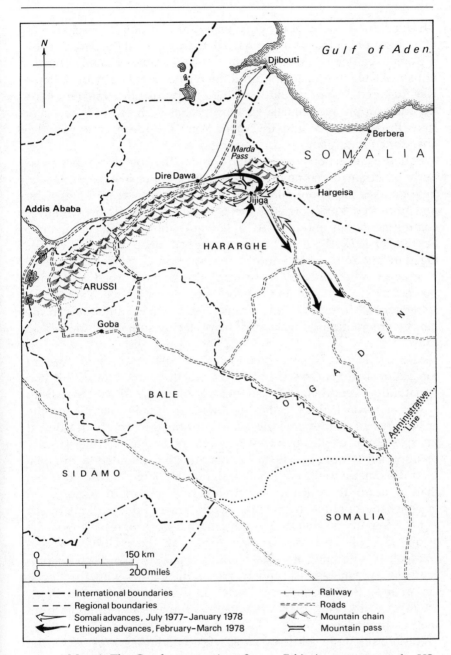

Map 6. The Ogaden campaign. *Source*: *Ethiopia: a country study*, US Government Printing Office, Washington D.C., 1981, p. 270.

'shocked' by the scale of the Ogaden fighting, promptly rescinded its offer to supply Somalia with arms. Belatedly aware of the participation of Somali regular forces in the conflict, the US argued it could not make arms available to Mogadishu until the territorial integrity of Ethiopia was 'restored'.[54] Nor would Washington approve the transfer of any US arms supplies to Somalia via third parties such as Saudi Arabia or Iran. Britain, France and the other West European countries also abandoned their plans to arm the Somalis.

Equally, the response of the Arab world to the Somali campaign was fairly constrained. While pro-Western Arab states like Saudi Arabia, Egypt and Sudan individually declared their support for Mogadishu and protested loudly against the US volte-face, their own military commitment was modest. At a Foreign Ministers' meeting on 5 September 1977, the Arab League expressed 'deep concern' over the Ogaden but refused to endorse the position of Somalia, an Arab League member since 1974. Instead, the League urged all foreign powers to 'stay out and let the peoples of the region reach a peaceful settlement'.[55] Ironically, only China, a state whose ambitions in the Horn were political rather than military, tacitly supported the Somali cause.[56]

Meanwhile, Moscow wobbled towards a position of all-out support for Ethiopia. Embarrassed by the Somali invasion – the USSR had apparently given Mengistu assurances in March 1977 that Mogadishu would not attack the Ogaden[57] – Moscow initially maintained the appearance of even-handedness and continued to arm both sides. It interpreted the conflict between Ethiopia and Somalia as a classic case of 'imperialist' intrigue. The tactic was probably intended to win time for a diplomatic solution. In this fashion, the Soviet media observed that in order to control this 'strategically important region', US imperialism sought to 'dismember revolutionary Ethiopia' and 'by the same token to disable and render harmless, progressive Somalia also'.[58] To this end, the US was 'using all the methods of neo-colonialism – fanning nationalism and separatism to discredit progressive African regimes and to smear their links with the Soviet Union and other socialist countries'[59] in the Red Sea area. In short, attempts were being made 'to separate Somalia and Ethiopia from their natural allies'.[60]

At the same time, Moscow indicated it had little sympathy for the 'so called Western Somali Liberation Front' and exerted considerable pressure on Siad to halt the fighting. This effort took several forms. Firstly, there was diplomatic pressure. On 6 August, the quasi-official

Soviet Afro-Asian Solidarity Committee deplored the 'alarming news' of armed clashes in 'Eastern Ethiopia' involving 'regular units of the Somali armed forces'.[61] The committee called for an immediate cease-fire and reaffirmed its support for Article 3 of the OAU Charter regarding the territorial integrity of each state:

> Practice has confirmed that violation of these principles and attempts to use force in recarving the existing frontiers, no matter what justification is made, damage the anti-imperialist unity of the African peoples and only assist the imperialist forces.[62]

Convinced that a 'political settlement' was 'the sole right and sensible way out', the USSR again floated its Marxist–Leninist federation proposal. Berhanu Bayeh, the PMAC's head of Foreign Affairs, secretly met a Somali delegation in Moscow in early August. As before, the talks ended in deadlock.[63]

Secondly, the USSR introduced selective military sanctions against Somalia. On the one hand, Moscow initiated a cut-back of its technical and military personnel in Mogadishu. In July 1977, about 1,200 Soviet advisers were directly airlifted to Addis Ababa from Somalia. It was reported that many of those who left took with them advanced weaponry such as Styx missiles and some MiG fighter-planes.[64] On the other hand, Moscow began to manipulate the supply of arms to Mogadishu. After the Somali invasion on 23 July 1977, the Kremlin suspended shipments of spare parts and military equipment. Then, on 7 August, the USSR suddenly resumed military supplies to Somalia. However, Moscow warned the Somali leadership that it would be further 'sanctioned' if the fighting with Ethiopia persisted. This was not an empty threat. By the end of August, the USSR was reportedly withholding small arms and, according to the Somali National Security Chief, Colonel Ahmed Suleiman Abdulle, had generally slowed down its arms deliveries to Mogadishu.[65]

Thirdly, Moscow sought to restrain Somalia through economic inducements. As if to remind Mogadishu that Soviet aid projects 'constitute the foundation of the state sector of the economy without which Somalia's further progress is inconceivable',[66] the USSR signed two new economic agreements with the Siad regime. On 17 August 1977 – almost a month after the Somali attack on the Ogaden – the two countries concluded an agreement which included continuation of work on the Fanole Dam project. Shortly afterwards, the USSR and Somalia reached an understanding on a water-location survey said to be worth 30 million Somali Shillings or nearly $5 million.[67]

These Soviet measures, however, required time to be effective. And time was running out. So long as the Somali forces were clearly winning the Ogaden war, Siad was in no mood to heed Soviet pleas to stop the fighting. Moreover, Mengistu was getting impatient with Soviet 'even-handedness'. In mid-August, the Ethiopian leader publicly questioned Soviet arms aid to Somalia:

> We had not suspected that they [the Somalis] would wage an attack against the Ethiopian revolution with the arms which the socialist countries had given them . . . We have found the situation extremely controversial, difficult to believe and one which perplexes genuine revolutionaries.[68]

With little or no room left for manoeuvre, the Soviet government decided to publicly commit itself. On 17 August 1977, *Izvestiya* condemned Somalia's 'armed intervention' in 'Ethiopia's domestic affairs' and said that even 'the noble pretext of exercising the principle of self-determination'[69] did not justify such an act. But, in what was a last-ditch Soviet effort to dissuade Somalia from the course it was taking, President Siad was invited to Moscow for consultations. All the evidence suggested the three-day visit (29–31 August) went badly. While Siad had talks with Kosygin, Suslov and Gromyko, he was not received by Brezhnev. A short *Tass* statement at the end of the talks merely said the two sides 'exchanged views on questions of mutual interest'. Nothing was said about the substance of the discussions. But it is safe to assume Soviet officials rejected Siad's contention that Somalis living in the Ogaden deserved self-determination as nationalist 'narrow-mindedness'.[70]

From then on, the USSR and Somalia were on a collision course. Although Moscow continued to profess goodwill towards both parties, the top Soviet priority now was to strengthen the military position of Ethiopia. After the Somali victory at Jijiga on 13 September, the Ethiopian Army was engaged in a desperate rearguard struggle to hang on to the last two strongholds in the Ogaden region – Harar and Dire Dawa. But increased delivery of Soviet arms and the arrival of a South Yemeni brigade began to turn the tide in Ethiopia's favour. In late September 1977, Addis Ababa for the first time received substantial quantities of crated MiG-21 jet fighters, 'Stalin Organs' (batteries of 40 122mm rockets mounted on lorries) and new T-55 tanks.[71] These arms, along with South Yemeni troops and a growing number of Soviet and Cuban military advisers, were rushed to the front-line. From mid-October 1977 onwards, this combination played a crucial role in denying Harar and Dire Dawa to the Somalis. The period of the rout was over. At this stage, though, Moscow was unwilling to publicly acknowledge Soviet bloc military involvement. This support also had an internal dimension. As previously noted, Addis Ababa and many of the major Ethiopian towns were in a virtual state of 'anarchy' during 1977 as the PMAC and EPRP waged urban guerrilla warfare. In September 1977, Mengistu's campaign against the 'counter-revolutionaries' was boosted by advisers from the German Democratic Republic (GDR).[72] They were given responsibility for organising the Dergue's internal security apparatus and instructing the Soviet-equipped 'People's Militia' in such techniques as house-to-house combat.

In contrast, the USSR systematically reduced its support for Somalia: fuel shipments were cut off; and arms deliveries were squeezed another notch. By mid-September 1977, Mogadishu was only receiving spare parts and some light arms. Delivery of heavy weapons ceased altogether.[73] Nevertheless, Mengistu remained uneasy about what remained of the Soviet–Somali connection. At a press conference on 18 September, the Ethiopian leader floated the idea of fresh American arms supplies and warned Moscow that 'if socialist countries are still supplying arms to Somalia, then this is not only violating one's principles, but also tantamount to complicity with the reactionary Mogadishu regime'.[74] This public rebuke had the desired effect.

On 18 October 1977, Anatoly Ratanov, the Soviet Ambassador to Ethiopia, announced that the USSR had completely stopped supplying arms to Somalia and was now providing Ethiopia with 'defensive weapons to protect her revolution'.[75] Five days later, in the clearest statement of policy since the war began in the Horn of Africa, Ratanov pledged total Soviet support for 'the Ethiopian side in the defence of its revolution and unity'.[76] To underline the message, the USSR and Cuba did not send the traditional greetings to President Siad on 21 October 1977, the eighth anniversary of the Somali revolution – a glaring omission – and, shortly afterwards, instructed the Somalis to cut their diplomatic mission in Moscow to just eight.[77]

By November 1977, the Somali offensive had lost momentum. The initial thrust had yielded large gains, but the Somalis became bogged down around the key towns of Harar and Dire Dawa. Over-extended supply lines, the aerial dominance of Ethiopian F-5 fighter planes,[78] the growing weight of Soviet armour behind Ethiopian resistance and, above all, an increasing shortage of weapons took its toll on the Somali campaign. Without military aid from the West, the Siad regime had to rely on slim pickings from the Arab states. Egypt and Iraq provided Somalia with some arms from their Soviet-supplied arsenals, but Saudi Arabia conditioned its promise of $300–$350 million to buy arms from the West on Mogadishu severing its ties with the USSR. In the meantime, the military initiative in the Horn was changing sides. This fact strained Soviet–Somali relations to breaking point.

Mogadishu had warned the USSR as early as 7 September 1977 that it would expel Soviet advisers from the country if the Soviets continued to back Ethiopia 'with experts and weapons'. On 21 October, Siad delivered a blistering attack on Soviet and Cuban support of Ethiopian 'black power colonialism' which, he said, placed their relations with Somalia in 'great jeopardy'. Ten days later, Siad claimed, for the first time, that between 7,000 and 15,000 Cuban combat troops were fighting on Ethiopia's side. The Somali President appealed to 'other world powers'[79] for help and, in an attempt to rally Western support, raised the spectre of a Soviet-inspired Cuban–Ethiopian invasion of his country:

> We are sure that Ethiopia with their friends are planning to attack Somalia. We are expecting it and are prepared. But will they stop at Somalia? I don't think so.[80]

Yet, despite the very real bitterness against the Soviets in Somalia, Moscow seemed to believe that its pressure tactics might succeed where negotiations had failed. At a luncheon for President Neto of Angola on 28 September 1977, President Brezhnev (now President after assuming the title from Podgorny), in a reference to the 'regrettable' war between Ethiopia and Somalia, argued that providing 'the principle of the inviolability of borders be universally observed in the interests of peace, security and the progress of peoples', then 'there is no doubt ... problems of this kind ... could be settled by mutual accord on the basis of good-neighbourliness'.[81] Similarly, on 21 October, *Tass* maintained that the withdrawal of Somali troops from Ethiopian territory – 'the only reasonable way' to 'eliminate the threat over the Horn of Africa' – would facilitate a settlement formula 'acceptable to both parties involved in the conflict'.[82] Soviet optimism that it would eventually dictate an Ogaden settlement was probably related to three considerations. Firstly, since Moscow cut off the arms flow, Mogadishu had failed to secure an alternative and comparable supplier from the West. Secondly, the Soviets knew Siad feared the potential destabilisation of his regime which an abrupt break with Moscow might bring. Thirdly, for all his anti-Soviet rhetoric, Siad declared in early November 1977 there was a 'mutual interest'[83] in Soviet–Somali co-operation. Indeed, this appeared to be confirmed by continued contacts between the two sides. In September 1977, a large group of Somali students were sent to study at Soviet educational institutions.[84] Then, on 7 November 1977, a Somali delegation led by Brigadier General Ali Hattan Hashi attended the Revolutionary Day celebrations in Moscow. In an address, Hashi paid tribute to Soviet–Somali friendship and asserted 'the USSR is assisting Somalia . . . the Somali people always remember the assistance given by the USSR'.[85]

However, as a British Prime Minister once remarked, 'a week is a long time in politics'. On 13 November 1977, the Siad government abrogated the 1974 Soviet–Somali Treaty of Friendship and Co-operation; expelled all of the remaining 1,678 Soviet technical and military advisers; revoked Soviet use of naval, air and ground military facilities in Somalia; and drastically reduced the size of Soviet diplomatic representation in Mogadishu. In addition, because 'Cuba deliberately sent its troops into the Horn of Africa to assist colonialism',[86] Mogadishu severed relations with Havana and ordered all Cuban diplomats and experts to leave the country within forty-eight hours. Thus, the USSR experienced a major blow and was forced to disengage from important strategic facilities such as the communications and submarine missile handling station at Berbera.

According to Mogadishu, the action was necessitated by the USSR's brazen interference. Despite 'numerous' warnings, Siad told the Somali nation on 14 November, the USSR armed and 'sanctioned the commitment of Cuban troops' to the Ethiopian side against the Somali liberation struggle. In doing so, the USSR had 'unilaterally terminated the supply of legitimate defensive arms to the SDR'[87] in direct contravention of the military co-operation clause of the Friendship Treaty between the two countries. The final straw, Somali officials revealed, was a Soviet message threatening 'grave consequences for Soviet–Somali relations' unless Somalia ended its 'interference in the internal affairs of Ethiopia'.[88] But there were other considerations behind the Somali decision. Mogadishu was anxious to remove what it increasingly saw as the Soviet impediment to enlisting the military aid of pro-Western states like Saudi Arabia and Iran, and perhaps the Western powers themselves. There was also the question of Soviet unpopularity in Somalia. Siad correctly anticipated that breaking with Moscow would enhance the popularity of his regime. In fact, Somalis even turned up at Mogadishu airport to jeer and jostle the Soviets and Cubans as they boarded planes to leave.

The USSR was not caught totally unawares by the Somali expulsion order. In the words of a Soviet spokesman, it followed 'a long period of hesitation, insincere assurances and downright blackmail'[89] by the Siad regime. A *Tass* statement on 15 November 1977 declared that 'essentially behind this action lies dissatisfaction because the Soviet Union did not support Somalia's territorial claims on a neighbouring state and refused to facilitate the stirring of a fratricidal war in the African Horn'.[90] It was argued, with breathtaking cynicism, that the Somali government knew full well 'the only purpose of Soviet military aid was to strengthen the defences of Somalia', and was 'not for an attack on neighbouring states'[91] such as Ethiopia. The Somali allegation of Soviet interference was dismissed as 'absurd' since 'Soviet assistance to revolutionary Ethiopia . . . in no way endangers any of the neighbouring states including Somalia'. *Tass* added that 'Judging from the present steps, chauvinist expansionist moods prevailed over common sense inside the Somali government.'[92] While still professing 'sentiments of friendship for the people of Somalia', Moscow warned the Somali leadership a price would have to be paid for its 'unfriendly line': 'The Soviet side has taken note of the Somali government's actions, the responsibility for which rests fully with the Somali side. Time will show what this rash action will cost Somalia.'[93]

The Soviet intervention

The expulsion of Soviet advisers from Somalia coincided with an important development in Ethiopia. On 11 November 1977, the last of Mengistu's prominent rivals and number two man in the Dergue, Vice-Chairman Atnafu Abate, was executed for 'opposing socialism'. The relief in Moscow was almost audible. Like previous purge victims, Atnafu had become disenchanted with Mengistu's hard-line policy toward Eritrea. He also questioned the wisdom of Mengistu's pro-Soviet policy. In September 1977, Atnafu apparently sounded out the US about the prospect of improving relations.[94] Then, in early November 1977, Atnafu tried to oust Mengistu. At the Dergue's Third General Congress, Atnafu accused Mengistu of 'handing Ethiopia over to the Russians'[95] and ridiculed the claim that Ethiopia could make a rapid transition to socialism. But this argument fell on deaf ears. Once again Mengistu carried the day and was able to mete out 'revolutionary justice' to a political rival. *Pravda* could not contain its satisfaction with the outcome. It applauded the 'resolute rebuff' administered to Atnafu who allegedly sought to establish 'a

Bonapartist military dictatorship' and end Ethiopia's 'close co-operation with the socialist countries'.[96]

Taken together, the demise of Atnafu and the expulsion from Somalia had the effect of removing any remaining restraint on the Soviet part. Previous aid to Addis Ababa, effective though it was, paled in comparison with what was to follow. On 26 November 1977, the Soviets launched a massive airlift of military equipment and personnel. The operation lasted for about six weeks. It involved some 225 Antonov-22s and Ilyushin-76s – about 15 per cent of the entire Soviet air transport fleet – in simultaneous flights to Addis Ababa from bases near Moscow, Tbilisi, Tashkent and Georgievsk.[97] Using Aden and Tripoli as staging posts, the Soviet transports overflew the air-space of a number of countries, sometimes without permission, and drew official protests on this score from Yugoslavia, Iraq and Turkey. This effort was backed up by a huge sealift. Scores of Soviet and East European cargo ships, protected by a record number of Soviet warships in the southern part of the Red Sea, travelled from the Black Sea through the Suez Canal to the Eritrean ports of Assab and Massawa where they unloaded supplies. Large Soviet transport vessels were also deployed to convey Cuban combat contingents from Angola and Cuba itself to Ethiopia. And, to co-ordinate and control the whole exercise, Moscow launched a military communications satellite, Cosmos 964.[98]

Overall, the USSR ferried in over $1 billions worth of armaments[99] (nearly four times the amount supplied to Ethiopia by the US over twenty-five years) including 'hundreds' of T-54 and T-55 tanks, around 50 MiG-21 and MiG-23 jets, a flotilla of giant M1-6 helicopters (capable of lifting tanks), multi-barrelled rocket launchers, artillery and mobile radar units; dispatched about 12,000 Cuban combat troops, 1,500 Soviet military advisers, 750 soldiers from South Yemen and 'several hundred' East German technicians;[100] and sent four Soviet generals, including V. I. Petrov, First Deputy Commander-in-Chief of Soviet Ground Forces, and G. Barisov, formerly head of the Soviet military mission in Somalia, to supervise the integration of sophisticated Soviet weaponry into the Ethiopian Army and direct the war against the Somalis.[101] Table 12 provides a breakdown of the Soviet weapons sent during this time.

Throughout the air- and sealift, Moscow doggedly denied any military involvement in Ethiopia. Despite mounting evidence to the contrary, the USSR insisted that all allegations of 'military intervention' were 'absolutely groundless'. On 17 November 1977, *Pravda*

Table 12. *Soviet arms- air- and sealift to Ethiopia during the Ogaden war, November 1977-January 1978*

Types of weapons	Amount sent
T-34 tanks	A few
T54/55 tanks	400–500
T-62 tanks	Some
Armoured personnel carriers (incl. BTR-152 APCs and BMP-1 AFVs)	300
MiG-17s	Some
MiG-21s	50–60
MiG-23s	20
Mi-6 helicopters	4–6
Mi-8 helicopters	25
SAM 7 missiles	Several hundred
Sagger antitank missiles	Thousands
BM21 122mm rocket launchers	30–35
Artillery guns, 100mm to 152mm	Over 300
Artillery guns, 155mm and 185mm	Some
Mortars	Substantial
Light arms	Thousands

Sources: adapted from Bruce D. Porter, *The USSR in Third World Conflicts* p. 200; *Strategic Survey* (1978) pp. 94–8; C. G. Jacobsen, *Soviet Strategic Initiatives* p. 124

noted that the Ethiopian government 'categorically rejects the statement by Somalia's President Siad Barre alleging that Cuban troops are fighting on the Ethiopian Army's side in the Ogaden'.[102] A subsequent *Tass* statement was more specific:

> Soviet military personnel are allegedly taking part in military operations on the side of Ethiopia along with 'thousands' of citizens of other socialist countries ... Provocative fabrications are being spread on the imaginary participation of Soviet ships and aircraft in military operations taking place in Ethiopia. *Tass* is authorised to state that all these fabrications are completely without foundation.[103]

Nevertheless, following the termination of the Soviet airlift to Addis Ababa in early January 1978, Moscow publicly acknowledged for the first time that it was giving some military aid. According to *Pravda*, 'when Somali troops invaded Ethiopian territory, the Soviet Union, as always in such cases, sided with the victim of aggression. At the request of the Government of Ethiopia, it is giving her appropriate

material and technical assistance for repelling the aggressor.'[104] Such
assistance, however, had nothing to do with what the Soviet media
called 'the canard about Soviet involvement'[105] in the Horn conflict.

In reality, Moscow argued, these 'irrelevant' allegations were
simply a 'propaganda smokescreen' to conceal Western interference in
the Ethiopian–Somali war. Convinced that revolutionary Ethiopia was
an 'obstacle' to imperialist plans to control the Red Sea basin, the US
and reactionary Arab regimes 'in league with them' purportedly
encouraged the 'chauvinistic, expansionist ambitions of the Somali
leaders'[106] against Addis Ababa. The objective was 'to smother the
Ethiopian national-democratic revolution' and thereby strengthen the
position of imperialism in North-east Africa. But to implement 'this
broad plot', the Western powers found it necessary to 'international-
ise' the dispute by arming the Somali 'aggressor'.[107] The fact that
President Carter had categorically barred arms supplies to both
Ethiopia and Somalia failed to impress the Kremlin. This was simply
deemed an imperialist manoeuvre.

The Soviet media repeatedly claimed during the conflict that NATO
arms were 'pouring into Somalia' via third countries like Saudi Arabia
and Egypt: 'This use of pro-imperialist circles enables American
diplomacy to don righteous garb, while local traitors to the national
liberation movement and capitulationists of various stripes do its dirty
work.'[108] However, apart from a couple of reports in February 1978
indicating Somalia had received a 25 million mark loan from West
Germany and 'military contingents' from conservative Arab states,[109]
Moscow was remarkably reticent in detailing its charges. It was only in
March 1978, with the Ogaden war virtually over, that Moscow shed
any light on the West's 'extensive military aid':

> The West German [newspaper] *Unsere Zeit* reported recently that 150
> persons had been recruited in Federal Germany to fight Somalia's
> war against Ethiopia . . . The Paris newspapers *Le Matin* and *Le Monde*
> report that over 100 tanks, including French and US tanks and also
> West German Leopard tanks in service with NATO forces, 300 Italian
> armoured vehicles and 600 French anti-aircraft and anti-tank missiles
> have been delivered to that country.[110]

Even if the above account was accurate – and a PMAC supporter
indicated it was not[111] – Moscow did not seem entirely confident that
its message was getting across. Perhaps because of this, *Izvestiya*
adopted a more subtle approach which seemed to recognise the dearth
of US weapons:

> The point is not that the US did not begin to deliver weapons to
> Somalia, which complicated the situation in this part of Africa, but

that promises of such deliveries were given which, it is now evident, actually did Somalia a disservice and caused bloodshed.[112]

Furthermore, Moscow accused China of playing 'an especially unsavoury role' in the 'alliance against the Ethiopian people's revolution'. During the Ethiopian–Somali war, Peking reportedly dispatched troops [sic] and weapons, including ground-to-air missiles, to Mogadishu. In this way, the Chinese leadership 'allied itself with reactionary Arab regimes' and acted 'hand in glove with the imperialists'.[113]

All this was accompanied by a determined Soviet campaign to discredit Siad's regime. Almost as soon as the Soviet airlift to Addis Ababa got under way, Moscow appeared to lose interest in a political solution to the Ogaden conflict. On 2 December 1977, V. N. Sofinsky, the head of the Soviet Foreign Ministry Press Department, savagely denounced the Somali invasion, particularly Mogadishu's justification that it was simply aiding a national liberation movement, the WSLF:

> In fact no WSLF exists – there is no such animal. There are subversive and terrorist groups which are formed in Somalia and transferred to Ethiopia. These groups, which mount sabotage, subversion and acts of terrorism are proclaimed the WSLF.[114]

Moreover, Moscow, for the first time since the 1969 Somali revolution, recalled that Mogadishu's territorial claims were not confined to the Ogaden. A Soviet commentator observed 'that even in the past Somalia had bourgeoise nationalists infatuated with ideas of a "Greater Somalia"', which would include 'the present Republic of Djibouti and the northeastern part of Kenya'.[115]

At the same time, Soviet commentators increasingly portrayed 'the expansionist policy of the Somali government' as proof that Mogadishu had become 'an instrument' of the 'imperialist powers':[116]

> The true pro-imperialist countenance of the Somali aggressors has come to light and is now visible to the entire world, especially since the Somalis have embarked on the well-trodden path of anti-Sovietism.[117]

According to Moscow, 'the fact that the Mogadishu leaders today claim sympathy and aid from those who not so long ago oppressed the Somali people . . . only shows the depths they have fallen to'. Such an 'adventurous course' had led to Somalia's 'isolation in Africa'. As the quarrel deepened, Moscow maintained that peace initiatives had 'no chance of success'[118] until Somali troops were removed from Ethiopian territory. This Soviet stand, it was argued, 'is fully consistent with the Charter and resolutions of the UN' and 'coincides with the OAU Charter, which calls for respect of the sovereignty and territorial integrity of each state . . . and also with the recommendations of the OAU committee for the settlement of the Somali–Ethiopian conflict'.[119]

Thus, between November 1977 and late January 1978, the Soviet media gradually constructed a scenario in which the political, legal and moral underpinning for Soviet intervention were set forth.

We must now return to our chronicle of the war. It did not take Ethiopia long to translate the massive injection of Soviet military aid into usable firepower. By the end of November, the newly reinforced and regrouped Ethiopian Army not only withstood a major Somali effort to take the key town of Harar, but actually pushed the Somalis back some twenty kilometres from their target. That proved a turning point. In December 1977, the Somalis found themselves pinned down by a combination of accurate long-range Ethiopian artillery and a series of limited but demoralising air-strikes on northern Somali towns, Hargeisa and Berbera. Suddenly, Somali officials began to adopt a more conciliatory stance. Siad was quoted on 26 December as saying he would welcome conciliation efforts by Madagascar's President Ratsiranka to achieve 'a peaceful solution'[120] to the conflict. Moscow was encouraged. Writing at this time, a Soviet observer declared:

> The Ethiopian revolution has proved that it can defend itself. Imperialist propaganda media are publishing fewer and fewer reports about the 'successes' of the so-called liberation fronts.[121]

Meanwhile, Somalia desperately searched in vain for a new military patron to replace her old Soviet ally. These efforts focussed once again on the US and other Western nations. While Siad admitted he had received no 'specific assurances' of Western support before the expulsion of the Soviets and Cubans, he certainly attempted thereafter to capitalise on Western anxieties in relation to the Soviet build-up in Ethiopia. On 23 November 1977, the Somali leader publicly deplored the US unwillingness to become involved in the conflict. A month later, Siad sent the Minister for Water and Mineral Resources, Abdulkadir Qasim, on a special mission to the US in a bid to improve relations. The visit signalled the resumption of US economic aid to Mogadishu. But no military aid was forthcoming.[122] On 16 January 1978, Siad called in the Ambassadors of the US, Britain, France, West Germany and Italy. He told them that his country faced 'an imminent invasion' by 'Warsaw Pact countries' backing Ethiopia.[123] Then, in February 1978, Siad accused the USSR of pursuing a 'grand design' in the Horn. He told a Western correspondent:

> What is puzzling is why the US allows the Soviets to spread their hegemony . . . Soviet leaders have convinced the Carter Administration not to react to the biggest Soviet airlift in history. Bigger than the October war. Bigger than Angola. They have moved to Ethiopia highly sophisticated equipment that the Ethiopians cannot possibly use themselves. At first the Cubans convinced Ambassador A. Young they were just sending a few doctors. Now their regular forces are in place. Moscow has hoodwinked you . . . We stood up to them. But who is with us?[124]

The response from the US was distinctly cool. Washington interpreted the expulsion of the Soviets as putting Somalia in 'a far better position to pursue a truly non-aligned policy'.[125] But it reiterated that no US military aid could be furnished so long as Somalia was in aggressive occupation of the Ogaden. This stand rested on at least two factors. First, the Carter government, unlike previous administrations, was initially disposed to seek 'African solutions to African problems'. Figures like Andrew Young, the US Ambassador to the UN, and Cyrus Vance, the US Secretary of State, believed that African nationalism was 'the surest barrier to external intervention'.[126] This approach seemed to be vindicated by the Soviet eviction from Somalia. As a consequence, the Carter administration at first took a fairly relaxed attitude to Soviet intervention in the Horn conflict[127] and maintained firm support for the OAU's principle concerning the sanctity of post-colonial boundaries.

Secondly, the Somali campaign in the Ogaden was strongly opposed by two of America's regional allies. Israel had traditionally supported the territorial integrity of Ethiopia, and continued to do so after the 1974 revolution. This policy was dictated by the Israeli fear that Ethiopian dismemberment would turn the Red Sea into an 'Arab lake'. Such a possibility prompted Tel Aviv to support the counter-insurgency efforts of the Mengistu regime in both Eritrea and the Ogaden. When, however, the Ethiopian–Somali war erupted, Israel stepped up its military aid. On 6 February 1978, the Israeli Foreign Minister, Moshe Dayan publicly confirmed that Tel Aviv was providing Ethiopia with 'certain kinds of arms'.[128] There were also reports that Israel sent teams of advisers in military aviation and logistics to Ethiopia.[129] Thus, Israeli opposition to 'Somali aggression' led to the apparently incredible situation whereby Tel Aviv briefly found itself on the same side as the USSR, Cuba, Libya and the PDRY. Similarly, pro-Western Kenya, conscious of Somali irredentist designs on its North-east territory, gave Addis Ababa strong political support during the Ogaden conflict. Linked to Ethiopia by a mutual defence pact, Kenya ridiculed President Siad's alarms about Soviet–Cuban threats to the region:

> It was Somalia who first invited the Soviet Union to secure a firm foothold in the Horn of Africa. Somalia has now fallen out with Moscow and Russia has switched horses, giving military and other assistance – in vast quantities – to Ethiopia. Let us not split hairs. It was Ethiopia which was aggressed in the Ogaden . . . Now that the tide has turned, the world is being fed this hysterical claptrap about invasions, unholy alliances and the like.[130]

More specifically, Nairobi repeatedly cautioned the West against arming Mogadishu. In February 1978, a high-powered Kenyan delegation, headed by the Vice-President Daniel Arap Moi, visited both London and Washington in a bid to drive the point home. The Kenyan Vice-President evidently told the Carter administration that it was imperative to stop the Somali aggression, and then worry about the Soviet and Cuban presence in Ethiopia.[131]

Nonetheless, despite the constraints on US policy, Washington became concerned that its 'wait and see' posture might convey an impression of political paralysis. By all accounts, the administration was taken aback by the scale and duration of the Soviet air- and sealift to Ethiopia. It was one thing to say leave Africa to Africans. Quite another to sit back and watch Moscow, hiding behind general African support for the doctrine of the inviolability of frontiers, impose its own military solution in the Horn. America's friends in the region, Saudi Arabia, Egypt and Iran were no less upset. Under pressure to 'do something' about the Soviet role in the Horn, the Carter administration adopted an increasingly outspoken approach to the area.[132]

The first major indication of American concern was a speech by Ambassador Andrew Young at the General Assembly of the UN on 6 December 1977. Young officially complained about the quantity of Soviet arms supplies to Addis Ababa. Then, on 14 December, President Carter's National Security Adviser, Zbigniew Brzezinski, delivered a warning to the Soviet Ambassador to the US, A. Dobrynin. Brzezinski said that if the USSR persisted in its support to Ethiopia, Washington would 'stop restraining'[133] regional allies like Iran, Egypt and Saudi Arabia. A month later, Carter himself roundly condemned the 'excessive quantities of weapons' sent to Ethiopia and accused the

Soviet Union of having 'contributed to the war presently taking place between Somalia and Ethiopia' through, *inter-alia*, 'dispatching Cubans into Ethiopia'.[134] Such rhetoric, however, did not change the substance of US policy. On 17 January 1978, the US restated that it would not supply arms to Somalia until the Ogaden fighting ceased. To further emphasise the point, a conference on 21 January of five Western states in Washington, convened on the initiative of the US to discuss the crisis in the Horn, concluded 'no lasting solution to the problems of the region can be found by force of arms'. The participants urged a negotiated settlement to the Ogaden conflict and reaffirmed their 'full support'[135] for the peace efforts of the OAU and its mediation committee.

In the circumstances, it was perhaps inevitable that a public split developed within the Carter administration over how to react to the Soviet intervention. The State Department under Cyrus Vance questioned what the US could do about the situation however much it disliked it, and tended to play down the extent of Soviet and Cuban involvement in the hope that the OAU would be able to effect a settlement. But Zbigniew Brzezinski disagreed. From January 1978 onwards, Brzezinski pressed for a much stronger response. He believed that 'if Soviet-sponsored Cubans determined the outcome of an Ethiopian–Somali conflict, there could be wider regional and international consequences . . . greater regional uncertainty and less confidence in the US'. To counteract this, Brzezinski advocated the sending of a US aircraft-carrier task-force to the Red Sea area to 'send a strong message to the Soviets'.[136] But President Carter, along with Vance, Harold Brown, the US Defence Secretary and the Joint Chiefs of Staff, opposed this move. They argued that if an American carrier was deployed and Somalia was then invaded by Soviet-supported Ethiopia, 'it would be perceived as a defeat for the US'.[137]

With Washington cautious and increasingly divided in its response to the conflict, Siad intensified the search for support in the Arab world. Between November 1977 and February 1978, he personally visited Saudi Arabia, Iran, Jordan and Egypt. These efforts bore some fruit. On 1 January 1978, the Shah of Iran announced that his country would intervene if Ethiopia invaded Somali territory: 'Iran will not remain indifferent in the face of any further aggression against the recognised borders of Somalia'.[138] This statement, which was condemned as foreign 'meddling' by an outraged OAU, was followed on 15 January by a promise from the Saudi Foreign Minister that his country would also go to Somalia's aid 'if it becomes a target of foreign aggression'.[139] Both pledges of support, however, were designed to protect Mogadishu's borders and not to recast African frontiers. Translated into material assistance, these Arab assurances fell very short of being enough to sustain the Somali Army's firepower in the Ogaden. The main problem was the lack of heavy weaponry. While Saudi Arabia and, to a lesser degree, Iran, provided petrodollars galore to purchase arms, Somalia found itself hamstrung by US-imposed restrictions on the re-export of American arms via third parties. It certainly managed to buy some light arms from France, Switzerland, Italy, Pakistan and Syria and something like 590 tons of Soviet-made weapons (including Kalashnikov rifles and ammunition) on the international arms market. It was also reported that Iran and Egypt air-lifted modest quantities of Soviet military equipment from their own stocks to Mogadishu.[140] But these dribs and drabs were no match for the flood of sophisticated Soviet arms and Cuban 'advisers' that poured into Addis Ababa.

Undersupplied and outgunned, the Somali Army in the Ogaden braced itself for the predictable blow. It was not long in coming. By mid-January 1978, the 50,000-strong Ethiopian Army, fitted out with its new Soviet equipment and supplemented by a huge People's Militia, had at last acquired a clear set of military priorities. The Ethiopian high command now found itself under the direction of a special defence committee or war council.[141] This consisted of Soviet, Cuban and Ethiopian officers with V. I. Petrov, First Deputy Commander in Chief of Soviet Ground Forces, in overall charge. In January 1978, the Cuban Defence Minister, Raoul Castro, secretly arrived in Addis Ababa and almost certainly participated in the proceedings of the committee.[142] One thing became plain. Moscow and its allies decided that the Ogaden conflict took priority over all others facing the Mengistu regime including the Eritrean insurrection. As *Pravda* put it at the time, the Ethiopian government was 'determined to achieve a peaceful settlement of the Eritrean question'.[143] Whether this was true, however, was another matter. The Somali problem, though, could not be deferred.

In late January 1978, the Ethiopian Army, assisted by Cuban troops and Cuban-flown combat aircraft, launched its long-awaited counter-offensive in the Ogaden. The assault took place on four fronts between Dire Dawa and Harar, and almost immediately scored major successes. The Somalis were rapidly driven back towards the key town of Jijiga. A Soviet war correspondent, writing in early March 1978 gave a graphic account of Ethiopia's progress on the battlefield:

> At the beginning of this year the Somali army was in control of a large part of Hararghe Province ... The situation was critical. [But] The Somali successes were not long-lived. In their recent counter-offensive, the Ethiopian armed forces and people's militia pushed the enemy back 60 kilometres from Dire Dawa, and 40 kilometres in the south, more than 30 kilometres in the north and 75 kilometres in the east in the Harar area. ... Life in the liberated areas is gradually coming back to normal. Thousands of peasants are returning to their homes ... The retreating Somali forces are abandoning their large amounts of materiel.[144]

The outcome of the war was no longer in doubt. On 10 February 1978, Mengistu solemnly called on Somalia to 'give up the battle or face annihilation'.[145] Coincidentally, this ultimatum was delivered on the very day that US Secretary of State, Cyrus Vance, publicly urged the Somalis to withdraw their troops from the Ogaden. But Siad remained deaf to both pleas. Instead, Mogadishu announced it was sending its regular army into the Ogaden – something which it claimed it had not done over the previous seven months of war – and ordered a general mobilisation. Ex-servicemen were called up and steps were taken to organise civilians for civil defence and other duties. Gradually, concern grew in the West that the Ethiopian–Cuban counter-offensive would spill over into Somalia. On 17 February, President Carter stressed that all parties in the Horn must respect recognised borders and warned Addis Ababa that the US would consider an invasion of Somalia 'a very serious breach of peace, endangering worldwide peace'.[146] In the event, Washington received an assurance on this point, but only because it also corresponded to Moscow's own political interests. The Soviet media stressed that the Ethiopian Army had 'no intention of crossing the Somali border'.[147] The logic was simple. If the Ethiopian Army entered Somalia, Ethiopia would be changed from victim into aggressor and this, in turn, would damage Soviet influence in the Horn, particularly any prospect of restoring relations with Mogadishu. That goal remained under active consideration. In late February, General Gaddafy presented a Soviet peace plan to Siad in Tripoli which, in essence, was a variation of the previous Marxist–Leninist confederation proposal.[148] But Siad rejected the scheme and vowed to fight on.

The final blow was delivered in early March 1978. Having retreated to Jijiga in mid-February, the main Somali force, consisting of four brigades of troops, waited for an attack through the Marda Pass mountain range. The attack never materialised. Instead, after several weeks of heavy aerial bombardment, the Tenth Ethiopian division supported by an entire Cuban armoured brigade of 60 to 70 tanks bypassed the Marda Pass in a helicopter-borne operation and attacked Jijiga from the unexpected direction of the north. Cuban-crewed tanks were also air-lifted behind the Somali lines and Cuban-piloted MiGs supported the attack in which the Soviets unveiled a weapon never before tested in combat – the BMP-I, a highly mobile armoured vehicle with a 73 mm gun, anti-tank missiles and heat-seeking anti-aircraft missiles.[149] The Somalis held out for three days; on the fourth, they were overwhelmed. In the closing stages of the battle, which ended with Ethiopia regaining control of Jijiga on 5 March, the Somalis committed their strategic reserve of 2,000 men to the struggle. This brigade only got a few miles inside the Ethiopian border before being decimated by a squadron of Ethiopian MiGs. On 9 March, Siad as good as admitted defeat by announcing the withdrawal of all regular Somali forces from the Ogaden. Two weeks later, Addis Ababa officially confirmed it had regained control of the disputed province.[150]

The Ethiopian–Cuban victory was the signal for Moscow to break its silence over its intervention in the Horn. Throughout the time of the counter-offensive, the USSR continued to deny any direct military involvement in the war. In mid-February a *Pravda* war correspondent derided Somali 'fabrications' and 'fables'[151] about the participation of Soviet or Cuban units in the fighting in the Ogaden. The same line was repeated by Deputy Defence Minister Marshal Moskalenko at a press conference in Moscow on 16 February.[152] All this was reinforced, as noted, by Soviet battle reports which consistently depicted advances by Ethiopian forces alone. Even after Mengistu's first public admission on 2 March 1978 that Cuban troops had participated in combat operations, Moscow remained silent. It did not report Mengistu's speech.

However, once it became plain that the 'expansionist' Siad regime had suffered a 'crushing defeat', Moscow relaxed its guard. In mid-March 1978, the USSR not only acknowledged that 'Soviet and Cuban military personnel' took part in the Ogaden war, but also contended that this resolute, 'internationalist aid' in 'no small measure'[153] shaped the outcome. A Soviet writer described the Soviet contribution as follows:

> The imperialist adventure [in the Ogaden] experienced defeat. Revolutionary Ethiopia, with the support of the Soviet Union and Cuba maintained its state and territorial integrity. 'Precisely thanks to the solidarity of the progressive forces' – declared Comrade L. I. Brezh-

nev at the 18th Congress of VLKSM [Leninist Young Communist League of the Soviet Union] – 'we have managed to destroy the attempts of imperialism and its protégés ... to dismember revolutionary Ethiopia.'[154]

Other Soviet observers paid tribute to the Soviet military input by stressing the scale of the Somali debacle. A *Pravda* correspondent, reporting 'the liberation of Jijiga' found the town 'destroyed and desolate' and 'a tragic witness to the adventure launched by reactionary African forces and their imperialist patrons'.[155] In this connection, Moscow rhetorically asked:

> What did this war bring to Somalia? The death of thousands of young people who laid down their lives for essentially alien interests, the undermining of the economy, the growth of prices and foreign debt, and the decline of the international prestige of the country.[156]

At the same time, in the immediate aftermath of the war, the USSR brushed aside rather confused US 'attempts to link the unconditional withdrawal of Somali units [from the Ogaden] to the presence in Ethiopia of military personnel invited by its government'. According to *Pravda*, 'it is obvious that this question can be resolved only by Ethiopia and the appropriate parties'[157] meaning the USSR and Cuba. This uncompromising stand was related to two factors. Firstly, the Soviet attitude towards the Ogaden question hardened after the Ethiopian victory. It should be recalled that during the Ethiopian–Somali conflict Moscow argued for a settlement based on mutual respect for the principles of territorial integrity and 'the unconditional and immediate withdrawal of Somali troops from Ethiopian territory'.[158] When, however, the Somalis withdrew, Moscow demanded that the Somali leaders completely 'renounce their claims to a portion of the territory of Ethiopia and Kenya, as well as their claims to Djibouti' and 'abandon the use of force in the resolution of international disputes'.[159]

Secondly, the USSR did not consider the defeat of Somalia as the end of its 'internationalist duty'[160] in Ethiopia. Soviet attention now switched to the second major battlefield, Eritrea. On 15 March 1978, *Pravda* observed:

> After the failure of their 'Ogaden operation', the imperialist forces are increasingly linking their plans for interference in the internal affairs of Ethiopia with the activities of separatist elements in the North East province of Eritrea. In supporting these elements, the imperialists and Arab reaction are striving to weaken Ethiopia and to deprive it of access to the sea.[161]

In a sense, Soviet anxieties were justified. By early 1978, virtually all of Eritrea, except for four isolated government strongholds, was in the hands of the local rebel movements, the ELF and the EPLF.[162] With its huge new investment under threat, Moscow indicated its readiness to back Mengistu's hard-line approach to Eritrea. It declared, amongst other things, that 'the real interests of the population of the province coincide with the interests of all the Ethiopian people' and its 'revolutionary leadership'.[163] Suffice it to say, by May 1978, the USSR and, to a much lesser extent, Cuba, supported the Dergue's new offensive in the province.

Soviet behaviour: an analysis

The Soviet realignment in the Horn of Africa was interpreted in the West in two broadly opposite ways. On the one hand, there were those such as Steven David who argued that the Soviet about-face was nothing more than a rational switch of support from a smaller country, Somalia, to a stronger one, Ethiopia.[164] On the other hand, other observers, like Fred Halliday and Maxine Molyneux, simply saw it as an energetic response to an unexpected and forced disengagement in Somalia.[165] Both interpretations, it must be conceded, bore some relation to the actual course of events. But neither constituted in themselves wholly adequate explanations. The first school of thought assumed the existence of a Soviet grand design for Africa and thus obscured the extent to which Soviet policy in the Horn was sometimes shaped by forces outside its control. The second posits that Soviet policy in the region had no hierarchy of objectives and falsely implies, therefore, that a 'blind' Russian bear stumbled into Ethiopia only after being pushed out by the Somalis on 13 November 1977. In reality, Soviet policy was neither entirely initiatory or responsive, but rather a combination of both. That is to say, the related processes of disengagement in Somalia and intervention on Ethiopia's behalf were the product of a complex interaction between defined Soviet interests and the operational environment of the Horn. The fact that these two elements in the equation did not always correspond indicates that contrary to the implications of the aforementioned approaches Soviet policy involved a degree of risk.

Why, then, did the USSR jeopardise and eventually lose its close relationship with Somalia by pursuing a military relationship with Ethiopia? The answer, it would appear, lay in a hard-headed *calculation* of interests in a region of not unlimited possibilities for the USSR.

Following the failure of the Marxist–Leninist confederation scheme in March 1977, the Soviet leadership was certainly aware of the strength of Somali nationalism. This was evident in what was otherwise a self-serving Soviet explanation for the switch of allegiance:

> After the entry of Somali forces into the Ogaden the Soviet leaders called for their immediate withdrawal and the cessation of armed activities. However, this sensible appeal unfortunately did not obtain any response.
> Led by Leninist principles of foreign policy, the USSR stood on the side of the victim of aggression ... The Soviet Union adopted the only possible principled and just position for it, although unfriendly actions of the Somali leadership in relation to the USSR could have followed and actually did follow from this.[166]

Thus, Moscow recognised that its armed support for Ethiopia was totally unacceptable to Mogadishu, but had apparently concluded it was a risk that had to be taken. In the words of the Soviet Ambassador to Somalia, G. Samsonov, Moscow by August 1977 was 'determined that the Ethiopian revolution will succeed at all costs'.[167] The implication was clear. Somalia, in the short term at least, was viewed as an expendable asset.

From our account above, it was evident that Moscow had demonstrated a degree of *decommitment* in Somalia *before* the expulsion order of 13 November 1977. It was Moscow, not Mogadishu, which first sought to redefine the relationship. As related, the USSR agreed to arm Addis Ababa at the end of 1976 and introduced selective military sanctions against Mogadishu in July 1977. Furthermore, Moscow publicly endorsed the Ethiopian stand toward the Ogaden from mid-1976 onwards. Some of the possible reasons for this drift away from Somalia have already been discussed – Mogadishu's mish-mash ideology, the obstacle of Islam ('The religious problem was our worst enemy'),[168] Siad's unrelenting demands for more Soviet economic aid and, of course, Somalia's obsessive nationalism. There were, however, several other factors which contributed to Soviet disenchantment.

In the first place, the *political impermeability* of the Siad government exasperated Moscow. Despite Soviet hopes to the contrary, the establishment of one-party rule in July 1976 did not make Somalia more amenable to Soviet influence. Like the military regime before it, the new Somali Revolutionary Socialist Party (SRSP) was subject to Siad Barre's brand of 'benign, despotic paternalism'.[169] Using a combination of tribal patronage and nepotism, Siad managed to concentrate an enormous amount of power in his hands. Many of the most prominent figures in the new ruling party were drawn from the old regime and, as before, nearly all of the important posts were occupied by members of Siad's minority Marehan clan (a branch of the Darod tribal family). Siad himself was President, Prime Minister and Secretary-General of the SRSP; his son-in-law, General Ahmed Suleiman, was head of the National Security Service (NSS); his nephew, General Omer Hagi Masala, was Commander of the Army; and Masala's brother, Colonel Abdullah Haji Masala, was number two man in the party.[170] Under the circumstances, there were few channels for Soviet influence on the decision-making process in Somalia other than through Siad. To be sure, a pro-Soviet faction was identified within the 74-man Central Committee of the SRSP,[171] but it was questionable whether this faction was capable of seriously challenging President Siad's authority. It was purportedly led by General Ali Mohammed Samantar, a Vice-President and Defence Minister, a man who owed everything to Siad's patronage and was, according to an opposition group in exile, 'totally dependent on Siad for his political existence'.[172]

In addition, the July 1977 Somali invasion of the Ogaden indicated to the Kremlin that Soviet policy had fallen prey to Somali *manipulation* and lost its *raison d'être*. Since 1969, Soviet readiness to arm the Siad regime was apparently based on the assumption that if necessary Moscow could keep the Somali military machine in check. Evidently, Moscow believed the large Soviet presence in the country would serve to restrain the 'chauvinistic, expansionist ambitions in the nationalist-minded section of the army officers'.[173] In the event, the USSR miscalculated. Thanks to Soviet arms, Mogadishu obtained a military capacity that provided it with at least a short-term independence from its backer. As a result, the Soviet Union was unable to prevent Somalia using its Soviet-supplied army to invade the Ogaden and thereby jeopardising the new Soviet position in Ethiopia. From a Soviet perspective, matters had clearly got out of hand:

> It should be mentioned that the present Somali leaders took no such action against the monarchy that existed [in Ethiopia] until 1974. At that time their claims did not go beyond verbal demands for the 'return' of the Ogaden ... The Somali leaders started preparing for aggression only when the revolution began in Ethiopia.[174]

Furthermore, Soviet policy-makers had good reason to believe that the Soviet political model would *function better* in Africa after decommitment in Somalia. Two considerations were paramount here. Firstly, if Moscow remained a close supporter of Somalia, it would inevitably be seen as a party to the Ogaden invasion because it had supplied and trained the Somali armed forces. And, since the Somali action was a clear violation of the OAU principle concerning the inviolability of established frontiers, Moscow would find itself seriously at odds with mainstream African opinion. Secondly, even in the event of a Somali victory in the Ogaden, the Soviets could not count on Somali gratitude for having supplied the necessary arms. Soviet suspicions on this score were fuelled by Siad's links with 'reactionary' Arab states like Saudi Arabia, and the Somali President's apparent willingness to entertain the idea of expelling the Soviet presence as early as July 1977. This, as far as Moscow was concerned, did not bode well for the future of Soviet–Somali relations, especially if and when Mogadishu's need for Soviet arms became less pressing.

Finally, and most importantly, the Soviets estimated that the *costs of decommitment* in Somalia would be more than fully recovered through an alliance with Ethiopia. While the phrase 'more than fully recovered' suggested a multiplicity of reasons, the vast majority of them fell under the following categories:

Strategic interests

The USSR had a geo-strategic interest in the Horn of Africa. But if Moscow had long valued the Indian Ocean coastline of Somalia, it considered Ethiopia in 1977–8 to be the greater prize by virtue of its access to the Red Sea. In the view of the *New Times* journal, the significance of the Red Sea basin needed no emphasising:

> The area has been allotted an exceptionally important place in the imperialist strategic plans because of its geographical location at the junction of two continents, Asia and Africa, its first-class ports in the Gulf of Aden and the Indian Ocean and, above all, its proximity to key sea lanes linking oil-producing countries with America and Europe. Some 70 per cent of the oil and other raw materials imported by Western Europe is carried over these sea routes.[175]

Many of the strands of Soviet strategic thinking with regard to Ethiopia were outlined in this revealing comment. The reference to 'imperialist strategic plans' in the Red Sea reflected Soviet concern that hostile Arab states like Egypt and Saudi Arabia, with the backing of the US, were trying to turn the region into 'a closed "Arab lake"'. This scheme would, amongst other things, 'close this region off from beneficial co-operation with the Soviet Union and other countries of the socialist commonwealth'.[176] Soviet fears along these lines were

Table 13. *Cumulative totals of Soviet naval port visits to Ethiopia and Somalia, 1953–1980*

Country	Total ship days
Ethiopia	4,812
Somalia	6,199

Source: adapted from Bruce W. Watson, *Red Navy at Sea: Soviet Naval Operations on the High Seas, 1956–1980*, Boulder, Colorado, Westview Press, 1982, pp. 224–5

further increased by a dramatic announcement in early November 1977 that President Sadat of Egypt would visit Israel. It was a move that torpedoed plans for multilateral talks on the Middle East at Geneva and suddenly removed the Soviets from playing a direct role in the Arab–Israeli peace talks. To Moscow, therefore, a strong position in Ethiopia, which is just across the Red Sea from Saudi Arabia, would answer the need to balance, in some degree, the loss of influence in Egypt and also counter US-supported efforts to exclude the USSR from the Middle East conflict zone altogether.

But Moscow's strategic motives were not entirely defensive in character. The observation that the Red Sea embraced 'key sea lanes linking oil-producing countries with America and Europe' indicated a Soviet awareness that an alliance with Ethiopia might have considerable anti-Western or 'anti-imperialist' potential. This, it would seem, rested not so much on Moscow gaining complete freedom of shipping or access to oil for itself ('There is no need to prove to the world that the Soviet Union's petroleum resources are sufficiently large...'),[177] but rather denying or at least acquiring a capability to deny these things to the West.

Moreover, the allusion to the Red Sea's 'first-class ports' suggested that Moscow did not view its military investment in Somalia as irreplaceable. The Soviet leadership probably calculated that if Soviet support for Ethiopia led to the loss of naval facilities at Berbera, the cost could be absorbed by access to the Ethiopian ports, Assab and Massawa. Both of these Red Sea ports possessed mechanised cargo-handling equipment and were capable of accommodating deep-sea vessels. However, it is known that not all Soviet officials, particularly in the Navy, shared this analysis. They were reportedly reluctant to trade an open oceanic position at Berbera for the sake of more congested ports like Assab and Massawa whose approach entails the use of the Suez Canal or the Straits of Bab el Mandeb.[178] Besides, by the spring of 1977, if not earlier, it was clear that access to the new facilities would be critically dependent on the cessation of the Eritrean rebellion. Table 13 seems to emphasise that Somali naval facilities were in no way inferior to those available in Ethiopia.

Thus, while strategic considerations played an important part in the Soviet shift to Ethiopia they alone cannot fully explain Soviet readiness to exchange good solid naval facilities in Somalia for less certain strategic returns in Ethiopia.

Ideological interests

According to Moscow, the 'ideological proximity' of Ethiopia 'to the socialist community' was 'of decisive importance'[179] for Soviet realignment in the Horn of Africa. Speaking in May 1977, President Podgorny declared that 'social processes in Ethiopia create favourable prerequisites for substantial headway in bilateral co-operation'.[180] Certainly, Soviet observers again and again stated their breathless admiration for what they called the 'genuine' nature of the Ethiopian revolution.[181] The latter, it was argued, was distinguished from other 'African events of the 1970s' by the fact that it 'strictly' belonged to 'the regular channel of Marxist–Leninist theory and politics'.[182] That is to say, Ethiopia was the first African state where conditions existed which 'in one or other way remind one at times of the distinctive features of the three Russian revolutions'.[183]

Soviet writers identified the following parallels: both the Soviet and Ethiopian revolutions swept aside centralised monarchic regimes backed by a landed aristocracy and a strong Christian Church;[184] both revolutions occurred at the feudal stage of historical development in which the great masses of the people were landless peasants; both countries were 'multinational empires, each with a particularly acute nationalities' question intensified by a motley ethnic pattern'[185] and, most important of all, as far as the Soviets were concerned, both revolutions initially experienced political turmoil and bloody 'Red Terror' as new radical dictatorships struggled to establish themselves. In this connection, a Soviet commentator enthused about the level of 'naked class conflict' in Ethiopia which 'puzzled even some progressive groups in African countries, whose path toward revolutionary democracy did not go through and is not going through deep class battles'.[186] Presumably, Somalia, with its relatively classless, nomadic society, fell into that category. Seen from Moscow, then, Ethiopia seemed to bear all the hallmarks of an authentic 'on-going' revolution. In comparison, the Somali commitment to socialism was only viewed as 'skin-deep'.

Such an explanation for Soviet decision-making, however, was not without its limitations. To be precise, the case for an ideological analogy was flawed in two respects. First, Ethiopia had no vanguard party in 1977–8. But Moscow did not allow this to deter it. Instead, the Kremlin attached the progressive label to the existing military regime in Addis Ababa, and indirectly participated in the ruthless extermination of the civilian Marxist–Leninist Ethiopian People's Revolutionary Party (EPRP). In fact, on the very weekend Podgorny made his speech praising favourable social trends in Ethiopia, nearly 500 students, mostly EPRP members, were slaughtered following a May Day demonstration.[187] The Soviet position was based on the cold, pragmatic recognition that the PMAC, not the EPRP, would facilitate Soviet penetration of the Ethiopian state machine.[188] Moreover, Moscow was suspicious of the EPRP because it consisted almost entirely of foreign-educated students, many of whom had links with the West European left. Soviet commentators ridiculed the 'students and various petty-bourgeois strata' which made up the EPRP, and claimed that its composition generated unstable, 'leftists tendencies [sic]'.[189] In other words, the EPRP was a difficult organisation for Moscow to control.

Secondly, unlike the Soviet example, the principal threat to the young Ethiopian revolution came not from 'imperialism', but from another self-proclaimed Marxist–Leninist state – namely Somalia. Moscow, of course, tried to square the circle by arguing that Mogadishu was already by July 1977 in the clutches of the 'imperialists and Arab reactionary regimes'.[190] But this analysis confused cause and effect. If there was any one factor which accelerated the Somali invasion of the Ogaden, it was the Soviet arming of Ethiopia. In this sense, Soviet policy was self-fulfilling. By embracing the Mengistu regime, Moscow repelled the Siad government and pushed it towards the anti-Soviet Arab states and the West, and in this way made Somalia, to use the Soviet jargon, more 'reactionary'. Furthermore, the Soviets knew as well as anyone that the Somali incursion into the Ogaden was the logical, some might say, inevitable outcome of an enduring desire to unite the Somali nation. It was certainly not the product of exterior 'imperialist' intrigue. Consequently, the USSR to some extent used ideology as a post-factum legitimising device for the shift in its own policy in the Horn.

On balance, Marxism–Leninism in Ethiopia probably attracted and encouraged Soviet support. But, in view of the fact that the Dergue's principal opponents, both internal and external, likewise claimed the Marxist mantle, it did not determine the stance the Soviets in fact took.

Regional interests

On the whole, Soviet policy-makers believed Ethiopia, rather than Somalia, was intrinsically the most important state in the Horn of Africa. Quite apart from purely strategic considerations, Moscow was convinced that the Ethiopian revolution was a major international event in its own right. This was underlined in an article in the influential journal, *World Marxist Review*. Berhanu Bayeh, a member of the PMAC's standing committee with overall responsibility for foreign policy, was quoted as saying:

> The Ethiopian revolution can have a very important international role to play. Its successes can largely promote the anti-imperialist struggle and not only in Africa. They will also be a contribution to the socialist transformation of the world . . . Imperialism is aware of this and that is why it has been using its agents within and outside the country to undermine the development of our revolution.[191]

Soviet spokesmen from the Politburo down endorsed this analysis, and declared that Soviet–Ethiopian contacts had 'implications' which 'go beyond Soviet–Ethiopian relations'.[192]

The Soviet assessment was linked to the physical and qualitative characteristics which distinguished Ethiopia. In the first place, Ethiopia was almost twice as large as Somalia and had about 35 million inhabitants. That constituted the second largest population in black Africa and was approximately ten times larger than that of Somalia. The significance of this disparity was not lost on Moscow. A Soviet specialist calculated that by the early 1980s, '83 per cent of the Horn of Africa's entire population will be living in Ethiopia'. As a result, 'a genuine socialist solution for Ethiopia's nationalities problem will with time logically affect the ethnopolitical issues of this entire trouble-bedevilled area'.[193] Secondly, Ethiopia, although very poor, had greater long-term economic potential than Somalia. It could offer the Soviets not only a greater market for its products but also more natural resources than could Somalia. It is noteworthy that around this time at least one Soviet observer claimed that the Ogaden area had oil resources.[194] Thirdly, Ethiopia, unlike Somalia, had long been a major force on the African diplomatic scene. As the first independent black

African state, Ethiopia was widely recognised as the inspiration behind the creation of the Organisation of African Unity (OAU) in 1963. This fact certainly impressed Moscow: 'Historically, Ethiopia, which enjoys high prestige among African countries as the ancient sovereign state, played a prominent role in uniting the newly-free African countries within the OAU' whose 'headquarters are in Addis Ababa'.[195] Seen from Moscow, involvement in Ethiopia provided a springboard to expand Soviet influence on the African continent. In contrast, Somalia was something of a diplomatic liability for the USSR. Isolated by its opposition to the OAU principle on the immutability of state boundaries established at independence, Mogadishu was reputed to be the 'Problem Child of Africa'.[196]

Institutional and elite group interests

During the spring and summer of 1977, the position of certain political and bureaucratic elite groups, resisting a policy of all-out support for Ethiopia, was systematically weakened. As previously mentioned, some Soviet high Navy officials were distinctly unenthusiastic about jeopardising the Somali connection. It is probable that the likes of Admiral Gorshkov, who had visited Somalia on a number of occasions, were reluctant to trade the Soviet-built naval complex at Berbera for the sake of uncertain returns in Ethiopia. This view was apparently shared by some senior Soviet military officials, responsible for arms transfers to the Somalis, and a prominent Politburo member, N. Podgorny.[197] The latter was intimately involved in making Soviet alliance policies with Somalia. Podgorny was said to have developed a close working relationship with President Siad, this being highlighted by his visit to Somalia in July 1974 to sign the Treaty of Friendship and Co-operation there. All this, however, might have counted for nothing if the Horn of Africa question had not become a pawn in a Kremlin power struggle.

In early 1977, Brezhnev encountered a final obstacle in his efforts to consolidate supreme power in his own hands. Administratively, Brezhnev's personalised draft of the new Soviet constitution cleared the way for him to assume the dual roles of head of state and party. But, when approached, Podgorny blocked the new constitution by refusing to stand down as Chairman of the Presidium of the Supreme Soviet.[198] Instead, he embarked on a goodwill and fact-finding mission to four African states lasting from 17 March to 2 April. The trip was probably an attempt by Podgorny to cover his political flank at home. As the man most responsible for Soviet African policy, he knew he was liable to be blamed by his old rival Brezhnev for setbacks in this area. This was particularly so in the Horn of Africa where the two Soviet leaders were identified with different sides in the Ogaden dispute. It should be recalled that Brezhnev associates such as Soviet Foreign Minister, Andrey Gromyko, and his son, Anatoly Gromyko, the Head of the African Institute, played a prominent role in pro-moting Soviet–Ethiopian ties in 1976–7. On the other hand, Podgorny was notable for his absence in the first high-level talks between Moscow and the Dergue in July 1976. As someone with first-hand experience of the Somali situation, Podgorny probably took the view that since Brezhnev had, in his own words, little grasp of foreign-policy 'intricacies',[199] it was wise to demonstrate caution in relation to Ethiopia.

The African tour was not an unqualified success for Podgorny. While his delegation was well received in each of the countries officially visited, Podgorny failed to silence his critics with respect to the Horn. An unscheduled visit to Mogadishu at the beginning of April 1977 did not succeed in bringing Siad into line. At the same time, Podgorny bypassed Ethiopia on his African trip and, in a speech in Tanzania, seemed to take issue with the relatively new pro-Ethiopian emphasis of Brezhnev. Soviet friendship and co-operation with African countries, he declared, was not 'of passing duration, tailored for the moment'.[200] It is not difficult to imagine that back in Moscow Brezhnev cited these actions or inactions to create the impression that Podgorny was unwilling to recognise and support the Ethiopian revolution. In any event, Podgorny found himself out-manoeuvred and up-staged. The Cuban President, Fidel Castro – with the apparent encouragement of Brezhnev – conducted his own whirlwind tour of Africa in March–April 1977. Unlike Podgorny, Castro visited both Somalia and Ethiopia during his African encounter, and flew immediately afterwards to Moscow to report his findings.[201] If, as seems likely, Brezhnev used Castro to embarrass Podgorny, the tactic worked well. Castro delivered a glowing account of Mengistu and the Ethiopian revolution ('I consider Mengistu to be a true revolutionary and the revolution currently unfolding in his country to be a true revolution')[202] and thus raised serious doubts about Podgorny's competence to conduct policy in the Horn.

Matters came to a head with Mengistu's state visit to Moscow in early May 1977. The Soviet media were almost uniformly enthusiastic about the Ethiopian guest. Indeed, General Secretary Brezhnev broke with protocol to see Mengistu.[203] It was left to Podgorny to temper the words of praise with words of caution. He told Mengistu:

> From the experience of our revolution we know that winning power is only the beginning of a long and difficult road. It takes, as Lenin taught, a stubborn struggle against the forces and traditions of the old society.[204]

And, in a comment which seemed to reflect a pro-Somali approach to the Ogaden issue, Podgorny argued that although 'colonialism' had 'grown deep roots' in Africa he was sure 'the new Ethiopia will serve to provide peaceful conditions for the country's development'.[205] The assumption being that Ethiopia had the means to confer peace in the region if it so wished. But Podgorny's views found no echo in Moscow. The writing was on the wall for Podgorny and Brezhnev was holding the pen. On 25 May 1977, N. Podgorny was 'freed from his duties'[206] as a member of the Politburo.

The removal of Podgorny seemed to give Soviet–Ethiopian relations a new impetus. It coincided, one may recall, with the signing of the second and hitherto most substantial arms deal between the two countries,[207] as well as a significant strengthening of the Cuban presence in Addis Ababa. Interestingly enough, Soviet sources confirmed that the 'development' of Soviet–Ethiopian ties were 'boosted', in particular, by 'personal contacts at the very highest level'. In this vein, a Soviet writer observed that Mengistu expressed 'deep gratitude' to the USSR and to Leonid Brezhnev 'personally'[208] for supporting the Ethiopian revolution. But, if the ousting of Podgorny had a positive effect, it also had its negative side. In Mogadishu, the event was conceivably viewed as an unfriendly act towards Somalia. With Podgorny no longer on the scene, the Somalis probably calculated that the Kremlin was fully committed to Addis Ababa and that there was no prospect whatsoever of securing a negotiated transfer of the Ogaden. This interpretation seemed to be corroborated by President Siad himself. In an interview, he asserted that until the time of Podgorny's dismissal:

> I was still hoping to influence events through quiet diplomacy. We didn't want any trouble. But Soviet leaders [Brezhnev?] got angry with us. They told us to mind our own business. We pointed out the dangers to them, but they . . . disagreed. So be it.[209]

To be sure, the triumph of Brezhnev over Podgorny – Brezhnev assumed the dual roles of head of party and state on 17 June 1977 – was not the most important factor shaping the Soviet switch towards Ethiopia – but nor was it one which can be discounted.

The foregoing suggests there were ample positive and negative reasons for the Soviets to support Ethiopia. What is less clear, however, is why Moscow pushed its support for Addis Ababa up to the point of military intervention against Somalia. The inadequacy of the other explanations forces one back to the residual answer – *political expediency*. This was not, though, a case of the USSR simply seizing a golden chance to project its power in the Horn without any appreciable risk or cost to itself. The reality of Soviet intervention was rather more complex and hazardous.

Moscow was aware at the outset of its intervention that it would not be easy to reverse the process of anarchy and disintegration in Ethiopia. Writing in August 1977, a Soviet commentator described the dimensions of Ethiopia's *overt crisis*:

> Ethiopia is, to all intents and purposes, in a state of siege. Crucial economic arteries have been blocked, food and raw materials are in short supply and the theatre of hostilities is expanding.[210]

The last point was truly prophetic. By the beginning of the Soviet air-lift to Addis Ababa in late November 1977, the Ethiopian Army found itself defending Harar, one of only two main towns that had not fallen to the Somalis in the Ogaden region. At this stage, Soviet commentators acknowledged that Ethiopia's 'territorial integrity was hanging in the balance' and that 'the outstanding question was – would the Ethiopian revolution survive or not?'[211] After all, 'revolutionary Ethiopia had to fight not only against internal counter-revolution, but also against an external aggression'. Such a task, according to Moscow, involved 'fighting against heavy odds'.[212]

But it was a challenge the USSR felt unable to refuse. The eviction of Soviet personnel from Somalia represented a humiliating blow to Soviet prestige in more ways than one. Coming as it did after comparable setbacks in Egypt in July 1972 and Sudan in May 1977, the Somali decision threatened Moscow's self-image as a great power and thus affected the *emotional disposition* of the Kremlin. In particular, the Soviets were enraged by the treatment meted out to departing Soviet officials at Mogadishu airport. It was reported that many Russian advisers and their families were forced to unpack their luggage for prolonged searches, which Soviet sources later claimed extended to some unnecessarily crude 'body frisking'.[213] As a result, Moscow was determined to demonstrate that it would not allow Somalia's example of *lèse-majesté* go unpunished. By the same token, the Soviet leadership probably believed that an Ethiopian victory in the Ogaden would sooner or later topple Siad Barre's regime[214] and bring a more amenable regime to Mogadishu.

In addition, Moscow, convinced that 'local imperialism' was directed and determined by 'global imperialism', saw the Somali expulsion episode as a victory for US policy in the Horn: 'No explanation by the US State Department can refute the fact that since the spring of 1977 Washington has been actively striving for a deterioration in relations between Somalia and the Soviet Union.'[215] Thus, the USSR perceived that it stood to lose a great deal in the Horn of Africa unless it intervened to protect its interests. A Soviet article on Ethiopia summed up the Kremlin's concern:

> Will the imperialist forces be able to continue to set the African and Middle East countries one against the other or will this policy be duly rebuffed?
> Much indeed – the future of the progressive forces in the area of the Red Sea and on the African continent in general and the evolution of the international situation as a whole – is at stake here.[216]

What is more, the Soviets, in the last analysis, were confident that they could tip the military balance in the Horn in Ethiopia's favour. In 1977, Moscow set out the prospects for Soviet 'internationalist aid' or intervention in the region. It was assumed that 'the PMAC alone could not cope with the tasks set by the [Ethiopian] revolution'.[217] Rather:

> It is a question of how much Ethiopia's progressive forces, leaning on world socialism and enriching themselves by its theory and practice, take advantage of the present international situation in the interests of the continued revolutionary struggle. It is precisely the existence of the socialist system that leads to a situation in which the 'imperialist powers cannot interfere, being paralysed', which was implied by V. I. Lenin when he wrote about the particularly favourable combination of international conditions which made it possible to wage successful national wars against the imperialist powers. This is what will lend particular importance in the future of the Ethiopian revolution.[218]

This remarkably 'bullish' *interventionary calculus* contained two key elements. First, it was implicitly stated that Moscow had a high degree of belief about the likely gains of intervening in Ethiopia. Such an assessment was shaped by the following variables:

Perceived utility of the Soviet military instrument The relationship between intentions and capabilities is a two-way street. In 1975–6, the USSR gave a practical demonstration of its new ability to project force in the Angolan civil war. Here, the Soviets successfully mounted a large-scale air and sea operation, involving the transportation of arms and thousands of Cuban troops, to ensure the victory of the Popular Movement for the Liberation of Angola (MPLA) over its Western-backed rivals. This episode undoubtedly increased Moscow's readiness to subsequently intervene in the Horn. Conscious that it had 'played the main role in repelling imperialist intervention and scoring victory in Angola',[219] Moscow concluded that proletarian internationalism had 'become the most important principle of policy of the socialist countries in their relations with the liberated countries'.[220] More specifically, Angola underlined to the Kremlin the value of Cuban proxies for achieving Soviet African objectives and provided useful logistical facilities for the eventual build up in Ethiopia. There was, however, an additional circumstance in the Horn which reinforced the military option. As the long-term arms supplier to the Siad regime, the USSR had gained extremely good intelligence on the Somali military machine. According to *Der Spiegel*, many of the Soviet military advisers directly transferred to Ethiopia from Mogadishu knew 'full well where the ammunition dumps are in Somalia and to what degrees the nomadic men can command their weapons'.[221] As a consequence, the Soviets probably reasoned they were exceptionally placed to promote a neat and surgical military operation against the Somali forces in the Ogaden.

On the other side of the coin, Moscow was optimistic about Addis Ababa's capacity to effectively absorb Soviet and Cuban military aid. This view rested, in part, on a Soviet respect for the tradition of centralised decision-making in Ethiopia. The latter was regarded as a positive legacy of the Haile Selassie era: 'the concentration of unlimited power in the hands of the Emperor helped to overcome feudal fragmentation and by that very fact strengthened the position of the state in the face of external danger'.[222] Likewise, under Mengistu, the Dergue responded to early reverses on the Ogaden battlefield by swiftly mobilising large numbers of peasants for belligerent duty and putting the Ethiopian state on a war footing. This ability to organise pleased Moscow:

> Only a regime confident in its own justness, in its authority and close links with the people can move towards the creation of almost half a million strong people's militia including, in particular, about 100,000 well trained and armed soldiers with modern [Soviet] weapons and equipment.[223]

Furthermore, Moscow was aware that the Ethiopian military, for all its problems of morale in 1977, had a sound infrastructure. Owing to a thirty-year association with the US, Addis Ababa had a regular army with competent officers and personnel versed in the use of sophisticated American weaponry, as well as one of the best quality air-forces in black Africa. This, of course, did not eliminate the general problem of converting to Soviet equipment. But it made it less difficult than it might otherwise have been. For example, it was estimated Ethiopian pilots used to flying US-built F-5s needed no more than about ten hours of flying to make the transition to Soviet MiGs.[224]

The lure of Ethiopian dependency   Seen from Moscow, the desperate position of the Mengistu regime in mid-1977 was perhaps the best guarantee that intervention in Ethiopia would pay political dividends. Certainly, as the media in the Soviet bloc acknowledged, there was no shortage of urgent Ethiopian requests for Soviet military aid. In February 1977, almost immediately after seizing supreme power, Mengistu told *Neues Deutschland*:

> We are now in a period in which our revolution consolidates itself. We call it a period of consolidation because we cannot lose the positions which we have already achieved. We must secure the revolution.[225]

At roughly the same time, another member of the PMAC, Berhanu Bayeh, reminded a Soviet audience that 'Ethiopia is fighting against imperialism and internal reaction, and this is a struggle that cannot be carried on single-handed'.[226] Finally, two Soviet writers quoted yet another call by Mengistu in a message to Brezhnev on the sixtieth anniversary of the October Revolution:

> In this critical period, when our revolution and territorial integrity are being menaced by imperialist-provoked aggression and counter-revolutionary schemes, the Ethiopian people and government, loyal to the spirit of international proletarian solidarity, expect the complete support of the progressive forces in general and of the people and government of the Soviet Union in particular.[227]

These appeals helped to persuade Moscow that Ethiopia had 'revolutionaries for whom the Soviets could do much'.[228] In this regard, it is likely that the Soviet leadership viewed the pro-Soviet foreign-policy posture of the PMAC as anything but a coincidence. Unlike Somalia's President Siad, whose commitment to socialism was always tempered by a pledge of neutrality between the superpowers, the Dergue asserted that 'anti-imperialism' was the foundation of the non-aligned movement. That is to say, Addis Ababa rejected 'the insidious concept of the "equidistance" of the non-aligned countries from Moscow and Washington'[229] and thus adopted a position broadly similar to Castro's Cuba. Such a willingness to identify with Moscow against both the West and China on international matters fuelled the expectation that Ethiopia could receive a 'kind of political "acceleration"' through Soviet 'internationalist aid'.[230] Here, Soviet attention centred on the establishment of a vanguard party.

In May 1977, while shopping for arms in Moscow, Mengistu forecasted the imminent birth of a ruling revolutionary party in Ethiopia. The significance of the timing of the announcement was not lost on Soviet observers:

> Understanding of this necessity was by no means a result of an armchair analysis made by members of the PMAC. It was dictated by the entire course of the revolutionary process . . . It is not by chance that precisely during the period of struggle against the Somalian expansionists the leaders of the PMAC began to stress that the creation of the party was a question of life or death for the revolution.[231]

Viewed in this way, it is not inconceivable that the Kremlin saw military intervention as a means of consolidating the trend towards a vanguard party in Ethiopia. The latter, it was argued, would prevent the revolution 'degenerating into one of the mostly surface-skimming military coups that are so frequent in the modern history of the developing countries of Africa, Asia and Latin America'.[232] At least one Soviet politician, however, cautioned against undue optimism about political returns in Ethiopia.[233]

The apparent popularity of the USSR in Ethiopia Moscow seemed to believe that Soviet intervention against the Somali forces would be welcomed in Ethiopia. This assessment reflected the perception that the USSR and Addis Ababa enjoyed a 'special' relationship:

> One should not forget . . . that Russia, Russians, called maskob in Ethiopia as a derivative of the word Moscow, for a whole number of factors had for many decades evoked the warmest feelings among Ethiopians.[234]

These factors included such 'historical and contemporary facts as the Ethiopian origins of one of the ancestors of the great Russian poet Alexander Pushkin'; the 'noble and dedicated work of Russian doctors in Addis Ababa hospitals during almost a century now'; Russian support for Ethiopia in 'the period of Italy's imperialist expansion in Northeast Africa at the end of the last century and again during fascist Italy's aggression in the 1930s';[235] and the purported upsurge of Ethiopian enthusiasm for the Soviet way of life after the 1974 revolution. Soviet visitors reported great interest in Russian language courses, Soviet films and in the classic works of Marxism–Leninism which, it was claimed, were repeatedly sold out within minutes of appearing in Addis Ababa bookshops.[236]

Under the circumstances, the Soviets anticipated little resistance inside Ethiopia to a supportive military operation and reasoned it could don the mantle of Ethiopia's national 'saviour' in the process.

The second aspect of Moscow's *risk calculus* in the Horn was the conviction that the West was unable to counteract Soviet intervention there. In early May 1977, when Mengistu paid his first official visit to Moscow, it was instructive that both sides 'discussed the world situation and agreed that the contemporary balance of forces favours progress, peace and socialism'.[237] And, although the Soviets always accused the NATO powers, especially the US and, to a lesser degree, China, of arming the Somali campaign in the Ogaden, they generally behaved as if such support was irrelevant or non-existent. A Soviet commentary on the eve of the massive Soviet air-lift to Addis Ababa was revealing in this respect:

> Today imperialist circles are promising arms, money and economic aid to the Somali leadership. But this will not help Somalia to extricate itself from this disastrous military conflict, nor will it help to strengthen the independence of that young African state or to overcome the economic difficulties, which have increased since the beginning of the reckless military operations against a neighbouring country.[238]

Soviet confidence derived, in part, from an image of America constrained in the international arena by domestic circumstances. It was evident to Moscow that Jimmy Carter assumed office in January 1977 at a time when the 'Imperial' style of Presidency was under critical scrutiny. Following the Watergate scandal and the Vietnam debacle, American public opinion was in no mood to countenance the possible further abuse of Presidential power. Congress had reasserted itself in the US political system and sought, amongst other things, to extend its role in the making of US foreign policy. Notably, on 19 December 1975, the US Senate had voted to prevent the Ford administration continuing its military assistance to the anti-MPLA forces in Angola. New constraints of this type persuaded Moscow that Carter's room for manoeuvre in the Horn, at least in comparison with many of his predecessors, was relatively limited. Thus, when Carter somewhat belatedly denounced Soviet activities in the Horn, *Pravda* crisply responded:

> What people in Washington were really after was the removal of restrictions imposed by Congress in 1975 on US armed intervention in Africa so that they could exercise the functions of a colonialist gendarme on the continent.[239]

But Moscow made it clear it did not take this particular prospect very seriously. A *New Times* commentary in March 1978 pointedly observed:

> At present loud calls are heard in Washington for US military advisers to be dispatched to Somalia to show the Somalis how to make effective use of NATO weapons.
> [But] This pattern of interference is all too reminiscent of Vietnam the spectre of which still hangs over the US Administration and the idea of a 'new Vietnam' is obviously unpalatable to Washington.[240]

At the same time, the actual conduct of the Carter administration in relation to the Horn of Africa did little to enhance Soviet respect. Early dealings with the administration probably convinced the Soviet leadership that they were dealing with an ambitious, yet still inexperienced President. The American decision to announce its readiness to supply arms to Somalia during the escalating Somali military offensive, followed by the sudden reversal and refusal to supply arms or even permit Arab allies to supply US arms was a 'major blunder'.[241] Not because, as Soviet and some Western critics alleged, it prompted the Somali invasion of the Ogaden.[242] But because it demonstrated, despite the availability of excellent intelligence and warnings from National Security Council staffer Paul Henze about the dangers of becoming involved with irredentist Somalia,[243] a political naivety on the part of the White House that frankly played into the Soviet's hands. To immediately and publicly retract the decision to supply arms to the Somalis – however misguided that original decision was – had the effect of critically weakening Siad's bargaining position *vis-à-vis* Moscow and was, therefore, tantamount to telling Moscow that it could back Ethiopia without fear of US involvement.

Moreover, it is fair to assume that Washington's inability to formulate a quick and coherent response to the Soviet intervention, starting in November 1977, emboldened Moscow to 'go for broke'. Confronted with a clear split between the likes of Secretary of State, Cyrus Vance, who argued that 'there is no linkage between the SALT negotiations and the situation in Ethiopia' and Carter's National Security Adviser, Zbigniew Brzezinski, who contended that a 'linkage' strategy in the region was necessitated by Moscow's 'unwarranted exploitation of local conflict for larger international purposes',[244] Moscow was predictably unimpressed. *Pravda* detected 'some contradictions'[245] as well as 'clear inconsistency'[246] in Washington's position. The problem of arms limitation, Moscow insisted, had 'no bearing whatsoever'[247] with the situation in the Horn of Africa. The Soviets were also aware that these divisions within the administration damaged Carter's domestic standing. It is interesting that *Pravda* dismissed Carter's warnings about a 'growing Soviet threat' in the Horn as an 'attempt to demonstrate, in another field, the firmness which he was being criticised for not showing in domestic policy'.[248] This takes us to the last element in Moscow's *interventionary calculus*.

The Soviets knew that any attempt to put the Ethiopian humpty-dumpty back together again would be protected by a fortuitous political environment. Because Ethiopia's position in the Horn conflict was sanctified by the OAU principle concerning the inviolability of established borders, Moscow could count on at least tacit support from the majority of black African countries for a Soviet–Cuban intervention there. This fact placed Moscow's class adversary, Washington, in a 'no-win' situation. Whatever particular shortcomings the Carter administration may have had, it was politically difficult for any US government to openly back a pro-forma aggressor which, in this case, was Somalia. Besides, the US had never questioned the validity of Ethiopia's insistence on preservation of its territorial integrity. Key African allies of the West such as Israel and Kenya also believed, in the words of the Soviet *New Times* journal, that Ethiopia was 'waging a just defensive war'.[249] Thus, the USSR reasoned 'the majority of African states will not accept the connivance of the West in the activities of intra-continental aggressive forces and the revision of borders', and would tolerate 'the collapse of the calculations of the imperialist and reactionary forces in the convulsions at the centre of the great conflict in the region of the African Horn'.[250]

Ultimately, then, the Soviet decision to intervene in Ethiopia's favour was essentially a political one. It is true that strategic, ideological, regional and elite group interests played a part in the Soviet realignment in the Horn of Africa. But none of these factors, either individually or collectively, fully explain the lengths to which the Soviets were prepared to go to support their new Ethiopian ally. More than anything else, Moscow was attracted by the opportunity to demonstrate a power to sustain a friendly government under threat from a Somali regime which had only recently defected from the Soviet fold. In this way, Moscow wanted to undermine the position of the West in a vital part of Africa and, just as important, to be seen to be doing so. Only this can account for the scale of Soviet intervention, for it far exceeded Ethiopia's immediate military requirements. Indeed, some of the Antonovs in the Soviet air-lift operation were reported to have been empty.[251] The strategy, of course, involved considerable risk. But, as Moscow saw it, the worst risk at that time was not to take any risk at all.

Conclusion

7   Soviet power without influence?

> What happened in the Ogaden should serve as an object lesson for the future, not only for imperialist fanciers of using others to pull the chestnuts out of the fire, but also for those who allow such imperialists to lead them by the nose.　　(*Pravda*, 19 March 1978)

> It is immoral to throw hundreds of millions of dollars into the development of homicide means when millions starve and are devoid of everyday necessities.
> (Mikhail Gorbachev, General Secretary of the CPSU cited in
> M. Volkov 'Militarisation Versus Development', *Asia and Africa Today*, No 5, 1987, p. 9)

At the outset of this study it was observed that the concept of intervention in international affairs described a situation where a state (or a combination of states) deviates from the norm of existing relations, and attempts to impose its will on an apparently weaker country in order to realise some political, moral or legal objective within a limited period of time. But for a state to intervene in the affairs of another it must have both the motive and opportunity to do so. While motivations and circumstances vary, the act of intervention is always distinguished by the exercise of power. To intervene is to use power. However, power is a very general concept and has many dimensions, only one of which is military force. That being so, an intervening state can rarely be certain in advance whether the resources at its disposal will be sufficient to secure compliance with its objectives in the target state. Thus, intervention involves risk. The decision 'to go in' is basically a political one. But interventions can and do go wrong.

Disengagement is the process which begins when intervention ends. It usually involves the withdrawal or the substantial reduction of a foreign presence – be it personnel or some form of assistance programme – from the target state. Again the precipitating factors are not usually identical, but at some stage in the proceedings the intervener concludes or is forced to conclude that the costs of leaving are less than that of trying to stay. Nevertheless, the transition from intervention to disengagement is seldom a tidy one. More often than not, it is a lamentably ragged process stretched over a considerable length of time.

Viewed through the lens of this framework, Soviet policy in the Horn of Africa has had mixed results.

The military juggernaut

From a purely military standpoint, the Soviet intervention on the side of Ethiopia was undoubtedly a tremendous success. Thanks to massive Soviet military aid and Cuban combat troops, the Ethiopians launched a 'text-book-perfect assault' to defeat the Somalis – a feat which had earlier looked impossible – and, by November 1978, had reduced the Eritrean threat to its lowest point in years. In the process, Moscow helped the Mengistu regime finally achieve 'a measure of stability',[1] and carved out for itself a position as the dominant external power in the area. There was no disguising Soviet satisfaction with the outcome. According to one Soviet account, 'the successful counteroffensive of Ethiopian troops and militia against Somali regular troops in the Ogaden . . . caused shudders among the NATO military and in the capitals of Arab states which are supplying arms to Mogadishu'.[2] The reasoning was simple. For Moscow, the Ogaden conflict demonstrated 'an enormous increase' in the capability of the USSR and its allies 'for immediate intervention, particularly by means of rapidly moving large military units and armaments over large distances'.[3] And this, as the then CPSU Central Committee Secretary Boris Ponomarev pointed out in a speech on Soviet–Ethiopian relations, gave a whole new meaning to 'the growing alliance of the forces of national liberation and of world socialism'.[4]

In the years since the Soviet–Cuban intervention of 1977–8, the view that the USSR fundamentally shifted the local military balance in Ethiopia's favour has remained valid. To be sure, the comprehensive defeat of the Somali Army in March 1978 did not end hostilities in the Ogaden. In May 1978, President Siad vowed to continue backing the 'independence' struggle of the WSLF. But, in the classic guerrilla campaign that followed, the pattern of Ethiopian military success repeated itself. The decisive ingredient in this has been Soviet assistance. On 20 November 1978, the USSR and Ethiopia signed a Treaty of Friendship and Co-operation. The treaty was broadly similar to the one previously renounced by the Somalis. Amongst other things, the agreement stressed the principles of 'sovereignty, territorial integrity and the inviolability of frontiers' and committed both parties to 'continue to co-operate in the military field'[5] in the interest of ensuring their defence capability (Article 10). In effect these provisions, given the difference in power between the signatories, provided a guarantee of Soviet military support for the Mengistu regime.

Between 1978 and 1987, the Soviets, according to the US Arms Control and Disarmament Agency (ACDA), supplied Addis Ababa with something like an additional $7 billion in military aid. As a consequence, the Ethiopian military machine became the largest and best equipped in sub-Saharan Africa. A recent assessment put the Ethiopian army at 313,000 strong, with an air-force of 138 combat aircraft. This compares with a Somali army of 61,300 men and an air-force possessing approximately 70 combat aircraft. Ethiopia enjoys the logistical support of 1,200–1,400 Soviet military advisers, some 4,000 Cuban troops – the figure was reduced from 12,000 in June 1984 – and 300 East German advisers[6](see Table 14).

Further, the Soviet commitment to Ethiopia was underlined by regular visits of top Soviet military officials. Many were unannounced. There were, however, some notable exceptions. In July 1980, Admiral S. Gorshkov, the then Commander of the Soviet Navy, paid an inspection visit to the Eritrean ports of Assab and Massawa; in April 1981, General A. A. Yepishev, the then CPSU Central Committee member and head of the Soviet army and navy main political directorate, led a military delegation to Addis Ababa; in early July 1981, the then Deputy Defence Minister, Marshal S. L. Sokolov, a key participant in previous arms negotiations in the Horn, held talks with the Ethiopian leadership in Addis Ababa; in February 1984, Rear Admiral R. L. Dymov, commander of the Soviet fleet in the Indian Ocean, paid a visit to Ethiopia and, in July 1984, Marshal V. Petrov, who had earlier directed the successful Ethiopian–Cuban counter offensive, visited Ethiopia's naval base at Massawa.[7]

As intimated, one of the main casualties of the Soviet military input has been the Somali cause. Fighting had broken out again in the Ogaden just nine months after the announcement of the Somali withdrawal in March 1978. By May 1980, the conflict had significantly escalated. For the first time since the 1977–8 war, Somali regular soldiers entered the fray alongside the WSLF guerrillas.[8] The Dergue's

Table 14. *The military balance in the Horn of Africa 1987–1988: A breakdown*

Category	Ethiopia	Somalia
Population	42,555,000	7,010,000
Estimated GNP 1985/6	US$ 5.47 billion	$ 1.00 billion
Total armed forces	320,000	65,000
Estimated defence budget	US$ 446.86 million	$134.22 million
Army		
Total strength	313,000 (incl. 150,000 People's Militia)	61,300
	22 infantry divisions	4 Corps, 12 div, HQ
	8 parachute commander brigades	4 tank battalions
	37 artillery brigades	45 mech. and infantry brigades
	12 air defence battalions	4 commando brigades
Equipment	Tanks: 750 incl. 600 T–54/–55 and 50 T–62	1 SAM brigade
	Armoured Fighting Vehicles: 165 BRDM–11–2,	3 field artillery brigades, 30 AA brigades
	600 BTR–40/–60/–152, 40 BMP–1	Tanks: 303 incl. 30 Centurion, 123 M–47
		and 110 T–54/–55
		Armoured Fighting Vehicles: 30 BRDM–2,
		15 AML–90, 64 BTR–40/–50/–60, 100
		BTR–152, 310 Fiat 6614/6616
Navy		
Total strength	3,000	1,200
Bases	Massawa, Assab	Mogadishu, Berbera, Kismayo
Equipment	2 Petya II frigates	2 Osa–11 with 4 SS–N–ZSSM
	Fast Att. Craft with missiles incl. 8 Sov Osa II	4 Soviet Mol Fast Att. Craft
	4 Soviet Mol Fast Att. Craft	5 Poluchat patrol craft
	5 large patrol craft incl. 3 118 ton Swiftships	1 Polnocy Amphibious craft
	2 Polnocny Amphibious craft	4 T–4 landing craft
	4 T–4 landing craft	
	1 US Barnegat	

Air Force

Total strength	4,000	2,500
Equipment	138 combat aircraft incl. 78 MiG–21, 20 MiG–17 and 40 MiG–23	71 combat aircraft incl. MiG 17, Hunter (FGA–76), MiG 21, 30 J–6, SF–260W
	11 AN–12 transp. pl.	3 AN–24 transp. pl.
	2 AN–26 transp. pl.	1 AN–26 transp. pl.
	Helicopters incl. 32 Mi–8, 22 Mi–24 and 10 Chetak	4 BN–2 Islander transp. pl.
		Helicopters incl. 6 Mi–4, 4 Mi–8, 5 Augusta-Bell
Defence expenditure as % of GNP	8.2	13.4

Note: Ethiopia's armed forces are supplemented by 1,200–400 Soviet advisers, 3,000–4,000 Cuban troops and about 300 East German military and technical personnel.

Source: Adapted from *The Military Balance, 1987–1988*, London, International Institute for Strategic Studies, 1987, pp.111–12 and p. 126

response was both immediate and devastating. It launched a series of air-strikes on northern Somali border towns, suspected of being stop-off points for Somali infiltrators and deployed newly imported Hind Mi24 helicopter gunships from the USSR against rebel held positions. The result was that, by August 1980, the second foray of Somali regular troops, perhaps 14,000-strong, collapsed.[9] To add insult to injury, Mogadishu also suffered a major reverse on the diplomatic front. An eight-nation OAU mediation committee, re-convened in Lagos between 18 and 20 August 1980 to consider the Ethiopian–Somali dispute, adopted a resolution which effectively recognised the Ogaden as an integral part of Ethiopia.[10]

Ironically, these set-backs qualified Somalia for defensive military aid from the United States. On 22 August 1980, the US and Somalia finally signed an agreement for the use of military facilities at the port of Berbera by the new US Rapid Deployment Force (RDF). In return, Somalia was to receive $20 million in military credits, $5 million in budgetary support and a further $20 million in general credits.[11] The agreement, however, was not implemented immediately and, in the meantime, did little to lessen tension between Addis Ababa and a much weakened Somalia.

The conflict entered a new stage in July 1982. In an attempt to end the almost permanent Somali threat to the Ogaden, Ethiopia launched a limited offensive in central Somalia. The operation involved about 7,000 Ethiopian troops and a dissident Somali group, the Somali Democratic Salvation Front (SDSF). There was probably Soviet involvement, too.[12] For several years prior to the incursion, the Soviet media had focussed on the 'opposition movement' inside Somalia to the 'pro-imperialist' regime of Siad Barre. The invasion itself was depicted in Moscow as a purely internal affair between the SDSF 'patriots' and a corrupt Mogadishu regime which, it was alleged, had 'turned its country into a bridgehead for the US military'.[13] But, contrary to Soviet and Ethiopian hopes, Siad's government survived the crisis. An airlift of US military equipment helped, as did wide-spread Somali antipathy towards Ethiopia.

After the flare-up in the summer of 1982, sporadic clashes in the Ethiopian–Somali border area continued. On each occasion, however, Ethiopia dominated the exchanges. Having captured two Somali border towns, Balamballe and Galdogob, in 1982 Ethiopia ensured that most of the action took place on Somali soil. In July 1983 and again in January 1985, Mogadishu announced that it had repulsed attacks from Ethiopian 'invaders'.[14] Then on 12 February 1987, a more serious incident occurred. It happened in the middle of Ethiopian–Somali peace discussions, about which more will be said later. An Ethiopian brigade and some guerrillas from the Somali National Movement (SNM) launched a joint offensive on six towns in the Togdheer region in North-west Somalia. The attack was supported by twenty-two T–55 tanks and a squadron of MiG-23 fighter bombers. But Somalia proved to be no push-over. Around 300 Ethiopian soldiers were killed and vast quantities of Soviet-supplied military equipment, including eleven T–55 tanks, were lost in what was a decisive rebuff.[15] Meanwhile, the Ogaden province itself remained comparatively quiet. The Ethiopian Army had squeezed the WSLF to little more than a nuisance value.

To a lesser degree, the security situation in Eritrea also improved. In 1978 Mengistu's Army forced the EPLF to retreat into the countryside after reoccupying all of the major urban centres in Eritrea. The rebels seemed to have bounced back in 1984–5 by capturing the important towns of Barentu and Tessenei. But this success proved to be only temporary. By September 1985, both of these towns were back in Ethiopian hands. In the months that followed the Ethiopian army in Eritrea launched one of its periodic 'final' offensives. It re-took many rebel-held areas including Mersa Tekla. But it failed to dislodge the EPLF from its stronghold at Nacfa and sustained heavy casualties into the bargain.[16] Moreover, the offensive failed to stem the guerrilla thrusts behind Ethiopian lines in the province. Seen from Moscow, Addis Ababa's protracted efforts on the battlefield confirmed that Eritrean 'separatist bands ... only operate in a limited area'.[17] Certainly there were signs of growing military confidence in Addis Ababa. At the beginning of 1984, Mengistu decided that more than half of the Cuban troops in Ethiopia – many of whom were stationed in the Ogaden – were surplus to requirements.[18] The Soviet role in this military equation in the Horn was paramount. As one Soviet commentator put it, Ethiopian officials knew 'that Ethiopia's contacts with the socialist countries ensures preservation of Ethiopian territorial integrity'.[19]

But did the Soviets invest so much just to consolidate the Mengistu government and maintain Ethiopia's sovereignty? The answer, of course, is an unequivocal no. It should be recalled that the original objective of Soviet policy was to establish a Pax Sovietica in which all states in the Horn would be linked through a confederation under Soviet political tutelage. That objective, however, foundered on the stony ground of Somali nationalism in 1977. Thus, while Soviet intervention on the side of Ethiopia was a successful demonstration of power, it was also an illustration of the limitations of Soviet influence in the area. This finding goes to the very heart of the question which prompted this study – if the USSR was one of the most powerful states in the world and able to project force in distant places like Ethiopia, why did it find it necessary to disengage in Somalia, a country where Soviet interests had long been established?

In Somalia, as we now know, Moscow found that generous military aid did not readily translate into an effective basis for political influence. The roots of this autonomy lay in the ambiguous nature of the Soviet-Somali relationship. While Mogadishu was linked to the USSR by its avowed loyalty to scientific socialism, the ideological bond was more symbolic than real. Rather, the Soviet–Somali alliance was basically an exchange arrangement whereby each side traded certain benefits in order to follow different, but for a time compatible objectives. Somalia actively sought the military backing of the USSR so that it could equip its army to pursue the liberation of the Ogaden. The USSR had a geopolitical interest in the Red Sea and Indian Ocean region. It was, therefore, interested in securing access to naval facilities at Berbera and generally expanding Soviet influence in the Horn. The snag, for Moscow, was that when these two sets of objectives finally collided in 1977 it was virtually powerless to revise the terms of the relationship to accommodate the growing Soviet interest in Ethiopia. After all, the Siad regime had initially defined the limits of the permissible by inviting Soviet support in an area dominated by the longstanding and ultimately irreconcilable conflict with Ethiopia. Consequently, when the Soviets started arming the Mengistu government, they wittingly challenged what the Somalis regarded as the rationale for Soviet–Somali ties. The upshot was predictable. Siad accused Moscow of rank disloyalty and acrimoniously ejected the Soviets from the country.

To some extent, the Soviet experience in Somalia was reproduced in Ethiopia after 1978. Despite the break with Mogadishu, Moscow still clung to the long-term goal of a Pax Sovietica in the Horn. It was remarkable that even in the wake of Somalia's devastating defeat in March 1978, Moscow refloated the idea of a diplomatic solution to the Ethiopian–Somali dispute. In this vein, *Pravda* asserted that 'the road to peace and good-neighbourly relations in the Horn of Africa is completely possible' since 'there exists no sense of enmity between the peoples of Ethiopia and Somalia'.[20] Six months later, Vasily Kuznetsov, the then First Vice-President of the Presidium of the USSR Supreme Soviet, was more specific:

> Our sentiments towards both the Ethiopian and the Somalia peoples are those of friendship and we are ready, as hitherto, to contribute to the establishment between them of friendly and good neighbourly relations'.[21]

In a sense, then, the Soviet commitment to Ethiopia has represented an attempt to gain a Marxist–Leninist confederation in the Horn by other means. But, if this strategy was to stand any chance of success, Moscow, in the short and medium term at least, had to politically bind revolutionary Ethiopia to itself.

At first sight, steady progress seems to have been made towards achieving this goal in the economic sphere. Article 8 of the Soviet–Ethiopian Treaty of Friendship and Co-operation pledged the two sides to 'expand and deepen co-operation' in the economy, trade and science.[22] Between 1978 and 1987, the USSR and Ethiopia signed over fifty agreements and other intergovernmental documents on specific matters of co-operation in the economy.[23] In agriculture, the Soviets helped to build a tractor-assembly plant at Nazret, a dam and irrigation scheme in the Baro-Akobo valley, a phytopathological laboratory at Ambo, thirty-one granaries, farm-machinery repair workshops, livestock-raising facilities (with veterinary services), a textile mill, knitwear factory and experimental farms. They developed cotton production in the Awash valley as well as assisting in the reclamation of Ethiopia's vast Gambela region.[24] In the fuel and power sector, Moscow expanded the capacity of the Soviet-built oil refinery at Assab, conducted geological prospecting for oil and gas in the Ogaden and participated in the construction of the recently completed hydro-electric power station at Melka-Wakana, which will nearly double the country's hydroelectric power output. It also contributed to the general infrastructure with a cement factory at Dire Dawa, a caustic-soda factory and cold-storage facilities.[25]

Furthermore, the USSR has given Addis Ababa technical and training assistance. Hundreds of Soviet specialists – doctors, engineers, technicians, geologists and agronomists – have worked in Ethiopia during this period. In March 1984, *Izvestiya* declared that 'there is perhaps no problem in the economic and social life of the country in the solution of which Soviet specialists do not now take part'.[26] The organisation of the Ethiopian mass media is a case in point. Newspapers and journals 'use the experience of party period-

icals of socialist countries'.[27] In 1982, GOSKOMIZDAT (Publishing
Affairs Committee of the USSR) and Kuraz (the Ethiopian state
publishing agency) signed a co-operation agreement for publishing,
translating, editing and distributing socio-political literature in Ethiopia. Soviet teachers and lecturers have also worked in Ethiopian
higher-educational establishments and, at the Yekatit 66 political
school, the institution responsible for the training of cadres in Marxist–
Leninist doctrine.[28] On the other side of the coin, about 3,000 Ethiopians are now studying in the USSR.[29] This intake is higher than from
any other African country. All this has been accompanied by an
expansion in Soviet–Ethiopian trade. If, in 1978, the volume of
bilateral trade was worth 68.5 million roubles, by the end of 1987 the
figure had risen to 177.4 million roubles.[30] This was almost a three-fold
increase in trade turnover.

Soviet aid has been supplemented by that of the Socialist bloc
countries. Their level of involvement in Ethiopia has broadly corresponded to their own relations with Moscow. It is symptomatic that
East Germany, Bulgaria, Czechoslovakia and Cuba were amongst the
most active aid supporters. Two of them, East Germany and Cuba,
have provided large training programmes for Ethiopian personnel and
substantial numbers of instructors in Ethiopian institutions of higher
learning.[31] They have also, along with Bulgaria, supplied technical
assistance and extensive programmes of university scholarships. For
its part, Czechoslovakia has participated in several of the major
Soviet-bloc projects, notably the Kokeb textile mill and the Melka
Wakana hydroelectric scheme. In addition, Prague has allocated 200
million birr (about $100 million) for various development projects and
sent technical experts to assist in their implementation.[32] On a slightly
lesser scale, Yugoslavia has been a partner in projects such as the
Nekemte agro-industrial complex in Welega (Western Ethiopia) and a
mining feasibility study in the Asmara region.[33] It, too, has sent
experts to Ethiopia and offered scholarships.

At the same time, the USSR claimed a major role in the international
relief effort mounted in Ethiopia during 1984–5. The emergency
operation was prompted by a horrendous drought and famine which
affected twelve of Ethiopia's fourteen provinces. Something like 7.9
million people had their lives threatened by starvation. According to
the Soviet media, which was initially reluctant to even report the
famine,[34] the USSR and the socialist countries were 'the first to
respond' [sic] to this 'natural calamity'.[35] Starting in November 1984,
the USSR supplied stricken Ethiopia with a variety of aid. It sent

foodstuffs, medicines, equipment to drill artesian wells, blankets and other necessities; donated a 100-bed fully equipped mobile hospital, together with its complement of 150 doctors, nurses and technical staff, for use at Asosa, Wollega province;[36] helped to distribute and deliver grain and other supplies inside Ethiopia by deploying twelve large An–12 transport planes, twenty-four MI–8 helicopters and a column of 340 Zil 131 trucks complete with crews; and, in what was an extended replay of the Somali resettlement operation of the mid-1970s, Soviet aircraft evacuated around 200,000 from drought-affected areas in northern Ethiopia to more fertile lands in the south of the country.[37] This controversial scheme was justified in Moscow as the 'only alternative' to starvation, strictly 'voluntary' in character and consistent with Lenin's decree on land.[38] All in all, Soviet assistance 'in eliminating the consequences of the severe drought' was, in the words of Yusaf Ahmed, the Ethiopian Minister of Transport and Communications, 'a manifestation of genuine internationalism'.[39] It was estimated by Moscow that its 'free, urgent aid' to Ethiopia exceeded $120 million in value.[40]

On the ideological level, Ethiopia has formally evolved towards what Moscow regarded as the orthodox model for a 'national-democratic' regime. In December 1979, Mengistu announced the formation of the Commission for Organising the Party of the Working People of Ethiopia (COPWE). However, the Commission, with Mengistu and six standing committee members of the ruling Dergue serving on its executive, developed slowly. It was not until 12 October 1982, amid signs of growing Soviet pressure, that the USSR and Ethiopia signed an agreement on co-operation between the CPSU and COPWE.[41] But Moscow was not fully satisfied.

In January 1983, a Soviet commentator, after examining the 'materials' of the Second Congress of COPWE, concluded that while COPWE had 'done much to lay foundations for the future party . . . a lot is to be done yet'.[42] To underline the point, Moscow sent a large consignment of Marxist–Leninist literature to the COPWE Central Committee and held 'business discussions' with a visiting COPWE delegation in March 1983.[43] For its part, Ethiopia symbolised its commitment to scientific socialism by becoming in October 1983 the first African country to erect a statue of Lenin in its capital. Then, on 12 September 1984, on the tenth anniversary of the Ethiopian revolution and nearly five years after the establishment of COPWE, the Mengistu regime finally honoured its pledge to establish a Marxist–Leninist vanguard party. Political power was to be officially transferred from the PMAC to the new Workers' Party of Ethiopia (WPE). The event was greeted with considerable fanfare in Moscow. Grigory Romanov, then a Politburo member and Central Committee Secretary, who led a CPSU delegation to the constituent congress of the WPE, described the development as 'a major milestone in the history of the Ethiopian revolution'.[44]

The next item on Mengistu's agenda was the establishment of constitutional rule in Ethiopia. In mid-1986, the Dergue distributed a million copies of a 1977 Soviet-style draft constitution across the country. After what was described as a 'truly nationwide'[45] discussion on the document, the final draft of the constitution was overwhelmingly approved in a national referendum on 1 February 1987. On 14 June, Mengistu and all Politburo and some central committee members of the ruling WPE were elected to the new 835-seat Shengo (National Assembly). Under the new constitution, the Shengo was defined as the supreme organ of government. On 9 September 1987, the newly elected Shengo unanimously chose Mengistu as Ethiopia's first civilian President and officially proclaimed the birth of the People's Democratic Republic of Ethiopia (PDRE). The new constitution made provision for the granting of 'autonomous' status to five regions, including the Ogaden and Eritrea. Lev Zaikov, Secretary of the CPSU Central Committee and guest at the thirteenth anniversary of the Ethiopian revolution, told his hosts that the establishment of the PDRE was 'an historic event'. Its significance 'goes way beyond the confines of your country'.[46]

In the international arena, the USSR and Ethiopia have pursued what one Soviet writer has called 'hand in hand'[47] diplomacy. The Mengistu government has generally sided with Moscow on most foreign-policy issues. Shortly after the Ogaden war, when it was the Soviet custom to do so, Addis Ababa adopted a fiercely anti-Chinese posture. It recognised the regime installed in Kampuchea by Vietnam and accused Peking of being 'one of 13 states that directly or indirectly supplied Somalia with weapons and ammunition'[48] during the Horn conflict. In addition, Ethiopia was one of only three African countries to vote against a UN resolution calling for the immediate withdrawal of Soviet troops from Afghanistan in January 1980. More generally, Ethiopia's voting record in the UN has consistently conformed with that of the Soviet Union. In June 1984, in a symbolic demonstration of solidarity, Ethiopia joined the Soviet boycott of the Los Angeles Olympics.[49] All this has been accompanied by regular and well-publicised contacts between Addis Ababa and the USSR. Exchanges of delegations have been frequent, as have Mengistu's visits to the USSR. The Mengistu regime has also expanded its ties with the 'socialist commonwealth'. It signed treaties of Friendship and Co-operation with East Germany on 13 November 1979, with South Yemen on 4 December 1979, with Bulgaria in 1981 and with North Korea on 23 October 1983.[50] Furthermore, Ethiopia signed a regional, tripartite agreement with Libya and South Yemen on 23 August 1981. This treaty, according to *Pravda*, was 'an important stage' in strengthening the solidarity of the local 'anti-imperialist forces'.[51] It should be added that Mengistu's visit to India in 1985 was his first to any non-socialist and non-African state.

The Ethiopian constraints

On closer inspection, however, the picture of Ethiopia as a Soviet satellite was, and still is, wholly misleading.[52] Relations between the two countries have been in reality more complex and less one-sided. If anything, the balance of advantage within the alliance has favoured the Mengistu regime. For the USSR, Ethiopia has presented a fundamental problem in that two of Moscow's objectives – establishing the Mengistu government firmly and making itself indispensible – have proved difficult to reconcile in practice. In particular, three factors have stood in the way of lasting Soviet influence in the country.

The first has been Ethiopian nationalism. As in Somalia, substantial Soviet military aid to Ethiopia has had the unintended effect of strengthening a popular sense of nationalism. The catalyst in this process was the military triumph of 1978 against the hereditary enemy, Somalia. The struggle revived memories of a proud history in which Ethiopia, sometimes with foreign assistance, successfully maintained its political independence for centuries, including during the era of nineteenth-century European colonialism in Africa. Such an independent tradition brought with it a deep sense of self-respect and an almost pathological distrust of foreigners. These strongly ingrained attitudes in Ethiopia have been internalised by the revolutionary government. It is not a coincidence, for example, that the Dergue has shown intense determination to hold on to every inch of territory inherited from the *ancien régime*. Indeed, Mengistu has cultivated nationalism as a source of domestic legitimacy even more than his Imperial predecessor. It is notable that even in the heady days of 1974 Mengistu tempered revolutionary rhetoric with praise for the past contributions of three Emperors, Tewodros, Yohannes IV and Menelik II, all of whom were associated with the rejection of foreign interference in Ethiopia's internal affairs.[53] Likewise, the adoption of Marxism–Leninism in Ethiopia also contained a national dimension. Mengistu told a Soviet audience of his pride in 'the historical uniqueness of the Ethiopian revolution'.[54] The latter, he noted, prevailed despite the initial absence of a vanguard party: 'Our nascent revolution which erupted spontaneously has achieved so many victories which were not attained by radical socialist revolutions under the leadership of famous communist parties.'[55]

There are a number of specific ways in which the Ethiopian revolution has been a natural extension of nationalist development, rather than Soviet experience. For one thing, Mengistu has preserved the political tradition of firm, one-man rule in Ethiopia. Like Emperor Haile Selassie before him, Mengistu has deliberately sought to exercise comprehensive control over all the major branches of government and policy. As noted, Mengistu resisted Soviet pressure to form a ruling political organisation for a long time. Moscow believed that 'a genuinely Leninist' party was vital to ensure that Ethiopia would progress 'all the way to socialism and not stop half way'.[56] That is, Moscow wanted a political structure which would devolve Mengistu's power, enhance the role of Soviet-trained political cadres[57] and thus institutionalise the USSR's position as political patron to Addis Ababa. But Mengistu and his supporters in the PMAC had other ideas.

In May 1978, the Ethiopian leader thwarted a Kremlin-inspired move to foist a party organisation on the Dergue. An exiled leader of the by then outlawed Meison (All Ethiopian Socialist Movement), Negede Gobeze, was smuggled back into Addis Ababa under the protection of the Cuban Embassy. However, an enraged Mengistu refused to negotiate with Negede and forced both Negede and the Cuban ambassador to leave the country by 14 May 1978.[58] The then Soviet ambassador departed soon afterwards. New Cuban and Soviet ambassadors were appointed later in the year. Nor was the decision to establish COPWE in December 1979 a significant concession on Mengistu's part. COPWE had no independent status and had an executive and central committee dominated by members of the Dergue. Its function was to screen potential members of the future party and, if eligible, provide them with political training. The process was a painstaking one. But Mengistu, the Chairman of COPWE, was prepared to wait to get the desired result. In the meantime, Ethiopian society found itself the subject of a personality cult. Mengistu moved in to Emperor Haile Selassie's palace and assumed the trappings of the Imperial style. On several public occasions, Mengistu was observed sitting alone on an elevated platform in the gold and red velvet eighteenth-century armchair favoured by the Emperor.[59] Elsewhere, on the street corners of Addis Ababa, Mengistu's brightly coloured portrait, far bigger than life, became a permanent feature.

Moscow was deeply troubled by Mengistu's behaviour. In February 1982, *Pravda* referred to the slow pace of change in Addis Ababa.[60] Another Soviet source, commenting on the process of party construction in Ethiopia, was blunter: 'It is impossible to forget with regard to this, that in the country there are still influential forces, resisting this process and coming out for the system of autocratic leadership.'[61] Moreover, it would appear that Moscow did not confine its disapproval to words. At the end of February 1984, two Soviet diplomats, one of whom was identified by Western diplomatic sources as the KGB station chief in Addis Ababa, were expelled from Ethiopia. While neither the Soviet nor the Ethiopian government commented on this unusual incident between 'fraternal allies', it was reported that the Soviet officials were involved in a plot to oust Mengistu and replace him with a more pro-Soviet figure, Feseha Desta, then ranked third in the PMAC.[62] One month later, Mengistu informed the USSR 'that we are now approaching the moment when we will witness the birth of the WPE.[63]

Whether Mengistu was spurred into action by Soviet subversion or fear of it is a moot point. In any event, the Ethiopian leader had prepared his ground well. Quite apart from the work done by COPWE, Mengistu had also consolidated his position through administrative changes. In 1982 the regime reorganised the All-Ethiopian Trade Union and the All-Ethiopian Peasant Association, and set up a National Workers' Control Committee which, in turn, established branches at factory level. In April 1983, Mengistu carried out an extensive reshuffle of the ruling PMAC hierarchy. This involved, *inter alia*, the appointment of new government ministers in the fields of agriculture, education and health. In addition, it is likely that Mengistu demanded extra Soviet economic and military support as a price for the introduction of a vanguard party.[64]

From Mengistu's standpoint, such manoeuvring certainly paid off. The WPE emerged in September 1984 as a hand-picked group of Marxist cadres. Mengistu was duly 'elected' the new party's General Secretary while the Political Bureau – the WPE's top decision-making body – consisted largely of the most prominent individuals of the

PMAC. By the same token, nearly all the new Party Secretaries in the provinces were old Dergue members. Thus, the new ruling party in Ethiopia was a thinly disguised military one and a Mengistu-dominated one at that. President Chernenko was not exaggerating when, in a message of congratulation to Addis Ababa, he declared that 'You personally Comrade Mengistu, made a great contribution to the creation of the Workers' Party of Ethiopia'.[65] But Mengistu's political 'contribution' did not end there.

The advent of the PDRE in September 1987 both legitimised and further entrenched Mengistu's power structure. While the political trappings undoubtedly changed, the distribution of power did not. Even a previously sympathetic observer like the Ethiopian historian, Aleme Eshete, who has been cited in Soviet writings on Ethiopia, con-demned the new constitution for institutionalising the position of the Mengistu regime.[66] This suspicion was well-founded. Firstly, the 343-strong commission, which drafted the new constitution, was appointed by the WPE. Secondly, the new constitution, all seventeen chapters and 120 articles of it, was adopted through the device of a referendum in a country where something like 40 per cent of the popu-lation are illiterate. Thirdly, all candidates for the National Assembly (Shengo) were either nominated or vetted by the WPE. Fourthly, the new Ethiopian consitution, by combining the main features of the Soviet and Romanian models, concentrated more power in the hands of its President than any other Marxist leader including Mikhail Gorba-chev.[67] It came as no great surprise, therefore, that Mengistu emerged as Head of State in the new Republic and Secretary-General of the country's only political party. The military government of Colonel Mengistu had become the civilian government of President Mengistu. The birth of the PDRE was not the Soviet success it seemed.

Furthermore, Ethiopian nationalism has played a part in frustrating Soviet strategic expectations. It should be remembered that the USSR sacrificed an important naval base at the Somali port of Berbera in the Indian Ocean for the sake of supporting Addis Ababa during the Horn conflict of 1977–8. Did the USSR then gain equal if not better facilities from Ethiopia? In December 1984, Goshu Wolde, the Ethiopian Foreign Minister (who subsequently defected in October 1986)[68] observed:

> We have no military bases here. We have a treaty of Friendship and Co-operation with the Soviet Union but that does not in any way mean we are subservient to Soviet foreign policy.[69] We do not belong to the Warsaw Pact, nor to any camp or sphere.

This statement was misleading. The Ethiopians permitted the Soviet Navy in 1978 to establish anchorage facilities in the Dahlac Islands off Massawa in the Red Sea.[70] It is also understood that the Soviet military were given access to air and land facilities at Makele, Tigre (south of Eritrea), Debre Zeit and Dire Dawa.[71]

Nevertheless, and here Goshu's words assumed greater meaning, Ethiopia steadfastly refused to give in to all of Moscow's military demands. This has been most strikingly shown in the case of the Soviet plea for a naval base at Massawa on mainland Ethiopia. On at least three occasions the Mengistu government has reportedly rejected approaches from senior Soviet military figures, including Admiral S. Gorshkov and Marshal V. Petrov, for such a base.[72] The Ethiopian attitude reflected an awareness of the general resentment in the country towards the Russian presence. There were reports, in particular, of friction between Ethiopian officers and their Soviet 'advisers' over the quality and reliability of Soviet equipment, as well as over the issue of tactics in Eritrea.[73] Such reports indicated that Mengistu courted political disaster if he compromised Ethiopian independence to appease the Soviets. Suffice it to say, Moscow was sometimes angered by what it regarded as Mengistu's 'international-ist' shortcomings. In 1981 the Deputy Director of the Soviet Africa Institute pointedly observed that the new generation of 'revolutionary democrats' which emerged in 'the political struggle scene' in Africa in the 1970s need *inter alia* 'to abandon the principles of nationalism and replace them with the principles of patriotism and ethno-national equality and in specific circumstances also of self-determination (Ethiopia)'.[74] This takes us to the other irritating facet of Ethiopian nationalism for Moscow.

In Eritrea, Mengistu refused to consider anything but a military solution. He made it clear that his regime would never negotiate with the Eritrean liberation movements unless it was on the basis of regional autonomy. This concept lay at the heart of the PMAC's Nine-Part Peace Plan of 1976 and, more recently, the provision in the new republic's constitution which granted Eritrea autonomy status within the framework of the Ethiopian 'unitary state'. Both initiatives, however, were swiftly rejected by the EPLF for failing to address the central question of Eritrean self-determination. Mengistu is resigned to the fact that 'the Eritrean war may continue for generations'.[75] This hard-line approach was spelt out in an interview with the Soviet *New Times* journal. Mengistu argued that 'to contend that the bandits of Eritrea are fighting for a righteous cause is to condone brigandage and terrorism ... against the national unity of Ethiopia'.[76] On this view, 'the idea of negotiating with [Eritrean] bandits and terrorists cannot be entertained'.[77]

Officially, Moscow endorsed the Mengistu line on Eritrea. Since 1978, the Soviet media regularly pointed out that the victory of the Ethiopian revolution removed any political justification for Eritrean secessionism. It was variously claimed that the 'subversive activities of the [Eritrean] separatists' were 'greatly weakening', that the province had 'in the main, returned to a normal situation' and that Eritrea had joined 'mainstream' life in revolutionary Ethiopia.[78] Indeed, one Soviet observer even went so far as to suggest that there was 'no insurgency in Ethiopia'.[79]

Yet, while Moscow was not prepared to jeopardise Soviet–Ethiopian ties over the Eritrean question, it certainly had some reservations about Mengistu's uncompromising posture. This was discernible in the way Moscow used diplomatic back-channels in an attempt to advance a political option in Eritrea. Having had some links with the ELF since 1968, the USSR set up a series of secret meetings between PMAC officials and leaders of the Eritrean movement. In February, March and June 1978 discussions involving the EPLF leadership were held in East Berlin. These talks ended in deadlock. Then, after several clandestine visits to Moscow by the ELF leader, Ahmed Nasser, between 1978 and 1980, a negotiating session was reportedly held in Beirut on 24 August 1980.[80] The participants included Soviet diplomats, PMAC representatives and ELF leaders. The meeting achieved little, except to worsen relations between the Soviet-leaning ELF and the self-reliant EPLF. It also nurtured the belief among some Ethiopians that the Soviets were secretly aiding the EPLF. Since then, the prospects for a negotiated settlement in Eritrea have been virtually non-existent. And that, as far as Moscow was concerned, constituted something of a diplomatic embarrassment, especially in the Arab world where Soviet allies like Syria actively supported the Eritrean cause.[81]

The second major stumbling block to Soviet influence in Ethiopia was an inability to satisfy the economic requirements of the African state. Since 1978, Ethiopia continued to receive less development assistance per capita than almost any other Third World country. In 1987, for example, it was estimated that the annual per-capita figure was only $9. Corresponding figures for neighbouring Somalia and Sudan were $65 and $51 respectively.[82] The paucity of this aid is all the more remarkable in that Addis Ababa had one of the lowest per-capita incomes – around $120 per annum – in the world throughout this period.[83] But if international development assistance remained relatively sparse, the Soviet contribution, official rhetoric notwithstanding, was no more than moderate.

In the three years ending 1986 (one of the recent years for which detailed figures are available), the Moscow-based Council for Mutual Economic Assistance (CMEA) supplied aid to the tune of $491.8 million.[84] That figure constituted about 22 per cent of the total aid received by Ethiopia. The bulk of the remaining aid came from international organisations or individual Western countries. The UN's organisations contributed $336.5 or 15.5 per cent of the total; the EEC provided some $294.3 million (13.5 per cent); and the Internatioal Development Association (IDA) weighed in with $163 million (8 per cent). On the bilateral level, the largest aid donors were Italy with $380.1 million (17.5 per cent), Sweden with $95.8 million (4.3 per cent) and West Germany with $93.2 million (4.1 per cent).[85] The Soviet-bloc share in development assistance has been a great disappointment to the Mengistu government. In October 1983, the Ethiopian Minister of Planning, Mersae Ejigu, attended the annual CMEA conference in East Berlin and complained 'that the level of co-operation [with CMEA] is not yet high'. This complaint, however, along with a request for $7.2 billion in aid, failed to evoke any response from the CMEA.[86]

But the scale of Soviet aid was not the only reason for Ethiopian dissatisfaction. The Mengistu government was unhappy about the quality of Soviet assistance. In agriculture, Soviet machinery was criticised for being antiquated, unreliable and lacking spare parts. Mengistu said as much when he informed Brezhnev in October 1982 'that Ethiopia will not come to socialism "by bull and wooden plough"'.[87] Subsequent efforts by Moscow and its allies to extend mechanisation had mixed results. Apparently reliable reports indicated that the much heralded Soviet-built tractor-assembly plant at Nazret had production problems, while East German tractors, operating under Ethiopian conditions, frequently needed repairs.[88] Collectivist prescriptions for Ethiopian agriculture were not a resounding success either. In September 1983, Mengistu, commenting on the steady fall in the country's grain production, cuttingly observed that Soviet-assisted state farms made a contribution of merely 4 per cent to the Ethiopian economy and occasionally consumed 'more than what is produced'.[89] Nationalised enterprises, where Soviet aid was channelled, were also criticised for waste, theft and 'laziness'.[90] For its part Moscow acknowledged some Ethiopian discontent. With regard to the

Soviet-assisted Melka-Wakana hydroelectric station, a Soviet broadcast frankly admitted that 'our Ethiopian friends have told us to speed up construction'.[91] What Moscow did not say, however, is that Soviet specialists were sometimes seen in Ethiopia as the main reason for slow progress. According to one account, Soviet experts frequently lacked the necessary linguistic skills, remained aloof from their Ethiopian counterparts and could be technically unqualified, particularly in plants containing American or West German machinery.[92]

In addition, Ethiopia has resented Moscow's commercial approach to bilateral economic relations. The question of debt repayment looms large here. Following the Ogaden war and its aftermath, Ethiopia has incurred a huge arms debt. On top of this, Addis Ababa has remained fully dependent on the USSR for the purchase of petroleum products. Altogether, it is estimated that Ethiopia owes Moscow in the region of $4 billion.[93] And while Moscow has apparently been willing to write off much of this debt, it has certainly tried to extract some repayment. On two occasions, such financial pressure led to serious strains in the already fragile Ethiopian economy. In early 1981 and again in February 1985, Mengistu was forced to ban or drastically curtail imports in order to scrape up enough hard currency to meet Soviet demands.[94] The latter might have been easier to accept if Ethiopia's foreign earnings were not so meagre and if there had not been the suspicion Moscow was profiteering through the manipulation of the rouble–dollar exchange rate.[95] Finally, the exorbitant cost of Soviet know-how has probably removed any illusions in Addis Ababa that the desire for profit was exclusive to the 'capitalist' countries.

With Soviet economic aid failing to match Ethiopian expectations, the Mengistu regime has looked to the West for additional support. According to Mengistu, Ethiopia has always been aware of 'the state of material and spiritual development in the West'.[96] Certainly, the revolution did not undermine the US's status as Addis Ababa's main trading partner. In June 1979, Ethiopian Airlines negotiated a $30.1 million loan from the Chase Manhattan bank to finance the purchase of two American Boeing 727 aircraft. In 1984, the Ethiopians purchased a new generation of Boeings for their national air-line.[97] These moves angered the Soviets. They wanted to equip Addis Ababa airport with a fleet of Ilyushins.[98] At the same time, the US has remained a major market for Ethiopian coffee, the country's main source of hard currency.

Commerical prospects with the West were further improved in 1987 when the Ethiopian government agreed to provide $7 million in compensation to US firms whose assets were nationalised during the 1974 revolution.[99] Similar compensation settlements had earlier been concluded with a number of Western states including the Netherlands, Italy, Japan and Britain. Of these countries, Italy has assumed the dominant role in aid provision. In July 1984, Italy pledged $275 million in development loans and grants and another $100 million in commerical credits.[100] Meanwhile, Britain donated well-drilling equipment, Austria agreed to build two health centres in Eastern Ethiopia, Sweden signed a research agreement with Addis Ababa University and Finland provided substantial financial and technical support for an electrification project at Hosa'ina, central Ethiopia.[101] But perhaps the potentially most significant step in Ethiopia's campaign to widen economic contacts came in February 1983. For the first time since 1974, a PMAC edict permitted the establishment of joint ventures with foreign partners in the Ethiopian economy. So far the initiative has failed to attract any substantial Western investment at all.[102]

These developments have been watched in the Kremlin with a mood of uneasy acceptance. After the death of Brezhnev in November 1982, the Soviet leadership has tried to face the unpalatable fact that foreign revolutions like Ethiopia's may demand more of Moscow than Moscow can hope to give. In June 1983, Yury Andropov made a significant statement on Soviet ties with socialist-oriented countries:

> It is one thing to proclaim socialism as one's goal, and it is quite another to build it. This requires a defined level of productive forces, and of culture, and of social consciousness. The socialist countries solidarize with these progressive states, give them aid in the sphere of politics and culture, and promote the strengthening of their defence. We also assist their economic development to the extent of our possibilities. But fundamentally that – as also the whole social progress of these countries – can of course only be the result of work by their own people, and of a correct policy on the part of their leadership.[103]

In other words, Andropov's message to countries such as Ethiopia was that they could not rely on Soviet resources for development and must, in the last analysis, be self-reliant.

In practice, though, Moscow has shown itself to be very nervous about the political implications of this stand, especially when, as in Ethiopia, it tacitly encourages links with 'the world capitalist market'. In this vein, the Soviet media exhibited a lukewarm attitude towards the PMAC's mixed companies decree of February 1983. A Soviet commentator drily observed that 'in the opinion of the Ethiopian leadership mixed foreign and state capital controlled by the state may play a positive role in the development of Ethiopia's national economy'.[104] While denying that the new law would turn Ethiopia 'into an appendage of the capitalist world', Moscow remains aware that in the economic sphere 'the imperialists have at their disposal fairly powerful levers and substantial possibilities for manoeuvre'.[105]

To a large degree, the strains in the Soviet–Ethiopian economic relationship have been focussed by the dreadful famine of 1984–5. So far we have only discussed the tragedy in terms of the Soviet perspective. Let us now broaden the picture. A Kenyan journalist, Mohammed Amin who shot the BBC film in October 1984 that shook the conscience of the world, described a scene at Korem in the Wollo province during the height of the famine:

> ... there was this tremendous mass of people, groaning and weeping, scattered across the ground in the dawn mist ... as if a hundred jumbo jets had crashed and spilled out the bodies of their passengers among the wreckage, the dead and the living mixed together so you couldn't tell one from the other.[106]

But the Ethiopian famine was not just a natural disaster. It was also a direct challenge to the political legitimacy of the Mengistu regime. The PMAC, it should be recalled, came to power on the back of a famine which affected one million people. In doing so, Ethiopia's revolutionaries claimed to have 'ended forever' the 'permanent hunger'[107] of the Haile Selassie regime. But, ten years on, the Soviet-backed Mengistu government found itself impotent against a famine seven times worse than the one that scuttled the *ancien régime*. Suddenly, the slogan, 'proletarian internationalism' had a hollow ring to it.

As things turned out, it was not Moscow but the Western governments and voluntary agencies which provided the bulk of emergency food aid for famine-stricken Ethiopia. Between 1984 and 1985, the EEC countries, either bilaterally or on a Community-wide basis, sent Addis Ababa some 280,000 tons of food aid. That constituted the biggest allocation of famine aid given to any African country by the EEC. At the same time, the US donated 432,000 tons of food – approximately one third of all Ethiopia's food aid in 1985 – which was estimated to be worth $243 million.[108] This compared with a contribution of 11,230 tons of food aid from the USSR in 1985.[109] Moreover, in early November 1984, the British RAF and the West German Luftwaffe, represented by four Hercules transport planes and full flying crews, initiated what was to become a highly efficient multinational air-lift of grain into Ethiopia's drought-affected interior. However, the energetic response of most Western governments to Ethiopia's plight did not mark a change in political attitude toward the Mengistu regime. Rather, it was a case of Western politicians bowing to the pressure of public opinion in their respective countries.

Assisted by the powerful medium of television, charitable organisations and prominent individuals, above all the rock star, Bob Geldof, appealed for public support to help famine victims in Ethiopia. The campaign inspired a climate of altruism in many countries. It was a climate which democratic politicians could not ignore. Altogether forty-seven non-government organisations administered famine relief in Ethiopia[110] and many were overwhelmed by public generosity. For instance, in Britain, the Oxfam organisation, raised £10.4 million just three months after the first pictures of starving Ethiopians appeared on television screens.[111] The fund-raising efforts of Bob Geldof were even more spectacular. In January 1985, Geldof promoted the Band Aid charity record, 'Do they know it's Christmas?'. This raised more than £8 million for Ethiopian famine relief. Then, in July 1985, Geldof organised a 'Live Aid' pop marathon, beamed world-wide via Wembley and Philadelphia. The 'Live Aid' project generated about £48 million for African countries like Ethiopia experiencing famine and drought. Clearly, for the man in the street, particularly in the West, humanitarian considerations took precedence over political ones, and the victims of the Ethiopian famine could not be ignored on account of the behaviour of the Mengistu government. At the time of the crisis, the government lavishly spent around £55 million on the celebrations marking the tenth anniversary of revolutionary power.[112] It continued to devote 43 per cent of the Ethiopian national budget to defence expenditure, sometimes gave priority to the unloading of Soviet military equipment over the delivery of food shipments at the congested port of Assab, did not negotiate its own first major purchase of grain on the world market until October 1984 and, according to foreign relief workers and Aid agencies, forcibly resettled 600,000 people from drought-afflicted areas at a cost of many thousands of lives.[113]

Despite this, the successful mobilisation of famine-relief aid from the West has been something of a political watershed. The relief operation ensured that the death toll was in the hundreds of thousands rather than millions. The net effect of the Western response – gratefully described by the then Ethiopian Foreign Minister, Goshu Wolde, as a gesture, 'unmatched perhaps in the last century'[114] – served to strengthen Ethiopia's hand in relations with the USSR.

While some embarrassed members of the Mengistu regime sought to minimise the Western role, it could not alter a universal public awareness inside the country concerning the main source of food aid. It is interesting that the Soviet relief effort, which was largely concentrated in the provision of transport, only materialised after the West appeared on the scene. According to an apparently reliable report, Moscow was galvanised into action by a stormy secret meeting in Addis Ababa on 11 October 1984. Apparently, Dawit Wolde Giorgis, the head of the Ethiopian Relief and Rehabilitation Commission, warned the Ambassadors of the Soviet bloc that American and West European aid efforts were casting the Eastern countries in a bad light.[115] Certainly, Moscow was alive to the prospect of 'political capital accruing to Washington from its grain deliveries'.[116]

The USSR acknowledged that 'Ethiopia receives food supplies from the West', but insisted 'consignments from that quarter' were invariably accompanied by a 'noisy propaganda clamour'[117]: 'The Washington Times has written, for instance, that the Soviet Union has been supplying chiefly weapons to Ethiopia while the West has been rendering it humanitarian aid.'[118] Such assertions, Moscow contended, were intended to conceal Western responsibility for Ethiopia's predicament: 'The fact remains ... that the West, which oppressed Africa for centuries and is still continuing to plunder it, is actually returning only an infinitesimal fraction of what it owes the continent.'[119] Further, Moscow denied that Western food aid was purely humanitarian. It alleged that some representatives of 'Western charity organisations' were aiding 'separatist bands' in Eritrea and Tigre by 'placing large consignments of grain at their disposal'. Actions of this type 'clearly bear the stamp of the CIA' and were nothing short of 'an attempt to use the grain deliveries to bring about a change in the "undesirable" Ethiopian regime, which the US has been trying to undermine ever since the 1974 revolution'.[120]

To sustain this disreputable image of the West, the Soviet media ignored events which might contradict it. For example, Moscow remained silent about a joint initiative called 'Operation Saint Bernard'. The latter, launched in February 1985, involved an unprecedented degree of co-operation between the Soviet, Polish, British and West German air forces in an exercise to drop food to starving Ethiopians in remote, mountainous regions. Equally, the USSR was one of the few countries in the world which declined to be a full participant in Bob Geldof's 'Live Aid' fund-raising pop concert.[121]

The Soviet media ignored the event and thus denied Soviet citizens the chance to contribute to the Live Aid relief fund.

Such defensive behaviour reflected Moscow's sense of vulnerability over the aid question. For, behind the repeated belittling of Western aid, lay the realisation, as President Chernenko put it to Mengistu, that while 'the Soviet people take to heart the ordeal that has befallen the population of Ethiopia' they could only 'render necessary help and support as far as possible'.[122] This meant, in the less sanitised language of an Ethiopian doctor, 'if the Russians want to send us food to help against the famine they will have to buy it from the West'.[123] It would not be an exaggeration to say, then, that the Ethiopian famine exposed the frailties of the Soviet position in the country. Confirmation of this came from Moscow itself, ironically, at the end of the emergency in October 1985. Writing on the newly formed WPE, the *New Times* journal observed, with undisguised relief, that: 'The party passed the acid test of famine, resisted counterrevolution, and did not abandon its course of socialist orientation in exchange for Western food supplies.'[124]

A third obstacle to Soviet penetration in Ethiopia has been the enduring strength of religious feeling there. Almost half of the Ethiopian population are followers of the Coptic Christian Church, which has a history of sixteen centuries of dominance behind it. The rest of the 46 million-strong population are largely Muslim. From the outset, the revolutionary regime has been forced to recognise the strength of religion in Ethiopia. An initial move to dis-establish the Ethiopian Orthodox Church in 1974 was balanced by the acknowledgement of Islamic holidays and a more relaxed approach towards the construction of mosques. In fact, the two principal religious dignitaries – the Orthodox Patriarch and the chief Muslim Mullah of Addis Ababa – have been present at all state functions, including revolutionary anniversaries. While Mengistu himself has not participated in any public religious ceremonies, his wife has attended annual pilgrimages to Kulubi for the feast of St Gabriel.[125]

Symbolic acts of this kind have alarmed 'socialist conservatives' in Moscow especially as, in the words of a secret Dergue position paper in 1981, 'the numbers of believers in both the churches and mosques is on the increase'.[126] Recent Western visitors to Addis Ababa have confirmed that this is indeed the case. Young people, in particular, have been very much in evidence at religious services.[127] For some Soviet observers and their hard-line supporters in Addis Ababa like Captain Legesse Asfaw, 'the religious question occupies a place of no small importance'. In their view, there remained the danger that 'adherence to various religions' in Ethiopia will be 'made use of by reactionary circles inside and outside the country'.[128] These elements, therefore, sought to marginalise religion. The effort bore some results. On 18 February 1977, the Patriarch of the Ethiopian Orthodox Church, Abuna Theophilos, was arrested for alleged financial crimes against the Ethiopian people.[129] A more compliant figure, Mersze Hazen Abeba, was installed in his place. A Dergue campaign against Protestant churches with Western missions followed. In early 1982, Sweden and Norway reported that the Ethiopian Evangelical Church had been seized by the government and that 600 Lutheran churches had been closed. Meanwhile, Ethiopian Archbishop Mattias fled and received asylum in Britain in late 1981. There were also reports of the sudden disappearance of several Coptic Church leaders, the public hanging of certain Muslim teachers and the persecution of Mekane Yesus supporters.[130]

At the same time, the Canadian Association for Ethiopian Jews and the Los Angeles-based Simon Wiesenthal Center accused the Mengistu regime of waging a campaign of repression against the Jewish community in Ethiopia, known as the Falashas. It is likely that these allegations played a part in the Israeli decision to mount a secret airlift, code-named 'Operation Moses'. For three months from November 1984, Tel Aviv airlifted around 7,000 Falashes out of the drought-stricken Gondar and Tigre provinces via Khartoum. The rescue operation halted in January 1985 amid much controversy.[131]

But, while the authoritarian Mengistu has demonstrated he is suspicious of religion both as a countervailing power and as a possible source of ammunition for his more ideological rivals within the government, he nevertheless retains a vested interest in ensuring some semblance of religious freedom in Ethiopia. As a leader with a strong sense of Ethiopian history, Mengistu understands only too well the tactical value of distancing himself from views synonymous with that of a foreign, atheist ally, the USSR. By the same token, Mengistu is also aware of the political risks attached to a strategy of unrestrained assault on what is part of the national heritage, namely, the Ethiopian Orthodox Church. In May 1985, an angry mob brutally thwarted an attempt to desanctify a small church in the Ethiopian capital. The mob beat to death the priest and the deacon caught in the act of removing the arc of the covenant from the church.[132] It is unlikely, therefore, that Mengistu will take the campaign against religion as far as some elements in Moscow would like. This realisation has already caused some frustration in the Soviet Union. A Soviet visitor to the country strongly hinted that religion was having a negative effect on political attitudes. He recounted an episode in which an Ethiopian policeman confiscated a camera from a diplomat, who was taking a picture of the Lenin monument in Addis Ababa, and exposed the film:

> When clearing up the matter, it turned out many Ethiopians, includ-
> ing policemen, decided that the monument to Lenin could not be
> photographed and even approached because it was sacred and
> therefore taboo. Well, there is no denying the fact that antiquated
> norms of life still persist.[133]

From the perspective of mid-1988, Soviet intervention on the side of Ethiopia is beginning to look a lot less decisive than it did in 1977–8. Although Moscow has helped the Mengistu government build up its military position and subdue the Somali threat, it has failed to establish the basis for a durable, political relationship with Addis Ababa. Lacking a reliable foothold, Moscow has made little progress toward its ultimate goal – the creation of a Pax Sovietica in the Horn of Africa. For much of the post 1978 period, relations between the USSR and Somalia have been decidedly frosty. As related, the Soviet media has identified with internal opposition groups, the Somali Democratic Salvation Front (SDSF) and the Somali National Movement (SNM), seeking to overthrow the Barre regime. This stance has reflected the Soviet conviction that Mogadishu had experienced 'a curious meta-morphosis'. From being an 'anti-imperialist' ally of the USSR, the Siad regime had 'succumbed' to collaboration with imperialism.[134] Amongst other things, the Barre government had placed the Berbera military base 'at the disposal of the Pentagon' and its RDF, signed a 'sinister' and secret arms agreement with South Africa in December 1984 and entered a similar arrangement with Israel in June 1985.[135] All of which meant, in the words of one Soviet commentator, there was 'not much to be pleased about'[136] in Somalia. The feeling was mutual. In the summer of 1982, Mogadishu accused the USSR of directing 'irresponsible anti-Somali elements' operating inside Somalia. These activities, it was alleged, were part of an 'expansionist' Soviet policy to 'seize control of this region of Africa'.[137] Clearly, in Ethiopia and in the Horn more generally, Soviet intervention seems to have become something of a blunt instrument.

The Soviet learning process

After the death of Brezhnev in November 1982, the first indications began to appear that Soviet experience in the Horn had contributed to a learning process with profound implications for future Soviet policy. Several Soviet Third World specialists vented their dissatisfaction with Moscow's permissive brand of internationalism of the 1970s. Writing in 1984, Karen Brutents, the CPSU Central Committee International Department's expert on Asian and African countries observed:

> One can hardly regard as valid the sort of approach encountered in some published studies in which, as if ignoring the big moves and changes that have taken place in the liberated countries, they carry on, as before [Russian: po-prezhnemu],* about the national liberation movement as such. The inadequacy of this approach is patent in light of these countries' real situation – both international and domestic – which has come about during the years of their independence.[138]

A similar, but more detailed criticism had been voiced by Georgiy Mirskiy, Director of the Middle East Department at the Institute of World Economy and International Relations in Moscow, in early 1986:

> More often than not, Soviet writings set forth outwardly logical but somewhat abstract and schematic structures of the revolutionary process in the developing world. According to them, there are (a) national liberation revolutions, i.e., anti-colonial national revolution; (b) national-democratic revolutions, i.e., purely social but somewhat intermediary and indeterminate, with the participation of the bourgeoise and under the guidance of revolutionary democracy; and (c) popular democratic revolutions led by vanguard parties embarking on the road of scientific socialism.
>
> The logic of this scheme, however (which theoretically is probably irreproachable) is vulnerable if one takes a look at real developments.[139]

What, then, are the 'real developments' to which Brutents and Mirskiy refer? In the Horn of Africa, four have been identified. First, Soviet writers have acknowledged that 'in socialist oriented countries revolutionary processes are not yet irreversible' and sometimes involve 'zigzags and backward steps'.[140] In Mirskiy's terms, 'the transition of type "b" revolution into type "c" revolution' is neither 'complete' nor 'straightforward'. Somalia is a prime example. In

---

* The Russian phrase, 'po–prezhnemu,' appears to be a code phrase – approximating 'po–Brezhevu' – to criticise the old order. I am indebted to David Morison, editor of the *USSR and Third World*, for alerting me to this point.

Mogadishu 'the socio-political forces that opted for socialism have been defeated. The state of national democracy (if one holds that it was set up there) has collapsed or degenerated.[141]

Secondly, the Somali defection and the behaviour of the Mengistu regime after 1978 has lent weight to those Soviet writers who have always been sceptical about the progressive potential of 'revolutionary-democratic' military regimes. As early as 1976, Mirskiy argued that 'to consider the army as the leading force of the anti-capitalist revolution and as the leader of society in the socialist-oriented countries would be a serious error', since 'the corporate interests of the privileged military elite will make it an opponent of radical trends'.[142] On this view, the military is unlikely to tolerate any force – like a genuine vanguard party committed to scientific socialism – under whose influence the revolution might escape its control. This analysis has been backed by at least one Soviet observer with first-hand experience of the Ethiopian revolution.

In September 1978, S. Kondrashov, an *Izvestiya* correspondent, attended the fourth anniversary celebration of the Ethiopian revolution in Addis Ababa. Curiously, Kondrashov described himself as a 'novice' to African affairs and one who had no 'pretence to fundamentalise'.[143] But Kondrashov was no stranger to the politics of the Horn.[144] In his account of the visit, the Soviet journalist discreetly challenged the Brezhnev government's assumption that the Mengistu regime had a clear political identity and was 'capable of playing the role of an advanced, conscious and organised vanguard of the working class'.[145] He did this by contrasting the 'somewhat different' Ethiopian responses to the question, 'how and why did the [Ethiopian] military arrive at socialism, at Marxist–Leninist views?' There were those like Goshu Haile Mariam, the chief editor of the government newspaper, the *Ethiopian Herald*, who contended 'that perhaps the military "drifted" to the direction of socialism under the pressure of the people and the strata of people who had been attracted by Marxist ideas'.[146] Others, such as Lieutenant Tamrat Ferede, a PMAC member responsible for Information and Public Relations, told Kondrashov that:

> The military is a cross section of the Ethiopian people ... When in 1974 there was created a Co-originating Committee of the Armed Forces, its composition reflected the stratification of Ethiopian society and the majority of the Committee belonged to representatives of the oppressed.[147]

Furthermore, Kondrashov questioned the extent to which Ethiopia had changed under revolutionary military rule. Walking through the streets of Addis Ababa, the Soviet journalist discerned a 'fleeting glimpse of the old way of life' in the country:

> On the one hand, there are revolutionary placards everywhere, everywhere there is the hammer and sickle and everywhere one hears the word 'international'. On the one hand, one can physically sense the link with the past from which you cannot tear yourself away by any kind of effort, however heroic and spontaneous.[148]

Kondrashov added that in Ethiopia, he encountered 'the most primitive economy, undeveloped mineral wealth and so many people who are unaware that in other towns of this very earth the last quarter of the twentieth century looks completely different'.[149] However, the problem was not just one of 'backwardness'. Kondrashov implied there was an unacceptable gulf between the comfortable lifestyle of the Ethiopian leadership – he referred to Mengistu's 'pink scarf' and his 'open red cadillac' – and that of the Ethiopian masses.

A third and not unrelated factor concerns what one Soviet writer has called the 'staggering diversity'[150] of developing countries. Ethiopia and Somalia have been no exceptions. While these countries share a common position 'in the structure of the struggle of the two systems' in international relations, they are differentiated on 'national, ethnic, tribalist, religious, caste and clientel' lines, rather than just by 'class character'.[151] But, according to M. Vol'pe, Soviet analysts in the Horn have often overlooked this fact. In this context, Soviet-Ethiopianists, using a 'class against class'[152] approach, sometimes neglect the 'perceptions' of 'Ethiopians themselves' in matters like 'the scientifically based dating' of the Ethiopian revolution. As a consequence, 'the traditional complexity in Ethiopian research' may well be 'buried in oblivion'.[153] At the same time, Professor V. Maksimenko has warned against the tendency in Soviet writings 'to rely too heavily on analogues and historical parallels' instead of examining 'in detail the present-day mechanism of revolutionary processes'[154] in developing countries. This warning, by implication, takes to task Soviet establishment figures such as Anatoly Gromyko, the Director of the Africa Institute, who has been inclined to draw something of a straight historical line from tsarist Russia's expeditions to Ethiopia at the end of the nineteenth century to the Soviet military intervention of 1977–8.[155]

The fourth consideration affecting the Soviet outlook was the advent of the Reagan administration in America. Unlike the 'more flexible' Carter government, the Reagan leadership 'wholly rejects the recognition of any kind of independence and self-determination of the national liberation movement (especially, in the contemporary "post-colonial" stage) and passes it off as a result of "the subversive activity" of the Soviet Union'.[156] This 'universal anti-Soviet strategy' of the Reagan administration has consisted of ' "from a position of strength" policy toward the socialist countries' and a concomitant readiness to use a 'crude element of force' against 'unwelcome regimes'[157] in the Third World. To some extent, the Soviet assessment is linked to the US decision to establish a 'rapid intervention' capability in the Red Sea, the Indian Ocean and the Horn of Africa region. While it should not be forgotten that President Carter took the first steps in this direction – in 1980 Washington negotiated access to air and naval bases at Oman, Kenya and, of course, Somalia, as well as developing existing military facilities at Diego Garcia – it was the Reagan government that implemented these agreements and thus gave the new RDF an operational expression. Moreover, in the case of Somalia, the Soviets are conscious that Reagan has expanded the original military agreement of August 1980.

Between 1980 and 1983, the US gave Somalia about $85 million in military and financial assistance.[158] Further, Washington spent about $24 million on developing facilities in the port of Berbera. In November 1983, the US played a prominent part in arranging a $1.5 billion international loan for the ailing Somali economy.[159] At the same time, the US signalled its resolve to act if necessary to defend its new Somali ally. As previously mentioned, in July 1982, the US air-lifted what Moscow called 'a large consignment of weapons'[160] into Mogadishu at a time of crisis. According to David Korn, the then US chargé d'affaires in Ethiopia, the airlift consisted of $15.5 million in military equipment. If, as seemed likely, Moscow had a hand in the limited Ethiopian incursion, the message was plain. The Barre regime was not 'without good strong friends'.[161] The same message was repeated in February 1987 when Ethiopia and the SNM launched an unsuccessful foray into North-west Somalia. Shortly afterwards, the US announced that it had agreed to strengthen Somalia's defence capability and also expand its naval facilities at the port of Kismayo at an estimated cost of $66 million.[162] These commitments came on top of a US military-assistance programme which, from 1983 to 1986, averaged $36–40 million per annum.[163]

Moscow was also struck by Washington's businesslike desire to involve 'Somalia's armed forces in its military exercises and war games'[164] in the region. Since 1982, US RDF troops and Somali forces have held regular joint exercises. These included a mock battle at Mogadishu, a marine amphibious landing at Berbera and, in August 1987, a combined sea and air operation at Alala and Wan-la-Weyn.[165] In addition, the Soviets were conscious of the Reagan administration's attempts to weaken the Mengistu regime. Starting in 1981, a London-based anti-communist opposition group, the Ethiopian People's Democratic Alliance (EPDA) received about $500,000 per year in aid from the US Central Intelligence Agency (CIA). This aid was limited to funding a propaganda campaign against Addis Ababa.[166] By 1987, hard-hitting radio broadcasts, outlining the EPDA's political stance, were regularly transmitted in Amharic to Ethiopia. Viewed from Moscow, then, the impact of the Reagan Presidency in this region was considerable. The Kremlin was no longer able to assume in advance that any further military venture in the Horn would be unopposed. Nor could it take for granted, with a reinvigorated CIA, that its own 'gains' were invulnerable to American challenge.

Taken together, the four strands of Soviet experience in the Horn outlined above seem to have buttressed a major revision in Soviet Third World thinking:

> It was proved – and this is one of the most important lessons in the past decade of the development of the liberated countries – that while there are vast anti-imperialist reserves there is no guaranteed 'automatic' revolutionary potential there, any more than anywhere else.[167]

This sober appraisal, which is a far cry from Moscow's military-based optimism of the 1970s, has been accompanied by an increasingly rigorous view of the standards expected of the USSR's African and Third World allies. It is not enough, as Andropov observed, for 'backward' countries to simply adopt the ideas of socialism. Rather, it is necessary for them to have a 'radical governing authority' to resolve outstanding, internal social 'tasks'.[168] The emergence of a more discriminating approach in Moscow reflects both disappointment with the political yield from huge military investments – as in Somalia and to a lesser degree, Ethiopia – and a recognition that military aid is no substitute for economic-aid deficiencies in regions where economic and social needs are so vast. It is no coincidence that since 1983 Soviet 'global foreign policy strategy' increasingly has reasserted 'the Leninist precept that we influence international development, the march of world history, above all through our economic achievements'.[169]

Epilogue: the diplomacy of perestroika

Since 1986, changing Soviet perceptions of the Horn have begun to obtain a policy expression. The impetus for this development has flowed from a momentous programme of reform known as perestroika or restructuring. Launched shortly after Mikhail Gorbachev's accession to power in March 1985, perestroika is basically a gargantuan drive to renovate Soviet socialism along Leninist lines. It is, in Gorbachev's words, 'a turning-point'[170] in Soviet history. Two principles are central to this process. Glasnost' (openness) and democratisation or 'socialist pluralism'. The application of perestroika to Soviet foreign policy is still in its early stages. But its effects are already significant and likely to be increasingly so in the future.

Convinced that the USSR's 'international prestige and influence' had been damaged by 'the stagnation and conservatism of the preceding period',[171] the Gorbachev regime has devised a new international approach. In the medium term, the new strategy seeks to improve relations with the technologically advanced West and with what is a rapidly modernising China. The objective is to reduce expenditure on defence – currently estimated to be 15 per cent of Soviet GNP[172] – and switch priorities from abroad to home so as to make the USSR economically competitive by the turn of the century. Such thinking reflects what Gorbachev has called the 'novelty of our time'. That is, while 'fundamental differences between states remain', the world today is 'interconnected and interdependent and ... a definite integral whole'.[173] The first fruits of the new Soviet foreign policy include the new Soviet commitment to the UN, the Soviet disengagement from Afghanistan and the INF treaty. In the long term, however, the Gorbachev strategy is ambitious and seeks to reassert the link between Soviet socialism and the political destiny of the planet:

> If the reform programme drawn up in the USSR is effectively carried out ... one may well expect a major shift of world public opinion in favour of socialism at the turn of the next millennium ... [But] if our policy of reform fails ... if capitalism rather than socialism succeeds in taking the new tidal wave of high technology in its stride; the world balance of forces may change in favour of capitalism.[174]

In relation to the Horn of Africa, one of the most striking features of the Gorbachev era has been a fresh emphasis on a peaceful solution to the Ethiopian–Somali dispute. A hint of what was to follow came during the tenth anniversary of the Ethiopian revolution. *New Times,* the Soviet world affairs journal, marked the occasion by observing 'that Ethiopia needs peaceful skies for its creative endeavours'.[175] Fourteen months later, in the course of Soviet–Ethiopian talks in Moscow, Gorbachev reminded Mengistu that the Ethiopian people 'had broad opportunities to display their constructive potential'.[176] Meanwhile, the Somali leader, Siad Barre, declared in February 1985 that Somali–US relations were 'limping' and that he would welcome the restoration of normal relations with the USSR.

It is against this background that the Ethiopian leader, Mengistu, and his Somali counterpart had their first face-to-face talks for nearly a decade in Djibouti in mid-January 1986. At the meeting, the sides agreed to set up a joint committee to improve bilateral relations. It is unclear what part, if any, Moscow played in arranging these talks. However, the USSR has acknowledged the important role of pro-Western Djibouti in this process.[177] Her efforts to reconcile the two antagonists dated back to July 1983. Whatever the facts, Moscow swiftly endorsed the new talks , and urged 'the speediest establishment of a stable peace and good-neighbourly relations between Ethiopia and Somalia'.[178] The reasoning was plain. For Gorbachev and his allies, the Horn conflict 'for more than a decade has remained a running sore' which has always contained 'within itself the danger of an explosion'.[179] And it is an 'explosion' of the superpower variety that has been most feared in Moscow.

Between January 1986 and April 1987, the newly formed Ethiopian–Somali joint ministerial committee met three times. But, in the words of a Soviet observer, 'the obstacles to a normalisation of bilateral relations appeared difficult to overcome'.[180] The main sticking point seemed to be procedural. Ethiopia insisted that Somalia recognise the existing international border before discussing other issues such as the re-establishment of diplomatic relations. The atmosphere was further strained by the ugly Ethiopian–Somali border clash on 12 February 1987. As related, around 300 Ethiopian soldiers died in the incident. It came as no great surpise, therefore, that the third round of peace talks in April 1987 was suspended. Predictably, each side blamed the other for the continuing deadlock.

At this point, Moscow stepped in to try and bolster the faltering peace talks. Gorbachev invited Mengistu to the Kremlin for consultations. This brief 'friendship visit' took place between 17 April and 19 April 1987. The indications are that the talks went badly. According to a *Tass* statement, the two leaders 'stressed their shared desire for the further development of Soviet–Ethiopian relations'.[181] In other words, there was plenty of room for more co-operation between the two sides. While Gorbachev formally endorsed the Ethiopian stand that regional co-operation in the Horn must be based on the principles of 'national sov ereignty ... territorial integrity, recognition of existing borders and non-interference in internal affairs',[182] he did not seem very impressed by Mengistu's plea for more Soviet arms (Ethiopia was 'exposed to continuous political, economic and ideological pressure on the part of imperialism' and had 'to fight armed counter-revolutionaries'). In fact, Gorbachev appeared to rebuke Mengistu for not showing enough diplomatic flexibility: 'It is important to proceed from realities and not to outrun stages of development. It is extremely important, too, not to grow complacent and stop in one's advance'.[183]

Over the next twelve months, the Gorbachev regime increased its pressure on Ethiopia for an accommodation with Somalia. On 24 July 1987, Karen Brutents, candidate member of CPSU Central Committee and a leading critic of the Brezhnevist Third World policy, delivered a personal message to Mengistu from Gorbachev.[184] The contents of the message are not known. But it coincided with persistent rumours in Addis Ababa that Mengistu had received an ultimatum from the Soviet leader. According to one well-informed source, Mengistu was basically told: 'Improve your relations with your neighbours and persuade them to withdraw support for insurgent movements. Establish internal peace so you can get on with the task of development.'[185] Then, on 10 September 1987, in a speech in Addis Ababa marking the proclamation of the PDRE, Lev Zaikov, Secretary of the CPSU Central Committee and member of the Politburo, spelt out the Gorbachev line:

> As has been repeatedly declared at the most authoritative level ... We are opposed to the transformation of Africa into an arena of confrontation. In this region of the world we firmly uphold the principle of political settlement of regional conflicts. We are resolutely opposed to the outbreak of so-called low-intensity wars on the African continent.[186]

In addition, Zaikov conveyed to Mengistu another personal message from Gorbachev and held talks in which the 'necessity for new political thinking'[187] was stressed.

The vigour of Moscow's campaign for a negotiated Ethiopian–Somali settlement has its roots in two factors. The first concerns the loosening of what Gorbachev has termed 'outdated sterotypes' in Soviet attitudes towards Somalia. Recognising that 'the old habit of seeking to satisfy one's rights and interests at other people's expense'[188] in regional conflicts like the Horn is inappropriate, Moscow since

1986 has sought a less partisan approach. This has meant, first and foremost, establishing a dialogue with President Siad. In early October 1986, the Soviet Foreign Minister, Eduard Shevardnadze, and the then Somali Foreign Minister, Abdurahman Jama Barre, met in New York while attending the United Nations General Assembly. The two men agreed that the friendly links which existed before 1977 should be restored. From 23 November to 2 December 1986 a large Somali delegation led by Dr M. A. Hamud, Minister of State for Foreign Affairs, visited the USSR at Moscow's invitation. The two sides discussed, in a 'constructive atmosphere', the strengthening of bilateral relations and international issues, including the situation in the Horn of Africa.[189] But, while the visit did not produce any tangible results, it nonetheless represented an important step in the thaw in relations between the two countries.

Why, then, has the Gorbachev leadership sought a better relationship with what some Soviet commentators describe as the 'reactionary'[190] regime of President Siad? The answer would seem to lie in the Soviet perception that Somalia is approaching the stage where it is ripe for political change. Since 1986, the Siad government has been rocked by a combination of domestic turmoil and political in-fighting. To a large extent, these problems have stemmed from the clan-based nature of Somali politics. In northern Somalia, the SNM, which draws its support largely from the Isaaq clan, has stepped up its guerrilla activities. In December 1986, the SNM assassinated the chief of security in the North Western regional capital of Hargeisa,[191] and, throughout 1986, waged a fierce military struggle in Hargeisa and other northern towns such as Burao. By early 1988, Siad's Army was both demoralised and isolated in many parts of northern Somalia. Meanwhile, for the first time since Siad seized power in 1969, Mogadishu in August 1987 experienced riots and mass demonstrations.[192] The disturbances were prompted by fuel shortages and price rises in essential commodities.

To make matters worse, a near-fatal car accident in May 1986 fuelled uncertainty about Siad's position as leader. Although Siad resumed the leadership after a month's convalescence, his new vulnerability served to trigger a power struggle within the ruling regime. On the one hand, there were elements from the President's own Marehan clan, including members of his immediate family. Prominent amongst these were the President's half-brother, Abdurahman Jama Barre, the then Foreign Minister, and his son, General Maslah Mohammed Siad, the head of the army's supply department. On the other hand, there was a 'constitutional' faction consisting of powerful non-Marehan figures headed by the First Vice-President, Mohammed Ali Samantar.[193] A graduate of the Moscow Military Academy, General Samantar is known to have been an able advocate of close association with the USSR during the 1970s. Despite close attention from the US in recent years, there are signs, documented below, that Moscow expects to re-establish that closeness should Samantar attain power. And that prospect cannot be dismissed. In January 1987, Samantar consolidated his number two status by being appointed to the newly created post of Prime Minister. Against this, Samantar has lost his defence portfolio and seen some of his supporters in the army demoted.

Many Soviet observers frankly admit that the 'present leadership' in Somalia is facing a severe crisis. According to one writer, the 'deformation of the socialist orientation ... is [now] clearly visible'.[194] For instance:

> In 1980 in exchange for American military and economic aid they [the Somalis] granted access to Somali territory to the Pentagon. But hopes for a mighty inflow of foreign capital were not realised. In these years the USA did not display especial generosity.[195]

But if 'tribalism, nationalism and Islam *for the time being* took precedence over the ideals of social class solidarity'[196] in Somalia, this need not always be the case. Two months after Samantar's appointment as Prime Minister, G. Sashin welcomed 'certain changes' for the better in Somalia which 'in part, corrected the drift to the West.[197] Similarly, I. Tarutin, the first Soviet journalist to visit Somalia for more than eleven years, strongly implied that an improvement in Soviet–Somali ties must look beyond the existing Siad regime. During his visit, Tarutin met many Somalis who had received a Soviet education and maintained an interest 'in everything that was going on in our country, especially with the processes of perestroika'. He added: 'Many of these people occupy responsible posts in the administration, the party apparatus and in the army'. Moreover, such people 'indicated the desire to lay foundations for *rapprochement*'[198] with the USSR. Other Soviet commentators, less sympathetic to the pragmatism of the Gorbachev era, have argued that radical changes in the Somali leadership must precede any improvement in Soviet–Somali ties.[199]

A further consideration in the new Soviet assessment has been the apparent strains in the Somali–US relationship. Tensions have centred on the reduction in US military support for Mogadishu. In 1987, US military aid was cut to $8.7 million.[200] That was approximately 70 per cent less than the preceding year, and way short of the $47 million the Somali government requested. In 1988, US military aid was not expected to exceed $5 million.[201] Evidently, Washington remains suspicious of Somali intentions towards the Ogaden. It does not want to do anything that might jeopardise the long-term objective of luring Ethiopia away from the Soviet fold. Suffice it to say, President Siad's loud protests to Washington have not gone unnoticed in Moscow. A Soviet commentator, amid expressions of regret over the US 'military base' in Somalia, observed that:

> military co-operation with the USA [had] substantially undermined the authority of the SDR in the international arena and in Africa especially. The Somali leaders themselves also are beginning to realise this more and more. Thus, in an interview in the journal 'Al Mustakbal' Siad Barre admitted that 'a big gulf exists between the words and deeds of the USA'.[202]

Equally, in March 1988, *Moscow Radio* highlighted the fact that Somalia had demonstrated its dissatisfaction with US military aid by declining to receive a US military delegation.[203] It is not unreasonable to assume, therefore, that some Soviet leaders believed they could exploit US–Somali tensions to Soviet advantage.

The second factor behind Gorbachev's push for a negotiated settlement in the Horn is a reluctance to underwrite Mengistu's burgeoning military needs indefinitely. From Gorbachev's standpoint, the 'defence problems' of Ethiopia cannot be divorced from 'the political, economic [and] social'[204] challenges facing the country. And these challenges are formidable. In September 1987, just two years after the great drought disaster of 1984–5, the Ethiopian Relief and Rehabilitation Commission (RRC) announced that Ethiopia would face another famine of similar proportions.[205] Insufficient rains during June and July had led to a severe shortage of crops. The worse affected areas were the parched northern provinces – Eritrea, Tigre and Wollo. Althogether, an estimated 5–6 million people were threatened with starvation.

Moscow is aware that the re-emergence of famine in Ethiopia has seriously dented the political credibility of the Mengistu regime. Many Western observers have forcefully argued that the disaster is largely self-inflicted. In fact, David Korn, the one-time US chargé d'affaires in Ethiopia, predicted in 1986 'it cannot be expected that the last has been heard of famine in Ethiopia'.[206] For Korn and other critics, Ethiopia's vulnerability has been linked to three aspects of its agricultural policy. The first is the resettlement of people from the drought-stricken north to the more fertile south-western region. However admirable in principle, this scheme has purportedly been implemented in such a coercive way that it has disrupted Ethiopian agriculture. The second aspect is 'villagisation' whereby peasants living in remote homesteads are relocated into huge, centralised villages. By 1994, Addis Ababa hopes to have moved 20 million people in this programme.[207] Officially, 'villagisation' is justified as a means of improving the peasants' life. But, according to recent visitors to Ethiopia, like Paul B. Henze, these new villages lack even basic facilities and seem to be part of a creeping collectivisation of agriculture.[208] Thirdly, Mengistu's neo-Stalinist marketing and pricing policy is widely believed to have reduced Ethiopia's capacity to feed itself. Until January 1988, the incentive for the peasants to grow more food was virtually non-existent. Forced to sell a proportion of their surplus to the Ethiopian state, they were paid as little as a third of the open market value. However, in early 1988, the Mengistu regime belatedly bowed to international pressure and, *inter alia*, raised state quota prices paid to the peasantry. As a direct result, the EEC and the World Bank unfroze $350 million in long-term development aid to Ethiopia.[209]

At the same time, a rash of high-level defections from the Ethiopian government in 1986–7 seemed to confirm the substance of international criticisms. Goshu Wolde, the former Ethiopian Foreign Minister, Dawit Wolde Giorgis, the former head of the RRC, his deputy, Berhane Deressa, and the former Ethiopian Ambassador to Japan, Abebe Kebede, were among those who cited opposition to Mengistu's agrarian dogmatism as a factor in their political defections. Dawit, in particular, said that the 1984–5 famine 'need never have happened' had it not been for 'the callousness' and 'indifference' of Mengistu. His policies, Dawit argued, 'have caused hundreds of thousands to die and brought unprecedented suffering to the entire population'.[210] Such claims may or may not be self-serving. The fact they were made, however, could not but embarrass Gorbachev and his radical supporters.

For some time, the reformist wing in the Kremlin had urged Mengistu to pursue more flexible and de-centralised agricultural policies. In September 1985, the Soviet advisory group to the Ethiopian Central Planning Commission produced a critical report on the Ethiopian economy. That report, amongst other things, recommended that Ethiopia should turn its attention away from expanding state farms and producer co-operatives and, instead, concentrate its limited resources on increasing the productivity of small farmers.[211] Why, then, has Mengistu, with his centralised programme of resettlement and villagisation, apparently ignored this advice? The answer, it would seem, lies in the fact that on this issue, as on others, Moscow has been unable to speak with one voice. A significant body of Soviet opinion, which includes the State Farm Director V. Paukov, has firmly rejected the view that 'agrarian Ethiopia' can be transformed 'into a small-scale, petty-bourgeois individual-based economy'.[212] According to this perspective, Mengistu's policies have been essentially correct in that they have advanced the key goal of gradual collectivisation. Despite 'imperialist propaganda', the resettlement programme and 'villagisation' are deemed to be 'voluntary' in character, and essential for guaranteeing the necessities of life for the peasantry. Moreover, these programmes provide 'stimuli toward a voluntary common labour'[213] while Western countries 'which give assistance to Ethiopia, are only interested in the technical modernisation of its agriculture . . . along capitalist lines'.[214]

In the event, the second famine has forced Mengistu to reluctantly accept the advice of the Kremlin reformers (and much of the international community). The announcement of the Ethiopian agricultural reforms in January 1988, though, must have provoked mixed feelings in Moscow. Indeed, it was a full six months before the Soviet media endorsed the reforms by declaring that they provide 'substantial grounds'[215] for increasing food production. In the meantime, however, the Gorbachev government has had to face the very problem that its reformist elements had tried to prevent – renewed famine in Ethiopia.

Its response has been, by Soviet standards, quite extraordinary. Despite its own shortage of food, the Soviet Union has perceived the political stakes in Ethiopia to be such that it has become a major food donor. This stands in direct contrast to the famine of 1984–5 when the USSR largely left the giving of food aid to Western countries and international voluntary organisations. On 26 January 1988, the Soviet ambassador to Ethiopia, A. Dimitriyev, announced that the USSR had agreed to send 250,000 tons of wheat to the drought-stricken country.[216] The wheat has been purchased on the open market, mainly from Turkey, at an estimated cost of around $80 million.[217] Altogether, it constitutes about a fifth of the 1.3 million tons in emergency food aid pledged to Ethiopia for 1988 by the international community.[218] Only the US, which has contributed something like 400,000 tons has donated more food aid on a bilateral basis. In addition, three Soviet An–12 planes and five Soviet MI–8 helicopters, and their crews, have participated in a UN famine-relief air-lift from Asmara (Eritrea) to Makele (Tigre).[219] The operation, which has also involved five Hercules aircraft chartered by the UN and the EEC, began in December 1987. It has helped to bridge the gap caused by the escalating northern conflicts, the EPLF attacks on food-relief truck convoys and the expulsion of most foreign aid workers in April 1988 from Tigre and Eritrea on 'security' grounds. Simultaneously, between January and June 1988, five Polish light cargo aircraft transported aid[220] from Addis Ababa to the Shoa region, central Ethiopia. Furthermore, the USSR decided to send a team of fifty experts to south-east Ethiopia to prospect for water, while the Soviet Red Cross, in January 1988, dispatched foodstuffs, baby food and medicines to the African country.[221]

Several factors seem to have prompted the generous reaction of the Gorbachev government. First, Moscow, conscious that the famine of 1984–5 had been the main factor in expanding Ethiopian relations with the West, feared a high political price would have to be paid if Ethiopia was once again left almost totally dependent on the West for food. The Mengistu regime has become more vulnerable than before. Not only has it lost credibility with a large section of the Ethiopian population and many of its own officials, but it has also lost some of its ability to intimidate and coerce. Signs of political unrest in Ethiopia have multiplied. In the armed forces, a clandestine group, the Free Ethiopian Soldiers Movement (FESM), was formed in October 1986 to establish a democratic government in Addis Ababa.[222] Twelve months later, students at Addis Ababa University clashed with police while demonstrating against poor living conditions.[223] Moscow, therefore, probably calculated that substantial food aid would reduce the leverage of the West, above all the US, at what was a very difficult time for Mengistu.

Secondly, the limited application of glasnost' to the Soviet media's foreign reporting has had some feedback for the policy-making process toward Ethiopia. In October 1987, Boris Asoyan, the former deputy Director of the Africa Institute and now a senior adviser in the Foreign Ministry, launched a savage attack on Soviet press coverage of Africa. He condemned Soviet journalism for a 'bureaucratic approach' which shamelessly 'concealed the truth' and promoted a slavish attitude to African leaders who include 'real murderers', 'maniacs' and 'dictators' within their ranks.[224] The exposure of such 'hack work' has, amongst other things, led to more candour in Soviet press coverage of

Ethiopia. Unlike the previous famine of 1984–5, the latest Ethiopian disaster has been treated in a fairly frank and detailed fashion. I. Tarutin, *Pravda's* correspondent in Addis Ababa, has written of the 'pain' of Ethiopia where hundreds of thousands of 'living people are standing human tragedies'.[225] In a visit to Asmara, Tarutin reports how he was shaken by 'the way a half-starved little boy grabbed a piece of a loaf' lying in a road. He also recorded the disturbing sight of thousands of hungry peasants converging on the town for food. 'I saw how they dragged themselves along the road, barefooted in dirty homespun clothing which had worn into holes.'[226] Such graphic reporting could not but affect Soviet 'public awareness'. This, in turn, may have influenced the Gorbachev leadership to respond to the famine in the way that it did. Certainly, in a Machiavellian sense, glasnost' enabled Gorbachev to de-emphasise the military focus of Soviet–Ethiopian relations.

Thirdly, and not unconnected with this, the present Soviet leadership has concluded that the old habit of relying heavily on military aid has cost the USSR dear in Ethiopia and must be reduced. A prominent Gorbachev supporter, Professor V. Dashichev, head of the department of International Relations at the Institute of Economics of the World Socialist System, has pinpointed the negative political effects. According to Dashichev, the 'incompetent approach' of the Brezhnev regime ignored the Leninist notion of 'political equilibrium'[227] in foreign policy. That is to say, the USSR tried to upset the international equilibrium in its favour without due attention to the countervailing consequences:

> Speaking before Soviet diplomats, Comrade Shevardnadze noted that we have often 'committed huge material investment to hopeless foreign political projects'. What have been the consequences of such 'expenditure-oriented' diplomacy? Feeling that it had to answer 'the Soviet challenge', the West [resorted] to military-economic pressure.[228]

Ethiopia clearly fits into this category to a 'T'. Between 1978 and 1988, the USSR has pumped over $7.5 billion in military aid into the country. Yet, despite such enormous expenditure, the main political effect has been to reinforce US efforts to establish a presence in this region. As noted, in the early 1980s, the US developed a Rapid Deployment Force (RDF) which, following military base agreements with Somalia, Kenya, Egypt and Oman, was capable of rapid military intervention. Such an outcome convinced Dashichev that 'we made mistakes in appraising the global situation in the world'.[229]

Viewed in this light, the USSR's energetic response to the Ethiopian famine crisis seems to be part of a long-term effort to project a new, less militarist image in the Third World. This is not to say, however, that the Gorbachev government has stopped arming Addis Ababa in the short term. On the contrary, the food initiative has been coupled with a new $2 billion arms agreement which, according to reliable sources, was signed in November 1987.[230] Under this agreement, it is understood that Ethiopia will receive something like $600 million per year in scheduled arms shipments from the USSR. What is distinctive, though, about this arrangement is its time frame. It is due to expire in 1991 and Deputy Foreign Minister A. Adamishin has apparently told Mengistu that this arms deal will be the last in its present form and scale. Arms supplies in the future will be more limited.[231] Presumably, these conditions have been intended to encourage Mengistu to negotiate in earnest with Somalia. At the same time, the Gorbachev leadership, by continuing to send military aid, has sought to protect the Soviet position in the country and thus parry charges from conservative internal opponents in the USSR that Moscow was making a concession to the forces of 'imperialism' in Ethiopia.

But, if the Gorbachev leadership has had good reasons for wanting an Ethiopian–Somali settlement, Mengistu did not appear greatly moved by Soviet pressure. Following the suspension of Ethiopian–Somali talks in April 1987, nearly a year went by before the two sides resumed top-level contacts. During that period, there were few signs of intense diplomatic activity, except for public statements by Presidents Mengistu and Barre, supporting the peace process. In January 1988, the Soviet Ambassador to Sudan reiterated the Soviet position: he called on all countries in the Horn to support 'the adoption of peaceful means for solving disputes'.[232] Mengistu, however, seemed almost impervious to such calls. His uncompromising attitude was probably linked, in part, to the fact that he had widened his supply of arms by signing a weapons deal with Yugoslavia in late 1987.[233] There are also indications that Mengistu has received discreet encouragement from certain elements in the Soviet establishment to pay no more than lip-service to Gorbachev's 'new thinking'. Several Soviet writers, for instance, have stressed, in time-honoured fashion, the 'class character of Soviet–Ethiopian relations'. According to this perspective, attempts 'to portray Ethiopia as a militaristic state' are 'malicious';[234] Ethiopia is one of the targets of 'international and regional reaction', and thus 'is compelled to expend significant amounts for the protection and defence of its revolutionary gains and territorial integrity'.[235]

In a similar vein, Yegor Ligachev, Gorbachev's conservative Politburo rival, declared that the pursuit of 'solutions to common human problems' – such as the peaceful political settlement of regional conflicts in the Horn – in 'no way means any artificial "deceleration" of social and liberation struggle'.[236]

In the end, Mengistu was forced to compromise in the talks with Somalia. But this was not due to Gorbachev's diplomatic skill. Rather, it was the direct result of what Moscow admitted were 'serious reverses'[237] for the Ethiopian Army on the battlefield. In fact, from 17 to 19 March 1988, the EPLF scored its single biggest military victory ever by routing the Ethiopians at Afabet. This town was the Ethiopian regional headquarters in Eritrea, and the main garrison for the country's crack troops. Altogether, the EPLF put out of action three Ethiopian divisions (about 18,000 men). The guerrillas also captured an enormous quantity of Soviet arms. These included BM–21 'Stalin organs' rocket-launchers, 130 mm artillery, 122 mm howitzers, anti-aircraft guns, light weaponry and 50–60 T–55 tanks. More embarrassingly, Moscow confirmed that the EPLF had, for the first time since the start of Soviet involvement, captured two Soviet officers, a colonel and a lieutenant, during the storming of Afabet.[238] As if that was not humiliation enough, the TPLF simultaneously extended its control of Tigre province. On 26 and 27 March 1988, the TPLF seized the key towns, Axum and Ende Selassie from Mengistu's army. On 28 and 31 March, it followed up by capturing Adwa and Adigrat respectively.

Mengistu himself was partially responsible for these disastrous defeats. Shortly before the Afabet debacle, Mengistu ordered the execution of the much respected Afabet commander, Brigadier-General Tariku Ayene. According to a reliable source, Tariku paid the price for candidly telling the Ethiopian leader during a tour of the region that the Eritrean situation was a 'mess' which could not be won by military means alone.[239] His execution apparently caused turmoil and demoralisation within the ranks of the Ethiopian army at Afabet. The subsequent crisis forced Mengistu to publicly concede, for the first time during his rule, that the 'northern problem' was no longer just a case of a few bandits. In an address to the nation, Mengistu admitted that the 'anti-people elements in Eritrea and Tigre' posed a major threat to his regime:

> ... the problem ... cannot be underestimated. If it is neglected and allowed to continue as at present, it should be properly understood that it will call into question the victory of our progress.[240]

The new slogan became 'Everything to the war front'. To give this slogan a practical expression, Mengistu knew that he had to improve relations with Somalia. Only then could he redeploy in the north a major part of the 50,000 to 70,000 troops based in the disputed Ogaden region bordering Somalia.

As it happened, the two leaders of Ethiopia and Somalia had their second face-to-face meeting in Djibouti on 21–22 March 1988. This meeting had been arranged several weeks before the sudden deterioration of the Ethiopian Army's position in the north. At the meeting, Mengistu and Barre apparently agreed a new framework for further discussions.[241] On 1–2 April, the Ethiopian Foreign Minister, Berhanu Bayeh, and Somalia's Deputy Prime Minister, Ahmed Mohammoud Farah continued negotiations in Mogadishu. The upshot was the announcement of a ten point Ethiopian–Somali agreement on 4 April. Under this plan, the two sides decided to restore diplomatic relations (after a break of eleven years). The two countries also agreed 'to prevent all acts of destabilisation and subversive activities against each other'; to implement a phased withdrawal of their troops at least six miles back from the existing border; exchange prisoners of war; 'refrain from using or threatening force against the territorial integrity and political independence'[242] of the other; and solve all issues by peaceful means. At the time of writing, it would appear that the provisions of this agreement are being honoured by both sides.

The Ethiopian–Somali peace accord confirmed that Mengistu had retreated on the basic issue dividing the two countries. Somalia has not been required to abandon its territorial claim to the Ogaden. According to the agreement, the two sides have merely agreed to discuss the boundary issue at some future, unspecified date.[243] Clearly, the paramount concern for the Mengistu government was to obtain an assurance of security on her eastern borders. Indeed, the ink on the agreement was hardly dry before Ethiopia started airlifting troops from the Somali border to the battle zones in the north in preparation for a counter-offensive there. For Somalia, too, the peace agreement has been something of an exercise in political expediency. The withdrawal of Ethiopian troops from the border zone has meant that the embattled regime of Siad Barre has automatically regained control of the towns of Galdogob and Balamballe for the first time since 1982. Additionally, the peace pact terminated all Ethiopian financial and logistical support for Somali rebel groups such as the SNM. This agreement, however, had an unexpected sting. It seemed to prompt an SNM invasion of the northern region of Somalia in May 1988 from bases previously used in Ethiopia. Fierce fighting, centred on the provincial capital of Hargeisa, ensued. Troops loyal to the Siad regime just about retained the upper hand but only at the cost of about 1,000 lives and the flight of more than 100,000 Somali refugees to Ethiopia. Finally, by reducing tension with Ethiopia, Siad would appear to have gained more scope to adjust Somalia's relations with the US and the USSR.

Not surprisingly, the news of the Ethiopian–Somali accord has been received with 'deep satisfaction'[244] by the Soviet leadership. The deputy Foreign Minister, V. Petrovskiy, observed: 'We regard the Ethiopian–Somalian agreement as a striking sign of the new political thinking, realism and responsibility of these two countries.'[245] Another Soviet official added:

> Military confrontation took too much of the effort and resources so badly needed for the development of the region. It has now become possible to eradicate age-old hostility and pool efforts in combatting the famine, drought and other calamities threatening the nations of the Horn of Africa.[246]

Some Soviet commentators also saw the agreement as a vindication of Gorbachev's new, warmer approach towards Somalia. President Siad was quoted as saying that the 'renewal of co-operation with the USSR may have shown a positive influence here'.[247] The political significance of this accord, however, is not confined to bilateral relations. The Deputy Minister for Foreign Affairs, A. Adamishin, said it is 'a good example to follow ... for other hot spots on the [African] continent'.[248] Nevertheless, Gorbachev has stressed the need for Ethiopia and Somalia to consolidate the accord by adhering to the principles of 'mutual respect' and 'territorial integrity'. That would safeguard the 'normalisation process' against 'outside [Western] interference'.[249]

The future

Notwithstanding Soviet optimism, the Ethiopian–Somali détente has mixed implications for the Soviet future in the Horn. If we assume that this rather fragile agreement survives for a reasonable time, two possible policy options face Moscow. First, there is the revival of the Pax Sovietica plan. This course tends to be favoured by Gorbachev's conservative opponents inside the USSR. They believe that alliances should be made on ideological rather than economic grounds. On this view, peace between Ethiopia and Somalia presents a major new opportunity to expand ties with 'progressive' figures in the Somali leadership such as First Vice-President General Moham-med Ali Samantar, and also to detach the country from the US. Writing in January 1988, a Soviet commentator on the Horn insisted that in the long term 'only Marxism, the class approach' based on the experience of 'the socialist community' makes it possible to 'regularise ancient disputes between various tribes and ethnic groups ... between Muslims and Christians'.[250]

The second and perhaps more probable option is one of gradual military disengagement. It is a course which Gorbachev and other 'realists' of the 'new thinking' are likely to favour. In essence, this perspective accepts that the situation in the Horn is 'extremely complex'[251] and not amenable to any quick-fix military or ideological solutions. According to this reasoning, the improvement in Eth-iopian–Somali relations will facilitate a cut in the USSR's huge military-aid bill in Ethiopia at apparently little or no political cost. Such a move will release badly needed resources for the 'radical economic reforms' in the USSR. This, in turn, will 'create favourable prerequisites for more effective economic co-operation'[252] between the Soviet Union and 'loyal friends' like Ethiopia, as well as 'mutually beneficial relations'[253] with developing countries presently oriented towards the Western capitalist model such as Somalia. In short, Gorbachev will strive to decrease the example of Soviet force in the Horn and increase the force of the Soviet economic example there.

So fundamental a change of political emphasis in Soviet policy in the Horn, however, has severe risks. First, without substantial progress on the core issue of the Ogaden, a Soviet military squeeze could alienate Mengistu and forestall an improvement in ties with Moga-dishu. The history of mutual suspicion between Ethiopia and Somalia cannot be erased by the stroke of a pen. If Addis Ababa does not receive what it considers to be an adequate supply of Soviet arms, relations with Moscow could quickly sour. Equally, it is doubtful that the Kremlin will be able to seriously develop relations with Somalia unless it is prepared to supply arms. According to one report, the Somalis have already made one request for Soviet arms.[254]

Secondly, reduced Soviet military involvement could exacerbate Soviet–Ethiopian differences over the rebellions in Eritrea and Tigre. While Gorbachev now believes it possible to arrive at a 'just [nego-tiated] solution of the Eritrean problem within the framework of the multinational Ethiopian state',[255] Mengistu does not fully share that view. In an important speech on 31 March 1988, Mengistu strongly implied that the USSR had a moral obligation to help him crush the 'comrade terrorists' in the north. He emphasised that the Ethiopian revolution 'inherited' the problem of 'terrorist activities' in Eritrea, which at the time of the *ancien régime*, 'received support from some progressive forces'.[256]

Thirdly, there is a danger that in the transition from a military to an economic-oriented policy in the Horn, Moscow will 'fall between two stools'. On the one hand, the Gorbachev government may find itself explaining to a besieged Mengistu regime that its military aid is limited for economic reasons. On the other hand, because of the inevitable gap between the initiation of Soviet economic reforms and their achievement of tangible results, Gorbachev would have little to offer Mengistu economically, except a promise of more aid in the distant future. All of which is little consolation to a leader like Mengistu who may well be fighting for his political survival. Already, there are signs that Mengistu has begun to explore the Western diplomatic option. During the past year, Addis Ababa has improved relations with Saudi Arabia, released seven women members of the Ethiopian Royal Family from fourteen years' detention and publicly called for better relations with the US.[257] Fourthly, an apparently poor personal relationship between Gorbachev and Mengistu could undermine Soviet efforts to reshape its policy. This is not just a question of chemistry, but also political style. From Gorbachev's standpoint, Mengistu is one of those socialist-oriented leaders whose political emergence in the 1970s was adversely affected by 'the period of stagnation' in the USSR. Such leaders very often assimilated 'everything we are resolutely renouncing today as a standard of socialism'. This included 'the consequences of the personality cult ... with its anti-democratic and authoritarian features'.[258] It is not difficult to imagine, therefore, that Mengistu's iron fist rule – with its summary executions, its intolerance of dissent and its Orwellian-like pronouncements on all matter of things – must seem to Gorbachev and his associates uncomfortably reminiscent of 'the Stalin–Brezhnev version of socialism'.[259]

For his part, Mengistu has shown little inclination to adjust to the Gorbachev era. In agricultural marketing policy and in relations with Somalia, Mengistu has only accepted the Gorbachev line when events have forced him to do so. Such behaviour reflects Mengistu's concern that Gorbachev's reformist ideas actually challenge his tight grip over Ethiopian society. The concept of glasnost', for example, has been doubly unwelcome. Not only has it exposed socialist-oriented countries like Ethiopia to barely veiled Soviet criticism – how long will it be before a Soviet writer criticises the Mengistu regime directly? – but also it has stimulated sympathetic political discussion within Ethiopia itself.[260] Such consequences may strengthen Mengistu's nationalist instincts. It is interesting that since 1986 Mengistu has started to pepper his speeches again with the old military slogan, Ethiopia Tikdem (Ethiopia First). At the same time, Mengistu's robust attitude towards the Gorbachev experiment has also been shaped by an awareness that the Soviet leader has yet to fully consolidate his power. At present, the USSR is witnessing what one Soviet writer has called a state of 'dual power',[261] an uneasy and unresolved tension between two main political factions. Recent comments by Gorbachev's former deputy and now Minister for Agriculture that the new Soviet foreign policy has sometimes sown 'confusion among Soviet people and among our friends abroad'[262] indicates that this struggle is far from over.

Today, the Soviet Union, under Gorbachev's leadership, has turned its back on the Brezhnev era. In the Horn of Africa, there now seems to be a general recognition by the new leadership that it has inherited a strong but precarious position. To Soviet observers familiar with the Somali scene during the 1970s, the Ethiopian experience after 1978 surely had a sense of *déjà vu* about it. After all, this was not the first time Moscow had encountered nationalist, economic and religious impediments in its bilateral dealings in the region. The Gorbachev government, however, has tried to end the 'period of stagnation' in the Horn by embracing the notion of 'new thinking'. The Ethiopian–Somali *détente* represents the first tentative step in this direction. It is an agreement, though, which does little to lessen the uncertainty of Moscow's future prospects. It is unlikely, for reasons of history and cost, to lead to the fulfilment of the old Pax Sovietica project in the Horn. But if, as is more likely, the Gorbachev regime sees the peace accord as a painless way of cutting the military costs of the Soviet alliance with Ethiopia, it could be heading for a showdown with Mengistu. The latter has made it quite clear that he will not compromise his determination to smash the Eritrean and Tigrean rebels 'whatever the cost'.[263] Perhaps, even more alarming for Moscow, should the Ethiopian–Somali accord prove a complete success and herald peace throughout the Horn – admittedly an improbable prospect – long-neglected considerations such as economic development would come to the fore. That would leave the USSR, perestroika notwithstanding, in a vulnerable position. In the circumstances, Mengistu, like Siad and Sadat before him, might just find the politics of the grand gesture irresistible and expel the Soviets. One thing is clear. The Soviet military intervention of 1977–8 has not insured Moscow against such an eventuality.

Appendix A Soviet–Somali treaty of 11 July 1974

Friendship and co-operation treaty between the USSR and Somali Democratic Republic: the text

The Union of Soviet Socialist Republics and the Somali Democratic Republic,

considering that the further development of friendship and all-round co-operation between them answers the basic national interests of the peoples of both states and serves the cause of strengthening peace throughout the world,

inspired by the ideals of the struggle against imperialism and colonialism, the constant aspiration to render support in every possible way to the peoples, the struggle for freedom, independence and social progress and the striving for the complete liquidation of colonialism in all its forms and manifestations,

filled with determination to contribute to the stabilisation of international peace and security in the interests of all nations of the world,

convinced that in the contemporary world international problems must only be resolved through peaceful means,

reaffirming their fidelity to the aims and principles of the Charter of the United Nations organisation,

moved by the aspiration to strengthen and consolidate the building of friendly relations and mutual co-operation between both states and peoples and to create the basics for its further development,

resolved to conclude a genuine Treaty of friendship and co-operation and have agreed on the following:

Article 1. The high contracting parties solemnly state that stable peace and friendship will exist between both countries and their peoples. The sides will continue to develop and strengthen their relations on the basis of the principles of respect for sovereignty, territorial integrity, non-interference in each other's internal affairs, and equality. They will co-operate in every way in ensuring conditions for the preservation and deepening of their people's socio-economic achievements.

Article 2. The USSR and SDR will continue to expand and deepen all-round co-operation and exchange of experience in the economic and scientific-technical spheres – in industry, farming and livestock raising, irrigation and water resources, the development of natural resources, the development of power engineering, the training of national cadres, and in other corresponding spheres of the economy. The sides will expand trade and maritime navigation between them on the basis of the principles of mutual benefit and most-favoured-nation status in accordance with the provisions of the trade and payments agreement between both countries concluded in Moscow on 2 June 1961.

Article 3. The high contracting parties will contribute to the further development of co-operation between them in the sphere of science, art, literature, education, health, the press, radio, the cinema, television, tourism, sport, and in other spheres. The sides will contribute to the expansion of co-operation and direct ties between the political and public organisations of the working people, enterprises, and cultural and scientific establishments with the aim of deeper mutual familiarisation with the life, labour and achievements of the people of the two countries.

Article 4. In the interests of strengthening the SDR's defence capability the high contracting parties will continue to develop co-operation in the military sphere on the basis of the corresponding agreements between them. Such co-operation will provide for, in particular, co-operation in the training of Somali military personnel and in the mastery of the arms and equipment supplied to the SDR for the purposes of enhancing the defence potential.

Article 5. Pursuing a peace-loving foreign policy, the USSR and the SDR will continue to contribute in every way to the preservation of peace and to advocate the easing of international tension, the settlement of international problems by peaceful means, and the achievement of general and complete disarmament and, primarily, nuclear disarmament.

Article 6. The USSR respects the policy of non-alignment pursued by the SDR, which constitutes a factor in maintaining international peace and security. The SDR respects the peace loving policy pursued by the USSR aimed at strengthening friendship and co-operation with all peoples.

Article 7. Guided by the ideals of freedom and equality of all peoples, the high contracting parties condemn imperialism and colonialism in all its forms and manifestations. They will continue to oppose the forces of imperialism and colonialism and to co-operate with each other and with other states in supporting the struggle of the peoples for freedom, independence, and social progress on the basis of the principle of equality and self-determination of the peoples, as expressed in the UN Charter.

Article 8. Expressing profound interest in safeguarding universal peace and security and attaching great significance to co-operation between themselves in the international arena for the purpose of achieving these objectives, the high contracting parties will consult regularly and exchange views with each other on important international issues. Such consultations and exchanges will encompass: International issues, including situations causing tension in various parts of the world, with a view to contributing to the relaxation of tension, developing co-operation, and strengthening security; issues which are the subject of multilateral negotiations, including those being examined by international organisations and at international conferences; and issues of a political, economic and cultural nature and other issues affecting relations between the two countries. Such consultations and exchanges of view will be effected through meetings between leading statesmen from the sides and visits by official delegations and special representatives and also through diplomatic channels.

Article 9. In the event of the emergence of situations creating a threat to or a violation of peace the high contracting parties will make contact without delay and consult with each other with a view to eliminating the threat which has arisen or restoring peace.

Article 10. Each of the high contracting parties states that it will not be party to military alliances or any groupings of states or to actions or undertakings directed against the other high contracting party.

Article 11. Each of the high contracting parties states that the commitments under existing international treaties are not at variance with the provisions of the current treaty and undertake not to become party to any international agreements incompatible with them.

Article 12. This treaty will be in force for a term of 20 years from the date of its validation. Unless either of the high contracting parties expresses its desire to terminate the treaty within one year prior to the expiration of this term, it will remain in force for the next five years and until such time as one of the high contracting parties gives written notice one year prior to the expiration of the five-year period of its intention to terminate the validity of the treaty.

Article 13. This treaty is subject to ratification and will come into force on the day of the exchange of the instruments of ratification, which will take place as soon as possible in Moscow. This treaty is made in two copies, one in Russian and one in Somali, both texts being of equal validity.

Done in Mogadishu this 11 July 1974.

(Signed) For the USSR, N. V. PODGORNY

For the SDR, MOHAMMED SIAD BARRE.

Source: *Pravda*, 30 October 1974.

Appendix B Soviet–Ethiopian treaty of 20 November 1978

Friendship and co-operation treaty between the USSR and Socialist Ethiopia: the text

The Union of Soviet Socialist Republics and Socialist Ethiopia, believing that the further development and strengthening of the relations of friendship and all-round co-operation that exist between them is in the fundamental national interests of the peoples of both countries and serves the cause of consolidating peace and security throughout the world,

desiring to make an appropriate contribution to the development of peaceful relations between states and fruitful international co-operation,

filled with determination to develop the social and economic achievements of the Soviet and Ethiopian peoples,

inspired by the ideals of consistent struggle against imperialism and expansionism, as well as colonialism, racism and apartheid in all their forms and manifestations, and guided by a desire to support peoples who are struggling for their freedom, independence and social progress,

reaffirming their fidelity to the goals and principles of the United Nations Charter, including the principles of respect for sovereignty, territorial integrity and non-interference in each other's internal affairs,

taking into consideration the May 6, 1977, Declaration of Principles of Friendly Relations and Co-operation Between the Union of Soviet Socialist Republics and Socialist Ethiopia, and motivated by a desire to consolidate still more these relations of friendship and mutually advantageous co-operation between the two states and peoples,

have agreed on the following:

Article 1. The high contracting parties will develop and deepen

311

relations of indestructible friendship and all-round co-operation in the political, economic, trade, scientific, technical, cultural and other fields on the basis of equality, non-interference in internal affairs, respect for sovereignty, territorial integrity and the inviolability of borders.

Article 2. The high contracting parties declare that they will co-operate closely and comprehensively to ensure conditions for the preservation and further development of the social and economic gains of their peoples and respect for the sovereignty of each party over all its natural resources.

Article 3. The Union of Soviet Socialist Republics respects the policy pursued by Socialist Ethiopia, based on the goals and principles of the Charter of the Organisation of African Unity and the non-aligned movement, which is an important factor in the development of international co-operation and peaceful co-existence.

Socialist Ethiopia respects the peace-loving foreign policy pursued by the Union of Soviet Socialist Republics, which is aimed at strengthening friendship and co-operation with all countries and peoples.

Article 4. The high contracting parties will continue to make every effort to protect international peace and the security of peoples, to deepen the process of the easing of international tension, extend it to all parts of the world and embody it in concrete form of mutually advantageous co-operation among states, and to settle disputed international questions by peaceful means without detriment to the legitimate right of states to defend themselves, on an individual or collective basis, against aggression in accordance with the United Nations Charter. They will actively promote the cause of general and complete disarmament, under effective international control.

Article 5. The high contracting parties will continue to work actively for the final elimination of colonialism, neo-colonialism, racism and apartheid and the full implementation of the UN Declaration on the Granting of Independence to Colonial Countries and Peoples.

Article 6. The high contracting parties will consult with each other on important international questions directly affecting the interests of the two countries.

Article 7. In the event that a situation arises that creates a threat to peace or breaks international peace, the high contracting parties will immediately seek to contact each other with a view to co-ordinating their positions in the interests of eliminating the threat that has arisen or restoring peace.

Article 8. The high contracting parties, attaching great importance to economic, trade and scientific co-operation between them, will
expand and deepen co-operation and exchanges of experience in these
fields. The parties will expand all-round co-operation on the basis of
the principles of equality, mutual advantage and most-favoured-
nation treatment.

Article 9. The high contracting parties will promote the further
development of ties and co-operation between them in the fields of
science, culture, the arts, literature, education, public health, the
press, radio, motion pictures, television, tourism, sports and other
fields, with a view to more thorough mutual familiarisation with the
life, labour, experience and achievements of the two countries'
peoples.

Article 10. In the interests of ensuring the defense capability of
the high contracting parties, they will continue to co-operate in the
military field.

Article 11. Each of the high contracting parties declares that it
will not enter into an alliance or take part in any grouping of states or
in actions or measures directed against the other high contracting
party.

Article 12. The high contracting parties declare that the provisions of this treaty are not at variance with their commitments under
existing international treaties, and they pledge not to conclude any
international agreements incompatible with this treaty.

Article 13. Any questions that may arise between the high
contracting parties with respect to the interpretation or application of
any provision of this treaty will be resolved bilaterally in a spirit of
friendship, and mutual respect and mutual understanding.

Article 14. This treaty will be in effect for 20 years from the day it
enters into force.

Unless one of the high contracting parties declares, no later than one
year before the expiration of the above term, its desire to terminate the
treaty, it will remain in force for the next five years and until such time
as one of the high contracting parties, no later than one year before the
expiration of the current five-year period, gives written notice of its
intention to terminate the treaty.

Article 15. This treaty is subject to ratification and will enter into
force on the day that instruments of ratification are exchanged, which
will take place in Addis Ababa at the earliest possible date.

This treaty is drawn up in duplicate, in the Russian, Amharic and
English languages, all three texts being equally authentic.

Done in Moscow on November 20, 1978 – [signed] For the Union of Soviet Socialist Republics – L. BREZHNEV; for Socialist Ethiopia – MENGISTU Haile Mariam.

Source: *Pravda*, 21 November 1978.

Notes

Preface

1 A. Bovin in *Soviet Weekly*, 19 September 1987.
2 D. E. Albright, 'Soviet Policy', *Problems of Communism*, 27: 1 (January – February 1978), p. 35.

1. From intervention to disengagement: a framework

1 *Tass*, 3 January 1980.
2 Nguyen Vinh, 'Vietnam to Withdraw Troops from Kampuchea' *New Times*, no. 30, 1988, p. 31.
3 Eduard Shevardnadze, *Tass*, 14 April 1988 cited in 'Afghanistan: Negotiating the Soviet Withdrawal' *USSR and Third World*, supplement to 18, 1–2, November 1987-April 1988, p. 9.
4 W. B. Gallie, 'Essentially Contested Concepts' in Max Black, ed., *The Importance of Language*, Englewood Cliffs, New Jersey, Prentice Hall, 1962, p. 121.
5 Quincy Wright, 'Intervention 1956', *American Journal of International Law*, 51, April 1957; C. G. Fenwick, 'Intervention by Way of Propaganda', *American Journal of International Law*, 35, October 1941, pp. 626–31; James N. Rosenau, *The Scientific Study of Foreign Policy*, New York, The Free Press, 1971, p. 281; Quincy Wright, 'The Munich Settlement and International Law' *American Journal of International Law*, 33, January 1939, pp. 12–32; K. J. Holsti, *International Politics: A Framework for Analysis*, Englewood Cliffs, New Jersey, Prentice Hall Inc., 1967, pp. 320–2; Michael H. Cardozo, 'Intervention: Benefaction as Justification', in Roland J. Stanger, ed., *Essays on Intervention*, Columbus, Ohio State University Press, 1964, pp. 63–85; L. Morley, 'Invasion and Intervention in the Caribbean Area', *Editorial Research Reports*, 2, July 1959, pp. 535–52.
6 L. Oppenheim cited in Hedley Bull, ed., *Intervention in World Politics*, Oxford, Oxford University Press, 1984, p. 1.
7 Mai Volkov, 'Militarisation Versus Development' *Asia and Africa Today*, 5, 1987, p. 7; Istvan Kende, 'Local Wars in Asia, Africa and Latin America, 1945–1969, Stockholm International Peace Research Institute (SIPRI) in *Armaments and Disarmaments in the Nuclear Age: A Handbook*, New Jersey, Humanities Press, 1976, pp. 174–5.

8 E. Korovin, 'Jungle Law Versus the Law of Nations', *New Times*, 1, 1957, p. 16.
9 James N. Rosenau, *The Scientific Study of Foreign Policy*, p. 292.
10 Richard Little, *Intervention: External Involvement in Civil Wars*, London, Martin Robertson, 1975, p. 8.
11 In a joint declaration, at the end of a state visit to Yugoslavia, Mikhail Gorbachev effectively repudiated the Brezhnev doctrine of limited sovereignty. The Soviet–Yugoslav declaration pledged 'consistent respect for the independence of parties to socialist countries in determining ways of their development'. This was based on 'the conviction that no one has a monopoly on the truth'. The declaration is reproduced in full in *Soviet Weekly* Supplement, 26 March 1988, p. vi.
12 G. Tunkin, *Osnovy Sovremennogo Mezhdunarodnogo Prava*, Moscow, Izdatel'stvo 'Mezhdunarodnyye Otnosheniya', 1967, p. 29.
13 Leonid Brezhnev's address at the Fifth Congress of the Polish Communist Party in November 1968, cited in Charles L. Robertson, *International Politics since World War II: A Short History*, second edition, New York, John Wiley and Sons, 1975, p. 323.
14 R. J. Vincent, *Nonintervention and International Order*, New Jersey, Princeton University Press, 1974, p. 13.
15 Samuel E. Finer, *The Man on Horseback: The Role of the Military in Politics*, second edition, Harmondsworth, Middlesex Peregrine Books, 1975, p. 63.
16 Ibid., pp. 62–3.
17 Charles L. Robertson, *International Politics since World War II*, p. 201.
18 'Crisis in Asia' *Survival*, International Institute for Strategic Studies (IISS), July-August 1980, 22, 4, p. 171.
19 Alvin Z. Rubinstein, 'Assessing Influence as a Problem in Foreign Policy Analysis' in Alvin Z. Rubinstein, ed., *Soviet and Chinese Influence in the Third World*, New York, Praeger Publishers, 1976, p. 10.
20 Robert E. Dowse and John A. Hughes, *Political Sociology*, London, John Wiley and Sons, 1972, p. 227.
21 Andrew Mack, 'Counterinsurgency in the Third World: Theory and Practice', in Andrew Mack, David Plant and Ursula Doyle, eds., *Imperialism, Intervention and Development*, London, Croom Helm, 1979, p. 131.
22 Samuel E. Finer, *The Man on Horseback: The Role of the Military in Politics*, p. 66.
23 Ibid., p. 69.
24 Ibid., pp. 70–1.
25 Jiri Valenta, 'The Soviet–Cuban Intervention in Angola, 1975', *Studies in Comparative Communism*, 1 and 2, 11, Spring-Summer 1978, p. 10.
26 James N. Rosenau, *The Scientific Study of Foreign Policy*, p. 245.
27 W. H. Riker's definition of rationality cited in Jan F. Triska and David Finley, *Soviet Foreign Policy*, New York, Macmillan, 1968, p. 346.
28 Philip Windsor, 'Superpower Intervention' in Hedley Bull, ed., *Intervention in World Politics*, pp. 47–8.
29 Christer Jönsson, 'The Paradoxes of Superpower: Omnipotence or Impotence?' in Kjell Goldmann and Gunnar Sjöstedt, eds., *Power, Capabili-*

ties, *Interdependence: Problems in the Study of International Influence*, London, Sage Publications Inc., 1979, p. 74.

30 Ibid., p. 75; Garry Wills, *The Kennedys: A Shattered Illusion*, London, Orbis, 1982, p. 278.

31 Klaus Knorr, 'On the International Uses of Military Force in the Contemporary World' *Orbis*, 1, 21, Spring 1977, p. 15.

32 Robert J. Art, 'To What Ends Military Power?', *International Security*, 4, 4, Spring 1980, p. 32.

33 John M. Kramer, 'Soviet–CEMA Energy Ties', *Problems of Communism*, 34, 4, July-August 1985, pp. 38–9.

34 *Izvestiya*, 5 November 1987.

35 John M. Kramer, 'Soviet–CEMA Energy Ties', pp. 39–40.

36 Garry Wills, *The Kennedys: A Shattered Illusion*, p. 257.

37 Hans J. Morgenthau, 'To Intervene or Not to Intervene', *Foreign Affairs*, 45, April 1967, pp. 425–6.

38 Arthur M. Schlesinger, Jun., *Robert Kennedy and His Times*, London, Futura, 1979, pp. 476–82.

39 Jan F. Triska and David Finley, *Soviet Foreign Policy*, p. 322.

40 Ibid., p. 321.

41 I am indebted to Professor Peter Nailer of The Royal Naval Staff College, Greenwich for bringing this point to my attention.

42 A. Gurnov, 'Washington's Grenada "Experiment" and its Meaning' *New Times*, 51, December 1984, p. 13.

43 This definition was coined by Professor Peter Nailor of The Royal Naval Staff College, Greenwich.

44 Colin Legum, *After Angola: The War over Southern Africa*, London, Rex Collings, 1976, p. 38.

45 Urs Schwarz, *Confrontation and Intervention in the Modern World*, New York, Oceania, 1970, p. 138.

46 Peter Dale Scott, 'The Death of Kennedy, Vietnam and Cuba' in Peter Dale Scott, Paul L. Hoch and Russell Statler, eds., *The Assassinations: Dallas and Beyond – A Guide to Cover-ups and Investigations*, London, Penguin, 1977, p. 366; Charles L. Robertson, *International Politics since World War II: A Short History*, p. 283.

47 Richard H. Ullman, *Intervention and the War*, Princeton, Princeton University Press, 1961, p. 253.

48 R. D. McLaurin, *The Middle East in Soviet Policy*, Lexington, Massachusetts, Lexington Books, 1975, pp. 47–66; Alvin Z. Rubinstein, *Red Star on the Nile: The Soviet–Egyptian Influence Relationship since the June War*, New Jersey, Princeton University Press, 1977, p. 190.

49 F. B. Weinstein, 'The Concept of Commitment in International Relations', *Journal of Conflict Resolution*, 13, 1969, pp. 39–56.

50 Richard Little, *Intervention: External Involvement in Civil Wars*, p. 136.

51 Ibid., p. 136.

52 David Dallin, *Soviet Foreign Policy after Stalin*, London, Methuen & Co, 1960, p. 110; Barry M. Blechman and Douglas M. Hart, 'Afghanistan and the 1946 Iran Analogy' *Survival*, IISS, 22, 6, November-December 1980, p. 252.

53 Charles L. Robertson, *International Politics since World War II: A Short History*, p. 220.
54 D. T. Campbell, 'Ethnocentric and Altruistic Motives' in D. Levine, *The Nebraska Symposium on Motivation*, 8, 1965, p. 298 cited in Richard Little, *Intervention: External Involvement in Civil Wars*, p. 181.
55 'Efficiency for the Common Good', *New Times*, 2, 1985, p. 1; 'An Eventful Year', *New Times*, 52, 1987, p. 2.
56 'Mikhail Gorbachev's answers to questions from the Washington Post and Newsweek', *New Times*, 22, 1988, p. 6.

2. The evolution of a Soviet interest

1 Colin Darch, *A Soviet View of Africa: An Annotated Bibliography on Ethiopia, Somalia and Djibouti*, Boston, G. K. Hall & Co, 1980, p. xiv.
2 Y. M. Kobishchanov, 'From the History of Relations between the Peoples of Russia and Ethiopia', in A. B. Davidson, D. A. Ol'derogge and V. G. Solodovnikov, eds., *Russia and Africa*, Moscow, 'Nauka' Publishing House, 1966, pp. 153–66.
3 Colin Darch, *A Soviet View of Africa: An Annotated Bibliography on Ethiopia, Somalia and Djibouti*, p. xiv.
4 Czeslaw Jesman, 'Early Russian Contacts with Ethiopia', in Third International Conference of Ethiopian Studies, 1966, *Proceedings*, Addis Ababa, 1, 1969, pp. 253–67.
5 S. L. Miliavskaia, 'Information about Africa in 18th century Russia', in A. B. Davidson, D. A. Ol'derogge and V. G. Solodovnikov, eds., *Russia and Africa*, p. 42.
6 Paul B. Henze, 'Christian Brothers and Imperial Ambitions: A Survey of Russian Interest in Ethiopia and the Horn of Africa from the mid-19th Century through the early Soviet Period', unpublished paper, Washington DC, October 1984, p. 3.
7 Edward T. Wilson, 'Russia's Historic Stake in Black Africa', in David E. Albright, ed., *Africa and International Communism*, London, Macmillan Press, 1980, p. 71.
8 'Abissinya', *Novyy Vostok*, 1, 1922, pp. 316–33, reproduced in Milene Charles, *The Soviet Union and Africa: The History of the Involvement*, Washington DC, University Press of America, 1980, p. 172.
9 Ibid., p. 172.
10 F. Volgin, *V Strane Chernykh Khristian*, St Petersburg, 1895, cited in Edward T. Wilson, 'Russia's Historic Stake in Black Africa', p. 73.
11 F. Volgin, *V Strane Chernykh Khristian*, St Petersburg, 1895, cited in Edward T. Wilson, 'Russia's Historic Stake in Black Africa', p. 73.
12 British indifference was reflected in Special Envoy Rennell Rodd's remark that Lord Salisbury, the then British Foreign Minister, was 'not much preoccupied by Abyssinian encroachments in Somaliland'. Cited in I. M. Lewis, *A Modern History of Somalia: Nation and State in the Horn of Africa*, second revised edition, London, Longman, 1980, p. 61.
13 Sergius Yakobson, 'The USSR and Ethiopia: A Case of Traditional

Behaviour' in Kurt London, ed., *New Nations in a Divided World*, New York, Praeger, 1963, p. 181.

14 Apollon Davidson, 'African Diary: Nikolai Gumilev', *Asia and Africa Today*, 4, 1988, p. 42.

15 M. V. Rayt, 'Russkiye ekspeditsii v Efiopiye v seredine XIX i nachale XX vekhov i ikh etnograficheskiye materialy' *Afrikanskiy Etnograficheskiy Sbornik*, 1, 1956, pp. 220–81.

16 Colin Darch, *A Soviet View of Africa: An Annotated Bibliography on Ethiopia, Somalia and Djibouti*, p. xv.

17 Grand Duke Aleksandr Mikhaylovich cited in Sergius Yakobson, 'The USSR and Ethiopia: A Case of Traditional Behaviour', p. 182.

18 Aryeh Yodfat, 'The Soviet Union and the Horn of Africa', Part One, *Northeast African Studies*, 1, 3, Winter 1979–80, p. 1.

19 G. A. Nersesov, 'The Soviet Union, Anti-Colonialism, Africa: From the Great October Revolution of 1917 to the Italo–Ethiopian War of 1935–36' *Africa in Soviet Studies*, 4, 1976, p. 238.

20 Ibid., p. 239.

21 Ibid., p. 239.

22 Ibid., p. 239.

23 A. E. Joffe, 'Nachalnyy etap vzaymootnosheniy Sovetskogo Soyuza s Arabskimi i Afrikanskimi stranami 1923–1932', *Narody Azii i Afriki*, 6, 1965, pp. 57–66. For a summary see *Mizan*, 8, 2, March-April 1966, pp. 90–1.

24 Edward T. Wilson, 'Russia's Historic Stake in Black Africa', p. 87.

25 Anatoly A. Gromyko, 'Sovetsko-Efiopskiye svyazy', *Narody Azii i Afriki*, 1, 1980, p. 8.

26 Lowell R. Tillett, 'The Soviet Role in League Sanctions Against Italy', *American Slavic and East European Review*, 15, 1, 1956, pp. 11–16.

27 The Soviet Foreign Minister, Max Litvinov, cited in J. Degras, ed., *Soviet Documents on Foreign Policy 1933–41*, Royal Institute of International Affairs, London, Oxford University Press, 1953, 3, pp. 194–5.

28 Milene Charles, *The Soviet Union and Africa: The History of the Involvement*, p. 37.

29 Isaac Deutscher, *Stalin: A Political Biography*, revised edition, Harmondsworth, Middlesex, Penguin Books, 1966, pp. 474–80.

30 Bereket Habte Selassie, *Conflict and Intervention in the Horn of Africa*, New York, Monthly Review Press, 1980, p. 102.

31 *Africa Research Bulletin* (ARB), May 1966, p. 530.

32 Rennell Rodd, the British Special Envoy in treaty negotiations with King Menelik II of Ethiopia, declared 'I succeeded in getting rid of any phraseology which necessarily implied a recognition of Abyssinian rights beyond our frontier'. Cited in *ARB*, May 1966, p. 530.

33 According to the terms of the Anglo–Somali Treaties, 1884–6, the territory in question, comprising the Haud and the Reserve areas, was placed under British protection, not jurisdiction. Therefore, it was not hers to abandon. *ARB*, May 1966, p. 530.

34 I. M. Lewis, *A Modern History of Somalia: Nation and State in the Horn of Africa*, p. 121.

35 Richard Greenfield, 'Pre-Colonial and Colonial History' in Basil Davidson, Lionel Cliffe and Bereket Habte Selassie, eds., *Behind the War in Eritrea*, Nottingham, Spokesman, 1980, p. 27.
36 Benjamin Rivlin, *The United Nations and the Italian Colonies*, New York, Carnegie Endowment for International Peace, 1950, pp. 11–13.
37 Andrey Zhdanov, *The International Situation*, Moscow, Foreign Printing Publishing House, 1947 cited in Alvin Z. Rubinstein, ed., *The Foreign Policy of the Soviet Union*, New York, Random House, 1972, third edition, p. 205.
38 For a balanced and authoritative account of Ethiopia's relations with the West during this period see Harold G. Marcus, *Ethiopia, Great Britain and the United States, 1941–1974*, California, University of California Press, 1983.
39 John Spencer, *Ethiopia, the Horn of Africa and US Policy*, Cambridge, Massachusetts, Institute for Foreign Policy Analysis, pp. 13–15.
40 D. R. Voblikov, 'Anglo-Amerikanskoye sopernichestvo v poslevoyennoy Efiopiye', *Sovetskoye Vostokovedeniye*, 4, 1957, pp. 27–38.
41 Marina Ottaway, *Soviet and American Influence in the Horn of Africa*, New York, Praeger, 1982, p. 26.
42 I. M. Lewis, *A Modern History of Somalia: Nation and State in the Horn of Africa*, p. 130.
43 Bereket Habte Selassie, *Conflict and Intervention in the Horn of Africa*, pp. 55–7.
44 Aryeh Yodfat, 'The Soviet Union and the Horn of Africa', Part one, p. 2.
45 Admasu Zike, *An Application of the Theory of Social Exchange to International Relations. The Kagnew Station as the Linchpin of the Ethiopian–United States Relationship*, Ph.D. dissertation, Northern Illinois University, 1979.
46 John Spencer cited in Raman G. Bhardwag, *The Dilemma of the Horn of Africa*, New Delhi, Sterling Publishers, 1979, p. 47.
47 John Foster Dulles cited in Bereket Habte Selassie, *Conflict and Intervention in the Horn of Africa*, p. 58.
48 Mohammed L. Ayoob, *The Horn of Africa: Regional Conflict and Superpower Involvement*, Canberra, Canberra Papers on Strategy and Defence, Australian National University, 1978, p. 11; Fred Halliday, *Threat from the East? Soviet Policy from Afghanistan and Iran to the Horn of Africa*, Harmondsworth, Middlesex, Penguin Books, 1981, p. 103.
49 In a speech at Qabradare in the Ogaden on 25 August 1956 Emperor Haile Selassie claimed that the Somali people were part of the 'Great Ethiopian Family'. See I. M. Lewis, *A Modern History of Somalia: Nation and State in the Horn of Africa*, pp. 151–2.
50 D. A. Ol'derogge, I. I. Potekhin and M. V. Rayt, 'Efiopiya i strany Krasnomorskogo poberezh'ya', in D. A. Ol'derogge and I. I. Potekhin, eds., *Narody Afriki*, Moscow, Izdatel'stvo Akademii Nauk SSSR, 1954, pp. 359–96.
51 D. R. Voblikov, 'Anglo-Amerikanskoye sopernichestvo v poslevoyennoy Efiopiye', pp. 27–38.
52 Ibid.
53 Ibid.

54 D. A. Ol'derogge, I. I. Potekhin and M. V. Rayt, 'Efiopiya i strany Krasno-morskogo poberezh'ya', pp. 359–96.
55 United Nations, *General Assembly Official Records*, First Committee, Third Session, Part 2, 1949, p. 18.
56 D. R. Voblikov, 'Anglo-Amerikanskoye sopernichestvo v poslevoyennoy Efiopiye', pp. 27–38.
57 David Dallin, *Soviet Foreign Policy After Stalin*, London, Methuen, 1960, p. 107.
58 The Ukraine delegate cited in Richard Greenfield, 'Pre-Colonial and Colonial History', p. 30.
59 Soviet Ambassador to UN, Andrey Gromyko, cited in *General Assembly Official Records*, First Committee, Third Session, Part two, 1949, p. 19.
60 Ibid., p. 23.
61 A. M. Khazanov, *Somaliyskaya Respublika: Istoricheskiy Ocherk*, Moscow, Izdatel'stvo Akademii Nauk SSSR, Institut Naradov Azii, 1961, p. 56.
62 Ibid., pp. 67–71.
63 A. M. Khazanov, *Osvoboditel'naya Bor'ba Narodov Vostochnoy Afriki Posle Vtoroy Mirovoy Voyny*, Moscow, Izdatel'stvo Sotsialisticheskoy Literatury, 1962, pp. 84–5.
64 D. R. Voblikov, 'Anglo-Amerikanskoye sopernichestvo v poslevoyennoy Efiopiye', pp. 27–38.
65 Ibid.
66 D. A. Ol'derogge, I. I. Potekhin and M. V. Rayt, 'Efiopiya i strany Krasno-morskogo poberezh'ya', pp. 359–96.
67 The text of the speech of the then Soviet Ambassador to the United Nations, A. Vyshinsky, is reproduced in Bereket Habte Selassie, *Conflict and Intervention in the Horn of Africa*, appendix 1, pp. 175–8; see also Lord Avebury's letter to the *Daily Telegraph*, 27 February 1979.
68 D. A. Ol'derogge, I. I. Potekhin and M. V. Rayt, 'Efiopiya i strany Krasno-morskogo poberezh'ya', pp. 359–96.
69 Ibid.
70 Ibid. D. R. Voblikov's review of *Economic Handbook of Ethiopia*, Addis Ababa, 1951, in *Sovetsoye Vostokovedeniye*, 4, 1955, pp. 185–7.
71 D. A. Ol'derogge, I. I. Potekhin and M. V. Rayt, 'Efiopiya i strany Krasno-morskogo poberezh'ya', pp. 359–96; D. R. Voblikov, 'Anglo–Amerikanskoye sopernichestvo v poslevoyennoy Efiopiye', pp. 27–38.
72 Karen Dawisha, *Soviet Foreign Policy Towards Egypt*, London, Macmillan, 1979, p. 6.
73 Soviet Foreign Ministry statement cited in J. Degras, ed., *The Communist International 1919–43*, 3, London, Oxford University Press, 1956, p. 347; Nikita Khrushchev cited in Alvin Z. Rubinstein, ed., *The Foreign Policy of the Soviet Union*, p. 429.
74 *Pravda*, 18 February 1956.
75 'Efiopiya' in *Bol'shaya Sovetskaya Entsiklopediya*, cited in *Mizan*, 4, 9, October 1962, p. 15.
76 Ibid.
77 Luba Anastasia Holowaty, *The Soviet Union and Countries of the African Horn:*

A Case Study of Soviet Perceptions and Policies, 1959–1968, Ph.D. dissertation, University of Pennsylvania, 1970, p. 130.

78 Robert F. Gorman, *Political Conflict on the Horn of Africa*, New York, Praeger, 1981, p. 34; *ARB*, May 1966, p. 531.

79 Andargachew Mesai cited in Bereket Habte Selassie, *Conflict and Intervention in the Horn of Africa*, p. 60.

80 Emperor Haile Selassie cited in the *New York Times*, 23 February 1958.

81 Luba Anastasia Holowaty, *The Soviet Union and Countries of the African Horn*, p. 133.

82 Y. Grigoryev, 'A West German Journalist in Ethiopia', *International Affairs* (Moscow), 6, 1958, p. 114.

83 Sergius Yakobson, 'The USSR and Ethiopia: A Case of Traditional Behaviour', pp. 183–6; *Mizan*, 4, 9, October 1962, pp. 17–18.

84 Y. Tomilin, 'Ethiopian–Soviet Friendship', *International Affairs* (Moscow), 7, 1959, p. 91.

85 'Novaya stranitsa traditsionnoy druzhby' *Sovremennyy Vostok*, 8, 1959, pp. 24–5.

86 Sergius Yakobson, 'The USSR and Ethiopia: A Case of Traditional Behaviour', p. 186; Marina Ottaway, *Soviet and American Influence in the Horn of Africa*, p. 27. It is noteworthy that a Soviet military delegation also attended the twenty-fifth anniversary of the Ethiopian Military Academy on 28 April 1960. See *Izvestiya*, 30 April 1960.

87 US Senate Investigating Sub-Committee on Security Agreements and Commitments Abroad, June 1970, cited in *Africa Contemporary Record* (ACR), 1970, p. B107.

88 V. G. Molchanov, *Efiopiya*, Moscow, Izdatel'stvo 'Znanie', 1960, pp. 28–31.

89 *Pravda*, 16 and 27 December 1960. It is ironic that the opposite version of events was probably true. According to the respected Ethiopian specialist, Richard Greenfield, there was strong evidence to suggest that the US played an active role in restoring Emperor Haile Selassie to the throne. See Richard Greenfield, *Ethiopia*, London, Pall Mall Press, 1965, pp. 412–13.

90 I. M. Lewis, *A Modern History of Somalia: Nation and State in the Horn of Africa*, note 17, p. 269.

91 Saadia Touval, *The Boundary Politics of Independent Africa*, Cambridge, Massachusetts, Harvard University Press, 1972, pp. 18–49.

92 Robert F. Gorman, *Political Conflict on the Horn of Africa*, p. 36.

93 Luba Anastasia Holowaty, *The Soviet Union and Countries of the African Horn*, p. 147.

94 *Izvestiya*, 2 July 1960.

95 Marina Ottaway, *Soviet and American Influence in the Horn of Africa*, p. 28.

96 *Mizan*, 5, 11, December 1963, p. 16; Saadia Touval, *Somali Nationalism*, Cambridge, Massachusetts, Harvard University Press, 1963, p. 175.

97 I. I. Potekhin, 'Somaliya' in *Yezhegodnik Bol'shoy Sovetskoy Entsiklopedii*, 1961, cited in *Mizan*, 4, 5, May 1962, p. 35; O. Gorovoy, 'Ya byl v Somaliye', *Aziya i Afrika segodnya*, 4, 1962, p. 40.

98 Y. Bochkarev, 'Somalia: Contours of the Future', *New Times*, 30, 1963, p. 28.

99 O. Gorovoy, 'Ya byl v Somaliye', p. 40.

100 President Aden Abdullah Osman cited in E. A. Bayne, 'Birthday for Somalia', *American University Field Service Report, Northeast Africa Series*, 8, August 1961, p. 14.

101 Abdarashid Ali Shermarke, Prime Minister of Somalia, cited in E. A. Bayne, 'Birthday for Somalia', p. 13.

102 Abdullahi Issa, the Somalian Foreign Minister, cited in Luba Anastasia Holowaty, *The Soviet Union and Countries of the African Horn*, pp. 191–2; Marina Ottaway, *Soviet and American Influence in the Horn of Africa*, p. 28.

103 That omission has been interpreted in different ways. Saadia Touval argued that the Soviet negotiator's purely verbal requests that the weapons should not be used against Somalia's neighbours was construed by Mogadishu as tacit support for pan-Somali aspirations. See S. Touval, *The Boundary Politics of Independent Africa*, p. 150. On the other hand, Professor I. M. Lewis of the London School of Economics and Political Science, in an interview with the author, contended that the Soviet request was a serious one.

104 Vijay Gupta, 'The Ethiopian–Somalia Conflict and the Role of the External Powers', *Foreign Affairs Reports*, 27, 3, 1978, p. 41; Charles B. McLane, *Soviet–African Relations*, 3 of Soviet–Third World Relations, London, Central Asian Research Centre, 1974, p. 125.

105 D. A. Ol'derogge, I. I. Potekhin and M. V. Rayt, 'Efiopiya i strany Krasnomorskogo poberezh'ya', pp. 359–96; M. V. Rayt and Ye G. Titov, *Efiopiya: Strana, Lyudy*, Moscow, Geografigiz, 1960, pp. 70–93.

106 S. Kondrashov, 'What the African Governments Discussed in Cairo', *New Times*, 15, 1961, pp. 3–5.

107 *Yezhegodnik Bol'shoy Sovetskoy Entsiklopedii*, 1962 and 1963, cited in *Mizan*, 5, 11, December 1963, p. 13.

108 A. M. Khazanov, *Somaliyskaya Respublika: Istoricheskiy Ocherk*, pp. 13 and 21.

109 A. M. Khazanov, 'Antikolonial'noye dvizheniye v Somali pod predvoditel'stvom Mukhammeda bin Abdally', *Problemy Vostokovedeniya*, 2, 1960, pp. 113–22.

110 I. D. Levin, ed., *Konstitutsiy Gosudarstv Bliznego i Srednogo Vostoka*, Moscow, Izdatel'stvo 'Mezhdunarodnyye Otnosheniya', 1956, p. 525.

111 G. V. Aleksandrenko, *Burzhauznyy Federalizm: Kriticheskiy Analiz Burzhauznykh Federatsiy i Burzhauznykh Teorii Federalizma*, Kiev, Izdatel'stvo Akademii Nauk Ukraynskoy SSSR, 1962, pp. 202–4.

112 Ibid., pp. 202–4.

113 Richard Sherman, *Eritrea: The Unfinished Revolution*, New York, Praeger Publishers, 1980, pp. 28–9.

114 L. Repina, 'Somaliya', in *Bol'shaya Sovetskaya Entsiklopediya*, cited in *Mizan*, 5, 11, December 1963, p. 12; A. M. Khazanov, *Somaliyskaya Respublika: Istoricheskiy Ocherk*, p. 127.

115 *Pravda*, 30 June 1963.

116 R. Avakov and G. Mirskiy, 'O klassovoy strukture v staborazvitykh stranakh', *Mirovaya Ekonomika i Mezhdunarodnyye Otnosheniya*, 4, 1962, pp. 68–92.

117 M. V. Rayt, *Narody Efiopii*, Moscow, Izdatel'stvo 'Nauka', 1965, pp. 154–5.
118 *Trud*, 2 February 1962, cited in *Mizan*, 4, 5, May 1962, p. 12.
119 US Congress, Senate Subcommittee on United States Security Agreements and Commitments Abroad of the Committee on Foreign Relations, *United States Security Agreements and Commitments Abroad: Ethiopia*, Hearings, 91st Congress, 2nd Session, 1 June 1970.
120 Testimony of Edward Kerry, the US Ambassador to Ethiopia between 1963 and 1967, during Senate Hearings of Subcommittee on African Affairs cited in Admasu Zike, *An Application of the Theory of Social Exchange to International Relations*, p. 132.
121 I. M. Lewis, *A Modern History of Somalia: Nation and State in the Horn of Africa*, pp. 200–1.
122 *Izvestiya*, 29 March 1963.
123 The Ethiopian Prime Minister, Aklilu Habte Wolde, cited in Saadia Touval, *The Boundary Politics of Independent Africa*, p. 149.
124 Ibid., pp. 85–6.
125 Khrushchev cited in I. I. Potekhin, 'Panafrikanizm i bor'ba dvukh ideologiy', *Kommunist*, 1, January 1964, p. 108.
126 I. M. Lewis, *A Modern History of Somalia: Nation and State in the Horn of Africa*, p. 201.
127 Text of N. S. Khrushchev's memorandum appeared in *Pravda*, 4 January 1964.
128 Ibid.
129 V. A. Zorin and V. L. Israelyan 'Marksistko–Leninskiy podkhod k resheniyu territorial'nykh sporov', *Kommunist*, 2, January 1964, p. 30.
130 Ibid., pp. 25–7.
131 Y. Tomilin, 'Territorial Problems in Africa', *New Times*, 4, 1964; I. I. Potekhin, 'Legacy of Colonialism', *International Affairs* (Moscow), 3, 1964.
132 *Pravda*, 1 February 1964.
133 Saadia Touval, *The Boundary Politics of Independent Africa*, p. 222.
134 The French authorities undercut the presence of the Somali plurality in the territory by redrawing the electoral boundaries to favour the less numerous Afar people, and by encouraging the immigration of the Danakil (ethnically related to the Afar) from Ethiopia to the territory. See Robert F. Gorman, *Political Conflict on the Horn of Africa*, p. 37.
135 Letter from Andrey Gromyko, the Soviet Foreign Minister, to the United Nations Secretary General U. Thant in *Pravda*, 24 September 1964.
136 R. N. Ismagilova in N. I. Gavrilov, ed., *Nezavisimyye Strany Afriki*, Moscow, Izdatel'stvo Institut Afriki Akademii Nauk SSSR, 1965, pp. 274–5.
137 *Pravda*, 29 June 1966.
138 Luba Anastasia Holowaty, *The Soviet Union and Countries of the African Horn*, p. 206.
139 Richard Sherman, *Eritrea: The Unfinished Revolution*, p. 74.
140 *ARB*, January 1971, p. 1957.
141 *ARB*, May 1966, p. 542.

142 *The Ethiopian Herald* (Addis Ababa), 12 May 1966.
143 Luba Anastasia Holowaty, *The Soviet Union and Countries of the African Horn*, p. 294.
144 *Izvestiya*, 14 October 1966.
145 A. N. Stepunin and O. L. Stepunina, *Efiopiya*, Moscow, Izdatel'stvo 'Mysl', 1965, pp. 18–19; M. V. Rayt, *Narody Efiopii*, p. 156.
146 I. S. Sergeyeva, *Somaliyskaya Respublika: Geograficheskaya Kharasteristika*, Moscow, Izdatel'stvo 'Mysl', 1965, pp. 96–8.
147 A. Abdurakhimov, 'Respublika Somalia – Nezavisimoye gosudarstvo Afriki', *Kommunist Uzbekistana*, 7, 1965, p. 91.
148 Marina Ottaway, *Soviet and American Influence in the Horn of Africa*, p. 37.

3. Entering the 1970s: The Soviet disposition

1 Winston Churchill cited in Richard M. Nixon, *The Real War*, London, Sidgwick and Jackson, 1980, p. 312.
2 Sh. Sanakoyev, 'Programme for the Strengthening of General Peace and Security in Action', *International Affairs* (Moscow), 10, 1970, p. 4.
3 A. A. Gromyko, V. Khvostov and B. Ponomarev, eds., *Istoriya Vneshnei Politiki SSSR*, Moscow, Izdatel'stvo 'Nauka', 1971, 2, p. 486.
4 V. I. Lenin, *Collected Works*, 27, February–July 1918, Moscow, Progress Publishers, 1965, p. 328.
5 Ibid., 27, p. 328; 32, December 1920-August 1921, p. 273.
6 A. Sergiyev, 'Leninism on the Correlation of Forces as a Factor of International Relations', *International Affairs* (Moscow), 5, 1975, pp. 100–1.
7 Karen Dawisha, 'The Correlation of Forces and Soviet Policy in the Middle East' in Adeed Dawisha and Karen Dawisha, eds., *The Soviet Union in the Middle East: Policies and Perspectives*, London, Heinemann, Royal Institute of International Affairs, 1982, p. 149.
8. D. G. Tomashevskiy, *Leninskiye Idei i Sovremennyye Mezhdunarodnyye Otnosheniya*, Moscow, Izdatel'stvo Politicheskoy Literatury, 1971, p. 97.
9 V. M. Kulish, ed., *Voyennaya Sila i Mezhdunarodnyye Otnosheniya*, Moscow, Izdatel'stvo 'Mezhdunarodnyye Otnosheniya', 1972, p. 113.
10 V. V. Zhurkina and Y. M. Primakova, *Mezhdunarodnyye Konflikty*, Moscow, Izdatel'stvo 'Mezhdunarodnyye Otnosheniya', 1972, p. 23.
11 *Pravda*, 4 May 1971.
12 G. Trofimenko, 'Political Realism and the "Realistic Deterrence" Strategy', *SShA: Ekonomika, Politika i Ideologiya* (hereafter referred to as SShA), 12, 1971, as cited in Vernon V. Aspaturian, 'Soviet Global Power and the Correlation of Forces', *Problems of Communism*, 29, 3, May–June 1980, p. 10.
13 G. Trofimenko, 'From Confrontation to Coexistence', *International Affairs* (Moscow), 10, 1975, p. 38.
14 President R. Nixon cited by V. Zorin, '200–letiye i "Konstitutsionnyy krizis"', *SShA* (Moscow), 7, July 1976, pp. 24–6.
15 V. Zhurkin, '"Doktrina Niksona" i mezhdunarodno-politicheskiye krizisy' in Y. P. Davydov, V. Zhurkin and V. S. Rudnev, eds., *Doktrina Niksona*, Moscow, Izdatel'stvo 'Nauka', 1972, p. 87.

16 G. A. Arbatov, 'O Sovetsko-Amerikanskikh otnosheniye', *Kommunist*, 3, 1973, pp. 101–3.
17 G. Trofimenko, 'Militarizm i vnutripoliticheskaya bor'ba' *SShA* (Moscow), 1, January 1972, p. 71.
18 G. A. Arbatov, '"Politicheskiy god" i problema politicheskikh prioritetov', *SShA*, 6, June 1972, p. 5.
19 Henry Kissinger as cited in Richard J. Barnet, *The Giants: Russia and America*, New York, Simon and Schuster, 1977, p. 25.
20 President R. Nixon cited in G. Trofimenko 'Voennostrategicheskiye aspekty "Doktriny Niksona"', in Y. P. Davydov, V. Zhurkin and V. S. Rudnev, eds., *Doktrina Niksona*, Moscow, Izdatel'stvo 'Nauka', 1972, pp. 54–80.
21 President J. F. Kennedy's inauguration speech, January 1961, cited in Arthur M. Schlesinger, jun., *Robert F. Kennedy and his Times*, London, André Deutsch, 1978, p. 455.
22 N. Fedulova, 'Mezhimperialisticheskaya bor'ba za vliyaniye v basseyene Tikhogo Okeana', *Mirovaya Ekonomika i Mezhdunarodnyye Otnosheniya* (hereafter referred to as MEiMO), 9, 1972, p. 37.
23 Ye. Novoseltsev, 'The Foreign Policy of Socialism and the World Revolutionary Process', *International Affairs* (Moscow), 10, 1970, p. 18.
24 *Pravda*, 26 September 1968.
25 Sh. Sanakoyev, 'Programme for the Strengthening of General Peace and Security in Action', p. 4.
26 Solzhenitsyn's phrase cited in Alayne P. Reilly, *America in Contemporary Soviet Literature*, New York, New York University Press, 1971, p. 3; V. Shumilin, 'The Capitalist Economy on the Threshold of the Seventies', *International Affairs* (Moscow), 2–3, 1970, p. 58.
27 N. Inozemtsev, 'Sovremennyye SShA i Sovetskaya Amerikanistika', *SShA*, 1, January 1970 cited in Morton Schwartz, *Soviet Perceptions of the United States*, Berkeley, University of California Press, 1978, p. 9.
28 V. Zorin, 'Vnutrennyye Amerikanskiye problemy 70kh godov', *SShA* (Moscow), 8, August 1971, p. 13.
29 *Pravda*, cited in Robin Edmonds, *Soviet Foreign Policy 1962–1973*, London, Oxford University Press, 1975 p. 86.
30 Ibid., p. 86.
31 L. I. Brezhnev, *Leninskim Kursom*, Moscow, Izdatel'stvo 'Progress', 1972, 3, p. 390.
32 A Soviet observer cited in David L. Morison, 'The Soviet Union and Africa 1968' in *ACR*, 1968–9, p. 42.
33 Richard M. Nixon, 'Asia After Vietnam', *Foreign Affairs*, 46, 1, 1967, p. 121.
34 B. Bulatov, 'Peking and Washington: A New Round', *Literaturnaya Gazeta* (Moscow), 11 December 1968.
35 D. L. Morison, 'The Soviet Union and Africa 1968', p. 42.
36 Robert C. Horn, 'Indian–Soviet Relations in 1969: A Watershed Year?', *Orbis*, 19, 4, Winter 1976, p. 1554.
37 *Pravda*, 8 June 1969.
38 *Krasnaya Zvezda*, 21 February 1967.

39 A. A. Gromyko, V. Khvostov and B. Ponomarev, eds., *Istoriya Vneshnei Politiki SSSR*, cited in Robin Edmonds, *Soviet Foreign Policy 1962–1973*, p. 47.

40 *Strategic Survey 1972*, International Institute for Strategic Studies (hereafter referred to as IISS), London 1973, p. 50.

41 V. L. Tyagunenko, *Vooruzhennaya Bor'ba Narodov Afriki za Svobodu i Nezavisimost'*, Moscow, Izdatel'stvo 'Nauka', 1974, p. 408.

42 L. I. Brezhnev, cited in Sh. Sanakoyev and N. I. Kapchenko, *Teoriya i Praktika Vneshney Politiki Sotsializma*, Moscow, Izdatel'stvo 'Mezhdunarodnyye Otnosheniya', 1973, p. 149.

43 Sh. Sanakoyev, 'Programme for the Strengthening of General Peace and Security in Action', p. 6.

44 L. I. Brezhnev, cited in Sh. Sanakoyev and N. I. Kapchenko, *Teoriya i Praktika Vneshney Politiki Sotsializma*, p. 87.

45 L. I. Brezhnev's speech at the Conference of the Communist and Workers' Parties of Europe, Berlin, 29 June 1976, in *Proletarian Internationalism – Our Banner, Our Strength!*, Moscow, Novosti Press Agency Publishing House, 1980, p. 15.

46 N. Lebedev, 'Proletarian Internationalism and Its Bankrupt Critics', *International Affairs* (Moscow), 8, 1970, p. 57.

47 V. Petrov, V. Belov and A. Karenin, *Leninskaya Vneshnyaya Politika SSSR: Razvitiye i Perspekitvy*, Moscow, Izdatel'stvo Politicheskoy Literatury, 1974, p. 94.

48 S. Vishnevsky, 'The Ideological Struggle and Current International Relations', *International Affairs* (Moscow), 2–3, 1970, p. 38.

49 V. Petrov, V. Belov and A. Karenin, *Leninskaya Vneshnyaya Politika SSSR: Razvitiye i Perspektivy*, p. 148.

50 *Pravda*, 27 October 1965.

51 I. I. Potekhin, 'Panafrikanizm i bor'ba dvukh ideologiy', *Kommunist*, 1, 1964, p. 111.

52 *Moscow Radio*, 23 September 1972.

53 Declaration of the 1960 Conference of Communist Parties cited in Fred Halliday and Maxine Molyneux, *The Ethiopian Revolution*, Manchester, Verso, 1981, pp. 274–5.

54 A. A. Lavrishchev, ed., *Razvivayushchiyesya Strany v Mirovoy Politike*, Moscow, Izdatel'stvo 'Nauka', Glavnaya redaktsiya vostochnoy literatury, 1970, p. 122.

55 R. A. Ul'yanovskiy, 'Leninism, Soviet Experience and the Newly Free Countries', *New Times*, 1, 1971, p. 20.

56 D. G. Tomashevskiy, *Leninskiye Idei i Sovremennyye Mezhdunarodnyye Otnosheniya*, p. 142.

57 V. M. Kulish, ed., *Voyennaya Sila i Mezhdunarodnyye Otnosheniya*, p. 136.

58 *Pravda*, 4 November 1967; A. Dinkevich, 'Principles and Problems of Socialist Orientation in the Countries of Africa and Asia', *Soviet News*, 16 October 1979, 5993, p. 337.

59 R. A. Ul'yanovskiy, 'O stranakh sotsialisticheskoy orientatsiy', *Kommunist*, 11, 1979, p. 118; R. A. Ul'yanovskiy, 'The "Third World" – Problems of Socialist Orientation', *International Affairs* (Moscow), 9, 1971, p. 27.

60 K. Brutents, 'Pravyashchaya revolyutsionnaya demokratiya: nekotoryye cherty prakticheskoy deyatelnosti', *MEiMO*, 11, 1972, pp. 104–17 and 12, pp. 115–29, cited in *USSR and Third World*, 3, 1, December 1972-January 1973, p. 1.

61 R. A. Ul'yanovskiy, 'The "Third World" – Problems of Socialist Orientation', p. 35.

62 V. M. Kulish, ed., *Voyennaya Sila i Mezhdunarodnyye Otnosheniya*, p. 135. Emphasis added.

63 Ye. Novoseltsev, 'The Foreign Policy of Socialism and the World Revolutionary Process', p. 16.

64 V. M. Kulish, ed., *Voyennaya Sila i Mezhdunarodnyye Otnosheniya*, p. 135.

65 V. G. Solodovnikov, *Afrika Vybirayet Put'*, Moscow, Izdatel'stvo 'Nauka', 1970, p. 179.

66 V. I. Lenin, cited in A. Sergiyev, 'Leninism on the Correlation of Forces as a Factor of International Relations', p. 104; D. G. Tomashevskiy, *Leninskiye Idei i Sovremennyye Mezhdunarodnyye Otnosheniya*, p. 142.

67 V. V. Zhurkina and Ye. M. Primakova, eds., *Mezhdunarodnyye Konflikty*, p. 37.

68 V. L. Tyagunenko, ed., *Vooruzhennaya Bor'ba Narodov Afriki za Svobodu i Nezavisimost'*, p. 410.

69 V. Petrov, V. Belov and A. Karenin, *Leninskaya Vneshnyaya Politika SSSR*, p. 210.

70 V. I. Lenin cited in ibid., p. 210.

71 R. A. Ul'yanovskiy, 'The "Third World" – Problems of Socialist Orientation', p. 29.

72 G. Mirskiy, 'Developing Countries: the Army and Society', *New Times*, 48, 1969, p. 16.

73 R. E. Sevortyan, *Armiya v Politicheskom Rezhime Stran Sovremennogo Vostoka*, Moscow, Izdatel'stvo 'Nauka', 1973 pp. 85–6; editorial, 'Armiya i osvoboditelnoye dvizheniye', *Aziya i Afrika Segodnya*, 9, 1966, p. 3.

74 R. E. Sevortyan, *Armiya v Politicheskom Rezhime Stran Sovremennogo Vostoka*, pp. 85–6.

75 Georgiy Mirskiy's scepticism about the sustained 'progressive' potential of military regimes is apparent in his book *'Tretiy Mir': Obshchestvo, Vlast' Armiya*, Izdatel'stvo 'Nauka', Moscow, 1976, pp. 378–85. This issue is examined at length in the Conclusion of this study.

76 R. A. Ul'yanovskiy, 'The "Third World" – Problems of Socialist Orientation', p. 28.

77 Aleksey Kosygin, the then Soviet Prime Minister, in his report to the twenty-fourth CPSU Congress in 1971 on foreign economic relations Moscow Radio, 7 April 1971, cited in *USSR and Third World*, 1, 4, March–April 1971, p. 156; V. Smirnov, 'Vazhnyy faktor ekonomicheskogo progressa razvivayushchikhsya stran', *Vneshnyaya Torgovlya*, 3, 1971, pp. 13–17.

78 K. Gerasimov, 'Ethiopia Forges Ahead', *New Times*, 51, 1971, p. 28.

79 Mary Kaldor, *The Disintegrating West*, Harmondsworth, Middlesex, Penguin, 1978, pp. 155–6; Malcolm Kerr, 'Soviet Influence in Egypt

1967–73' in Alvin Rubinstein, ed., *Soviet and Chinese Influence in the Third World*, New York, Praeger, 1976, p. 96.
80 Jon D. Glassman, *Arms for the Arabs*, Baltimore, John Hopkins University Press, 1975, pp. 65–67.
81 Cecil Eprile, *Sudan: the Long War*, Conflict Studies, Institute for the Study of Conflict Ltd, London 21, 1972, p. 12.
82 *Izvestiya*, 20 October 1968; *Pravda*, 1 June 1969; *Pravda*, 5 November 1969.
83 Charles B. McLane, *Soviet–African Relations*, 3 of Soviet–Third World Relations, London, Central Asian Research Centre, 1974, p. 141.
84 Ibid., p. 136; Cecil Eprile, *Sudan: The Long War*, pp. 1–19.
85 *Izvestiya*, 26 May 1970.
86 M. V. Rayt, 'Mezhafrikanskiye Otnosheniya v Severo-Vostochnoy Afrike', in Anatoly A. Gromyko, ed., *Afrika v Mezhdunarodnyye Otnosheniya*, Moscow, Izdatel'stvo 'Nauka', 1970, p. 344.
87 Helen Desfosses, 'Naval Strategy and Aid Policy: A Study of Soviet–Somali Relations' in W. Weinstein, ed., *Chinese and Soviet Aid to Africa*, New York, Praeger, 1976, pp. 183–201; Robin Edmonds, *Soviet Foreign Policy 1962–1973*, p. 60.
88 V. F. Davydov and V. A. Kremenyuk, 'Strategiya SShA v rayone Indiyskogo Okeana', *SShA*, 5, May 1973, p. 14.
89 Richard E. Bissell, 'Soviet Use of Proxies in the Third World: The Case of Yemen', *Soviet Studies*, 30, 1, January 1978, p. 99.
90 Michael McGwire, ed., *Soviet Naval Developments: Capability and Context*, New York, Praeger, 1973, p. 429; Richard Remnek, *Soviet Policy in the Horn of Africa: The Decision to Intervene*, Professional Paper 270, Arlington, Virginia, Center for Naval Analyses, January 1980, p. 5.
91 Admiral S. G. Gorshkov, cited in R. G. Weinland, R. W. Herrick and J. M. McConnell, 'Admiral Gorshkov's "Navies in War and Peace"', *Survival*, IISS, 17, 2, March–April 1975, p. 57.
92 Y. Tomilin, 'Indiyskiy Okean v agressivnykh planakh imperializma', *MEiMO*, 8, 1971, p. 27.
93 V. F. Davydov and V. A. Kremenyuk, 'Strategiya SShA v rayone Indiyskogo Okeana', pp. 14–15.
94 Y. I. Dolgopolov, ed., *U Karty Indiyskogo Okeana*, Moscow, Voennoye Izdatel'stvo Miniserstva Oborony SSSR, 1974, p. 60.
95 Admiral Gorshkov cited in C. G. Jacobson, *Soviet Strategic Initiatives: Challenge and Response*, New York, Praeger, 1979, p. 18.
96 Captain K. Titov, 'Indiyskiy Okean na karte Pentagona', *Morskoy Sbornik*, 7, 1973, p. 96.
97 Captain K. Titov, 'Indiyskiy Okean na karte Pentagona', p. 93.
98 Ibid.
99 Y. P. Davydov, V. Zhurkin and V. S. Rudnev, eds., *Doktrina Niksona*, p. 71.
100 John Madeley, *Diego Garcia: A Contrast to the Falklands*, report no 54, London, Minority Rights Group Ltd, 1982, p. 4.
101 V. Kudryavtsev, 'The Indian Ocean in the Plans of Imperialism', *International Affairs* (Moscow), 11, 1974, p. 117.

102 Y. P. Davydov, V. Zhurkin and V. S. Rudnev, eds., *Doktrina Niksona*, p. 71.
103 V. F. Davydov, 'Voyennoye – politicheskoye sotrudnichestvo SShA i Britannii: "Vostok Suezy"', *SShA* (Moscow), 11, 1971, p. 71.
104 Y. I. Dolgopolov, ed., *U karty Indiyskogo Okeana*, p. 4; G. G. Drambyants, *Persidskiy Zaliv bez Romantiki*, Moscow, Izdatel'stvo 'Mezhdunarodnyye Otnosheniya', 1968, pp. 3–4.
105 Charles B. McLane, *Soviet–African Relations*, p. 12.
106 *Africa Contemporary Record* (ACR), 1970–1, p. B56.
107 Richard E. Bissell, 'Soviet Use of Proxies in the Third World: The Case of Yemen', p. 100.
108 Captain K. Titov, 'Indiyskiy Okean na karte Pentagona', p. 07.
109 Tom J. Farer, *War Clouds on the Horn of Africa: The Widening Storm*, second revised edition, New York, Carnegie Endowment for International Peace, 1979, p. 35.
110 It is noteworthy that the USSR had only ever given military aid to the Eritrean movement indirectly through its Arab allies and, after the Six Day War, Syria, in particular, 'could spare little for the Eritreans'. See Haggai Erlich, *The Struggle Over Eritrea, 1962–1978: War and Revolution in the Horn of Africa*, Stanford, Hoover Institution Press, 1983, p. 60.
111 At the end of Emperor Haile Selassie's visit to Moscow in March 1967, the USSR and Ethiopia issued a joint communique which, amongst other things, expressed respect for 'national sovereignty, equality and noninterference in the internal affairs of other states, respect for their sovereign equality and territorial integrity and renunciation of the use of force or the threat of its use in settling international disputes'. *Pravda*, 3 March 1967.
112 Aryeh Yodfat, 'The Soviet Union and the Horn of Africa', part one, *Northeast African Studies*, 1, 3, Winter 1979–80, p. 5.
113 Tom J. Farer, *War Clouds on the Horn of Africa*, p. 35; Robert L. Hess, *Ethiopia: The Modernization of Autocracy*, New York, Cornell University Press, 1970, p. 216; Aryeh Yodfat, 'The Soviet Union and the Horn of Africa', part one, note 51, pp. 15–16.
114 Paul B. Henze, *Rebels and Separatists in Ethiopia: Regional Resistance to a Marxist Regime*, Santa Monica, The Rand Corporation, R-3347-USDP, December 1985, p. 32; Saadia Touval, *The Boundary Politics of Independent Africa*, Cambridge, Massachusetts, 1972, p. 236.
115 Saadia Touval, *The Boundary Politics on Independent Africa*, p. 230; I. M. Lewis, *A Modern History of Somalia: Nation and State in the Horn of Africa*, revised edition, London, Longman, 1980, p. 203.
116 The then Somalian Prime Minister, Mohammed Ibrahim Egal, cited in *Africa Research Bulletin* (ARB), October 1967, p. 882.
117 Saadia Touval, *The Boundary Politics of Independent Africa*, p. 234.
118 *Moscow Radio*, 24 November 1967.
119 G. Viktorov, 'Somalia, The Coup: Causes and Consequences', *International Affairs* (Moscow), 2–3, February–March 1970, p. 112.
120 ACR, 1968–9, p. B202; Luba Anastasia Holowaty, *The Soviet Union and Countries of the African Horn: a Case Study of Soviet Perceptions and Policies 1959–1968*, Ph.D. dissertation, University of Pennsylvania, 1970, p. 303.

121 Y. Y. Etinger, *Mezhgosudarstvennyye Otnosheniya v Afrike: Politicheskiye Problemy, Evolyutsiya, Organizatsionnyye Formy*, Moscow, Izdatel'stvo 'Nauka', 1972, p. 82.
122 *ACR*, 1968–9, p. B206.
123 *ACR*, 1969–70, p. B178.
124 Richard M. Nixon, *The Memoirs of Richard Nixon*, London, Sidgwick and Jackson, 1978, p. 400.
125 Aryeh Yodfat, 'The Soviet Union and the Horn of Africa', part one, p. 11.
126 Richard Sherman, *Eritrea, the Unfinished Revolution*, New York, Praeger, 1980, p. 78.
127 *Ethiopian Herald* (Addis Ababa), cited in *ARB*, March 1969, p. 1352; *New York Times*, 18 August 1970; *ARB*, November 1969, p. 1585.
128 *The Observer*, 30 March 1969.
129 Paul B. Henze, 'Getting a Grip on the Horn: The Emergence of the Soviet Presence and Future Prospects' in Walter Laquer, ed., *The Pattern of Soviet Conduct in the Third World*, New York, Praeger, 1983, p. 158.
130 Emperor Haile Selassie declared that: 'The current situation in Czechoslovakia has deeply saddened us. What has happened to Czechoslovakia has already happened to other small nations and is likely to happen again in the future. Although there are misunderstandings between Czechoslovakia and her immediate neighbours, we urge all involved in Czechoslovakia to reach a peaceful settlement, and we urge the immediate withdrawal of foreign troops from Czechoslovakia.' See *ACR*, 1968–9, p. 145.
131 E. Borisov, 'Problemy tysyacheletney strany', a review of A. Elyanov's book, *Efiopiya*, Moscow, Izdatel'stvo 'Mysl' 1967, in *Aziya i Afrika Segodnya*, 2, 1969, p. 63.
132 G. Galperin, 'Lyudy v zelennykh shinelyakh', *Aziya i Afrika Segodnya*, 9, 1966, p. 15.
133 M. V. Rayt, *Mezhafrikanskiye Otnosheniya v Severo-Vostochnoy Afrike*, p. 347.
134 G. Viktorov, 'Somalia: Toward Progress', *International Affairs* (Moscow), 12, December 1970, p. 85.
135 *ARB*, December 1969, p. 1626; Paul B. Henze, formerly a member of the US Embassy staff in Addis Ababa, 1969–72 and now a resident consultant at the Rand Corporation, interview with author, 17 June 1988.
136 Gary D. Payton, 'The Somali Coup of 1969: the Case for Soviet Complicity', *Horn of Africa*, 4, 2, 1981, p. 18.
137 *Pravda*, 24 October 1969.
138 *Izvestiya*, 27 November 1969.
139 *ACR*, 1969–70, p.B179.
140 *ARB*, April 1970, p. 1730; Mohammed Heikal, *The Road to Ramadan*, Glasgow, Fontana, 1976, p. 92.
141 V. Yermashev, *Moscow Radio*, 1 July 1970.
142 *Soviet News*, 27 October 1970, No 5566, p. 39.
143 P. Manchkha, 'Somalia – A Year of Progress', *Za Rubezhom*, 49, December 4–10, 1970, pp. 16–17.
144 *ACR*, 1969–70, p. B159–B163.
145 G. Viktorov, 'Somalia: Towards Progress', p. 85.

146 Christopher Clapham, 'Ethiopia and Somalia', in *Conflicts in Africa*, Adelphi Papers, 93, IISS, London, December 1972, pp. 16–17; Gary D. Payton, 'The Somali Coup of 1969', pp. 11–20; Paul B. Henze, interview with author, 17 June 1988.

147 P. Manchkha, 'Somalia – A Year of Progress', pp. 16–17.

148 Y. Y. Etinger, *Mezhgosudarstvennyye Otnosheniya v Afrike*, p. 82.

149 Gary D. Payton, 'The Somali Coup of 1969', p. 17.

150 *Pravda*, 24 October 1969; G. Viktorov, 'Somalia, The Coup: Causes and Consequences', p. 112.

151 Saadia Touval, *The Boundary Politics of Independent Africa*, p. 238.

152 I. M. Lewis, 'The Politics of the 1969 Somali Coup', *The Journal of Modern African Studies*, 10, 3, October 1972, pp. 397–400.

153 Marina Ottaway, *Soviet and American Influence in the Horn of Africa*, New York, Praeger, 1982, p. 39.

154 Ibid., p. 37; E. S. Sherr, 'Ekonomicheskaya "Pomoshch" imperialisticheskikh gosudarstv Somali', *Narody Azii i Afriki*, 3, 1970, pp. 134–40.

155 *ACR*, 1969–70, p. B181.

156 *ACR*, 1969–70, p. B177; G. Viktorov, 'Somalia, The Coup: Causes and Consequences', p. 112.

157 Mohammed Siad Barre, *My Country and My People*, 1, Mogadishu, Ministry of Information and National Guidance, 1974, p. 53.

158 *October Star* (Mogadishu) cited in *ARB*, October 1969, p. 1551.

159 Mohammed Siad Barre, *My Country and My People*, 1, pp. 67–71.

160 Y. Y. Etinger seemed to have little doubt about the nationalist orientation of the Somali upheaval: 'The fact of the matter is that the Egal government, overthrown by a military coup in October 1969, was for a long time subjected to sharp criticism from the side of opposition for its "moderate" approach toward the problem of Somali re-unification into a single national state. The Egal course directed at reconciliation with Ethiopia and Kenya aroused dissatisfaction, above all, amongst the most radically inclined groups of Somali nationalists, who accused the Prime Minister of a Somali "sell-out" and with the renunciation of the aims of the Republic set forth in the constitution for re-unifying all Somalis into a single state.' Y. Y. Etinger, *Mezhgosudarstvennyye Otnosheniya v Afrike*, pp. 81–2.

161 Mohammed Siad Barre, *My Country and My People*, 1, p. 55.

162 Siad Barre interviewed in *Pravda*, 20 December 1969.

163 Ibid.

164 *Mogadishu Radio*, cited in *ARB*, December 1969, p. 1622.

165 Mohammed Siad Barre, *My Country and My People*, 1, p. 166.

166 Siad Barre cited in *ACR*, 1970–1, p. A60.

167 Y. Y. Etinger, *Mezhgosudarstvennyye Otnosheniya v Afrike*, p. 82.

168 *ARB*, March 1970, p. 1703; *ARB*, October 1970, p. 1895.

169 *ACR*, 1970–1, p. 163.

170 *The Times*, 30 December 1970.

171 Haggai Erlich, *The Struggle Over Eritrea, 1962–1978*, pp. 27–31.

172 *ACR*, 1970–1, p. B106.

173 *The Guardian*, 10 March 1972.

174 *The Arms Trade with the Third World*, London, Elek, Stockholm International Peace Research Institute (SIPRO), 1971, pp.650–1.

175 Colin Legum and Bill Lee, *Conflict in the Horn of Africa*, London, Rex Collings, 1977, p. 23; Richard Sherman, *Eritrea: The Unfinished Revolution*, p. 79; Paul B. Henze, *Rebels and Separatists in Ethiopia*, p. 36.

176 *Soviet News*, 3 November 1970, 5567, p. 52.

177 *Pravda*, 31 May 1970.

178 Y. Y. Etinger, *Mezhgosudarstvennyye Otnosheniya v Afrike*, p. 69.

179 M. V. Rayt, *Mezhafrikanskiye Otnosheniya v Severo-Vostochnoy Afrike*, p. 342.

180 Y. Y. Etinger, *Mezhgosudarstvennyye Otnosheniya v Afrike*, pp. 69–92.

181 G. V. Fokeyev, *Vneshyaya Politika Stran Afriki*, Moscow, Izdatel'stvo 'Mezdunarodnyye Otnosheniya', 1968, p. 122.

182 M. V. Rayt, *Mezhafrikanskiye Otnosheniya v Severo-Vostochnoy Afrike*, p. 346.

183 G. Tsypkin, 'Gorod Budushchego', *Aziya i Afrika Segodnya*, 6, 1969, pp. 58–60.

184 G. V. Fokeyev, *Vneshyaya Politika Stran Afriki*, pp. 119–22.

185 Y. Y. Etinger, *Mezhgosudarstvennyye Otnosheniya v Afrike*, p. 82.

186 M. V. Rayt, *Mezhafrikanskiye Otnosheniya v Severo-Vostochnoy Afrike*, pp. 348–350. Emphasis added.

187 Y. Y. Etinger, *Mezhgosudarstvennye Otnosheniya v Afrike*, pp. 70–84.

188 M. V. Rayt, *Narody Efiopii*, Moscow, Izdatel'stvo 'Nauka', 1965, pp. 157–8.

189 G. Galperin, 'Lyudy v zelennykh shinelyakh', p. 15.

190 Ibid. p. 15.

191 A Polish observer described Emperor Haile Selassie in the following terms: 'His venerable Majesty was no reader. For him, neither the written nor the printed word existed; everything had to be relayed by word of mouth. His Majesty had had no schooling.' Ryszard Kapuscinski, *The Emperor: Downfall of an Autocrat*, London, Quartet Books, 1983, p. 7.

192 Richard M. Nixon cited in Admasu Zike, *An Application of the Theory of Social Exchange to International Relations: The Kagnew Station as the Linchpin of the Ethiopian-United States Relationship*, Ph.D. dissertation, Northern Illinois University, 1979, p. 105.

193 *ARB*, March 1970, p. 1710.

194 *New York Times*, 13 February 1970.

195 *Africa Confidential*, 2, 12, 1970, p. 8.

196 *ARB*, May 1970, p. 1764.

197 *Soviet News*, 2 June 1970, 5545, p. 108.

198 Between 1965 and 1973, in what was one of the least glorious chapters of British history, the UK systematically and forcibly removed all of the 2000 or so Ilois people who inhabited Diego Garcia and deposited them in exile in Mauritius without any workable resettlement scheme. See John Madeley, *Diego Garcia: A Contrast to the Falklands*, p. 4.

199 Senator Stuart Symington cited in Admasu Zike, *An Application of the Theory of Social Exchange to International Relations*, pp. 105–15.

200 David Newson cited in *ACR*, 1970–1, p. B107.
201 Paul B. Henze, interview with author, 17 June 1988.
202 David L. Morison, Alan Berson and Klaus Luders, *Soviet Aims and Activities in the Persian Gulf and Adjacent Areas: Report on an Investigation of Soviet Media Output*, Washington DC, Abbot Associates, Inc., November 1976, p. 61.
203 V. M. Kulish, ed., *Voyennaya Sila i Mezhdunarodnyye Otnosheniya*, p. 136.
204 A. A. Lavrishchev, ed., *Razvivayushchiyesya Strany v Mirovoy Politike*, p. 22.
205 Andrey Gromyko, the Soviet Foreign Minister, in *Pravda*, 13 July 1969.
206 O. M. Borbatov and L. Y. Cherkasskiy, *Sotrudnichestvo SSSR so Stranami Arabskogo Vostoga i Afriki*, Moscow, Izdatel'stvo 'Nauka', Glavnaya Redaktsiya Vostochnoy Literatury, 1973, pp. 73–4. Emphasis added.
207 V. L. Tyagunenko, ed., *Vooruzhennaya Bor'ba Narodov Afriki za Svobodu i Nezavisimost'*, p. 408.
208 *Diplomaticheskiy slovar'*, 2, Moscow, Izdatel'stvo, Politicheskoy Literatury, 1971, pp. 296–8.
209 V. M. Kulish, ed., *Voyennaya Sila i Mezhdunarodnyye Otnosheniya*, p. 136.

4. The budding alliance: Marx, Lenin and Mohammed

1 President Siad Barre interviewed in *Izvestiya*, 2 June 1971.
2 Irving Kaplan, *Area Handbook for Somalia*, Washington DC, US Government Printing Office, 1977, pp. 221–2.
3 Marina Ottaway, *Soviet and American Influence in the Horn of Africa*, New York, Praeger, 1982, p. 67.
4 David E. Albright, 'The Horn of Africa and the Arab–Israeli Conflict', in Robert O. Freedman, ed., *World Politics and the Arab–Israeli Conflict*, New York, Pergamon Press, 1979, p. 154; David D. Laitin and Said S. Samatar, *Somalia: Nation in Search of a State*, Colorado, Westview Press, 1987, p. 140.
5 V. Shmarov, 'New Stage in Soviet–Somali Relations', *New Times*, 29, 1974, p. 6.
6 *Pravda*, 30 October 1974.
7 Brian Crozier, 'The Soviet Presence in Somalia', *Conflict Studies*, 54, February 1975, pp. 3–19.
8 *Pravda*, 31 July 1971.
9 Aryeh Y. Yodfat, 'The Soviet Union and the Horn of Africa', *Northeast African Studies*, part one, 1, 3, Winter 1979–90, p. 12.
10 Charles B. McLane, *Soviet–African Relations*, Soviet–Third World Relations, London, Central Asian Research Centre, 3, 1974, p. 125.
11 The Chinese Premier, Chou En-lai quoted in *USSR and the Third World*, 2, 5, 1972, p. 292.
12 *African Contemporary Record* (ACR), 1970–1, p. B56.
13 'Strong Ties', *New Times*, 48, 1971, p. 17.
14 *ACR*, 1971–2, p. B196.
15 *Pravda*, 23 November 1971.
16 'Strong Ties', *New Times*, p. 17.

17 Mogadishu Radio cited in *Africa Research Bulletin* (ARB), November 1971, p. 2297.
18 *Krasnaya Zvezda*, 19 February 1972.
19 Robert G. Weinland, 'Land Support for Naval Forces: Egypt and the Soviet Escadra 1962–1976', *Survival*, 20, 2, March-April 1978, p. 77, note 17.
20 *Krasnaya Zvezda*, 19 February 1972.
21 Mohammed Heikal, *The Road to Ramadan*, Glasgow, Fontana/Collins, 1976, p. 174.
22 *Krasnaya Zvezda*, 20 July 1972.
23 Ibid., 20 July 1972.
24 *The Military Balance 1973–1974*, London, The International Institute for Strategic Studies (IISS), 1974, p. 41.
25 J. Bowyer Bell, 'Strategic Implications of the Soviet Presence in Somalia', *Orbis*, 19, 2, Summer 1975, p. 404.
26 *Strategic Survey 1976*, London, IISS, 1976, p. 60; Brian Crozier, 'The Soviet Presence in Somalia', p. 9.
27 Richard Remnek, *Soviet Policy in the Horn of Africa: The Decision to Intervene*, Professional Paper 270, Arlington, Virginia, Center for Naval Analyses, January 1980, pp. 10–11.
28 *Strategic Survey 1976*, p. 60; Mohammed Ayoob, *The Horn of Africa: Regional Conflict and Superpower Involvement*, Canberra Papers on Strategy and Defence, 18, Canberra, Australian National University, 1978, p. 11; *The Times*, 19 May 1972; Richard Remnek, *Soviet Policy in the Horn of Africa: The Decision to Intervene*, p. 12.
29 V. Sofinsky, 'Somalia on the Path of Progress', *International Affairs* (Moscow), 11, November 1974, p. 64.
30 *Izvestiya*, 7 September 1972.
31 V. Gorodnov, N. Kosukhin, 'In the Somali Democratic Republic', *International Affairs* (Moscow), 5, May 1972, p. 102.
32 E. F. Chernenko, 'Osnovnyye napravleniya ekonomicheskoy politiki Somaliyskoy Demokraticheskoy Respubliki', *Narody Azii i Afriki*, 5, 1975, p. 19.
33 E. Sherr, 'Veter peremen nad Somali', *Aziya i Afrika Segodnya*, 11, 1971, p. 12.
34 *The Daily Telegraph*, 10 April 1973.
35 Charles B. McLane, *Soviet–African Relations*, pp. 124–5.
36 E. Sherr, 'Veter peremen nad Somali', p. 13.
37 E. Denisov, 'Vazhnyy etap razvitiya', *Aziya i Afrika Segodnya*, 9, 1972, p. 28.
38 President Siad cited in E. F. Chernenko, 'Osnovnyye napravleniya ekonomicheskoy politiki Somaliyskoy Demokraticheskoy Respubliki', p. 20.
39 I. M. Lewis, *A Modern History of Somalia: Nation and State in the Horn of Africa*, revised edition, London, Longman, 1980, p. 210.
40 *ARB*, January 1972, p. 2345; Mohammed Siad Barre, *My Country and My People 1969–1974*, Mogadishu, Ministry of Information and National Guidance, 1974, p. 75.
41 Marina Ottaway, *Soviet and American Influence in the Horn of Africa*, pp. 65–6.
42 V. Sofinsky, 'Somalia on the Path of Progress', p. 63.

43 A. Rachkov, 'Uardigli-tsentr orientatsii', *Aziya i Afrika Segodnya*, 3, 1973, p. 10.
44 E. Sherr, 'Somalia: Socialist Orientation', *International Affairs* (Moscow), 2, February 1974, p. 87.
45 *Soviet Objectives in the Middle East*, a special report, Institute for the Study of Conflict, London, January 1974, pp. 14–15; David D. Laitin and Said S. Samatar, *Somalia: Nation in Search of a State*, p. 81.
46 Brian Crozier, 'The Soviet Presence in Somalia', pp. 5–6; for a Somali account of the KGB role in Somalia see Nurruddin Farah, *Sweet and Sour Milk*, London, Allison and Busby, 1979, pp. 116–17.
47 E. Sherr, 'Veter peremen nad Somali', p. 14.
48 *ACR*, 1971–2, p. B184.
49 'Somalia: How Much Soviet Influence?', *Africa Confidential*, 14, 6 July 1973, p. 3.
50 E. Denisov, 'Vazhnyy etap razvitiya', pp. 25–7.
51 V. Sofinsky, 'Somalia on the Path of Progress', p. 64.
52 *Pravda*, 30 June 1971.
53 V. Gorodnov, N. Kosukhin, 'In the Somali Democratic Republic', p. 103.
54 *Pravda*, 30 June 1971.
55 Marina Ottaway, *Soviet and American Influence in the Horn of Africa*, p. 76.
56 E. F. Chernenko, 'Osnovnyye napravleniya ekonomicheskoy politiki Somaliyskoy Demokraticheskoy Respubliki', p. 22.
57 *ACR*, 1972–3, p. B254.
58 According to one observer, the results of the co-operative movement were not commensurate with the government's rhetoric. By 1980, there were 315 agricultural co-operatives, with some 34,000 members, and a few others in areas such as fisheries, transport and crafts. See Marina Ottaway, *Soviet and American Influence in the Horn of Africa*, p. 75.
59 'Contribution to Somali Development', *New Times*, 32, 1973, p. 7; *ACR*, 1974–5, p. B278.
60 Tom J. Farer, *War Clouds on the Horn of Africa: The Widening Storm*, Washington DC, Carnegie Endowment for International Peace, 1979, p. 112.
61 I. M. Lewis, *A Modern History of Somalia: Nation and State in the Horn of Africa*, p. 216.
62 Tom J. Farer, *War Clouds on the Horn of Africa: The Widening Storm*, p. 112.
63 *ACR*, 1973–4, p. B246.
64 E. Sherr, 'Somalia: Socialist Orientation', p. 86.
65 President Nyerere cited in T. Farer, *War Clouds on the Horn of Africa: The Widening Storm*, p. 113.
66 I. M. Lewis, *A Modern History of Somalia: Nation and State in the Horn of Africa*, pp. 214–5.
67 Marina Ottaway, *Soviet and American Influence in the Horn of Africa*, p. 74.
68 Mohammed Siad Barre, *My Country and My People 1969–1974*, p. 126.
69 It was reported that nomads in Burao, northern Somalia, rioted in October 1973 when called upon to take part in a street-cleaning self-help operation and pay taxes. See 'Somalia: A Sort of Marxism', *Africa Confidential*, 14, 25, 14 December 1973.

70 E. Denisov, 'Vazhnyy etap razvitiya', p. 26.

71 *ACR*, 1971–2, p. B184.

72 President Siad's assessment cited in *ACR*, 1971–2, p. B197.

73 *ACR*, 1972–3, p. B238; *ACR*, 1971–2, p. B197.

74 *ACR*, 1972–3, p. B238.

75 E. F. Chernenko, 'Osnovnyye napravleniya ekonomicheskoy politiki Somaliyskoy Demokraticheskoy Respubliki', p. 25.

76 Ibid., pp. 25–6.

77 N. D. Kosukhin, E. S. Sherr, 'Sovetsko-Somaliyskaya ekspeditsiya', *Narody Azii i Afriki*, 5, 1972, pp. 222–7.

78 E. F. Chernenko, 'Osnovnyye napravleniya ekonomicheskoy politiki Somaliyskoy Demokraticheskoy Respubliki', p. 21.

79 V. Sofinsky, 'Somalia on the Path of Progress', p. 64.

80 *Vneshnyaya Torgovlya SSSR*, 1971 and 1974, Moscow, 'statistika'.

81 Charles B. McLane, *Soviet–African Relations*, p. 131.

82 E. F. Chernenko, 'Osnovnyye napravleniya ekonomicheskoy politiki Somaliyskoy Demokraticheskoy Respubliki', p. 26; V. Sofinsky, 'Somalia on the Path of Progress', p. 63.

83 E. F. Chernenko, 'Osnovnyye napravleniya ekonomicheskoy politiki Somaliyskoy Demokraticheskoy Respubliki', p. 20; E. S. Sherr, 'Vazhnyy shag k progressu', *Aziya i Afrika Segodnya*, 5, 1974, p. 40.

84 E. F. Chernenko, 'Osnovnyye napravleniya ekonomicheskoy politiki Somaliyskoy Demokraticheskoy Respubliki', p. 20.

85 E. S. Sherr, 'Somalia: Socialist Orientation', p. 88.

86 N. Kosukhin, 'The Soviet–Somalian Scientific Expedition and its Early Results', a paper presented at the *International Conference of Africanists*, Addis Ababa, December 1973. See *ACR*, 1973–4, pp. B251–2.

87 One Soviet writer argued that the 'heavy task' of abolishing tribalism in Somalia required more than 'just a campaign'. See E. F. Chernenko, 'V. Somaliyskoy stepi', *Aziya i Afrika Segodnya*, 8, 1974, p. 31.

88 E. S. Sherr, 'Somali: Religiya i Politika, *Narody Azii i Afriki*, 4, 1987, pp. 52–3.

89 E. S. Sherr, 'Somalia: Socialist Orientation', p. 87.

90 Ibid., p. 87.

91 E. F. Chernenko, 'V. Somaliyskoy stepi', p. 32.

92 N. D. Kosukhin, E. S. Sherr, 'Sovetsko–Somaliyskaya ekspeditsiya', pp. 222–7.

93 E. Sherr, 'Somalia: Socialist Orientation', p. 88; Harry Brind, 'Soviet Policy in the Horn of Africa', *International Affairs*, 60, 1, Winter 1983–4, pp. 82–3.

94 See the *Washington Post*, 18 December 1973.

95 E. S. Sherr, 'Somalia', *New Times*, 11, 1971, p. 31. Having discussed Soviet economic co-operation with Mogadishu, Sherr observed that to 'seek examples of mutually advantageous co-operation of a similar kind between Somalia and the Western countries would be a waste of time'.

96 One Soviet writer observed that 'the Peking leaders simply do not have the material and technical base or adequate financial resources . . . to solve the cardinal problems of economic development in the African countries'. See

Yu. Mikhailov, 'What Peking Wants in Africa', *Sovetskaya Rossiya*, October 31, 1974.

97 Mohammed Siad Barre, *My Country and My People*, p. 60.

98 Harry Brind, 'Soviet Policy in the Horn of Africa', p. 83.

99 *The New York Times*, 6 September 1970.

100 President Siad cited in I. M. Lewis, *A Modern History of Somalia: Nation and State in the Horn of Africa*, p. 217.

101 I. M. Lewis, *A Modern History of Somalia: Nation and State in the Horn of Africa*, pp. 220–1.

102 Mohammed Siad Barre, *My Country and My People*, p. 195.

103 Ibid., p. 75.

104 Ibid., p. 105.

105 Ibid., p. 126.

106 I. M. Lewis, *A Modern History of Somalia: Nation and State in the Horn of Africa*, p. 225.

107 E. Denisov, 'Vazhnyy etap razvitiya', p. 28; E. S. Sherr, 'Veter peremen nad Somali', p. 12.

108 E. S. Sherr, 'Somalia: Socialist Orientation', p. 85; E. S. Sherr, 'Veter peremen nad Somali', p. 12.

109 *ACR*, 1973–3, p. B252; G. Nadezhdin, 'Somali Democratic Republic', *International Affairs* (Moscow), 8, 1973, p. 118.

110 *ACR*, 1971–2, p. B195.

111 *ACR*, 1972–3, pp. B223–4.

112 Moscow Radio, 26 May 1973, cited in *USSR and Third World*, 3, 5, 1973, p. 362.

113 During the Yom Kippur war, Somalia informed Egypt that it would send its entire supplies of meat, preserved fish and livestock to Egypt and Syria to help them overcome shortages. In fact Somalia did not do it. Patrick Gilkes, *Private communication*, 1 May 1988; *ACR*, 1973–4, p. B250.

114 *ACR*, 1973–4, p. B251.

115 Mohammed Siad Barre, *My Country and My People*, p. 102; Siad cited in *ACR*, 1973–4, p. B253.

116 The GDR signed a co-operation agreement with Mogadishu in January 1971 concerning economic, technical, cultural and information affairs. North Korea and Bulgaria rendered agricultural assistance, particularly in the areas of mechanisation and irrigation. Finally, in 1974, Cuba started to train Somalis in the field of sugar technology, livestock and fisheries, as well as medical aid. See under the Somali Democratic Republic in *ACR*, from 1971 to 1974.

117 Mohammed Siad Barre, *My Country and My People*, p. 88.

118 *ACR*, 1972–3, p. B142; Mohammed Siad Barre, *My Country and My People*, p. 147.

119 *ARB*, October 1971, p. 2250.

120 Haggai Erlich, *The Struggle Over Eritrea*, Stanford, Hoover Institution Press, 1983, p. 67.

121 I. M. Lewis, *A Modern History of Somalia: Nation and State in the Horn of Africa*, p. 232.

122 *ACR*, 1972–3, p. B234.
123 Colin Legum, *Ethiopia: The Fall of Haile Selassie's Empire*, London, Rex Collings, 1975, pp. 19–20.
124 *ACR*, 1973–4, pp. B248–9.
125 *ACR*, 1973–4, p. B249.
126 *ACR*, 1973–4, p. B249.
127 Emperor Haile Selassie cited in Colin Legum, *Ethiopia: The Fall of Haile Selassie's Empire*, p. 20.
128 *The Daily Telegraph*, 13 April 1973.
129 Mohammed Siad Barre, *My Country and My People*, p. 34.
130 *The Military Balance 1970–1971*, London, International Institute for Strategic Studies (IISS), pp. 48–52; *1973–1974*, pp. 39–41.
131 *ACR*, 1973–4, pp. B161–2; *The Financial Times*, 2 October 1973.
132 Adapted from *The Military Balance 1970–1971*, pp. 48–52; *1973–1974*, pp. 39–41.
133 Colonel Gaddafy expressed complete support for Somalia's 'national demands'. See *ARB*, January 1972, p. 2338.
134 *Soviet News*, 22 November 1977, 5907, p. 408.
135 R. N. Ismagilova, *Etnicheskiye Problemy Sovremennoy Tropicheskoy Afriki*, Moscow, Izdatel'stvo 'Nauka', 1973, pp. 334–5.
136 These comments were made during a review of Luigi Pestalozza's book, *Somalia, a Chronicle of the Revolution*. See N. Kosukhin, L. Obukhov, 'On the Road of Social Progress', *International Affairs* (Moscow), 10, October 1974, pp. 129–31; E. F. Chernenko, 'Osnovnyye napravleniya ekonomicheskoy politiki Somaliyskoy Demokraticheskoy Respubliki', p. 26.
137 *The Guardian*, 13 March 1975; Harry Brind, 'Soviet Policy in the Horn of Africa', p. 83; Brian Crozier, 'The Soviet Presence in Somalia', p. 12.
138 Tom J. Farer, *War Clouds on the Horn of Africa: The Widening Storm*, p. 17.
139 Jonathan Dimbleby's film for British television revealed the full horrors of the Ethiopian famine. See C. Legum, *Ethiopia: The Fall of Haile Selassie's Empire*, p. 12; Robert F. Gorman, *Political Conflict on the Horn of Africa*, New York, Praeger, 1981, p. 41.
140 Donald Petterson, 'Ethiopia abandoned? An American perspective', *International Affairs*, 62, 4, Autumn 1986, p. 628.
141 C. Legum, *Ethiopia: The Fall of Haile Selassie's Empire*, p. 2.
142 *ARB*, March 1971, p. 2036; Haggai Erlich, *The Struggle Over Eritrea*, p. 66.
143 *ACR*, 1973–4, p. B156. In October 1972, Mohammed Heikal, the Egyptian journalist, argued the case for 'a new strategy that will guarantee full Arab sovereignty over the Red Sea'. See Haggai Erlich, *The Struggle Over Eritrea*, pp. 63–4.
144 *ARB*, May 1973, p. 2849.
145 Haggai Erlich, *The Struggle Over Eritrea*, p. 59.
146 N. Tarasov, 'The Pentagon's Plans for the Red Sea', *Asia and Africa Today*, 4, July–August 1983, p. 17.
147 A. Kokiev, 'Puti razvitiya Efiopskoy derevni', *Aziya i Afrika Segodnya*, 2, 1972, p. 20.
148 Ibid., p. 20.

149 Moscow Radio, 12 June 1973, cited in *USSR and Third World*, 3, 5, May-July 1973, p. 351.
150 Moscow Radio, 15 June 1973.
151 A. Kokiev, 'Puti razvitiya Efiopskoy derevni', p. 20; K. Gerasimov, 'Ethiopia Forges Ahead', *New Times*, 51, 1971, p. 29.
152 It was estimated, for example, that the total value of US assets nationalised after the revolution in Ethiopia was about $50 million. Even this figure was probably inflated by the claim of the dispossessed owners. See Marina Ottaway, *Soviet and American Influence in the Horn of Africa*, p. 30.
153 A. Kokiev, 'Puti razvitiya Efiopskoy derevni', p. 21.
154 *Izvestiya*, 13 February 1971.
155 Addis Ababa Radio, 31 August 1971, cited in *USSR and Third World*, 1, 8, 1971, p. 471.
156 Charles B. McLane, *Soviet–African Relations*, p. 46.
157 *Sovetskaya Rossiya*, 24 April 1973.
158 Charles B. McLane, *Soviet–African Relations*, p. 47.
159 *Izvestiya*, 26 January 1974.
160 Oleg Shitov in *Tass*, 2 November 1971, cited in *USSR and Third World*, 1, 10, 1971, p. 628.
161 V. Shmarov, 'Traditional Friendship', *New Times*, 45–6, 1973, p. 36.
162 Donald Petterson, 'Ethiopia Abandoned? An American Perspective', p. 628; Paul B. Henze, private communication, 31 May 1988; Patrick Gilkes, private communication, 1 May 1988.
163 'The Horn of Africa and The Middle East', *Africa Confidential*, 14, 22, 2 November 1973, pp. 1–2.
164 Donald Petterson, 'Ethiopia Abandoned? An American Perspective', p. 628; *ACR*, 1973–4, pp. B161–2.
165 Donald Petterson, 'Ethiopia Abandoned? An American Perspective', p. 628.
166 *Tass*, 16 October 1973, cited in *USSR and Third World*, 3, 8, October-December 1973, p. 577.
167 Marina Ottaway, *Soviet and American Influence in the Horn of Africa*, p. 51.
168 *ACR*, 1973–3, p. B160.
169 US Congress Senate Subcommittee on United States Security Agreements and Commitments Abroad, *United States Security Agreements and Commitments Abroad: Ethiopia*, Hearings, 91st Cong., 2nd Session, 1 June 1970, p. 1913–47.
170 Charles B. McLane, *Soviet–African Relations*, p. 46; *The Times*, 2 November 1972.
171 *ACR*, 1972–3, p. B141.
172 O. Vladimirov, M. Kuranin, *New Times*, 46, 1972, cited in *USSR and Third World*, 2, 10, 1972, pp. 559–60.
173 Moscow Radio, 28 February 1973.
174 K. Gerasimov, 'Ethiopia Forges Ahead', p. 30; Yu. Rytkheu, 'V Efiopii pozdney osen'yu', *Aziya i Afrika Segodnya*, 7, 1972, p. 39.
175 Yu. Rytkheu, 'V Efiopii pozdney osen'yu', p. 39.
176 Addis Ababa Radio, 3 May 1972.

177 Charles B. McLane, *Soviet–African Relations*, p. 46.
178 *The Egyptian Gazette*, 31 August 1973.
179 *Tass*, 14 September 1973.
180 *Izvestiya*, 3 October 1973; *Pravda*, 3 October 1973.
181 K. Gerasimov, 'Ethiopia Forges Ahead', p. 28.
182 A. Dolgov, Moscow Radio, 3 January 1971.
183 'The Horn of Africa and The Middle East', *Africa Confidential*, p. 4.
184 Haggai Erlich, *The Struggle Over Eritrea*, note 9, pp. 134–5.
185 *Pravda*, 1 November 1973.
186 *Pravda*, 1 November 1973.
187 *Pravda*, 1 November 1973.
188 *Soviet News*, 6 November 1973, 5712, p. 464.
189 *Pravda*, 13 July 1974.
190 *The Egyptian Gazette*, 4 March 1974.
191 Mohammed Siad Barre, *My Country and My People*, p. 50.
192 *ACR*, 1974–5, p. B274.
193 E. S. Sherr, 'Somali: Vneshnyaya politika strany sotsialisticheskoy orien-
     tatsii', *Aziya i Afrika Segodnya*, 1, 1975, p. 43.
194 Tom J. Farer, *War Clouds on the Horn of Africa: The Widening Storm*, p. 117.
195 *Pravda*, 17 March 1974.
196 'Events in Ethiopia', *New Times*, 21, 1974, p. 9.
197 *ARB*, January 1974, p. 3102.
198 The book in question was Luigi Pestalozza's *The Somali Revolution*. See
     ARB, June 1974, pp. 3256–7; *ACR*, 1974–5, p. B273.
199 Brian Crozier, 'The Soviet Presence in Somalia', pp. 4–5; *The Daily
     Telegraph*, 9 July 1974.
200 President Podgorny's party included I. V. Arkhipov, Deputy Chairman
     of the Soviet Council of Ministers; V. V. Kuznetsov, First Deputy Foreign
     Minister; General S. L. Sokolov, First Deputy Defence Minister; V. A.
     Ustinov, Head of the African Department of the Soviet Foreign Ministry
     and V. N. Sofinsky, Head of the Foreign Ministry Press Department. See
     Ian Greig, *The Communist Challenge to Africa*, London, Foreign Affairs
     Publishing Co. Ltd., 1977, p. 105.
201 *Pravda*, 30 October 1974.
202 Brian Crozier, 'The Soviet Presence in Somalia', pp. 3–5.
203 *The Daily Express*, 6 September 1974; Aryeh Yodfat, 'The Soviet Union and
     the Horn of Africa', *Northeast African Studies*, part two, 2, 1, 1980, p. 34.
204 *Pravda*, 30 October 1974.
205 *Izvestiya*, 16 July 1974.
206 Addis Ababa Radio, 13 July 1974, cited in *USSR and Third World*, 4, 5,
     June–July 1974, p. 329.
207 V. Sofinsky, 'Somalia on the Path of Progress', p. 66.
208 'New-Type Treaty', *New Times*, 45, 1974, p. 17.
209 *Izvestiya*, 16 July 1974.
210 *ARB*, July 1974, p. 3315; Mogadishu Radio, 9 July 1974; *ARB*, July 1974,
     p. 3315.
211 *ARB*, July 1974, p. 3315.

212 Brian Crozier, 'The Soviet Presence in Somalia', p. 4.
213 Marina Ottaway, *Soviet and American Influence in the Horn of Africa*, p. 71.
214 Brian Crozier, 'The Soviet Presence in Somalia', p. 5.
215 *USSR and Third World*, 4, 7, September-October 1974, p. 428.
216 G. Nadezhdin, 'Somali Democratic Republic', p. 117.
217 President N. Podgorny, cited in V. Shmarov, 'New Stage in Soviet–Somali Relations', *New Times*, 29, 1974, p. 6.
218 *The Sunday Times*, 14 July 1974.

5. The Ethiopian revolution and the quest for a Pax Sovietica

1 *Africa Research Bulletin* (ARB), September 1974, p. 3361.
2 Moscow Radio, 5 October 1974.
3 *Washington Post*, 5 March 1978.
4 Marina Ottaway, *Soviet and American Influence in the Horn of Africa*, New York, Praeger, 1982, p. 107.
5 Mogadishu Radio, 19 June 1975, cited in *USSR and Third World*, 5, 5, May-July 1975, p. 259.
6 *Moscow News*, 3 October 1976, 44, p. 6.
7 C. Legum, *Ethiopia: The Fall of Haile Selassie's Empire*, London, Rex Collings, 1975, pp. 33–5.
8 René Lefort, *Ethiopia: An Heretical Revolution?*, London, Zed Press, 1983, p. 54.
9 I. Doronin, 'Efiopiya smotrit vpered', *Nauka i Religiya*, 9, 1975, p. 77.
10 Alexis de Tocqueville, *The Old Regime and the French Revolution*, cited in Anthony Parsons, *The Pride and the Fall: Iran 1974–1979*, London, Jonathan Cape, 1984, p. 60.
11 René Lefort, *Ethiopia: An Heretical Revolution?*, p. 55; *ARB*, March 1974, p. 3171.
12 *ARB*, April 1974, p. 3203.
13 C. Legum, *Ethiopia: The Fall of Haile Selassie's Empire*, p. 45.
14 *ARB*, August 1974, pp. 3328–9.
15 *ARB*, August 1974, pp. 3330–1.
16 C. Legum, *Ethiopia: The Fall of Haile Selassie's Empire*, p. 51.
17 F. Halliday and M. Molyneux, *The Ethiopian Revolution*, London, Verso, 1981, p. 88.
18 Donald Petterson, 'Ethiopia Abandoned? An American Perspective', *International Affairs*, 62, 4, Autumn 1986, p. 631; *ARB*, November 1974, p. 3433.
19 *ARB*, December 1974, p. 3459.
20 René Lefort, *Ethiopia: An Heretical Revolution?*, pp. 94–100.
21 F. Halliday and M. Molyneux, *The Ethiopian Revolution*, p. 99; Marina Ottaway, *Soviet and American Influence in the Horn of Africa*, p. 93.
22 F. Halliday and M. Molyneux, *The Ethiopian Revolution*, p. 99.
23 Yu Ustimenko, 'Novaya zhizn'drevney Efiopii', *Aziya i Afrika Segodnya*, 4, 1977, p. 15; René Lefort, *Ethiopia: An Heretical Revolution?*, pp. 134–8.
24 *ARB*, April 1976, pp. 3391–2.
25 *ARB*, April 1976, pp. 3991–2.

26 René Lefort, *Ethiopia: An Heretical Revolution?*, pp. 159–60.
27 Bereket Habte Selassie, *Conflict and Intervention in the Horn of Africa*, New York, Monthly Review Press, 1980, pp. 34–40; Aryeh Yodfat, 'The Soviet Union and the Horn of Africa', *Northeast African Studies*, part two, 2, 1, 1980, p. 32.
28 C. Legum and B. Lee, *Conflict in the Horn of Africa*, London, Rex Collings, 1977, pp. 50–2; Haggai Erlich, *The Struggle Over Eritrea, 1962–1978: War and Revolution in the Horn of Africa*, California, Hoover Institution Press, 1983, pp. 73–4.
29 Haggai Erlich, *The Struggle Over Eritrea*, pp. 48–71; René Lefort, *Ethiopia: An Heretical Revolution?*, pp. 71–2.
30 *ARB*, May 1976, p. 4025.
31 C. Legum and B. Lee, *Conflict in the Horn of Africa*, p. 55; René Lefort, *Ethiopia: An Heretical Revolution?*, p. 178.
32 David D. Laitin and Said S. Samatar, *Somalia: Nation in Search of a State*, Colorado, Westview Press, 1987, pp. 140–1; Patrick Gilkes, private communication, 1 May 1988.
33 Marina Ottaway, *Soviet and American Influence in the Horn of Africa*, p. 83; *International Herald Tribune*, 23 October 1977.
34 Michael Imru, the Dergue's Minister of Information, cited in *The Egyptian Gazette*, 17 December 1974.
35 *The Guardian*, 13 March 1975.
36 *ARB*, July 1977, p. 4509.
37 René Lefort, *Ethiopia: An Heretical Revolution?*, p. 191.
38 E. Sherr, 'Flag nezavisimosti nad Dzhibuti', *Aziya i Afrika Segodnya*, 8, 1977, p. 13.
39 C. Legum and B. Lee, *Conflict in the Horn of Africa*, p. 74.
40 Haggai Erlich, *The Struggle Over Eritrea*, p. 74; *African Contemporary Record* (ACR), 1976–7, p. B331.
41 F. Halliday and M. Molyneux, *The Ethiopian Revolution*, p. 198.
42 Pliny the Middle-Aged, 'The PMAC: Origins and Structure', *Northeast African Studies*, part two, 1, 1, 1978, p. 1; R. F. Gorman, *Political Conflict on the Horn of Africa*, New York, Praeger, 1981, p. 57.
43 René Lefort, *Ethiopia: An Heretical Revolution?*, pp. 151–2; *ARB*, April 1975, p. 3597.
44 C. Legum and B. Lee, *Conflict in the Horn of Africa*, p. 40; Parick Gilkes, private communication, 1 May 1988.
45 R. F. Gorman, *Political Conflict on the Horn of Africa*, p. 57; *New York Times*, 29 February 1976.
46 C. Legum and B. Lee, *Conflict in the Horn of Africa*, p. 40.
47 René Lefort, *Ethiopia: An Heretical Revolution?*, p. 166.
48 Bereket Habte Selassie, *Conflict and Intervention in the Horn of Africa*, pp. 36–7.
49 C. Legum and B. Lee, *Conflict in the Horn of Africa*, p. 54.
50 *Pravda*, 10 March 1974.
51 *Pravda*, 12 March 1974.
52 *Pravda*, 26 February 1974.

53 'Events in Ethiopia', *New Times*, 21, 1974, p. 9.
54 *Pravda*, 10 March 1974.
55 Moscow Radio, 7 May 1974.
56 Moscow Radio, 27 April 1974, cited in *USSR and Third World*, 4, 4, April-June 1975, p. 243.
57 V. G. Solodovnikov's letter to the editor, entitled 'Classics of Marxism and Non-Capitalist Development', in *Africa in Soviet Studies Annual*, 1972, USSR Academy of Sciences, Africa Institute, Moscow, 'Nauka' Publishing House, 1975, p. 195.
58 *Izvestiya*, 6 July 1974; *Pravda*, 27 July 1974.
59 Moscow Radio, English-language Africa broadcast, 18 December 1974.
60 A. Kokiev, 'Efiopiya: po puti obnovleniya', *Aziya i Afrika Segodnya*, 2, 1975, p. 19.
61 Moscow Radio, English-language Africa broadcast, 18 December 1974; E. I. Doronin, 'Ethiopia Without the Emperor', *New Times*, 38, 1974, pp. 12–13.
62 Moscow Radio, 5 October 1974.
63 K. Gerasimov, 'Ethiopia Without the Crown', *New Times*, 51, 1974, p. 27.
64 V. S. Yag'ya, 'Revolyutsionnyye peremeny v Efiopii (1974–1975)'. *Narody Azii i Afriki*, 6, 1975, p. 17.
65 *Izvestiya*, 29 May 1975; A. Kokiev and V. Vigand, 'National Democratic Revolution in Ethiopia: Economic and Socio-Political Aspects' in *Modern Ethiopia from the Accession of Menelik II to the Present*, Proceedings of the Fifth International Conference of Ethiopian Studies, Nice, 19–22 December 1977, Rotterdam, 1980, p. 421; V. S. Yag'ya 'Revolyutsionnyye peremeny v Efiopii (1974–1975)', p. 18.
66 A. Kokiev and V. Vigand, 'National Democratic Revolution in Ethiopia: Economic and Socio-Political Aspects', p. 420.
67 V. Shmarov, 'Reform in Ethiopia', *New Times*, 7, 1975, p. 22.
68 G. Galperin, 'Natsional'no-demokraticheskiye preobrazovaniya v Efiopii', *Asiya i Afrika Segodnya*, 8, 1976, p. 9; G. Galperin, 'Revolyutsiya v Efiopii: osobennosti razvitiya', *Aziya i Afrika Segodnya*, 3, 1978, p. 11; V. S. Yag'ya, 'Revolyutsionnyye peremeny v Efiopii (1974–1975)', p. 20.
69 A. Kokiev and V. Vigand, 'National Democratic Revolution in Ethiopia: Economic and Socio-Political Aspects', p. 421.
70 Ibid., p. 421.
71 G. Galperin, 'Natsional'no-demokraticheskiye preobrazovaniya v Efiopii', p. 9.
72 A. Kokiev and V. Vigand, 'National Democratic Revolution in Ethiopia: Economic and Socio-Political Aspects', p. 421.
73 G. Galperin, 'Revolyutsiya v Efiopii: osobennosti razvitiya', p. 10.
74 V. Korovikov, 'A New Life Comes to Ethiopia', *International Affairs*, (Moscow), 3, 1977, p. 128.
75 V. S. Yag'ya, 'Revolyutsionnyye peremeny v Efiopii (1974–1975)', p. 19.
76 *Pravda*, 25 May 1975.
77 A. Kokiev and V. Vigand, 'National Democratic Revolution in Ethiopia: Economic and Socio-Political Aspects', p. 420.

78 V. S. Yag'ya, 'Revolyutsionnyye peremeny v Efiopii (1974–1975)', p. 19.

79 Ibid., pp. 19–20.

80 *Pravda*, 25 May 1975; K. Gerasimov, 'Ethiopia: The Reactionaries Resist', *New Times*, 15, 1975, pp. 12–13.

81 *Pravda*, 24 April 1976; V. Korovikov, 'A New Life Comes to Ethiopia', pp. 127–8.

82 Yu. Ustimenko, 'Efiopiya: trudnosti, sversheniya, perpsektivy', *Aziya i Afrika Segodnya*, 5, 1977, p. 8.

83 Berhanu Bayeh, 'From Feudalism to People's Democracy', *World Marxist Review*, 8, 1976, p. 38.

84 G. Galperin, 'Natsional'no-demokraticheskiye preobrazovaniya v Efiopii', p. 12.

85 'Programme of the Revolution', *New Times*, 18, 1976, pp. 9–11.

86 'Ethiopia: Policy Statement', *New Times*, 52, 1974, p. 9.

87 *Pravda*, 16 August 1975; *Pravda*, 6 November 1975.

88 V. S. Yag'ya 'Revolyutsionnyye peremeny v Efiopii (1974–1975)', p. 20. Parenthesis added.

89 'Changing Ethiopia', *New Times*, 14, 1976, p. 25.

90 A. Kokiev and V. Vigand, 'National Democratic Revolution in Ethiopia: Economic and Socio-Political Aspects', pp. 422–3.

91 G. Galperin, 'Natsional'no-demokraticheskiye preobrazovaniya v Efiopii', p. 11; G. Galperin, 'Ethiopia: Some Aspects of the Nationalities' Question', *The African Communist*, 83, 4th Quarter, 1980, p. 58.

92 G. Galperin, 'Ethiopia: Some Aspects of the Nationalities' Question', p. 59.

93 V. S. Yag'ya, 'Revolyutsionnyye peremeny v Efiopii (1974–1975)', p. 9.

94 G. Galperin, 'Natsional'no-demokraticheskiye preobrazovaniya v Efiopii', p. 10.

95 V. Korovikov, 'A New Life Comes to Ethiopia', p. 132; G. Galperin, 'Ethiopia: Some Aspects of the Nationalities' Question', pp. 54–56.

96 G. Galperin, 'Ethiopia: Some Aspects of the Nationalities' Question', p. 57.

97 Berhanu Bayeh, 'People's Gains in the Ethiopian Revolution', *The Africa Communist*, 74, 1978 cited in G. Galperin, 'Ethiopia: Some Aspects of the Nationalities' Question', pp. 57–9.

98 V. S. Yag'ya, 'Revolyutsionnyye peremeny v Efiopii (1974–1974)., p. 9; *Izvestiya*, 9 February 1975.

99 Moscow Radio, Somali-language broadcast, 22 January 1975, cited in *USSR and Third World*, 5, 2, January-February 1975, p. 76; *Izvestiya*, 9 February 1975; D. Borisov, 'The Developments in Ethiopia', *New Times*, 8, 1975, pp. 10–11.

100 Radio 'Peace and Progress', Arabic-language broadcast, 1 March 1975, cited in *USSR and Third World*, 5, 3, February-March 1975, p. 117; Moscow Radio, 22 May 1976; *Izvestiya*, 9 February 1975.

101 G. Galperin, 'Eritreyskaya problema – fakty i domysli', *Novoye Vremya*, 5, 1979, p. 28; V. S. Yag'ya, 'Revolyutsionnyye peremeny v Efiopii (1974–1975)'. p. 21; D. Borisov, 'The Developments in Ethiopia', p. 11.

102 Radio 'Peace and Progress', Arabic-language broadcast, 1 March 1975, p. 117; D. Borisov, 'The Developments in Ethiopia', p. 11.
103 G. Galperin, 'Ethiopia: Some Aspects of the Nationalities' Question', p. 56; Moscow Radio, 22 May 1976.
104 G. Galperin, 'Eritreyskaya problema – fakty i domysli', pp. 26–7.
105 G. Galperin, 'Ethiopia: Some Aspects of the Nationalities' Question', p. 57; G. Galperin, 'Eritreyskaya problema – fakty i domysli', p. 27.
106 Radio 'Peace and Progress', Arabic-language broadcast, 1 March 1975, p. 117.
107 Yu. Ustimenko, 'Efiopiya: trudnosti, sversheniya, perspektivy', p. 9.
108 Moscow Radio, Amharic-language broadcast, 14 June 1976, cited in C. Legum and B. Lee, Conflict in the Horn of Africa, p. 12; Moscow Radio, 22 May 1976.
109 Moscow Radio, English-language broadcast, 3 May 1975.
110 Ibid.; Moscow Radio, 24 October 1975, cited in USSR and Third World, 6, 8, July-December 1975, p. 414.
111 A Tass dispatch cited in D. Morison, 'The Soviet Union's Year in Africa', in ACR, 1975–6, p. A108.
112 Moscow Radio, English-language African broadcast, 3 May 1975; V. S. Yag'ya, 'Revolyutsionnyye peremeny i Efiopii (1974–1975)', p. 21.
113 Pravda, cited in ARB, September 1974, p. 3363.
114 Pravda, 23 March 1976; I. Doronin, 'Efiopiya smotrit vpered', p. 79.
115 V. S. Yag'ya, 'Revolyutsionnyye peremeny i Efiopii (1974–1975)', p. 17.
116 Ibid., p. 21; See also I. Doronin, 'Efiopiya smotrit vpered', p. 79.
117 V. S. Yag'ya, 'Revolyutsionnyye peremeny i Efiopii (1974–1975)', p. 21.
118 Yu. Ustimenko, 'Efiopiya: trudnosti, sversheniya, perspektivy', p. 9; The Guardian, 6 January 1975.
119 'Changing Ethiopia', p. 25.
120 A. Kokiev and V. Vigand, 'National Democratic Revolution in Ethiopia: Economic and Socio-Political Aspects', p. 424.
121 Pravda, 4 April 1975.
122 Moscow Radio, 16 May 1974; V. S. Yag'ya, 'Revolyutsionnyye peremeny i Efiopii (1974–1975)', p. 21.
123 C. Legum, 'Angola and the Horn of Africa', in Stephen S. Kaplan, ed., Diplomacy of Force: Soviet Armed Forces as a Political Instrument, The Brookings Institution, Washington DC, 1981, p. 613; The Observer, 1 December 1974.
124 Bruce D. Porter, The USSR in Third World Conflicts: Soviet Arms and Diplomacy in Local Wars 1945–1980, Cambridge, Cambridge University Press, 1984, p. 192.
125 Paul B. Henze, The Rand Corporation, interview with author, 17 June 1988.
126 Bruce D. Porter, The USSR in Third World Conflicts, p. 192.
127 Milene Charles, The Soviet Union: The History of Involvement, Washington DC, University Press of America, 1980, p. 135; David A. Korn, Ethiopia, the United States and the Soviet Union, London, Croom Helm, 1986, p. 17; Paul B. Henze, The Rand Corporation, interview with author, 17 June 1988.

128 Confidential source cited in Bruce D. Porter, *The USSR in Third World Conflicts*, p. 193.

129 Ibid., p. 193.

130 *Pravda*, 6 February 1976.

131 C. Legum and B. Lee, *Conflict in the Horn of Africa*, p. 70.

132 'Changing Ethiopia', p. 25.

133 Moscow Radio, 21 June 1974; Moscow Radio, 22 January 1975; Moscow Radio, 26 May 1974, cited in *USSR and Third World*, 4, 4, April-June 1974, p. 244; Moscow Radio, 12 March 1975; *Pravda*, 3 January 1976.

134 *Vneshnyaya Torgovlya za SSSR*, Moscow, 'Statistika', 1971 and 1976.

135 René Lefort, *Ethiopia: An Heretical Revolution?*, p. 184.

136 *Vneshnyaya Torgovlya za SSSR*, 1975 and 1976.

137 *Pravda*, 25 February 1976.

138 Paul B. Henze, 'Russians and the Horn: Opportunism and the Long View', *European American Institute For Security Research*, paper 5, Summer 1983, pp. 32–3.

139 Paul B. Henze, private communication, 31 May 1988; Donald Petterson, 'Ethiopia abandoned? An American Perspective', *International Affairs*, 62, 4, Autumn 1986, p. 630.

140 *ARB*, September 1974, p. 3364.

141 Donald Petterson, 'Ethiopia Abandoned? An American Perspective', p. 632; René Lefort, *Ethiopia: An Heretical Revolution?*, p. 207.

142 Marina Ottaway, *Soviet and American Influence in the Horn of Africa*, p. 102.

143 Donald Petterson, 'Ethiopia Abandoned? An American Perspective', pp. 632–3, *ARB*, March 1975, p. 3562.

144 Negussay Ayele, 'The Horn of Africa: Revolutionary Developments and Western Reactions', *Northeast African Studies*, 3, 1, 1981, p. 17.

145 Ibid., p. 18.

146 'The Horn: Ethiopia and Somalia', a paper written jointly by the US Bureau of African Affairs and the Policy Planning Staff cited in Donald Petterson, 'Ethiopia Abandoned?', p. 630; C. Legum, 'Angola and the Horn of Africa', in Stephen S. Kaplan, ed., *Diplomacy of Power: Soviet Armed Forces as a Political Instrument*, p. 613.

147 *ACR*, 1975–6, p. B308.

148 *The Financial Times*, 18 July 1975.

149 *ACR*, 1975–6, p. B302.

150 United States Government, Department of Defense, Security Assistance Agency, *Foreign Military Sales and Military Assistance Facts*, December 1978, pp. 5, 15, 20, 24; Bruce D. Porter, *The USSR in Third World Conflicts*, p. 207.

151 *Strategic Survey 1977*, London, International Institute for Strategic Studies (IISS), p. 19; C. Legum, 'Angola and the Horn of Africa', in Stephen S. Kaplan, ed., *Diplomacy of Power*, p. 613.

152 Paul B. Henze, 'Getting a Grip on the Horn', in Walter Laqueur, ed., *The Pattern of Soviet Conduct in the World*, New York, Praeger, 1983, p. 168; Paul B. Henze, 'Arming the Horn 1960–1980', working paper 43, International Security Series, Woodrow Wilson Center for Scholars, Smithsonian Institution, Wahington DC, July 1982, p. 653.

153 David A. Korn, *Ethiopia, the United States and the Soviet Union*, p. 16.
154 *Pravda*, 5 March 1975.
155 Moscow Radio, English-language Africa broadcast, 3 May 1975.
156 *Pravda*, 16 May 1976.
157 Kola Olufemi, 'Sino–Soviet Rivalry in the Horn of Africa', *Horn of Africa*, 5, 3, 1983–4, p. 18; René Lefort, *Ethiopia: An Heretical Revolution?*, p. 186.
158 *Jeune Afrique*, 17 January 1975, cited in Aryeh Yodfat, 'The Soviet Union and the Horn of Africa', note 6, p. 50.
159 *New China News Agency* (NCNA), 3 May 1975; NCNA, 23 August 1976; *Addis Ababa Radio*, 5 September 1976, cited in *USSR and Third World*, 7, 4, p. 195; *NCNA*, 9 July 1975.
160 Morris Rothenberg, *The USSR and Africa: New Dimensions of Soviet Global Power*, Miami, Advanced International Studies Institute 1980, p. 35. See also *NCNA*, 12 March 1976.
161 *NCNA*, 1 December 1976.
162 Bruce D. Porter, *The USSR in Third World Conflicts*, p. 211.
163 C. Legum and B. Lee, *Conflict in the Horn of Africa*, p. 13.
164 *NCNA*, 21 March 1976.
165 E. Sherr, 'Novyye rubezhi Somali', *Aziya i Afrika Segodnya*, 1, 1977, p. 14.
166 *Pravda*, 21 October 1975; E. Sherr, 'Novyye rubezhi Somali', p. 14.
167 Bruce D. Porter, *The USSR in Third World Conflicts*, p. 193.
168 *International Herald Tribune*, 21 June 1975.
169 Yuri Kuritsin, 'Somalian Encounters', *New Times*, 38, 1975, p. 26.
170 Ibid., p. 26; A. Dolgov, 'Somali: puteshestviye na yug', p. 30; David D. Laitin and Said S. Samatar, *Somalia: Nation in Search of a State*, Colorado, Westview Press, 1987, p. 112.
171 A. Dolgov, 'Somali: puteshestviye na yug', pp. 30–1; Yuri Kuritsin, 'Somalian Encounters', p. 27.
172 B. Asoyan, 'In the New Somalia', *New Times*, No 44, 1976, p. 25.
173 A. Dolgov, 'Somali: puteshestviye na yug', p. 32.
174 B. Asoyan, 'In the New Somalia'. p. 24.
175 A. Dolgov, 'Somali: puteshestviye na yug', p. 32.
176 Ibid.
177 *ACR*, 1975–6, pp. B310–11; then, 1 US dollar = 6.75 Somali Shillings.
178 *Pravda*, 10 July 1975.
179 *The Military Balance 1976–1977*, London, International Institute for Strategic Studies (IISS), p. 44.
180 *Strategic Survey 1976*, p. 59.
181 *The Military Balance 1976–1977*, pp. 42–4.
182 *The Guardian*, 13 March 1975.
183 *The Observer Foreign News Service*, 30 April 1975; *The Guardian*, 24 February 1975.
184 *Pravda*, 3 March 1976; E. Sherr, 'Novyye rubezhi Somali', p. 15.
185 According to E. Sherr, Siad's speech at the 25th Congress of CPSU confirmed that: 'The Somali leaders are attentively learning the pronouncements of Lenin, the documents of international communism and the workers' movement.' E. Sherr, 'Novyye rubezhi Somali', p. 14.

186 *Tass*, 4 March 1976.
187 D. D. Laitin, 'Somali's Military Government and Scientific Socialism', in C. Rosberg and T. Callaghy, eds., *Socialism in Sub-Saharan Africa*, California, Institute of International Studies. 1979, p. 197.
188 President Siad Barre, 'Revolutionary Resolve', *World Marxist Review*, 19, 5, 1976, p. 26; President Siad Barre's interview, *US News and World Report*, 21 July 1976, p. 32.
189 E. Sherr's review of President Siad's book, *My Country and My People*, (the Collected Speeches 1969–71), Mogadishu, Ministry of Information, 1971, in *Narody Azii i Afriki*, 1, 1974, p. 189.
190 E. Sherr, 'Novyye rubezhi Somali', p. 15.
191 President Siad Barre, 'Revolutionary Resolve', pp. 25–6.
192 G. V. Kazakov, *Somali na Sovremennon Etape Razvitiya*, Moscow, Izdatel'stvo 'Mysl', 1976, pp. 96–7.
193 Yu. Ivanov's review of G. V. Kazakov's book, *Somali na Sovremennon Etape Razvitiya*, in *Aziya i Afrika Segodnya*, no. 2, 1977, p. 60. At the same time, Y. Kuritsin spoke of 'cardinal changes' in Somalia (Y. Kuritsin, 'Somalian Encounters', p. 25) while B. Asoyan observed that the Somali revolution 'has already passed the transitional stage', (B. Asoyan, 'In the New Somalia', p. 25).
194 G. V. Kazakov, *Somali na Sovremennon Etape Razvitiya*, p. 100.
195 A. Dolgov, 'Somali: puteshestviye na yug', p. 32.
196 *Pravda*, 10 July 1975.
197 *The Guardian*, 19 March 1975.
198 President Siad Barre, 'Revolutionary Resolve', p. 25.
199 D. D. Laitin, 'The War in the Ogaden: Implications for Siyaad's Role in Somali History', *Journal of Modern African Studies*, 17, 1, 1979, pp. 96–7.
200 *The Guardian*, 12 June 1975.
201 The Somali Ambassador to the US, Abdullahi Ahmed Addou, quoted in *International Herald Tribune*, 27 June 1975; *New York Times*, 4 July 1975.
202 *New York Times*, 8 July 1975.
203 *New York Times*, 7 July 1975; *New York Times*, 8 July 1975.
204 President Siad Barre, 'Revolutionary Resolve', p. 26. Emphasis added.
205 A. Dolgov, 'Somali: puteshestviye na yug', pp. 30–2.
206 T. Farer, *War Clouds on the Horn of Africa: The Widening Storm*, second revised edition, New York, Carnegie Endowment for International Peace, 1979, p. 117.
207 *NCNA*, 2 June 1976; Kola Olufemi, 'Sino–Soviet Rivalry in the Horn of Africa', p. 17; *NCNA*, 16 November 1976; *NCNA*, 9 July 1976; *NCNA*, 26 May 1976.
208 *The Times*, 3 March 1975.
209 *ACR*, 1975–6, p. B310.
210 Former US Ambassador to Saudi Arabia, James Akins, told a Senate Sub-Committee on 5 May 1976 that the State Department turned a deaf ear to a Saudi proposal to finance a military and economic aid programme to Somalia as a means of eliminating the Soviet presence there. According to Akins' testimony, the non-response was due to the Administration's

preoccupation with establishing a case for a major US naval base at Diego Garcia. A member of the Senate Armed Services Committee, Senator Symington, described the episode as 'the most dishonest thing I have heard in thirty years in Congress'. See *International Herald Tribune*, 6 May 1976.

211 A. Dolgov, 'Somali: puteshestviye na yug', p. 32.

212 Ibid., p. 32.

213 Ibid., pp. 31–2.

214 *ACR*, 1976–7, pp. B325–6. Marina Ottaway, *Soviet and American Influence in the Horn of Africa*, p. 82.

215 *Tass*, 3 May 1976.

216 A. Zhigunov, 'Somalia: A Major Landmark', *New Times*, 29, 1976, p. 28.

217 B. Asoyan, 'In the New Somalia', p. 25; *Moscow News*, 44, October 1976, p. 6.

218 *Pravda*, 14 July 1976.

219 Marina Ottaway, *Soviet and American Influence in the Horn of Africa*, p. 106.

220 *Soviet News*, 20 July 1976, 5842, p. 271.

221 *Pravda*, 14 July 1976.

222 Negussay Ayele, 'The Horn of Africa: Revolutionary Developments and Western Reactions', p. 19.

223 Haggai Erlich, *The Struggle Over Eritrea*, pp. 103–4.

224 C. Legum and B. Lee, *Conflict in the Horn of Africa*, p. 42; Pliny the Middle Aged, 'The PMAC: Origins and Structure', part two, *Northeast African Studies*, 1, 1, 1978, p. 5.

225 Addis Ababa Radio, 13 July 1976.

226 US Congress, Senate, Committee on Foreign Relations, Subcommittee on African Affairs, *Ethiopia and the Horn of Africa*, 94th Cong., 2nd sess., August 4–6, 1976, p. 94. See also David A. Korn, *Ethiopia, the United States and the Soviet Union*, p. 19.

227 Y. Tsaplin, 'Ethiopia: Fighting the Reactionaries', *New Times*, 47, 1976, p. 14.

228 G. Galperin, 'Revolyutsiya v Efiopii: osobennosti razvitiya', p. 11.

229 Yu. Irkin, 'Efiopiya na puti sotsialisticheskoy orientatsii', *Kommunist Voruzhennykh Sil*, 2, January 1979, p. 82.

230 Paul B. Henze, 'Getting a Grip on the Horn', in Walter Laqueur, ed., *The Pattern of Soviet Conduct in the World*, p. 163.

231 An. Gromyko, 'SSSR–Efiopiya: traditsii i sovremennost', *Aziya i Afrika Segodnya*, 10, 1979, p. 5.

232 Paul B. Henze, 'Russians and the Horn', paper prepared for the *Council on Foreign Relations*, New York, February 1979, p. 13.

233 G. Galperin, 'Revolyutsiya v Efiopii: osobennosti razvitiya', p. 11.

234 V. S. Yag'ya observed: 'Already in December 1973 there was a mutiny in one of the units of the Fourth Infantry Division, stationed in Shoa.' See V. S. Yag'ya, 'Revolyutsionnyye peremeny v Efiopii (1974–1975)', p. 11.

235 In the early 1970s, the Soviet press depicted Sekou Touré's regime in Guinea as 'an example to the rest of Africa' (*Pravda*, 31 October 1971). Such coverage coincided with Anatoly Ratanov's spell as Soviet Ambassa-

dor to Guinea, between 1970 and 1973. See Borys Lewytzkyi, ed., *Who's Who in the Soviet Union*, London, K. G. Saur, 1984, p. 271.

236 Alexei Bukalov has observed that in view of the Emperor's 'great authority with the majority of Ethiopians' the 'Dergue planned and carried out a series of measures to isolate the monarch politically, measures that prepared public opinion in the country for the dethronement of Haile Selassie I'. See A. Bukalov 'From Monarchy to Republic', *New Times*, 36, 1987, p. 20.

237 K. Gerasimov, 'Ethiopia Without the Crown', p. 26.

238 V. Korovikov, 'A New Life Comes to Ethiopia', p. 127; V. S. Yag'ya, 'Revolyutsionnyye peremeny v Efiopii (1974–1975)', p. 16.

239 A. Kokiev, 'Efiopiya: po puti obnovleniya', p. 21.

240 F. Halliday and M. Molyneux, *The Ethiopian Revolution*, pp. 117–18.

241 Pliny the Middle-Aged, 'The PMAC: Origins and Structure', p. 10.

242 René Lefort, *Ethiopia: An Heretical Revolution?*, p. 206.

243 F. Halliday and M. Molyneux, *The Ethiopian Revolution*, p. 116. See also Haggai Erlich, *The Struggle Over Eritrea*, pp. 102–3.

244 C. Legum and B. Lee, *Conflict in the Horn of Africa*, pp. 46–7; *ARB*, September 1976, p. 4157.

245 C. Legum and B. Lee, *Conflict in the Horn of Africa*, pp. 45–7.

246 According to Paul B. Henze, the USSR engineered the de-stabilisation of Ethiopia during this period through a 'spoiling policy' of encouraging and funding a wide variety of political movements including Meison, EDRP and the EPLF. Paul B. Henze, The Rand Corporation, interview with author, 17 June 1988; Paul B. Henze, 'Getting a Grip on the Horn', in Walter Laqueur, ed., *The Pattern of Soviet Conduct in the World*, pp. 165–6.

247 William Schaufele's assessment of the Dergue was communicated during an appearance before the US Senate Foreign Relations sub-committee on African Affairs on 8 August 1976. See *Keesings Contemporary Archives (KCA)*, 27 August 1976, 22, p. 27912.

248 G. Galperin, 'Natsional'no-demokraticheskiye preobrazovaniya v Efiopii', p. 10.

249 *Pravda*, 20 November 1976; *Pravda*, 30 November 1976; *Pravda*, 6 January 1976; *Izvestiya*, 18 November 1976.

250 *Pravda*, 10 October 1976.

251 *Izvestiya*, 18 November 1976; G. Galperin, Natsional'no-demokraticheskiye preobrazovaniya v Efiopii', p. 10; Yu. Irkin, 'Efiopiya na puti sotsialisticheskoy orientatsii', p. 84; *Pravda*, 30 November 1976.

252 *Pravda*, 4 October 1976; G. Galperin, 'Natsional'no-demokraticheskiye preobrazovaniya v Efiopii', p. 10.

253 *Pravda*, 4 October 1976.

254 *Washington Post*, 5 March 1978; David A. Korn, *Ethiopia, the United States and the Soviet Union*, p. 19.

255 Paul B. Henze, 'Getting a Grip on the Horn', in Walter Laqueur, ed., *The Pattern of Soviet Conduct in the World*, pp. 169–70.

256 An. Gromyko, *Through Russian Eyes: President Kennedy's 1036 Days*, Washington DC, International Library Inc., 1973, p. 70.

257 E. Sherr, 'Novyye rubezhi Somali', p. 15.
258 Ibid., p. 15.
259 E. Sherr, 'Flag nezavisimosti nad Dzhibuti', p. 13.
260 *The Manchester Guardian*, 10 July 1977.
261 *Pravda*, 18 January 1976.
262 *Pravda*, 14 July 1976.
263 Y. Ivanov, 'Productive Visit', *New Times*, 33, 1976, p. 16; *Pravda*, 10 August 1976.
264 *ARB*, September 1976, p. 4157.
265 E. Sherr, 'Novyye rubezhi Somali', p. 15.
266 *ARB*, September 1976, p. 4157.
267 Haggai Erlich, *The Struggle Over Eritrea*, p. 81.
268 *ARB*, January 1977, p. 4282.
269 Haggai Erlich, *The Struggle Over Eritrea*, p. 77.
270 C. Legum and B. Lee, *Conflict in the Horn of Africa*, p. 68.
271 *ARB*, January 1977, p. 4282; C. Legum and B. Lee, *Conflict in the Horn of Africa*, p. 48.
272 *The Financial Times*, 29 December 1976.
273 C. Legum and B. Lee, *Conflict in the Horn of Africa*, p. 87.
274 David D. Laitin, 'Somalia's Military Government and Scientific Social-ism', p. 194.
275 *The Sunday Times*, 22 May 1977.
276 Y. Ivanov, 'Productive Visit', p. 16.
277 The Soviet negotiating team included A. Kirilenko, member of the Politburo and Secretary of the CPSU Central Committee; B. N. Pono-marev, candidate member of the Politburo and Secretary of the CPSU Central Committee; I. V. Arkhipov, member of the CPSU Central Com-mittee and Vice-Chairman of the USSR Council of Ministers, and V. V. Kuznetsov, member of CPSU Central Committee and USSR First Deputy Minister of Foreign Affairs. *Pravda*, 10 August 1976.
278 *Pravda*, 10 August 1976.
279 *The Guardian*, 13 March 1975.
280 Bruce D. Porter, *The USSR in Third World Conflicts*, p. 194.
281 René Lefort, *Ethiopia: An Heretical Revolution?*, pp. 193–5.
282 *ARB*, January 1977, p. 4282.
283 Yu. Ustimenko, 'Efiopiya: trudnosti, sversheniya, perspektivy', p. 9.
284 *Pravda*, 27 February 1977.
285 *Pravda*, 15 February 1977; *Pravda*, 5 February 1977; *Pravda*, 27 February 1977.
286 C. Legum and B. Lee, *Conflict in the Horn of Africa*, p. 70.
287 A. Kokiev and V. Vigand, 'National Democratic Revolution in Ethiopia: Economic and Socio-Political Aspects', p. 423.
288 *ARB*, March 1977, p. 4361 and p. 4373; *ARB*, April 1977, p. 4396.
289 *New York Times*, 16 May 1977.
290 *The Observer*, 8 May 1977.
291 *ARB*, April 1977, p. 4396; *The Daily Telegraph*, 17 May 1977.
292 Andrey Gromyko, 'Leninskaya strategiya mira: yedinstvo teorii i prak-tiki', *Kommunist*, 14, September 1976, pp. 11–32.

293 Mohammed Ayoob, *The Horn of Africa: Regional Conflict and Superpower Involvement*, Canberra Papers on Strategy and Defence, 18, Canberra, Australian National University, 1978, p. 23.
294 President Numeiry of the Sudan cited in *The Guardian*, 2 June 1977.
295 *Daily Nation* (Kenya), 17 March 1977.

6. War, realignment and the enforcement of proletarian internationalism

1 *Pravda*, 9 May 1977.
2 *The Financial Times*, 3 September 1977, Colin Legum and Bill Lee, *Conflict in the Horn of Africa*, London, Rex Collings, 1977, p. 94. A confidential Ethiopian source has placed the value of the arms deal to be much higher than Western estimates suggest. See Bruce D. Porter, *The USSR in Third World Conflicts: Soviet Arms and Diplomacy in Local Wars*, Cambridge, Cambridge University Press, 1984, p. 196.
3 *The Guardian*, 17 May 1977; *Pravda*, 8 May 1977.
4 *Izvestiya*, 17 August 1977.
5 Dimitri K. Simes, 'Imperial Globalism in the Making: Soviet Involvement in the Horn of Africa', *The Washington Review, Special Supplement*, May 1978, p. 35.
6 Siad Barre cited in K. Weiss, *The Soviet Involvement in the Ogaden War*, Professional Paper 269, Arlington, Virginia, Center for Naval Analyses, February 1980, p. 5.
7 *ACR*, 1977–8, p. B246; *Newsweek*, 9 May 1977, p. 16; *Africa Research Bulletin* (ARB), April 1977, p. 4396.
8 G. Galperin, 'In and Around the Horn of Africa', *New Times*, 32, 1977, p. 24; V. Sidenko, 'Washington's Crooked Mirror', *New Times*, 21, 1977, p. 17.
9 M. Ottaway and D. Ottaway, *Ethiopia: Empire and Revolution*, New York, Africana, 1978, p. 168; *ARB*, April 1977, p. 4394; 'Cubans in Africa', *Newsweek*, 20 March 1977, p. 22.
10 *Pravda*, 5 May 1977.
11 *Pravda*, 9 May 1977.
12 *Pravda*, 9 May 1977.
13 *Soviet News*, 10 May 1977, 5881, pp. 158–9.
14 Morris Rothenberg, *The USSR and Africa: New Dimensions of Soviet Global Power*, Miami, Advanced International Studies Institute, 1980, p. 38; *Pravda*, 7 May 1977.
15 *The Financial Times*, 3 September 1977; C. Legum and B. Lee, *Conflict in the Horn of Africa*, p. 94; Bruce D. Porter, *The USSR in Third World Conflicts*, p. 200.
16 *International Herald Tribune*, 22 July 1977; C. Legum and B. Lee, *Conflict in the Horn of Africa*, p. 94.
17 Moscow Radio, 25 May 1977.
18 Moscow Radio, 10 June 1977, cited in *USSR and Third World*, 7, 3, May–June 1977, p. 66; Moscow Radio, 6 July 1977.
19 Kiev Radio, 27 June 1977, cited in *USSR and Third World*, 7, 4, July–August 1977, p. 86.

20 Anatoly A. Gromyko, 'Sovetsko–Efiopskiye svyazy', *Narody Azii i Afriki*, 1, 1980, p. 11; *Tass*, 22 July 1977.
21 *Vneshnyaya Torgovlya SSSR, 1976 and 1977*, Moscow, 'Statistika'.
22 René Lefort, *Ethiopia: An Heretical Revolution?*, London, Zed Press, 1983, p. 211; *ACR*, 1977–8, p. B374.
23 *ACR*, 1977–8, pp. B374–375; Patrick Gilkes, private communication, 1 May 1988; Siad Barre cited in *International Herald Tribune*, 21 June 1977.
24 *ACR*, 1977–8, p. B374.
25 *Pravda*, 3 and 4 April 1977.
26 Siad Barre cited in *Afrique–Asie*, 13–25 June 1977.
27 *Al Yaqsa* (Kuwait), 27 June 1977; *The Daily Telegraph*, 27 May 1977.
28 *The Sunday Times*, 22 May 1977.
29 *New China News Agency* (NCNA), 21 January 1977; *NCNA*, 22 and 29 June 1977; *International Herald Tribune*, 4 June 1977; *ARB*, February 1978, p. 4741.
30 *Dawn* (India), 3 May 1977; *ACR*, 1977–8, p. B388.
31 *ACR*, 1977–8, p. B388; *Hsinhua News Agency* (HNA), 31 May 1977.
32 *The Daily Telegraph*, 27 May 1977; *HNA*, 5 August 1977.
33 David E. Albright, 'The Horn of Africa and the Arab–Israeli Conflict', in Robert O. Freedman, ed., *World Politics and the Arab–Israeli Conflict*, New York, Pergamon Press, 1979, p. 164.
34 *The Sunday Times*, 19 April 1977.
35 Paul B. Henze, The Rand Corporation, interview with author, 17 June 1988; Paul B. Henze, private communication, 31 May 1988.
36 *ACR*, 1977–8, p. A74.
37 Cyrus Vance, 'The United States and Africa: Building Positive Relations', *Department of State Bulletin*, 76, 1989, 8 August 1977, pp. 169–70.
38 *ACR*, 1977–8, p. A74.
39 *Izvestiya*, 16 April 1977.
40 Dimitri K. Simes, 'Imperial Globalism in the Making: Soviet Involvement in the Horn of Africa', note 7, p. 39.
41 Y. Tsaplin, 'Playing with Fire', *New Times*, 25, 1977, p. 12; G. Galperin, 'In and Around the Horn of Africa', p. 23.
42 *Pravda*, 28 April 1977.
43 *Tass* statement, *Pravda*, 6 June 1977.
44 Moscow Radio, 4 February 1977; *The Guardian*, 2 May 1977.
45 *Pravda*, 29 May 1977; *Pravda*, 8 May 1977; *Pravda*, 24 March 1977.
46 Moscow Radio, 6 May 1977.
47 *Afrique–Asie*, 13 June 1977, cited in René Lefort, *Ethiopia: An Heretical Revolution?*, p. 210.
48 Aryeh Yodfat, 'The Soviet Union and the Horn of Africa', *Northeast African Studies*, part two, 2, 1, 1980, p. 40.
49 Moscow Radio, home service, 1 June 1977 and 2 June 1977.
50 Moscow Radio in Somali, 2 June 1977, in Foreign Broadcasting Information Service (FBIS), Soviet Union, 3 June 1977, pp. H2–H3.
51 On 8 July 1977, only two days after the EPLF took Decarnere, it captured Keren – the key to control of western and northern Eritrea. Exactly a week later, the EPLF pulled off another spectacular success by freeing 800

political prisoners from the largest prison in Asmara, the provincial capital. July 1977 was indeed a bleak time for the Dergue in Eritrea. See Haggai Erlich, *The Struggle Over Eritrea, 1962–1978: War and Revolution in the Horn of Africa*, California, Hoover Institution Press, 1983, p. 77: *The Guardian*, 17 July 1977.

52 *ACR*, 1977–8, p. B375; *ACR*, 1977–8, p. B227.

53 *ARB*, August 1977, p. 4526.

54 *ACR*, 1977–8, p. B383; David A. Korn, *Ethiopia: the United States and the Soviet Union*, London, Croom Helm, 1986, p. 33.

55 C. Legum, 'Angola and the Horn of Africa', in Stephen S. Kaplan, ed., *Diplomacy of Power: Soviet Armed Forces as a Political Instrument*, Washington DC, the Brookings Institution, 1981, p. 619; *The Daily Telegraph*, 3 October 1977; *ACR*, 1977–8, p. B388.

56 *ARB*, August 1977, p. 4527.

57 Donald R. Katz, 'Children's Revolution: A Bloodbath in Ethiopia', *Horn of Africa*, 1, 3, July–September 1978, p. 9; Paul B. Henze, private communication, 31 May 1988.

58 *Soviet News*, 9 August 1977, 5893, p. 289; *Izvestiya*, 2 August 1977.

59 *Izvestiya*, 2 August 1977.

60 *Pravda*, 14 August 1977.

61 *Pravda*, 30 July 1977; *Pravda*, 7 August 1977.

62 *Pravda*, 7 August 1977.

63 *Pravda*, 14 August 1977; René Lefort, *Ethiopia: An Heretical Revolution?*, p. 211; Paul B. Henze, *Flexible Opportunism*, Wisconsin, Foreign Area Research Inc., December 1986, p. 115.

64 *New York Times*, 19 July 1977; *Daily Express*, 14 July 1977; *The Observer*, 14 August 1977; *The Sunday Telegraph*, 17 July 1977.

65 *International Herald Tribune*, 8 August 1977; *The Sunday Times*, 14 August 1977; *The Guardian*, 30 August 1977.

66 Y. Tsaplin, 'Road of Friendship', *New Times*, 28, 1977, p. 14.

67 *The Daily Telegraph*, 18 August 1977; Mogadishu Radio, 5 October 1977, cited in *USSR and Third World*, 7, 5–6, September–December 1977, p. 142.

68 Mengistu cited in *ARB*, August 1977, p. 4528.

69 *Izvestiya*, 17 August 1977.

70 *Pravda*, 1 September 1977; Moscow Radio, English-language Africa broadcast, 1 September 1977.

71 Paul B. Henze, 'Flexible Opportunism', p. 116; *ARB*, September 1977, pp. 4558–9; *International Herald Tribune*, 22 September 1977; *The Daily Telegraph*, 3 October 1977.

72 *The Financial Times*, 20 October 1977; *International Herald Tribune*, 5 September 1977.

73 *October* (Cairo), 11 September 1977; *International Herald Tribune*, 27 September 1977.

74 *The Washington Post*, 27 September 1977.

75 Ratanov cited in *The Guardian*, 20 October 1977.

76 Ratanov cited in *The Daily Telegraph*, 25 October 1977.

77 *The Daily Telegraph*, 25 October 1977; *Qatar News Agency*, 7 November 1977.

78 From the outset of the Ogaden conflict, the Ethiopian US-made F-5 fighter planes were, in the words of one Ethiopian official, 'running rings around the MiGs', belonging to Somalia. See 'War on the Horn', *Newsweek*, 29 August 1977, p. 15.

79 Riyadh Radio, 7 September 1977; *The Financial Times*, 22 October 1977; *The Daily Telegraph*, 22 October 1977; *The Guardian*, 3 November 1977; *ARB*, October 1977, p. 4592.

80 Siad Barre cited in *The Daily Telegraph*, 3 November 1977.

81 *Pravda*, 29 September 1977.

82 Moscow Radio, 21 October 1977.

83 *ACR*, 1977–8, p. B381; *The Guardian*, 3 November 1977.

84 *Tass*, 5 September 1977.

85 Moscow Radio in Somali, 11 November 1977, cited in *FBIS*, Soviet Union, 14 November 1977, pp. H3–4.

86 *ACR*, 1977–8, pp. B381–2.

87 *ACR*, 1977–8, p. C81.

88 *The Economist*, London, June 1978, cited in *ACR*, 1977–8, p. B382.

89 *Soviet News*, 22 November 1977, 5907, p. 408.

90 *Pravda*, 16 November 1977.

91 *Soviet News*, 22 November 1977, 5907, p. 408.

92 *Soviet News*, 13 December 1977, 5910, p. 431; *Pravda*, 16 November 1977.

93 *Soviet News*, 22 November 1977, 5907, p. 412; *Izvestiya*, 22 November 1977; *Soviet News*, 13 December 1977, 5910, p. 431.

94 Paul B. Henze, who at the time was a member of the US National Security Council staff, met both Berhanu Bayeh and Atnafu Abate at a reception in the second week of September 1977 in Addis Ababa. Apart from general expressions of good will, the main weight of the conversation centred on a request for resumed US military assistance. The request was turned down by President Carter. At that stage, Atnafu was doing no more than Mengistu himself in exploring the US arms option. Paul B. Henze, private communication, 31 May 1988. Nevertheless, the meeting may have influenced Atnafu's subsequent political thinking. By November 1977, Atnafu was convinced that Ethiopia had 'to be friendly with the East and with the West'. See Pliny the Middle-Aged, 'The PMAC: Origins and Structure', *Northeast African Studies*, 1, 1, part two, 1978, p. 14.

95 Atnafu cited in Pliny the Middle-Aged, 'The PMAC: Origins and Structure', p. 14.

96 *Pravda*, 21 November 1977.

97 C. Legum, 'Angola and the Horn of Africa', pp. 620–2; 'On the Wings of a Bear', *The Economist*, 21 January 1978, p. 14; J. Mayall, 'The Battle for the Horn: Somali Irredentism and International Diplomacy', *The World Today*, September 1978, p. 341; Steven David, 'Realignment in the Horn: The Soviet Advantage', *International Security*, 4, 2, Winter 1979–80, p. 80.

98 *Dawn* (India), 28 January 1978; *NCNA*, 12 January 1978; *ACR*, 1977–8, p. B388; *International Herald Tribune*, 8 January 1978; Richard Remnek, *Soviet Policy in the Horn of Africa: The Decision to Intervene*, Professional Paper 270, Arlington, Virginia, Center for Naval Analyses, January 1980,

pp. 35–6; *Daily Express*, 6 February 1978; *The Financial Times*, 20 January 1978; *New York Times*, 8 January 1978.

99 This figure refers to the value of Soviet armaments transferred during the airlift period only. Tom J. Farer, *War Clouds on the Horn of Africa*, New York, Carnegie Endowment for International Peace, second revised edition, 1979, p. 125. Altogether, for the years 1977 to 1978, the USSR delivered arms to Ethiopia worth a total of $2.05 billion. US Arms Control and Disarmament Agency (ACDA), *World Military Expenditures and Arms Transfers 1987*, Washington, March 1988, p. 100.

100 C. G. Jacobsen, *Soviet Strategic Initiatives: Challenge and Response*, New York, Praeger, 1979, pp. 123–4; *ACR*, 1977–8, pp. B228–9; *The Daily Telegraph*, 7 March 1978; 'The Battle for the Horn', *Newsweek*, 13 February 1978, p. 15; Dimitri K. Simes, 'Imperial Globalism in the Making: Soviet Involvement in the Horn of Africa', p. 35; Bruce D. Porter, *The USSR in Third World Conflicts*, pp. 200–4.

101 *International Herald Tribune*, 27 February 1978; *ARB*, February 1978, p. 4740.

102 *Pravda*, 18 and 20 November 1977.

103 *Pravda*, 19 January 1978.

104 *Pravda*, 19 January 1978.

105 *Pravda*, 23 January 1978.

106 *Soviet News*, 17 January 1978, 5914, p. 21; *Izvestiya*, 25 February 1978; *Izvestiya*, 29 January 1978; V. Sofinsky and A. Khazanov, 'The Imperialist Design for the Horn of Africa', *New Times*, 7, 1978, p. 4.

107 'The Facts about the Conflict in the Horn of Africa', *Soviet News*, 14 February 1978, 5918, p. 63; *Moscow Radio*, 11 January 1978; Y. Tsaplin, 'Who is Fanning the Flames?', *New Times*, 5, 1978, p. 8.

108 'The Facts about the Conflict in the Horn of Africa', *Soviet News*, 14 February 1978, 5918, p. 63; V. Kudryavtsev, 'Dark Spots on the Globe', *Nedelya*, 4, 23–9 January 1978, p. 5.

109 Y. Tsaplin, 'Who is Fanning the Flames?', p. 5; *Pravda*, 6 February 1978.

110 Y. Tsaplin, 'The Ogaden Fighting', *New Times*, 9, 1978, p. 15.

111 Negussay Ayele observed that, while the US and its allies were 'not disinterested observers' of the Horn conflict, Washington 'had not been able to make significant arms deliveries to Somalia during the seven months of the war'. See N. Ayele, 'The Horn of Africa: Revolutionary Developments and Western Reactions', *Northeast African Studies*, 3, 1, 1981, pp. 26–7.

112 *Izvestiya*, 24 January 1978.

113 Yu. Irkin, 'Efiopiya na puti sotsialisticheskoy orientatsii', *Kommunist Voruzhennykh Sil*, 2, January 1979, p. 84; V. Sofinsky and A. Khazanov, 'The Imperialist Design for the Horn of Africa', p. 5; Radio Peace and Progress, 16 December 1977; Y. Tsaplin, 'Who is Fanning the Flames?', p. 8.

114 Moscow Radio, 2 December 1977, cited in *USSR and Third World*, 7, 5–6, September–December 1977, p. 142.

115 V. Kudryavtsev, 'Dark Spots on the Globe', p. 5.

116 V. Nekrasov, 'God 1977-y', *Kommunist*, 18, December 1977, p. 93; A. Khazanov, 'Problema mezhgosudarstvennykh konfliktov v Afrike i soby-tiya na Afrikanskom Roge', *Aziya i Afrika Segodnya*, 7, July 1978, p. 22.
117 V. Kudryavtsev, 'Dark Spots on the Globe', p. 5.
118 Moscow Radio, 30 January 1978; Moscow Radio, 5 January 1978; *Pravda*, 25 January 1978; *Pravda*, 24 November 1977.
119 Y. Tsaplin, 'Who is Fanning the Flames?', p. 8.
120 Siad cited in *The Daily Telegraph*, 28 December 1977.
121 V. Shubin, 'Revolution Square', *New Times*, 50, 1977, p. 23.
122 *New York Times*, 17 November 1977; *ACR*, 1977–8, p. B384; Robert F. Gorman, *Political Conflict on the Horn of Africa*, New York, Praeger Publishers, 1981, p. 121.
123 *ACR*, 1977–8, p. B384.
124 President Siad interviewed by Arnaud de Borchgrave in *Newsweek*, 13 February 1978, pp. 16–17.
125 President Jimmy Carter cited in *Hindu* (India), 16 November 1977.
126 A. Lake, 'Africa in a Global Perspective', *Department of State Bulletin*, 77, 2007, 12 December 1977, p. 843.
127 The Carter administration's assessment was reinforced at the time by sentiments expressed by US military officials who left Ethiopia in April 1977 – many felt the USSR had made a grave miscalculation in backing the Mengistu regime; see *The Daily Telegraph*, 26 April 1977 – and by the general consensus amongst Western diplomats in Addis Ababa that the new Soviet strategy was both risky and vulnerable. See *New York Times*, 14 November 1977.
128 *ARB*, February 1978, p. 4739.
129 *ACR*, 1977–8, p. B252.
130 *The Daily Nation* (Kenya), 18 January 1978.
131 Michael A. Ledeen, 'The Israeli Connection', *The Washington Review Special Supplement*, May 1978, pp. 46–7.
132 *Washington Post*, 5 March 1978; T. J. Farer, *War Clouds on the Horn of Africa: The Widening Storn*, p. 127.
133 *New York Times*, 7 December 1977; Z. Brzezinski, *Power and Principle*, London, Weidenfield and Nicolson and Son, 1983, p. 179.
134 *ARB*, January 1978, p. 4701; *Soviet News*, 17 January 1978, 5914, p. 21.
135 *ACR*, 1977–8, p. B384; *ARB*, January 1978, p. 4703.
136 Z. Brzezinski, *Power and Principle*, pp. 182–3.
137 C. Vance, *Hard Choices: Critical Years in America's Foreign Policy*, New York, Simon and Schuster, 1983, p. 87.
138 *ACR*, 1977–8, p. B389.
139 *ARB*, January 1978, p. 4702; *ACR*, 1977–8, p. B389.
140 'The Battle for the Horn', *Newsweek*, 13 February 1978, p. 16; *ACR*, 1977–8, pp. B388–9; Robert F. Gorman, *Political Conflict on the Horn of Africa*, p. 121.
141 L. Bondestam, 'External Involvement in Ethiopia and Eritrea', in B. Davidson, L. Cliffe and B. Habte Selassie, ed., *Behind the War in Eritrea*, Nottingham, Spokesman, 1980, p. 70; 'The Battle for the Horn', p. 14.

142 *ARB*, January 1978, p. 4704.
143 *Pravda*, 15 October 1977.
144 Y. Tsaplin, 'The Ogaden Fighting', p. 15.
145 *ACR*, 1977–8, p. B378.
146 President Carter cited in C. Legum, 'Angola and the Horn of Africa', p. 624.
147 'Horn of Africa', *New Times*, 8, 1978, p. 9.
148 *ACR*, 1977–8, p. B392.
149 *The Sunday Times*, 19 March 1978; 'The Ogaden Debacle', *Newsweek*, 20 March 1978, p. 21; Bereket Habte Selassie, *Conflict and Intervention in the Horn of Africa*, New York, Monthly Review Press, 1980, pp. 121–2; *ACR*, 1977–8, p. B379.
150 *The Sunday Times*, 19 March 1978; René Lefort, *Ethiopia: An Heretical Revolution?*, p. 260.
151 *Pravda*, 15 February 1978.
152 Moscow Radio, African Service, 16 February 1978.
153 N. Tarasov, 'The Pentagon's Plans for the Red Sea', *Asia and Africa Today*, 4, 1983, p. 17; 'Horn of Africa', *New Times*, 12, 1978, p. 11; Moscow Radio, English-language Africa broadcast, 15 March 1978; E. Sherr and O. Dolgova, 'From a Monarchy to a People's Democratic Republic', *Asia and Africa Today*, 5, 1984, p. 43.
154 Yu. Irkin, 'Efiopiya na puti sotsialisticheskoy orientatsii', p. 84.
155 *Pravda*, 16 March 1978.
156 A. Khazanov, 'Problema mezhgosudarstvennykh konfliktov v Afrike i sobytiya na Afrikanskom Roge', p. 22.
157 *Pravda*, 19 March 1978.
158 *Pravda*, 19 January 1978.
159 *Pravda*, 19 March 1978.
160 L. Davydov, 'The USSR and Ethiopia: Close Friendship and Co-operation', *International Affairs* (Moscow), February 1979, p. 94.
161 *Pravda*, 15 March 1978.
162 Christopher Clapham, 'The Soviet Experience in the Horn of Africa', in E. J. Feuchtwanger and P. Nailor, eds., *The Soviet Union and the Third World*, London, Macmillan Press, 1981, p. 214; *The Times*, 4 January 1978.
163 *Pravda*, 15 March 1977.
164 S. David, 'Realignment in the Horn: The Soviet Advantage', pp. 69–90.
165 F. Halliday and M. Molyneux, *The Ethiopian Revolution*, London, Verso, 1981, pp. 237–50.
166 A. Khazanov, 'Problema mezhgosudarstvennykh konfliktov v Afrike i sobitiya na Afrikanskom Roge', p. 22.
167 G. Samsonov cited in *The Observer*, 14 August 1977.
168 The remark of a departing Soviet official to a foreign colleague in Mogadishu. See 'Somalia: Sending Moscow a Message', *Newsweek*, 29 August 1977, p. 16.
169 I. M. Lewis, *A Modern History of Somalia: Nation and State in the Horn of Africa*, revised edition, London, Longman, 1980, p. 223.

170 *International Herald Tribune*, 31 August 1977; I. M. Lewis, *A Modern History of Somalia: Nation and State in the Horn of Africa*, pp. 219–23.

171 It is interesting that President Castro in a speech at the end of the Ogaden conflict drew a distinction between the 'rightist faction' and 'progressive, leftist forces' inside the Somali government. Havana Radio, 15 March 1978; see also *ACR*, 1978–9, p. B384.

172 *International Herald Tribune*, 31 August 1977.

173 V. Sofinsky and A. Khazanov, 'The Imperialist Design for the Horn of Africa', p. 4.

174 Ibid., p. 5.

175 V. Sofinsky and A. Khazanov, 'The Imperialist Design for the Horn of Africa', p. 4.

176 G. Afanasyev, 'Gunboat Diplomacy in the Red Sea', *Za Rubezhom*, 9, 24 February–2 March 1978, p. 7; *Izvestiya*, 25 February 1978.

177 *Izvestiya*, 25 February 1978.

178 Irving Kaplan et al., *Area Handbook for Ethiopia*, Washington DC, American University Press, 1971, p. 417; Paul B. Henze, private communication, 31 May 1988; Jiri Valenta, 'Soviet–Cuban Intervention in the Horn of Africa: Impact and Lessons', *Journal of International Affairs*, 34, 2, Winter 1980–1, p. 358; A. Gavshon, *Crisis in Africa: Battleground of East and West*, Middlesex, Penguin Books, 1981, p. 272.

179 M. Barinov, 'Socialist Ethiopia Moves Confidently Ahead', *International Affairs* (Moscow), 11, November 1980, p. 28.

180 N. Podgorny cited in *The Egyptian Gazette*, 6 May 1977.

181 Aryeh Yodfat, 'The Soviet Union and the Horn of Africa', Part Three, p. 70; a Soviet diplomat in Addis Ababa reportedly told an Arab colleague that 'we feel the Ethiopian revolution is more genuine' than the Somali one. See D. Ottaway and M. Ottaway, *Ethiopia: Empire in Revolution*, p. 204.

182 S. Sergeyev, 'Ethiopia Starts a New Life', *International Affairs* (Moscow), 5, May 1979, p. 16; G. Galperin, 'Revolyutsiya v Efiopii: osobennosti razvitiya', *Aziya i Afrika Segodnya*, 3, 1978, p. 9.

183 G. Galperin, 'Revolyutsiya v Efiopii: osobennosti razvitiya', p. 9.

184 Soviet sources quoted in *The Daily Telegraph*, 25 October 1977.

185 G. Galperin, 'Ethiopia: Some Aspects of the Nationalities' Question', *The African Communist*, 83, 4th Quarter, 1980, p. 58.

186 G. Galperin, 'Revolyutsiya v Efiopii: osobennosti razvitiya', p. 9.

187 C. Legum and B. Lee, *Conflict in the Horn of Africa*, p. 82; *The Egyptian Gazette*, 6 May 1977.

188 This observation was drawn from a series of personal interviews with Ethiopian citizens who lived through the events of 1974–8 in Addis Ababa. The author, however, must respect their desire for anonymity.

189 G. Galperin, 'Revolyutsiya v Efiopii: osobennosti razvitiya', p. 11; *Pravda*, 12 December 1977.

190 V. Sofinsky and A. Khazanov, 'The Imperialist Design for the Horn of Africa', p. 5.

191 B. Bayeh, 'The Ethiopian Revolution: A Hard Period', *World Marxist Review*, 4, April 1978, p. 55.

192 S. Sergeyev, 'An Important Landmark in Soviet–Ethiopian Co-operation', *International Affairs* (Moscow), 12, December 1979, p. 91.

193 G. Galperin, 'Ethiopia: Some Aspects of the Nationalities' Question', p. 61.

194 *Sovetskaya Belorussiya* (Minsk), 17 February 1978.

195 M. Barinov, 'Socialist Ethiopia Moves Confidently Ahead', p. 26.

196 Mesfin Wolde-Mariam, *Somalia: The Problem Child of Africa*, Addis Ababa, Artistic Printing Press, 1977.

197 Jiri Valenta, 'Soviet–Cuban Intervention in the Horn of Africa: Impact and Lessons', pp. 358–9.

198 *New York Times*, 4 June 1977; *The Times*, 25 May 1977.

199 Fyodor Burlatsky, political adviser to Mikhail Gorbachev and formerly consultant to the International Department of the CPSU Central Committee during Brezhnev's time, described Brezhnev as 'the least competent of all men that ever ruled the country' and said that Brezhnev openly conceded his own shortcomings in the sphere of foreign policy. Fyodor Burlatsky, 'A Hero of Times Past', *Literaturnaya Gazeta*, 1988. Reproduced in English in *The Guardian*, 17 December 1988.

200 N. Podgorny cited in *ARB*, March 1977, p. 4375.

201 *Tass*, 5 April 1977.

202 René Lefort, *Ethiopia: An Heretical Revolution?*, p. 270.

203 Brezhnev received Mengistu on 6 May 1977. *New York Times*, 7 May 1977.

204 *Pravda*, 5 May 1977.

205 *Soviet News*, 10 May 1977, 5881, pp. 159 and 167.

206 *Pravda*, 25 May 1977.

207 It would appear that Podgorny did not participate in the discussions concerning the Soviet–Ethiopian arms deal which was signed during Mengistu's visit to Moscow. His name does not feature in the bilateral talks on 'the international situation'. *Pravda* and *Izvestiya*, 7 May 1977.

208 L. Davydov, 'The USSR and Ethiopia: Close Friendship and Co-operation', pp. 90–1; Anatoly A. Gromyko, 'Sovetsko–Efiopskiye svyazy', p. 10.

209 Siad's interview in *Newsweek*, 13 February 1978, p. 17.

210 G. Galperin, 'In and Around the Horn of Africa', p. 24.

211 M. Barinov, 'Socialist Ethiopia Moves Confidently Ahead', p. 28; E. Denisov and V. Sharayev, 'Efiopiya: stroitsya avangardnaya partiya', *Aziya i Afrika Segodnya*, 11, 1980, p. 12.

212 S. Sergeyev, 'Ethiopia Starts a New Life', p. 17.

213 *The Guardian*, 11 December 1977; David A. Korn, *Ethiopia, the United States and the Soviet Union*, pp. 41–2.

214 *The Financial Times*, 19 January 1978. A Soviet commentary observed that 'these Mogadishu functionaries will not be saved by their statements that they are defending the interests of national minorities in Ethiopia'. Moscow Radio, 30 January 1978.

215 N. Tarasov, 'The Pentagon's Plans for the Red Sea', p. 17; *Izvestiya*, 24 January 1977.

216 V. Larin, 'Who Gains by the Tension?', p. 10.

217 E. Sherr and O. Dolgova, 'From a Monarchy to a People's Democratic Republic', p. 44.

218 A. Kokiev and V. Vigand, 'National Democratic Revolution in Ethiopia: Economic and Socio-political Aspects', in *Modern Ethiopia From the Accession of Menelik II to the Present*, Proceedings of the Fifth International Conference of Ethiopian Studies, Nice, 19–22 December 1977, Rotterdam, Balkema, 1980, pp. 423–4.

219 Comment of the editor of the *World Marxist Review* in an interview with Berhanu Bayeh, the PMAC's head of Foreign Affairs. See 'From Feudalism to People's Democracy', *World Marxist Review*, 8, August 1976, note 2, p. 39.

220 G. K. Shirokov and A. Khazanov, 'Sovetskiy Soyuz i natsional'no osvoboditel'noye dvizheniye', *Narody Azii i Afriki*, 1, 1978, p. 9.

221 The German magazine, *Der Spiegel*, cited in *HNA*, 26 February 1978.

222 This view was expressed in M. L. Volpe's sympathetic review of V. S. Yag'ya's book, *Efiopiya v Noveyshee Vremya*, Moscow, Izdatel'stvo 'Mysl', 1978. See M. L. Volpe, 'Novyye raboty Sovetskikh Efiopistov', *Narody Azii i Afriki*, 1, 1983, pp. 170–1.

223 G. Galperin 'Revolyutsiya v Efiopii: osobennosti razvitiya', p. 12.

224 René Lefort, *Ethiopia: An Heretical Revolution?*, pp. 212–18; 'War on the Horn', *Newsweek*, 29 August 1977, p. 15; *The Daily Telegraph*, 22 September 1977.

225 Mengistu interviewed in *Neues Deutschland*, 25 February 1977. Reprinted in 'Ethiopia Under Fire', *The African Communist*, 71, 4th Quarter, 1977, pp. 92–6.

226 Berhanu Bayeh, 'The Ethiopian Revolution: A Hard Period', p. 55.

227 A. Kokiev and V. Vigand, 'National Democratic Revolution in Ethiopia: Economic and Socio-political Aspects', p. 424.

228 Soviet Foreign Minister, Andrey Gromyko, cited in 'The Battle for the Horn', *Newsweek*, 13 February 1977, p. 18.

229 *Soviet News*, 20 July 1976, 5842, p. 271; 'Responsibility for the Future', *New Times*, 11, 1983, p. 1.

230 K. Brutents, 'Osvobodivshyesya strany v nachale 80-kh godov', *Kommunist*, 3, 1984, p. 113.

231 E. Sherr and O. Dolgova, 'From a Monarchy to a People's Democratic Republic', p. 44.

232 Ibid., p. 42.

233 A. Dzasokhov, the Deputy Chairman of the Soviet Afro–Asian Solidarity Committee, visited Ethiopia in October 1977. Upon his return to Moscow, Dzasokhov, while declaring that 'the Ethiopian people were deeply interested in scientific socialism' (Moscow Radio, 1 November 1977), strongly hinted that he found the Ethiopians no less nationalistic than the Somalis. To illustrate his point, Dzasokhov recited an Ethiopian parable: 'In present day Ethiopia, swept up by revolutionary events into a new stage of its history, they told us of an old legend. At one time, guests arrived in this country. They were joyfully received. But when they were getting ready to leave [then] the Ethiopians asked them to remove their

shoes, carefully shook the dust and sand from them, knocked off the earth that had dried on them and, turning, explained to the surprised guests. "This earth is the dearest thing we have, we cannot give it away to you even the tiniest grain of it".' See *Pravda*, 12 December 1977.

234 E. Sherr and O. Dolgova, 'From a Monarchy to a People's Democratic Republic', p. 43.

235 E. Sherr, 'Lenin in Ethiopia', *Asia and Africa Today*, 2, 1985, p. 51; S. Sergeyev, 'An Important Landmark in Soviet–Ethiopian Co-operation', pp. 88–9.

236 Yu. Irkin, 'Efiopiya na puti sotsialisticheskoy orientatsii', pp. 83–4; Yu. Ustimenko, 'Efiopiya: trudnosti, sversheniya, perspektivy', *Aziya i Afrika Segodnya*, 5, 1977, p. 11.

237 *Soviet News*, 10 May 1977, 5881, p. 158.

238 *Soviet News*, 22 November 1977, 5907, p. 408.

239 *Pravda*, 17 June 1978.

240 P. Mezentsev, 'Covering up the Tracks', *New Times*, 11, 1978, p. 12.

241 David A. Korn, *Ethiopia, the United States and the Soviet Union*, p. 34.

242 Soviet observers like V. Sofinsky and A. Khazanov ('The Imperialist Design for the Horn of Africa', p. 5) claimed that the Somali invasion was the result of 'a direct deal' with US 'imperialism'. Similarly, some Western correspondents such as V. Zorza argued that without Washington's support, 'Somalia might never have moved against Ethiopia' (*International Herald Tribune*, 18 January 1978). These arguments, however, strain credulity. First, Somalia was militarily involved in the Ogaden campaign long before there was any suggestion of US support. Secondly, for a state which was allegedly counting on US support, Somalia treated Washington in a rather cavalier fashion. For instance, during the critical May-June period of 1977, President Siad kept the US Ambassador, J. Loughran, waiting for nearly three weeks for a requested audience (*International Herald Tribune*, 4 June 1977; B. Habte Selassie, *Conflict and Intervention in the Horn of Africa*, p. 120).

243 Paul B. Henze, private communication, 31 May 1988; David A. Korn, *Ethiopia, the United States and the Soviet Union*, p. 36.

244 C. Vance cited in Z. Brzezinski, *Power and Principle*, p. 185.

245 *Pravda*, 3 March 1978.

246 *Pravda*, 4 March 1978.

247 *Pravda*, 5 March 1978.

248 *Pravda*, 10 June 1978.

249 Y. Tsaplin, 'The Ogaden Fighting', *New Times*, 9, 1978, p. 15.

250 V. Nekrasov, 'God 1978-y', *Kommunist*, 18, 1978, p. 116.

251 *New York Times*, 8 January 1978.

7. Soviet power without influence?

1 Mengistu cited in *Pravda*, 28 October 1980.

2 P. Mezentsov, 'Covering Up the Tracks', *New Times*, 11, 1978, p. 12.

3 M. Maksimova, 'Vsemirnoye khozyaystvo: nauchno – tekhnicheskaya revo-

lyutsiya i mezhdunarodnyye otnosheniya', *Mirovaya Ekonomika i Mezhdu-narodnye Otnosheniya* (MEiMO), 4, April 1979, pp. 23–4.

4 *Pravda*, 8 February 1979.

5 *Pravda*, 21 November 1978.

6 Military data derived from *The Military Balance 1987–1988*, London. The International Institute for Strategic Studies (IISS), pp. 111–12 and p. 126; David A. Korn, *Ethiopia, the United States and the Soviet Union*, London, Croom Helm, 1986, p. 91; Christopher Clapham, *Transformation in Revolutionary Ethiopia*, Cambridge, Cambridge University Press, 1988, p. 229; US Arms Control and Disarmament Agency (ACDA), *World Military Expenditures and Arms Transfers 1977–1986*, Washington DC, March 1988, p. 100; Paul B. Henze, private communications, 31 May 1988 and 9 December 1988. *Reuters*, 24 January 1984; *The Sunday Times*, 29 November 1987.

7 *The Observer*, 20 July 1980; Addis Ababa Radio, cited in *USSR and Third World*, 11, 5–6, July–November 1981, p. 92; *Africa Contemporary Record* (ACR), 1984–5, p. A249; Addis Ababa Radio, 19 July 1984.

8 *Africa Research Bulletin* (ARB), June 1980, p. 5701.

9 *The Guardian*, 8 August 1980; *ARB*, August 1980, p. 5762.

10 The resolution included *inter alia* 'the recognition, affirmation, implementation and application' of the principle of the inviolability of frontiers of member states as attained at the time of independence. *ARB*, August 1980, p. 5764.

11 *ARB*, August 1980, p. 5764.

12 Richard Greenfield, Oxford University, visited the scene of the conflict and found discarded Soviet military manuals in abandoned Ethiopian trucks, 'The Spreading War for a Wasteland' *Newsweek*, 30 August 1982, p. 16.

13 *Krasnaya Zvezda*, 13 July 1982; Y. Bochkarev, 'Metamorphosis of the Regime', *New Times*, 14, 1983, p. 15.

14 Mogadishu Radio, 17 July 1983; *The Guardian*, 3 January 1985.

15 *The Guardian*, 16 February 1987; *The Daily Telegraph*, 26 March 1987. *ARB*, March 1987, p. 8391.

16 Lionel Cliffe 'Eritrea: How the War Feeds the Famine', *The Observer Magazine*, 31 January 1988; David A. Korn, *Ethiopia, the United States and the Soviet Union*, pp. 159–60.

17 Y. Bochkarev, 'A Pack of Lies' *New Times*, 11, 1987, p. 16.

18 *Reuters*, 24 January 1984; David A. Korn, *Ethiopia, the United States and the Soviet Union*, pp. 93–4.

19 Moscow Radio, English-language Africa broadcast, 12 April 1985.

20 *Pravda*, 19 March 1978.

21 *Soviet News*, 19 September 1978, 5946, p. 320.

22 *Pravda*, 21 November 1978.

23 Y. Makeyev, 'USSR–Ethiopia: Economic and Technical Co-operation', *Foreign Trade*, 6, 1985, p. 30.

24 Ibid. pp. 30–1; 'With Soviet Assistance', *Foreign Trade*, 7, 1984, p. 56.

25 'With Soviet Assistance', p. 56; 'Facts and Figures' *Socialism: Principles*,

Practice, Prospects, 9, September 1984, p. 31; Y. Makeyev, 'USSR–Ethiopia: Economic and Technical Co-operation', p. 30.

26 *Izvestiya*, 28 February 1984.
27 E. S. Sherr 'Ways of Disseminating the Ideas of Scientific Socialism in Ethiopia' *Africa in Soviet Studies Annual 1986*, Nauka Publishers, Moscow, 1987, p. 78.
28 Ibid., pp 78–80.
29 'Facts and Figures', p. 31.
30 *Vneshnyaya Torgovlya za SSSR, 1978 and 1987*, Moscow, 'Statistika'.
31 Christopher Clapham, *Transformation in Revolutionary Ethiopia*, p. 234; David A. Korn, *Ethiopia, the United States and the Soviet Union*, p. 93.
32 Addis Ababa Radio, 5 September 1986.
33 Addis Ababa Radio, 10 October 1986.
34 The Soviet media did not report the Ethiopian crisis until the end of October 1984 (*Izvestiya* 30 October 1984; Moscow Radio, English-language Africa broadcast, 30 October 1984). In contrast, the famine made news in the West in July 1984 following Michael Buerk's first harrowing film in Ethiopia. Michael Buerk, private communication, 20 July 1988; *The Guardian*, 13 July 1984; *The Evening Echo*, 5 November 1984.
35 Moscow Radio, English-language Africa broadcast, 12 November 1984; *Soviet Weekly*, 16 March 1985.
36 *Tass*, 9 November 1984; *Soviet News*, 14 November 1984, 6250, p. 309; *Soviet News*, 21 November 1984, 6251, p. 404; 'Friendly Aid In Coping With the Elements', *Asis and Africa Today*, 2, March–April 1985, p. 56; *Soviet Weekly*, 12 January 1985.
37 *Pravda*, 3 December 1984; *Soviet Weekly*, 14 December 1985; 'Friendly Aid in Coping With the Elements', p. 56. G. Gabrielyan, 'Novaya Stranitsa Istorii' *Aziya i Afrika Segodnya*, 12, 1987, p. 18.
38 *Soviet Weekly*, 11 January 1986.
39 *Soviet News*, 14 November 1984, 6250, p. 399.
40 Moscow radio cited in *ACR*, 1984–5, p. A250.
41 *Krasnaya Zvezda*, 11 September 1982; *Pravda*, 13 October 1982.
42 Moscow Radio, English-language Africa broadcast, 8 January 1983.
43 *Pravda*, 13 October 1982; Moscow Radio, English-language Africa broadcast, 22 March 1983.
44 *Tass*, 5 September 1984.
45 G. Gabrielyan, 'Rebirth of a Nation' *New Times*, 35, 1986, p. 22.
46 Addis Ababa Radio in Russian, 10 September 1987.
47 An. A. Gromyko, 'Ruka ob ruku', *Aziya i Afrika Segodnya*, 1, 1987, p. 12.
48 Mengistu cited in *Pravda*, 18 November 1978.
49 David A. Korn, *Ethiopia, the United States and the Soviet Union*, p. 101.
50 *ARB*, November 1979, p. 5495; *ARB*, December 1979, p. 5520; P. Schwab, *Ethiopia: Politics, Economics and Society*, London, Frances Pinter, 1985, p. 98; *Korean Central News Agency* (KCNA), 23 October 1983.
51 *Pravda*, 23 August 1981.
52 David A. Korn, US Chargé d'affaires in Ethiopia from June 1982 to July 1985, disagrees. In his informative book, Korn observes that 'all but the

most deluded optimist would after a time have to conclude that Mengistu and those closest to him had chosen the Soviet side' (David A. Korn, *Ethiopia, the United States and the Soviet Union*, p. xv). Yet, Korn weakens the consistency of his argument by conceding that Mengistu 'is a figure in the mainstream of Ethiopian tradition' (David A. Korn, *Ethiopia*, p. 107) and someone that the Soviets 'had to learn' that they could not 'order around' (David A. Korn, *Ethiopia*, p. 97).

53 *ARB*, November 1974, p. 3429.
54 *Pravda*, 18 November 1978.
55 Mengistu Haile Mariam, *Towards Party Formation*, Addis Ababa, Ministry of Information and National Guidance, December 1979, p. 35.
56 Yury Andropov in *Pravda*, 23 April 1982.
57 Aryeh Yodfat, 'Ethiopia: Pressure for Political Reorganisation', *Soviet Analyst*, 27, October 1982, pp. 2–3.
58 Haggai Erlich, *The Struggle Over Eritrea 1962–1978*, California, Hoover University Press, 1983, p. 113.
59 *The Guardian*, 14 March 1981; David A. Korn *Ethiopia, the United States and the Soviet Union*, p. 107.
60 *Pravda*, 27 February 1982.
61 E. Denisov and V. Scharayev, 'Efiopiya: stroitsya avangardnaya partiya', *Aziya i Afrika Segodnya*, 11, 1980, p. 13.
62 *United Press International* (UPI), 8 March 1984; *The Times*, 16 February 1985.
63 Mengistu Haile Mariam, 'Ethiopia: A Course for Socialist Construction', *Socialism: Principles, Practice, Prospects*, 9, September 1984, p. 26.
64 Six months before the creation of the WPE, Mengistu told Moscow that 'the key task today is to ensure the viability of the vanguard party of the working people in Ethiopia, to strengthen the people's defence forces . . . to accelerate the creation of an independent and strong socialist economy'. See Mengistu Haile Mariam, 'Ethiopia: A Course for Socialist Construction', p. 26. It is interesting therefore, that the promulgation of the WPE in September 1984 coincided with the signing of a long-term economic co-operation agreement which, according to Addis Ababa, 'guaranteed the party's future development' and 'would play a vital role in Ethiopia's economy'. Addis Ababa Radio, 8 September 1984.
65 *Soviet Weekly*, 15 September 1984.
66 Aleme Eshete wrote an article, 'Betrayal of the Revolution' in *The Guardian*, 13 September 1986.
67 *ARB*, October 1987, p. 8624.
68 *The Daily Telegraph*, 29 October 1986.
69 Goshu Wolde interviewed in *The Daily Telegraph*, 7 December 1984.
70 Marina Ottaway, *Soviet and American Influence in the Horn of Africa*, New York, Praeger, 1982, p. 149; Richard Sherman, *Eritrea: The Unfinished Revolution*, New York, Praeger, 1980, p. 93.
71 R. Sherman, *Eritrea: The Unfinished Revolution*, p. 93; Mogadishu Radio, 13 August 1983; *The Guardian*, 8 November 1984.
72 In July 1980, it was reported that Ethiopia turned down a Soviet request for a naval base at Massawa during the visit of Admiral S. Gorshkov (*Hsinhua*

News Agency – HNA – 23 August 1980; *Emirates News*, 29 September, 1980). Then, in March 1981, another Soviet attempt to obtain base facilities at Massawa failed (*The Guardian*, 31 March 1981). Finally, the Soviets appeared to experience a further rebuff in July 1984 when Marshal V. Petrov, the then Soviet Deputy Defence Minister, visited what Addis Ababa pointedly called the 'Ethiopian naval base' at Massawa (Addis Ababa Radio, 19 July 1984).

73 *The Observer*, 18 November 1984; *ACR*, 1985–6, p. A275.

74 G. B. Starushenko, ed., *Ideologiya Revolyutsionnykh Demokratov Afriki*, Moscow, Izdatel'stvo 'Nauka', 1981, p. 285.

75 Lars Bondestam, 'External Involvement in Ethiopia and Eritrea' in Basil Davidson, Lionel Cliffe and Bereket Habte Selassie, eds., *Behind the War in Eritrea*, Nottingham, Spokesman, 1980, p. 79.

76 Mengistu interview, 'Considerable Progress Already', *New Times*, 48, 1985, pp. 10–11.

77 Ethiopian Relief and Rehabilitation Council (RRC) chief, Berhanu Jembere, cited in *The Times*, 3 December 1987.

78 Moscow Radio, English-language Africa broadcast, 12 February, 1986; *Pravda*, 15 January 1982.

79 Y. Bochkarev, 'What a Hope!', *New Times*, 20, 1986, pp. 16–17.

80 *Africa Confidential*, 19, 14, 7 July 1984, pp. 3–4; *The Times*, 29 February 1980.

81 *The Christian Science Monitor*, 6 March 1978.

82 Figures derived from 'Ethiopia: Is There Any Hope?', *The Save The Children Magazine*, March 1988, pp. 5–6; *The Observer*, 3 January 1988; *The Guardian*, 2 February 1988; *The Sunday Times*, 29 November 1987.

83 *The Times*, 11 October 1985.

84 *Geographical Distribution of Financial Flows to Developing Countries 1983–1986*, Organisation for Economic Co-operation and Development (OECD), Paris, 1988, p. 103; Ian Greig, 'Third World: Moscow Changes Direction', *Soviet Analyst*, 17, 2, January 1988, p. 4; *Yezhegodnik 1987*, Moscow, Izdat'stvo 'Sovetskaya Entsiklopediya', 1987, p. 419.

85 *Geographical Distribution of Financial Flows to Developing Countries 1983–1986*, p. 102.

86 *Allgemeine Deutscher Nachrichten* (ADN), 19 October 1983; *The Financial Times*, 1 November 1983.

87 Mengistu's comments were repeated by the then Soviet leader in 'Leonid Brezhnev's Speech', *Supplement, Moscow News*, 44, 31 October 1982, p. 2.

88 David A. Korn, *Ethiopia, the United States and the Soviet Union*, p. 92; Paul B. Henze, 'Ethiopia – Contrasts and Contradictions', The Rand Corporation, Santa Monica, California, paper 7389, October 1987, p. 8.

89 Addis Ababa Radio, 13 September 1983; Mengistu cited in Paul B. Henze, 'Communism and Ethiopia', *Problems of Communism*, 30, 3, May–June 1981, note 48, p. 71.

90 Addis Ababa Radio, 13 September 1983.

91 Moscow Radio, English-language Africa broadcast, 27 February 1984.

92 Lars Bondestam, 'External Involvement in Ethiopia and Eritrea', p. 76. For a recent, candid account of the shortcomings of Soviet specialists in Africa

see G. Polyakov, 'USSR–Africa: Economic Co-operation from the Viewpoint of Perestroika', *Asia and Africa Today*, 5, 1988, p. 8.

93 Paul B. Henze, *Eritrea – The Dilemmas of Marxism*, p. 49; David A. Korn, *Ethiopia, the United States and the Soviet Union*, p. 91.

94 *Observer Foreign News Service* (OFNS), 28 May 1981; *The Guardian*, 11 February 1985.

95 The Kenyan newspaper, *The Standard*, accused the USSR of taking advantage of the fact that both the Ethiopian birr and the Soviet rouble are inconvertible currencies. According to *The Standard*, the USSR was being repaid in US dollars at an artificially high rouble–dollar exchange rate. See *HNA*, 20 March 1981.

96 Mengistu interview in *OFNS*, 6 March 1980.

97 *The Financial Times*, 1 June 1979; Christopher Clapham, *Transformation in Revolutionary Ethiopia*, pp. 229–30.

98 This information is derived from an Ethiopian source who wishes to remain anonymous.

99 'War and Hunger: Ethiopia', *Africa News*, 30 November 1987, p. 5.

100 David A. Korn, *Ethiopia, the United States and the Soviet Union*, p. 59.

101 Addis Ababa Radio, 9 December 1986; Addis Ababa Radio, 21 October 1986; Addis Ababa Radio, 13 December 1986; Addis Ababa Radio, 10 September 1986.

102 *The Times*, 15 February 1983. Christopher Clapham, private communication, 6 November 1988.

103 *Pravda*, 12 July 1983.

104 Moscow Radio, English-language Africa broadcast, 16 February 1983.

105 Karen Brutents, 'Osvobodivshyesya strany v nachale 80-kh godov', *Kommunist*, 3, 1984, p. 108.

106 Graham Hancock, *Ethiopia: The Challenge of Hunger*, London, Victor Gollancz Ltd, 1985, p. 9.

107 The then Ethiopian acting Chargé d'affaires and Press Counsellor to Britain, Tesfaye Demeke, interviewed in *The Morning Star*, 26 October 1979.

108 *The Guardian*, 22 February 1985; *The Guardian*, 26 April 1986.

109 *Soviet Weekly*, 21 September 1985.

110 *The Guardian*, 6 December 1985.

111 *The Times*, 25 January 1985.

112 That is the estimate of Dawit Wolde Giorgis, head of the Ethiopian Relief and Rehabilitation Commission until his political defection in early 1986. See Dawit's account in *The Guardian*, 2 July 1987.

113 *The Guardian*, 24 October 1985; *The Times*, 8 March 1985; *The Daily Telegraph*, 5 October 1984; G. Gabrielyan, 'Novaya Stranitsa Istorii', p. 18; David A. Korn, *Ethiopia, the United States and the Soviet Union*, p. 141.

114 Goshu Wolde cited in *The Guardian*, 11 February 1985.

115 *The Daily Telegraph*, 2 November 1984; David A. Korn, *Ethiopia, the United States and the Soviet Union*, p. 127.

116 Y. Bochkarev, 'Grain and Slander', *New Times*, 21, 1985, p. 21.

117 Y. Bochkarev, 'Fighting Hunger', *New Times*, 48, 1984, p. 11.

118 G. Galperin, 'Aid: Facts and Fictions', *New Times*, 2, 1985, p. 12.

119 Y. Bochkarev, 'Fighting Hunger', p. 11.

120 Y. Bochkarev, 'Grain and Slander', p. 21.

121 *The Daily Telegraph*, 15 July 1985.

122 *Tass*, 17 December 1984.

123 *The Observer*, 18 November 1984.

124 V. Sharayev, 'Despite the Difficulties', *New Times*, 44, 1985, p. 21.

125 Paul B. Henze, 'Communism in Ethiopia', p. 68.

126 The document apparently originated from the Ethiopian Ministry of Information and National Guidance. It was partially reproduced in 'Disestablishing the Church', *Africa Now*, 8, November 1981, p. 43.

127 Paul B. Henze, 'Ethiopia – Contrasts and Contradictions', p. 6.

128 E. Sherr, 'Islam v Somali i Efiopii', *Aziya i Afrika Segodnya*, 1, 1988, pp. 58–9.

129 P. Schwab, *Ethiopia: Politics, Economics and Society*, p. 93.

130 Mary Dines (then General Secretary of the War on Want organisation), *The Times*, 12 August 1982; P. Schwab, *Ethiopia: Politics, Economics and Society*, p. 93.

131 When the airlift became public knowledge on 3 January 1985, an embarrassed Ethiopia immediately condemned it as a 'gross interference in the internal affairs of Ethiopia' (*The Guardian*, 5 January 1985). However, it is unlikely that Addis Ababa was unaware of the three-month airlift. Despite the absence of diplomatic relations, Ethiopia and Israel maintained a close military relationship throughout the years of the Ethiopian revolution. According to the *International Monetary Fund*, Israeli arm sales to Ethiopia have averaged about $5 million a year since 1980. It is possible, therefore, as the Sudanese government alleged, that Addis Ababa and Israel had entered a secret understanding whereby the Ethiopian government turned a blind eye to the airlift in exchange for Israeli arms. See *The Guardian*, 8 January 1985.

132 David A. Korn, *Ethiopia, the United States and the Soviet Union*, p. 170.

133 E. Sherr, 'Lenin in Ethiopia', *Asia and Africa Today*, 2, March–April 1985, pp. 50–1

134 Y. Bochkarev, 'Metamorphosis of the Regime', *New Times*, 14, 1983, pp. 14–15; Moscow Radio, English-language Africa broadcast, 22 October 1983.

135 Y. Bochkarev, 'Metamorphosis of the Regime', p. 14; Moscow Radio, English-language Africa broadcast, 15 February 1985; Moscow Radio, English-language Africa broadcast, 10 June 1985.

136 Moscow Radio, 17 September 1984.

137 Mogadishu Radio, 19 July 1982; Mogadishu Radio, 1 September 1983.

138 Karen Brutents, 'Osvobodivshyesya strany v nachale 80-kh godov', p. 111.

139 'Revolution and Reform in the National Development of Eastern Countries' (a Round Table discussion), *Asia and Africa Today*, 1, 1986, p. 58.

140 Y. Pavlov, 'Socialist Orientation: Inventions and Reality', *Socialism Principles, Practice, Prospects*, 2, February 1983, p. 27; Karen Brutents, 'Osvobodivshyesya strany v nachale 80-kh godov', p. 104.

141 'Revolution and Reform in the National Development of Eastern Countries', p. 58.

142 G. Mirskiy, *'Tretiy mir': obshchestvo, vlast', armiya*, Izdatel'stvo 'Nauka', Moscow, 1976, p. 378.
143 S. Kondrashov, 'Efiopskiye zarisovki', *Asiya i Afrika Segodnya*, 2, 1979, p. 32.
144 Kondrashov wrote about the Ethiopian–Somali dispute during the early 1960s ('What the African Governments Discussed in Cairo', *New Times*, 15, 1961, pp. 3–5) and also penned a profile of Somalia (*Pervyy raz v Somali*, Izdatel'stvo 'Izvestiya', Moscow, 1961).
145 *Voyna i Armiya*, Moscow, Voenizdat, 1977, pp. 334–5.
146 S. Kondrashov, 'Efiopskiye zarisovki', p. 34.
147 S. Kondrashov, 'Efiopskiye zarisovki', p. 34.
148 Ibid., p. 34.
149 Ibid., p. 34.
150 Karen Brutents, 'Osvobodivshyesya strany v nachale 80-kh godov', pp. 104–6.
151 Ibid., p. 105; 'Revolution and Reform in the National Development of Eastern Countries', p. 58.
152 'Revolution and Reform in the National Development of Eastern Countries', p. 58.
153 M. L. Volpe, 'Novyye raboty Sovetskikh Efiopistov', *Narody Azii i Afriki*, 1, 1983, pp. 171–5.
154 'Revolution and Reform in the National Development of Eastern Countries', p. 56.
155 Anatoly Gromyko's writings seem to mirror a conviction that the precedent of Imperial Russian involvement in nineteenth-century Ethiopia served as a preconditioner for contemporary Soviet–Ethiopian relations. Boris Bogdanov, for example, has written that 'Russia was then the only country whose position helped Ethiopia preserve its sovereignty' ('The Russian Traveller's Feat', *Asia and Africa Today*, 4, July–August 1983, p. 59). Gromyko agreed. In 1979, the Director of the Soviet Africa Institute dwelt on the lingering sense of manifest destiny in Soviet–Ethiopian relations: 'I. Zalkind published (during the early 1920s) a piece, "Abyssinia", in the journal "The New East" ... which concluded with truly prophetic words. Before Ethiopia, he wrote, lie "2 paths, the choice of which to a large extent depends" more on the country itself "than in the pressure and influence of Europe. One path is through the scorching furnace of capitalism ... to experience all stages ... covert or overt colonisation, or to be introduced into the epoch of the growth of the productive forces under the aegis of worker's power, with minimum sacrifice and with maximum aid from those countries where new forms of social construction have already been victorious."' (An. Gromyko, 'SSSR-Efiopia: traditsii i sovremennosti', *Aziya i Afrika Segodnya*, 10, 1979, pp. 3–4.

To be sure, there has been a remarkable degree of historical continuity in the official Russian attitude towards Ethiopia. In 1897, the head of the Russian Diplomatic Mission in Ethiopia, P. M. Vlasov, observed: 'We do not pursue in Abyssinia any selfish or mercantile interests and wish well the actions of the Emperor to strengthen his power and create calm and prosperity in his country ... our main and direct objective is to win the trust of the Emperor and protect him as much as possible from the intrigues of our political rivals' (Alexander Khrenkov, 'Deep Roots', *Asia and Africa Today*, 1, 1985, p. 60).

Boris Orekhov, a *Pravda* journalist, defended the Soviet interest in not totally dissimilar terms eighty-one years later: 'Our country has not pursued and is not pursuing any sort of self-seeking interests in the area of the Horn of Africa. It is guided exclusively by the interests of peace and friendship among the countries of the region, by a desire to strengthen the positions of the progressive forces in both Somalia and Ethiopia. All who are open-minded know this to be the case.' (*Pravda*, 19 March 1978)

156 Karen Brutents, 'Osvobodivshyesya strany v nachale 80-kh godov', p. 107.
157 Ibid., pp. 103, 107.
158 *New York Times*, 22 April 1983.
159 'Somalia: Last-minute deal with IMF', *Africa Now*, 38, June 1984, p. 22.
160 Y. Bochkarev, 'Metamorphosis of the Regime', p. 15.
161 An official of the Barre government quoted in *Newsweek*, 30 August 1982, p. 16.
162 *ARB*, May 1987, p. 8486; Addis Ababa Radio, 16 July 1987.
163 David D. Laitin and Said S. Samatar, *Somalia: Nation in Search of a State*, Westview Press, Boulder, Colorado, 1987, p. 144.
164 Moscow Radio, 14 June 1983.
165 *ARB*, December 1982, p. 6688; *The Times*, 6 August 1983; *ARB*, September 1987, p. 8611.
166 *The Guardian*, 26 April 1986; 'War and Hunger: Ethiopia', p. 5.
167 Karen Brutents, 'Osvobodivshyesya strany v nachale 80-kh godov', p. 104.
168 *Pravda*, 23 April 1982; Karen Brutents, 'Osvobodivshyesya strany v nachale 80-kh godov', p. 113.
169 'Efficiency for the Common Good', *New Times*, 2, 1985, p. 1. The same theme was repeated in the Editorial, 'An Eventful Year', *New Times*, 52, 1987, p. 2.
170 M. Gorbachev's interview in the Chinese newspaper *Liaowang* reproduced in *Soviet Weekly*, 16 January 1988.
171 A. Bovin, 'The Policy of Reform and the Destiny of Socialism', *Asia and Africa Today*, 1, 1988, p. 18; M. Gorbachev cited in A. Karpychev, 'Revolution Means Action ... ', *New Times*, 46, 1987, p. 5.
172 *The Independent*, 23 April 1988.
173 Report on 'Great October and the World Today', by M. Gorbachev in *Izvestiya*, 3 November 1987.
174 A. Bovin, 'The Policy of Reform and the Destiny of Socialism', p. 19.
175 G. Gabrielyan, 'The People Will Have Their Own Party', *New Times*, 36, 1984, p. 21.
176 Soviet Weekly, 9 November 1985.
177 Moscow Radio, English-language Africa broadcast, 27 June 1988.
178 V. Sharayev, 'Signs of a Thaw', *New Times*, 22, 1986, p. 10.

179 *Pravda*, 9 April 1988.
180 *Pravda*, 9 April 1988.
181 *Soviet News*, 22 April 1987, 6371, p. 141.
182 *Soviet News*, 22 April 1987, 6371, p. 141.
183 *Soviet News*, 22 April 1987, 6371, p. 141.
184 Addis Ababa Radio, 24 July 1987.
185 Paul B. Henze, 'Ethiopia – Contrasts and Contradictions', p. 4.
186 Addis Ababa Radio, in Russian, 10 September 1987.
187 Moscow Radio, 12 September 1987.
188 'Mikhail Gorbachev's Answers to Questions from the *Washington Post* and *Newsweek*', *New Times*, 22, 1988, p. 7.
189 Mogadishu Radio, 2 December 1986.
190 E. Sherr, 'Somali: Religiya i Politika', *Narody Azii i Afriki*, 4, 1987, p. 55.
191 'Somalia: Siad Barre Shaken By Bombs' *Africa Now*, January 1987, p. 18; *ARB*, February 1987, p. 8374.
192 *ARB*, September 1987, p. 8603.
193 David D. Laitin and Said S. Samatar, *Somalia: Nation in Search of a State*, pp. 168–9; 'Somalia: A Regime in Troubled Waters', *The African Communist*, 3rd Quarter, 1987, 110, p. 86.
194 E. Sherr, 'Somali: Religiya i Politika', p. 48.
195 *Pravda*, 27 June 1988.
196 E. Sherr, 'Somali: Religiya i Politika', p. 55. Emphasis added.
197 Moscow Radio, English-language Africa broadcast, 17 March 1988.
198 *Pravda*, 27 June 1988.
199 E. Sherr has observed: 'The country [Somalia] will be able to return to a progressive course only when its people and leaders understand the hopelessness of a development along the path of a self-imposed isolation from the contemporary revolutionary forces.' See E. Sherr, 'Somali: Religiya i Politika', p. 55.
200 *ARB*, September 1987, p. 8603.
201 Paul B. Henze was given that figure during a visit to Mogadishu in March 1988. The author is indebted to Paul B. Henze for sharing that information with him.
202 E. Sherr, 'Somali: Religiya i Politika', p. 55.
203 Moscow Radio, English-language Africa broadcast, 24 March 1988.
204 *Soviet News*, 22 April 1987, 6371, p. 141.
205 Addis Ababa Radio, 14 September 1987.
206 David A. Korn, *Ethiopia, the United States and the Soviet Union*, p. xvi.
207 *The Financial Times*, 27 October 1986; *The Sunday Times*, 29 November 1987.
208 Paul B. Henze, 'Ethiopia – Contrasts and Contradictions', pp. 12–15.
209 *The Guardian*, 2 February 1988.
210 Dawit cited in *The Sunday Times*, 29 November 1987; see also Dawit's own account in *The Guardian*, 2 July 1987.
211 Paul B. Henze, who has produced an important study of the Gosplan advisers' critique, generously drew my attention to this development. See also *The Guardian*, 15 September 1987.

212 V. Paukov and G. Polyakov, 'Ethiopia. The Cooperative Movement: Theory and Practice', *Asia and Africa Today*, 1, 1987, p. 61.
213 G. Gabrielyan, 'Novaya Stranitsa Istorii', p. 20.
214 V. Paukov and G. Polyakov, 'Ethiopia. The Cooperative Movement: Theory and Practice', p. 60.
215 Moscow Radio, English-language Africa broadcast, 16 June 1988.
216 Addis Ababa Radio, 27 January 1988; *Soviet Weekly*, 6 February 1988.
217 This information is derived, in part, from interviews with Paul B. Henze of The Rand Corporation on 17 June 1988 and Harold Jenkins of the East Africa Desk in the British Foreign Office on 5 May 1988.
218 *The Financial Times*, 9 June 1988.
219 *Pravda*, 1 February 1988; Addis Ababa Radio, 27 January 1988; *The Daily Telegraph*, 9 February 1988.
220 Addis Ababa Radio, 31 January 1988.
221 *Tass*, 30 December 1987; *Soviet Weekly*, 6 February 1988.
222 'Ethiopia: Mengistu Soldiers On', *Africa Confidential*, 1 July 1988, 29, 13, p. 2.
223 Radio Voice of Ethiopian Unity (Radio station of opposition group, the Ethiopian People's Democratic Alliance, the EPDA), 21 October 1987.
224 Boris Asoyan, 'Africa is not so far away: How we looked at that continent and what we see there today', *Literaturnaya Gazeta*, 7 October 1987.
225 *Pravda*, 8 February 1988.
226 *Pravda*, 8 February 1988.
227 V. Dashichev, 'Vostok-Zapad: Poisk Novykh Otnosheniy', *Literaturnaya Gazeta*, 22 May 1988.
228 V. Dashichev in 'October Revolution, Peace, Peaceful Coexistence' (a Round Table discussion), *New Times*, 44, 1987, p. 6.
229 V. Dashichev, 'Vostok-Zapad:Poisk Novykh Otnosheniy'.
230 Information derived from interviews with Paul B. Henze and Harold Jenkins.
231 'Ethiopia: Mengistu Soldiers On', *Africa Confidential*, p. 2.
232 Suna Radio, English-language broadcast, 19 January 1988.
233 Details of the Yugoslav–Ethiopian arms deal remain scant. According to the BBC2 TV programme, 'Rough Guide to Europe', 15 August 1988, the arms agreement was revealed in an article by Gorazd Suhadolnik in *Mladina*, February–March 1988.
234 Y. Bochkarev, 'A Pack of Lies', pp. 16–17.
235 An. Gromyko, 'Ruku ob ruku', p. 12.
236 *Soviet News*, 10 August 1988, No 6437, p. 317.
237 Moscow Radio, English-language Africa broadcast, 9 June 1988.
238 Moscow Radio, English-language Africa broadcast, 23 March 1988; *The Financial Times*, 24 March 1988.
239 A confidential source provided this information.
240 Addis Ababa Radio, 31 March 1988.
241 *ARB*, May 1987, p. 8838.
242 The full text of the Ethiopian–Somali agreement was reproduced in *ARB*, May 1987, p. 8837.

243 *The Indian Ocean Newsletter*, 9 April 1988.
244 *Pravda*, 8 April 1988.
245 *Tass*, 6 April 1988.
246 A. Adamishin, USSR Deputy Minister of Foreign Affairs, interviewed in 'Peace Be With You, Africa!', *New Times*, 21, 1988, p. 19.
247 *Pravda*, 27 June 1988.
248 'Peace Be With You, Africa!', p. 19.
249 *Soviet News*, 27 July 1988, 6435, p. 302.
250 E. Sherr, 'Islam v Somali i Efiopii', p. 59.
251 Moscow Radio, English-language Africa broadcast, 2 June 1988.
252 Y. Etinger, 'Socialist Orientation: Deeds and Slogans', *Moscow News*, 18, 1988.
253 'Peace Be With You, Africa!', p. 18.
254 President Siad's opponents, the SNM, made this claim in a broadcast through their station Radio Halgan, 25 November 1986.
255 *Soviet News*, 27 July 1988, 6435, p. 302.
256 Addis Ababa Radio, 31 March 1988.
257 *ARB*, May 1988, p. 8837; *The Times*, 25 May 1988; Mengistu, interview in *New York Times*, 28 November 1988.
258 Y. Etinger, 'Socialist Orientation: Deeds and Slogans'.
259 Ibid.
260 Mersha Assefa of Addis Ababa and Afewerk Tekle, Deputy to the Ethiopian National Assembly, are among those Ethiopian personalities who have heaped praise on Gorbachev's perestroika campaign. See Y. Shevchenko, 'Glasnost Needs No Translation', *New Times*, 26, 1987, p. 16 and 'Highlight of the Week', *New Times*, 26, 1988, p. 4.
261 A. Nuikin, 'Idealy ili interesy', *Novyy Mir*, 1, Yanvar', 1988, pp. 190–211.
262 *Soviet News*, 10 August 1988, 6437, p. 317.
263 Mengistu, interview in *New York Times*, 28 November 1988.

Bibliography

Books, documents and articles

Abdi, Said Yusuf, 'Cuba's Role in Africa: Revolutionary or Reactionary?', *Horn of Africa*, 1:4 (October-December 1978), pp. 17–24.

'Self-determination for Ogaden Somalis', *Horn of Africa*, 1:1 (1978), pp. 20–5

Abdurakhimov, A, 'Respublika Somalia-Nezavisimoye gosudarstvo Afriki', *Kommunist Uzbekistana*, 7 (1965), pp. 90–92.

Adamishin, A, Interview in *New Times*, 21 (1988), pp. 18–19.

Adomeit, Hannes, 'Soviet Risk Taking and Crisis Behaviour: A Theoretical and Empirical Analysis', Ph.D Dissertation, University of Columbia, (1977).

Albright, David E., ed., *Africa and International Communism* (London: Macmillan Press Ltd, 1980)

Aleksandrenko, G. N., *Burzhuaznyy Federalizm; Kriticheskiy Analiz Burzhuaznykh Federatsiy i Burzhuaznykh Teorii Federalizma* (Kiev: Izdatel'stvo Akademii Nauk Ukraynskoy SSSR, 1962).

Alekseyev, L A, *Africa: Struggle for Political and Economic Liberation* (Moscow: 'Znanie', 1978).

Amin, Samir, *Imperialism and Unequal Development* (Hassocks: The Harvester Press, 1977).

'An eventful year', *New Times*, 52 (1987), p. 2.

Arbatov, G A, 'O Sovetsko-Amerikanskikh otnosheniye', *Kommunist*, 3 (1973), pp. 101–13.

'Politicheskiy god i problema politicheskikh prioritetov', *SShA: Ekonomika, Politika i Ideologiya* (hereafter referred to as *SShA*), 6 (June 1972), pp. 3–15.

Armaments and Disarmaments in the Nuclear Age: A Handbook (New Jersey: Humanities Press, 1976).

'Armiya i osvoboditelnoye dvizheniye', *Aziya i Afrika Segodnya*, 9 (1966), p. 3.

The Arms Trade with the Third World (London: Elek and Stockholm International Peace Research Institute (SIPRI), 1971).

Art, Robert J., 'To What Ends Military Power?', *International Security*, 4:4 (Spring 1980), pp. 3–35.

Asoyan, B., 'Africa is Not so Far Away: How We Looked at that Continent and What We See There Today', *Literaturnaya Gazeta* (7 October 1987).

'In the new Somalia', *New Times*, 44 (1976), pp. 24–25.

Aspaturian, Vernon, V., 'Soviet Global Power and the Correlation of Forces', *Problems of Communism*, 29:3 (May-June 1980), pp. 1–18.

Avakov, R., 'Novoye myshleniye i problema izucheniya razvivayushchikhsya stran', *Mirovaya Ekonomika i Mezhdunarodnyye Otnosheniya* (hereafter referred to as MEiMO), 11 (1987), pp. 48–62.

Avakov, R. and G. Mirskiy, 'O klassovoy strukture v staborazvitykh stranakh', *MEiMO*, 4 (1962), pp. 68–82.

Ayele, Negussay, 'The Horn of Africa: Revolutionary Developments and Western Reactions', *Northeast African Studies*, 3:1 (1981), pp. 15–29.

Ayoob, Mohammed L., 'The Horn of Africa: Regional Conflict and Superpower Involvement', *Canberra Papers on Strategy and Defence* (Canberra: Australian National University, 1978), pp. 1–41.

Barber, James and Michael Smith, eds., *The Nature of Foreign Policy: A Reader* (Milton Keynes: Open University Press, 1974).

Barinov, M., 'Socialist Ethiopia Moves Confidently Ahead', *International Affairs* (Moscow), 11 (November 1980), pp. 22–8.

Barnet, Richard J., *The Giants: Russia and America* (New York: Simon and Schuster, 1977).

Bayeh, Berhanu, Interview in *World Marxist Review*, 19:8 (1976).

Interview in *World Marxist Review*, 21:4 (1978).

Baylis, John and Gerald Segal, ed., *Soviet Strategy* (London: Croom Helm, 1981).

Bayne, E. A., 'Birthday for Somalia', *American University Field Service Report, Northeast Africa Series*, 7:9 (August 1961).

Bell, J. Bowyer, 'Strategic Implications of the Soviet Presence in Somalia', *Orbis*, 19:2 (Summer 1975), pp. 402–11.

Bereket Habte, Selassie, *Conflict and Intervention in the Horn of Africa* (New York: Monthly Review Press, 1980).

'Political Leadership in Crisis: The Ethiopian Case', *Horn of Africa*, 3:1 (1980), pp. 3–13.

Bhardwag, Raman G., *The Dilemma of the Horn of Africa* (New Delhi: Sterling Publishers, 1979).

Bissell, Richard, E, 'Soviet Use of Proxies in the Third World: The Case of Yemen', *Soviet Studies*, 30:1 (January 1978), pp. 87–106

Black, Max, ed., *The Importance of Language* (Englewood Cliffs, New Jersey: Prentice Hall, 1962).

Blechman, Barry M. and Douglas M. Hart, 'Afghanistan and the 1946 Iran Analogy', *Survival*, 22 (International Institute for Strategic Studies), pp. 248–253.

Bochkarev, Y., 'Ethiopia: Looking to the Future', *New Times*, 38 (1984), p. 11.

'Fighting Hunger', *New Times*, 48 (1984), pp. 10–11.

'Grain and Slander', *New Times*, 21 (1985), p. 21.

'Metamorphosis of the Regime', *New Times*, 14 (1983), p. 14–15.

'A Pack of Lies', *New Times*, 11 (1987), pp. 16–17.

'What a Hope!', *New Times*, 20 (1986), pp. 16–17.

Bogdanov, B., 'Ethiopia: The Russian Traveller's Feat', *Asia and Africa Today*, 4 (July-August 1983), p. 59.

Borbatov, O. M. and L. Y. Cherkasskiy, *Sotrudnichestvo SSSR so Stranami Arabskogo Vostoga i Afriki* (Moscow: Izdatel'stvo 'Nauka': Glavnaya Redaktsiya Vostochnoy Literatury, 1973).

Borisov, D., 'The Developments in Ethiopia', *New Times*, 8 (1975), pp. 10–11.

Bovin, A., 'The Policy of Reform and the Destiny of Socialism', *Asia and Africa Today*, 1 (1988), pp. 16–19.

Brezhnev, L. I., *KPSS i Bor'be za Yedinstvo vsekh Revolyutsionnykh i Mirolyubivykh Sil* (Moscow: Izdatel'stvo 'Mysl', 1979).

Leniniskim Kursom, 3 vols. (Moscow: Izdatel'stvo 'Progress', 1972).

On the Policy of the Soviet Union and the International Situation (New York: Doubleday, 1973).

Brind, Harry, 'Soviet Policy in the Horn of Africa', *International Affairs*, 60:1 (Winter 1983–4), pp. 75–95.

Brown, Neville, 'Soviet Naval Expansion – The Global Scene Assessed', *New Middle East*, 30 (March 1971), pp. 17–21.

Brutents, K., 'Osvobodivshyesya strany v nachale 80-kh godov', *Kommunist*, 3 (1984), pp. 102–13.

'Pravyashchaya revolyutsionnaya demokratiya: nekotoryye cherty prakticheskoy deyatelnosti', *MEiMO*, 11 (1972), pp. 104–17 and 12 (1972), pp. 115–29.

Brzezinski, Zbigniew, *Power and Principle* (London: Weidenfield and Nicolson and Son, 1983).

Bukalov, A, 'A Far-away Land', *Asia and Africa Today*, 4 (1987), pp. 78–80.

'From Monarchy to Republic', *New Times*, 36 (1987), pp. 20–2.

Bull, Hedley, ed., *Intervention in World Politics* (Oxford: Oxford University Press, 1984).

Chaliand, Gérard, 'The Horn of Africa's Dilemma', *Foreign Policy*, 30 (Spring 1978), 116–31.

Charles, Milene, *The Soviet Union and Africa: The History of Involvement* (Washington DC: University Press of America, 1980).

Chernenko, E. F., 'Osnovnyye napravleniya ekonomicheskoy politiki Somaliyskoy Demokraticheskoy Respubliki', *Narody Azii i Afriki*, 5 (1975), pp. 19–27.

'V Somaliyskoy stepi', *Aziya i Afriki Segodnya*, 8 (1974), pp. 31–3.

Chubin, Shahram, 'Repercussions of the Crisis in Iran', *Survival* (IISS), 21:3 (May–June 1979), pp. 98–106.

Clapham, Christopher, 'Conflicts in Africa', *Adelphi Papers, No 93*, (London: IISS, December 1972), pp. 1–23.

Transformation in Revolutionary Ethiopia (Cambridge: Cambridge University Press, 1988).

Clay, Jason W. and Bonnie K. Holcomb, 'Politics and the Ethiopian Famine 1984–1985', *A Cultural Survival Inc. Occasional Paper* (Cambridge), 20, pp. 1–199.

Cliffe, Lionel, Basil Davidson and Bereket Habte Selassie, eds., *Behind the War in Eritrea* (Nottingham: Spokesman, 1980).

'Contribution to Somali Development', *New Times*, 32 (1973), p. 7.

'Crisis in Asia', *Survival* (IISS), 22:4 (July-August 1980), pp. 171–6.

Crozier, Brian, 'The Soviet Presence in Somalia', *Conflict Studies*, 54 (February 1975), pp. 3–19.

Dallin, David, *Soviet Foreign Policy After Stalin* (London: Methuen and Co., 1960).

Darch, Colin, *A Soviet View of Africa: An Annotated Bibliography on Ethiopia, Somalia and Djibouti* (Boston: G. K. Hall & Co., 1980).

Dashichev, V., 'Vostok-zapad: poisk novykh otnosheniy', *Literaturnaya Gazeta* (22 May 1988).

David, Steven, 'Realignment in the Horn: The Soviet Advantage', *International Security*, 4:2 (Winter 1979–89), pp. 69–90.

Davidson, A., 'African Diary: Nikolai Gumilev', *Asia and Africa Today*, 4 (1988), pp. 39–42.

Davidson, A. B., D. A. Ol'derogge and V. G. Solodovnikov, eds., *Russia and Africa* (Moscow: 'Nauka' Publishing House, 1966).

Davidson, B., 'Somalia Beats the Drought', *West Africa*, 3039 (22 September 1975), 1115–16.

Davydov, L., 'The USSR and Ethiopia: Close Friendship and Co-operation', *International Affairs* (Moscow), 2 (February 1979), pp. 90–4.

Davydov, V. F., 'Voyennoye-politicheskoye sotrudnichestvo SShA i Britanii: 'Vostok Suezy'', *SShA* (Moscow), 11 (1971).

Davydov, V. F. and V. A. Kremenyuk, 'Strategiya SShA v rayone Indiyskogo Okeana', *SShA* (Moscow), 5 (May 1973).

Davydov, Y. P., V. Zhurkin and V. S. Rudnev, eds., *Doktrina Niksona* (Moscow; Izdatel'stvo 'Nauka', 1972).

Dawisha, Adeed and Karen Dawisha, eds., *The Soviet Union in the Middle East: Policies and Perspectives* (London: Heinemann and Royal Institute of International Affairs, 1982).

Dawisha, K., *Soviet Foreign Policy Towards Egypt* (London: Macmillan Press, 1979).

Degras, Jane, ed., *Soviet Documents in Foreign Policy*, 3 vols. (London: Oxford University Press, 1953).

Denisov, E., 'Vazhnyy etap razvitiya', *Aziya i Afrika Segodnya*, 9 (1972), pp. 25–8.

Denisov, E. and V. Sharayev, 'Efiopiya; stroitsya avangardnaya partiya', *Aziya i Afrika Segodnya*, 11 (1980), pp. 10–13.

Deutscher, Isaac, *Stalin: A Political Biography*, revised edition (Harmondsworth, Middlesex: Penguin Books, 1966).

Diplomaticheskiy slovar', 2 vols. (Moscow: Izdatel'stvo Politicheskoy Literatury, 1971).

Dolgopolov, Y. I., ed., *U Karty Indiyskogo Okeana* (Moscow: Voennoye Izdatel'stvo Ministerstva Oborony SSSR, 1974).

Dolgov, A., 'Somali: puteshestviye na yug', *Aziya i Afrika Segodnya*, 6 (1976), pp. 30–2.

Donaldson, Robert H., ed., *The Soviet Union in the Third World: Successes and Failures* (London: Croom Helm, 1981).

Doronin, I., 'Efiopiya smotrit vpered', *Nauka i Religiya*, 9 (1975), pp. 75–9.

'Ethiopia Without the Emperor', *New Times*, 38 (1974), pp. 12–13.

Dougherty, James E, *The Horn of Africa: A Map of Political Strategic Conflict* (Washington DC: Institute for Foreign Policy Analysis Inc., Special Report, April 1982).

Dowse, Robert E. and John A. Hughes, *Political Sociology* (London: John Wiley and Sons, 1972).

Drabek, Anne Gordon and Wilfrid Knapp, *The Politics of African and Middle Eastern States: An Annotated Bibliography* (Oxford: Pergamon Press, 1976).

Drambyants, G. G., *Persidskiy Zaliv bez Romantiki* (Moscow: Izdatel'stvo 'Mezdunarodnyye Otnosheniya', 1968).

Duncan, W. Raymond, ed., *Soviet Policy in the Third World* (New York: Pergamon Press, 1980).

Edmonds, Robin, *Soviet Foreign Policy 1962–1973: The Paradox of Super Power* (London: Oxford University Press, 1975).

'Efficiency for the Common Good', *New Times*, 2 (1985), p. 1.

Elyanov, A., *Efiopiya* (Moscow: Izdatel'stvo 'Mysl', 1967).

Eprile, Cecil, 'Sudan; The Long War', *Conflict Studies*, 21 (London: The Institute for the Study of Conflict Ltd, 1972), pp. 1–20.

Erlich, Haggai, *The Struggle over Eritrea, 1962–1978: War and Revolution in the Horn of Africa* (Stanford, California; Hoover Institution Press, 1983).

'Ethiopia: Policy Statement', *New Times* 21 (1974), p. 9

Etinger, Y. Y., *Mezhgosudarstvennyye Otnosheniya v Afrike: Politicheskiye Problemy: Evolyutsiya i Organizatsionnyye Formy* (Moscow: Izdatel'stvo 'Nauka', 1972).

Evans, John David, Jr, 'The Dilemma of the Horn: A Study of Conflict in Northeast Africa', *Ph.D Dissertation, University of Georgetown* (1967).

'Events in Ethiopia', *New Times*, 21 (1974), p. 9.

Farah, Nuruddin, *Sweet and Sour Milk* (London; Allison and Busby, 1979).

Farer, Tom J., *War Clouds on the Horn of Africa: The Widening Storm*, 2nd revised edition (New York: Carnegie Endowment for International Peace, 1979).

Fazlov, M., Interview in *New Times*, 14 (1976).

Fedulova, N., 'Mezhimperialisticheskaya bor'ba za vliyaniye v basseyne Tikhogo Okeana', *MEiMO*, 9 (1972), pp. 33–50.

Fenwick, C. G., 'Intervention by way of Propaganda', *American Journal of International Law*, 35 (October 1941), pp. 626–31.

Feuchtwanger, Edgar J. and Peter Nailor, eds., *The Soviet Union and the Third World* (London: Macmillan, 1981).

Filippov, A., 'Sovetsko-Efiopskiye Torgovye Svyazi' *Vneshnyaya Torgovlya*, 9 (1987), pp. 42–3.

Finer, Samuel E., *The Man on Horseback: The Role of the Military in Politics*, 2nd edition (Harmondsworth, Middlesex: Peregrine Books, 1975).

Fitzgerald, James F., 'Gunboat Diplomacy and the Horn', *Horn of Africa*, 2:2 (1979), pp. 49–53.

FitzGibbon, Louis, *The Evaded Duty* (London: Rex Collings, 1985).

Fokeyev, G. V., *Vneshnyaya Politika Stran Afriki* (Moscow: Izdatel'stvo 'Mezdunarodnyye Otnosheniya', 1968).

Freedman, Robert O., ed., *World Politics and the Arab–Israeli Conflict* (New York: Pergamon Press, 1979).

'Friendly Aid in Coping with the Elements', *Asia and Africa Today*, 2 (March–April 1985), p. 56.

Gabrielyan, G., 'Novaya Stranitsa Istorii', *Aziya i Afrika Segodnya*, 12 (1987), pp. 18–20.

'The People Will Have Their Own Party', *New Times*, 36 (1984), p. 21.

'Rebirth of a Nation', *New Times*, 35 (1986), 22.

Galperin, G, 'Aid: Facts and Fictions', *New Times*, 2 (1985), pp. 12–13.

Efiopiya: Revolyutsiya i Dereviya (Moscow: Izdatel'stvo 'Nauka': Glavnaya Redaktsiya Vostochnoy Literatury, 1985).'

'Eritreyskaya problema – fakty i domysli', *Novoye Vremya*, 5 (1979), pp. 26–8.

'Ethiopia: Some Aspects of the Nationalities' Question', *The African Communist* 83:4th quarter (1980), pp. 53–61.

'Lyudy v zelennykh shinelyakh', *Aziya i Afrika Segodnya*, 9 (1966), pp. 14–15.

'In and Around the Horn of Africa', *New Times*, 32 (1977), pp. 22–4.

'Natsional'no-demokraticheskiye preobrazovaniya v Efiopii', *Aziya i Afrika Segodnya*, 8 (1976), pp. 9–12.

'Revolyutsiya v Efiopii: osobennosti razvitiya', *Aziya i Afrika Segodnya*, 3 (1978), pp. 9–12.

Gavrilov, N. I., ed., *Nezavisimyye Strany Afriki* (Moscow: Izdatel'stvo Institut Afriki Adademii Nauk SSSR, 1965).

Gavrilov, N. I. and G. B. Starushenko, ed., *Africa: Problems of Socialist Orientation* (Moscow: 'Nauka', 1976).

Gavshon, Arthur, *Crisis in Africa: Battleground of East and West* (Harmondsworth, Middlesex: Penguin Books, 1981).

Geographical Distribution of Financial Flows to Developing Countries 1983–1986, (Paris: Organisation of Economic Co-operation and Development, 1988).

Gerasimov, K., 'Ethiopia Forges Ahead'. *New Times*, 51 (1971), pp. 28–30.

'Ethiopia: The Reactionaries Resist', *New Times*, 15 (1975), pp. 12–13.

'Ethiopia Without the Crown', *New Times*, 51 (1974), pp. 26–8.

Gilkes, Patrick, *The Dying Lion: Feudalism and Modernization in Ethiopia* (London: Julian Friedmann Publishers Ltd, 1975).

Glassman, Jon D., *Arms for the Arabs* (Baltimore: John Hopkins University Press, 1975).

Goldman, Kjell and Gunnar Sjöstedt, eds., *Power, Capabilities, Interdependence: Problems in the Study of International Influence* (London: Sage Publications Inc., 1979).

Gonzalez, Edward, 'Complexities of Cuban Foreign Policy', *Problems of Communism*, 26:6 (November-December 1977), pp. 1–15.

Gorelick, Robert E., 'Pan-Somalism vs Territorial Integrity', *Horn of Africa*, 3:4 (1980), pp. 31–5.

Gorman, Robert F., 'The Anatomy of an International Hot Spot: The Determinants of Conflict, Foreign Policy Change and Intervention on the Horn of Africa', Ph.D Dissertation, University of Oregon (1979).

Political Conflict on the Horn of Africa (New York: Praeger, 1981).

'Prospects for Reconciliation in the Horn of Africa', *Horn of Africa*, 4:4 (1981–2), pp. 3–14.

Gorodnov, V. and N. Kosukhin, 'In the Somali Democratic Republic', *International Affairs* (Moscow), 5 (May 1972), pp. 102–6.

Gorovy, O., 'Ya byl v Somaliye', *Aziya i Afrika Segodnya*, 4 (1962), pp. 40–1.

Greenfield, Richard, *Ethiopia* (London: Pall Mall Press, 1965).

Greig, Ian, *The Communist Challenge to Africa* (Richmond: Foreign Affairs Publishing Co. Ltd, 1977).

'Third World: Moscow Changes Direction', *Soviet Analyst*, 17:2 (27 January 1988), pp. 3–4.

Grigoryev, Y., 'A West German Journalist in Ethiopia', *International Affairs* (Moscow), 6 (1958), pp. 112–14.

Gromyko, A., V. Khvostov and B. Ponomarev, eds., *Istoriya Vneshnei Politiki SSSR*, 2 vols. (Moscow: Izdatel'stvo 'Nauka', 1971).

Gromyko, A., 'Leninskaya strategiya mira: yedinstvo teorii i praktiki', *Kommunist*, 14 (September 1976), pp. 11–31.

Gromyko, An. A., 'Ruka ob ruku', *Aziya i Afrika Segodnya*, 1 (1987), pp. 12–13.

Sovetsko-Efiopskiye Otnosheniya Izucheniye Efiopii v SSSR, (Moscow: Izdatel'stvo 'Nauka', 1979).

'Sovetsko-Efiopskiye svyazy', *Narody Azii i Afriki*, 1 (1980), pp. 3–13.

'SSSR-Efiopiya: traditsii i sovremennost'', *Aziya i Afrika Segodnya*, 10 (1979), pp. 2–6.

Through Russian Eyes: President Kennedy's 1036 Days (Washington DC: International Library Inc, 1973).

Gromyko, An. A., ed., *Afrika v Mezhdunarodnykh Otnosheniyakh* (Moscow: Izdatel'stvo 'Nauka', 1970).

Gupta, Vijay, 'The Ethiopia–Somali Conflict and the Role of the External Powers', *Foreign Affairs Reports*, 27:3 (1978), pp. 39–57.

Gurnov, A., 'Washington's Grenada "Experiment" and its Meaning', *New Times*, 51 (December 1984), pp. 12–13.

Halliday, Fred, 'The Soviet Union and the Horn of Africa', in *Das Horn von Afrika vom 'Scramble for Africa' zum Ost-West Konflikt* (Bonn: Friedrich Ebert Stiftung, 1983), pp. 163–9.

Threat from the East? Soviet Policy from Afghanistan and Iran to the Horn of Africa (Harmondsowrth, Middlesex: Penguin Books, 1981).

Halliday, Fred and Maxine Molyneux, *The Ethiopian Revolution* (London: Verso, 1981).

Hancock, Graham, *Ethiopia: The Challenge of Hunger* (London: Victor Gollancz Ltd, 1985).

Hansen, Robert W., 'Soviet Images of American Foreign Policy 1960–1972', Ph.D Dissertation, University of Princeton (1975).

Heikal, Mohammed, *The Road to Ramadan* (Glasgow: Fontana, 1976).

Hensel, Howard M., 'Soviet Policy in the Persian Gulf: 1968–1975', Ph.D Dissertation, University of Virginia (1976).

Henze, Paul B., 'Arming the Horn 1960–1980', Washington DC, Working Paper 43, International Security Series, Woodrow Wilson Center for Scholars, Smithsonian Institution (July 1982), pp. 637–56.

'A Challenging Decade – The Economic Development of Ethiopia and Kenya, 1975–1984', Paper prepared for the third Annual Conference on the Horn of Africa, New York (May 1988).

'Christian Brothers and Imperial Ambitions', Washington DC, unpublished paper (October 1984), pp. 1–32.

'Communism and Ethiopia', *Problems of Communism*, 30:3 (May-June 1981), pp. 55–74.

Eritrea – The Dilemmas of Marxism (Philadelphia: Foreign Policy Research Institute, 1988).

'Eritrea: The Endless War', *The Washington Quarterly*, 9:2 (Spring 1986), pp. 23–36.

'Ethiopia – Contrasts and Contradictions', *Paper 7389* (Santa Monica, California: The Rand Corporation, October 1987), pp. 1–32.

Flexible Opportunism (Wisconsin: Foreign Area Research, December 1986), pp. 1–120.

'Getting a Grip on the Horn' in Walter Laqueur, ed., *The Pattern of Soviet Conduct in the Third World* (New York: Praeger, 1983).

'History and the Horn', *Problems of Communism*, 32:3 (January-February 1983), pp. 66–75.

'Marxism-Leninism in Ethiopia: political impasse and economic deterioration' in Michael Clough, ed., *Reassessing the Soviet Challenge in Africa, Policy Papers in International Affairs*, 25 (Berkeley, California, Institute of International Studies: University of California, June 1985), pp. 31–47.

'Rebels and Separatists in Ethiopia: Regional Resistance to a Marxist Regime' (Santa Monica: The Rand Corporation, R-3347-USDP, December 1985), pp. 1–94.

'Russians and the Horn: Opportunism and the Long View', Paper no. 5 (California: European American Institute for Security Research, Summer 1983), pp. 1–53.

'The Soviet Impact on African Political Dynamics'. Paper prepared for conference sponsored by Hoover Institution, Washington DC (July 1988).

'Highlight of the Week', *New Times*, 26 (1988), p. 4.

Holowaty, Luba Anastasia, 'The Soviet Union and the Countries of the African Horn: A Case Study of Soviet Perceptions and Policies, 1959–1968', Ph.D Dissertation, University of Pennsylvania (1970).

Holsti, K. J., *International Politics: A Framework for Analysis* (Englewood Cliffs, New Jersey: Prentice Hall Inc., 1967).

Horn, Robert C., 'Indian–Soviet Relations in 1969: A Watershed Year?', *Orbis*, 19:4 (Winter 1976), pp. 1539–63.

Hough, Jerry F. *Soviet Leadership in Transition* (Washington DC: The Brookings Institute, 1980).

Hunt, Kenneth and Uwe Nerlich, eds., *The Flanking Strategy: Regional Instability and Soviet Power Projection* (London: Macmillan, 1981).

Inozemtsev, N., 'Sovremennyye SShA i Sovetskaya Amerikanistika', *SShA* (Moscow), 1 (January 1970), pp. 6–14.

Irkin, Yu., 'Efiopiya na puti sotsialisticheskoy orientatsii', *Kommunist Voruzhennykh Sil*, 2 (January 1979), pp. 81–5.

Ismagilova, R. N., *Etnicheskiye Problemy Sovremennoy Tropicheskoy Afriki* (Moscow: Izdatel'stvo 'Nauka', 1973).

Ivanov, Y., 'Productive Visit', *New Times*, 33 (1976), p. 16.

Jacobsen, C. G., *Soviet Strategic Initiatives: Challenge and Response* (New York: Praeger, 1979).

Jansson, Kurt, Michael Harris and Angela Penrose, *The Ethiopian Famine* (London: Zed Books, 1987).

Jesman, Czeslaw, *The Russians in Ethiopia: an Essay in Futility* (London: Chatto & Windrus, 1958).

Joffe, A. E., 'Nachalnyy etap vzaymootnosheniy Sovetskogo Soyuza s Arabskimi i Afrikanskimi stranami 1923–1932', *Narody Azii i Afriki*, 6 (1965), pp. 57–66.

Kaldor, Mary, *The Disintegrating West* (Harmondsworth, Middlesex: Penguin Books, 1978).

Kaplan, Irving, *Area Handbook for Somalia* (Washington DC: US Government Printing Office, 1977).

Kaplan, Irving et al., *Area Handbook for Ethiopia* (Washington DC: American University Press, 1971).

Kaplan, Morton A., ed., *Great Issues of International Politics* (Chicago: Aldine Publishing Company, 1970).

Kaplan, Stephen S., ed., *Diplomacy of Power: Soviet Armed Forces as a Political Instrument* (Washington DC: The Brookings Institution, 1981).

Kapuscinski, Ryszard, *The Emperor: Downfall of an Autocrat* (London: Quartet Books, 1983).

Karpychev, A., 'Revolution Means Action . .', *New Times*, 46 (1987), p. 5.

Katz, Donald R., 'Children's Revolution: A Bloodbath in Ethiopia', *Horn of Africa*, 1:3 (July-September 1978), pp. 3–11.

Kazakov, G. V., *Somali na Sovremennom Etape Razvitiya* (Moscow: Izdatel'stvo 'Mysl', 1976).

Kelemen, Paul, 'The Politics of the Famine in Ethiopia and Eritrea', *Manchester Sociology Occasional Papers*, 17 (University of Manchester, March 1985), pp. 1–34.

Keohane, R. O., 'The Big Influence of Small Allies', *Foreign Policy*, 2 (Spring 1971), pp. 161–82.

Khazanov, A., 'Antikolonial'noye dvizheniye v Somali pod predvoditel'stvom Mukhammeda bin Abdally', *Problemy Vostokovedeniya*, 2 (1960), pp. 113–22.

'Problema mezhgosudarstvennykh konfliktov v Afrike i sobytiya na Afrikanskom Roge', *Aziya i Afrika Segodnya*, 7 (July 1978), pp. 21–2.

Khazanov, A. M., *Osvoboditel'naya Bor'ba Narodov Vostochnoy Afriki Posle Vtoroy Mirovoy Voyny* (Moscow: Izdatel'stvo Sotsialisticheskoy Literatury, 1962).

Somaliyskaya Respublika: Istoricheskiy Ocherk (Moscow: Izdatel'stvo Akademii Nauk SSSR, Institut Narodov Azii, 1961).

Khrenkov, A., 'Deep Roots', *Asia and Africa Today*, pp. 59–61.

Knorr, Klaus, 'On the International Uses of Military Force in the Contemporary World', *Orbis*, 21:1 (Spring 1977), pp. 5–27.

Kokiev, A., 'Efiopiya: po puti obnovleniya', *Aziya i Afrika Segodnya*, 2 (1975), pp. 19–21.

'Puti razvitiya Efiopskoy derevni', *Aziya i Afrika Segodnya*, 2 (1972), pp. 20–1.

Komarova, L. A., 'O printsipe nevmeshatel'stva', *Sovetskoye Gosudarstvo i Pravo*, 6 (1967), pp. 129–32.

'Printsip nevmeshatel'stva i narody Afriki', *Uchenyye Zapiski Instituta Mezhdunarodnykh Otnosheniy*, 16 (1963), pp. 40–1.

Kondrashov, S., 'Efiopskiye zarisovki', *Aziya i Afrika Segodnya*, 2 (1979), 32–35.

Pervyy Raz v Somali (Moscow: Izdatel'stvo 'Izvestiya', 1961).

'What the African Governments Discussed in Cairo', *New Times*, 15 (1961), 3–5.

Korn, David A., *Ethiopia, The United States and The Soviet Union* (London: Croom Helm, 1986).

Korovikov, V. I., *Efiopiya-Gody Revolytsii* (Moscow: Izdatel'stvo 'Mysl', 1979).

Korovikov, V., 'A New Life Comes to Ethiopia', *International Affairs* (Moscow), 3 (1977), pp. 127–34.

Korovin, E., 'Jungle Law versus the Law of Nations', *New Times*, 1 (1957), pp. 15–17.

Kosukhin, N. D. and E. S. Sherr, 'Sovetsko-Somaliyskaya ekspeditsiya', *Narody Azii i Afriki*, 5 (1972), pp. 222–7.

Kozhevnikov, F., *Sovetskoye Gosudarstvo i Mezhdunarodnoye Pravo* (Moscow, Yuridicheskoye: Izdatel'stvo Ministerstva Yustitsii SSSR, 1947).

Kramer, John M., 'Soviet-CEMA Energy Ties', *Problems of Communism*, 34:4 (July-August 1985), pp. 32–47.

Kudryavtsev, V., 'The Indian Ocean in the Plans of Imperialism', *International Affairs* (Moscow), 11 (1974), pp. 114–18.

Kulish, V. M., ed., *Voyennaya Sila i Mezhdunarodnyye Otnosheniya* (Moscow: Izdatel'stvo 'Mezhdunarodnyye Otnosheniya', 1972).

Kuritsin, Yu., 'Somalian Encounters', *New Times*, 38 (1975), pp. 25–7.

Laitin, David, 'The Political Economy of Military Rule in Somalia', *Journal of Modern African Studies*, 14:3 (1976), pp. 449–70.

'The War in the Ogaden: Implications for Siyaad's Role in Somali History', *Journal of Modern African Studies*, 17:1 (1979), pp. 95–115.

Laitin, David D. and Said S. Samatar, *Somalia: Nation in Search of a State* (Boulder, Colorado: Westview Press, 1987).

Larin, V., 'Who Gains by the Tension?', *New Times*, 19 (1977), p. 10.

Lavrishchev, A. A., ed., *Razvivayushchiyesya Strany v Mirovoy Politike* (Moscow: Izdatel'stvo 'Nauka', Glavnaya redaktsiya vostochnoy literatury, 1970).

Lebedev, N., 'Proletarian Internationalism and its Bankrupt Critics', *International Affairs* (Moscow), 8 (1970), pp. 57–64.

Ledeen, Michael A., 'The Israeli connection', *The Washington Review* (Special Supplement), (May 1978), pp. 46–9.

Lefort, René, *Ethiopia: An Heretical Revolution?* (London: Zed Press, 1983).

Legvold, Robert, 'The Nature of Soviet Power', *Foreign Affairs*, 56:1 (October 1977), pp. 49–71.

Legum, Colin, *After Angola: The War Over Southern Africa* (London: Rex Collings, 1976).

Ethiopia: The Fall of Haile Selassie's Empire (London: Rex Collings, 1975).

Legum, Colin and Bill Lee, *Conflict in the Horn of Africa* (London, Rex Collings, 1977).

The Horn of Africa in Continuing Crisis (New York: Africana Publishing Company, 1979).

Lenin, V. I. *Collected Works*, vols. 1–45 (Moscow: Progress Publishers, 1965).

Levin, I. D. ed., *Konstitutsiy Gosudarstv Blizhnego i Srednogo Vostoka* (Moscow: Izdatel'stvo 'Mezhdunarodnyye Otnosheniya', 1956).

Lewis, I. M. *A Modern History of Somalia: Nation and State in the Horn of Africa*, 2nd revised edition (London: Longman, 1980).

'The Politics of the 1969 Somali coup', *Journal of Modern African Studies*, 10:3 (October 1972), pp.383–408.

Lewis, I. M., ed., *Nationalism and Self-Determination in the Horn of Africa* (London: Ithaca Press, 1983).

Lewytzkyi, Borys, ed., *Who's Who in the Soviet Union* (London: K. G. Saur, 1984).

Light, Margot, *The Soviet Theory of International Relations* (London: Wheatsheaf, 1988).

Lisovskiy, V., *Mezhdunarodnoye Pravo* (Kiev: Izdatel'stvo Gosudarstvennogo Universiteta, 1955).

Little, Richard, *Intervention: External Involvement in Civil Wars* (London: Martin Robertson, 1975).

Lobachenko, V., 'Efiopiya pyat' let spustya posle krusheniya monarkhii', *Za Rubezhom*, 37 (September 1979), pp. 12–13.

Lobban, Richard, 'The Eritrean War; Issues and Implications', *Canadian Journal of African Studies*, 10:2 (1976), pp. 335–46.

London, Kurt, ed., *New Nations in a Divided World* (New York; Praeger, 1963).

Macfarlane, Neil, 'Intervention and Regional Security', *Adelphi Papers* (IISS), 196 (Spring 1985), pp. 1–66.

Mack, Andrew, David Plant and Ursula Doyle, eds., *Imperialism, Intervention and Development* (London: Croom Helm, 1979).

Madeley, John, *Diego Garcia: A Contrast to the Falklands*, report no. 54 (London: Minority Rights Groups Ltd, 1982), pp. 1–16.

Makeyev, Y., 'USSR–Ethiopia: Economic and Technical Co-operation', *Foreign Trade*, 6 (1985), pp. 30–2.

Makinda, Samuel, 'Shifting Alliances in the Horn of Africa', *Survival* (IISS), 28:1 (January-February 1985), pp. 11–19.

Maksimova, M., 'Vsemirnoye khozyaystvo nauchno-tekhnicheskaya revolyutsiya i mezhdunarodnyye otnosheniya', *MEiMO*, 4 (April 1979), pp. 36–44.

Mangold, Peter, 'Shaba I and Shaba II', *Survival* (IISS), 21:3 (May-June 1979), pp. 107–15.

Marcus, Harold G. *Ethiopia, Great Britain and the United States, 1941–1974* (California; University of California Press, 1983).

Mariam-Wolde, Mesfin, *Somalia: The Problem Child of Africa* (Addis Ababa: Artistic Printing Press, 1977).

Markakis, John, *National and Class Conflict in the Horn of Africa* (Cambridge; Cambridge University Press, 1987).

Markakis, John and Nega Ayele, *Class and Revolution in Ethiopia* (Nottingham: Spokesman, 1978).

Mastny, Vojtech, 'Kremlin Politics and the Austrian settlement', *Problems of Communism*, 31:4 (July-August 1982), pp. 37–51.

Mayall, James, 'The Battle for the Horn: Somali Irredentism and International Diplomacy', *The World Today*, 34:9 (September 1978), pp. 336–45.

'The National Question in the Horn of Africa', *The World Today*, 39:9 (September 1983), pp. 336–43.

McGwire, Michael, ed., *Soviet Naval Developments: Capability and Context* (New York: Praeger, 1973).

McLane, Charles B., *Soviet–African Relations*, vol. 3 of Soviet–Third World Relations (London: Central Asian Research Centre, 1974).

McLaurin, R. D., *The Middle East in Soviet Policy* (Lexington, Massachusetts: Lexington Books, 1975).

Mengistu, Haile Mariam, 'Ethiopia: A Course for Socialist Construction', *Socialism: Principles, Practice, Prospects*, 9 (September 1984).

Interview in *Neues Deutschland* (25 February 1977).

Interview in *New Times*, 38 (1979).

Interview in *New Times*, 48 (1985).

Interview in the *New York Times*, (28 November 1988).

Toward Party Formation (Addis Ababa: Ministry of Information and National Guidance, December 1979).

Mezentsev, P., 'Covering up the Tracks', *New Times*, 11 (1978), p. 12.

'Mikhail Gorbachev's Answers to Questions from the Washington Post and Newsweek', *New Times*, 22 (1988), pp. 4–13.

Mirskiy, G., 'Developing Countries: The Army and Society', *New Times*, 48 (1969), pp. 15–17.

'Newly Independent States: Way of Development', *Africa and Asia Today*, 5 (1987), pp. 53–6.

'Tretiy mir': Obshchestvo, Vlast', *Armiya* (Moscow: Izdatel'stvo 'Nauka', 1976).

Molchanov, V. G., *Efiopiya* (Moscow: Izdatel'stvo 'Znanie', 1960).

Moore, John Norton, eds., *Law and Civil War in the Modern World* (Baltimore: The John Hopkins University Press, 1974).

Morgenthau, Hans J., 'To Intervene Or Not To Intervene', *Foreign Affairs*, 45 (April 1967), pp. 425–46.

Politics Among Nations: The Struggle for Power and Peace, 3rd edition (New York: Alfred A. Knopf Inc., 1960).

Morison, David L., 'Patterns of Russian Aggrandizement,' *Common Cause Report*, 2 (February 1983), pp. 1–4.

'Two Decades of Soviet Involvement in Africa,' *Common Cause Report*, 12 (December 1979), pp. 1–4.

Morison David L., Alan Berson and Klaus Luders, *Soviet Aims and Activities in the Persian Gulf and Adjacent Areas: Report on an Investigation of Soviet Media Output* (Washington DC: Abbot Associates Inc., November 1976).

Morley, L., 'Invasion and Intervention in the Caribbean Area', *Editorial Research Reports*, 2 (July 1959), pp. 535–52.

Nadezhdin, G., 'Somali Democratic Republic', *International Affairs* (Moscow), 8 (1973), pp. 117–18.

Nekrasov, V., 'God 1977–y', *Kommunist*, 18 (December 1977), pp. 89–102.
'God 1978–y', *Kommunist*, 18 (December 1978), pp. 105–18.
Nersesov, G A, 'the Soviet Union, Anti-Colonialism, Africa: From the Great October Revolution of 1917 to the Italo-Ethiopian War of 1935–36', *Africa in Soviet Studies*, 4 (1976), pp. 214–46.
'New-type Treaty', *New Times*, 45 (1974), p. 17.
Nixon, Richard M., 'Asia After Vietnam', *Foreign Affairs*, 46:1 (1967), pp. 111–25.
Memoirs of Richard Nixon (London: Sidgwick and Jackson, 1978).
The Real War (London: Sidgwick and Jackson, 1980).
'Novaya stranitsa traditsionnoy druzhby', *Sovremennyy Vostok*, 8 (1959), pp. 24–5.
Novik, Nimrod, *On the Shores of Bab al Mandab: Soviet Diplomacy and Regional Dynamics* (Philadelphia: Foreign Policy Research Institute, Monograph No. 26, 1979).
Novoseltsev, Y., 'The Foreign Policy of Socialism in the World Revolutionary Process', *International Affairs* (Moscow), 10 (1970), pp. 16–18.
Nuechterlein, Donald E., 'National Interests and Foreign Policy: A Conceptual Framework for Analysis and Decision-making', *British Journal of International Studies*, 2 (1976), pp. 246–66.
Nuikin, A., 'Idealy ili interesy', *Novyy Mir*, 1 (Yanvar' 1988), pp. 190–211.
Nurthen, William, 'Russia's Abyssinian Gambit: The Soviet Decision to Support Ethiopia Over Somalia: a Dual Analysis', Paper presented at US Naval Postgraduate School, Monterey, California, September 1979.
'October Revolution, Peace, Peaceful Coexistence (a Round Table discussion)', *New Times*, 44 (1987), pp. 4–7.
Ol'derogge, D. A. and I. I. Potekhin, eds., *Narody Afriki* (Moscow: Izdatel'stvo Akademii Nauk SSSR, 1954).
Olufemi, Kola, 'Sino–Soviet Rivalry in the Horn of Africa', *Horn of Africa* 5:3 (1983–4), pp. 16–24.
Osman, Mohamoud, 'Somalia: Crisis and Decay in an Authoritarian Regime', *Horn of Africa*, 4:3 (1981), pp. 7–11.
Ottaway, Marina, *Soviet and American Influence in the Horn of Africa* (New York: Praeger, 1982).
Ottaway, Marina and David Ottaway, *Ethiopia: Empire in Revolution* (New York: Africana, 1978).
Parsons, Anthony, *The Pride and the Fall: Iran 1974–1979* (London: Jonathan Cape, 1984).
Patman, Robert G., 'Ideology, Soviet Policy and Realignment in the Horn', in Adeed Dawisha and Karen Dawisha, eds., *The Soviet Union in the Middle East* (London: Heinemann, Royal Institute of International Affairs, 1982), pp. 45–61.
'Talking Peace, Preparing for War in the Horn', Special Reports, *Africa*, 148 (December 1983), pp. 40–2.
Paukov, V. and G. Polyakov, 'Ethiopia. The Co-operative Movement; Theory and Practice', *Asia and Africa Today*, 1 (1987), pp. 58–61.
Pavlov, Y., 'Socialist Orientation: Inventions and Reality', *Socialism: Principles, Practice, Prospects*, 2 (February 1983), pp. 27–9.

Payton, Gary D., 'The Somali Coup of 1969: The Case for Soviet Complicity', *Horn of Africa*, 4:2 (1981), pp. 11–20.

Petrov, V., V. Belov and A. Karenin, *Leninskaya Vneshnyaya Politika SSSR: Razvitiye i Perspektivy* (Moscow: Izdatel'stvo Politicheskoy Literatury, 1974).

Petterson, Donald, 'Ethiopia Abandoned? An American Perspective', *International Affairs*, 62:4 (Autumn 1986), pp. 627–45.

Pliny the Middle-Aged, 'The PMAC: Origins and Structure', *Northeast African Studies*, Part 2, 1:1 (1978), pp. 1–20.

Polyakov, G., 'USSR–Africa: Economic Co-operation from the Viewpoint of Perestroika', *Asia and Africa Today*, 5 (1988), pp. 8–11.

Porter, Bruce D., *The USSR in Third World Conflicts: Soviet Arms and Diplomacy in Local Wars 1945–1980* (Cambridge: Cambridge University Press, 1984).

Potekhin, I. I., 'Legacy of Colonialism', *International Affairs* (Moscow), 3 (1964), pp. 15–20.

'Panafrikanizm i bor'ba dvukh ideologiy', *Kommunist*, 1 (January 1964), pp. 104–13.

'Programme of the Revolution', *New Times*, 18 (1976), pp. 9 and 11.

Proletarian Internationalism – Our Banner, Our Strength! (Moscow: Novosti Press Agency Publishing House, 1980).

Pushkov, K., 'Ethiopia: The Programme for Restructuring Society', *International Affairs* (Moscow), 9 (September 1975), pp. 132–3.

Rachkov, A., 'Uardigli-tsentr orientatsii', *Aziya i Afrika Segodnya*, 3 (1973), p. 10.

Rapoport, Louis, 'There's Hope for Ethiopia', *Horn of Africa*, 2:1 (1979), pp. 2–6.

Rayt, M. V. *Narody Efiopii* (Moscow: Izdatel'stvo 'Nauka', 1965).

'Russkiye ekspeditsii v Efiopiye v seredine XIX i nachale XX vekhov i ikh etnograficheskiye materialy', *Afrikanskiy Etnograficheskiy Sbornik*, 1 (1956), pp. 220–81.

Rayt, M. V. and Ye. G. Titov, *Efiopiya: Strana, Lyudy* (Moscow: Geografgiz, 1960).

Rees, David, 'Soviet Strategic Penetration of Africa', *Conflict Studies*, 77 (November 1976), pp. 1–20.

Reilly, Alayne P., *America in Contemporary Soviet Literature* (New York: New York University Press, 1971).

Remnek, Richard, 'Soviet Policy in the Horn of Africa: The Decision to Intervene', Professional Paper 270, Arlington, Virginia, Center for Naval Analyses, January 1980, pp. 1–52.

'Revolution and Reform in the National Development of Eastern Countries', (a Round Table discussion), *Asia and Africa Today*, 1 (1986), pp. 54–61.

Reynolds, P. A., *An Introduction to International Relations* (London: Longman, 1971).

Rivlin, Benjamin, *The United Nations and the Italian Colonies* (New York: Carnegie Endowment for International Peace, 1950).

Robertson, Charles L., *International Politics since World War II: A Short History*, 2nd edition (New York: John Wiley and Sons, 1975).

Rosberg, C. and T. Callaghy, eds., *Socialism in Sub-Saharan Africa* (Berkeley, California: Institute of International Studies, 1979).

Rosenau, James, ed., *International Aspects of Civil Strife* (Princeton: Princeton University Press, 1964).

Rosenau, James N., *The Scientific Study of Foreign Policy* (New York: The Free Press, 1971).

Rothenberg, Morris, *The USSR and Africa: New Dimensions of Soviet Global Power* (Miami: Advanced International Studies Institute, 1980).

Rubinstein, Alvin Z., *Red Star on the Nile: The Soviet–Egyptian Influence Relationship since the June War* (New Jersey: Princeton University Press, 1977).

   Soviet Foreign Policy since World War II (Cambridge, Massachusetts: Winthrop Publishers Inc., 1981).

   ed., *The Foreign Policy of the Soviet Union* (New York: Random House, 1972), 3rd edition.

   ed., *Soviet and Chinese Influence in the Third World* (New York: Praeger, 1976).

Rytkheu, Yu., 'V Efiopii pozdney osen'yu', *Aziya i Afrika Segodnya*, 7 (1972), pp. 37–9.

Sanakoyev, Sh., 'Programme for the Strengthening of General Peace and Security in Action', *International Affairs* (Moscow), 10 (1970), pp. 3–7.

Sanakoyev, Sh. and N. I. Kapchenko, *Teoriya i Praktika Vneshney Politiki Sotsializma* (Moscow: Izdatel'stvo 'Mezhdunarodnyye Otnosheniya', 1973).

Schlesinger, Arthur M., Jr, *Robert F. Kennedy and His Times* (London: Futura, 1979).

Schwab, Peter, *Ethiopia: Politics, Economics and Society* (London: Frances Pinter, 1985).

Schwartz, Morton, *Soviet Perceptions of the United States* (Berkeley: University of California Press, 1978).

Schwarz, Urs, *Confrontation and Intervention in the Modern World* (New York: Ocenia Publications, 1970).

Scott, Peter Dale, Paul L. Hoch and Russell Stetler, eds., *The Assassinations: Dallas and Beyond – A Guide to Cover-ups and Investigations* (London: Penguin Books, 1977).

Seabury, Paul, *The United States in World Affairs*, (New York: McGraw-Hill, 1973).

Sergeyev, S., 'An Important Landmark in Soviet–Ethiopian Co-operation', *International Affairs*, (Moscow), 12 (December 1979), pp. 87–91.

   'Ethiopia Starts a New Life', *International Affairs* (Moscow), 5 (May 1979), pp. 16–24.

Sergeyeva, I. S., *Somaliyskaya Respublika: Geograficheskaya Kharasteristika* (Moscow: Izdatel'stvo 'Mysl', 1965).

Sergiyev, A., 'Leninism on the Correlation of Forces as a Factor of International Relations', *International Affairs*, (Moscow), 5 (1975), pp. 99–107.

Sevortyan, R., *Armiya v Politicheskom Rezhime Stran Sovremennogo Vostoka* (Moscow: Izdatel'stvo 'Nauka' 1973).

Sharayev, V., 'Ethiopia: Despite the Difficulties', *New Times*, 44 (1985), p. 21.

   'Signs of a Thaw', *New Times*, 22 (1986), p. 10.

Sherman, Richard, *Eritrea: The Unfinished Revolution* (New York: Praeger, 1980).

Sherr, E., 'Ekonomicheskaya 'Pomoshch'' imperialisticheskikh gosudarstv Somali', *Narody Azii i Afriki*, 3 (1970), pp. 134–40.

'Flag nezavisimosti nad Dzhibuti', *Aziya i Afrika Segodnya*, 8 (1977), pp. 12–15.

'Islam v Somali i Efiopii', *Aziya i Afrika Segodnya*, 1 (1988), pp. 57–9.

'Lenin in Ethiopia', *Asia and Africa Today*, 2 (1985), pp. 50–1.

'Novyye rubezhi Somali', *Aziya i Afrika Segodnya*, 1 (1977), pp. 14–16.

'Somali: Religiya i Politika', *Narody Azii i Afriki*, 4 (1987), pp. 49–55.

'Somalia', *New Times*, 11 (1971), pp. 30–1.

'Somalia: Socialist Orientation', *International Affairs* (Moscow), 2 (February 1974), pp. 84–8.

'Somali: vneshnyaya politika strany sotsialisticheskoy orientatsii', *Aziya i Afrika Segodnya*, 1 (1975), pp. 42–3.

'Vazhnyy shag k progressu', *Aziya i Afrika Segodnya*, 5 (1974), p. 40.

'Veter peremen nad Somali', *Aziya i Afrika Segodnya*, 11 (1971), pp. 12–14.

'Ways of Disseminating the Ideas of Scientific Socialism in Ethiopia', *Africa in Soviet Studies Annual 1986* (Moscow: Nauka, 1987), pp. 75–85.

Sherr, E., and O. Dolgova, 'From a Monarchy to a People's Democratic Republic', *Asia and Africa Today*, 5 (1984), pp. 42–5.

Shevchenko, Y., 'Glasnost Needs No Translation', *New Times*, 26 (1987), p. 16.

Shmarov, V., 'New Stage in Soviet–Somali Relations', *New Times*, 29 (1974), pp. 6–7.

'Reform in Ethiopia', *New Times*, 7 (1975), p. 22.

Shubin, V., 'Revolution Square', *New Times*, 50 (1977), pp. 22–3.

Shumilin, V., 'The Capitalist Economy on the Threshold of the Seventies', *International Affairs* (Moscow), 2–3 (1970), pp. 57–64.

Siad Barre, Mohammed, Interview in *Afrique-Asie* (13 June 1977).

Interview in *The Independent* (6 January 1987).

Interview in *Izvestiya* (2 June 1971).

Interview in *Newsweek* (13 February 1978).

Interview in *Pravda* (20 December 1969).

Interview in *Pravda* (27 June 1988).

Interview in *US News and World Report* (21 July 1975).

Interview in *World Marxist Review*, 19:5 (1976).

My Country and My People 1969–74, 2 vols. (Mogadishu: Ministry of Information and National Guidance, 1974).

'The Only Way for Somalia: Scientific Socialism', *New Era*, (Mogadishu), 5 (March 1972).

Sidenko, V., 'Growing Friendship', *New Times*, 20 (1977), p. 7.

'Washington's Crooked Mirror', *New Times*, 21 (1977), p. 17.

Simes, Dimitri K., 'Imperial Globalism in the Making; Soviet Involvement in the Horn of Africa', *The Washington Review, Special Supplement* (May 1978), pp. 31–9.

Smirnov, V., 'Vazhnyy faktor ekonomicheskogo progressa razvivayushchikh-sya stran', *Vneshnyaya Torgovlya*, 3 (1971), pp. 13–17.

Sofinsky, V., 'Somalia on the Path of Progress', *International Affairs* (Moscow), 11 (November 1974), pp. 62–6.

Sofinsky, V. and A. Khazanov, 'The Imperialist Design for the Horn of Africa', *New Times*, 7 (1978), pp. 4–6.

Solodovnikov, V. G., *Afrika Vybirayet Put'* (Moscow: Izdatel'stvo 'Nauka', 1970).

'Somalia: A Regime in Troubled Waters', *The African Communist*, 3rd quarter, 11 (1987), 84–87.

'Somalia: Siad Barre Shaken by Bombs', *Africa Now* (January 1987), 18.

Soviet News (London: Press Department of the Soviet Embassy).

The Soviet Union and the Third World: A Watershed in Great Power Policy? Report to the Committee on International Relations, House of Representatives, Congressional Research Service, Library of Congress, US Government Printing Office, Washington, 1977.

Spencer, John, *Ethiopia, the Horn of Africa and US Policy* (Cambridge, Massachusetts: Institute for Foreign Policy Analysis, 1977).

Stanger, Roland J., ed., *Essays on Intervention* (Columbus: Ohio State University Press, 1964).

Starushenko, G. B., *Natsiya i Gosudarstvo v Osvobodayushchikhsya Stranakh* (Moscow: Izdatel'stvo 'Mezhdunarodnyye Otnosheniya', 1967).

Uprocheniye Zavoevaniy Revolyutsii v Efiopii i Opyt Stran Sotsialisticheskoy Orientatsii (Moscow: Izdatel'stvo 'Nauka', 1979).

ed., *Ideologiya Revolyutsionnykh Demokratov Afriki* (Moscow: Izdatel'stvo 'Nauka', 1981).

Stepunin, A. N. and O. L. Stepunina, *Efiopiya* (Moscow: Izdatel'stvo 'Mysl', 1965).

'Strong Ties', *New Times*, 48 (1971), p. 17.

Tarabrin, Ye. A., ed., *The USSR and the Countries of Africa* (Moscow: 'Mysl', 1976).

Tarasov, N., 'The Pentagon's Plans for the Red Sea', *Asia and Africa Today*, 4 (July–August 1983), pp. 15–17.

Thornton, Richard, 'Soviet Strategy and the Vietnam War', *Asian Affairs: An American Review*, 4 (March–April 1974), pp. 198–208.

Thurston, Raymond L., 'The United States, Somalia and the Crisis in the Horn', *Horn of Africa*, 1:2 (April–June 1978), pp. 11–20.

Tikhomirov, I. and A. Panasenko, 'Zakhvat Aviabazy', *Voyennyy Vestnik*, 2 (1975), pp. 50–2.

Tillett, Lowell R., 'The Soviet Role in League Sanctions Against Italy', *American Slavic and East European Review*, 15:1 (1956), pp. 11–16.

Titov, K., 'Indiyskiy Okean na karte Pentagona', *Morskoy Sbornik*, 7 (1973), pp. 91–8.

Tomashevskiy, D. G., *Leninskiye Idei i Sovremennyye Mezdunarodnyye Otnosheniya* (Moscow: Izdatel'stvo Politicheskoy Literatury, 1971).

Tomilin, Y., 'Ethiopian–Soviet Friendship', *International Affairs* (Moscow), 7 (1959), pp. 91–3.

'Indiyskiy Okean v agressivnykh planakh imperializma', *MEiMO*, 8 (1971), pp. 19–29.

'Territorial Problems in Africa', *New Times*, 4 (1964), pp. 10–12.

Touval, Saadia, *The Boundary Politics of Independent Africa* (Cambridge, Massachusetts: Harvard University Press, 1972).

Somali Nationalism (Cambridge, Massachusetts: Harvard University Press, 1963).

Triska, Jan F., and David Finley, *Soviet Foreign Policy* (New York: Macmillan, 1968).

Trofimenko, G., 'From Confrontation to Coexistence', *International Affairs* (Moscow), 10 (1975), pp. 33–41.

'Militarizm i vnutripoliticheskaya bor'ba', *SShA*, (Moscow), 1 (January 1972), pp. 65–72.

Tsaplin, Y., 'Ethiopia: Fighting the Reactionaries', *New Times*, 47 (1976), p. 14.

'Playing with Fire', *New Times*, 25 (1977), p. 12.

'The Ogaden Fighting', *New Times*, 9 (1978), p. 15.

'Who is Fanning the Flames', *New Times*, 5 (1978), p. 8.

'Road to Friendship', *New Times*, 28 (1977), pp. 14–15.

Tsypkin, G., 'Gorod budushchego', *Aziya i Afrika Segodnya*, 6 (1969), pp. 58–60.

Tubiana, Joseph, ed., 'Modern Ethiopia from the Accession of Menelik II to the Present', Proceedings of the 5th International Conference of Ethiopian Scholars, Rotterdam, Balkema (1980).

Tunkin, G., *Osnovy Sovremennogo Mezhdunarodnogo Prava* (Moscow: Izdatel'stvo 'Mezhdunarodnyye Otnosheniya', 1967).

'V I Lenin i printsipy otnosheniy mezhdu sotsialisticheskimi gosudarstvami', *Sovetskiy Yezhegodnik Mezhdunarodnogo Prava* (1970), pp. 16–32.

Tyagunenko, V. L., ed., *Vooruzhennaya Bor'ba Narodov Afriki za Svobodu i Nezavisimost'* (Moscow: Izdatel'stvo 'Nauka', 1974).

Ullman, Richard H., *Intervention and the War* (Princeton: Princeton University Press, 1961).

Ul'yanovskiy, R. A., 'Leninism, Soviet Experience and the Newly Free Countries', *New Times*, 1 (1971), pp. 18–21.

'O stranakh sotsialisticheskoy orientatsii', *Kommunist*, 11 (1979), pp. 114–23.

'The "Third World" – problems of socialist orientation', *International Affairs* (Moscow), 9 (1971), pp. 26–35.

United Nations, *General Assembly, Official Records*, Plenary Meetings, 1st Session, 2 (1946).

General Assembly, Official Records, First Committee, 3rd Session, Part 2, (1949).

United States, Congress, House, *War in the Horn of Africa: A Firsthand Report on the Challenges for United States Policy*, Report to the Committee on International Relations, 95th Congress, 2nd Session, 12–22 December 1977.

United States, Congress, Senate, Subcommittee on African affairs of the Committee of Foreign Relations, *Ethiopia and the Horn of Africa*, Hearings, 94th Congress, 2nd Sessions, 4, 5, and 6 August 1976.

United States, Congress, Senate, Subcommittee on United States agreements and commitments abroad of the Committee on Foreign Relations, *United States Security Agreements and Commitments Abroad*, Ethiopia Hearings, 91st Congress, 2nd Session, 1 June 1970.

United States, *Department of State Bulletin*, Washington DC (1960–1988).

Ustimenko, Yu., 'Novaya zhizn' drevney Efiopii', *Aziya i Afrika Segodnya*, Part 1:4 (1977), pp. 12–15, 29.

'Efiopiya: trudnosti, sversheniya, perspektivy', *Aziya i Afrika Segodnya*, Part 2:5 (1977), pp. 8–11.

Valenta, Jiri, 'From Prague to Kabul: The Soviet Style of Invasion', *International Security*, 5:2 (Winter 1980), 114–141.

'Soviet–Cuban Intervention in the Horn of Africa: Impact and Lessons', *Journal of International Affairs*, 34:2 (Winter 1980–1), pp.353–67.

'The Soviet–Cuban alliance in Africa and the Caribbean', *The World Today*, 37:2 (February 1981), pp. 45–53.

'The Soviet–Cuban intervention in Angola, 1975', *Studies in Comparative Communism*, 11:1 and 2 (Spring/Summer 1978), pp. 3–33.

Vance, Cyrus, *Hard Choices: Critical Years in America's Foreign Policy* (New York: Simon and Schuster, 1983).

Vanneman, Peter and Martin James, 'Soviet Thrust into the Horn of Africa: The Next Targets', *Strategic Review*, 6:2 (1978), pp. 33–40.

Vestal, Theodore M., 'Ethiopia's Famine: A Many-dimensioned Crisis', *The World Today*, 41:7 (July 1985), pp. 125–8.

Vigand, V. and N. Topuridze, 'IX mezhdunarodnyy congress po Efiopskim issledovaniyam', *Narody Azii i Afriki*, 2 (1987), pp. 124–7.

Viktorov, G., 'Somalia: The Coup: Causes and Consequences', *International Affairs* (Moscow), 2–3 (February-March 1970), p. 112.

'Somalia: Toward Progress', *International Affairs* (Moscow), 12 (December 1970), pp. 84–5.

Vincent, R. J., *Nonintervention and International Order* (New Jersey, Princeton University Press, 1974).

Vinh, Nguyen, 'Vietnam to Withdraw Troops from Kampuchea', *New Times*, 30 (1988), p. 31.

Vishnevsky, S., 'The Ideological Struggle and Current International Relations', *International Affairs* (Moscow), 2–3 (1970), pp. 38–45.

Vivo, Raul Valdes, *Ethiopia: The Unknown Revolution* (New York: International Publishers, 1978).

Vneshnyaya Torgovlya SSSR (Moscow: 'Statistika', 1960–88).

Voblikov, D. R., 'Anglo-Amerikanskoye sopernichestvo v poslevoyennoy Efiopiye', *Sovetskoye Vostokovedeniye*, 4 (1957), pp. 27–38.

Volkov, M., 'Militarisation Versus Development', *Asia and Africa Today*, 5 (1987), pp. 7–9.

'War and Hunger: Ethiopia', 2 parts, *Africa News* (16 November 1987), pp. 6–9; (30 November 1987), pp. 5–8.

Weeks, Albert L., 'Chauvinism and Russian Expansion', *Horn of Africa*, 1:3 (July–September 1978), pp. 65–9.

Weinland, Robert G., 'Land Support for Naval Forces: Egypt and the Soviet Escadra 1962–1976', *Survival* (IISS), 20:2 (March-April 1978), pp. 73–9.

Weinstein, F. B., 'The Concept of Commitment in International Relations', *Journal of Conflict Resolution*, 13 (1969), pp. 39–56.

Weinstein, W., ed., *Chinese and Soviet Aid to Africa* (New York: Praeger, 1976).

Weiss, Kenneth G., 'The Soviet Involvement in the Ogaden War', *Professional Paper 269* (Arlington, Virginia: Center for Naval Analyses, February 1980), pp. 1–42.

Whitaker, Jennifer Seymour, ed., *Africa and the United States: Vital Interests* (New York: New York University Press, 1978).

Wills, Garry, *The Kennedys: A Shattered Illusion* (London: Orbis, 1982).

Wilson, Daniel, 'Class and Revolution in Ethiopia', *Horn of Africa*, 4:4 (1981–2), pp. 15–22.

Winfield, Percy H., 'Intervention', *Encyclopedia of the Social Sciences* (New York: Macmillan, 1932), p. 236.

'With Soviet Assistance', *Foreign Trade*, 7 (1984), p. 56.

Wright, Quincy, *International Law and the United Nations* (Bombay: Asia Publishing House, 1960).

'Intervention 1956', *American Journal of International Law*, 51 (April 1957), pp. 257–76.

'The Munich Settlement and International Law', *American Journal of International Law*, 33 (January 1939), pp. 12–32.

Yag'ya, V. S., *Efiopiya v Noveyshee Vremya* (Moscow: Izdatel'stvo 'Mysl', 1978).

'Revolyutsionnyye peremeny v Efiopii (1974–1975)', *Narody Azii i Afriki*, 6 (1975), pp. 7–21.

Yeremeyev, D., 'Roots of Interconfessional Conflicts', *Asia and Africa Today*, 1 (1987), pp. 58–61.

Yodfat, Aryeh, 'Ethiopia: Pressure for Political Reorganisation', *Soviet Analyst*, 27 (October 1982), pp. 2–3.

'The Soviet Union and the Horn of Africa', 3 parts, *Northeast African Studies*, 1:3 (Winter 1979–80), pp. 1–17; 2:1 (1980), pp. 31–57; 2:2 (1980), pp. 65–81.

Zawadzka, Hannah Josephine, 'The USSR's Path to Global Power via the Soviet Bloc and the Third World', Ph.D Dissertation, The John Hopkins University, Maryland (1974).

Zhigunov, A., 'Somalia: A Major Landmark', *New Times*, 29 (1976), p. 28.

Zhurkina, V. V. and Y. M. Primakova, *Mezhdunarodnyye Konflikty* (Moscow: Izdatel'stvo 'Mezhdunarodnyye Otnosheniya', 1972).

Zike, Admasu, 'An Application of the Theory of Social Exchange to International Relations: The Kagnew Station and the Linchpin of the Ethiopian–United States Relationship', Ph.D Dissertation, University of Northern Illinois (1979).

Zorin, V., '2oo-letiye i 'Konstitutsionnyy krizis'', *SShA* (Moscow), 7 (July 1976), pp. 24–6.

'Vnutrennyye Amerikanskiye problemy 70-kh godov', *SShA* (Moscow), 8 (August 1971), pp. 3–13.

Zorin, V. A. and V. L. Israelyan, 'Marksistsko-Leninskiy podkhod k resheniyu territorial'nykh sporov', *Kommunist*, 2 (January 1964), pp. 28–39.

Zuniga, Fred Joseph, 'Soviet Naval Diplomacy: Naval Suasion for Political Effect', Ph.D Dissertation, The George Washington University, 1979.

Newspapers and periodicals

Africa (London)
Africa Confidential
Africa Contemporary Record
Africa in Soviet Studies
Africa Research Bulletin
African Affairs
The African Communist
Afrikanskiy Etnograficheskiy Sbornik
American Slavic and East European Review
Aziya i Afrika Segodnya
British Broadcasting Corporation: Summary of World Broadcasts
British Journal of International Affairs
Canadian Journal of African Studies
Christian Science Monitor
Current Digest of the Soviet Press
The Daily Nation (Nairobi)
The Daily Telegraph
Dawn (Delhi)
The Economist
The Egyptian Gazette
The Ethiopian Herald (Addis Ababa)
The Financial Times
Foreign Affairs
Foreign Affairs Reports
Foreign Policy
Foreign Trade (Moscow)
The Guardian
Hindu (Delhi)
Horn of Africa
Hsinhua News Agency
International Affairs (Moscow)
International Affairs (R.I.I.A)
International Herald Tribune
International Security
Izvestiya
Journal of Modern African Studies
Keesings Contemporary Archives
Kommunist
Kommunist Uzbekistana
Kommunist Voruzhennykh Sil
Krasnaya Zvezda

Literaturnaya Gazeta
The Los Angeles Times
The Military Balance (London: IISS)
Mirovaya Ekonomika i Mezhdunarodnyye Otnosheniya
The Mizan Newsletter
The Morning Star
Morskoy Sbornik
Moscow News
Narody Azii i Afriki
Nauka i Religiya
Neues Deutschland
New China News Agency
New Middle East
Newsweek
New Times
New York Times
Northeast African Studies
The Observer
The Observer Foreign News Service
October Star (Mogadishu)
Orbis
Pravda
Problems of Communism
Problemy Vostokovedeniya
Socialism: Principles, Practice, Prospects
Sovetskoye Vostokovedeniye
Soviet Analyst
Soviet Studies
Soviet Weekly
Sovremennyy Vostok
SShA: Ekonomika, Politika i Ideologiya
The Standard (Nairobi)
Strategic Survey (London: IISS)
Studies in Comparative Communism
Survival (London: IISS)
The Times and *Sunday Times*
USSR and Third World
The Washington Post
The Washington Review
World Marxist Review
World Military Expenditures and Arms Transfers (Washington: ACDA)
The World Today
Za Rubezhom

Index

Abdirazak Haji Hussein, 89
Abdullah Haji Masala, 237
Abdurahman Jama Barre, 292
Abebe Kebede, 295
Abiye Abebe, 153
Abu Dhabi, 130, 144, 181
Abuna Theophilos, 282
Abyssinian crisis, 31–2
Adair, Ross, 175
Adamishin, A., 299, 302
Aden
  and the Suez canal closure, 80
Aden Abdullah Osman, 47
advisers, Soviet
  in Ethiopia, 191, 205, 210, 265, 273
  expulsion from Egypt, 16, 18–19, 114,
    166
  expulsion from Somalia, 220, 221–2,
    223, 227, 246–7
  in Somalia, 95, 96, 117, 118, 126,
    127–8
  transferred from Somalia to Ethiopia,
    217, 248
Afghanistan
  Soviet intervention in, 3–4, 15, 18, 21,
    268, 289
Agnew, Spiro, 65
agriculture
  in Ethiopia, 138, 275, 294–5, 304
  in Somalia, 122
  Soviet–Ethiopian co-operation, 265
Ahmed Mohammoud Farah, 301
Ahmed Mahgoub, 114
Ahmed Nasser, 274
Ahmed Suleiman Abdulle, 120, 121, 217,
  237
air force
  Ethiopian, 103, 135, 183, 184, 261
  Somali, 103, 135, 183, 261
aircraft, Ethiopian purchases of, 276
Aklilu Habte Wolde, 152, 153
Aleksandrenko, G. B., 51

Alemayehu Haile, 201
Aleme Eshete, 272
ALF (Afar Liberation Front), 159
Algeria, 100, 130
Algerian crisis (1958), 20
Ali Hattan Hashi, 221
Allende, Salvador, 10
Aman Andom, General, 154, 156, 160,
  175, 193, 194
Amin, Hafizullah, 3
Amin, Idi, 5, 16
Amin, Mohammed, 278
Andropov, Yuri, 121, 277, 288
Angola, 130
  and Ethiopia, 171
  Soviet–Cuban military intervention
    (1975–6), 11, 16, 151, 185, 248
  and the United States, 251
animal health care
  in Somalia, 123
Arab League
  and Somalia, 143–5, 181, 216
Arab states
  and Eritrea, 142, 198, 274
  and Ethiopia, 169, 170
  and the Ethiopian–Somali war, 230–1
  and the Red Sea, 238
  and Somalia, 130, 189, 211, 212, 220
Arab–Israeli War, see Six Day War
Arap Moi, Daniel, 229
Arbatov, G., 64
Aremetev, A., 94
Argentina
  intervention in the Falklands (1982), 8
Arkhipov, I., 191
armed forces
  Ethiopian, 92, 101–3, 107, 133, 134–5,
    182–3, 184, 192–3, 194, 248–9,
    260–1
    and the Ethiopian Revolution, 152,
      153
    in the Ogaden conflict, 231–3

Soviet and East European Studies

The following series titles are now out of print:

49.50